English Electric
CANBERRA

Ken Delve • Peter Green
John Clemons

Midland Counties Publications

This work
is dedicated to the
manufacturers, crews and maintainers
of the Canberra,
world wide.

Copyright © 1992
Ken Delve, Peter Green, John Clemons

First published in 1992 by
Midland Counties Publications
24 The Hollow, Earl Shilton
Leicester, LE9 7NA
England

North American trade distribution by
Specialty Press Publishers & Wholesalers Inc
123 North Second Street
Stillwater, MN 55082, USA

ISBN 0 904597 73 3

Editorial Layout by
Chris Salter and Vanessa Piper

Printed and bound in the United Kingdom by
The Alden Press
Oxford

Photograph on opposite page:
**This close formation shot of a
31 Squadron PR.7 over north east France
will recall many memories of the use of the
Canberra in the low level role.**
Group Captain G.Pitchfork

English Electric
CANBERRA

Ken Delve • Peter Green
John Clemons

William Edward Willoughby Petter
Chief Engineer, English Electric Company's Aircraft Division, July 1944 to February 1950
The creative genius behind the Canberra.

Contents

Front cover from a specially commissioned painting by Keith Woodcock GAvA.

Introduction and Acknowledgements

The English Electric Canberra has now seen over forty years of sterling and varied service, in many guises and with many air arms around the world. Our aim in producing this book has been to record comprehensively the history of this well-loved aircraft – even though it cannot be the final word because the type seems set to be around for some time yet.

The basis of the research for this book is the individual squadron and unit Operational Record Books (ORBs) from which the outline histories of the squadrons have been obtained; many thanks to the staff at AHB for obtaining source material. We also wish to place on record our thanks to the Officer Commanding and staff of RAF Quedgeley for their help with access to stored records.

Having established the historical framework it was the patience and co-operation of the many ex-Canberra aircrew and groundcrew who answered questionnaires or who sat through interviews that put the flesh on the bare historical bones. Everyone has their favourite story of the Canberra and many books could be filled with such tales; we have included all too few, but space is always a problem.

The list of people who have helped is too long to produce in full but special mention must be made of a number of individuals: R.C.B. (Chris) Ashworth, Mrs Pauline Bacon, Philip Birtles, Roy Bonser, M.J.F. (Mike) Bowyer, Tony Bridges, Dudley Brown, Bill Davies, Chris Donne, Roger Evans, Bill Fisher, Tony Foster, Malcolm Freestone, T. Neil Gaunt for the entry on Rhodesian Canberras, R.B. (Rob) Glover, John Hart, John Hale, Ron Henry for much assistance and with RRE notes, Group Captain C. Herbert, Paul Jackson, Captain John Kemp, Roger McLeod, Mrs

Wendy Mills (Airwork Ltd), Rick Pearson, Arthur Pearcy, Dave Pells, Peter Pountney, Rev J.D.R. Rawlings, Flt Lt Norman Roberson, Bruce Robertson, David Sargent, Philip Spencer, Captain Ken Styles, Gordon Swanborough, G.S. Taylor, Wing Commander W.J. (Bill) Taylor, Flt Lt A.S. (Andy) Thomas – many of whom have helped over a long period of time. Hopefully we shall be forgiven for not mentioning anyone who thinks that they ought to have been included!

The bulk of the data in the Appendices was painstakingly compiled by Peter Green from personal observation and research over a period of forty years. However special mention must be made of the considerable assistance rendered by Phil Butler, Robert Fairclough and Chris Salter to this section at the eleventh hour, also to the staff of the Air Historical Branch (AHB) for their help in obtaining reference to material, particularly to Richard King and Graham Day for their help in obtaining the serial allocation dates and related contract information. Access to the MoD(PE) files in the RAF Museum was via Ken Hunter of the Department of Aviation Records and the good offices of Richard Searle, Chief Librarian of the Royal Aerospace Establishment, Farnborough. As a result, the information in this section is, without question, far more comprehensive than anything else that has previously appeared in print.

When it came to photograph selection we were fortunate in having a pool of several thousand from which to choose. A prime objective was to employ a high proportion of previously unpublished images, whilst another was to feature as many of the British Services user-operators as possible. In spite of this vast

choice, our selection was restricted by what was to hand and as a consequence photographs of aircraft of one or two British units have still eluded us. In several instances priority for inclusion has been given to historical significance over technical perfection and we hope readers will be understanding of this necessity. A number of photographs that proved difficult to incorporate elsewhere in the book have been gathered in an appendix we have called 'Candid Canberra'.

The original sources of many of the photographs are now nearly impossible to trace and we have credited images to the immediate source of supply unless the name of the original photographer has been ascertained. Uncredited photographs are from the authors' collections. If we have misapplied any credits we apologise, as it was not our intention to do so. We thank the many people who have contributed photographs and only regret we have not been able to use even more!

We are also indebted to various sources of published material including specialist work done by Air-Britain members and in particular we have been glad to make use of information appearing in Air-Britain publications as well as *British Aviation Review* and *Roundel*, the house magazines of the British Aviation Research Group. Additionally and over many years, individual copies of the magazines *The Aeroplane, Air Enthusiast, Air International, Air Pictorial, Aircraft Illustrated, Flight, Flypast* and *Military Aviation Review* have been gleaned for the minutiae that provide such an essential component of the story.

However, as we said at the beginning, the Canberra story is not at an end and the authors would be delighted to hear from anyone with Canberra connections.

List of Abbreviations

AAA	Anti-Aircraft Artillery
A&AEE	Aircraft and Armament Experimental Establishment
acft	Aircraft
AEW	Airborne Early Warning
AHU	Aircraft Handling Unit
AHQ	Air Headquarters
AI	Airborne Interception (radar)
AIEU	Armament and Instrument Experimental Unit
Air Min	Air Ministry
APC	Armament Practice Camp
APS	Aircraft Preservation Society
ARDU	Aircraft Research and Development Unit (Australia)
ARS	Aerospace Research Squadron
AS	Armstrong-Siddeley
ASW	Akrotiri Strike Wing
ATAF	Allied Tactical Air Force
ATDU	Air Torpedo Development Unit
att	Attached
ATU	Air Trials Unit
Aw/cn	Awaiting collection
AWRE	Air Weapons Research Establishment
BAC	British Aircraft Corporation
BAe	British Aerospace
BCAMS	Bomber Command Acceptance and Modification Section
BCAMU	Bomber Command Acceptance and Modification Unit
BCDU	Bomber Command Development Unit
BCHU	Bomber Command Holding Unit
BDRF	Battle Damage Repair Flight
BLEU	Blind Landing Experimental Unit
BoB	Battle of Britain
(B)OCU	Bomber Operational Conversion Unit (RAAF & RNZAF)
BP	Boulton Paul
BS	Bristol-Siddeley
BTU	Bombing Trials Unit
B/u	Broken up
C(A)	Controller (Aircraft)
CAMU	Command Acceptance and Modification Unit
CAS	Close Air Support
Cat.3	Damage category. Repairable on site
Cat.4	Damage category. Repairable at MU or manufacturer
Cat.5	Damage category. Write off or total loss
CAW	College of Air Warfare
CCAS	Civilian Craft Apprentices School
CEPE	Central Experimental and Proving Establishment

CEV	Centre d'Essais en Vol
CF	Communications Flight
CFE	Central Fighter Establishment
CFS	Central Flying School
CIT	Cranfield Institute of Technology
c/n	Constructors number
CNCS	Central Navigation and Control School
CO	Commanding Officer
conv	Converted / Conversion
CPE	Central Proving Establishment
cr	Crashed
CRE	Central Reconnaissance Establishment
CRT	Crash and Rescue Training
c/s	Call-sign
CS(A)	Controller Supply (Aircraft)
CSDE	Central Servicing Development Establishment
CSDU	Central Servicing Development Unit
CSE	Command Signals Establishment
CSF	Central Servicing Flight
CTTS	Civilian Technical Training School
DEODS	Defence Explosive Ordnance Disposal School
del	Delivered / Delivery
det(s)	Detached / Detachments
dev	Development
DFVLR	Deutches Forschungs und Versuchsanstalt fur Luft und Raumfahrt (German Aerospace Research Institute)
DH Props	De Havilland Propellers Ltd.
doc	Diverted off contract
ECM	Electronic Counter Measures
EE Co	English Electric Company
EFS	Experimental Flying Squadron (or Department)
Emc	Electromagnetic Capability
EOKA	Ethniki Organosis Kyprion Agoniston
ETPS	Empire Test Pilot's School
FAA	Fuerza Aerea Argentina
FAE	Fuerza Aerea Ecuatoriana
FAP	Fuerza Aerea del Peru
FAV	Fuerza Aerea Venezolana
FCT	Flying Crew Training
FDS	Fighter Direction School
FEAF	Far East Air Force
FECS	Far East Communications Squadron
f/f	First Flight
FFS	Fire Fighting School
FFU	Ferranti Flying Unit
FLIR	Forward Looking Infra-Red

FOB	Forward Operating Base
FRADU	Fleet Requirements and Air Direction Unit
FRADTU	Fleet Requirements and Air Direction Training Unit
FR Ltd	Flight Refuelling Ltd.
FRU	Fleet Requirements Unit
FTB	Flying Test-bed
FTU	Ferry Training Unit
FU	Ferry Unit
GCA	Ground Controlled Approach
g/g	Gate Guard
g/i	Ground Instructional Airframe
GW(A)	Guided Weapons (Air)
HSD	Hawker Siddeley Dynamics
IAM	Institute of Aviation Medicine
IFF	Identification, Friend or Foe
ILS	Instrument Landing System
INAS	Inertial Navigation and Attack System
ITF	Instrument Training Flight
IWM	Imperial War Museum
IRLS	Infra Red Line Scan
JCF	Jet Conversion Flight
JCU	Jet Conversion Unit
JSODS	Joint Services Ordnance Disposal School
JSTU	Joint Services Trials Unit
k	Killed (refers to aircrew loss in crash)
LABS	Low Altitude Bombing System
LRMTS	Laser Ranger and Marked Target Seeker
LABS	Low Altitude Bombing System
MEAF	Middle East Air Force
MECS	Middle East Communications Squadron
Met Flt	Meteorological Research Flight
MB	Martin Baker Ltd.
MCP	Malayan Communist Party
MinTech	Ministry of Technology
MoA	Ministry of Aviation
mod	Modification
MoD	Ministry of Defence
MoD(PE)	Ministry of Defence (Procurement Executive)
MoS	Ministry of Supply
MPC	Missile Practice Camp
MRLA	Malayan Races Liberation Army
MU	Maintenance Unit
NARIU	Naval Air Radio Installations Unit
NAS	Naval Air Station (US Navy)
NATIU	Naval Air Trials Installation Unit
N/e	Non Effective
Nea	Non Effective Aircraft
NEAF	Near East Air Force

NECS	Near East Communication Squadron	RN	Royal Navy	ss	Sold as Scrap
NGTE	National Gas Turbine Establishment	RNAY	Royal Navy Air Yard	TANS	Tactical Air Navigation System
NMIM	New Mexico Institute of Mining and Technology	RNZAF	Royal New Zealand Air Force	TR	Tactical Recce
		ros	Repair on Site	TASF	Transit and Aircraft Servicing Flight
npw	Not proceeded with	RR	Rolls-Royce		
nr	Near	RRAF	Royal Rhodesian Air Force	tb	Test-bed
ntu	Not taken up	RRE	Radar Research Establishment	TDP	Target Director Post
NWTC	Nuclear Weapons Training Compound (at Catterick)	RRF	Radar Reconnaissance Flight	TDU	Tactical Development Unit
		RRFU	Rolls-Royce Flying Unit	TFF	Target Facilities Flight
o/c	On Charge	RS	Radio School	TFS	Target Facilities Squadron
OCU	Operational Conversion Unit	RSRE	Royal Signals and Radar Establishment	t/i	Trials Installation
o/h	Overhaul			TI	Target Indicator
PEE	Proof & Experimental Establishment	r/w	Runway	t/o	Take off
		RWR	Radar Warning Receiver	TRE	Telecommunications Research Establishment
PRU	Photo-Reconnaissance Unit	SAAF	South African Air Force		
R&D	Research and Development	SAH	School of Aircraft Handling	TSR	Tactical Strike & Reconnaissance (role)
RAAF	Royal Australian Air Force	SDB	Shallow Dive Bombing		
RAE	Royal Aircraft Establishment	SF	Station Flight	TT	Target Towing (role)
RAFC	Royal Air Force College	SGB	Shallow Glide Bombing	u/c	Undercarriage
RAFEF	RAF Exhibition Flight	SLAR	Sideways Looking Airborne Radar	u/s	Unserviceable
RAFFC	RAF Flying College			VA	Vickers Armstrong
RAFG	Royal Air Force Germany	soc	Struck off Charge	wfu	Withdrawn from use
ret	Returned	SoTT	School of Technical Training	w/o	Written off
riw	Repair in Works	SPE	Special Proving Establishment	WRE	Weapons Research Establishment
		Sqn	Squadron		
		SR	Strategic Recce		

Select Bibliography

Air War South Atlantic
Jeffrey Ethell & Alfred Price
Sidgwick & Jackson, London, 1983.

B-57 Canberra at War 1964-1972
Robert C.Mikesh
Ian Allan Ltd, Shepperton, 1980.

B-57 Canberra in Action
Aircraft in Action 77
Jim Mesko
Squadron Signal, Carollton Tx, USA, 1988.

British Military Aircraft Serials 1878-1987
Bruce Robertson
Midland Counties Publications
Leicester, 1987.

Eastward
Sir David Lee
HMSO, London, 1984.

*Encyclopedia of US Aircraft
& Missile Systems vol.2:
Post-World War II Bombers 1945-73*
Marcelle S.Knaack
USGPO/Office of AF History.

*English Electric Aircraft
and their Predecessors*
Stephen Ransom & Robert Fairclough
Putnam/Conway Maritime Press, 1987.

English Electric Canberra: Inside Story
Roland Beamont & Arthur Reed
Ian Allan, Shepperton, 1984.

Falklands: The Air War
British Aviation Research Group
Arms & Armour Press, London, 1986.

Guide to Aviation Museums in Australia
Graham Potts
Australian Academic Press Pty Ltd
Bowen Hills, Queensland, 1990.

*Lincoln, Canberra & F-111
in Australian Service*
Stewart Wilson
Aerospace Publications Pty Ltd
Western Creek, ACT 2611, 1989.

The Malayan Emergency
(AP3410)

*The Martin B-57 Night Intruders
& General Dynamics RB-57F*
Aircraft in Profile 247
David A.Anderton
Profile Publications Ltd, Windsor, 1973.

Pilots Notes
and
Flight Reference Cards
for each Canberra mark.

Suez: The Double War
Roy Fullick & Geoffrey Powell
Hamish Hamilton, 1979.

Winged Bomb: History of 39 Squadron
Ken Delve
Midland Counties Publications
Leicester, 1985.

Wings in the Sun
Sir David Lee
HMSO, London, 1989.

*Wrecks & Relics (13th edition) –
The biennial survey of preserved
instructional and derelict airframes
in the UK & Ireland*
Ken Ellis
Midland Counties Publications
Leicester, 1992.

Wrecks & Relics (1991 Pocket edition)
Ken Ellis
Midland Counties Publications
Leicester, 1991.

Chapter One

Concept and Development

The Canberra design was the brainchild of one man, W. E. W. 'Teddy' Petter who in 1944 was working at Westlands and had turned his attention to a Ministry of Aircraft Production (MAP) requirement for a jet-powered aircraft to replace the Whirlwind/Typhoon/Mosquito genre of aircraft. This proposal had stemmed from Air Staff and MAP meetings the previous year to discuss the feasibility of a high-speed day jet bomber. In 1944 Petter left Westlands to join English Electric at Preston; he took his new ideas with him but found he had no staff and very limited facilities, initially based in a bus garage in Corporation Street, Preston. As Chief Engineer of the English Electric Aircraft Division at Preston, Petter set about building up a team to work with him on the development of his jet bomber. The Division had completed its production run of Halifax bombers and was tooling-up for production of Vampire fighters for which de Havilland had no spare production capacity. As this required little design work the team was able to apply itself to investigations of designs to meet requirements for a high-altitude jet bomber.

The initial Ministry specification was for a high speed, high altitude unarmed (i.e. no self-defence armament) bomber. The unarmed criterion was debated because American jet bomber research still favoured the provision of heavy self-defence armament. However, Petter and his team were convinced that they could design an aircraft that would not require such protection and would thus reap the benefits of saving space and weight. By June 1945 the design had evolved into a mid-wing monoplane to be powered by a single large turbojet, with provision for a basic crew of two, pilot and navigator, and alternative side-by-side or back-to-back seating arrangements. Such a design depended on a suitable engine to power an aircraft that was likely to be in the 40,000 lb AUW (all up weight) class. Discussions with Rolls-Royce suggested that a single engine of 66" diameter appeared

feasible and with a two-stage centrifugal design could produce the estimated 12,000 lb static thrust needed to meet the proposed specification of 500 mph at 40,000 ft. Such an engine layout would allow a neat circular fuselage - ideal for a pressurised crew compartment - and clean wings with the consequent aerodynamic advantages. The state of engine design also meant that a twin engine option would require power plants of 48" diameter to meet the thrust requirement and would have necessitated a very large fuselage section.

It seemed that the first RAF jet bomber would be a clean-looking straight-winged affair powered by a single engine. However, within a month of the concept being formalised ideas changed again, partly because of problems of bomb and fuel storage in the single engine layout, but also because of advances in jet engine design. In July a new design layout was agreed which would use two of the new Rolls-Royce Avon AJ.65 axial engines, forerunners of the excellent Avon series. With the smaller intake size the plan was to semi-bury the engines in the wing roots. Although no-one had voiced doubts on jet engine reliability after the first proposal, the manufacturer's brochures now spoke of 'twin engine reliability and safety'. The

other main advantage was that it freed the neat circular fuselage for bomb bay and fuel tanks. There was even an overall theoretical weight saving as the smaller, lighter engines gave a lower fuel consumption through increased efficiency and it now seemed likely that the design would come out under 40,000 lb AUW.

The design team had started virtually from scratch with little background 'concept basis' (i.e. known parameters and characteristics). In a lecture in the early 1950s D. L. Ellis, one of the chief design engineers on the project, outlined the thoughts of the initial design team, '.. an analysis based on low wing loading and low power loading in order to give high performance and manoeuvrability at the extreme altitude required and to allow for future development.' He also stated that consideration had been given to the use of wing sweep for improved performance but that doubts on stability had led them to keeping the design fairly traditional and not trying to be too clever, and, as Petter had earlier stated to *Flight* magazine 'sweepback was not needed at the Mach numbers attainable when carrying a useful military load with the thrust likely to be available from two Avons.' Nevertheless, the aircraft was to feature a number of innovations.

The ex-Barton Motors premises in Corporation Street, Preston - known as 'TC' after its wartime role as a training centre - and home of the Canberra development team. *via Bruce Robertson*

The design was crystallizing nicely and in Autumn 1945 the Company submitted a brochure to the Ministry of Supply for an aircraft to meet the recently issued Specification B3/45. The second draft for this Specification, dated September/October 1945, details criteria to 'meet the Air Staff Requirement for a high speed, high altitude bomber.'

The following extracts from this second draft outline the key elements:

1.01　*This specification is issued to cover the design and construction of prototype high speed, high altitude, unarmed bomber.*

2.01　*The aircraft shall be fitted with two RR AJ.65 jet propulsion units.*

2.09　*Means shall be provided to ensure that the crew can abandon the aircraft safely at all flight conditions.... the means provided shall ensure that the crew can cause themselves to be positively ejected from the bulk of the aircraft.*

APPENDIX B.

The Air Staff require a high speed, high altitude bomber capable of being operated in any part of the world.

02　*The normal continuous cruising speed is to be not less than 440 kts at 40,000 ft. The maximum speed at 40,000 ft is to be as high as possible.*

03　*Speed is the prime requirement for this bomber and in order that this shall be as high as possible short range will be accepted but this must not be less than 1,400 nautical miles in still air at 440 kts.*

05　*The service ceiling must not be less than 50,000ft.*

08　*The aircraft must be capable of completing take-off with one engine stopped and of climbing on one engine at 2,000 ft per minute with full war load at sea level.*

09　*Provision is required for carrying a full range of the most modern types of bombs that are likely to be designed within the service life of the aircraft.*

13　*The aircraft is to be laid out for bomb aiming by radar and other mechanical vision systems and for the use of guided projectiles.*

17　*Provision is to be made for a crew of two - one pilot and one radar operator/navigator.*

18　*It is essential that the radar operator/navigator shall have the best possible all round view, particularly to the rear, in order to direct the pilot in the event of rear attack.*

20　*A pressure cabin is to be provided for the pilot and radar/navigator.*

There were a number of other elements detailing equipment fit, test flying and performance envelope – amongst the latter a required full-load take-off run of approx 1,400 yards and a landing run of 1,000 yards. Within the framework of these basic requirements, the designers had a great deal of leeway unlike modern Specifications which dot every 'i' and cross every 't'. Item 18 is interesting. Of the initial design configurations only the back-to-back seating arrangement would have met this requirement and even then it was not envisaged that the navigator would sit in a raised canopy so his view would have been very limited. It appears at first sight to be a hang over from the heavy bomber days when other crew members called the twists and turns for fighter evasion. In the 1950s and 1960s such a notion would have been laughable, consider for example the TSR-2 design with its small forward-vision windows, but by the 1970s it was back in vogue and is now a major consideration in the design of tactical aircraft when every pair of eyes counts. A covering letter to the Air Staff Requirement (ASR) of 15th November stated that the B3/45 was 'intended to be a replacement for the Mosquito unarmed bomber... complementary to a long range, high speed armed bomber.'

By mid 1945 the first contract had been signed for several prototypes to meet the outline specification and in the latter part of the year the project was beginning to take firm root. The basic design concept for a twin-engined, circular fuselage, straight-wing aircraft was agreed and Petter had almost completed gathering his team together. Amongst the first to join the team were three aerodynamicists, Dai Ellis, Ray Creasey and Freddie Page, all of whom went on to have long and successful associations with the Canberra.

On 7th January 1946 a contract was signed for four prototype English Electric A1 aircraft and as the team moved to the former USAF Maintainance Unit at Warton on the northern edge of the River *Ribble*, detailed design work was at full swing. A problem which soon became apparent was the lack of any specialised equipment and testing facilities, especially wind tunnels. A good deal of funding was allocated to these priorities and eventually three tunnels were built: a 9 ft x 7 ft low-speed unit, a jet-induced high-speed tunnel and a water tunnel. It was a few years before they were ready, the low-speed tunnel becoming operational in May 1948 followed by the high-speed tunnel in July of that year and the water tunnel the following March. Other specialist equipment included a structural test rig and a hydraulics rig. All became invaluable in the development of the Canberra but also proved to be a wise investment as the basis of the continued successful development of British aircraft designs at Warton. During 1945 the design moved ahead rapidly. Provision was made for powerful longitudinal trimming using a variable incidence tailplane to counter the strong trim changes, and for spring-tab controls all round to cope with the 500 kts speed. Towards the end of the year Petter gave thought to the setting up of the necessary flight test organisation and recruited Wing Commander Roland Beamont as test pilot. Beamont was a very experienced aviator with two operational fighter tours and development flying, including the Gloster Meteor IV, behind him. He eventually joined the team in May 1947 and in the ensuing years quickly earned the epithet 'Mr Canberra' for his work with the project and his inspired flying sequences. Having established a good basic design, the team made a study in October 1946 for a civil transport version of the A1. This proposed a thirty-four passenger aircraft for stage lengths of 490-930 miles but with a maximum range of 1600 miles with only sixteen passengers. It was to be a straightforward adaptation of the basic A1 but with an enlarged fuselage giving an interior diameter of 10 feet and paired rows of seats.

The aircraft would have had two Rolls-Royce AJ.65s of 6500 lb st, boosted by 1000 lb for take-off and with the probability of more powerful engines becoming available later. The AJ.65s would have given it a cruise speed of 450 mph and it would, therefore, have been a quantum leap forward on the airliners available at the time – similar in its effects to Concorde when it entered service. Although it came to nothing, the project was not finally laid to rest until 1948 when work on the military bomber version speeded up.

A full-scale wood and cardboard mock-up of the basic A1 was built in 1947 and this enabled details of control runs, flaps and undercarriage and the positioning of internal equipment to be worked out. Details of the A1 had been kept fairly secret but the existence of the project was officially revealed when George Strauss, Minister of Supply, made a statement about the project, including the comment that it would have 'about twice the speed of current bombers'.

In the latter part of the year there were murmurings of problems with the Rolls-Royce engines. The new axial compressor was proving troublesome and there was concern over the big single-stage turbine that drove it. As an insurance against delay, the second prototype was re-engineered to take two Rolls-Royce Nene centrifugal engines of 5,000 lb st each. This presented an engine nacelle problem and the team had to settle for wing-mounted engines à la Meteor rather than the neat semi-buried wing-root arrangement. Nevertheless, work progressed steadily and by late 1948 component assembly was almost complete and early the following year final assembly and testing in No.25 hangar at Warton pointed to a Spring first flight. Another revolutionary

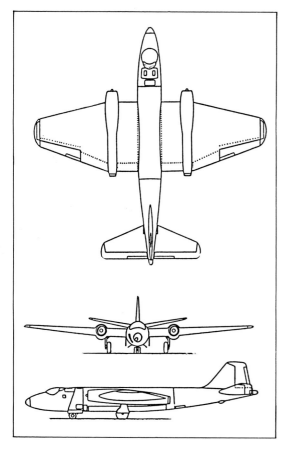

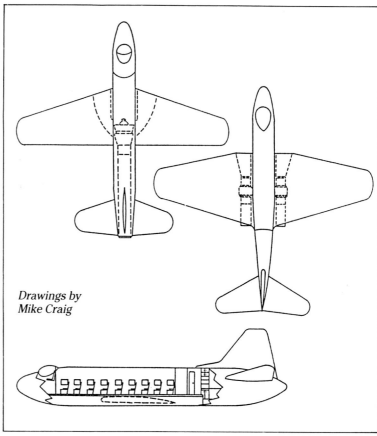

*Drawings by
Mike Craig*

English Electric Canberra B.2 three-view.

Early ideas for the A1 - including a 34 seat passenger variant.

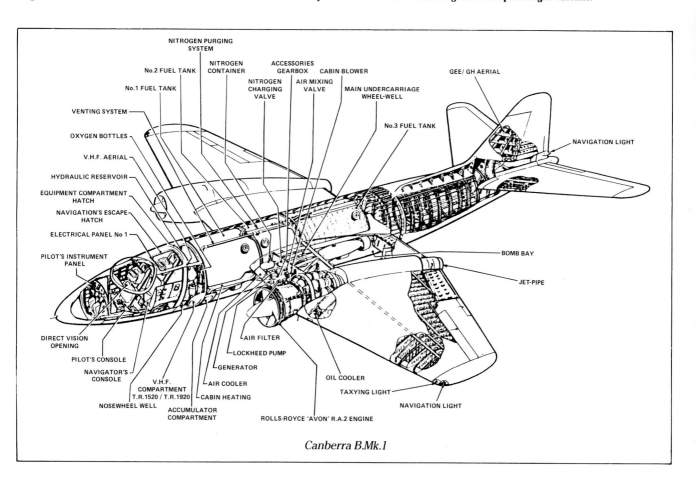

Canberra B.Mk.1

move was the adoption of jigging and tooling from the outset, hardly anything was handmade. Although this meant that the first prototype took some time to complete, development was rapid. The envisaged hiccup with the Avon engines did not occur but a more serious problem arose when it became obvious that the radar bombing system, in many ways the nub of the original idea, was a long way behind schedule and not likely to be available on time. With the increased desire to replace outdated types it was decided to modify the design to prevent delay in entry to service. Specification B5/47 was written to cover the changes – primarily the provision of a visual bombing system (clear nose with prone crew position) using the T2 bomb sight, and the presence of a third crew member to act as bomb aimer. At the time doubts were expressed in some circles over the accuracy of visual bombing from 30,000 to 40,000 ft and over the 'operational validity' of the concept. This was highlighted in a series of memos that declared that the H2S Mk.9 radar system was not going to be retrofitted to the B3/45 as it now fitted the time scale of the B9/48 and B35/46 bombers. It was even suggested that the B3/45 was no longer needed and that the whole project should be scrapped!

However, no such decision was taken and in March 1949 the unusual step was taken of placing a production order before the prototype had made its first flight. An Air Council Memo of a note from the Vice Chief of the Air Staff (VCAS) dated 1st March 1949 gave the details:

'It is not anticipated that there will be any inherent faults in it (the English Electric twin-jet) which will not be impossible of elimination in the production version and that in order to ensure early delivery of the aircraft into service, a pilot order should now be placed. This would enable the firm to set up production lines and prepare the way for large scale production when required. Five versions have been designed: Tactical bomber (B5/47), Blind bomber (B3/45), Target marker bomber (B22/48), Long range PR aircraft (PR31/46), Trainer (T11/49).

'The most urgent need is for a jet bomber for Bomber Command for high speed, high altitude operations and a PR aircraft to replace the Mosquito PR.34. Thus the initial requirement is for the B22/48, PR31/46 and the T11/49. We are relying on this type for the early re-armament of squadrons equipped with aircraft which are already outmoded; and if at all possible we wish to avoid placing orders for delivery in 1951 of obsolete aircraft to maintain our squadrons until new production can give satisfactory numbers of jet types. I propose an order of thirty B22/48, thirty PR31/46 and fifteen T11/49.'

Other sources have specified the initial order as ninety B5/47 (became the B.2), thirty-four PR31/46 (became the PR.3) and eight dual-control trainers T11/49 (became the T.4). There is also a variation in the Specification numbers with some recording the T.4 as the T2/49 and the PR.3 as the PR31/47, the company designators were T2/49 and PR31/46. The original trainer specification was called for on T11/47 and it would seem that the official memo was in error in mentioning T11/49. T2/49 was a developed trainer specification to cover production aircraft.

First Flight

The Rolls-Royce RA.2 engines arrived in March and the tempo of work increased. The first prototype English Electric A1, VN799, was rolled out of the hangar at Warton on 2nd May, resplendent in its 'Petter blue' paint scheme, for engine runs. The engine no's were A13/A617963 and A14/A617964. Taxying tests took place on 8th May, and the following day Beamont took the aircraft for a series of short straight 'hops' to check the responses from the flying controls. Three 'hops' were made, bringing the nose off the ground at 55 kts and the main wheels (unstick) at 75-80 kts. The first hop was to check the elevator feel and response, the second to check the ailerons and the third the rudder. All went well and so the first flight was scheduled for the first day that conditions proved favour-able - visibility 10 miles, nil or less than half cloud cover, less than 20 kts wind with less than 10 kts crosswind over the runway. The morning of Friday 13th May 1949 met the required conditions and despite what some considered an inauspicious date the flight went ahead. In the early morning Beamont took-off accompanied by a Vampire chase aircraft and climbed to 10,000 ft; all was going well and he viewed it as a 'smooth and quiet aeroplane'. However, he found a problem with the rudder as small inputs gave an abrupt lurch in yaw. Beamont took the aircraft back to Warton for an uneventful landing after what had been otherwise a very successful first flight. However, one of his comments is interesting – he found the heat through the canopy rather uncomfortable. The one-piece blown canopy had been another innovation in the aircraft design and despite various modifications over the years this 'greenhouse' effect and its consequent crew discomfort has been the main criticism, if such it can be called, by generation after generation of Canberra aircrew.

English Electric A1 (Canberra) prototype VN799 with its original rounded fin and rudder. After the first flight this was modified to a squared-off shape to reduce the balance area - the only major modification required to the airframe.

Beamont was of the opinion that the rudder problem was overbalance and that the rudder would have to be modified before the next flight. Despite initial objections from the design office it was decided to modify the rudder by reducing the horn balance area in stages, this being comparatively easy as it was a wooden component.

Above: **First prototype VN799 on one of its short hops, conducted to test control response, the day before its official first flight, which was on 13th May 1949.** *BAC AW/FA.8*

The Rt Hon R.G.Menzies, Prime Minister of Australia, performing the naming ceremony on WD929 the first production B.2, at RAF Biggin Hill, Kent, 19th January 1951.

This led to the 'squaring-off' of the original rounded fin which had until then been of very conventional shape.

Throughout May the test flights with VN799 continued and problems with vibration and 'snaking' were all that hindered an otherwise faultless test programme. The vibration and rudder problem was cured by reducing the size of the elevator horns, mass balances and rudder horns. The 'snaking' (directional oscillation) had been wake turbulence behind the canopy and was cured by the addition of a fairing. By the end of August the aircraft had covered the performance envelope to 42,000 ft, Mach 0.8 and 470 kts IAS and in the period 6th July to 31st August a series of thirty-six flights had given handling clearance throughout the initial design envelope. On 31st August the initial design

speed of 470 kts was achieved, giving the required margin of 20 kts over the proposed initial service limit of 450 IAS (Indicated Air Speed). Seldom had such a new aircraft suffered so few problems. As one indication of confidence the go-ahead was given for the aircraft to be displayed at the Farnborough Show in September and Beamont set about putting together a six-minute routine; he had already come to see his bomber as an aircraft with more of a fighter performance and this would be reflected in his handling of the Canberra at this and other displays.

A Name is Chosen

During the test programme the aircraft had been given the name *Canberra*, following the practise of naming British bombers after cities. It was not until 19th January 1951 that the official naming ceremony took place at Biggin Hill when Mr R. G. Menzies, Prime Minister of Australia, did the honour. It has been suggested by some that the name Canberra was chosen to encourage the Australian Government to choose the aircraft to replace its Lincoln bombers. However, *Flight* in January 1952 ascribes the choice of name to Sir George Nelson, chairman and managing director of English Electric, who was asked by the Air Ministry to suggest a name. 'Being a fervent believer that the peace and happiness of the world depend on the unity and understanding of the British Commonwealth, I sat down to think of a suitable name for this machine to further that object, and chose Canberra, the capital of its farthest flung country, the Commonwealth of Australia. This was immediately accepted by the Air Council.' For whatever reason, in the summer of 1949 the Australians had chosen the Canberra to be licence-built at the Government Aircraft Factories at Melbourne.

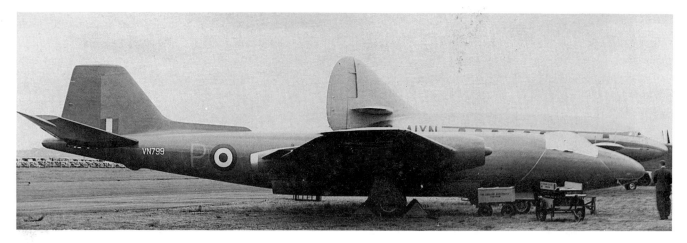

VN799 with modified squared fin/rudder, and fin fillet. *E. J. Riding.* **VN799 with fillet removed, Farnborough Sept 1951.** *F. G. Swanborough*

Below: **Leading members of the design team. Left to right: F.D.Crowe (chief structure designer), D.I.Ellis (chief aerodynamacist) S.C.Harrison (chief draughtsman), A.E.Ellison (chief designer), W.E.W.Petter (chief engineer), R.P.Beamont (chief test pilot), D.B.Smith, F.W.Page (chief stressman), H.S.Howatt.** *via Bruce Robertson*

Farnborough Impressions

Beamont took VN799 to Farnborough on 4th September, freshly painted blue and highly polished for its public debut. On the first day of the show, 6th September, VN799 taxied out with a light fuel load of only 3,000lb and Beamont prepared to show the aircraft to the world. Unfortunately, the port engine flamed-out on the runway, starved of fuel when the tanks were not switched in time. The aircraft was given a later slot in the display - the last. This time there were no problems and Beamont put the sleek blue aircraft

through its paces with tight turns, steep climbs and high-speed low level runs. At the end of the sequence he noticed that the starboard engine instruments and the test instruments were dead; the Air Traffic tower called that bits were dropping off the aircraft. An inspection after landing showed that the test instrument package in the bomb bay had torn loose. Amongst all the other great British aircraft at this SBAC show the Canberra was a great success and the aviation press was ecstatic.

'The biggest military surprise of the show was the English Electric Co. sky-blue

Canberra jet bomber. US observers were not impressed with the Canberra's straight wing and somewhat conventional configuration on the ground. But in the air, the combination of the test pilot R. P. Beamont and the 12,000 lb thrust from the two axial Avons made the Canberra behave in spectacular fashion. Its speed range from 500 mph to less than 100 mph was ably demonstrated by Beamont, who followed the high speed passes on the deck with an approach using full flaps, gear down and bomb bay doors open that slowed the Canberra to less than 100 mph. At this speed he rocked the big bomber violently to show the full control available as it approached stalling speed. Beamont whipped the bomber, designed to carry a 10,000 lb bomb load, around the deck like a fighter, flying it through a series of slow rolls, high-speed turns and remarkable rates of climb.' So ran a report in the American journal *Aviation Week*.

The European press was equally enthusiastic with *Flight* reporting 'Wing Commander Beamont's introductory performance in our first jet bomber was historic. The initial climb, with the Avons roaring and rumbling far into the distance, would not have shamed a Meteor. Then the beautiful medium bomber bore down fast along the runway and rolled away (one roll in each direction), its blue shape seeming, chameleon-like, to change its hue against the varicoloured clouds.... A new aircraft has never been more convincingly demonstrated.'

For the next five years the Canberra was a frequent headline item.

VX165 in Bomber Command colours.
EE Co AW/FA/46

VN813 the second prototype, was fitted with Rolls-Royce Nene engines and is seen here at Burnaston in June 1951.

VN828 the third prototype, with dorsal fin removed, at Warton on test with English Electric Co. *EE Co AW/FA/36*

VN850 the fourth prototype, seen during wing-tip tank tests, May 1950, Warton.

Development Continued

The initial flourish of publicity over, the flight test team got down to completing the contractors handling trials in preparation to handing the aircraft to A & AEE at Boscombe Down for service trials. VN799 was duly delivered in October and over the next month was put through its paces and thoroughly tested. The initial report was favourable .. '.. has proved its worth as a first-class flying machine and the criticisms which have come to light are of only a minor nature.'

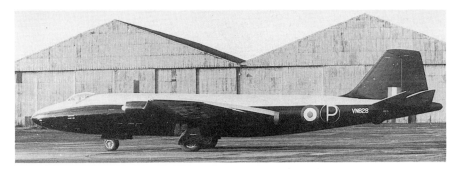

By the end of the year the other three B.1 prototypes had made their first flights:
9th November 1949 – VN813
2nd Prototype, Nene engines.
22nd November 1949 – VN828
3rd Prototype, Avon engines.
20th December 1949 – VN850
4th Prototype, Avon RA.2 engines.

The fourth prototype was the first of the series to be fitted with jettisonable tip tanks, cylindrical tanks each holding 250 gallons of fuel, positioned at the extreme underside of each wing tip. Tip tanks gave

Above: **VX169, second B.2 prototype, refuelling at Warton in 1952. WE135, the first production PR.3, is in the foreground.**

Bottom: **WJ971, the first Avro produced Canberra, on its first flight 25th Nov 1952.**

Below: **This shows the cylindrical fuselage so beloved by Petter. WP514 was a B.2 built as a replacement for WD939 which was diverted to RAAF service; in spite of its later serial it was delivered in August 1951 to 101 Squadron at Binbrook.**

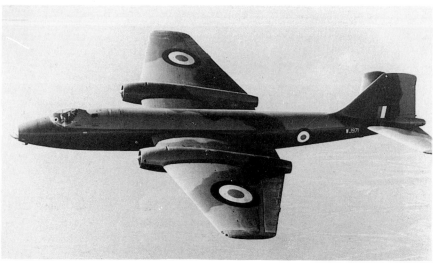

the aircraft an appreciable increase in fuel which at high level and with low fuel consumption, a feature of the Avons, gave a significant increase in range. However, it also meant an IAS limit of 365 kts – although many crews, including the authors, can vouch for the fact that the tips don't come off if you exceed 365! VN850 gave the first overseas showing of the Canberra with a display at Paris Orly on 11th June 1950, once again to rapturous enthusiasm. The sleek lines and fighter-like performance made it a winner wherever it went. 1950 saw the start of the Canberra's long string of records when, on 16th January, VN828 reached 50,000 ft. By the end of the 1950s the Canberra held nineteen distance and three height records. As the world was hailing the new jet bomber, work was going ahead on the B.2 and two prototypes were built. The first, VX165, made its maiden flight on 23rd April 1950 followed on 2nd August by VX169. Both were fitted with Avon 101 (RA.3) engines of 6,500 lb st, the production standard engine unit. The first production aircraft, WD929, flew from Samlesbury on 8th October 1950 beginning a long era of Canberra flight testing from that airfield.

In the midst of this activity came the stunning news that the world was at war again. On 25th June 1950 war broke out in Korea.

Production Surge

The run-down of military capability and the low level of Government interest in military projects after the Second World War had left the RAF and the aircraft industry in a poor state. What re-equipment programmes there were were based on long-term development and gradual replacement. Now the crunch had come and it was decided to increase arms production by every possible means. It was out of the question for English Electric to produce more than five or so Canberra airframes a month and so contracts were placed with other companies to produce the aircraft. A. V. Roe, Handley Page and Short Bros & Harland were roped-in to produce airframes and Bristol, Napier and Standard Motors to produce engines. The Avro works at Chadderton and Woodford tooled up and their first aircraft, WJ971, flew on 25th November 1952. Handley page at Cricklewood had WJ564 airborne on 5th January 1953 but Shorts at Queens Island, Belfast had beaten them all, having WH853 airborne on 30th October 1952. The somewhat outdated, even farcical notion of rushing extra factories into 'wartime' production of an advanced aircraft became obvious when within two years of the production lines starting they were closing again (an armistice had been signed in Korea in 1953). Avro and Handley Page had each produced seventy-five aircraft, the maximum rate for all lines combined had been thirteen aircraft a month, an excellent achievement considering the difficulties and a testament to the simplicity and excellence of the design. However, despite the 'standard' design of the Canberra there were problems later when trying to fit, for example, an HP door to an EE built aircraft! The Shorts line continued its involvement with the Canberra for many more years and from its stable came the ultimate Canberra – the PR.9. In the midst of all this activity the B.2 received its CA release (clearance into service) in the spring of 1951. A series of Air Council Memoranda for 1950-51 give details of initial orders and costings. The provisional cost of a B.5 varied from £101,973 to £78,000 depending on the size of the order and for a PR.3 from £95,454 to £88,888.

Structural Details

All Canberra marks, except the PR.9, had essentially the same airframe; the major differences between marks being with engines, fuel systems and internal equipment (see Appendices). The fuselage, as Petter intended, was of circular section assembled from standard frames and longitudinals making production easier. The front fuselage incorporated the pressure cockpit for the crew with a sloping pressure bulkhead to which the rear ejection seat rails were attached. This was one of the weak spots of the airframe and in a crash-landing the aircraft was likely to break apart at this point – no bad thing as it put the engines and the fuel apart from the crew. The main entrance door was positioned on the starboard side just forward of the wing and was hinged upwards. Clambering in and out through this door was a frequent cause of complaint and a great many sore knees! If you were really lucky the groundcrew would search out a set of steps, which generally meant a bang on the head from the door for climbing too high. This door arrangement on the starboard side was standard to all marks of Canberra except the PR.9 which was unique in being the only RAF Canberra to have two access points – hinged canopy and nose.

Internally the arrangement of aircraft varied from mark to mark and even within marks depending on modification state. The pilot, in all marks, sat on an ejection seat on the left hand side of the aircraft under a blown, or, in later interdictor marks, bubble, canopy. In all marks but the PR.9 this canopy was fixed but could be blown off by a series of explosive bolts. The canopy jettison system was selected 'Live' before take-off although it could be blown at any stage, and was not infrequently done so by accident. The Navigator(s) seating arrangement varied greatly , when ejection seats were provided these were attached to the pressure bulkhead. There was no canopy just a selection of small windows, depending on the mark. Above the seat was a 'frangible' hatch which could, like the pilot's canopy, be blown off by explosive bolts. Alternatively, the nav could eject through the in-place hatch which would break-up under the impact of the seat. For those with no Martin Baker rapid exit system it was a case of leaping out of the normal entry door. Some versions had a wind-break fitted which shielded the 'jumper' from the wind effects as he followed the advice 'to dive under the leading edge!' There were a number of successful aircraft abandonments using this procedure – and a chest parachute. No less than eight ejection seat marks, seventeen different seats if variants are taken into account, have been fitted to Canberra aircraft. These ranged from the very basic and simple Martin Baker 1C seat used on the prototypes and early marks – up to B(I)8 – to the somewhat more sophisticated seats of later marks such as the 3CS and 4QS fitted to pilot and nav stations respectively in the PR.9. The following list gives a complete breakdown of seats as fitted to the various marks of Canberra.

Seat Type	Aircraft Mark
1C	Prototype, B1 (all positions) B2, B6, (all positions) B(I)8 (pilot only)
1CN	B2, PR3, B6, B(I)6, B15, B16, (all positions) T.4 (navigator only)
2CA1 Mk.1 & 2	B2, PR3, B6, PR7, B15, B16 (pilot)
2CA2 Mk.1, 2, 3, 4	B2, PR3, B6, PR7, B15, B16 (navigator/bomb aimer) T4 (navigator only)
2CB Mk.1 & 2	B(I)8 (pilot only)
3CS Mk.1 & 2	PR9 (pilot)
3CT 1/2 Mk.1, 2, 3	T4 (right-hand pilot)
4QS Mk.1 & 2	PR9 (navigator)
Special facility aircraft:	
2CA1 Mk.2	E15, T17, TT18, T19, T22 (pilot)
2CA2 Mk.4	E15, T17, TT18, T19, T22 (rear positions)

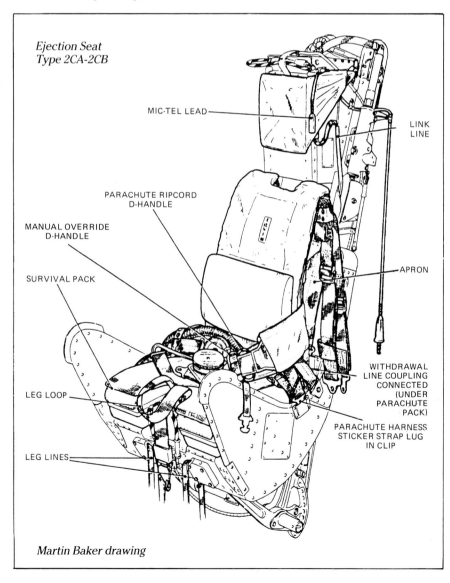

Ejection Seat Type 2CA-2CB

MIC-TEL LEAD

LINK LINE

PARACHUTE RIPCORD D-HANDLE

MANUAL OVERRIDE D-HANDLE

APRON

SURVIVAL PACK

LEG LOOP

WITHDRAWAL LINE COUPLING CONNECTED (UNDER PARACHUTE PACK)

PARACHUTE HARNESS STICKER STRAP LUG IN CLIP

LEG LINES

Martin Baker drawing

Modifications and improvements were introduced at regular intervals as ejection seat technology advanced to meet the increased demands of operational flying. The early seats fulfilled the requirement of ejecting the crew from the body of the aircraft and were designed to do no more than that. Operation of the seat was by means of the single 'face screen' handle on top of the seat which, when pulled sharply down, brought a protective blind over the face and at the same time fired the main seat cartridge which pushed the seat up the rail and clear of the aircraft. A line attached to the aircraft then deployed a drogue parachute to slow the seat down and stop it tumbling so that the occupant could release himself from the seat and operate his parachute. All ejection seats were eventually modified to be fully automatic in that separation from the seat and deployment of the parachute was automatic as soon as certain parameters had been met. A further improvement was the addition of a second firing handle between the legs, the 'seat pan' handle, which was both an alternative and a back-up to the face-screen handle, indeed in the low level environment this became the preferred handle as it was quicker and easier to use.

The entrance door was also the way out for a crew member whose ejection seat had failed to fire, an almost unheard of occurrence. In this circumstance it was a case of operating the manual separation handle to get free of the seat harness which left you attached to the parachute, waddle to the door and leap out. If the hatch had been blown and it was too difficult to get to the door then another alternative was to get the pilot, if he was still

there, to roll the aircraft inverted and let gravity do the rest. The problem with this technique was the better than evens chance of being hit by the fin!

One pilot had the 'misfortune' to return without his navigator. The aircraft had gone out of control during a handling exercise and, entering cloud, the crew had decided that the navigator would eject if the aircraft had not recovered by a certain height. In due course out went the nav, at the same instant the pilot yelled 'don't go! It's alright.'. . . Silence. One sheepish pilot went back to the OCU with the ejection seat 'pole' sticking up from the nav's cockpit. Fortunately the nav was picked up from his dinghy; his barnacle-encrusted bone-dome was fished out of the sea years later.

The only problem with the canopy was its tendency to mist up during rapid descents or on humid days and many an approach was made with nil visibility through the front of the canopy. On the left front of the canopy was the DV, or 'direct vision' panel window which was electrically heated to keep it clear. It could also be opened in flight if the aircraft was not pressurised and the speed was not too great. Because of its offset position it did entail a somewhat crabbed approach to the runway before kicking the rudder central just before touchdown.

The centre fuselage had provision for the bomb bay with the three fuel tanks above. The front and centre tanks were flexible self-sealing cells with internal bracing and the rear tank a crash-proof collapsible bag. Tank capacities were 512 gallons (4000 lbs) No.1 tank, 317 gallons (2500 lbs) No.2 tank and 545 gallons

(4250 lbs) in No.3 tank, giving a total internal fuel of 1374 gallons (10750 lbs). To this could be added the 250 gallons (1900 lbs) for each underwing tip tank when these were fitted. There were two electrically driven pumps in each fuselage tank with the port side feeding the No.1 engine and the starboard side feeding the No.2 engine via collector tanks. Thus any or all the fuel tanks could be used to feed either engine. Later marks had more tanks and therefore carried greater quantities of fuel, the PR.7 and PR.9 having 22,184 lbs internal fuel.

Despite the incorporation of many and various prevention devices on the throttle/fuel controls, the early Avons were prone to surging if even half-way mishandled. It was important to open the throttles smoothly and avoid the temptation to slam the throttles forward in the search for instant power. Engine surge could vary from the light 'pop' surge which could be easily cured by throttle manipulation to the quite heavy banging of a 'locked-in' surge which meant that the engine would have to be shut down and relit. According to the *Pilot's Notes* it was only above 3000 ft, as the effect of the acceleration control unit was reduced, that rapid acceleration of the engine to 5000 rpm could 'promote overheating and surging', but in fact one of the most likely times for a surge was during a touch and go 'roller' landing or on overshoot.

Avon engine cutaway illustration, courtesy of Rolls-Royce. Powerplant afficionados will realise that this particular variant would be more at home in a Hunter, than in a Canberra!

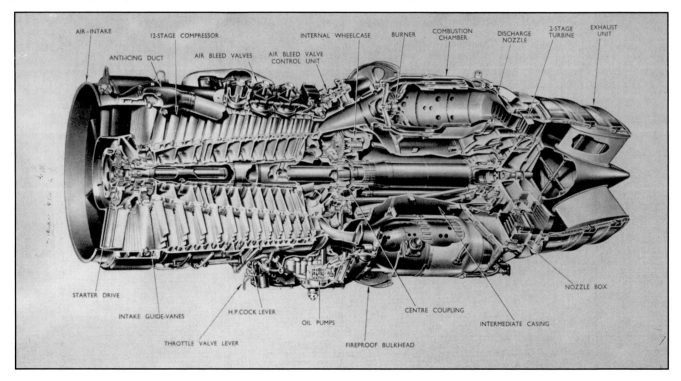

Apart from this perhaps unfortunate trait, the Avon series proved remarkably efficient and reliable. It was a durable engine quite capable of disposing of the odd over-adventurous bird without too much difficulty. Birdstrikes are a fact of life when flying low level and the Canberra, engine and airframe, dealt well with the hazard. With luck the bird would pass through the engine, giving the tell-tale smell of 'burning chicken' in the cockpit, without causing any major damage or at least not causing the engine to pack up. Subsequent ground inspection of post-bird Avons revealed some horrendous degrees of damage to the turbine blades but the engine had happily carried on working!

Engine starting was by means of a single – in later marks triple – breech cartridge starter in the intake 'bullet'. Pressing the starter button fired the cartridge which wound the engine up rapidly to 1500-1800 rpm which was enough for it to reach self-sustaining rpm, light up and settle down to idle at 2750 ± 100 rpm. Sitting in the aircraft could become quite unpleasant when the starboard engine started because the interior of the aircraft often filled with the fumes from the cartridge – an unforgettable smell and taste, which often prompted a quick burst of 100% oxygen. The starter cartridges were good solid chunks of brass and were in great demand worldwide either for their metal content or as souvenir ashtrays. At some

overseas airfields it was difficult to get service from the groundcrew until a used starter cartridge was offered up! This caused the odd problem for PR.9 crews who with their Avpin starter system had no cartridges to barter!

The Avon was also reasonable from the engineering point of view with engine changes being quite straightforward. ECU (Engine Change Unit) replacement involved removing the detachable engine cowlings, which also gave good access to the engines for routine servicing and maintenance, and then lifting the entire engine on a sling. Engines could not usually be repaired on base but had to be returned to the manufacturers. This is an appropriate place to take a more detailed

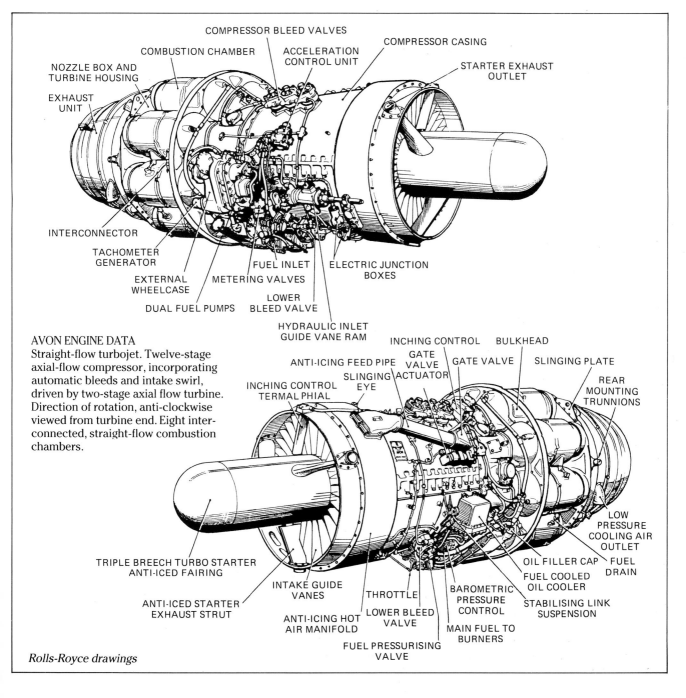

AVON ENGINE DATA
Straight-flow turbojet. Twelve-stage axial-flow compressor, incorporating automatic bleeds and intake swirl, driven by two-stage axial flow turbine. Direction of rotation, anti-clockwise viewed from turbine end. Eight interconnected, straight-flow combustion chambers.

Rolls-Royce drawings

look at the Avon series of engines as used in the Canberra. The Avon resulted from the belief held by Rolls-Royce designers that an axial-flow, rather than centrifugal, compressor would result in a smaller diameter and lighter engine as well as giving a lower Specific Fuel Consumption (SFC) because of its higher efficiency and pressure ratio. This led to a concentration of effort to produce an engine with a design thrust of 6500 lb for the proposed high-altitude light bomber. The outcome was the RA.1 engine weighing 2400 lb and with a single stage compressor. However, from its first run in March 1947 the RA.1 gave problems and was not able to meet its specifications.

Improvements were made and the next engine, the RA.2, began testing in January 1948 with features such as air bleed valves and inlet-guide vanes to improve the running efficiency of the compressor. The RA.2 took to the air in Lancastrian VM372 in August in place of the outboard Merlins and, with a rating of 6000 lb, went on to power the prototype Canberra on its first flight in May 1949. By that time the RA.3 was under test (April) and after flight trials in a Lancastrian at the end of the year went into production as the Avon Mk.1 in July 1950. This engine met the specification for 6500 lb with an acceptable SFC.

Towards the end of 1950 the pace of Canberra production, and thus the requirement for engines, increased and the Engine Division of Bristol Aeroplane Co and that of Napiers were given contracts to build the Avon. In the period 1953-55 Bristols built 240 engines for the Canberra whilst Napiers constructed 200 between 1953-56. Within months, bench tests had taken the RA.3 to 7500 lb and with a requirement for more powerful engines for the new generation of fighter aircraft the RA.7 was developed.

The RA.7 incorporated the developments used in the high-rated bench test RA.3s but one of its more important features was the incorporation of an engine anti-icing system. This utilized hot air bled from the compressors to heat the intake struts, inlet guide vane and starter fairing. The air intake lip had a separate hot air bleed. As the Avon 109 it was used in the production run of Canberra B.6s, PR.7s and B(I)8s. The final production Avon engine for the Canberra was the RA.24 (Avon 206) developed for the PR.9. The first of this series went on test in February 1955 and almost doubled the thrust of previous Canberra Avons by producing 11,250 lb thrust. Avon production for Canberras, amounted to a total of 1361 RA.3s, 690 RA.7s and 92 RA.24s between 1950 and 1959. See the Canberra Variants and Technical Details Appendices.

Hardly any two Canberras were alike inside. So many minor and major mods and changes were made even to the same mark that no single description of a Canberra interior can really be given. One thing they did, and do have in common is the smell. This is an indefinable quality but all aircraft types seem to have a particular smell and it is something they do not lose, even the PR.3 in the RAF Museum still has a typical Canberra smell about it! However, some items did not change or changed very little. The pilot end of the flying controls was not a stick but a 'control column handwheel', known as the 'spectacles'. This carried various switches and buttons and moved fore and aft to pitch, or turned like a steering wheel to roll the aircraft. In the early B.2s the handwheel carried the wheelbrake lever in the centre, the tailplane incidence (trim) control switch, a press-to-transmit switch and the airbrake switch. Controls and their positions changed mod to mod and mark to

mark, with weapons controls appearing on the stick in the inderdictor marks and camera controls in the recce marks, but the basics stayed the same. Internal equipment likewise varied depending on the role of the aircraft and the modification state but there was nothing startlingly new in the early bomber versions.

Aircraft performance was another variable depending on aircraft mark and fit. For the standard B.2s a full power take-off would give an unstick speed of 95-110 kts and a safety speed of 140 kts. This was the Canberra killer gap – the difference between the speed at take-off and the speed at which the aircraft could safely be flown on one engine. Lose an engine between the two and you had a major problem. If it was not possible to plonk it back down on the runway or if the aircraft had started to roll under asymmetric power there was only one alternative – eject.

Climbing speed was 330 kts becoming Mach 0·72 at around 20,000 ft. The flight planning chart below shows various climb/cruise/descent profiles for a B.2 related to fuel consumption and still air (i.e. no wind) range. This gives a maximum range for an aircraft with internal fuel of nearly 1600 miles, cruising at 48,000 ft and running the fuel down to the operational minimum of 250 gallons. However, if the aircraft operated at 360 kts at sea level the range reduced to a mere 500 miles, although this compares favourably with modern strike/attack aircraft capability.

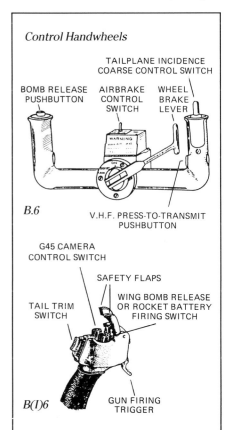

Control Handwheels

BOMB RELEASE PUSHBUTTON
AIRBRAKE CONTROL SWITCH
TAILPLANE INCIDENCE COARSE CONTROL SWITCH
WHEEL BRAKE LEVER
B.6
V.H.F. PRESS-TO-TRANSMIT PUSHBUTTON

G45 CAMERA CONTROL SWITCH
SAFETY FLAPS
TAIL TRIM SWITCH
WING BOMB RELEASE OR ROCKET BATTERY FIRING SWITCH
B(I)6
GUN FIRING TRIGGER

The rear fuselage was conventional with fin and tailplanes, the tailplane having a 10 degree dihedral. The straight wing tapered sharply outboard of the engines to a rounded tip. Load was taken by a single main spar which was a built-up beam with light alloy booms, virtually a single-spar structure in port and starboard units mounted direct on the fuselage side. The structure was covered with constant-thickness alloy sheet flush-riveted for aerodynamic effect. Wings are funny things – the 13 Squadron engineers could not work out why a particular PR.7 would not fly correctly. Many air tests and investigations later the problem was solved – the aircraft had been given one PR.7 wing and one B(I)8 wing! The fin was unconventional in that it was largely built of laminated spruce with a plywood skin, although the rudder post was metal.

Control surfaces were conventional with ailerons, elevators and rudder, the latter two having balance horns. Split flaps were fitted in four positions under the wings. The airbrakes were unusual, consisting of 21 'spokes', nine above the wing and twelve below. To quote from the *Pilots Notes* for the B.2 'the airbrakes are effective at high IAS but below 300 kts they are ineffective and do not help to reduce speed for the approach and landing. At high mach numbers their use promotes increased buffeting with little decelerating effect and their use above Mach 0·82 is not recommended.' The best 'airbrake' at lower speeds was the bomb doors and these could be used quite effectively to slow the aircraft down, this was especially useful during fixed power approaches when the throttles could not be used for speed control. It was, however, vital to remember to close the bomb doors before touchdown or risk scraping them along the runway. However, the most important aspect to remember with the bomb bay/bomb doors was the presence of a pannier. This 'metal box' was fastened to the bomb beam and used to carry all manner of items – not least being the crew's personal kit. Opening the bomb bay with a pannier full of kit led to the inevitable shower of shoes', shreddies' etc!

Opposite page: **Avon RA.7 being lowered back into a 98 Squadron E.15. Note the triple starter cartridge. An engine change was a major task but routine maintenance was easily carried out through numerous inspection panels.** *98 Squadron records*

231 OCU B.2 WH637 broken down into its main component parts after an accident at Rufforth in September 1952. These three views highlight the main Canberra details of circular fuselage (note bomb bay cut-out), engine mounting on slender wing, and dihedral tailplane. The aircraft had made a successful wheels-up landing and was being recovered by 60 MU.

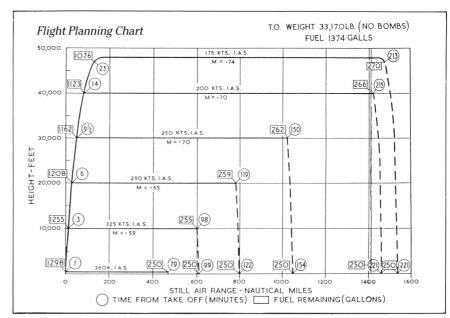

Flight Planning Chart

T.O. WEIGHT 33,170LB. (NO BOMBS)
FUEL 1374 GALLS

First Delivery to RAF
On 25th May 1951 Roland Beamont delivered the first Canberra to the RAF when he flew WD936 to RAF Binbrook for handover to 101 Squadron. The arrival was his standard sharp display and beat-up, an eye-opener to the assembled 'bomber' personnel. The formality over, Beamont was persuaded to let the Station Commander, Group Captain 'Wally' Sheen, fly the aircraft in the afternoon while he observed and instructed from the rumble seat. This fold-away seat positioned to one side of the entry door was used either by instructors to observe what the student pilot was doing, another crew member as an alternative to his normal crew station, or an extra passenger. It is said that the masters of Bomber Command were quick to react to this impromptu display and a letter was sent to Warton stating that there were to be no more aerobatics at RAF stations and that such antics were not suitable for bomber aircraft. A sad comment but the bomber barons of multi-engine background knew nothing else – after all, a bomber was a bomber. The Canberra had been designed to be a quantum leap from the Lincolns and Washingtons of Bomber Command and so it was, it now remained to see how it would be employed.

Other features of the airframe and systems will be examined in later chapters. In essence the Canberra airframe was both simple and robust, an ideal combination for a multi-role aircraft. It is said that many a true word is spoken in jest and when the 'new' NATO aircraft was designated MRCA (Multi Role Combat Aircraft) it was said in many circles that this stood for 'Must Refurbish Canberra Again!'

101 Squadron's first Canberra, WD936, arrives at Binbrook on 25th May 1951, following a typically impressive impromptu display by Roland Beamont.

Early production Canberra B.2s WD929, WD930 and WD931 at Warton, along with 3rd prototype VN828 and a 101 Squadron Lincoln, early 1951. *BAC/AW/8*

Chapter Two

Bomber Command - The New Era

The build-up of the Binbrook Canberra Wing meant that Bomber Command had entered the jet age. It is worth looking at the aircraft which were replaced by the Canberra. The Main Force element of Bomber Command consisted primarily of the Avro Lincoln B.2 and the Boeing Washington B.1 (B-29) and it was these two types that were replaced first. The Lincoln B.2, powered by four 1750 hp Merlins, had a service ceiling of 22,000 ft and top speed of 290 mph, carried a bomb load of 14,000 lbs and had a range of about 3,250 miles. The type entered service in late 1945 and eventually equipped twenty-three squadrons, seeing active service in Malaya before the last aircraft left service in 1963. The Washington, a MAP (Military Aid Program) aircraft from America was more advanced, powered by four 2200 hp Wright R-3350-23 engines, giving a maximum speed of 350 mph and a ceiling of 35,000 ft. It carried a bombload of 17,000 lbs for 1,000 miles or 6,000 lbs for 3,000 miles. It had a crew of 10 in pressurized compartments and had a great deal of self defence armament. The comparable figures for the Canberra show a much greater performance envelope with speed 450 mph plus and ceiling 45,000 ft, but a much reduced bombload of only 6000 lbs and 1600 mile range. A crew of three as against the seven of the Lincoln and the ten of the Washington, also implied the need for a radical re-think on operational employment and aircrew establishment. It must be borne in mind, however, that in sections of the Air Ministry the Canberra was looked on as a stopgap measure pending delivery of new large jet bombers in the classic tradition.

This was to be far too radical for many senior officers to accept and there was an active lobby against the Canberra in its early years who would have jumped at any major fault in the aircraft as an indication that the days of the heavy bomber were not dead.

The overall plan of Canberra re-equipment within Main Force was for twenty-four squadrons each with a Unit Establishment (UE) of ten Canberra B.2s to be organised in Wings of four squadrons at each of six bases, thus giving a total bomber force of 240 aircraft. Initial Air Staff thoughts were for a total force of 560 Canberras, of all marks, in the UK, all for the support of SHAPE (Supreme HQ Allied Powers Europe) in the European theatre.

The basic concept of employment of this essentially medium bomber force did not change from that of the post-war heavies, that is, Main Force tactics of mass formations of bombers passing over the target at medium level. The hope was that the blind bombing capability of the new type would prove decisive when the planned radar bombing systems entered service. However, in the meantime the Canberra would have to rely on visual bombing and on Gee-H as the primary blind-bombing aid.

The transition period is aptly illustrated in this Hemswell formation, circa 1954. Although a little short on contrast, it features three Lincoln B.IIs (RA672, RA662 and RE415) and three indecipherable Canberra B.2s of 139 Squadron (note the fin flashes).

The other main type being replaced was the Washington B.1 (B-29), seen here as part of a display at Hemswell, 19th September 1953, which also includes Mosquito T.3 VA928, plus it is thought, NF.36 RL239. This view shows the B-29, Lincoln and Canberra together - an interesting comparison.

Blind Bombing - Gee-H

Gee-H was a logical development of the wartime Gee system which had been developed in the early 1940s to provide accurate location information to aircraft and enable blind bombing of targets in Germany. The G stood for the Grid of position lines which fixed the aircraft's position but this was changed to Gee for security reasons. In essence, the aircraft receiver picked up pulses from three ground stations, one Master station linked by radio to two Slave stations, simultaneously. This enabled the navigator to read off the distance between the stations on the CRT timebase and compare these readings with a chart overprinted with a lattice grid based on the transmitting stations. There were two major drawbacks: firstly, the relative ease with which the radio pulses could be jammed and made unusable by the enemy; and, secondly, the limitation of range of each of the stations and the need to have an adequate number of suitably placed sites to cover the area of operations. None of these problems were overcome by Gee-H. The major difference between the two systems was the use of only two ground stations, the 'Cat' as the beacon used to provide a radius to fly to the target, and the 'Mouse' as the beacon cutting the radius and giving an exact position along it (see diagram). Lengthy pre planning was done, often modified in the air, to calculate positions equating to sighting angles for the bombsight and a typical bomb run would involve using 7-10 such check points. The system was given a very mixed reception when it entered operational service on the Canberra.

The Jet Conversion Unit lined up for inspection at Binbrook in January 1952. The Canberra B.2 is WD951, Meteor F.4s are VT179 and VT142, and the nearest Meteor T.7 is WG 942. *Flight 26731s*

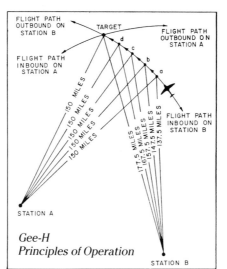

Gee-H
Principles of Operation

Aircraft on bombing run using 'cat' (A) and 'mouse' (B) with four check points.

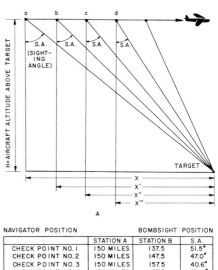

NAVIGATOR POSITION	BOMBSIGHT POSITION		
	STATION A	STATION B	S.A.
CHECK POINT NO.1	150 MILES	137.5	51.5°
CHECK POINT NO.2	150 MILES	147.5	47.0°
CHECK POINT NO.3	150 MILES	157.5	40.6°
CHECK POINT NO.4	150 MILES	167.5	33.2°

Vertical representation with check points equated to sight angle.

Build-up and Conversion

With the advent of the single pilot bomber aircraft came the problem of conversion to type. Specification T11/49 had been issued for a dual control trainer but this was not due to enter service until mid 1953. In the meantime, the Jet Conversion Unit (or Flight) at Binbrook undertook the task of pilot conversion using Meteors for basic jet conversion and handling together with Canberra B.2s for on-type instruction with a 'watch what I do and then do it yourself' technique. The JCU, or JCF as it was often called, was very much a part of the build-up of the Canberra force at Binbrook. As early as January 1951, 101 Squadron had two Meteor F.4s (VT179 and VT142) on charge as part of the run down of Lincoln strength ready for the concentration on jet re-role. By early July the two Meteor F.4s had been joined by two Meteor T.7s (and a Tiger Moth!) and the

crews were introduced to the 'joys' of jet asymmetric flying. Meanwhile, the first Canberras had made their visits to Binbrook when WD931, flown by Wing Commander Mahaddie, paid a quick call on the 27th March en route from Warton to RAE Farnborough. In early May a B.2 (WD930) from Handling Squadron, Manby spent a few days at Binbrook while crews were given lectures on aspects of Canberra flying performance - and a chance to crawl all over the aircraft. A few weeks later Beamont flew the first Canberra for 101 Squadron into Binbrook.

The JCU remained in association with 101 Squadron, as a unit within and administered by the Squadron, until the end of the year. In early January administration of the JCU was handed over to 617 Squadron as they were the next unit to re-equip. The first 617 Squadron aircraft, WD961, arriving on 21st January 1952.

WD938, the second aircraft for 101 Squadron arrived 28th June 1951 and the Squadron launched into an intensive flying programme of familiarisation and continuation training (CT).

After a slight hiccup in July when WD938 had a wheels-up landing after running out of fuel, the Squadron commenced bombing in August. By the end of the year, with eight aircraft on strength, intensive flying, exercises and tests were underway as the Squadron took on the development role for Canberra operations. This was a mixed blessing as although it allowed crews to get up to unusual aerial antics in the name of experimentation, it also meant that the Squadron was under the spotlight and was inundated with visits from military teams, press and politicians.

On the 22nd March 1952 the squadron took part in the Bomber Command exercise, *Bullseye* - one of the standard round

of Command exercises. The Squadron diary noted that the highlights of the aircraft were: '. . ability to fly in formation at 42,000 ft without undue difficulty and without much variation in fuel consumption and the clarity of the photographs taken from 42,000 ft. Attacks made by Meteors were largely ineffective and would have been avoided had not the formation been required to fly straight and level for the exercise.' The latter comment holds true for almost every exercise the Canberra took part in with height and speed restrictions being imposed to give the fighters a chance! Nothing changes, it was still the same in 1980; if you rang a fighter squadron to offer them a PR.9 as a high level target at 60,000 ft, the reception tended to be abject splutterings about prior commitments!

As the first station to re-equip, Binbrook became the guinea-pig for station organi-

sation. It was decided to adopt a simpler organisation to support the four flying units with a HQ squadron, flying support squadron (ops, air traffic and armoury), equipment and servicing squadron. Each of the flying squadrons was 'to undertake more servicing than had hitherto been possible with the Lincoln with all servicing up to and including Minors done at squadron level, the aim being to draw the unit into a more compact, independent and self-reliant unit.' This was an excellent

10 Squadron B.2 WH668 at Honington, September 1955, wearing the interim finish of Medium Sea Grey/Light Sea Grey upper surfaces with PRU Blue undersurfaces - introduced on production at WD987. *Honington Records*

101 Squadron B.2 complement at end of 1951. WD948, WD936 and WD934 are nearest the camera. *101 Squadron records*

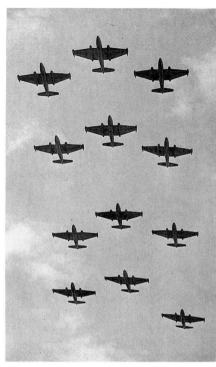

arrangement and was soon working very well because that desired element 'squadron feeling' began to develop.

The original plan for six stations each having four squadrons was modified as the need arose and Binbrook had five by the end of 1952 with the original two being joined by 12 Squadron (March), 9 Squadron (May) and 50 Squadron (August). Coningsby followed suit and had an establishment of five squadrons by the end of 1953 – 44 Squadron (March), 149 Squadron (March), 15 Squadron (March), 57 Squadron (May) and 40 Squadron in October. At the same time Scampton was building up with 10 Squadron arriving in January 1953 to be followed by 27 Squadron (June), 18 Squadron (August) and 21 Squadron (September). Marham also took a complement of four with 90 Squadron (November 1953), 115 Squadron (February 1954), 207 Squadron (March) and 35 Squadron (April). In the meantime the two target-marker units at

Hemswell had re-equipped with Canberras, 109 Squadron in August 1952 and 139 Squadron in November 1953, these were joined by the trials unit, 199 Squadron, which arrived in August 1954 from Watton where their first Canberra had been on strength since March 1954. Lastly, Wittering was given only three flying units with 76 Squadron arriving in December 1953, 100 Squadron in the first part of 1954 and 61 Squadron in August 1954. A further modification to the plan arose with a shortage of suitable airfields in the UK for more Canberra units. The decision was taken to send the last 'Wing' to a suitable airfield in Germany rather than uprate another UK airfield. 149 Squadron moved from Coningsby to Ahlhorn in August 1954 as part of this wing which included the newly reformed 102, 103 and 104 Squadrons. They were to be a lodger unit in 2ATAF remaining part of Main Force while under day to day administration of 2 ATAF.

B.2 WJ625 of 100 Squadron, October 1955, enjoying itself in the upper air on a rare clear day. Although not cleared for aerobatics, the Canberra was good at most of the standard aeros! *Flight 32731s*

Six B.2s of 35 Squadron (WH909, WH910, WH913, WH916, WH911 and WJ636) lead six B.2s of 50 Squadron (WJ727, WJ731, WJ733, WJ641, WJ676 and WK133).

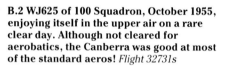

WJ611 at Binbrook. Note the Binbrook Wing flash on the nose - in the black and white colours of 101 Squadron. The aircraft is in the later overall silver finish.

Fg Off Watling, Fg Off John Hart and Flt Sgt Brown pose in front of their 50 Squadron B.2, 1955. Note the flying kit - especially the fur-lined boots (it was incredibly cold in a B.2 at 50,000ft!) *John Hart*

Operational Conversion Unit

The large numbers of new aircraft entering service made it obvious that 'on-squadron' conversion would have to give way to a proper Operational Conversion Unit (OCU) and so in the latter part of 1951, No.231 OCU was formed at RAF Bassingbourn, a place that became synonymous with the Canberra.

A draft paper on the 'Training Aspects of Re-equipment' expressed the view that 'conversion of aircrew to new equipment has seldom previously given rise to trouble and is not expected to do so in this instance. It is anticipated that when the first re-equipment is begun, complete squadrons will be sent through the OCU as courses. Before this stage is reached, however, the OCU should have been enabled to build-up a certain amount of experience in jet handling in dual Meteors, and of course sufficient experience in the B3/45 to enable the staff to teach the squadrons.'

In October Bassingbourn had become the home of 231 (Mosquito) OCU and 237 (Meteor) OCU and it was on the Meteors that the initial staff work up was done because the first Canberras did not arrive until the following February. 237 OCU disbanded on 1st December and became 'C' Squadron (the PR element) of 231 OCU, 'A' and 'B' Squadrons being the bomber squadrons. 231 was not simply a resident unit at Bassingbourn it *was* Bassingbourn and vice-versa. The entire station was the OCU with a complement of three squadrons and all the standard engineering and admin support. The unit operated as the Bomber Command OCU, training pilots,

A new Canberra crew at the OCU, May 1953. Left to Right: Pilot Officers J.Harvey, W.Swettenham and J.Aldred – all aged 20.
J.D. Aldred

Early days at Bassingbourn as trainee crews watch 231 OCU B.2 WE114 get airborne. The first B.2s arrived at Bassingbourn in February 1952 to be joined by PR.3s and, the following year, T.4s.

navigators and radar operators to reinforce PR and light bomber squadrons at home and overseas. Initially the OCU had a mixed complement of Mosquitos (T.3 and PR.34) and Meteors (T.7 and PR.10), plus assorted Tiger Moths and Ansons. For the first few months of 1952 flying concentrated on standardising the instructors and from February, with the arrival of the first B.2s, type conversion for the staff. The initial Unit Establishment (UE) was set at twenty-six B.2s and four PR.3s. By mid-February there were only two B.2s and one PR.3 on strength and it was not until the end of the year that B.2 strength reached a reasonable figure with twenty-five aircraft. By early summer the OCU was ready to receive its first students and No.1 course, of five crews, assembled at Bassingbourn on 27th May to herald the Canberra era. This first course passed out on 26th August.

The OCU ran three main courses: the light bomber course, a 'long' course of conversion to type and weaponry; the short course of conversion to type; and, the photo-recce course. The Meteors remained an important element in the training providing dual control sorties until the arrival of the Canberra T.4, the first of which arrived with the OCU in August 1953. From then on the relative UE and strength of each type varied almost month by month! UE started at thirty-seven B.2s, five PR.3s and six T.4s in early 1954 with the T.4 element increasing to eighteen by January 1956. The actual strength of each type very rarely reflected this establishment – at one stage no less than forty B.2s were in use! In July 1955 the PR element of the OCU moved to Merryfield with the PR.3s, eventually moving on to Wyton before returning to Bassingbourn in January 1958 when it once again became 'C' Squadron of 231 OCU with six PR.3s.

The pilots who were selected for the early courses were from very varied backgrounds; some were converting from the 'heavies' such as the Lincoln and Washington, others from the recce and

light bomber Mosquito squadrons. However, there were some who had been destined for fighters, especially Meteors, who found themselves headed for a dreaded bomber tour. It took only one or two flights in the Canberra to convince them that what they were getting was a bomber with a fighter performance!

The OCU was responsible for training all three crewmen – pilot, navigator/radar and navigator/plotter and a new course commenced every four weeks. The first two weeks of the course were spent in the classroom on the groundschool phase and then it was into the flying phase with a daylight jet refresher on the Meteors for the pilots before going on to the B.2s. The introduction of the T.4 saw the end of the Meteors, much to the regret of some of the pilots. Bombing was introduced towards the middle of the course and the student crew started to work together. In the early years about 50% of the aircrew going through the course were National Servicemen who would only serve some three months or so on a squadron before their commitment was ended. It was, therefore, proposed in 1953 to introduce a form of 'boost' training for trained crews on reserve status whereby they could return to a squadron to undertake two weeks of intensive refresher flying.

An excellent summary of life at the OCU appeared in the RAF magazine, *Air Clues.*

'At first the pilots and navigators will mostly go their separate ways and concentrate on the subjects peculiar to their own calling, but after about a week they will be crewed up – one pilot, one nav/observer, and one nav/plotter to a crew on the bomber side and a pilot and navigator on the P.R - and from then on will attend lectures and do drills as crew members. This first stage of the course will last about three weeks (ten days for the short courses) and during that time the crews will complete about 84 hours of lectures covering eight different subjects. Thus the pilots may be found in the Engines Section absorbing the means whereby the aviation

'For the next three weeks flying will alternate daily with the final phase of ground school which includes such subjects as aircraft recognition, intelligence and tactics, and from then on flying is the order of the day. On the flying side the early trips will be in a dual Canberra and all the sequences that make up a general handling exercise will be demonstrated and practised. There will also be some IF and an introduction to the let-down procedure. This will be followed by a demonstration flight in the bomber or PR version and the student's first solo.

'There follow two general handling trips to accustom the pilot to the feel of the aircraft and he is ready to start his operational exercises. For the bomber these include cross-country flights, simulated and live bombing, and for the PR, cross-country flights and photographic exercises. A dual check half-way through the operational flying and an instrument rating test at the end will complete the day flying syllabus. At night the sequence is repeated, but to a lesser extent. On the short courses only one of each exercise is completed after the initial conversion and familiarisation flight.'

Courses had an average failure rate of 10% but most failed students were simply recoursed to have another go. There were a number of pilots who for one reason or another were never able to come to terms with the asymmetric problems of the Canberra but generally it was considered to be a pleasant aircraft to fly with few vices. On average the OCU would fly 1400 hours a month(!), mostly in the B.2s, a typical breakdown being that for May 1953 with 745 hours B.2 by day and 385 B.2 at night, 111 T.4 day and 15 night and 116 hours day PR.3. As the number of T.4s increased so these hours increased and the B.2 hours decreased.

The T.4 entered service at the planned date with an original total order for 65 aircraft. This was continually increased over the lifetime of the Canberra force, with several B.2s being converted to T.4s. The initial concept of the T.4 was for a 'dual-control trainer with as few changes as possible.' The prototype, WN467, made its first flight on 12th June 1952 and entered service with the OCU a year later. Prior to the introduction of the T.4 there had been a number of fatal accidents with aircraft crashing short of the runway on approach; this was attributed to lack of familiarity

spirit and flames arrive at the right place at the right time to produce the urge for forward movement, or they may be watching in some fascination an array of lights and switches on a board known as 'electrics' which behave themselves so well under the persuasion of the engines instructor, but which flash and fail to respond in such heart-breaking fashion when the student is urged to demonstrate that he has 'got it'. Perhaps they are learning a little more about airmanship or the way they should behave at 40,000 ft and above from the medical point of view. They may even be found in the Link trainer or, perhaps, in the Navigation Section! And with two navigators in the crew!

'Meanwhile, the navs will probably be found either navigating an aircraft on a 1,000 mile cross-country while firmly rooted to the earth in a cubicle in the D.R.I or lying full length on a mock-up bombing platform aiming imaginary bombs at a

projected picture on the earth's surface which moves sedately beneath them. They may be in the radar demonstration room learning the art of manipulating radar devices which surely must be beyond the comprehension of all but the bespectacled gentry who invented them, or maybe they, too, are learning something of "behaviour at height" and the "ways of jetstreams". At the same time the P.R navs, who, at heart, are quite snooty about this bombing business, will be learning about cameras and how to take pictures and, having taken them, how to interpret them. Theirs is a nice little empire ...

'Towards the end of the three weeks' period the crews will be found together in the dummy cockpits where they will remain until, suitably hooded, they are able to lay fingers on any tap or switch that the instructor may mention. It is only then that they will be deemed ready to report to the flying squadron.

with the effects of acceleration. Rapid acceleration gave pilots a false nose-up sense and they were correcting this with nose-down on the flying controls and flying into the ground. Since its introduction in 1953 the T.4 has been known and 'loved' by generations of Canberra aircrew! The design of the cockpit left a lot to be desired because in order to meet the requirement of 'as few changes as possible' the front cockpit was identical to the B.2 in size and shape. A second seat was added on the right hand side of the cockpit for the instructor pilot. This seat was on a swivel mount and was pushed forward to allow the navigator to 'squeeze' through the hatch and into his black hole. The seat was then swung back again and locked in place as the pilots fought for elbow room in the cramped conditions with helmets pressed against the sides of the cockpit. In this environment the all-important instruction took place with at squadron level the never-ending round of check rides and 'trappers' (CFS Agents). The T.4 had two saving graces: it did not carry a great deal of fuel so sortie lengths were reasonably short and the rudder lines ran beneath the navigator's seat and for a fee could be manipulated in favour of your own pilot when he was being checked! Eventually most squadrons had one or more T.4s on strength with another one or two held by the 'Station Flight'.

As with any OCU, the main aim was to teach new crews the basic elements of the aircraft, develop flying skills with the particular type and teach operation of the aircraft systems, be it bombing or reconnaissance. The intention was that at the end of the course crews could be posted to squadrons fully capable of performing the operational task. On the squadron they would gain experience, learn squadron procedures and techniques as well as generally sharpen their performance. For the navigators it was primarily a case of learning to use the navigation and bombing/recce equipment in addition to operating as part of a crew. For the pilots it was the same plus learning the idiosyncrasies of the Canberra.

After hoisting aboard the almost wondrous performance of the aircraft probably the most important single element to master was asymmetric flying.

If the Canberra had emerged with wing-root mounted engines it would have dispelled its only major flying problem. Asymmetric refers to the problems caused when the aircraft is flying on one engine, i.e. asymmetric thrust. With engines close to the centre of the aircraft body there is very little asymmetric force being exerted when only one engine is producing thrust but with engines widely spaced in the wings, as they are on the Canberra, there is a great deal of thrust on one side and nothing on the other to counterbalance it. The pilot has to provide the balancing force by keeping the rudder fully deflected to oppose the turning moment of the live engine. The *Pilot's Notes* advice on single engine flying says 'the aircraft has a very good single-engine performance and the rudder trimmers are powerful enough to trim out all the foot load at normal cruising speeds. At 7400 rpm on one engine the aircraft will maintain a speed of approx 330 kts in level flight below 5,000 ft.' However, if insufficient force is maintained, or relaxed for a moment, the aircraft will try to turn which will produce a roll and in next to no time the aircraft is inverted and on its way down. Over the years this has killed a great many Canberra aircrew. Thus, the pilot has to rapidly identify which engine has failed, not always as easy as it sounds, and lock his leg onto the rudder pedals to counter the forces produced by the live engine. The word 'lock' means what it says, the leg must be locked at the knee and kept locked. Needless to say this is a very tiring position and long serving Canberra pilots tend to develop substantial leg muscles! For his part, the navigator keeps an eagle eye, almost a stare, on the air speed indicator to ensure that the aircraft does not drop below the minimum approach speeds. At certain stages of flight, especially take-off, to lose an engine means the almost inevitable loss of the aircraft as there is insufficient speed to get the aircraft into a safe condition. There is only one course of action – a very rapid ejection.

By the mid 1950s the OCU was also training the first of the foreign aircrew

whose governments had bought various marks of Canberras. Over the years the OCU became a truly cosmopolitan empire and hardly a month went by without a new uniform or flying suit making an appearance. The 231 formation team of four aircraft, was soon in great demand and was thrilling all and sundry with deft displays of close formation flying, a highlight being a very 'tight' box. One aircraft would also do a solo display at some stage of the demonstration.

Staff crews frequently flew on major exercises and enjoyed the change from the routine of training flying. The PR element normally deployed to and operated from Wyton during exercises. The Valiant OCU, 232 OCU at Gaydon, also made use of a number of Canberras from the mid 1950s for instrument training. An average of 100 hours a month were flown in the Canberras with ILS approaches being the most frequent event. The last Canberra left this OCU in June 1960.

Increased Production

The increase in production rates and delivery of B.2s made the early 1950s a hectic period as more and more squadrons re-equipped, new marks entered service and numerous equipment trials were carried out by squadrons as well as specialist units. OR302 for a single navigator version of the B.2 was cancelled at the end of 1952 and English Electric were told to stop work on the project.

After the B.2 and T.4, the next version on the operational scene was the PR.3 reconnaissance variant, No.540 Squadron at Benson received its first aircraft in December 1952 and four aircraft had been delivered to the Squadron before the mark had been cleared for service in an attempt to get the Squadron 'worked-up' as soon as possible. However, after a few minor snags, delivery was stopped until English Electric produced aircraft to the required spec. In the meantime, 540 continued its work-up using a pair of borrowed B.2s.

The first delivery had been expected in October from an initial total order for 109 aircraft to form the backbone of the RAF's recce force for the next ten years. Continuing the policy of adapting the basic airframe wherever possible, the PR.3 was a B.2 with a 14 inch extension in the front half of the fuselage for an extra fuel tank and camera bay while the bomb bay was redesignated as a flare bay to carry the flare-crate of 1.75 inch flares necessary for night photography. The prototype, VX181, made its first flight on 19th March 1950. The aircraft was at first rejected by Boscombe Down on trials because of excessive airframe vibration. This was traced to the fuselage extension and was compensated for by overslabbing the rear fuselage to stiffen it. The aircraft was configured for a basic camera fit of six F52 oblique cameras and an F49 vertical (survey) camera. There were variations on this basic fit depending on the requirement. For night photography two F89 cameras were used.

Star of Stage and Screen

It is almost impossible now to envisage the great impact the Canberra had on the aviation press and the public following its first showing at Farnborough in 1949 and throughout the 1950s. Hardly a week went by when the Canberra was not in the news for one reason or another – breaking yet another record or taking part in a display or world tour. A look at the aviation magazines of the period shows the great interest and enthusiasm for the aircraft.

Before long, Canberras became the stars at the many open days and flying displays held at various RAF stations and most squadrons found time to 'work-up' a formation team, usually of four aircraft, to show-off Canberra's capabilities. At some stage in the display one aircraft would normally break away from the formation and thrill the crowd with a spell of high speed runs and tight turns. Those squadrons which took part in the series of overseas tours were the first to 'work-up' team and solo displays but at some time almost

Opposite page: **PR.3 WE141, which served with 540 Squadron in 1953.**

Prototype PR.3 VX181 being refuelled at Warton. Note the wing-tip camera bulge.
EE Co / SG396

Bomber Command rehearsals for the 1953 Coronation Review.

every Canberra squadron has taken part in 'At Home' days and the like and are still doing so.

15th July 1953 was a great day for the Royal Air Force, one of the greatest shows of air power ever staged – the Coronation Royal Review at RAF Odiham when some six hundred aircraft flew past the reviewing stand in just 20 minutes! There was an equally impressive display of aircraft arranged on the hardstandings for inspection by the Royal couple - including six Canberras - five B.2s painted in the grey-green-/blue scheme and a grey/blue PR.3 (WE144). The B.2s were presumably chosen to represent each producer: WH639 and WH673 both of RAFFC Manby (and both EE built); WH856 of 10 Squadron (fourth Short example); WJ568 from RAF Coningsby (off the Handley Page line) and WJ973 (Avro built) from an un-noted MU.

In the latter part of the flypast were twenty-four Canberras from Binbrook and twenty-four from Hemswell/Scampton led by Group Captain N. Hyde and Squadron Leader J. Hill respectively. The numerous rehearsals and the actual display itself provided aviation enthusiasts with some of the best 'spotting' they have ever had. Typical was Binbrook where for weeks before the event the Canberras had been taking off in streams and carrying out close formation flying so as to be perfect on the day. Peter Green remembers the welcome occupation during the summer of 1953 of watching the Canberras at Binbrook practicing formation flying in ever increasing numbers. 'As the rehearsals

advanced one could watch from the good vantage point at Caistor the 36 Lincolns flying northwards from Waddington and Upwood, to turn at Hemswell and be joined by another nine aircraft before flying eastwards and passing directly overhead. There was then time to travel the six miles to Binbrook to wait for the twenty-four Canberras of the five Binbrook squadrons to start up, taxy out, and all take off in rapid succession. It was a very impressive performance.'

Flight was one of the aviation magazines lucky enough to have a reporter airborne with the Canberras en route to Odiham . . . '1544/35 at the "gate" and after this it's a seven-minute straight run to Odiham. Somebody says over the R/T that he's got a compressor stall, but immediately rights it. All play stops at a cricket match near Denham; groups of people stare up from every vantage point . . . The airfield comes into view. There are lines of aircraft; there, for a fleeting second, is the dais . . . three . . two . . .one. The time runs out. Binbrook has done it again. We have saluted the Queen!'

540 Squadron at Benson had three PR.3 aircraft at this time which were involved in taking film of the Coronation of Queen Elizabeth II across the Atlantic for Canadian and American television, which to quote the ORB 'was considered to be good operational training for both aircraft and aircrew'. These operation *Pony Express* flights were made on 3rd June 1953 (the day after the Coronation) and involved WE136, WE140 and WE142.

New Zealand Air Race

The PR.3, because of its superior range had been chosen as the RAF candidate in the great London to New Zealand Air Race of October 1953, in which, eventually, five Canberras comprising two PR.3s, WE139 (Race No.3) and WE142 (No.2), one PR.7 WH773 (No.1) and 2 RAAF Mk.20s A82-201 (No.5) and A85-202 (No.4), a Douglas DC-6, a Hastings and a Viscount took part. The original staff meetings of early 1952 which were called to decide on what RAF involvement, if any, there should be, had given thought to using the new Avro or Handley Page B.35/46 bomber, the Valiant, or the Canberra. By November the decision had been taken to enter three PR.7s and one Valiant but for a variety of reasons this changed to the list given above. The reasons given for entering at all were 'national and service pride' and the 'operational benefits of the experience gained'.

The main aim of the race was for contestants to achieve the shortest elapsed time journey from London to Christchurch, New Zealand, with routing and stopping points left to individual contestants to decide. There was also a handicap section which ran concurrently. After a number of withdrawals only the Canberras were left in the speed section and the other three aircraft for the handicap section. The RAF Canberra team was based at Wyton and in the month leading up to the race a great

deal of organisational work was carried out. The Air Race Flight, under Wing Commander L.M. Hodges, had formed at Wyton in June 1952 and production standard PR.3s were taken on strength although B.2s were borrowed for much of the crew work-up. One of the first jobs, however, was to modify the aircraft. Each one was given sufficient nav aids to cover all areas of the route – Marconi radio compasses, 'Rebecca' and periscopic sextant for astro navigation.

The main navigational aid was the Radio Compass which was used to obtain radio bearings up to 800 miles distant from the beacons (depending on transmitter power). The main problem was accuracy at extreme range, but in general terms the crews were impressed with the performance of this equipment. Each aircraft also carried a periscopic sextant for astro navigation and checks on the heading references. Accuracy was good if the autopilot was in use but a little suspect if the aircraft was being flown manually! Estimation of range from visual features – an island or a piece of coastline for example – was difficult because of the canopy shape as the pilot could only see clearly to the sides and front. So, an instrument called a 'Dangleometer' was devised to give an accurate estimation of range from visual features using the principles of geometry where angles and known height

allow a calculation of lateral distance to be made. With the autopilot engaged so that the pilot could use both hands to set up the gizmo, accuracy was very good!

Specialist camera equipment was removed and replaced by extra fuel tanks, including one in the flare bay, and the tip tanks were wired on. All this meant an increase in the take-off weights and so the RA.3 engines were 'tweaked' to give an extra 1000 lb thrust, and larger wheels were fitted to cope with the extra weight. With the altitudes and high temperatures of some of the planned airfields every bit of thrust would be needed and there was no safety margin.

There were three stages in the training routine, starting with B.2 sorties around the UK to practise nav techniques using the sextant (astro) and radio compass. The B.2s were then used for longer range nav exercises to Malta and Cyprus with the same aim in mind and, finally, the PR.3s were used to test parts of the actual race route. The race date was set for Thursday

8th October and the crews and aircraft were ready.

The planned route for the PR.3s was carefully thought out to make use of the maximum range of the aircraft: London – Shaibah (2875 miles), Shaibah (Iraq) – Ceylon (2634 miles), Ceylon (now Sri Lanka) – Cocos Islands (1771 miles), Cocos Islands – Perth (1840 miles) and Perth – Christchurch (3150 miles), a total of 12,270 miles. Specialist teams were positioned at each of these staging posts so that the aircraft could be refuelled and sent on its way again as soon as possible. Invariably the crew stayed strapped-in while their aircraft was turned-round (refuelled and serviced) rather than get out and stretch their legs, the time and effort involved in getting back into the aircraft was not considered a good trade for the few minutes leg stretch! Staying awake for the 24 hours was no problem as all the crews had undetaken 30-hour practise flights, and during the actual race there was the added element of competition. .

The final placings saw the Canberras fighting it out and results were dictated by the good or bad luck of serviceability. The winning aircraft was No.3, PR.3 WE139, crewed by Flight Lieutenant R. Burton and Flight Lieutenant D. H. Gannon, who completed the course in 23 hours and 51 minutes, an average speed of 514 mph. This aircraft is now preserved at the Royal Air Force Museum at Hendon. The other PR.3 had been delayed at Shaibah and was pipped by the RAAF Mk.20 (A84-201) of Squadron Leader P. Raw who had also been delayed, at Woomera for an hour, but still managed to complete the course in 24 hours 32 minutes. The longer range PR.7, perhaps the favourite, had been delayed 12 hours at Perth with generator trouble but had achieved a single stage of 3610 miles at an average speed of 538 mph by

missing out the Cocos Islands staging post which gave it the London to Colombo (Ceylon) record. The five Canberras had times within nine minutes of each other if only actual flight times are considered – from 22 hours 22 minutes to 22 hours 31 minutes. The final placings looked like this:

Crew Captains	Total time	Airborne time
Flt Lt Burton	23h 51m	22h 25m
Sqn Ldr Raw RAAF	24h 31m	22h 27½m
Flt Lt Furze	24h 33m	22h 31m
Wg Cdr Hodges	35h 31m	22h 22m
Wg Cdr Cumming RAAF	delay 2 days Cocos Island	22h 23½m

The whole event was a great achievement by the aircrew, support crew and the aircraft. The Canberra had shown itself to be remarkably reliable and the Avon engines had performed well. In theory at least the RAF could send squadrons from one side of the world to the other in 24 hours!

Air Race No.2, PR.3 WE142, refuelling at Cocos Islands. *via Bruce Robertson*

Air Race Canberras line up at Harewood (Christchurch, NZ) after the race. *via Bruce Robertson*

109 Squadron's WH640 at Boscombe Down in February 1953. The Hemswell fin flash was yellow for 109 Squadron and red with white outline for 139 Squadron.

WH649 of 139 Squadron, 1953. Along with 109 Squadron, 139 trained in the target marker role, the aircraft being equipped with flares and 250 lb TIs as a standard load. After sale to BAC in March 1965, this aircraft had a long career with the Venezuelan Air Force. *MAP*

'mark' the target area with coloured indicators. The Canberra Marking force comprised a mixed force of flare and TI aircraft with a standard format being two marker aircraft, Marker 1 and 2, and two or four flare aircraft, Flare 1 to 4. With a six aircraft team the following tactics would apply, H meaning the time at which the target would be clear for bombing and the times being minutes before this time (H minus so many minutes):

H –10	*Marker 1* and *2*, timed runs
to	from an Initial Point (IP) to
H –2	mark target then orbit the area to re-mark as required.
H –10	*Flare 1*, drop flares at end of timed run from IP to illuminate target for *Marker* aircraft.
H –7	*Flare 2*, drop flares as directed by *Marker 1*.
H –4	*Flare 3*, as 2.
H –3	*Flare 4*, as 2.
H	Target cleared for bombing.

Target Markers

Two of the Hemswell squadrons formed as dual-role units with a commitment to Main Force as bombers and as Target Markers. Both squadrons, 109/105 and 139, were ex Mosquito B.35 units and from July to December 1952 had converted to the Canberra B.2 via the standard Meteor route. By the early part of the following year both units were undertaking regular marking exercises using 250 lb TIs (Target Indicator Markers) and trials with 1000 lb TIs to determine release parameters. The latter trials included level release and up to 40 degree dive(!) with speed between 250 and 350 kts. The principle of target marking had changed little since the great bomber offensives of 1942-45 when a team of specialist target marking aircraft preceded the Main Force bomber stream to

This was the 'ideal' arrangement with the flares of the first aircraft providing sufficient light for the first Marker aircraft to drop its TIs, the rest of the formation was under the control of the Marker 1 captain to refine or re-mark the target as required.

The flares used were of two variants, both parachute types, the Mk.1/No.1 which ignited when the parachute opened and the Mk.1/No.2 which had a delay of two minutes from parachute opening. A normal load was twelve of these 4.5 inch flares on light series carriers thought it was not a particularly reliable piece of equipment with a high proportion of failures and inconsistent igniting height. The TIs were also not particularly reliable with some total failures and others not burning for the nominal 20 minutes.

A typical combined Markex/Bombex (marking and bombing exercise) would involve the Canberras marking a target with red or green TIs or acting as markers to 'centre' with red TIs previously dropped green proximity markers. This done, the bombing element would then appear to bomb the target.

Further Developments

The basic B.2 had been a modified concept from the original blind bomber/target marker originally specified and work continued to find a design to fulfil Specification B22/48 for such an aircraft. The second prototype PR.3, VX185, was converted before completion into what was referred to as the B.5 – an aircraft intended to fill the target marking role with an improved radar system and better low level performance. Once again the radar system was not available so the prototype B.5 (VX185) was built with three crew stations and provision for visual bomb/flare aiming through a flat panel under the nose. There were a number of important improvements to the airframe – an extra 900 gallons of fuel in wing leading-edge integral tanks, 'Maxaret' anti-skid braking system and Avon 109 (RA7) engines of 7,500 lb st.

The aircraft made its first flight on 15th July 1952 and then began a series of flight trials and long range flights. A month later it captured yet another record for the Canberra by becoming the first aircraft to make a double crossing of the Atlantic in one day. On 26th August 1952 the aircraft flew Aldergrove-Gander-Aldergrove in a total elapsed time of 10 hours and 3 minutes.

The aircraft/role was not taken up by the RAF but the basic improvements to the airframe (wing fuel, Maxaret brakes and Avon 109 engines) were incorporated into a production series of B.2s, though designated B.6, and eventually one hundred and nine aircraft were built by English Electric and Shorts. The new mark began re-equipping Bomber Command squadrons from June 1954, 101 Squadron being first in line.

The B.6 was just as sturdy and reliable as the B.2, having changed none of the basic airframe characteristics. Its main advantage was that the extra fuel in the wings gave it 'longer legs' although this was to some extent offset by the extra fuel weight. The fuel/range balance in the Canberra was always up for argument, especially regarding the pros and cons of the tip tanks. They could only hold 250 gallons each and yet provided extra weight and drag as well as giving a max speed limitation of 365 kts. Unless the tips were blown off as soon as they were empty they would be of no value as far as extra range was concerned at low level. Range could be further increased by fitting an overload fuel tank in the bomb bay which could hold 300 gallons. Ejection seats were provided for a basic crew of three and the prone bomb-aiming position was retained in the nose as the B.6 continued the roles of the B.2.

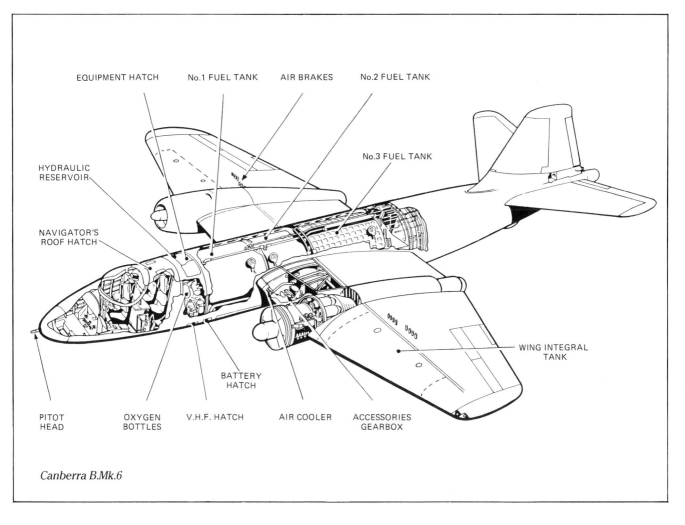

Canberra B.Mk.6

Classification

As we have already described, Gee-H was the primary blind bombing aid and some 60% of sorties were flown with simulated and live Gee-H bombing as the climax of a two and a half hour cross country navigation exercise. Gee-H proved very troublesome. The first problem was the ease with which the system could be jammed, aptly demonstrated during major Command exercises, but the major drawback was the unreliability of the system with frequent failures of the ground stations or the airborne equipment. The average failure rate seems to have been 15-18%, i.e. occasions when adequate Gee-H signals could not be obtained. However, having made this comment to ex-Canberra aircrew who operated Gee-H it was on the whole considered to be unfair to the kit which was remembered as being fairly good. With the cancellation of plans to put a true radar into the Canberra, the blind bombing capability bordered on a joke.

The 35 Squadron ORB reflects general squadron feeling: 'considerable effort is being wasted on unsuccessful Gee-H attacks, both during exercises and routine training. Much of this is caused by poor ground signals, the transmitter has on occasions functioned at only half power, and the inability of the ranges to plot our bombs.'

This meant that great reliance was still placed on visual bombing with, as ever, the bomb aimer doing the 'good things' with his optical bombsight – a T2,T3 or T4 sight.

The following table of 'Bomber Command Current Bombing Capability' is taken from a Bomber Command Operational Research Branch paper of October 1953:

Aircraft	Method	Bombing Height	Bombing error (50% Zone) Range*	Operational
Lincoln	H2S.4A	20,000 ft	500 yds	1,800 yds
Lincoln	Visual	20,000 ft	250 yds	500 yds
Lincoln	Gee-H	20,000 ft	250 yds	400 yds
Canberra	Visual	25,000 ft	350 yds	700 yds
Canberra	Visual	40,000 ft	700 yds	900 yds
Canberra	Gee-H	25,000 ft	325 yds	475 yds
Canberra	Gee-H	40,000 ft	450 yds	575 yds

*ie under ideal bombing range conditions

For accuracy there was little to choose between the Canberra and the Lincoln, which was only to be expected as they were basically using the same kit. However, bear in mind the 101 Squadron comment concerning the inability of fighters to attack the Canberras and it is apparent that operationally the Canberra was a far more valuable aircraft. Add to this the great tactical advantages of speed and reaction times and the Canberra comes into its own. The 61 Squadron crews who re-roled from the Mosquito B.35 to the Canberra viewed the visual bombing as little different – 'the bombing technique differs little from the Mosquito, enter attacks at 150 kts, bomb doors open early in the run and build the speed up to no more than 260 kts by the time the bombs are dropped. Results are generally good and no hang-ups.' 150 kts! Either 61 were doing it differently to everyone else or the author of this piece mis-read his ASI. 150 kts would not have been a good speed to fly around in a fully laden Canberra. Nevertheless, crews seemed to have been reasonably happy with the medium level bombing capability of the aircraft especially after the old T2 bombsights had been replaced.

The Canberra era of Bomber Command was not destined to last for long, the aircraft being considered a 'stop-gap' until the real jet bombers, the V-bombers, much more to the liking of the Bomber Chiefs, could enter service.

In the meantime, however, the Canberra bomber squadrons took part in the endless series of station, Wing, Group and Command exercises. Most of these had changed little, if at all, from the pre Canberra days with Main Force taking to the air in all its glory for major Command exercises such as the annual *Skyhigh*. Each squadron would be called on to contribute five to eight aircraft for each phase of such an exercise. *Skyhigh* was one of the better ones with jamming and spoofing of RT and Gee to add to the normal difficulties of night navigation. During Phase 1 the cross-country navex ended with simulated Gee-H attacks on Continental targets. In Phase 2 it was full load take-offs for live Gee-H on UK ranges such as Theddlethorpe, Luce Bay, Jurby, Donna Nook and the Wash ranges (not all these were Gee-H ranges, some were primarily for visual bombing). Nordhorn was a frequent victim for live bombing on the continent as it still is. *Skyhigh* also included a fighter element, no real problem to the Canberras except for the restrictions imposed on height and speed by the exercise instructions and the 365 kt speed limit for the carriage of tip tanks. Frequent fighter affiliation exercises increased the crew's confidence in the performance and capability of their aircraft. One such exercise by 139 Squadron against the Canadian Sabres from North Luffenham, the Meteors and Venoms from Coltishall and the Meteor F.8s from Horsham St.Faith brought the following, typical, comments: 'against the Sabres a steep climbing turn towards the fighter gave the Sabre great difficulty as it virtually stalled out of the turn. At height it was best to outrun it. Against the Venoms and Meteors, speed alone was sufficient.'

The fighter affiliation and major exercises also gave an operational test to a piece of equipment that was greeted with mixed feelings – the 'Orange Putter' tail warning radar. This equipment was fitted to Canberra and Valiant aircraft to provide audio-visual warning of any aircraft about one and a half miles astern, the position for an attacking fighter closing in for a guns kill. It was a short range active radar system and as such was vulnerable to such things as homing, a failing that made similar active systems unpopular on bombers in the Second World War. Its main problem was its unreliability and even when the kit appeared to be serviceable it seemed to give warning of only one in five night intercepts.

Skyhigh was the largest annual exercise and the more regular series were monthly Bombexs such as *Kingpin*. This followed the standard format of route to target with astro and dead-reckoning (DR) navigation for simulated or live Gee-H bombing and return to base for a stream landing to practise the recovery of large numbers of aircraft in the shortest possible time. Other exercises included *Coronet*, *Foxpaw*, with aircraft detached to Germany to attack the UK; *Phoenix*, an air defence exercise (ADEX) for the Home Fleet, *Marshmallow*, to test the German Gee chain and West European air defence and *Carte Blanche*, a 2ATAF and 4ATAF ADEX.

Added to these were the more spectacular NATO Mediterranean exercises such as *Medflex Epic*, *Green Pivot* and *Medflex Fort*, during which Bomber Command squadrons detached to Luqa to take part in attacks on the US Sixth Fleet and Mediterranean land targets.

Even so, these altogether were but a small part of the workload of a Bomber Command Canberra squadron. Most time and effort was expended on the Bomber Command Classification Scheme which was introduced in 1953 to provide a series of standards for crews and squadrons to attain. This table states the Bomber Command required standards for the various categories: (FRA - First Run Attack)

VISUAL BOMBING

Classi-fication	Minimum Number of Bombs	50% Zone (yds)	Simulated
Combat	12 (3 FRA)	T2-600 T4-500	3 runs in 1000 yds
Select	12 (3 FRA)	T2-500 T4-400	3 runs in 1000 yds
Select Star	12 (3FRA)	T2-500 T4-400	50% zone 600 yds

RADAR

Classi-fication	Minimum Number of Bombs	Minimum Success Rate	50% Zone (yds)
Combat	24	80%	900
Select	36	90%	600
Select Star	24	90%	500

Errors approximated to bombing height of 40,000ft. 50% zone means 50% of bombs to fall within the stated area.

Black and grey B.2 WD965 at Bovingdon in May 1957, sporting a 10 Squadron red 'speedbird' on the nose, although this was believed to be a 44 Squadron aircraft at the time. Note the Honington 'rising pheasant' on the fin. *A. Pearcy*

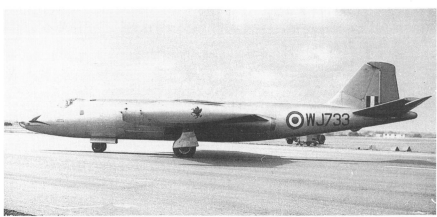

WJ733 of 18 Squadron, Upwood, July 1955, on display for the visit by the Sultan of Muscat and Oman. Note squadron badge only on the tip tank. *M. Freestone*

The Honington Wing parades for the visit by the Soviet team which included Mr Kruschev and Marshal Bulganin, April 1956. Nearest aircraft are WK107, then WK131, WH720, WJ645. *XV Squadron*

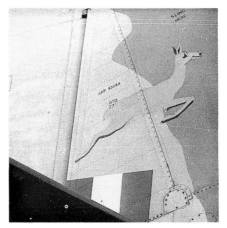

B.2 WK130 in 35 Squadron markings. *MAP*

B.6 WH948 of 101 Squadron, at Blackbushe in September 1956.

Hazy 'snap' of 90 Squadron detachment to Gibraltar in May 1955 for exercise 'Hannibal'. Close-up of the 'Golden Hind' fin marking that was prepared specially for the event by Fg Off Cliff.

57 Squadron B.2 WK141 at Bovingdon, May 1958. *A. Pearcy*

Innumerable 25 lb practice bombs were dropped on the UK ranges as crews 'climbed' the Command Classification ladder. Typically, a squadron would have five 'Select', five 'Combat Star', seven 'Combat' and five 'unclassified' crews. It was a continual struggle as it was a *Crew* classification and postings led to crew changes and the need for re-classification. It was a moan of squadron commanders that short-notice postings caused them great heartache!

B.6 WH972 of 9 Squadron provides a rare view of its spacious bomb-bay, over Coventry, July 1957.

Checking out the normal load of eight 25lb practice bombs, used in great numbers to simulate the ballistics of the 'real' 500/1000lb bombs.

Superb shot of 9 Squadron B.6 WH977, being flown by Squadron Leader Bastard, January 1956.

There were remarkably few incidents, one of the most unusual was set to poetry by 9 Squadron following an occasion when a Squadron aircraft dropped a 25 lb practice bomb outside of the range area. Unfortunately, it fell straight and true and totally demolished the outside toilet of a pub near the range – there were no occupants at the time! . . .

'Oh Dear? What can the matter be
Three old ladies locked in the lavatory
Hiding from bombs from Monday to Saturday
9 Squadron knew they were there.

The first one's name was Elizabeth Bonner
She moved away, for safety from Donna
But the bombs that were dropped still fell upon her
For 9 Squadron knew she was there.

The second one's name was Mary Lou Giles
She thought she was safe by four or five miles
Till down came the bomb
which banished her smiles
For 9 Squadron knew she was there.

Our third victims name was Mrs O'Conner
The other two ladies, they blamed it upon her
But Flavell knew better upstairs in his bomber,
for he knew those ladies were there.

Our story's nearly over, and I'm sorry to say
That 9 Squadron's aircraft are bombing today
So the ladies of Saltfleetby are moving away
For the Prussian Queen's 'Bog' is their target today.'

A normal load of practice bombs would be eight or twelve, dropped singly or in pairs. The bombs were remarkably reliable with a high release/detonation rate. There were a few instances of bombs exploding in the bomb bay, usually on landing after the aircraft had returned to base with a 'hang-up' (non-release) which then fell off onto the closed bomb doors with the jolt of landing.

Most live 1000 lb bombing (live meaning bombs that go bang rather than sand-filled inert weapons) were dropped at Theddlethorpe in Lincolnshire or Sandbanks, on the northern bank of the Elbe estuary, in northern Germany, but live bombing was a fairly rare event. The favoured location for visual bombing from 45,000 ft was El Adem in Libya and squadrons sent detachments to Luqa at frequent intervals for intensive periods of high level bombing in an attempt to get crews cleared to 45,000 ft.

On very rare occasions, such as *Skyhigh* in April 1955, some aircraft carried, and dropped, two 4,000 lb bombs. The maximum bomb load of the Canberra was six 1,000 lb bombs in the bomb bay although this was primarily an attachment point and wiring limitation. However, in August 1953, 57 Squadron armourers carried out bombing-up trials and successfully fitted nine 1,000 lb bombs in the bomb bay – with the doors able to close. Furthermore, if wing tip tanks were not carried, or left empty, it stayed within the maximum AUW. The only problems were that the aircraft system was only wired for six bombs and, more importantly, it would cause centre of gravity problems.

In and around the classification and exercises came such events as the Bomber Command Bombing Competition. This was competed for over a number of days by all Bomber Command squadrons with marks awarded for navigation, visual bombing and Gee-H bombing. No one squadron seems to have dominated the competition and it was often a matter of luck on the night with some crews varying from the rare Direct Hit (DH) to a 2000 yarder on the same target on different nights.

Squadron Personnel

Although a number of squadrons at each station had exactly the same role and equipment there was generally very little mixing operationally or socially. Operationally it was more competition than anything else with each seeking to head the bombing ladder and perhaps win the Bomber Command Efficiency Trophy for the best all-round bomber squadron. Each squadron, however, was essentially a well-knit organisation. Most of the aircrew were young Pilot Officers and Flying Officers, except for the flight commanders and the Squadron Leader CO. Most lived in the Officers Mess or in the Married Quarters on the station and social life centred on the Mess for station and squadron parties, plus the odd 'thrash' at one of the local pubs!

It was the same for the groundcrew and some squadrons ran special funds to pay for all-ranks parties when a coach would be hired and the squadron 'invade' a local pub. Working conditions were not too bad although there was a distinct hierarchy ranging from the dispersal teams up to the hangar teams and movement to a 'better' job was by way of experience and length of time on the squadron. Bearing in mind that the early days of the Canberra were the days of National Service it is remarkable how well the system ran. Canberra squadrons were happy squadrons.

The size of squadrons varied in the 1950s from the eight UE (Unit Establishment) at the beginning, rising quickly to ten UE and then towards the latter part of the decade to sixteen to twenty UE for those squadrons not re-equipping with V-bombers. Obviously, the number of crews per squadron varied according to the number of aircraft but a general ratio of 1.5:1 crews:aircraft was aimed for. Almost every squadron had at least one RAAF, RCAF or USAF aircrew officer on strength. Likewise, the number of groundcrew varied depending on the number of aircraft and the amount of servicing being done at squadron level, but the average for a sixteen UE unit was 80-100 groundcrew. There was never any shortage of flying, except during periods of grounding for technical defects, and aircrew averaged 300-400 hours a year, a monthly squadron total of 400-500 hours, although this increased to 700-800 hours a month for the higher UE squadrons!

Serviceability

Generally, the Canberra was a practical aircraft on which to work and its serviceability was good, the B.6 being better than the B.2 in this respect. The main recurrent problems came from the hydraulic system with leaking of the pneumatic accumulators and cracking pipes. Otherwise the aircraft had a good reputation from a First Line Servicing point of view.

The first major technical problem which arose was one that was to plague the Canberra for many years – the tailplane actuator. This first showed itself in early 1952 and 'runaway' tailplane trims were attributed as the cause of a number of fatal crashes including the loss of WD991 on test from Preston on the 25th March 1952. The fault was traced to the single-pole trim switch sticking on, causing the actuator to run to full travel and consequent loss of control. All aircraft were retrofitted with a dipole switch, improved wiring and a stop on the actuator to reduce the amount of travel. The problem did not totally go away and in late 1955 aircraft were restricted to 250 kts below 10,000 ft because of runaway tail trim actuators. It came to a head the next year and from January to April 1956 all aircraft were grounded until the tailplane actuator system could be modified. The fine trim control switch was moved to the spectacles and the coarse trim switch on the console made inoperative. This, it was hoped, would give the pilot better control of the tailplane actuator. Although it did not dispel all the tailplane problems, the mod certainly ended the rash of accidents that were blackening Canberra's reputation.

Low Level

As early as mid 1952, within a year of the first aircraft entering service, trials were started on the suitability of the Canberra as a low level interdictor. In June 1952, 101 Squadron formed an 'Intruder Flight' of four B.2s and began an intensive programme of low level flying and Shallow Dive Bombing (SDB). By August enough results were available for a planning conference to be held in Germany – the intruder role being designed for use in Germany – and the following month the Intruder Flight went to Fassberg to conduct a series of night intruder sorties. The details of this role rightly belong to the next chapter which deals with RAF Germany.

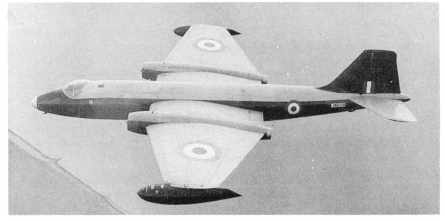

***Opposite page:* 9 Squadron line-up, 1956. WH973 is inscribed with details of the Squadron's hectic year.** *Tony Bridges*

Four-ship of B.6(BS)s from 109 and 139 Squadrons, including WJ778 and WT371, south of Cleethorpes in May 1955.

Canberra B.2 WD980 of 617 Squadron also seen flying over the Lincolnshire coast near its home base of Binbrook in 1952. The aircraft displays its red nose flash on the early black/grey colour scheme.

This was only one of many experiments/ trials to improve or diversify the capability of the Canberra. Many of the ideas, such as an automatic 'window' launcher, never got off the drawing board. Most revolved around equipment changes and the most important were those seeking to find an alternative blind navigation/bombing aid. Of these the most persistent was the introduction of the 'Blue Shadow' sideways-looking radar system.

The first squadron to have 'Blue Shadow' fitted was 109 who sent aircraft to TRE Defford in January 1953. The first aircraft arrived back in June, being the first 'Blue Shadow' equipped aircraft in the RAF. Of the initial ten sorties, eight went well with good results while the remaining two were aborted with unserviceable equipment. The first impressions were favourable – 'easy to master the technique and a good aid to navigation, especially as it is the first self-contained aid used by this squadron', said the initial reports by 109 Squadron.

In August 139 Squadron sent aircraft to Samlesbury, and later Colerne, for 'Blue Shadow' fitting and the two squadrons carried out service trials leading to Bomber Command Trial 237 in early 1954, a determined effort to discover the pros and cons of the equipment.

During the second part of the trial, the aim was to make recommendations on: the best method of navigation, the reliability of the equipment, modifications for its future use and any other notable aspects. Initial flights were made around the UK and Germany but this was extended to the Mediterranean area and the value of Blue Shadow as an aid to Marker aircraft was to be specifically examined. The conclusions reached showed 'Blue Shadow' to be a mixed blessing. It was considered valuable because it was self-contained and difficult to jam, it was also easy to operate and usable in most weather conditions. However, the list of disadvantages was formidable with the most important being the general poor quality of the trace produced and the problem of identifying anything other than distinctive coastal features. Also, it only looked one way, and over a small sector, and this imposed limitations on where it could be used. Finally, it required the use of pre-prepared strip maps and these took quite a time to produce, thus reducing the tactical flexibility of the squadron. The overall conclusion was that the system was a useful aid but should be limited to a 'pathfinder' Marker force with the rest of Main Force carrying out visual bombing. This would require that the 'Blue Shadow' sets to be removed from those aircraft that did not need them and another ejection seat installed to bring the crew back up to three. As we shall see in later chapters, this good advice was not adhered to and most of the later period Canberra bomber squadrons were equipped with 'Blue Shadow'.

World Tours Inc.

The Canberra had already established a reputation, in a peaceful scenario, on the international scene with a series of overseas tours in the period 1952-56. These were a mix of flag-waving and sales promotion. The main three such 'tours' were those by 12 Squadron in October 1952 (Exercise *Round Trip*) to South America, 139 Squadron in August 1955 (Operation *New World*) around the Caribbean and 9 Squadron's tour of West Africa in January 1956. Others included the European tour by 27 Squadron in June 1954 around Greece, France, Italy, Yugoslavia and Por-

tugal, and the Middle East tour by 57 Squadron in October 1954 of Iraq, Jordan and Libya.

The schedules for these tours were punishing on the aircraft with long stage lengths followed by display flying by formations and individuals. It was great credit to the aircraft and to the work of the groundcrew that very few problems arose in some quite remote areas. There was, however, the odd 'hairy' moment. On the South American tour Air Vice Marshal Boyle ran his aircraft off the runway at Maracay, in Venezuela, and had to swing the aircraft round to avoid a twenty foot

drop over a cliff. The aircraft suffered no damage and was soon on its way. On the same tour an aircraft flying a display at Rio hit a vulture which shattered the perspex nose but fortunately did no other damage. In just seven weeks 12 Squadron visited ten countries and flew some 24,000 miles.

The six-aircraft tour by 27 Squadron, Operation *Med Trip* was led by AVM J R.Whitley, AOC 1 Group, and was unique in including a Communist country in its schedule. The Squadron's silver aircraft acquired new transfers of the Squadron elephant badge plus Union Jacks, and were fitted with additional nav aids in the

form of Radio Compasses. The first stop was the French fighter base at Champagne and the routine of parties, flying demonstrations and VIP flying began. The 27 Squadron display routine was fairly typical. It was planned to last about 25 minutes and began with a mass start-up of the six Canberras, which then taxied out together and then split up into two teams. The first, of four aircraft, would take-off and form up into a box formation for the first flypast. The other two would follow three minutes later. They would go independently, the first doing a max rate climb from a steep take-off, the other going straight into a steep turn round the airfield. Next, the formation team would make a run across the airfield at 800 feet after which the two individuals would make a medium-speed run low over the crowd before splitting up for another run from opposite directions – one fast, one slow, the aircraft passing each other in front of the spectators. The 'slow' aircraft would then make a steep turn inside the airfield boundary while his opposite number positioned for a high-speed run.

Opposite page: **27 Squadron lines up at Scampton, June 1954, prior to its European tour to Greece, France, Italy, Portugal and even Yugoslavia.**

The 12 Squadron South American tour was led by AVM Dermot Boyle (centre), AOC No.1 Group; his navigator was Flt Lt B.Brownlow (right). Binbrook 20 October 1952, prior to departure.

Improvised planning at Abu Sueir by Julian Saker with his 90 Squadron B.2 - and 'helpful' pilot Keith Nunn, December 1955.

139 Squadron at Hemswell, August 1955, ready to depart on their goodwill tour of the Caribbean.

21 Squadron at Khormaksar, March 1955. Squadron visits to the Middle East were a regular feature of the mid 1950s. Note the red crossed keys insignia on the nose. WJ609 later went to Argentina as a B.62, delivered in May 1971.

While he was preparing for this the formation team would return, this time in line astern. After his fast run, the first lone Canberra would come back to the airfield for a demonstration of slow turns with undercarriage, bomb-doors, flaps and airbrakes extended while the other aircraft would do the same manoeuvres 'clean'. It was then the latter's turn for a high-speed run after which the two single Canberras would join up for steep formation turns until the main team arrived for a low, fast box formation pass. The team would then sweep up in a climbing turn from near-ground level to circuit height downwind where they would be joined by the two singletons. The concluding piece was a fly-past by all six aircraft in two echelons starboard from which they would break and land. It must be borne in mind that in the early 1950s, jet aircraft were a new thing and for Bombers to do this sort of thing was unheard of! After France it was on to Rome and, in quick succession, Greece, Turkey, Yugoslavia and Portugal. As with all such tours it was a punishing schedule (although enjoyable) on aircrew and groundcrew and the detachment was glad to get back to Scampton for a rest.

The 9 Squadron tour was planned to coincide with a Royal visit to Nigeria so was given special attention by the press. The Reuters correspondent in Lagos reported events in dramatic terms . . . 'Thousands believed they were being visited by beings from another planet as the high-pitched scream of the jet engines jarred their ear drums and mysterious trails of condensation spread across the sky, from apparently nowhere. The more sophisticated found the right explanation, but were no less awed and fascinated by the flashing, silvery and graceful bombers which hurtled over their heads.'

An opportunity was taken to fly local dignitaries and military VIPs if possible and many converts were won. 'Ricky' Richardson recalls a two-aircraft tour of the world when he was on 9 Squadron in January 1956: 'The itinerary flown by WH954, Air Marshal Sir Dermot Boyle, and WH955, myself, was impressive and a tribute to the hard work of the airframe and engine fitter who accompanied us – along with a bomb bay full of spares from wheels to radios. We did the odd impromptu display and at Sek Kong the CO of 28 Squadron elected to come along. I had no particular display plan in mind so I ran in for a low level beat up, vertical climb and stall turn.' The authors can appreciate how tricky a display at Sek Kong can be as John Clemons and Ken Delve had the problem of displaying a PR.9 in this bowl in the mountains to the north of Hong Kong in 1979 even with the much greater power of the PR.9! A great many more overseas tours were undertaken by the UK squadrons during the 1950s as well as frequent Lone Ranger training sorties to a wide variety of overseas locations around Europe and the Mediterranean.

Cameras Around the UK

The first Canberra PR.3s arrived at Benson to equip 540 Squadron in December 1952 and after the initial airframe problems the Squadron began a series of trials on cameras and film. The Squadron held on to three or four B.2s until mid 1954 for crew training and limited PR duties, the aircraft being fitted with a forward-facing F.95 camera.

Within a year two more PR squadrons had formed in the UK with 58 and 82 Squadrons at Wyton, both with PR.3s. Both units had previously been at Benson, 58 Squadron using Mosquito PR.35s and Anson C.19s and 82 Squadron using Spitfire XIXs and Lancasters. Both now

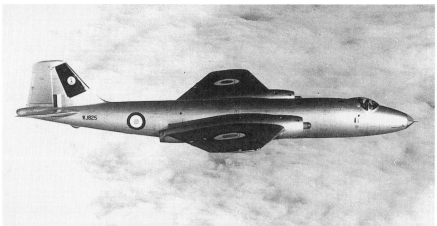

PR.3 WE137 of 540 Squadron - the first Canberra recce squadron.

82 Squadron PR.7 WJ825 over very unsuitable PR weather. Yet another shot showing the remarkable clean lines of the Canberra without tip tanks.

542 Squadron pose in front of their first PR.7, WH796, May 1954. CO was Sqn Ldr A.J.Picknett DFC.

Opposite page: **82 Squadron PR.7 at Abu Sueir, Sqn Ldr Young on the left. The Squadron re-equipped with PR.7s in October 1954 having previously flown PR.3s since reforming at Wyton as a Canberra unit the previous year.**

received a complement of PR.3s as 'part of the operational establishment for PR within Bomber Command.' Selected Lancaster crews from 82 Squadron went to 231 OCU to do the short PR Canberra conversion course before returning to the Squadron. The first operational Canberra sorties were made in December, the same month that the last Lancaster, PA427, went to Llandow for scrapping. 58 Squadron had been at Wyton since March 1953 and received its first PR.3, WE143, in December. Although a standard eight UE Squadron, it was May 1954 before the Squadron had even seven aircraft on strength because of the shortage of PR.3s.

The PR.3 was equipped as a medium to high level reconnaissance aircraft, ideal for the Bomber Command primary task of pre- and post attack photography. It was in this capacity that the squadrons took part in the routine of exercises, which provided an additional burden for the ever struggling air defences. With the likelihood that newly developed fighter aircraft would be able to get at the previously untouchable high-flying Canberra, attempts were made to 'cover' the blindspot at the rear of the aircraft. Most early Canberra marks had a mounting unit for a periscopic sextant, normally used for 'shooting' the stars for astro navigation, and 58 Squadron ran trials in 1955 with a 'Periscope Type KPG 6501' fitted so that the nav could observe the area to the rear of the aircraft – à la submarine! They found it was quite easy to track the contrails of attacking aircraft and thought the idea useful. Unfortunately, the trial was curtailed when English Electric asked for their periscope back! However, like all PR squadrons before and since, an important part of the day-to-day workload was 'task work' such as vertical photo cover for Town and Country Planning and the Ordnance Survey for map making. A variety of vertical and oblique cameras were available so there was little that the squadrons could not do. There was never a shortage of tasks, vertical pinpoints or area covers, oblique point targets or feature lines.

Basic PR techniques are discussed in the next chapter. Although the PR.3s had a high-level night capability it was not considered a suitable aircraft for low level night ops because the standard 4.5 inch flares were not good enough to use with the normal F.89 camera. The K.19 camera was usable with these flashes but was not used as it 'would not fit' in the Canberra - until 540 Squadron tried it in September 1953 and found it fitted quite well! Little came of it as the flares were not generally available to the recce squadrons and the squadrons were more than fully occupied with their normal tasks. A true low level night capability was not available until the F.97 camera system was introduced some time later. 'Flashing' had its dangers, it was not uncommon for photo-flashes to drop out of the flash crate and roll around on the flare doors. WF928 of 58 Squadron, was destroyed in mid air on 3rd June 1954 when a flash burst prematurely during a night photo run at 6000 ft over Sandbanks range.

Detachments went to various parts of the world on photo or other special tasks, such as Australia in March 1954 and Gibraltar in June the same year. The following month 82 Squadron acquired three B.2s for a special task, Operation *Dream*, an air sampling task, and kept the aircraft until September. In the same month, most of the PR.3s were handed to other units in preparation for re-equipment with PR.7s in October.

82 Squadron were not the first squadron to acquire the more powerful PR.7. 542 Squadron had reformed at Wyton on 17th May 1953 and received its first PR.7 in June with the same operational role as the other units. As the first PR.7-equipped squadron it then became involved with service trials on the mark, especially on the Avon 109 engines. WH796 was tasked to fly 300 hours in 28 days in June, on a 24 hours a day, seven days a week basis of up to six sorties a day. As no problems were encountered it was increased to 400 hours before the engines were stripped and sent back to the manufacturers. Like all Avon

engines, the 109s proved to be reliable and sturdy. The other Wyton squadrons also re-equipped with PR.7s in 1954, 540 getting its first aircraft in May and 58 their first in December. Most of the squadrons held a mix of PR.3s and PR.7s for some months until enough PR.7s were available and the PR.3s went for storage. Although all had the nominal eight aircraft, at one stage in early 1956 82 Squadron had thirteen aircraft on line.

By this time Wyton had a very impressive Canberra PR force – no less than four squadrons and a special flight, 1323 Flight. All the squadrons had the same range of duties and operational roles and sent detachments around the world. This included operational theatres with detachments by Wyton Squadrons to FEAF in the 1950s to reinforce the resident recce unit, 81 Squadron, and all the squadrons took part in Operation *Planters Punch* at one time or another. 542 Squadron started the ball rolling with a detachment in May 1955, followed by 540 then 82 Squadron in November and 58 Squadron the following January. The November detachment by 82 Squadron was typical with two aircraft, three crews and about twenty groundcrew deploying to Changi for four tasks – *Firedog* (anti-guerilla operations), Siam survey, Malay survey and Borneo/Sarawak survey. This was increased to four aircraft for a short period. The FEAF reinforcement remained a major task for the UK squadrons throughout the 1950s.

Many other overseas tasks were forthcoming, 58 squadron even sent two aircraft to Eastleigh, Nairobi for PR duties during the 'Mau Mau' troubles, the only Canberras involvement in this 'campaign'.

It was a very different existence on a PR squadron, the so-called 'PR or recce mystique' which once acquired made the PR aircrew a breed apart. No doubt this was partly due to the individualistic nature of most of the work – the lone recce aircraft flying either very high or very low. Visit almost any airfield in the world and there was a better than even chance that a PR Canberra would be there or would suddenly appear! It was too good to last and as financial constraints began to bite it was, as ever, the recce force that was the first to suffer.

The PR force decreased by one squadron in October 1955 when 542 Squadron disbanded, amalgamated with 1323 Flight and reformed, as 542 Squadron, as a Special Duties unit before moving to Weston Zoyland. The following year two of the PR squadrons were axed, 540 being disbanded in March 1956 and 82 in September. This left only 58 Squadron to shoulder the PR burden although they acquired the aircrew and aircraft of 82 Squadron pending the transfer of six of those crews to 100 Squadron to form a recce flight within that squadron for special duties.

Low Altitude Bombing System (LABS)
It was soon realised that a more practical technique would be required for the delivery of nuclear weapons to allow an acceptable degree of accuracy but also a safe escape for the aircraft. In the early 1950s development work on such a system was being done by the USAF and Minneapolis-Honeywell as the Low Altitude Bombing System (LABS). Deliveries of the system to the USAF began in 1954 and by the following year work was urgently progressing on a LABS system in the UK. Inevitably, delays and problems arose and in January 1956 a number of the Honeywell systems were bought to fill the gap.

The technique of low level penetration and 'toss' attack gave the Canberra a new lease of life in the bomber role as part of the balanced nuclear force. The B.6s of 9 Squadron were the first to go to the MU (at Colerne) to be modified for the LABS system, the first aircraft started the refit in mid 1957 and did not return to the Squadron until the following March. For a year or so aircraft were sent away in small batches to be modified and although the Squadron had a notional strength of 19 B.6s, up to four old B.2s had to brought back into service so that normal training could continue. It was not until February 1959 that 9 had enough of the modified aircraft to seriously make a start on LABS training, being the first squadron in Bomber Command to receive the system and the first to drop bombs using the LABS kit and technique. LABS became one of the primary roles for all strike/attack Canberra squadrons at home and abroad so it is worth examining the system in some detail.

The precise nature of flying required in this bombing technique and the stresses incurred through low level high speed flight necessitated certain new equipment and the strengthening of the Canberra airframe. This included a new inverter up the rear hatch, a LABS timer, 'G' meter and angle of release selector; also, detachable perforated baffle plates across the bomb bay to reduce buffeting. The bomb doors were strengthened to withstand wind speeds 80 kts above the original clearance limit. The approach to the target was at the lowest height at which it was possible to map read accurately. A calculation of how far a bomb would be projected (tossed) forward when released at a given speed and angle, dependent on the ballistics of the weapon, gave a bomb release point at a range from the target. To get to the release point the crew flew a timed run from a conspicuous landmark of known distance from the target. The pilot started an automatic timer from this point which then indicated the precise moment when the aircraft had to be pulled up to obtain the pre-selected angle of release. The bomb release mechanism operated when this angle has been reached and the aircraft then completed a half loop followed by a roll off the top.'

The basic parameters to ensure a good delivery were an entry speed of 420 kts from 250 ft, with a pull-up of 3g and release angle of either 45 degrees or 60 degrees depending on selection of primary or alternate mode. The bomb left the aircraft and peaked at about 5500 ft before descending to its forward throw distance of some 3700 yards. The aircraft reached 7000 ft and only 170 kts on recovery.

To try out the new system, 9 Squadron detached half its aircraft to Idris to carry out live LABS bombing with 25 lb practice bombs. By the end of the detachment in March 1959 over 1400 bombs had been dropped and the average error had reduced to 200 yards!

As the first modified aircraft arrived back on 9 Squadron, 139 Squadron were making a tentative start on training for this role with a programme of low level exercises. In July 1957 a number of aircraft were sent to Marshalls at Cambridge for LABS mods but none ever returned to the Squadron and 139 continued in a conventional role. A year later 12 Squadron were sending aircraft to Colerne for LABS work and by April 1959 the Squadron was flying its first LABS sorties, again at Idris, the favoured location for live bombing. By the summer they were settling into the new low level role and in July moved from Binbrook to Coningsby to join 9 Squadron who had been there since the 2nd June. These two squadrons were the only UK based units to receive the LABS system at a time when the UK Canberra force was continuing to contract. Both squadrons were now flying regular low level routes around Britain as well as trial sorties against naval targets up to 500 miles off Lands End. As an incentive to stay on track, and to record target accuracy, aircraft were fitted with short focal length F95 cameras. 12 Squadron seem to have 'perfected' the alternate or 'over the shoulder' delivery technique of a pull-up over the target and bomb release at 120 degrees (i.e. inverted)! This technique was useful if for any reason the planned run did not work, the aircraft could carry on to the

Opposite page: **9 Squadron B.6s pose in this classic echelon formation. 9 Squadron was the first to have its aircraft modified for the LABS technique.**

B.6 WT211 of 12 Squadron in the hands of the CO, Wg Cdr Blythe. 12 Squadron was another of the LABS units and developed the 'over the shoulder' release.

B.6 WJ764 of 12 Squadron. The later version of the squadron crest is superimposed on a green fin.

target and still get away with a safe delivery. The technique was suspended for a short while after a series of mishaps with the bomb not leaving the bomb bay cleanly but simply falling out when the aircraft recovered!

This was not the first problem which had arisen with LABS. the safety of the delivery technique had been questioned following the loss of two aircraft in Germany during LABS manoeuvres. As a result aircraft were restricted to 250 kts and later to not below 500 ft. The restrictions were lifted after short while but during an Idris detachment in November 1960 9 Squadron lost WJ759 and its crew during a LABS manoeuvre into cloud. Again the technique was suspended only to be reinstated in March 1961. It was inevitable that such a violent manoeuvre, often in marginal weather, would mean aircraft losses through crew disorientation.

Two further problems arrived with the nuclear LABS role. The first was the requirement to maintain aircraft on Quick Reaction Alert (QRA), which was introduced at Coningsby in October 1960. The second was the problem of aircraft fatigue in the low level role, for which the Canberra was not originally designed. A Bomber Command report of 1958 on Canberra fatigue life stressed the need to operate aircraft 'with due regard to fatigue' and to monitor the fatigue consumption. This was one of the main reasons for the fitting of 'G' meters as part of the LABS modifications as one of the main techniques of fatigue monitoring was 'g' counting. This can be used to estimate the percentage damage (or proportion of flying life) absorbed e.g if 100 hours of flying give 'g' equivalent to 10% of safe life then the safe life of the structure (aircraft) would be 1000 hours. The 'g' consumed on each sortie is recorded after landing from the fatigue meters and the life of the airframe monitored. The trick was to keep the fatigue consumption of

each sortie as low as possible. The Bomber Command report put forward four directives:

1. Speed to be kept as low as possible, consistent with the training or operational requirement.
2. Fuel drills to be arranged to keep wing integral fuel during low level or manoeuvring flight if possible.
3. Restrict low level and manoeuvre to latter stages of flight when fuel weight (aircraft weight) low.
4. No excessive 'g' to be pulled, exceed 4g as rarely as possible.

With these considerations the Report concluded 'unless the service life of the Canberra in this role continues for a very long time, say ten years from now, it is unlikely that any serious restriction of flying will be necessary as a result of fatigue damage.

Some of these same aircraft are still flying today and still getting hammered at low level!

B.6 (Mod) WJ775 of 51 Squadron. As a 'special' unit, 51 Squadron's aircraft underwent a number of modifications and at various times had different noses carrying different equipment.

B.2 WJ616 of 199 Squadron at Habbaniya 1954. This aircraft was eventually converted to a B.62 for Argentina and delivered in 1970. *via R.C.B. Ashworth*

Very rare shot of 51 Squadron B.2s at Watton, late 1950s. *RAF Museum P022115*

WJ616 of 199 Squadron, 1958, with new fin markings. *R.C.B.Ashworth*

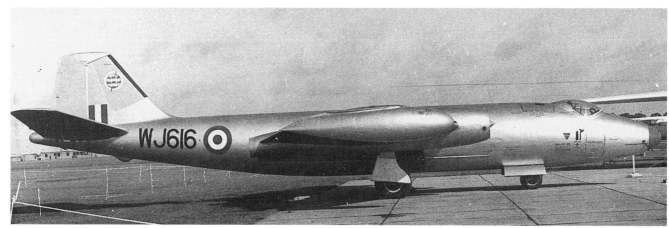

Wiggly Amps

Although the bomber and recce versions of the Canberra attracted the most attention, the type was already performing other roles, primarily with Signals Command and as 'special duties' squadrons. One of the earliest such was 527 Squadron which was formed out of the Calibration Squadron, Central Signals Establishment (CSE) at Watton on 1st August 1952 for the calibration of Control and Reporting (C & R) stations. Having used Lincolns, Ansons and Mosquitos, the Squadron re-equipped with a mix of Meteors and Canberras, plus a few Varsities. The great variety of calibration duties kept the Squadron very busy on routine sorties for airfield, air defence and naval radars, communications and navigation aids. The main aim of calibration sorties was to ensure that ground equipment, radar or nav, was functioning correctly and by means of the aircraft flying a series of pre-determined tracks, enabling the radar to be 'set-up' or calibrated correctly. By March 1956 the Squadron was operating only Canberras -

five B.2s plus two PR.7s, the latter being on loan from Bomber Command while the B.2s were grounded for tailplane mods. The PR.7s had gone by June as the B.2s returned to service. However, two aircraft, WJ620 and WJ647, were borrowed from the MU from April to July 1958 during a particularly hectic period. The following month, August, 527 was renumbered as 245 Squadron, still at Watton with no change in role – 'to provide the flying effort required for the air calibration and performance testing of C & R radar installations in 2 ATAF.' Four days later the unit moved to its new home at Tangmere although it was usual for aircraft to operate as small detachments from other airfields for calibration duties if required. Although not the most exciting flying job possible it was both necessary and quite demanding on the crew. Nevertheless, it is primarily remembered for its repetitive and boring nature.

'Special Duties' is one of those strange terms often used about events or tasks that are cloaked in secrecy or simply

unknown. It was inevitable that the Canberra would get involved in such work as it was such an adaptable and capable airframe. At Watton, the home of 'Signals' Canberras just as Wyton was the home of recce Canberras, 192 Squadron operated Washingtons and Lincolns on special duties and calibration up until February 1953 when 'B' Flight handed over its Lincolns in favour of two B.2s, WH670 and WH698.

245 Squadron B.2 WJ681, thought to have been photographed at Tangmere, 13 January 1959. As a 'special' squadron, 245 had a variety of aircraft - some shown here. Like so many Canberras, WJ681 had a long life but sadly went to Brawdy in January 1982, as 8735M, for crash rescue training. *Flight 38287s*

Canberra B.6 (Mod) WT305 'X' of 51 Squadron is seen here at Wyton on 20th April 1976, showing off its ESM 'dustbin'.

WJ640 of 51 Squadron. 51 took over from 192 Squadron as the 'Special Duties' squadron in August 1958, a role which it still holds although the Canberras were phased out in 1976. Note squadron marking on fin. *MAP*

Both aircraft went into the installation flight to have special equipment fitted and were not available for operations until September. It is still not certain exactly what 'operational tasks' the Air Ministry, the direct tasking authority, sent 192 on but they almost certainly included intelligence gathering. Aircraft were detached to European and Middle East bases from time to time with an average of one or two Canberra ops a month. Aircraft usually carried a crew of three including a 'Specialist Operator' for the kit.

The Squadron's B.2s were the first Canberras to be fitted with 'Green Satin' doppler, in June 1954, and as such conducted proving trials, accurate navigation being vital to the Squadron's work. The 'Green Satin' went on to become the main doppler fitted to most marks of Canberra and when combined with a GPI.4 (Ground Position Indicator) served the Canberra force in its worldwide ops for many years.

At the end of the year two B.6s, WT301 and WJ775, were acquired but the scale of operations continued as before. In August 1958 the Squadron was renumbered as 51 Squadron.

Another of the unusual squadrons was 199 at Hemswell which operated Lincolns and Canberras, usually two B.2s, WJ616 and WK188, as part of the ECM force. The first Canberra mention is July 1954 and from then on the aircraft took part in ECM training exercises for Fighter Command, Anti-Aircraft Command, Royal Navy, C & R and 2ATAF. Special jamming equipment

was fitted and it was the job of the Squadron to make life as difficult as possible for the 'defenders' by jamming radars and comms and generally making a nuisance of themselves! By late 1957 the squadron was at Honington operating Valiants and just one Canberra, WJ616. With disbandment in December the aircraft landed at Finningley from their last sorties to become 18 Squadron. The role remained the same but WJ616 left the squadron in February 1960 bringing the Canberra involvement to an end.

Other special squadrons, flights or units existed and many of these are covered in Chapters 6 and 9 which deal with Trials use of the Canberra but include other subjects such as Canberra use in the series of nuclear tests in the 1950s. Many other units had Canberras on strength at one time or another, some, like the 1 Group Communications Flight operating just a single aircraft acting as a 'run-around'; and others operating a few aircraft for specific duties.

Run-Down of Squadrons
From the end of 1956 the UK Canberra force entered a period of flux with the loss of crews to the V-bomber OCUs increasing. The first squadron had already said farewell to its Canberras when 617 Squadron disbanded in December 1955, to be followed in the last half of 1956 by the Germany Wing which had 'lodged' with 2ATAF since 1954. This was followed in January 1957 by the first of the UK wings when 101, 10 and 18 Squadrons disbanded. Although these units had only had Canberras for a few years, the disbandments were as scheduled but most did not reform on the V-bombers for a year or so.

As squadrons disbanded it freed aircraft, and to some extent spare crews, for other duties. The aircraft had a mixed fate.

A great many were sent to other Canberra squadrons and UEs were increased to sixteen to twenty aircraft, at times some squadrons had as many as twenty five aircraft. Others went to RAF squadrons overseas, some went into storage and some back to the manufacturers for refurbishing and overseas sales. This surplus of airframes also paved the way for the many conversions of mark that were to be such a feature of the Canberra in the late 1960s and 1970s.

The same year that saw the start of the run down of Canberra strength also saw the Canberra's greatest single operational involvement as the crisis over Egyptian Nationalism and the fate of the Suez Canal led Britain and France into conflict with Egypt. Most UK squadrons had been involved with detachments to the Middle East (Operation *Sun Tour*), to Luqa or Nicosia, which often included good-will visits to other countries, including Egypt. The full story of the Canberra's involvement in the Suez conflict of 1956 is told in Chapter 4. It was, however, not the first operational task undertaken by the UK Canberra squadrons as they had been involved, on a rotational basis, with anti-terrorist operations in the Far East, the Malayan Emergency, since the previous year. Details of this episode of the Canberra story are in Chapter 5. Although these events are covered in subsequent chapters they are very much an integral part of the Bomber Command Canberra story.

The Canberra equipped twenty six Bomber squadrons, including the four in Germany, at the peak of its service with Bomber Command. During this period it moved the Command into the jet age, doubled the height and speed of Lincoln operations, and prepared the way for the introduction of the new 'V' aircraft.

Chapter Three

Royal Air Force Germany

The Bomber Wing
The planned peak for the Canberra in service as a pure bomber was 1954/5 when a total of twenty four squadrons each with ten aircraft was envisaged.

By the middle of 1953 it became increasingly apparent that there were not sufficient airfields in the UK to house all the planned squadrons. At a meeting of the Expansion and Re-equipment Policy (ERP) Committee towards the end of 1953 two alternative courses of action were outlined: either another UK airfield would have to be brought up to Class 2 standard (Class 2, as required by the Canberras, stipulated a 9,500 ft runway, Class 1, as required by the V-bombers, an 11,000 ft runway) at an estimated cost of £100,000, the choice being either Full Sutton or

Worksop; or, the 'overflow' squadrons could go to an RAF station in Germany where Class 2 facilities already existed. The latter course of action had the added advantage that it would be seen as tangible support for NATO's forces in Europe.

149 Squadron B.2s in the hangar at Gutersloh, July 1956. Note the 551 Wing motif on the nose of the nearest aircraft. In January 1957 WH713 was delivered to the Bristol Aeroplane Co for installation of Olympus 104 engines and was eventually scrapped at Filton in Sept 1959.

Various staff papers were prepared during the remainder of the year and early in 1954 to discuss the pros and cons of both ideas, with the recommended number of squadrons for such deployment being agreed on as four, a standard bomber wing. Finally, on 29th March, the CAS, Air Chief Marshal Sir William Dickson, announced the decision that 'we should go ahead and form these squadrons in 2nd TAF.' By June the designations of the four squadrons were announced and further that a new wing, No 551, would be formed to control them. It was envisaged that the deployment would be only temporary until the run down of the Canberra force in the UK due to the V-bomber build up, then the Germany squadrons could withdraw to the UK or disband.

Because of the temporary nature of the deployment it was decided that the squadrons would remain under overall control of Bomber Command as part of the Main Force and would be withdrawn to the UK in the event of hostilities. HQ 2nd TAF would provide local operational control and administrative support to the new wing which would lodge at Gutersloh. This station was somewhat of a strange choice as it was only 70 miles from the East German border and in the North German Plain, long considered the most likely axis of any thrust from the east. Perhaps the plan to withdraw on the outbreak of hostilities was a sound one as Gutersloh would have been far too close for a strategic bomber unit to the front line, and at this stage the Canberras were purely envisaged in strategic terms.

Regarding terminology for the RAF organisation in Germany there has been some confusion as various records use differing titles. Some records refer to 2nd TAF (Tactical Air Force) while others refer to 2 ATAF (Allied Tactical Air Force), one even refers to 2nd ATAF. The confusion ends in 1959 when 2nd TAF was renamed as Royal Air Force Germany and from that date 2 ATAF refers to NATO units in northern Germany and 4 ATAF to those in the south. For simplicity, the terms should be considered interchangeable for the remainder of this chapter.

The first of the lodger squadrons was due to deploy 'ready made' with the other three to form in theatre. However, the plan was altered slightly as the runway at Gutersloh was being resurfaced and so in order to meet the date promised to SAC-EUR (Supreme Allied Commander Europe) the first squadron moved to Ahlhorn. Thus, Canberra B.2 WJ626 of 149 Squadron touched down at Ahlhorn at 1130 on 25th August 1954 and became the first aircraft of the first British bomber squadron to be based in Germany since the First World War. 1954 was a very mobile year for 149 Squadron; originally formed at Coningsby in April 1953 it moved to Cottesmore in June 1954 before deploying to Ahlhorn in August. This was only a short sojourn as the Squadron moved to the wing base at Gutersloh on 17th September. Established with ten B.2s, 149 was to be the experienced nucleus around which 551 Wing would form. Its operational policy and training requirements were the same as for any of the UK squadrons of Bomber Command and revolved around exercises and crew classification. There appears to have been the odd period of relief from high level navexs and bombing, as recorded in the ORB for October which reported that 'WJ567 had a birdstrike on a low level reconnaissance, the navigator in the bomb aimer's position was injured.' Low level was still the exception rather

than the rule as the roles did not require low level penetration, a technique that was to develop in the face of improved air defence systems. The incident did serve to highlight what was to become a major 'problem' for all low level aircraft – birdstrikes, of which more later.

Although the withdrawal from Germany of the 'temporary Canberra force' was continually being discussed, there was no doubt in the mind of the writer of the 149 Squadron ORB for the month of its arrival, 'the Squadron remains part of the Main Force Bomber Command, lodging in 2nd ATAF. Bomber Command continues to exercise policy control; day to day operational and administrative control is by HQ ATAF through HQ 2 Group.'

Within a few months the other squadrons had begun to form at Gutersloh, 102 Squadron on 30th October and 103 Squadron on 30th November. The final squadron, 104, did not form until 15th March 1955. All received the standard UE of ten B.2s and took part in all the same exercises that their UK counterparts were involved with; Gee-H was the main bombing system along with visual bombing and the continental ranges received a due pounding of 25 lb practice bombs and the odd 1,000 lb bomb or two. By making use of UK ranges as well, the Squadrons were able to work up very quickly, as evidenced by the fact that 102 Squadron had nine of

Opposite page: **Box of four 69 Squadron PR.3s, Laarbruch March 1958 - practising for the farewell flypast as 69 moved to Malta in April. Note broad white Vs on a blue background on nose-wheel doors.**

B.2 WK146 of 102 Squadron - a rare shot of this squadron's aircraft. As the second squadron of 551 Wing, 102 formed at Gutersloh in October 1954. *J.D.R. Rawlings*

17 Squadron pose for the camera. *Everley*

its eleven crews 'Combat' classified within seven months of formation. By the middle of 1955 the Wing had settled into a routine with each squadron flying some 400 hours a month, about 25% of this at night and dropping about 250 bombs, mainly 25 lb practice bombs, split equally between Gee-H and visual deliveries with bombing averages of 300 and 400 yards respectively.

Each squadron had one aircraft away each month to the Med, Middle East or even Nairobi on Lone Ranger flights and there were frequent trips back to the UK for competitions and exercises, added to this were the delights of an overseas tour. All this was obviously too good to last and so no one was surprised when early in 1956 it was announced that the Gutersloh Wing would disband on the original time scale. The four squadrons were disbanded in the summer of 1956, 104 in July and the other three in August. The medium bomber force had been as temporary as promised, but it was by no means the end of the Canberra in Germany.

Photo Recce
From the initial discussions of 1953/54 it was intended that 2nd ATAF in Germany should have its own Canberra force in the PR and NI (Night Interdictor) roles. The first of these in-theatre squadrons was 69 Squadron which formed at Gutersloh on 1st October 1954 with eight PR.3s. Early in

December the Squadron moved to Laarbruch. Situated close to the Dutch border, and therefore much less vulnerable than Gutersloh, Laarbruch had been designated as the home of the Germany PR assets and during 1955 another two recce squadrons were formed there, 31 Squadron (March) and 80 Squadron (June), both with PR.7s. A fourth squadron, 17 Squadron, was subsequently formed at Wahn on 1st June 1956, moving to Wildenrath nine months later, bringing the Canberra recce force up to full strength.

Although officially designated PR(MR) squadrons, the Maritime Recce aspect for the Germany based squadrons was virtually non-existent. Although they practised shipping photography when detached to the Med, the number of times they were actually tasked with this role was negligible as there were squadrons based in the UK and the Med who had more experience of such things.

As with the UK based PR squadrons the original camera fit for the PR.3 and PR.7 allowed for only medium to high level photography. The PR.3 for example with its fan of up to six F.52 cameras fitted with either 20 or 36 inch focal length lenses plus a vertically mounted K.17 with 6 inch lens or F.49 with a choice of 6 or 12 inch lenses. Although usually limited by the height of the cloud base, the squadrons used the outstanding performance of their

aircraft whenever possible. In June 1955 for example 69 Squadron took part in Exercise *Carte Blanche* and reported heights over the target in excess of 48,000 ft which was way out of reach of most of the defences. Earlier in the year the ORB refered to 'long-range PR sorties introduced by the Squadron' which consisted of cross-country exercises 'taking in the three practice photographic areas – South West France, North East Italy and Corsica/Sardinia/Sicily' during which 'photographs were taken under simulated operational conditions and at operational heights of 43 – 48,000 ft.' These trips obviously covered vast distances and although the Canberra was much faster than its contemporaries such sorties were frequently of 6 hours duration, the longest recorded being 6 hours 20 minutes – in a PR.3! The primary purpose of such photography operationally was to obtain pre-strike recce of targets, such as airfields or major installations, or post-strike recce to assess the damage state of the target.

Not all high level work was of pin-point targets. The aircraft could fly a tasked line to provide continuous cover of a strip or several runs could be flown so that the strips overlapped laterally giving coverage of an area, this being referred to as the SAC (Small Area Cover). This latter type of sortie could be flown at any height depending on the scale of photography required and the size of the area, but the lower the height the smaller the area covered by each exposure so to cover a given area required more overlapping lines. Frequently work of this nature required more than one sortie and to complete a survey of a country the size of Denmark or Holland could involve dozens of sorties over several months.

As well as providing vertical cover of a target the aircraft could use the oblique mounted cameras to provide stand-off photography of areas or installations which were too sensitive, or too heavily defended, to overfly, this technique being especially useful when looking over a border into unfriendly territory.

All vertical, and a lot of oblique, photo work was done with the navigator lying in the prone position in the nose and map reading along a line on a map. The recce sight was a very basic affair consisting of a banana-shaped blade (hence 'banana sight') approximately a foot long and 1.5 inches deep mounted horizontally. By squinting across the width of the blade so that he could see neither side, the navigator could see what was exactly below the aircraft – providing of course that the wings were level; 10 degrees of bank at 40,000 ft would represent a huge error on the ground! This technique of map reading and passing 'right a bit, left a bit' instructions to the pilot was the well

proven one used by bomb aimers for years, but things became more difficult for the recce crew when the camera was switched on. If the pilot banked the aircraft in response to a demand from the navigator just as an exposure was taken the resulting photograph would be a 'throw out' from the required line and might cause a gap. To combat this the pilot had a series of lights which illuminated to tell him that a photograph was about to be taken and therefore to level the wings quickly. This was fine at high level where there would be some 20 seconds between exposures but lower down the time interval between exposures reduced to as little as 2 seconds and so the system evolved of steering the aircraft with the rudder while keeping the wings level with aileron and all the while flying a very accurate height. The prolonged concentration required of both members of the crew on a survey sortie, perhaps 3 hours of navigating and flying to an accuracy only demanded of bomber crews for a few minutes at a time, made such a mission extremely tiring but the job satisfaction was immense.

Oblique photography of a pre-planned target could be flown in exactly the same way, indeed if the navigator map-read to the correct stand-off position then the photographs could be taken with neither crew member actually seeing the target! Targets of opportunity however were the domain of the pilot because he had a better view to the sides than the navigator. The problem of sighting the cameras – long focal length cameras with a very small field of view – produced many and varied solutions ranging from highly complex 'bolt-on' affairs that had to be squinted through, to annotated pieces of perspex that clipped to the side of the canopy. The simplest and – as it is still used by PR.9 pilots – probably the best system, was to draw two horizontal lines, one inside and the other outside the canopy. A tape measure and a formula (all sums done by the nav of course) produced a mark on the concrete of the dispersal which the pilot lined up with his normal sitting height, two chinagraph lines and all was ready.

Although very basic this method of sighting proved to be very accurate and it could even be used for navigation. The authors were once 'ever so slightly'

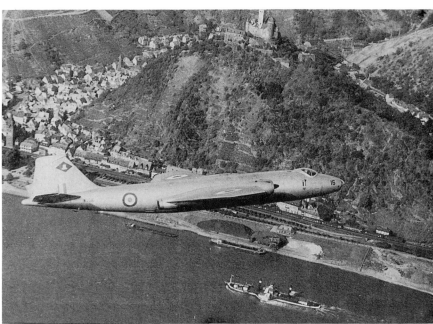

80 Squadron PR.7 WT516 doing the Rhine castles tour, 1958. This castle, like so many along the Rhine, became a favourite recce target!

Preparing the F.46 cameras for loading into a 69 Squadron PR.3, Laarbruch 1957.

unsure of their position over the sea en route to Hong Kong. The pilot noticed that an island some distance to port was going to pass through the sight lines so a quick look by the nav in the recce data book (tables of height to lateral distance) gave the actual stand off distance for that height, a call abeam and the result was an accurate fix that even the Squadron nav leader accepted!

In the spring of 1957 the recce Canberras started operating in a 'new low level role' as a counter tactic to the increasing threat at high levels. In the previous year, 80 Squadron had undertaken trials of a low level camera fit using F95 cameras with various focal length lenses. The trials concluded that the best all round results came

PR.7 WT534 of 17 Squadron. Recce Canberra plus a typical industrial target. In the TR role the Canberra squadrons were tasked against anything from a small bridge to a giant industrial complex - to come back with a Visual Report (Visrep) of a target such as this was no mean feat.

PR.7 WH798 of 80 Squadron, Laarbruch, seen here at Odiham, September 1960. After its operational life. WH798 remained in Germany as a decoy aircraft at Bruggen, as 8130M, from 1971 to 1977. *J.D.R. Rawlings*

from a 4 inch lens but with a 6 or 12 inch lens for special sorties where a greater stand off was advisable, for example when photographing a hostile airfield or ship.

Although the trial was essentially complete by the end of 1956, indeed in August of that year an 80 Squadron crew flew to Cyprus with cameras and a modification kit to brief 13 Squadron on low level techniques, it was not until March 1957 that a standard low level camera fit was decided upon. In November of that year the 80 Squadron ORB records that low level cross country flights were being flown at speeds between 300 and 360 kts at 250 ft while further trials had cleared the F95 for use up to 450 kts. At low level the navigator either lay in the nose or sat beside the pilot depending on personal preference. As with high level oblique work it was the pilot's job to aim and operate the cameras.

31 Squadron PR.7 WH775 doing the rapid film display in September 1964. A visiting VIP would be photographed as he arrived and a print would be presented to him within minutes of his arrival.
Gp Capt G. Pitchfork

It is interesting that in 1959 the role of the 2 ATAF Canberra recce force changed from 'photo reconnaissance backed up by visual reporting to visual reporting backed up by photography, with the proviso that no additional risk be taken to obtain photo cover.' In view of this, the CO of 80 Squadron put forward a proposal for two-nav crews in the PR.7s, his reasoning being that an extra nav makes planning quicker and more accurate and provides an extra set of eyes to look at the target for the visual report. With two navs on board one could do the map reading and pass visual fixes to the other who could monitor the nav kit and feed information back from the doppler. Furthermore, on the target run it was important to write down the target details as soon as possible so one nav could act as 'secretary' while the other nav and the pilot passed details of what they saw. With four or more targets on one sortie it was essential to complete the 'VISREP' as soon as possible, often accompanied by a little sketch of the target if the navigator felt so inclined!

Getting to know the standard terminology required for each different category of target was by no means easy, the number of different types of bridge for example is amazing with such variations as bowstring truss, cantilever and beam-and-deck to name but a few. The crew also had

to develop the ability to estimate the dimensions of the target, a procedure that usually involved calculating, or guessing, how many 'standard' cars would fit on the bridge! These are only two small elements of one target category from a list of almost twenty categories.

A third role for the PR force which evolved in the 1950s was that of night reconnaissance. Night photography obviously required a light source and at high level this was provided by Second World War 8 inch photo flashes designed to be dropped from 40,000 ft to ignite at 20,000 ft. However, this was a role which was not given to the Germany squadrons but was the exclusive prerogative of the two Mediterranean recce squadrons, who would happily have ditched the role if they could. Of more use in the Central Region was a low level system consisting of the F97 camera and a flash crate. This was first mooted in 1957 but did not arrive with 80 Squadron until November 1959. Carrying up to 256 1.75 inch photoflashes, the crate was fitted in the flare bay, as the truncated bomb bay of PR Canberras was known, and fired the flares downwards and slightly backwards. The flares exploded 2 seconds after leaving the aircraft and produced enough light for the F97 camera to take a photograph. The main problem with using this system was that the Canberra's

nav kit was not accurate enough to do away with the need of running from an easily found feature, then using stopwatch and compass to overfly the target. At night the requirement was for a lit ground feature, or bright moonlight, and the prospects of finding many lit features in wartime would be slim. The other problem was the tactical one of throwing out flares which lit up not only the ground but also, momentarily, the aircraft and as the flares were dropped in sticks of five to twelve it would not take long for someone to predict where the aircraft was! Only with the introduction of the passive Infra Red Line Scan (IRLS) equipment to the PR.9 in the late 1970s was this problem overcome.

The original Germany-based recce squadron, 69 Squadron, moved to Malta in April 1958 leaving three PR.7 units, 17, 31 and 80 Squadrons, as the recce element of RAF Germany.

Daily life on the squadrons was very varied, from the three hour low level sorties with five targets to the five hour high

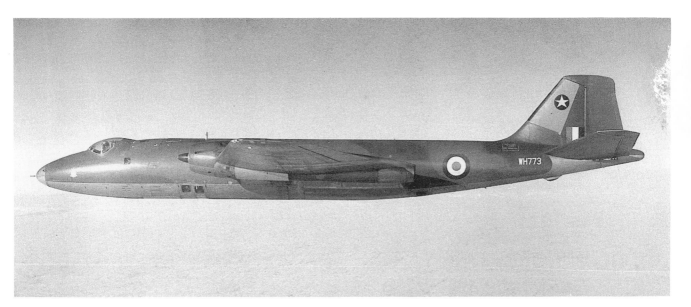

level extravaganzas on the 'round Europe tour'. There were numerous exercises, from the regular monthly 'Guest' where the purpose was to test regional air defences to one-off major exercises such as *Stronghold* to test the UK air defences. These, plus squadron and station exercises, were also good practice for the highlight of the recce year, the competition season. There were two main competitions, the Sassoon Photographic Trophy which was open to all RAF recce squadrons and Royal Flush where the best of 2ATAF took on the best of 4ATAF in a test of 'operational efficiency'. Royal Flush was open to all NATO recce squadrons based in the two regions with guest appearances from air forces from other regions or even a few non-NATO units. It was arguably the most intensive competition of its time and the stories of cheating and spoofing are legion. John Clemons was acting as Distaff (Directing Staff - the umpires of an exercise) one year when the competition was being flown out of the USAF base at Ramstein and a French squadron was invited to take part. On the particular day in question the weather was appalling in the target area and every aircraft reported a weather abort on one army target except the French pilot who produced a perfect visual report on what was supposed to be there but had failed to get photo cover because of 'marginal weather'. Subsequent investigation by the umpires discovered that the weather had been so bad that the army unit concerned, commanded by a friend of the erring pilot, had not even left the barracks!

Although not getting away so frequently or so far afield as their UK or Med based counterparts, the RAFG squadrons had their share of 'Lone Rangers' and 'Round Robins', the latter being designed to check the cross servicing capabilities at other NATO airfields. The main operating area however remained the Central Region of

PR.7 WH773 of 31 Squadron.
Gp Capt G. Pitchfork

80 Squadron PR.7 WT522, January 1960, showing the after-effects of a high-speed bird strike.

PR.7 WH792 of 31 Squadron. Typically the lone recce aircraft would be tasked to cover targets far and wide and a low level sortie lasted three hours and included five or six targets.

NATO and as the tactical environment changed with the advent of SAMs and the increasing complication of the NATO strike plans, the recce squadrons became ever more tied to the strictures and limitations of quick reaction, dispersal of forces, NBC and Taceval.

By the end of the 1960s it was obvious that the Canberra was becoming less and less viable in the Central Region as it was too slow and not manoeuvrable enough

against the modern threats. So, in September 1969 80 Squadron disbanded, followed at the end of 1969 by 17 Squadron. The last one, 31 Squadron, soldiered on until 31st March 1971 and like the others was never directly replaced in role in RAFG. The TR role was taken over by the Phantom FGR.2 with its excellent dual capability of recce and ground attack but the flexibility provided by the Canberra force was lost.

VX185 as the B(I)8 prototype - note belly bulge of the gun pack also the underwing pylons.

WT307, the first production B(I)6 in the early silver finish. Gun pack fitted plus 500lb bombs on underwing pylons.
EE Co. AW/FA/123

The Strike Squadrons
The first of the Germany Night Intruder squadrons, 213 Squadron, formed at Ahlhorn in July 1955 with B(I)6s and moved to Bruggen 2 years later. This was the only squadron to receive what was really an interim mark of aircraft; the B(I)6 was a basic B.6 equipped with a ventral 4 x 20 mm gunpack and underwing pylons for bombs or rocket launchers. The B.6 and B(I)6 Pilot's Notes are the same manual and the introduction states that the B(I)6 is 'a B.6 modified for conversion to an interdictor role. Special doors are fitted to the bomb bay which accommodate a gun pack at the rear; flares may be carried in the front of the bay. A Mk.3N reflector gun sight is above the pilot's instrument panel. An F.24 camera is carried in the rear

fuselage aft of the bomb bay and a G.45 gun camera is in the starboard wing leading edge. The control column handwheel is modified and carries gun, bomb and camera controls on its right grip.'

The B(I)6 therefore continued to suffer from the major drawback of all B.2s and B.6s at low level – poor visibility from the cockpit, although this did not stop the only B(I)6 Squadron, 213, from winning the RAFG bombing competition, the Salmond Trophy more than once. The true interdictor version, the B(I)8, which followed was a response to an early Air Staff requirement (Specification 1B/22D&P) for a 'specialised interdictor version for low level operation in visual ground contact armed with a wide range of conventional bombs, rockets and guns.' This required

substantial redesign of the nose area and at the same time the decision was taken to give the pilot a raised 'fighter-type' canopy for better all round vision. The 'punch' was provided by a Boulton Paul gun pack (4 x 20 mm Hispano) fitted into the rear of the bomb bay and carrying 525 rounds per gun, enough for 50 seconds firing, and the underwing pylons as on the B(I)6. The combination of four 20 mm cannon was a well proven one that had performed well in the past and was to bring the Canberra into the ground attack game in a new departure for the aircraft. Although not used operationally by RAF interdictor Canberras it did see active service with the Indian Air Force and was given a good write-up by the pilots. The 'good book' exhorted the pilot to 'confine firing to bursts not exceeding 3 seconds, with a minimum interval of 10 seconds between bursts'; even this short burst put over 100 rounds in the direction of the target! Although there was no speed limit on firing the guns, micro switches prevented the guns being fired with either the undercarriage down or the flare doors open – just as well really! VX185 was modified, yet again, into the new design and first flew on 23rd July 1954.

The B(I)8 was a popular aircraft with crews despite its obvious shortcoming of having no ejection seat for the navigator. This was partly due to the requirement for the aircraft to be produced with as few changes as possible from the basic Canberra. In order to revamp the pilot's cockpit and give him a bubble canopy it meant that the standard layout of navigator behind pilot had to go and so there was no room to fit in a second bang seat. So, the nav was given a little sideways facing table with a small window as his view on the world. However, he also had his home in the glazed nose which, with its additional side windows, gave him excellent visibility at low level and this became the standard position for the nav. With the increased amount of low level came an increase in the number of high-speed birdstrikes including a number of instances of birds impacting the perspex nose and coming through causing facial injuries to the navigator. Toughened macron panels were fitted which stopped the problem with the nose but airframe damage was still a factor, a bird the size of a seagull, impacted at 300 kts, is capable of causing severe airframe damage to wings and there are recorded instances of birds ending up inside tip tanks. Added to this, of course, was the danger of a bird going into the engine and causing the engine to pack-up - with consequent asymmetric problems. Fortunately the Avon is a sturdy engine!

The navigators wore special flying suits with a harness for the chest parachute which was stored on the wall by the entrance hatch. If the time came to leave the aircraft then the pilot had to convert aircraft speed into height with a zoom climb to give enough time, and height, for the nav to leap out. This entailed the nav clipping on the parachute, opening the door and 'tucking in the head and rolling out of the door', a large panel in front of the door was projected into the airflow to act as a windbreak. A static line attached to the aircraft operated the parachute. The system was used and it did work but it was by no means ideal in an aircraft that was designed to operate at low level. Although it was a subject of crewroom debate, the navs were resigned to the situation and, besides, very few aircraft at the time had ejection systems for rear crew so it was not really expected.

Following the disbandment of the four Bomber Command lodger squadrons at Gutersloh, some of the crews were retained there to form a new squadron, No.59, still equipped with B.2s. However, this squadron was the second to equip with the B(I)8, a process that took place in the summer of 1957 before the Squadron moved to Geilenkirchen on 15th November. The first of the new B(I)8 units was 88 Squadron which had reformed at Wildenrath in January 1956, having disbanded in October 1954 in the Far East as a Sunderland unit! The last of the B(I)8 squadrons, No.16, eventually reformed at Laarbruch on 1st March 1958 thus completing the four squadron strike force. RAFG had its medium range nuclear strike force, although at first relying on American weapons (Project E) as there was no suitable British weapon. This meant that all strike bases had an American 'presence' which controlled the weapons at each of the chosen sites. The Canberra strike force remained a vital part of the NATO deterrent force until mid 1972 when the last operational squadron, No.16, disbanded before re-equipping with Buccaneer S.2Bs.

With strike as the primary role, the squadrons spent much of their time perfecting the LABS techniques, the system being identical to that used by the LABS squadrons of Bomber Command. A detailed account of the technique is in Chapter 2. The Germany squadrons soon overtook their home-based counterparts, so much so that when a 213 Squadron crew attended a LABS instructors course

A member of 88 Squadron trying out modified survival equipment - reinforced elbows, new dinghy attachments and parachute quick release.

WT340 of 88 Squadron - the first of the B(I)8 units - over Germany, showing off the black undersurfaces of the early years of service of this variant. *88 Squadron records*

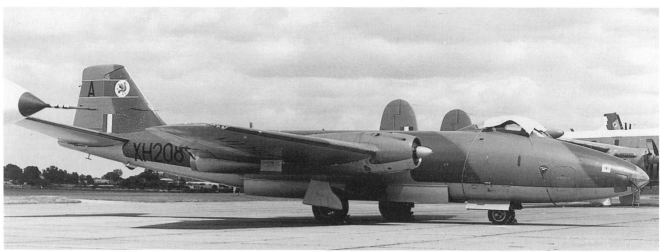

B(I)8 XM263 of 16 Squadron in pre sharks-tooth days. The bubble canopy enhanced the lines of the Canberra and made it look even better. This is a classic undercarriage-on-the-way-up shot. Like many B(I)8s, '263 made its way to Peru as a B(I)68.

B(I)8 XH208 of 3 Squadron, 1967. After 11 years of B(I)8 ops, 3 Squadron bade fare-well to its aircraft at Laarbruch in January 1972 and converted to Harriers. *MAP*

B(I)8 of 16 Squadron at Ghedi, included to show the hydraulic door 'wind break' which deployed so that the Nav could leap out of the main door. *Dudley Brown*

B(I)8 of 14 Squadron on QRA at
Wildenrath. Built for the low level ground
attack role, the B(I)8s in RAFG were soon
involved with nuclear LABS and so began
the round of Canberra QRA. *14 Squadron*

B(I)6 WT323 of 213 Squadron, 1969. The
squadron received its B(I)6s in March 1956
and operated the type as the sole RAF user
of the mark until the end of 1969. *MAP*

88 Squadron's mascot 'Fred Aldrovandi'
with Wally Meers at 40,000ft on the way to
Gibraltar. 'Fred has never shown any signs
of anoxia and is perfectly happy at altitude
provided the sun is on the nose cone.'

at Wittering in July 1958 they reported back that 'it would appear that knowledge of this subject is more advanced in 2 ATAF than in Bomber Command.' This state of affairs may have been partly due to a difference in training methods whereby in Germany a ground trainer (the LABS caravan) did the rounds of the strike squadrons so that all the crews could practise with the equipment, whereas in the UK selected crews went to the Bomber Command Development Unit (BCDU) for training and then had the job of disseminating the information to their squadrons. Another important factor was the emphasis placed on the low level role. However, some of the RAFG units did not commence serious LABS training until 1959, partly because of a lack of facilities and also because of other commitments. In mid 1958 this included a period of 'high readiness' for 88 Squadron and 59 Squadron for possible deployment to the Middle East. 88 Squadron took a photograph of their ops board showing eleven out of twelve aircraft serviceable and ready to go. The twelfth was the proverbial 'christmas tree' having been robbed for spares for the other aircraft and didn't fly for some time! The Middle East commitment remained in force until the early 1960s and although the squadrons did not deploy to the Persian Gulf, 'pioneer' trips were sent from time to time to inspect certain airfields.

88 Squadron was typical with its roles in early 1958 including low altitude nuclear bombing, medium/high level all-weather bombing using Gee-H (with nuclear weapons), and low level and shallow-dive bombing with conventional weapons. Earlier the Squadron had relinquished its declared roles of air to ground support for the army and visual reconnaissance so that concentrated LABS training could commence.

However, from the mid 1960s onwards the Canberra was almost solely devoted to the strike role and the majority of sorties were singleton sorties in the strike configuration flashing around Germany at 250 ft, 270 kts for two and a half hours or so. Target runs were flown at 360 kts although for competitions the tips were often removed and the attack speed increased to 420kts. One of the nav's main jobs on a LABS sortie was working out the LABS computer settings from the forecast met winds. Having used a 'gizmo' to get the numbers, he went into the back hatch to set the 'x' and 'y' co-ordinates. After that it was fly the sortie and keep your fingers crossed that you had got it right! On the LABS run itself there was nothing to do except time the run with a stopwatch and keep a very close eye on the altimeter during the recovery from the procedure.

As with all the Canberra squadrons, the RAFG units went on frequent excursions to Libya (Idris) to 'throw bombs at a bunch of oil cans at the Tarhuna range' – so said 88 Squadron! This was usually a double-squadron detachment with two squadrons going at the same time which, of course, led to 'healthy' competition... 88 Squadron had snakes, the Squadron motif, painted on their flying helmets to counter the black flying suits and yellow helmets worn by 16 Squadron!

The Tarhuna range target was a 40 yard triangle of oil cans which was considered too easy as it could be seen from miles away. However, this did not stop the local Arabs, who earned a shilling for recovering bombs from the sand, from sheltering in the centre of the target as this was considered the safest place!

bombs or flares to complement the bombs or rocket pods on the wing pylons. The original specification for the two marks required that 'the aircraft shall be capable of easy conversion to the normal bomber role. They shall therefore be delivered with a set of normal bomb doors, and any other fittings necessary to effect the conversion. It must be possible to effect the change under operational conditions in the field in less than 24 hours.'

Medium and high level bombing techniques were no different from those employed by Bomber Command but were practised 'just enough to keep one's hand in'. The LABS technique could be used to 'toss' conventional bombs but was not considered accurate enough for pinpoint targets, it would only be used on heavily defended 'area targets' such as vehicle parks or rail yards. The more accurate methods favoured by the crews were skip and dive bombing. In the former the bomb was released from level flight close to the ground and was fitted with a time delay fuse, the idea being for the bomb to 'skip' along the ground maintaining its forward speed until it came up against a target with vertical extent, a building or bridge abutment for example, and after burying itself in the side of the target, explode. To enable the accuracy of such deliveries to be assessed on the range an area the size of a tennis court was marked out on the ground and a large net was stretched vertically across the far end; to score a 'hit' the bomb had to skip in the court and penetrate the net. For dive bombing and rocketry a target circle was marked on the ground and the scores obtained by two widely spaced observers plotting the bearing of the impact and then comparing

the readings, where the bearings crossed was where the bomb had hit. Dive angles varied from a shallow 5° or 10° to a steep 20°. Angles as high as 40° were tried from time to time but were not very practical in the low cloud conditions of Europe as recovery from the dive would almost certainly be above the cloud! Rocketry and dive bombing were really pilot 'sports' and so he was given a reflector gun sight which was suitably modified. Originally a Mk.3N sight was used but this proved troublesome and inaccurate and was eventually replaced by the French SFOM sight. The SFOM sight was considered to be quite good although most pilots have remarked that it had an expiry date on it which was earlier than many were actually installed!

It was very much a day only sight but at one stage 16 Squadron took advantage of a change in the target at Nordhorn to use the sight at night. Vince Robertson, a pilot on 16 Squadron, remembers that the scrub and rubbish were cleared away from the target area at Nordhorn leaving a light-coloured sand circle which showed up from miles away – even at night. An intrepid crew decided to take advantage of this and use the sight for a night attack rather than rely on the standard technique of a Decca attack, a 'blind' bomb. However, the sight was too bright even with the light turned right down – the answer was to stick bits of red cellophane in front of the sight to dim the light enough for it to be of use. The first bomb dropped with this new 'system' went within a few feet of the target rather than the usual hundreds of feet of a Decca bomb. The crew was caught out because they were recorded as being at 500 ft and not the briefed minimum of 600 ft! On future sorties crews

Opposite page: **59 Squadron B(I)8s in earth revetment hide-aways.**

The pilot's ejection seat in 213 Squadron B(I)6 WT316 fired when the aircraft was hit by a runaway 80 Squadron aircraft!

B(I)8 XM275 of 3 Squadron over Germany 1968. The 'environment' for the interdictors was low level with a 'sneak up and hit them hard' philosophy, a task which the B(I)8 was well equipped to carry out.

213 Squadron B(I)6 WT323 - excellent shot of the upper surfaces of the aircraft.

All LABS training was done with practice bombs and despite the stated policy of having no secondary role each squadron carried out conventional weapons training using the full capability of the interdictor versions. Both marks had ventral gun packs fitted in the rear of the bomb bay with modified doors that enclosed the front half of the bomb bay so that the aircraft could also carry an internal load of

Checking the two practice bombs on the underwing pylon of a 213 Squadron B(I)6.

Groundcrew get to grips with a B(I)6 gun pack - not the easiest of places to work.

Opposite page, bottom: **213 Squadron B(I)6 over Tarhuna range. Height can be assessed by the size of the shadow.**

adjusted the readings on the sight to work at 600 ft and results were excellent! As with all spheres of military aviation, individuals devised their own additional techniques or 'gizmos', such as putting chinagraph marks on the canopy to denote crucial phases of an attack. It was standard practice for the navs to put chinagraph marks in the nose to assess if the dive was too steep or too shallow although the main job was still that of altimeter monitor to call descent heights and yell 'recover' when it was time to pull out of the dive. Vince Robertson again, 'having put the aircraft into what you thought was the correct dive angle you asked the nav to check it – the navs drew chinagraph marks on the nose at 5°, 10°, etc and could assess how the horizon sat and therefore the dive angle. "Only 10°" would come the reply so steepen the dive, "how's that now. . ." and so on until you achieved the correct angle. This often felt extreme and it seemed as if you were hanging in your straps even at 20 degrees!'

The target for strafe (guns) consisted of a 20 ft square panel of hessian sacking suspended from two poles; the scoring system was the same as that used on small arms ranges – after the shoot the range officer went down and counted the holes, if any!!

The conventional roles flown by the Canberra squadrons could be categorised as follows:

a. *Visual and armed recce.* Operating singly or in pairs the crews would search an area or line for enemy activity and either report back or, if armed, attack in a manner similar to the fighter sweeps of the Second World War. Daytime only.

b. *Close Air Support (CAS).* Called up by the ground forces the aircraft would be diverted to a target by a FAC, either airborne or ground, to give direct fire support to the ground forces. This required good co-operation between the crew and the FAC (Forward Air Controller) and the Canberra with its good manoeuvrability and weapons load proved an excellent aircraft for this job. CAS missions could be flown at night with the target area lit by flares fired by the ground troops.

c. *Interdiction.* Pre-planned sorties against important targets deep behind enemy lines, straight in and out sorties. A night capability for this role was highly desirable and since not many potential opponents were likely to leave the lights on, various methods of 'self illumination' were tried. This was where the front half of the bomb bay was utilised to carry flares, an aircraft could either toss a flare over the target area and then dive in to attack beneath it or, more common, one aircraft would toss the flares while a second aircraft made the attack run; the roles could then be reversed on another target.

By the late 1960s the primary role was still strike with LABS and laydown delivery; the CAS and recce roles had to all intents and purposes gone although the interdictor element was maintained. Night flying was the most boring aspect because of the limitations imposed on night flying in Germany which restricted the squadrons to a very few set routes. It was of far more value to fly across to the UK and make use of the UK low flying system where realistic sorties could be flown at 600 ft.

The four Germany squadrons saw limited operational action in the conventional role. In 1958 59 Squadron was sent to British Honduras (now Belize) in a show of strength to discourage Guatamalan advances and in mid-1961 213 Squadron deployed to Sharjah in the Persian Gulf during the Kuwait crisis. When their four aircraft arrived there on 2nd July they joined the four B(I)8s of 88 Squadron which had been there a few days. The rest of 88 Squadron, plus six aircrew from 3 Squadron, were based at Akrotiri to back-up the detachment at Sharjah. By 22nd July all the aircraft were back in Germany but the groundcrew stayed in Cyprus to look after 16 Squadron's aircraft which had taken over the reinforcement role.

16 Squadron went even further afield when eight aircraft went to Borneo in 1965 to reinforce the FEAF squadrons during 'Confrontation'. They were based at Kuantan for three months and on at least one occasion 'fired war ammunition against Indonesian terrorists in western Malaysia', this being the only reference the authors can find to the Germany squadrons firing their guns in anger.

These excursions abroad were by no means unusual, the Germany squadrons regularly went on Armament Practice Camp (APC) to Akrotiri, Exercise *Citrus Grove*, and to Idris, Exercise *Orange Grove*. The latter exercise was primarily for LABS training on Tarhuna range and was moved to Malta in 1966 when Idris closed. The Libyan detachments were particularly well-liked because of the opportunity they gave for a bit of ultra low level flying over the desert – climbing to avoid the herds of wild camels. A standard competition, especially for the recce squadrons, was to pass between two trucks going opposite ways on one of the desert roads – for a PR aircraft the trick was to get one truck on the port camera and one on the starboard camera!

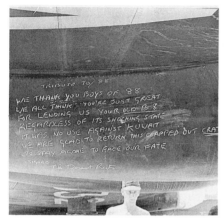

Top left: **The 213 Squadron hornet zaps the 88 Squadron snake on the fin of WT339 during detachment to Sharjah.**

213 Squadron poem on 88 Squadron B(I)8.

Above: **59 Squadron B(I)8 on APC. Note the bomb on pylon and posing groundcrew.**

88 Squadron B(I)8 over the Alps 1960. Highlights the offset canopy.

Top right: **The wire strike by XM265 in 1968 during 16 Squadron sortie out of Ghedi, Italy. The damage shown here is a testament to the sturdy nature of the Canberra!** *Dudley Brown*

In the early 1970s they used the newly opened range facilities at Decimomannu in Sardinia. Beside the APCs, the squadrons roamed the world on 'Lone Rangers' getting as far south as Nairobi and Aden and to Gan in the Maldives. The other 'good deal' was the frequent squadron exchanges, a practice they adopted from the fighter squadrons. The system was that a squadron would deploy for a couple of weeks to the base of an equivalent squadron of another NATO, or sometimes non-NATO, air force to operate in their airspace and compare operating procedures and tactics. On one such exchange by 16 Squadron in 1968 one crew got a little 'too familiar' with the new terrain. During a sortie from the Italian Air Force base at Ghedi, XM265 'became CAT 3 after a collision with some power cables. The navigator was ordered to abandon the aircraft and the pilot executed a skilful landing with a ton and a half of cable attached to the aircraft...'!

After a short break to regain breath, squadron exchanges being very hectic social events, the roles would reverse and the other squadron would visit an RAF base. The training value of these exchanges was, and is, enormous.

As with the recce squadrons, there was no shortage of competitions, often 'in house' like the Salmond Trophy for bombing, which was won for the first time by 213 Squadron in 1964. It then went between 213 Squadron and 3 Squadron (59 Squadron renumbered in 1961) until 1970 when 16 Squadron won it. In 1962 a major competition between 2 ATAF and 4 ATAF was instituted, with one of the four Canberra squadrons participating in the 2 ATAF team. This Tactical Weapons Meet was designed to test the teams skills in the four disciplines of simulated nuclear bombing, skip bombing, rocketry and strafe, and the Canberras participated in every meet until their withdrawal.

The list of exercises was as long and varied as in Bomber Command with *Whipsaw, Topweight, Cenobite* and the SACEUR exercise *Checkmate* to name but a few.

Some were 'non-aircrew' exercises because they involved a great deal of running about and playing with aircraft but very little flying, others enabled the squadrons to roam far and wide throughout Europe.

Apart from routine sorties and exercises the squadrons were sometimes tested by assessors from the station or HQ and these tests gradually evolved into the 'Evaluation' system still used. Once or sometimes twice a month the squadron would go to 'war' and would borrow observers from another squadron to act as umpires (Distaff – Directing Staff), whose job it was to inject inputs to which the squadron had to respond, and to assess the overall performance. It was soon realised that these 'Mini-Evaluations' (Minevals) could only be realistic if the rest of the station was involved providing back-up and support facilities. Thus came longer station exercises, 'Maxevals', of a few days duration during which all parts of the station and not just the flying units went onto a war footing. The culmination of the exercise system was the periodic,

roughly every 15 months, NATO 'Taceval', (Tactical Evaluation). This was as close to war as you could get and its purpose was to 'assess for SACEUR against prescribed criteria the operational potential of NATO

Opposite page: **213 Squadron on parade May 1967, while their B(I)6s sit it out in the readiness shelters.**

Line-up of 14 Squadron B(I)8s at Wildenrath. For 14 Squadron the B(I)8 game gave way in June 1970 to the Phantom FGA role. Of the aircraft here, WT362 went to the FFS at Catterick while WT368 became a B(I)68 for Peru. XM278 also went to Marshalls for conversion but was broken up and used as spares for the Peru contract.

Below (left): **213, 88 and 16 Sqns at the 1962 Tactical Weapons Meet at St Dizier, France.**

59 Squadron on APC, Cyprus late 1958.

88 Squadron B(I)8s in the ground attack role beating up a group of redundant Hunters at Larkhill Range, Salisbury Plain. 8th June 1962.

Command and assigned units and to award ratings to a common standard, to indicate deficiencies and to make recommendations where necessary.' The assessment was broken down into four categories, each rated 1 to 4, a 2 being 'satisfactory'. Training for 'Taceval' required a great deal of hard work by everyone on the station if good ratings were to be obtained. It is a sad fact that morale often suffered because of a surfeit of exercises in pursuit of a '1' but there is no doubt that the 'Taceval' system brought about and maintained a very high standard of operational efficiency in Germany.

This then was the lifestyle of the four Canberra squadrons who together with the three Valiant squadrons based at Marham provided the contribution to SAC-EUR's nuclear bombing force. With the phasing out of the Valiants with fatigue problems in 1965 the Canberra squadrons alone provided the tactical nuclear deterrent until 1969 when the Vulcans handed over strategic responsibility to the Polaris force and became part of the tactical force.

There is sometimes disagreement over the number of strike Canberra squadrons that were stationed in Germany; there were only ever four at any one time, but early in the 1960s two of them renumbered and then one of the new ones moved thus adding to the confusion. The facts are:

16 Squadron. Formed at Laarbruch in March 1958 with B(I)8s. Re-equipped with Buccaneers June 1972.

59 Squadron. Formed at Gutersloh in August 1956 using B.2s until first B(I)8s arrived April 1957. Moved to Geilenkirchen November 1957. Renumbered as 3 Squadron 1st January 1961, moved to Laarbruch January 1968 and disbanded December 1971.

88 Squadron. Formed at Wildenrath in March 1958 with B(I)8s. Renumbered as 14 Squadron December 1962 and disbanded June 1970.

213 Squadron. Formed at Ahlhorn in July 1955 with B(I)6s, moved to Bruggen August 1957 and disbanded December 1969.

As with the PR Canberras, the strike/attack aircraft were never directly role replaced. In the nuclear strike role the Buccaneer took over but although faster and with greater range lacked the versatility of the Canberra. On the attack side the Phantom and Harrier took over but it was not until the advent of the Jaguar that an aircraft appeared which could fulfil all three roles, albeit at shorter range. There can be no doubt that for many years the Canberra was the mainstay of the RAF's presence in Germany.

XH209 of 16 Squadron at Gutersloh as a decoy aircraft. Note the later 'Sharkmouth' marking.

Following disbandment in December 1969, many 213 Squadron aircraft were sold to BAC and went into storage at Samlesbury for possible resale overseas.

Chapter Four

Middle East Air Force

The deployment of Canberra aircraft to Cyprus was a direct result of the Baghdad Pact agreement of 1955 between the UK, Iran, Pakistan, Turkey and Iraq on the security of the Middle East. This organisation later became the Central Treaty Organisation (CENTO) following the withdrawal of Iraq after a coup.

It was agreed that a bomber force with a nuclear capability was needed and in 1956 the British Government offered to provide a force of four light bomber squadrons and one PR squadron to be based in Cyprus. This scheme was approved by the Chief of Staff in July 1956 and wheels were set in motion for the re-equipping or reforming of earmarked squadrons with Canberras.

Suez

However, events were to bring the Canberra into active operations within the theatre before the planned build-up commenced. From mid-1951 the fervour of Nationalism rose in Egypt, leading to a campaign of terror and non co-operation to put pressure on Britain to withdraw from her bases in Egypt. In 1952 Nasser came to power and the restlessness grew as Britain suggested a phased withdrawal and guarantees of intervention rights should the Suez Canal be threatened. The Anglo-Egyptian Agreement of October 1954 led to the gradual withdrawal of British forces, the last troops leaving in June 1956.

Despite withdrawal, the virulent anti-British propaganda of Egypt, in the form of Cairo Radio's 'Voice of the Arabs' continued unabated. Nasser increased his drive for Egyptian control of Egypt and its resources and in a fiery and dramatic speech on 26th July 1956 announced that the Suez Canal had been nationalised and that Egyptian forces were taking control 'as he spoke'.

Intervention was almost inevitable in one form or another following this 'slap in the face by a Hitlerite bandit', a phrase used in Parliament and taken up by the press. France and the UK as the most directly affected countries sought a diplomatic solution whilst at the same time examining military options. During September and October joint Anglo-French military planning took place and Operation *Musketeer*, the plan to occupy the Canal Zone, emerged. After frequent changes and arguments the air plan was formulated with three specific phases:

1. Neutralisation of the Egyptian Air Force.
2. Psychological warfare programme for a continual air offensive to disrupt the Egyptian economy, morale and armed forces.
3. Domination of the Canal Zone and its occupation by land, sea and air forces as might be neccessary.

The primary task of the Air Task Force of Air Marshal Barnett was the neutralisation phase. In late 1955 Egypt had received substantial amounts of modern weapons from Czechoslovakia including MiG-15 fighters and Il-28 bombers. British estimates put total Egyptian strength as 80 MiGs, 57 Vampires, 25 Meteors and 45 Il-28s – Israeli estimates suggested about half of this total.

Fullock and Powell in their analysis of the Suez war (*Suez, the Double War,* Hamish Hamilton, 1979) give details of the October secret protocol of Sèvres at which the Israelis expressed their fear of retaliation by the Egyptian Air Force on Israeli civilian targets should there be an Israeli advance on the Canal. France agreed to station fighters on Israeli airfields but it was considered vital that the British bombers act to destroy the offensive capability of the Egyptian Air Force at the earliest opportunity.

It was agreed that bombing would be selective to avoid civilian casualties or excessive material damage and so phase two, the aero-psychological phase, was virtually abandoned.

The bomber element of the Air Task Force was to comprise Canberra and Valiant squadrons from Bomber Command and plans were rapidly laid to deploy selected squadrons to the operational area. An immediately obvious problem was one of airfield space – where were all the squadrons going to go? Cyprus had only two fully operational stations, Nicosia and Tymbou and the latter was allocated to the French air elements. Akrotiri, on the southern tip of the island, was in the process of construction and was the home of the Command's only resident Canberra unit, 13 Squadron, with its PR.7s.

13 Squadron had started exchanging its Meteor PR.10s for Canberras in May 1956 at the new but rapidly growing airfield, receiving its first PR.7 on the 10th of the month. However, it was some months before the Meteor flight was finally disbanded as delivery of PR.7s was slow and erratic with only three on strength, plus a Command reserve, almost a year later! There was also a shortage of Canberra aircrew and in August a detachment of four PR.7s and crews of 58 Squadron from Wyton arrived at Akrotiri to strengthen the PR force during the 'present emergency'. During August and September this combined unit flew trials on the new F95 low level oblique camera. As the pace of reinforcement increased and airfield space was at a premium the Squadron flew landing trials at Tymbou airfield to assess its suitability for Canberra operations.

Nicosia was earmarked as the major airfield for the operation and it soon became overcrowded as the resident squadrons 'moved over' to make room for the great influx of fighter, bomber and support aircraft. At the height of the conflict a great many squadrons were operating from this airfield, a prime target should the Egyptian Air Force be capable of attacking it.

The next suitable location from which to mount bomber ops was Malta and the RAF station at Luqa and the RNAS station at Hal Far prepared to be inundated with Canberras and Valiants.

As early as August 1956 six Canberra squadrons (139, 15, 12, 101, 109, 9) had been ordered to restrict training flying and prepare personnel and aircraft for deployment to the Middle East. For 101 Squadron this came as quite a shock as they had just started to settle in at Butterworth, Malaya for their second stint of Operation *Mileage* in FEAF when orders arrived recalling the Squadron to Binbrook. Binbrook at this time was chaotic as the squadrons sorted out aircraft for possible hostilities. Air tests were frequent on the *Orange Putter* tail warning radar, a piece of equipment that had given a poor showing on exercises but might now be called on to produce accurate information in a real situation. Some aircraft required extra nav kit such as radio compasses to be fitted and teams from 49 MU arrived to do this work. For most of the designated units the net result of the warning order was to place them on a 96 hour standby and gradually, as nothing happened, the last bits and pieces of equipment were crated and the recalled personnel trooped in for their medicals and inoculations. Nevertheless, some missed out - Tony Bridges returned to 9 Squadron after a course to find the Squadron, and the whole of Binbrook, long gone!

For other units it was not so sedate. 15, 44 and 21 Squadrons were given the task of taking 1000 lb bombs to Luqa to build up stocks there, while 139 and 109 Squadrons, the target marker squadrons at Hemswell worked hard to sharpen-up their marking skills. Since re-equipping with the Canberra, Bomber Command had concentrated on Gee-H bombing as the blind delivery or night technique but without ground stations the system was unusable and there was no way to get adequate Gee cover of the operational area over Egypt. The entire Main Force would have to rely on Second World War techniques of visual bombing on a marked target – the old Pathfinder and Master Bomber technique. 139 Squadron was given the extra navigators it needed to make up two-nav crews as required by the marker role. The workup commenced, culminating in a Command exercise on 28th August when the target was marked by Valiants dropping green proximity markers for the Canberras to 'centre' with red TIs for the Main

Force to drop on. The exercise went well and it was the first time the Squadron had carried a mixed load of 4.5 inch flares and TIs. The general pace increased in September and two other squadrons, 61 and 18, were ordered to train in the marker role as soon as possible, concentrating on Shallow Dive Bombing (SDB) delivery techniques with their B.2s.

A joint 139/109 Squadron detachment, with 139 Squadron groundcrew, went to Malta towards the end of the month and waited for something to happen. However, within a matter of days it all changed again and some crews returned to the UK. At the same time, 101 Squadron were ordered to 'redeploy to Luqa as the vanguard of any air action which might be required in connection with the Suez crisis.' A few days later, the 22nd September, they were joined by 12 Squadron although on the 25th this squadron moved up the road to Hal Far.

The situation had become a little clearer by October and squadrons were shuffled around to meet the likely commitment. By the latter half of the month seven squadrons (139, 15, 18, 61, 10, 27 and 44) had arrived at Nicosia under the force commander Group Captain Key. Amidst the chaos, aircraft were prepared and crews sat through briefings on met, nav,

escape and evasion as well as the Egyptian air and ground threat. All aircrew were armed with ·38 revolvers slung in a webbing holster and looking a little incongruous over flying overalls. At Malta it was not quite so hectic as 101 and 109 waited at Luqa and 12 at Hal Far, being joined at the last minute by 9 Squadron who did not arrive until the 30th October.

Meanwhile, the aircraft were given a set of invasion stripes on fuselage and wings, in some cases white and black and in others yellow and black.

On the 30th October the BBC broadcast a warning to Egyptian civilians to keep away from all military targets as these were now under threat of bombing, an endeavour to keep civilian casualties low in order to avoid an international outcry.

Opposite page: **12 Squadron B.6s on dispersal at Hal Far, October 1956.**

101 Squadron crew at Hal Far, October 1956. Fg Off Nicholson, Fg Off Hart, W/O Ross. Note the ·38 revolvers carried as the standard aircrew weapon. *John Hart*

12 Squadron B.6 WH951 being bombed up.

The Hal Far line-up in October 1956. 9 and 101 Squadrons in the front row with 12 Squadron behind. *John Hart*

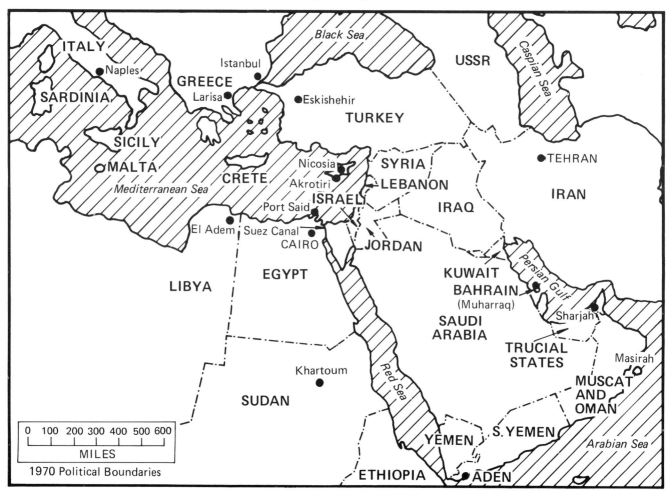

At Nicosia crews were briefed for attacks on Cairo West airfield and Almaza barracks but these were postponed by 24 hours. The Luqa target for the night was Kabrit, the old RAF base on the shore of the Bitter Lake, but this raid too was cancelled. The following day, squadrons from Nicosia and Malta carried out their first bombing missions, although the first Luqa wave was recalled after 20 minutes as Cairo West, the target airfield, was being used by the Americans as an evacuation point.

By the time that the first bombing ops were taking place, the recce Canberras had already flown five operational sorties of medium level photography. The 'enemy' had been encountered three times, once as light and ineffectual anti-aircraft fire and twice during rare appearances by Egyptian MiG-15s. On the 30th, in two separate incidents aircraft had been intercepted. One aircraft received cannon-shell damage to the elevator; in the other incident the pilot had been shocked to see explosive shells flying past the cockpit on both sides from behind! A smart piece of evasive flying threw off the not very persistent attacker and the PR.7 returned unscratched. By the end of active operations the Squadron had flown 44 operational sorties for the loss of one aircraft shot down. In this incident a 58 Squadron aircraft (WH799) with a 13 Squadron crew, was shot down by a MiG-17 over Syria (6th November), the pilot and one nav survived the attack and spent some time in Beirut Military Hospital but the other navigator was killed. In July 1987 the authors received a letter throwing a different light on this incident. It mentioned a converstion with a senior Syrian officer who in his younger days was a Fighter Controller during the Suez Crisis. He claimed that the Canberra had been tracked for some time before a Meteor was sent up to intercept. The Meteor climbed above the Canberra, identified its target and then shot it down.

Other than the loss of a PR.7, only two Canberras suffered battle damage during the Suez campaign: B.2 WH860 of 27 Squadron was hit by a shell splinter whilst cruising at 25,000 ft – the fragment made a 3 inch hole through the starboard tailplane, and B.6 WT371 was hit by light flak which caused damage to the main spar and integral tank. After a temporary repair the aircraft was scheduled to return to the UK to be replaced; unfortunately it crashed on take-off from Nicosia, killing the crew.

Detailed raid by raid analysis can be found in an Appendix. Raid composition was often complex with squadrons putting two or three aircraft into a joint raid with other squadrons rather than as a 'massed' squadron element within the Main Force, although the latter method was also

employed. Over the six days from 30th October, 18, 109 and 139 Squadrons flew day and night sorties marking airfields, barracks and gun batteries for the Main Force Valiants and Canberras. 139s marking ops were typical of the technique ... on the 31st the crews were briefed to mark Cairo West but as mentioned above this was cancelled and the target changed to Almaza airfield instead. The standard technique of *Marker 1 and 2* (each with eight 4.5 inch flares and two 1000 lb TIs) and *Flare 1 and 2* (each with twelve 4.5 inch flares) was used. Taking off at 1715 the aircraft flew out at 30,000 ft aiming for a distinctive bend in the Nile and from there to find the IP for a timed run and descent to 8,000 ft for the final run-in and release for ignition at 3,000 ft. With the target identified in the light of the flares, the TIs were dropped on the east and west hard-standings. As soon as the flares ignited the ground defences opened fire with continuous but ineffective AA fire.

WH799, of 82 Squadron, the RAF's only operational Canberra loss.

27 Squadron B.2s taxy out from a crowded Nicosia during Suez ops. Valettas of 114 Squadron parked on the left.

The CO, Squadron Leader Mallone, led a similar detail 45 minutes later with roughly the same results.

Having not expected to get airborne on this mission because his pilot was sick, Flight Sergeant Mike Heather had retired to his tent when he was called to replace a nav who had gone sick. He rushed to the briefing and duly took his place in one of the aircraft ... 'Strict RT silence was maintained during start-up, taxy and take-off. As we were taxying out to the runway each of the four aircraft was flagged down by one of the briefing officers who passed a note to each pilot. This said that information had been received that the Americans were evacuating their nationals through

Cairo West and we were to attack Almaza airfield instead. We got airborne in WT369 at 1715 and set course. We crossed the Egyptian coast as it was getting dark and when we arrived over Cairo all the lights were still on. We had little difficulty in finding Almaza airfield but in spite of this we went through the full procedure of dropping flares over the target and then into a shallow dive to place the TIs. The Egyptian AA gunners seemed to shoot at the flares rather than us so marking the target was easy, although by the time we had finished all the lights had been turned off.'

On the clear, moonless nights the green and red TIs were visible to the following bombers from 100 miles away and with only light opposition each aircraft dropped its load onto the TIs or as directed. Canberras operating from Nicosia carried the standard war load of six 1000 lb bombs but the Malta-based aircraft were restricted to four 1000 lb bombs because of the extreme range. Even with this limitation they were averaging five-hour sorties which most crews remember for their boredom and the numbing cold at 40,000 ft. On arrival back at Malta aircraft were very short of fuel after the round trip. Most Main Force bombing was done from 40 – 45,000 ft and accuracy and effectiveness suffered accordingly.

Not all were Main Force night sorties, there being a call for a number of day marking and bombing raids. 18 Squadron and 139 Squadron were involved on the 5th November with marking DZs at Port Said for the paratroop drop. 61 squadron, having trained at short notice in the marking role, were never called on to target mark but did more than their fair share of daylight ops with raids on Inchass airfield, Luxor airfield, Nifisha marshalling yards (all from 25,000 ft), Huckstep tank park (15,000 ft) and Cairo Radio (3,000 ft). The Cairo Radio sortie was an attempt to put the 'Voice of the Arabs' out of action and was unique in its 'low level' format for the Canberras. The target was marked by two aircraft of 18 Squadron and attacked by four aircraft from 61 Squadron and three from 15 Squadron. The TIs were hard to see and quickly obscured by dust and haze and the station was only damaged and was back on the air in a matter of days. French aircraft provided fighter cover during this raid of 2nd November but there was little likelihood of defending aircraft intervening because 260 Egyptian aircraft had been destroyed on the ground by British and French air attacks, most of them in the first 36 hours and the Egyptian Air Force had ceased to exist as an effective force by this time.

A total of 72 operational sorties were flown from Malta and 206 from Cyprus, plus a further 49 by the Valiants from Malta. Over the short operational period a

15 Squadron's B.2 XA536 at Luqa on its way back to Honington 8th November 1956. 15 Squadron sent three aircraft on the most successful of the Canberra bombing missions, the day low level attack on Cairo Radio Station. XA536 was built as a replacement aircraft for WD991 which crashed on test before delivery. Note the Valiants in the background. *15 Squadron records*

total of 283 1000 lb bombs were dropped by the Malta units and 1156 1000 lb bombs by the Cyprus squadrons. There has been continual debate since Suez on the relative value of the bombing by various aircraft types and overall the Canberra has been given a bad press. The Bomber Command report stated that visual bombing standards were low because of lack of practice following prolonged grounding for airframe modifications and a concentration of effort on flypasts for VIP visits. However, certain of the sorties, especially those against Cairo Radio were notable successes and the overall value of the medium bomber contribution should not be doubted. Most of the direct destruction of enemy aircraft, however, was due to the dive bombing aircraft, especially the carrier-borne units.

With the end of direct action the Squadrons maintained Standby for a few weeks, although 10, 15 and 44 departed Nicosia on the 7th. On the 18th the Readiness State was relaxed to 24 hours notice and routine training commenced. A week later a high-speed courier service from Cyprus to UK was established with the Canberras carrying urgent despatches. All squadrons, except 61 Squadron, left for the UK on 22nd December. A month later 61 also left and the Canberra part of Suez came to an end. By early 1957 13 Squadron was the only Canberra unit still in theatre although within a month the build-up of the Akrotiri strike wing commenced.

Akrotiri Strike Wing

While 32 Squadron was busily operating from RAF Mafraq with its Venoms in late 1956, word came through that another 32

Squadron was forming at RAF Weston Zoyland with Canberra bombers in preparation for a move to Nicosia, Cyprus! At Weston Zoyland the new Squadron received a directive from AHQ Levant to the effect that the unit was to be 'a light bomber squadron, crews to become familiar with Middle East air routes and to attain a high standard of visual bombing as soon as possible and with a SDB marker element to train within the Squadron.'

While awaiting delivery of their own aircraft from Wroughton, crews borrowed a couple of B.2s from 542 Squadron and also managed to get their hands on a T.4. Aircraft for the Squadron began to arrive in late January 1957, the first on the 29th, and the first flight left for Nicosia on the 15th February. The whole Squadron was in place by the 6th March only to be told to up-sticks and move to Akrotiri, this being completed by the 19th - the Akrotiri strike wing was on its way.

It was a similar story for the next squadron of the wing when 73 Squadron said goodbye to its Venoms in March and collected B.2s from the MU. After a short period at Weston Zoyland for aircraft familiarisation and acceptance, the Squadron moved to Akrotiri, via Idris, arriving one day after 32 Squadron, although the second four aircraft were not in place until the 30th. The last two squadrons of the wing, 6 Squadron and 249 Squadron, followed the same path giving up Venoms for Canberra B.2s, 6 Squadron arriving in July and 249 in October.

Life at Akrotiri was chaotic at first as it was still very much a new airfield and the sudden presence of so many squadrons brought formidable problems, not least of which was accommodation. Typically, 249 Squadron was allocated a rocky section of the airfield for its very own and told to get on with it. Very little progress could be made in erecting tents until a pneumatic drill was 'borrowed' from the Royal Engineers! Over a period of time the tented areas took on an aura of ordered permanence and it was not until the early 1960s that all the squadrons had more substantial buildings provided.

Above: **32 Squadron B.2 WH638, which eventually went to Ethiopia as a B.52.** *MAP*

Below: **'Moby Dick', WD988 of 73 Squadron at El Adem 1960.**

Bottom: **B.2 WK109 of 6 Squadron, 1958, in fully laden (fuel) tail-down attitude.**

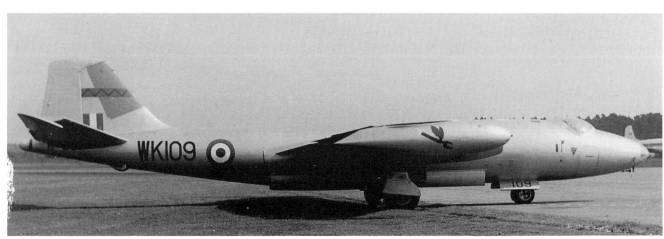

B.6 (BS) WT372 of 6 Squadron, Akrotiri. Early view of the aircraft in non camouflage finish shows well the 'flying can opener' motif of 6 Squadron. *MAP*

B.2 WK111 of 73 Squadron, October 1964. Note the clip-on canopy sun shade.

B.6 (BS) WT374 of 249 Squadron sits baking in the sun at Akrotiri.

Target markers on the El Adem range, Libya, late 1958.

One of the lessons of Suez was that accurate target marking was still vital for successful visual bombing in certain circumstances; even more essential in an area where blind night bombing was impracticable for lack of ground stations. In early November 1959, 249 Squadron re-equipped with eight B.6s ready for its new role as a target marker unit, the Squadron's operational role being defined as 'part of the NEAF tactical light bomber force supporting CENTO and to provide target marking facilities for this force and other operational units.' Three experienced crews were posted in from 139 Squadron to form the nucleus of the marking team and training concentrated on SDB and TI exercises using 4.5 inch flares and 250 lb TIs at El Adem range. The Squadron was declared operational in the new role on the 18th December with two *Marker 1* crews, two *Marker 2* crews and three *Flare* crews.

Basic techniques were as developed by 139 Squadron and Bomber Command although over the ensuing months trials were conducted to determine the best employment methods and tactics for use in the Middle East. By April 1960 the Squadron was conducting trials dropping standard 1000 lb TIs, along with a series of trials to determine the best drop height for burn time and accuracy, the suggested ideal being 1800 feet.

With the advent of a marker unit, the Akrotiri strike wing had all the elements it needed for its own mini Main Force. In the early years a typical markex/bombex would involve a high level navex to El Adem where 249 Squadron would mark the target with 1000 lb TIs for the other squadrons to attack with up to six 1000 lb bombs per aircraft. This was very much a follow-on from the Suez experience and the old style of bomber operations. However, in the mid 1960s changes in tactical employment were introduced and the Canberra entered the era of flexibility of roles and weapons as previously described for RAFG.

With the introduction of RP (Rocket Projectile), with 2 inch rockets, came CAS (Close Air Support) and interdiction – a 'whole new ball game'. The marker squadron was not so vital now as it was possible for aircraft to drop their own package of 4.5 inch flares and then carry out an RP attack by their light. The same basic concept was used with Canberra markers putting down flares for Hunters to run in and RP the target. We will return to the RP a little later, after dealing with the decline of marking. By August 1966, 249 Squadron was the only remaining official marker squadron in the RAF and they put forward a case for replacing the 4.5 inch type with the much more reliable and efficient 8 inch Lepus flare which gave a greater area of light thus making target ident easier. The Squadron had carried out a trial two years earlier on the Lepus and were impressed. It then became a regular routine to pester 'higher authority' for a change especially as the old flares seemed to be getting more and more unreliable with numerous incidences of aircraft not carrying through an RP attack because of the insufficient light generated. Ironically, the Lepus was finally released to the Squadron one month before disbandment.

Life was never completely straightforward for the Cyprus squadrons because of the continued internecine strife between Greeks and Turks that afflicted the otherwise paradisiacal island. Four centuries of Turkish rule had been ended by the British take-over of the island in 1878 but in those 400 years there had been little intermixing of the racial groups. Until the mid 1950s Britain gave very little thought to the future of the island and treated the Greek Cypriot desire for 'Enosis' (Union with Greece) with disinterest. However, from 1955 onwards the situation changed as Cyprus took on a more vital role in the strategic balance of the area following British withdrawal from the Suez bases. The value of this base was well proven in the ensuing Suez crisis. The extremist Greek Cypriots realised the importance of this hardening of attitudes and the terrorist organisation EOKA was born under the leadership of Colonel (General) Grivas and the political direction of Archbishop Makarios. The terror campaign of bombing, sabotage and murder began in 1955 and continued for three years and had a profound effect on both the operational and social life of the island-based squadrons. The most direct threat was that of sabotage; the bombing of aircraft, and this was a major problem during the Suez ops when the airfields were crowded with aircraft. During this period there were a number of incidences of aircraft being damaged by time-pencil bombs. On 26th November 1957 a bomb destroyed the ASF hangar with the loss of five aircraft, including WF886 of 6 Squadron, B.2 WP514 and PR.7 WT508.

This led to yet another tightening of security which also placed a strain on squadron resources by demanding more airmen as guards.

To ease the security problem a dispersal plan was implemented in early 1958 whereby ten aircraft from the wing 'evacuated' Cyprus from dusk to dawn every day, dispersing to El Adem, Idris and Habbaniya. By the latter part of the year the dispersal plan had changed so that all serviceable aircraft were dispersed every night, to such diverse places as El Adem, Luqa, Tehran, Eastleigh, Gibraltar, Mauripur and even Upwood. In November, as one 249 crew put it, 'we had become a jet medium range ferry pool with 60% of flying being to-and-fro and very little real training.'

The terrorist threat obviously affected life-style as well, especially for those families living away from Akrotiri particularly in Limassol. Plans were laid to move them to the comparative safety of the Sovereign Base Areas (SBAs) and for their husbands to be detached away for a maximum of two consecutive nights, an ideal that did not always work in practice. 1958 saw an increase in violence between the two racial groups, as well as EOKA attacks. The leaders of Turkey and Greece saw the dangers of escalation and agreed to a series of three-cornered meetings between themselves and Britain which eventually led to the Zurich and London agreements of 1959. These proposed independence for the island in the following year but with Britain retaining its SBAs and with all parties guaranteeing the collective security of the island and its racial groups.

Despite a carefully thought-out scheme of power sharing, a series of deadlocks had paralysed the new government by 1963 and intercommunal conflict erupted again, made worse by Makarios's proposed constitutional changes. This precipitated a major crisis and led to serious outbreaks of fighting in December 1963 in which the small garrisons of regular Greek and Turkish troops took sides while the British forces tried to enforce local cease-fires and general negotiation. Turkish warships sailed towards the island and Turkish aircraft flew low over the divided city of Nicosia.

The aftermath of the EOKA bomb in one of the hangars at Akrotiri. *C. Herbert*

Akrotiri became a hive of activity. Restrictions were placed on the movements of personnel whilst families were moved to the base areas. Shipping recce sorties were flown by the Canberras and with the increased possibility of a major intervention by one side or the other, the squadrons were placed on standby. Part of the evacuation plan for families was to move them to the UK and one reason for the standby was to enable one of the resident squadrons to fly out at short notice and make room for evacuation aircraft. Tension remained high in the first few months of 1964 and the hoped-for relaxation with the arrival of a UN peace-keeping force in March did not materialise as both sides continued fighting. Aircraft flew regular shipping recces – 'dusker' patrols – looking for likely gun-running ships as well as maintaining armed standby with full pods of 2 inch RPs for possible CAS of British troops maintaining the security of the SBAs, there being no suggestion that British forces would intervene unless under direct threat. At one stage aircraft were brought to 90 minutes readiness but the threat, whatever it was, never materialised and readiness was gradually relaxed until by July a feeling of 'normality' had returned and normal training and Rangers resumed.

When the squadrons were on initial work-up, operational training was a little difficult due to a lack of Avro Triple Carriers for the 1000 lb bombs and a lack of T3 bombsights. Also, the only bombing range was at El Adem, a long 'flog' of 500 miles each way. However, by February 1958 most aircraft had been fitted with the bombsights and on the 3rd of the month the range at Episkopi Bay was opened for live bombing. As this was only two miles from the 2-9 end of the runway it gave the squadrons a greater flexibility in their training! The smoke-float targets at this range were primarily for (Shallow Guide Bombing) SGB and SDB bombing with 25 lb practice bombs while the El Adem range was the primary night target as well as day bombing above 35,000 ft. Most practice bombing was done with a load of eight 25 lb practice bombs although on occasions twelve such bombs were carried.

WH961, the first B.15 conversion - seen here at Filton.

B.16 WT303 of 249 Squadron. This aircraft was a converted B.6 (BS), as evidenced by the 'wave guide' strake on the starboard fuselage side, which was part of the *Blue Shadow* fit.

As with all Canberra bombing squadrons, crews had to gradually work-up in bombing height from the 20,000 ft bracket,which was easy to attain, to the max height of 45,000 ft. This was all part of the great Command Classification scheme which is described more fully in the chapter on Bomber Command. There was no *Gee* bombing requirement for the NEAF squadrons which meant that greater reliance had to be placed on the only other so-called blind aid, the *Blue Shadow* radar system which was discussed in the previous chapter with the Middle East trials carried out by 109/105 Squadron in July 1954 . It was not given a particularly good reception by the crews who used it, the general feeling being that it was no more accurate than a map and stopwatch and probably a good deal less accurate unless you happened to be near a suitable piece of coast. There were some who were prepared to give the system a fair trial but even they found that it required a large amount of effort to get good results. Graham Logan, a nav-plotter of 249 Squadron recalled: 'The main problem was that you were looking at things that you were already going past and unless it was a very distinctive piece of coast it was often hard to determine what you were looking at. Some towns showed up but generally the results were considered so poor that most navs didn't spend too much time using the equipment.' This same comment was later applied to another 'modern' piece of equipment the aircraft were given, the Decca roller map – a moving map display. This was driven by the doppler and as this itself was not particularly accurate it meant that the roller map was also inaccurate. The nav-observer sat with the display unit in his hand and was able to use it as a map-reading aid should he wish to do so,

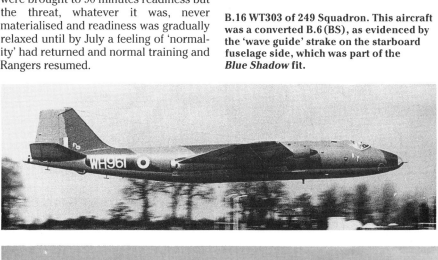

although most preferred to rely on the old method of map and watch. Another drawback with the roller map was the time taken to produce maps for it and unless it was for a standard route it was seen as a waste of time.

Thus, on the training side of things there was the standard round of Squadron, Wing and Command 'Bombexs' as well as more specific events such as the Sassoon Bombing Competition. This was competed for each year by the four light bomber squadrons, over a number of day and night bombing phases. Over a period of time the honours seem to be even between the squadrons! The MEAF Bombing Competition was quite similar, with a 'navex' around the island followed by FRAs and academic bombs at Episkopi and El Adem. Average bombing errors were similar to those of Bomber Command with visual deliveries at 350 to 400 yards from high level using Mk.6 or Mk.7 1000 lb bombs.

A typical squadron exercise would comprise a full-load take-off with six 1000 lb bombs – sometimes a bit tricky if not impossible on a hot day at Akrotiri – then a high-low-high profile with a live stick drop at El Adem at two minute intervals and then a return to Akrotiri for a stream landing. This, and the special exercises mentioned above comprised the vast majority of squadron training. A new technique introduced in September 1958 involved Shackletons and B.6s in the target mark phase. The Canberras would lead the wave to rendezvous at the IP for the drop and the Shackleton, with its more accurate nav kit, would pass the target bearing and distance to the stream while the B.2s orbited at 40,000 ft. As soon as the Shackleton started his run-in the B.2s descended to 15,000 ft over the IP and waited for the Shackleton to drop flares for the B.6s to mark the target with TIs. This seemed to work out far better than any previous technique but was for some reason not adopted as standard. In a good month, particularly if it included a detachment to El Adem, a single squadron might drop 500∓ practice bombs.

Re-equipment, B.15/B.16

A major change came about in late 1961 when the strike wing squadrons prepared to re-equip with new aircraft and take on the low level role with RPs, a much more realistic employment for the aircraft. 32 Squadron was first to start re-equipping and in August 1961 received the first six of its new UE of eight B.16s. The Squadron lost one of its B.2s (WD995) in a tragic mid-air accident with Javelin XH906 near Akrotiri on 26th November 1961.

Re-equipment was not complete until February 1962 and in the meantime the Squadron handed its B.2s to 73 Squadron from September onwards. 249 Squadron was next to get new aircraft, giving up its

B.6s for B.16s from November 1961 onwards but taking until April 1963 to get the full set of eight. The first B.16 for 6 Squadron arrived in February 1962, completing in late 1963 when the last B.2 was scrapped and taken to the range at Larnaca for use as a target. 73 Squadron were last in line to start the swop but had a complete set of B.15s by the end of 1962.

In essence, the B.15s and B.16s were B.6s with modified equipment, navigational and weapons. The main difference between types was that the B.16 had one of the rear ejection seats removed to make room for the *Blue Shadow* radar system. The rear ejection seat was used by the nav plotter so the nav observer had to wear a special flying suit with a built-in harness for a chest parachute and an oxygen bottle.

It also meant that the 2 inch RP had arrived at Akrotiri. Low level RP, described by some as the 'sport of kings' required either a shallow dive delivery or an ultra low-level level delivery. The crews were cleared down to 50 ft for level RP although the ideal height was 59 ft. Some who took part in this 'sport' remember this figure so well because of the novel way it was arranged at one of the ranges for crews to be certain of their height. There was a particular tree on the run-in to the target and some intrepid individual decided to cut the top off this tree so that it was exactly 59 ft tall – simple, all you had to do was get level with the top of the tree, aim at the target and let rip! Live firing began in July with Larnaca range being one of the favoured venues although El Adem and Episkopi were used as well. RP became a regular feature of squadron training with quarter, half and full pod (72 rockets) shoots, the latter being particularly impressive and a favourite at the frequent weapons-effects displays given to VIP visitors.

WJ756, a B.15 of ASW on a full pod shoot of RPs during the annual CENTO firepower demonstration.

Opposite page: 73 Squadron B.15 displaying the range of weapons options for the B.15/16, also the underwing hard points.

B.16 XH570 of 6 Squadron, 1968.

Average RP errors were 12 to 15 yards for all the squadrons although this is based on single or double projectile firing and the effect of even a half pod was to obliterate the target area. There was very little for the nav to do during RP attacks except to monitor *very* carefully the heights, especially in any dive, and some chose to sit on the rumble seat to watch the show. The 2 inch RP was a reliable weapon with only 7% hang-ups and 4% malfunctions; although not particularly accurate as it was unguided. The changeover to RP, whilst also maintaining standard free-fall bombing, did place a large extra workload on the armourers. One of the most dramatic 'shows' was the CENTO firepower demo in April 1964 when the target was three five-ton trucks plus 150 jerry-cans of petrol and the 'punch' delivered by three aircraft with 400 rockets with AP heads!!

These low RP deliveries carried a number of dangers not least of which was that of richochet damage from debris flung up from the target area. Also, at Larnaca particularly, birdstrikes seem to have been a frequent problem.

In January 1967, 73 Squadron gave up the 2 inch RP in favour of the more advanced SNEB system. This weapon was normally delivered in a shallow dive at about 100 ft and had greater reliability and accuracy.

The basic sight on the aircraft was the good old chinagraph mark on the canopy but after years of sterling service this gave way, after a series of trials, to the French SFOM sight. The advantage of this was that it had a depression-setting knob and graduated scale that allowed the pilot to match the sight to particular targets while airborne.

With RP work came an increase in low level tactical flying and formation, usually pairs, and CAS. The latter role involved the squadrons in numerous exercises with the army and with FAC work.

Nuclear LABS
With the new aircraft came another new role, that of LABS, the fulfilment of the promised nuclear capability of the British forces committed to CENTO. LABS was the same for the Akrotiri strike wings squadrons as it was in RAFG - the procedures and training were identical. To pass it off in such few words does not, unfortunately, provide an insight into how important or how much of a training commitment it was to the squadrons. It became, effectively, the primary role of the squadrons and, as such, occupied a large proportion of the ground and flying programme. Most LABS work was done at either El Adem or Tarhunna ranges in Libya.

The final role, a minor one, was skip bombing for the delivery of napalm, and

for conventional bombs against targets with 'vertical' extent such as hangars and buildings. This role was simulated by dropping tanks full of coloured water from 50ft in a high speed (350 knots) delivery. With such a wide variety of roles it was hard for crews to keep current, or to fulfil their training quotas for each role. Squadrons therefore tended to have periods concentrating on a single role, be it visual bombing, LABS or RP. LABS details were sometimes flown with practice bombs on the wing pylons. Pity the poor engineers and armourers who had to keep up with whatever aircraft/weapon fit the aircrew called for, and, as was typical of aircrew, they were likely to change their minds at short notice!

A few years before the re-equipment programme took place a paper from the AOC-in-C MEAF, Air Marshal W. L. M. MacDonald, recommended that the Akrotiri strike force should be replaced by two squadrons of TSR2s for the strike role and three FGA squadrons in the period 1961-4 to give a more balanced force. However, with the cancellation of the TSR2 programme in 1965 and insufficient numbers of the planned buy of F-111s to go round, the NEAF squadrons were to re-equip with V-bombers although this was seen as a temporary measure pending arrival of the Anglo-French Variable Geometry (AFVG) aircraft – also cancelled in 1967!

Needless to say, Cyprus provided a great social life and there was never a shortage of things to do, from the great 'bun fight' squadron kebabs at one of the numerous excellent kebab houses around Akrotiri and Limassol to the quiet, sedate family BBQ. Akrotiri had just about every conceivable outdoor facility from water skiing and scuba diving to 'Go-karts'. There were numerous clubs and beaches within the base area so it was virtually like a holiday camp - away from the EOKA troubles. The normal working day was from 7am to 3pm with some flying on Saturday mornings from time to time. There was even the chance of good skiing at Mount Troodos, with the difference that après-ski could be taken on the beach with a dip in the sea! Apart from the local area there was a wide selection of both social and historical places to visit around the island and a tour in Cyprus was, and still is, much sought after!

To ensure that the Officers Mess Summer Ball was outstanding, the squadrons' were tasked to send aircraft far and wide to obtain 'goodies' - the main destinations being Leuchars in Scotland for beef, Malta for ham, Germany for champagne and wine and Masirah for crayfish!

Cameras Over the Med

In the three years following Suez 13 Squadron suffered from a lack of serviceable aircraft and a surplus of tasks. With only two or three aircaft available at any time it was impossible to answer the clamours for operational and survey photography. The problem was eased a little when 69 Squadron moved with its PR.3s from Wildenrath to Luqa in early 1958. This was in fulfilment of an agreement made in July 1956 in answer to a SACEUR request for PR resources to be made available from 2 ATAF to fill the PR gap on the Southern Flank of the 6 ATAF area. It was at first agreed to maintain an RAFG recce squadron at Naples (Capodicino) on a rotational basis and from January to May 1956 a squadron deployed to Luqa to carry out C-in-C South tasks. At the same time a counter proposal was made to reduce by one the PR squadrons in RAFG and put one at Luqa, this would provide the requirement and would also be more cost effective as a Shackleton squadron at Luqa could be disbanded. Thus, 69 Squadon moved south and on 1st July was renumbered as 39 Squadron.

In the years that the two squadrons were based in the Med/ME area they had very similar 'modus operandi', the major difference being that 39 Squadron was a NATO and 6 ATAF assigned unit while 13 Squadron was a CENTO assigned unit. Both operated widely throughout the Mediterranean area, in its loosest sense, and as early as March 1958 13 Squadron had over 95% of its tasks outside the immediate area of Cyprus with surveys of Oman, the Arabian peninsula, Kenya and the Seychelles. There was no shortage of customers for vertical survey and the Squadron demonstrated the potential of such survey by covering the whole of Cyprus, some 3500 square miles, on a single sortie from 40,000 ft. It was very much the same for 39 Squadron, 'have camera will travel', although NATO exercises tended to be more frequent and involved than CENTO exercises.

WH971 B.15 of 73 Squadron, ASW, April 1968. The aircraft bounced on landing and swung off the runway. The crew, Joe Hickmet and Piet Lishman, walked away.

Opposite page: **PR.3 WF926 of 69 Squadron near the volcanic island of Stromboli, Spring 1958.**

Fitting a tip tank to 69 Squadron PR.3 WE144 at Luqa. The tip tank was held in place by explosive bolts and so could be purposely jettisoned if required.

Below: **73 Squadron B.15 dropping tip tanks filled with coloured water in a low level 'skip' bombing demonstration.**

Until the early 1960s both squadrons had been concentrating on survey work, border surveillance and shipping, all primarily medium to high level work using F49 and F52 cameras. During 1962 there was an increased appreciation of the value of low level TR (Tactical Reconnaissance) and trials were conducted on the F95 low level optical camera and the F97 night camera system using photoflashes carried in the aircraft flare bay.

With trials being done at squadron level there were the inevitable demos for visiting VIPs. A standard format for such a 'show' was a flypast as the VIPs arrived or at some other suitable time; the aircraft landed and the film was rushed off to be processed and printed against the clock so that the finished prints could be handed to the recently photographed visitors. On one of the first such demos by 13 Squadron the prints were in a helicopter and en route to the VIPs within 16 minutes of being taken! This 'trick' has never ceased to amaze the recipients and was a favourite at families days at Wyton where the aircraft would stop in front of the crowd and the navigator would leap out and rush across to the waiting Land Rover and speed off. Minutes later, copies of the photograph would be on display and the crowd would gather to find themselves on the picture!

F97 trials proceeded at Episkopi range and 13 Squadron became operational in the role during the first months of 1962. A year later the Squadron carried out the first operational night flashing sortie when the CO was tasked to carry out a photo run over an area of the island where it was thought that arms caches were being dug up at night. This 'sound and light' extravaganza was duly reported by many Cypriots as 'parachutists dropping with torches' or 'an engagement between fighters with searchlights'.

PR.3 WE139 of 39 Squadron in the dispersal at Luqa. The aircraft still carries the 'Winner' nose plaque from its victory in the London to New Zealand Air Race. *E.Keeler*

13 Squadron PR.7 WT540. In the early 1960s both Canberra PR squadrons added low level operations to their already heavy tasking and Tactical Recce became a primary role.

Changing the F.95 on a 13 Squadron PR.7 at Luqa. These cine cameras were primarily used for low level TR and were fitted with either a 4in or 12in lens.

At about the same time 39 Squadron tried their hand at the same role with most sorties being flown over Filfla island, just off the main island, or over the RAF rescue launch. 13 Squadron was content to stick with the 1.75 inch flash but 39 Squadron was given the task of experimenting with old Second World War 8 inch photoflashes for high level night PR, the idea being to use the normal day vertical cameras with the target illuminated by a series of these monster flashes, in effect mini-suns. Standard fit was for five of these flashes to be dropped from 40,000 ft in a stick at 20 second intervals to explode at 20,000 ft. They proved notoriously unreliable and as El Adem was the only range where they could be dropped it proved almost impossible for crews to remain current in this somewhat dubious role. The RAF withdrawal from Libya following the seizure of power by Qaddafi meant that El Adem was no longer available and the role was thankfully abandoned.

As 13 Squadron had blazed the way with night flashing, so 39 Squadron took the lead in low level TR after the CO, Wing Commander F. G. Agnew, had pinned AFSOUTH down on the Squadron's role in war and peace. The outcome was to make 39 a SR/TR (Strategic Recce/Tactical Recce) Squadron for 6 ATAF, with FOBs in Greece (Larissa) and Turkey (Eskishehir).

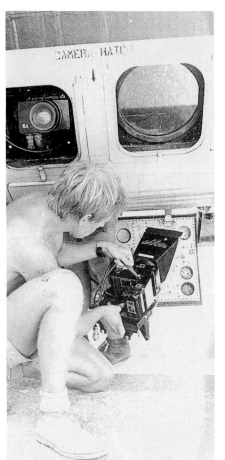

In essence, this was nothing new as both places, especially Eski, had already been used by the Squadron but it did define and emphasise the low level role. The Squadron then concentrated on flying low level routes around Libya (before withdrawal), Sicily and Turkey; and, after a bit of string pulling, Germany. It was mid-1964 before 13 Squadron launched itself into a similar low level programme.

Continuing Crises in the Middle East

The recurring political problems of Cyprus have already been discussed but these immediate troubles were not the only Middle East crises which affected the Akrotiri squadrons. In the midst of the Cyprus trouble came the Kuwait crisis. Negotiations began between the UK and Kuwait to end the original 1899 treaty and in June 1961 Britain agreed a number of long term plans, one of which was the guarantee of military aid should Kuwait, an up-and-coming oil state, be attacked. In mid-1961 the Iraqi Prime Minister, General Kassim, proclaimed Kuwait to be part of Iraq and moved troops towards the border.

An air and land task force was proposed, much of it only on paper, to include the interdiction capability of the Akrotiri Canberra squadrons and a reinforcement of RAFG Canberras. The official request for aid was made by Kuwait on the 30th June

and by the 9th July the immediate build-up in Kuwait was complete. The Cyprus strike squadrons stayed put but were placed on six hours standby for two weeks in July with normal flying curtailed. RAFG sent four B(I)8s from 88 Squadron and four B(I)6s from 213 Squadron all of which were in place at Sharjah by 2nd July.

The standby was gradually relaxed for the bomber squadrons when it became obvious that no action was likely. The RAFG Squadrons left Sharjah at the end of July and returned to their bases. It had been a 'sporty' little detachment as aircraft operated from the old hard sand runway at Sharjah, which, while not the best surface in the world, presented few problems to the rugged Canberra undercarriage.

13 Squadron with a line-up of brand new PR.9s. The Squadron's first PR.9, XH135, was taken on strength on 13th June 1961, but nearest the camera on this occasion are XH165, XH137 and XH130.

For 13 Squadron it was a much more hectic involvement and from June 1961 to May 1963 the Squadron was involved with PR ops around the Gulf area. This started as a permanent detachment of one PR.7 at Bahrein but at times involved no less than three permanent aircraft at Bahrein and Nairobi. During the early part of this period, the Squadron re-equipped with the more powerful PR.9, the first aircraft (XH135) arriving on the 13th June 1961 and the full establishment of eight aircraft being operational within a year. During the same period, 39 Squadron at Luqa gave up its PR.3s in favour of PR.9s, the first aircraft arriving in November 1962 after crews had converted to type under the guidance of 58 Squadron at Wyton. By April 1963 the last PR.3 (WE135) had been ferried back to the UK and the Squadron settled in with its new establishment of nine PR.9s and a T.4.

It was to be a 15 year love affair with the PR.9 for 13 Squadron but the unit had to give up its aircraft as part of rationalisation when 39 Squadron returned to the UK in 1970. The decision was taken to allocate all remaining PR.9s to 39 Squadron and for 13 to re-equip with PR.7s once more. The process started in May 1972 but was not completed until August 1976 when the last aircraft (XH136) went back to the UK. The PR.9 years had seen their share of tragedy

Opposite page, top: **A 13 Squadron PR.9, XH130, at Luqa. This view shows the inset position of the wing tip tanks on the PR.9.**

Opposite page, bottom: **XH169 'on the break' at Luqa.** *via Bill Corser*

Above: **XH170 in service with 39 Squadron.** *Bill Corser*

Below: **58 Squadron PR.9 XH170. This underside view highlights the filled-in wing area between wing and fuselage.**

for 13 Squadron with three fatal crashes; XH164 in January 1969, XH130 in March 1969 and XH172 in October 1972. In all instances the crashes occured as the aircraft was making a steep turn on approach to the airfield. After the first two accidents all aircraft were grounded for control integrity checks but no obvious faults were found and the PR.9 acquired a name as a dangerous aircraft in the circuit. The most worrying factor in each case was that the crew had been unable to eject safely; although most had initiated ejection they were either too close to the ground or outside the design limits of the seat, a problem for which there was no solution.

By no means all the crises were confined to the Mediterranean/Gulf area. In late 1963, 73 Squadron was declared as part of a Tactical Air Reserve and brought to 24 hours notice to deploy with six aircraft – destination, the Caribbean! They were stood down after three days when the planners were happy that the system would have worked if required.

The same was not true of the 'call to arms' at the end of 1964. In September, 73 Squadron deployed to the Far East as reinforcement for the FEAF Canberra squadrons. They in turn were relieved by the other Akrotiri strike wing squadrons in rotation up to late 1965. Details of this episode are in the next chapter which deals with FEAF.

RAF Persian Gulf

Within the NEAF area the Akrotiri squadrons had a major commitment to exercises and operational support of RAF Persian Gulf (RAFPG). Invariably, these detachments were based at Sharjah, a NEAF deployment airfield on the west coast of the promontory of the Trucial States which projects into the Persian Gulf and forms the southern shore of the Straits of Hormuz. As *Pottage* or Exercise *Kennoway* these detachments became a regular part of life for each of the strike squadrons. Conditions were by no means ideal at Sharjah but the airfield was modernised in the late 1960s and was given a 9000 ft tarmac runway. Masirah, on an island off the east coast of Oman was improved at the same time as part of the post-Aden realignment of resources, British forces having left Aden in 1967. To some people the improvements at Sharjah spoilt the character of the place with the end of the pre-fab accommodation and the building of new messes. However, these detach-

ments did enable squadrons to undertake a period of intensive training, usually with an emphasis on tactical air operations and RP at Jebajib or Rashid range with full, half and quarter pod shoots. Because no permanent range staff were available, the squadron would send one of the aircrew off to the range as Safety Officer, either by helicopter or by car, the latter being a pretty tortuous journey. On arrival at the range it was not unusual for the RSO to have nothing to do so he would take to the water for a quick swim keeping a watchful eye out for sharks!

Whilst at Sharjah it was quite usual for aircraft to go down to Masirah for a change of scenery, although this was a place you either liked or hated. On one 73 Squadron detachment to Masirah, for Exercise *Biltong* the aircrew lived in tents while the groundcrew had the luxury of huts! There were also occasional operational detachments to the area, especially in the mid 1960s when there was an insurgent problem in Oman. In May 1966 aircraft were

tasked with low level visual and photographic recce of likely supply routes for arms and supplies.

By the end of the decade Britain was planning to withdraw permanent forces from the Gulf area and 1971 was set as the rundown year. Sharjah was duly closed on the 14th December and Muharraq on the 15th although Masirah kept going for a while as it was used as a staging post on the route to the Far East.

Heat Stress!

This is a good time to look once more at a problem which beset the Canberra in this theatre - heat in the cockpit. During his early flight trials Beamont had criticised the 'greenhouse effect' beneath the canopy. It was very soon realised that this was going to be a major snag in the heat of the Med and in January 1958 WD988 was used in a trial to find a solution to the problem. The aircraft was painted all-over white instead of the usual silver; temperatures of crew and cockpit were recorded and compared to readings from a normal aircraft. Whatever the result nothing came of it and the only notable white Canberra in the theatre was WH727 *Queen of the Arabian Skies*, a B.2 used as the personal aircraft of AOC Aden. Sir David Lee in his time as AOC Aden has very fond memories of flying this aircraft with its very un-Canberra like pristine interior and white colour scheme, and he took every opportunity he could to fly it. His Command

13 Squadron PR.9 XH136 takes on fuel at Muharraq, March 1964.

73 Squadron at Sharjah on exercise 'Pottage', May 1968. This was one of the regular series of exercises held throughout the operational area covered by the ASW (Akrotiri Strike Wing) squadrons.

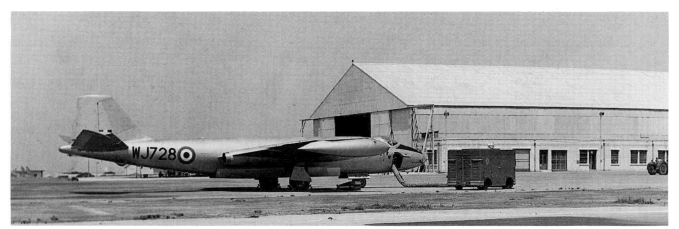

covered a vast geographical area but by using the Canberra the AOC could travel to the various regions in hours rather than half-a-day or more which it would have taken in an Andover or Hastings.

The heat problem for NEAF ops was never solved despite attempts to provide coolers for aircraft and personnel. It became very much a matter of acclimatisation to the theatre. One of the squadron record books notes that on a detachment to Sharjah in September 1966 cockpit temperatures were 106°F with Mk.5 coolers and 112°F with Mk.3 coolers and comments that 'they were surprisingly low'! Standard dress was a flying suit and as little else as possible and still the crew would emerge wringing wet from a low level sortie.

One attempt to ease the heat problem was the provision of AVSs (Air Ventilated Suit). The AVS is a nylon undergarment designed to be worn over a string vest and pants and under a normal flying suit. Sewn into it, in such a way that their open ends protrude inside the suit, are numerous small air tubes connected by various slightly larger tubes to a main inlet tube situated on the left hip and which protrudes through a slit in the flying suit. Air is taken under pressure from one of the engine compressor stages, cooled and fed through tubing to the main inlet. Thus a flow of air is produced which has a cooling effect on the body.

The AVS had been introduced in the mid 1950s after a series of trials, one of which was a round trip to Singapore by a 21 Squadron aircraft and crew to test the new system under varied 'operational conditions'. One section of their report reflects the scale of the problem . . 'Leaving Aden the cockpit temperature was 91°F and the rear crew set the control to hot at 17,000 ft whereas the pilot kept his selected to cold throughout the sortie. Typically, all the crew suffered profuse sweating before take-off, a rapid climb to altitude before the sweat had time to evaporate, followed by a long and uncomfortable spell in an icy-cold moisture-laden cabin with frost forming on walls, instruments and shoes.' The reference to 'hot' selected was the incorporation of a means of shutting off the heat exchanger so that hot air was fed in from the engines. Tearing around the Near East, or the Far East, at low level in

high temperatures was the test of the system and it worked quite well although the suit was not all that comfortable. Early AVS suits were made of cotton which had a tendency to rot but were comfortable and therefore liked. To prevent rotting, nylon suits were produced but these were uncomfortable next to the skin. It was very much personal preference and some aircrew never did get on with it, some prefered to carry a length of tubing to stick into the AVS connector to give a general blast of cold air!

As well as RAFPG and further afield, the squadrons ranged far and wide in the CENTO countries bordering the Med and associated areas with regular exercises and detachments to Greece, Turkey, Iran and Pakistan. On average, squadrons took part in three or four major exercises with the Turks and Greeks each year, usually operating out of Eskishehir for the former.

Various attempts were made to keep cockpit temperatures down while aircraft were on the ground. The simplest was the bolt-on or wheeled sunshade, the other was a cooler unit, as seen here plugged into WJ728, which blew cold air into the cockpit.

Not only cool the aircraft but cool the crew. Here 149 Squadron crews 'model' the Air Ventilated Suit (AVS).

Top: **PR.7 WH794 of 13 Squadron at Luqa. After 25 years of Canberra PR ops throughout the Med, 13 Squadron left Malta and returned to the UK in October 1978.**

Above: **A fine nose study of a Canberra PR.7** *B.A. Crook*

WH966 of the ASW, Akrotiri 1967. *MAP*

The other regular exercise was the annual CENTO Air Defence Exercise (Adex), *Shabaz,* for which the squadrons operated from Tehran, Iran or Peshawar, Pakistan. This followed the standard 'canned' pattern of Adexs with high level routes flown over Iran and Pakistan and set target attacks with no live bombing. This, in the opinion of the Canberra units, greatly reduced the value of the exercise and the only realistic air threat, on the few occasions that intercepts were made, came from the Iranian F-5s.

However, attitudes changed a little when low-level legs were introduced and on one exercise during November 1961, 73 Squadron conceded that the air threat was too great – in the form of a plague of locusts: 'air superiority was given to the locusts, they filed no flight plans and shed not a tear as wingmen and companions were sucked into RR engines or ended their lives as a smear in a dent on a tip tank.'

Up to four raids a day by five aircraft meant hard work for the groundcrew, especially if temperatures rose above 100°F, which they frequently did, making the metal skin of the aircraft untouchable. For the Tehran detachments at least, the crews stayed in luxurious hotels so free time was enjoyed and the social life hectic. As Piet Lishman of 73 Squadron recalls: 'The international hotels in Tehran were excellent. Vodka and fresh lime was the "in-drink" and the only ones who missed out on the great social life were those who didn't drink and who ate only English food.'

Despite all the limitations imposed by the exercise, the opportunity to work closely with the Iranian and Pakistan Air Forces was of obvious benefit in the CENTO context. After a hectic few weeks aircraft returned to Akrotiri laden with copper-ware, paintings and carpets!

While the strike squadrons were caught up in the interminable round of exercises and detachments, the recce squadrons

The Khormaksar Station Flight line-up including B.2 WH860. *via A. Thomas*

B.2 WH727 'Queen of the Arabian Skies', the all white aircraft of AOC Aden. *via Chris Ward*

B.15 WJ774 of 249 Squadron, 1962, shortly after the squadron had exchanged its B.6s for B.15s although it was not until April the following year that the full UE of eight had arrived. *E. Taylor*

Gulf area. The following year 13 Squadron sent a detachment of three aircraft to reinforce the overworked crews of 81 Squadron at Tengah during *Confrontation*. Up to the end of the Confrontation period, regular, usually three-monthly, detachments from 13 Squadron and 39 Squadron took it in turns to reinforce the FEAF theatre, adding yet another burden to the already hard-pressed resources. In between two of their Tengah stints, 13 Squadron moved to Luqa because of overcrowding at Akrotiri and from September 1965 until the rundown of MEAF the two PR units operated side by side, continuing the standard squadron rivalry. For the next five years both units had the same basic workload and commitments but also maintained their own specific operational areas.

As early as January 1967 it was rumoured that one of the squadrons would have to go as part of the general run-down of forces on Malta, but it was not until late 1969 that it was announced that 39 Squadron would move back to the UK 'sometime in 1970'.

Meanwhile, it was business as usual with 13 Squadron doing surveys of Gan and Sierra Leone and 39 Squadron taking its share of the other surveys. However, the NATO commitment and QRA occupied much of the Squadron's time and resources. Both squadrons, when time, aircraft and crews permitted, continued the excellent Canberra tradition of *Lone Rangers* with singleton detachments far and wide throughout Europe, Africa and the Middle East. Almost any airfield that had a suitable runway received a visit from a Canberra on more than one occasion! At last the day came, 39 Squadron bade a sad farewell to Malta and flew to its new home at Wyton on the 1st October.

Once again 13 Squadron was the only Canberra squadron in the MEAF/NEAF area although 39 Squadron maintained an operational interest in the area and flew frequent detachments 'and *Rangers* back to its old haunts.

were busy with operational PR. It is easy to see why it was virtually unknown to have a squadron all together in one place at one time. Life on a Canberra PR squadron was certainly not boring! As soon as one regular task was cancelled or reduced, another was proposed or extended. In February 1964 the 13 Squadron detachment returned to Akrotiri from the Gulf bringing to an end a seven year rotated detachment! At the same time, 39 Squadron took on the Gulf and Aden commitment to give 13 time to collect their thoughts and carry out training flying. From then on it was 39 Squadron's turn to keep a virtually standing detachment in Aden (Khormaksar) and Bahrein (Muharraq) for SR of the Persian

AS.30

Meanwhile the Akrotiri strike wing was at operational standby in the mid 1960s. With quite a range of weapons already available to the Canberra it was decided to add another for two of the squadrons when 73 Squadron and 32 Squadron were scheduled to equip with the AS.30 guided missile. In January 1965 73 Squadron started training its first six crews with the new system after a number of observers had returned from an instructional course in Paris the previous year. Only three Canberra squadrons were scheduled to receive the weapon, the third one being 45 Squadron in the Far East.

The AS.30 missile was built by Aerospatiale (Nord Aviation) to a French requirement for a guided air to surface missile (ASM) with a range greater than six miles and an accuracy of less than 33 ft. The company scaled-up the existing AS.20 missile to produce a weapon just under 13 ft long, weighing 1,146 lbs and carrying a warhead of 529 lbs. The missile had a two-stage solid propellant power plant and radio command guidance with fixed wings and cruciform 'flip out' fins. With a launch speed range of Mach 0.45 to Mach 1.5 it was only just suitable for the Canberra although early trials were conducted by French Canberras and Vautours. The system exceeded its specifications both in its range of seven miles and its accuracy of less than 30 ft. The missile was not roll stabilised but had a sustainer motor with two nozzles, one on each side and the operator 'flew' the missile by tracking its flare tail with cross-hairs in the aircraft and sending commands by radio link which biased two vibrating spoilers that intermittently interrupted the jets from the nozzles, thus causing the missile to change course. The autopilot interpreted the interupt commands into steer left/right or up/down.

The first few months of 1965 were spent on intensive ground training to prepare for the arrival of the new weapon while in March a number of B.15s were sent to Samlesbury for airframe modifications to make them missile capable, the first such aircraft being WH974. By July the Squadron had an AS.30 simulator rigged up in the crewroom and crews had to complete six hours a month on this machine getting used to the controls and basic techniques. One aircraft, WH966, was eventually fitted out as an airborne AS.30 trainer and had fixed cross hairs in the nose which the navs could use to track almost anything as a simulated target.

Normal launch range was seven miles and the missile was then held high to track above the target; while the nav plotter called out range and time, the nav observer 'flew' the missile and the nearer the missile got to the target so it was progressively steered down to the impact point. There was a hold up on the live firing programme because there was no suitable range, but eventually El Adem was cleared for use and a 73 Squadron crew fired the first live round at this range in November – with an

error of just nine yards. One story says that a brand new target was built at a cost of £40,000 at El Adem and that on one of the very first missile attacks it was blown to pieces! The AS.30 programme gathered speed and in March 1965 32 Squadron received its first modified aircraft and both units began regular simulated and live firing attacks at El Adem. The system proved to be very reliable with very few failures and an accuracy overall of some 18 yards. AS.30 firing was seen as a bit of light relief from the routine sorties and greatly enjoyed by the crews.

In November 1966, the Canberra Tactical Evaluation Flight (CANTAC) ran a programme of test firings at El Adem which culminated in a simultaneous shoot by three aircraft in battle formation! For the early firings only one missile was carried and as the missile was not jettisonable a dummy or alternative store had to be carried on the other pylon to prevent any imbalance if the aircraft lost an engine and went asymmetric. It was not long, however, before aircraft were cleared to carry two missiles and double-firings took place soon afterwards.

73 Squadron B.15 lets loose the first AS.30, February 1966.

A typical pose – Gerry Crombie checks the rear hatch of a 13 Squadron PR.7 in Malta. The rear hatch not only gave access to the large format cameras but also provided extra storage space, for such things as detachment bicycles! *Steve Norrie*

A year after the introduction of the AS.30, two aircraft from 73 Squadron were modified by 103 MU for trial firings of the AS.12 wire-guided missile, which was much smaller and lighter. The object of the trial was to see if the guidance wire would break at speeds from 180 to 250 knots. Some ten launches were made by an operator from Nord Aviation and the Squadron heard no more about it. Although the system was never intended for the Canberra, it must have been a very interesting trial to have a great length of cable attached to a high-speed aircraft!

No developments were made to the AS.30 although numerous updates such as laser guidance were suggested, and in fact adopted by the French in the AS.30L for the Jaguar.

In the midst of these developments it was decided to replace the squadron markings on the aircraft with a Strike Wing design of a Flamingo above crested waves over a lightning flash, a move that was given a cool reception by the squadrons. Worse was to follow when in July 1966 centralised servicing was introduced which meant that all aircraft and groundcrew were taken away from the squadrons to form a central pool. A 'wake' was held for the groundcrew who lost their squadron identity, and dire predictions were made for the future. Lo and behold the predictions proved true and aircraft serviceability dropped dramatically, although this was partly attributed to the aircrew not being able to 'carry snags', i.e. pass on details of minor aircraft problems on aircraft because they did not know which squadron would get the aircraft next and could not therefore brief the new crew.

Top: **Nord AS.30 ASM under a B.15. 'Mac' MacDonald and Gordon Campbell prior to winning the champagne on a 73 Squadron AS.30 shoot at El Adem, June 1968.**

Detail of Akrotiri Strike Wing marking on fin - a Flamingo above crested waves over a Lightning flash. *MAP*

B.16 WT303 of 32 Squadron. Only two of the ASW squadrons, 73 and 32, acquired the AS.30 role.

Disbandment

All four of the strike squadrons took on a nomadic life for the last four months of 1968 as the runway at Akrotiri was resurfaced yet again. Each squadron went its own way, spending a month here and a month there – to such places as Nicosia, Luqa, El Adem and the UK. One bonus was that each squadron was given its own groundcrew and one of the first jobs on leaving Akrotiri was to repaint the squadron insignia on the aircraft!

By the time they were back at Akrotiri it was in tablets of stone that they were all soon to disband as part of the run-down of NEAF. The Akrotiri Strike Wing held its disbandment parade and flypast on 10th January 1969, a very sad but colourful occasion. 6 Squadron was the first to say goodbye to its aircraft, re-equipping with Phantoms in mid January and moving to Coningsby. 32 Squadron continued for another few weeks, disbanding on 3rd February. 249 Squadron continued ferrying aircraft right up to the last day on 24th February, after a tremendous final Squadron party at Symelledes in Limassol! 73 Squadron held on the longest and carried on its primary role with ever diminishing numbers of aircraft until they too 'shut up shop' and brought another Canberra era to an end.

That left only the two PR squadrons on Malta and within a year 39 had left to return to the UK leaving 13 Squadron on its own – the first Canberra squadron in the theatre and destined to be the last. The task increased as the Squadron picked up commitments in Italy, Greece and Turkey to add to its existing ones for the Middle East, Gulf and East Africa. On the 4th January 1972 the Squadron moved back to Akrotiri following a bad patch in Anglo-Maltese relations but this was only for a few months and by October they were back at Luqa. In February 1974 the Squadron had the shock of being declared to SACEUR and started taking a more active part in NATO exercises and being subjected to TACEVAL. This simply added to the pace of life in the remaining years at Malta. The continued contraction of overseas forces caught up with 13 and in October 1978 the Squadron bade farewell to Malta and moved to Wyton. The last Mediterranean Canberra squadron had gone.

WJ777 painted as last NEAF Strike Canberra with badges of all four ASW squadrons. The flypast and disbandment parade was held on 10th January 1969 although the squadrons continued to operate until the end of February. *MAP*

WH960 of ASW/249 Squadron. In the latter half of 1968 the squadrons took the opportunity to repaint squadron markings on the aircraft, the move to a 'Wing' mentality had proved very unpopular.

Chapter Five

Far East Air Force

On 19th February 1955 the South East Asia Collective Defence Treaty was signed by eight nations: Australia, Britain, France, New Zealand, Pakistan, Philippine Republic, Thailand and the United States. Under the terms of this Manila Treaty they agreed 'separately and jointly, by means of continuous and effective self help and mutual aid, to maintain and develop their individual and collective capacity to resist armed attack and to prevent any counter-subversive activities directed against their territorial integrity and political stability.'

This was very much a response to the take-over in China by Mao Tse Tung's hard-line regime and the spread of Communist 'terrorism' in the SE Asia and West Pacific area, Malaya being a classic example. The permanent HQ of SEATO was set up at Bangkok with C-in-C FEAF maintaining a watching brief over RAF affairs in SEATO on behalf of the Chief of the Air Staff (CAS). SEATO had no standing forces or command structure but each of the signatory nations undertook to provide forces for the regular exercises and, of course, in time of tension. This normally utilised in-theatre forces but Home Commands also took part. However, at this time there were no Canberra units in the FEAF inventory and none were earmarked for deployment to the theatre before 1957 at the earliest. Thus, the first appearance of the Canberra in this theatre came about as a result of the political situation in Malaya and during the latter part of the 'Malayan Emergency' (1948-60) squadrons from Bomber Command deployed to Malaya and Singapore for active operations.

Malayan Emergency
In many ways the Malayan crisis was a legacy of the Second World War when Britain had armed, and encouraged, communist guerilla groups to act against the Japanese. The post-war re-establishment of control and the forming of a Malayan Union caused internal upheaval as the Communists sought greater influence. This led to a period of 'peaceful agitation' of non-co-operation and strikes. However, there was dissatisfaction within the Malayan Communist Party (MCP) over progress towards power, despite virtual control of most unions, and a new General Secretary, Chin Peng, was elected in

March 1947. He immediately instituted more vigorous action, stepping up strikes and increasing the level of violence and intimidation. This in turn caused a reaction amongst the urban population and some unions who were fed up of the dictatorial attitudes of the communist groups. In June 1948 the government decided to introduce legislation to curb the communist influence and within two weeks the MCP abandoned 'peaceful' action and took to the jungle to take up the armed struggle.

Operating the typical 'cell' structure of a communist guerilla organisation, the Malayan Races Liberation Army (MRLA) soon had control of much of the interior of Malaya. Villages and isolated rubber plantations became the targets for collection or extortion of money or supplies. The government campaign was orientated at preventing the guerillas having access to such supplies by a 'hearts and minds' campaign and by enclosing and policing villages. Area by area this policy was enforced and as each area was closed down the military campaign would take place to eliminate the guerilla bands.

During the 'intensive period' of operations, 1952-55, Communist Terrorist (CT) camps were attacked from the air and the CT's forced into prepared ambush areas where ground forces were waiting. The main weight of bombing had been provided by the Lincolns of Bomber Command and the RAAF and it was only towards the end of this period that the first jet bombers, Canberras, appeared in the theatre with the arrival of a detachment from 101 Squadron with four B.6s.

Over a period of 15 months the Binbrook wing rotated its squadrons in theatre until the first resident FEAF Canberra squadron appeared on the scene in December 1957. By the end of the 'Emergency' the deployment schedule looked like this:

101 Sqn	Tengah/Changi/ Butterworth	Feb - Jun 1955
617 Sqn	Butterworth	Jun - Oct 1955
12 Sqn	Butterworth	Oct 55 - Mar 56
9 Sqn	Butterworth	Mar - Jun 1956
101 Sqn	Butterworth	Jun - Sep 1956
45 Sqn	Tengah	Dec 57 - end
75 Sqn, RNZAF	Tengah	1958 - end

101 Squadron had started training for the Operation *Mileage* detachment to Malaya early in January 1955 and on the 9th of the month the Sunday papers announced that four aircraft from RAF Binbrook were 'going to Malaya for operations against the terrorists'. Low level navigation and bombing sorties were flown ready for the difficult task of finding targets in the jungle. On 7th February the aircraft left Binbrook for Idris, Habbaniya, Mauripur, Negombo and finally Changi where they arrived on the 11th. Local area flying, bombing up trials and practice bombing on China Rock range soon gave way to operational tasks. The first 'simulated attack on a static target' was flown on the 18th and five days later, 23rd, Squadron Leader Robertson in WH948 made the first live jet bomber attack when he led a formation of three aircraft to bomb a static target. A static target was defined as a known terrorist area but with no friendly troops in the immediate vicinity. Over the ensuing weeks the detachment undertook many 1,000 lb bomb raids, including a number of night attacks, and details of these sorties are listed in an Appendix. In mid March 1,000 lb ops were halted because of a fault in the Avro triple carriers which had resulted in bombs falling off the carrier and onto the bomb bay doors! The armament officer of 1 Squadron, RAAF, arrived with a modification and the aircraft started operating with a load of six 500 lb bombs. As the first of the Canberra squadrons in the theatre, 101 tried a variety of attack techniques, many adopted from those used successfully by the Lincolns. However, the two main techniques adopted at first were 'Austermark' (Auster Target Marking) and 'Datum Point'. Pinpoint targets were usually attacked by three aircraft in vic to ensure a good distribution of bombs over the target area. Having been given the target position as a six-figure map reference it was plotted on a 1:1 million scale map and a circle 10 minutes radius flying time at 200 kts drawn around it. The area was then examined for the best run-in taking into consideration terrain, navigation features etc. Planning complete, the formation would head for the target area, set itself up for the pre-planned run and check-in with the Auster marker aircraft. At the ten minute point the Canberra leader would

call 'bombing in 10'. As the formation ran-in the navigators would time with stop-watches, resetting these at regular check features to reduce timing error, and the leader call 'bombing in 9' and so on down to 'bombing in 2' A final call of 'bombing in 90 (seconds)' and the Auster would drop his marker flare on the target and call 'target marked, target height 'n ft'. The Auster would stay in the area to call the results of the bombing, give further assistance or re-mark the target if required. Target runs were done at 200 kts because of the limited range of the Auster radio.

'Datum Point' was when the lead aircraft navigated at a pre-determined height and speed along a carefully seleted track to a final pin-point fix (The Datum Point), after

which a timed run was made – releasing the bombs on the lead nav's timing mark (stopwatch). As this technique was used for 'area attack' targets only, it was accurate enough!

The other Bomber Command squadrons took their turns in theatre, operating along the same lines. Some, like 9 Squadron, had a reasonably quiet time and others found it quite hectic. During their three months of active ops (June - August), 617 Squadron flew twenty-four ops, mainly in concentrated periods of 2-3 days in support of ground forces. Most sorties were in the standard three-ships with six 1,000 lb or 500 lb bombs per aircraft but 25 lb practice bombs were dropped during some practice (static) strikes. Night sorties were flown with aircraft over the target in stream. In order to keep the element of surprise it was suggested that a new offset technique be used whereby the flare was dropped on a known bearing and distance from the target and with a time delay fuse so that it burst after several hours. As well as the difficulty of finding targets in the dense jungle, weather proved no small problem as one 617 squadron crew recalled, 'the aircraft were confronted with almost continuous lightning and at times St Elmos fire completely blinded the vision.' On this particular occasion discretion won the day and the aircraft turned back!

101 Squadron was unique in that it was the only squadron to do two tours of duty in the campaign, the second one (in mid-1956) being cut short when the Squadron was recalled to standby for ops in the Middle East.

By early 1957 active operations had decreased as the number of terrorists had been reduced to an estimated 2,500. These were the hard-core 'professionals' and they were scattered throughout the country in small cells.

The overall anti-terrorist campaign in Malaya has been hailed as one of the few successful such campaigns ever undertaken by security forces and the 'air control' policy played an important part in the outcome. With the concentration of ops against the MRLA forces in Central Malaya, the existing command and control system was modified and AHQ Malaya was concentrated at Kuala Lumpur. This was a short-lived arrangement because on 31 August 1957 Malaya gained its independence and responsibility for law and order devolved on the Governments of Malaya and Singapore. They immediately requested assistance from the UK, Australia and New Zealand until the end of the 'Emergency'. This tied-in with the deployment of the first resident FEAF Canberra units although it was not until October 1957 that the decision was taken on which of the FEAF airfields should be developed for the jet bomber era. An Air Council Memorandum of October 1957

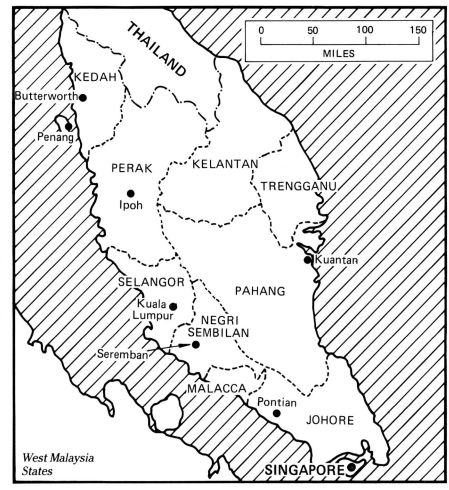

West Malaysia States

outlined the decision to develop Tengah rather than Butterworth, Seletar or Paya Lebar and plans were made to expand the existing facilities and to provide a 9000 ft all-weather runway for two permanent Canberra squadrons and a reinforcement of two V-bomber squadrons. The original mid 1950s plan was for only one squadron of B.2s and a half squadron of PR.7s but the vital importance of recce had been realised early on in the *Firedog* operations.

WJ758 of 101 Squadron dropping a stick of bombs over Malaya during Operation *Mileage*, 1955. Most bombing was by single aircraft or by formations of three aircraft. *A. Bridges*

Above: **45 Squadron B.2 WJ630. This aircraft began its operational career with 100 Squadron and was loaned to 75 Squadron RNZAF in between two periods of service with 45 Squadron. It was later converted to T.17 standard and is still serving with 360 Squadron at Wyton.** *MAP*

Below: **58 Squadron dispersal at Butterworth during** *Planters Punch* **April- May 1956. Note the presence of the Vickers Valetta C.1s of the Far East Transport Wing, which dropped over 2,000 tons of supplies to troops in the jungle, as well as hundreds of millions of leaflets.**

Bottom: **WH948 of 101 Squadron at Butterworth during the Malayan Emergency 1955. 101 was unique amongst the Bin- brook Wing squadrons, doing two tours of Operation** *Mileage,* **the second curtailed by the Suez Crisis and the squadron's redeployment to Malta.** *A.Bridges*

45 Squadron were no strangers to Butter- worth and the FEAF area, having operated Venoms from Butterworth for some time before disbandment in March 1957. How- ever, the squadron reformed at Coningsby in November 1957 with B.2s ready to return to Butterworth and become the first resident FEAF Canberra squadron. As the squadron reformed, crews were checked on the T.4 by pilots of the BCHU (Bomber Command Holding Unit) pend- ing arrival of the Squadron's own aircraft from MU, the plan being for a 10 hour 'shakedown' of aircraft and crews before the long haul to the Far East. It was not until early December that aircraft began to arrive at Coningsby and it was the 9th before the first wave of four aircraft took- off to fly the route Idris-Akrotiri-Karachi- Katunayake-Tengah. Preparations for the ferry flight were extensive with a series of lectures on aircraft servicing, navigation and met, while the aircraft were fitted with Marconi sub-miniature radio compasses to give some semblance of navigation kit to the otherwise poorly-equipped B.2. By the 13th three of the aircraft from the first wave were on the final leg to Tengah when tragedy struck. In the descent to Tengah two of the aircraft collided in cloud (WJ983 and WH882) and although two crew members managed to eject safely, the other four were killed as the wreckage fell in the Pontian area of South Malaya. This was a tragic start to the Squadron's new life in FEAF. The following day with two aircraft safely on the ground, the crews were flown to the Joint Operations Centre (JOC) at Kuala Lumpur for an HQ brief on the Malayan crisis and *Firedog* operations by the staff of HQ 224 Group.

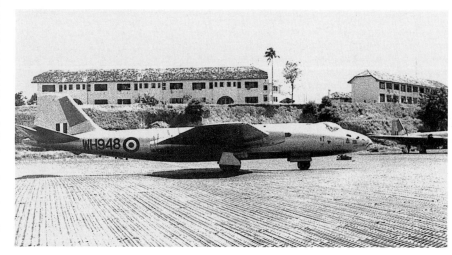

Meanwhile, the groundcrew were carrying out acceptance checks on the two aircraft and within a couple of days both were ready for their first sorties. Most of the groundcrew were ex 45 Squadron (Venom) from Butterworth although a nucleus of Canberra trained personnel had been posted in from the UK. The first few sorties consisted of local area famil flying and orientation but soon included initial trials for *Firedog* operations which were expected in the near future as the government forces prepared to deal with the remaining hard-core cells. A number of bombing and marking techniques had been devised during previous *Firedog* ops and one of these, Target Director Post (TDP) became the subject of an early 45 Squadron trial to decide on the best speeds and techniques for this type of bombing. After a few dry runs crews were sent off to drop practice bombs on Raffles range using this technique and also visual bombing.

While the first two crews were settling in to this routine, plus the odd ride on active ops in the Lincolns of No.1 Squadron RAAF, the rest of the Squadron's aircraft were getting ready to leave the UK. A short stop at Waddington to be disinsectisized and four aircraft left the UK on the 11th arriving at Singapore a few days later to go through the same briefings and work-up flying as the earlier arrivals. 45 Squadron now had a reasonable strength of aircraft and crews in theatre and so began a programme of intensive tactical and *Firedog* training which aimed to get the Squadron operational by 1st May 1958.

Thus, the Squadron slotted into its routine of training sorties with a typical profile being a 20 second stream take-off by six or seven aircraft, a climb to 15,000 feet to clear the airways in the Singapore terminal area, a bit of formation practice, a descent to low level for map reading training and perhaps a 25 lb practice bomb or two at Raffles range to conclude the exercise before going back to Tengah. The low level map reading element was vital as very few of the crews had done much of this before and, anyway map reading over the jungle was a definite art to be acquired with practice. By early February, night flying had been added to the agenda as night operations in one form or another were seen as a distinct possibility. Formation bomb runs using TDP became fairly standard as did the adoption of another well-proven technique, Auster Target Marking.

A number of crews were allowed the dubious pleasure of an op with the Austers to watch target marking at first hand or simply on a general jungle recce. While none doubted that this helped them to gain a feeling for the operational area, most preferred the comfort and security of their Canberras!

With training progressing so well, the Squadron was called on to start operations before the notional 1st May date, with a series of strikes for Operation *Ginger*, a large-scale harassing operation in support of 28 Commonwealth Brigade in the Chemor Hills west of Ipoh. For these missions the Squadron detached to and operated from their old base at Butterworth. The first strike, by four aircraft, was led by the CO, Squadron Leader C. C. Blount, on the 18th March, against jungle targets marked by an Auster. All four aircraft carried the standard load of six 500 lb bombs, which were dropped in a single pass over the target giving a complete straddle of the marked area and an assessed overshoot of only 70 yards - a good start. Between the 19th and 22nd March six more raids were flown, four very similar to that above and two by single aircraft acting as lead aircraft to formations of No.14 (RNZAF) Venoms. A four-day break back at Tengah and then into the fray again with another round of ops from Butterworth over a three day period with five four-aircraft raids and another two Venom-lead details. This time the formation attacks were made by dropping two 500 lb bombs on each of three passes over the target to ensure better coverage of the target area. March had seen the Squadron arrive operationally in FEAF with two hundred and twenty 500 lb bombs dropped. Great credit was due to the groundcrew, and especially to the armourers, who not only kept the aircraft flying but were turning four aircraft round to full load in only 86 minutes – good going for a full refuel and re-arm.

April and May proved just as hectic. Sorties during the period 10-15th April, were a

continuation of Operation *Ginger* plus ops in the Yong Peng area to harass small bands of CTs and move them into ambush areas. This, as mentioned previously, was fairly standard practice with aircraft used to 'herd' the enemy into prepared ambush areas for ground forces to round them up and prevent any stragglers escaping, as it was important to eliminate the cell completely.

At the same time and continuing into May, the Squadron took part in Operation *Bintang* in support of No.2 Federal Infantry Brigade. By May the Squadron was getting into its stride and trying new techniques and procedures. Experience had shown that a five aircraft formation was the maximum practical size for formation bombing and even then each crew must be aware at all times of their rôle and place. Then began a series of 1000 lb bombing sorties referred to as 'practice strikes in an operational area', live bombing of likely terrorist areas but not counted as operational strikes. To improve the aircrew understanding of the Target Director Post (TDP) technique, the system was set up at Tengah so that TDP radar operators and squadron aircrew could exchange ideas and discuss procedures.

This was followed by a trial whereby the system was set up to give a projected release point at Pin Point Island which the bomb aimers could check in the bomb sight. In the next series of ops, July to August, TDP became the favoured technique as it gave a blind capability with reasonable accuracy - 180 yards average error overshoot and 150 yards right, quite a good straddle of bombs from a formation release.

The blind delivery capability was important because of the frequent problems with cloud obscuring the target, thus negating 'Auster Mark' and visual delivery.

Having taken care of blind delivery training, the Squadron took time to concentrate on visual bombing at the China Rock range to calibrate the bombsights by using strike photos and plotted results.

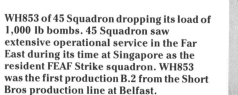
WH853 of 45 Squadron dropping its load of 1,000 lb bombs. 45 Squadron saw extensive operational service in the Far East during its time at Singapore as the resident FEAF Strike squadron. WH853 was the first production B.2 from the Short Bros production line at Belfast.

Any aiming system requires calibration of one sort or another and this particularly applied to a fairly simple 'steam-driven' sight such as that fitted to the Canberra. The second reason for the intensive training was to prepare the Squadron to take an even bigger slice of the action when the Lincolns of 1 Squadron RAAF returned to Australia in July. June and July were to prove the busiest months for active operations with a mix of 500 lb and 1000 lb raids and 45 Squadron was in action on no less than seventeen days, including one night

formation attack. This period is summarised in the Canberra Operations Appendix. Most of the sorties were flown with the standard load of six 1000 lb bombs which meant a reduced fuel load on take-off and a refuel stop at Butterworth if the Squadron was operating out of Tengah. In mid June the formation tactic changed to improve TDP accuracy, the aircraft formed up at half a spans length, fanning to 75 yards about 8000 yards before bomb release point to give the TDP radar blips time to settle down, rather than fanning

out later which caused the TDP control screen to 'hunt' with consequent loss of accuracy. With this technique the bombing height was usually in the 10-15,000 ft bracket, although on occasions aircraft did drop from lower if weather or other factors dictated. The standard night technique was to use TDP with aircraft in 2,000 yard line astern or with a 30 minute spacing over the target. The psychological effect of a night attack on the terrorists was out of proportion to the physical damage or casualties caused. Out of the dark silent night the Canberras appeared without warning - one of the attributes of the Canberra was its silent approach, there being no appreciable noise until the aircraft was overhead.

In order to achieve some semblance of normality and allow crews an element of freedom, the Squadron operated a weekly-rotated standby system whereby five crews were at six hours readiness on working days and at eight hours readiness outside normal working hours. This also allowed the non-standby crews some continuity in the normal training routine although the latter was difficult to arrange because of a lack of aircraft with five on armed standby.

Operations for *Firedog* became less and less frequent after the hectic summer but were still called for until the official end of the Malayan Emergency in July 1960. This declaration brought an end to twelve years of anti-terrorist operations.

The value of the Canberra contribution has often been disputed. One FEAF report stated '...both from the point of view of maintenance and flying conditions, Lincolns were preferable to Canberras in the type of campaign that prevailed in Malaya.' It is true that the Lincoln carried

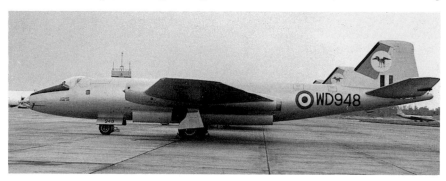

A pristine WD948 of 45 Squadron, ready for air test after a Major inspection at Tengah, 1959. The Squadron's camel motif went through a number of transformations. *R. Evans*

Refuelling 45 Squadron B.2s after a morning raid in 1960. Working on the aircraft in the heat of the Far East could be quite painful as the aircraft's skin became too hot to touch. *R. Evans*

WJ567 on a detachment to Kai Tak, 21st April 1960. Hong King was a frequent venue for squadron detachments or single aircraft 'Lone Rangers'. *Roger Evans*

Opposite page: **45 Squadron T.4 WH706 sporting the 'Camel Air' legend.**

a greater load and with its slower speed could attack jungle targets under direction quite accurately. The only real advantage with the Canberra was the speed of reaction and this paid dividends at times with the CT being caught in the camps.

With the departure of the Australian Lincolns, another Canberra unit replaced them in the theatre when No.75 (RNZAF) Squadron arrived at Tengah with its Canberra B.2s as part of the Commonwealth Strategic Reserve. This RNZAF unit's aircraft were on loan from the UK pending delivery to the RNZAF of the interdictor Canberras it had ordered. The Commonwealth Strategic Reserve was a somewhat nebulous 'formation' being a result of the Commonwealth agreements following the independence and granting of Commonwealth status to Malaya in October 1957. It was by this arrangement that Australia assumed command of Butterworth for use by its own Sabre, and later Canberra, squadrons, plus other Commonwealth units. The RAF units at Singapore were notionally part of the Strategic Reserve.

For 45 Squadron, ops continued at the rate of one or two a month up until August 1959 with the last sorties being TDP attacks on CT camps 30 miles to the NE of Kuala Lumpur. As on many other occasions, ground troops moved into the area after the bombing and were able to assess the results, in this case two camps flattened, one only a few hours after it had been abandoned.

To summarise this last phase:

1 Aug 58	5 acft	´ 500 lb	Johore area
3 Sept 58	3 acft	1000 lb	Ipoh area
30 Sept 58	5 acft	1000 lb	N Perak area
9 Nov 58	1 acft	500 lb	S Johore area
14 Nov 58	5 acft	500 lb	Rasah
8 Dec 58	2 acft	500 lb	N of Selangor
13 Aug 59	3 acft	1000 lb	30 miles NE Kuala Lumpur
17 Aug 59	3 acft	1000 lb	as 13 Aug '59

The raid of 30th September is of note as it was made in company with aircraft of No 75 (RNZAF) Squadron and No 2 (RAAF) Squadron, which had arrived at Butterworth in 1958. This was the first combined Commonwealth Canberra op, which became a pattern for many of the later raids and also in the training routine when the three squadrons worked very closely together. From October 1958 onwards the notional plan was for each of the squadrons to take turns on monthly standby for 'Firedogs' although this did not always prove possible in practice. The year ended on a tragic note for 45 with the loss on the 18th November of WH853. The aircraft suffered an engine failure after take-off and the 'deadly gap' claimed another victim as the heavy aircraft crashed with the loss of two of the crew, the third being injured.

With the easing of the operational commitment the Squadron settled into a much more normal bomber squadron routine. Instead of ops, flying revolved around crew classification, a subject which had not been given much consideration during the hectic months of *Firedog*. HQ 224 Group soon issued instructions aimed at bringing 45 Squadron into line with the bomber 'norm', adopting the standard Bomber Command classification scheme of Combat, Select and Select Star. Thus also began the routine of 'Lone Rangers' and 'Bombexs'. The 'Bombexs' followed the standard pattern of navigation and bombing often in company with other Commonwealth squadrons with two or three exercises a month, some flown from Butterworth.

However, life was not quite so routine and orderly as on a UK Bomber Command squadron because the area of operation allocated to 45 Squadron within FEAF was large and diverse. This led to frequent squadron exchanges and Lone Rangers. One of the regular exchange detachments was *Joss Stick* which took place to the Philippines, often to the USAF base at

Clark Field which operated B-57s. The first such visit took place in April 1959 when the Squadron sent four aircraft to work with the B-57s of 13th Tactical Bombardment Squadron (TBS), part of 3rd Tactical Bombardment Group at Clark to 'familiarise crews with USAF operating methods and techniques.' If not the best detachments from the operational point of view they were certainly high on the entertainment scale and the Americans proved excellent hosts. Another of the favoured locations for these exchanges was Kadena air base in Japan, notable for the cocktail parties held every night!

Regular 'Lone Rangers' (LRs) were flown throughout the FEAF area but especially to Kai Tak (Hong Kong) and Katunayake (Ceylon), while day trips to Bangkok for a lunch stop were quite popular! On average a crew could expect one 'decent' ranger per year plus, starting in late 1959, one ranger per tour to Australia/ New Zealand. The latter were normally flown in loose company with aircraft from 75 Squadron and 2 Squadron, the Australian B.20s acting as navigation advisors and 'windfinders' as they were equipped with the 'Green Satin' doppler equipment.

1960 saw two new elements enter the Squadron programme with trials in April on SDB. Initial results suggested a 30 degree dive from approx 6000 ft at 170 kts entry speed with bomb release at 2700 ft and 300 kts with aiming and release done by the pilot using a fixed sighting head and the navigator calling heights from the altimeter, with particular attention being paid to the recovery height! At roughly the same time, low level (500 ft) laydown delivery was introduced, followed a few months later by low level navexs to assess the best place for the nav to sit/crouch whilst working. Some preferred to lie in the usual bomb aimer position of prone in the nose, exhilarating low over the trees if you resisted the temptation to shut your eyes! Others preferred to stand, or rather stoop, beside the pilot to try to look out of the rather unsuitable canopy. The nose position had its own dangers at low level, not least of which was the prospect of a birdstrike on the perspex nose and the consequent danger of serious injury from shattered perspex and high speed bird remains.

The other problem was the need to scramble back to the rear ejection seat should a major problem occur. Ken Delve's own experience as a nav at 231 OCU years later flying around in the B.2 at low level, showed how tricky this could be. Some 30 seconds was 'allowed', the time the pilot could gain by a zoom climb if he suffered a catastrophic loss of power, to wriggle out of the nose, leap into the seat and put on 'minimum strapping' (i.e. parachute harness and ejection seat lap strap) only. That was on a good day!

The Recce Squadron Arrives

The other major event of 1960 was the much awaited arrival of the Canberra PR squadron long-promised to FEAF. No.81 Squadron had moved to Tengah in March 1958 with its Meteor PR.10s and Pembroke C.1(PR)s and proceeded to take a very active part in recce ops for *Firedog*. Rumours of Canberra re-equipment eventually proved to be true with the arrival in January 1960 of a single T.4 which was used for refresher flying by the crews awaiting their PR.7s. The first PR.7 did not arrive until March and promptly flew two weather-aborted *Firedogs*, the first operational Canberra recce and a not too auspicious start. The Meteors and Pembrokes continued to shoulder the burden. The situation got worse, and for the rest of the year there were only two PR.7s on strength and they spent much of their time unserviceable. At last, in March 1961, the Squadron had the majority of its strength made up of PR.7s - a year after the official change in UE which had ordered six PR.7s and one T.4. Nevertheless, it was the end of the year before 81 could feel happily settled with reasonable aircraft serviceability and with crews 'up to speed'. The standard medium level recce sorties had been supplemented by low level PR using a 12 inch F95 and 48 inch F52, the delay having been caused by prolonged delays in the PR.7 low level fatigue trials. Few problems arose from now on and the Squadron settled to its tasks which for the next few years were primarily *Firedog* ops of one sort or another despite the official end to the Emergency. No-one now doubted the value of PR and the Squadron was never short of work, especially when it started work on the survey of Borneo. This was a mammoth task requiring vertical cover of the whole of Borneo and was to prove a thorn in the side of this and other PR squadrons for some time.

Tracking over the jungle was as difficult as tracking over the desert with distinct lack of good features, so it was a case of starting from a good reference point, usually coastal, and taking up a heading hoping to emerge roughly where you expected to be. Off you went over the great green expanse while the other nav read off drift informa-

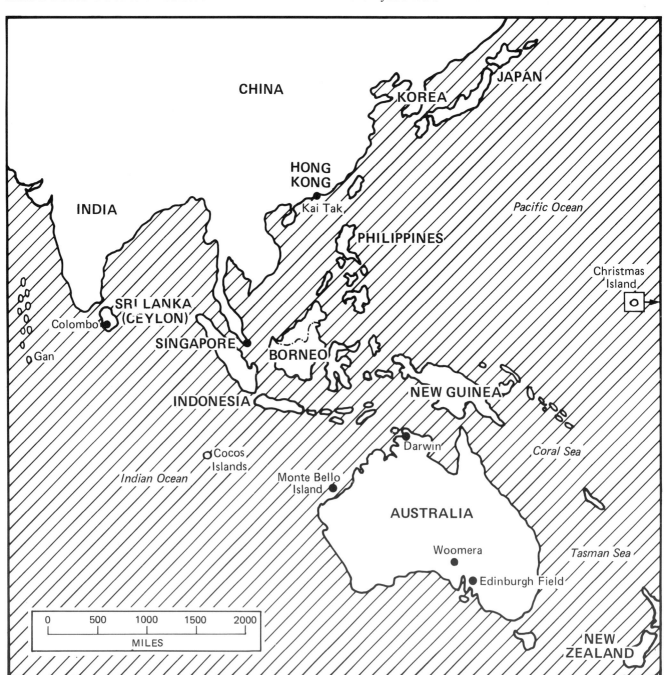

tion to keep the aircraft on track as you looked hopefully downwards for the few and far between check features. Even rivers were of little use unless they were very large because they would be hidden by trees; the best aids were the occasional hills sticking out of the forest.

As always with survey photography, the weather played a major factor in the success rate and the trick was to be on task well before the cloud built-up in the late morning, which, of course, meant some very early starts. The best weather conditions over Borneo came when typhoons were raging in the China Seas as this tended to give clear skies over Borneo and Malaya. The survey was to remain unfinished for the next few years and various methods of 'cracking the problem' were tried. For instance, aircraft detached to and operated from Labuan to save transit time and were thus able to make full load five hour sorties to take advantages of any breaks in the weather. At other times the Squadron received help from aircraft detached from other Canberra squadrons, this was particularly true during the period of 'Confrontation' in the mid 1960s when Borneo survey became a secondary task to the operational sorties.

Even with all this effort expended, the tropical rain-forest covered mountains of Borneo defied all attempts to obtain decent photography. In a last-ditch effort to complete the task sorties were mounted in the late afternoon until last photo light when gaps began to appear in the cloud, the hope being that the gaps would be large enough to allow a decent length of survey line to be run, a bit like trying to complete a jigsaw puzzle with holes in it. By late 1967 rumours were rife of an earlier rather than a later withdrawal from the Far East and a detachment to Labuan in May 1968 was the final major attempt by 81 Squadron to finish the survey before Labuan reverted to the Royal Malaysian Air Force (RMAF). A total of 25 sorties were flown, half of which produced usable photography giving 266 square nautical miles ground cover - a good indication of the flying effort required to fill in the difficult bits. Aircraft continued to

PR.7 WH797 of 81 Squadron, jacked and trestled. The 'back hatch' hangs down giving access to the rear half of the aircraft, including most of the SR sensors (long focal length cameras).

operate from Labuan with groundcrew-supported detachments after the handover to the RMAF and in May 1969 81 Squadron, with a degree of pride, and a great sense of relief, declared the Borneo survey to be 'virtually' complete.

Not all the Squadron's survey tasks had proved so difficult or drawn out. As with all Canberra PR squadrons, survey was very much a bread-and-butter job and 81 undertook a great many such tasks in and around the FEAF area. The Thailand survey of November 1961 was particularly pleasing as over half of the area was covered in the first few weeks and by March the following year over 5,000 square miles had been accepted. There were also a number of standing survey and SR tasks for the Squadron plus a quarterly detachment to Gan.

It would be impossible to consider FEAF without a word about Gan, an 'outpost' frequented at one time or another by almost every Canberra unit! It was decided that there was a need for a staging post on the route to the Far East because of overflying difficulties and facilities. A look at the map pointed to the Maldives, a group of coral islands some 400 miles south-west of Sri Lanka which already had a small airfield.

Addu Atoll was the most southerly of the group and consisted of a circle of small islands around a lagoon, Gan lay at the southern end of the string, next to the main deep water entrance to the lagoon. The full development of the airfield began in 1957 with work on the runway and support facilities and it came under the control of HQ FEAF. Gan never had any permanent squadrons, apart from the SAR Shackletons, but was one of the busiest transit airfields around with a never ending flow of transport aircraft as well as the 'V' bombers and Canberras. It was essential for aircraft to have a Radio Compass as this was often the only way of finding the island; the radio beacon sent out a very strong signal which the aircraft could home to. Gan suffered two major problems - darkness fell very early and the weather was very changeable. The latter often caused difficulties as aircraft, especially Canberras, would arrive short of fuel to find a thunderstorm raging over the airfield. With not enough fuel to go anywhere else and the prospect of the storm staying put for hours, some very hairy approaches ensued!

The island itself was looked on as something of a paradise by those who only passed through, but it was not so appealing for those on an unaccompanied posting. The staging post prospered in the 1960s and with the run down of FEAF remained under the control of HQ NEAF until finally abandoned in 1976.

81 Squadron had a number of other roles as well, starting in September 1961 with the introduction of low level PR followed in January 1962 by night low level navexs in preparation for night photo-flash work. A few months later the first photo flashing sorties were flown and a case was put forward by the Squadron for IR photography instead of photo flash for training purposes to reduce the servicing workload. This was granted, partly in response to the arguments given but also because there was a shortage of 1.75 inch photo flashes, which was not resolved until late 1963. From early 1964 the Squadron formed a number of two-nav crews for the night low level role, specifically for Exercise *Air Boon Choo* in April. The extra effort was rewarded by excellent night photo results and praise from the Air Task

commander in Thailand although no doubt the use of these flashes must have terrified some of the natives!

Tengah was now a very busy station having five resident squadrons, the three Canberra units plus the Javelins of 60 Squadron and the Hunter FGA.9s of 20 Squadron. As it was the best of the four airfields around Singapore (Tengah, Changi, Seletar and Kallang) it was also the scene of frequent detachments of visitors both RAF and Commonwealth. The other units were also busy and so the Singapore airspace was chaotic especially as the civil side developed. Tengah was continually undergoing expansion and improvement and was considered to be an excellent station. It was also seen as a great place for a tour, especially if that tour was on one of the Canberra squadrons with a diverse life-style and very active social life. It was exactly the same for the groundcrew although conditions were often difficult with high temperatures and very high humidity making working on the aircraft tiring.

In the meantime tension flared in the area again.

81 Squadron PR.7 with display of cameras, outside the squadron hangar at Tengah. Note the squadron badge on the hangar door.

The 81 Squadron dispersal at Tengah, June 1962. The 'U'-shaped building was the Squadron offices.

Opposite page: **81 Squadron PR.7 WH778 at Labuan, September 1962.**

Confrontation

In the early 1960s Britain was working towards greater independence for the area and with thoughts of incorporating North Borneo and Singapore into a 'Greater Malaysia' within the Commonwealth. However, President Sukarno of Indonesia had dreams of incorporating the whole of Borneo into a greater Indonesia. In 1962 the 'British' area of North Borneo consisted of the Crown Colonies of Sabah and Sarawak and the British Protectorate of Brunei. Rebellion broke out in Brunei, inspired by the Communist elements but supported by the Indonesians and it quickly spread into Sarawak as active terrorist units infiltrated the area. British forces moved into the area and Indonesian 'forces', at first irregulars but later elements of the Indonesian army, made raids across the border.

In December 1962 limited ground operations were undertaken by British and Gurkha forces supported by transport aircraft of 209 Squadron (Twin Pioneers) and 34 Squadron (Beverleys) with the 'teeth' provided by 45 Squadron who detached to Labuan. Twenty miles off the coast of North Borneo, Labuan had been a small staging post with a detachment of airmen from Changi to look after its periodic visitors. However, because of its good runway and its secure island position it became the main RAF base in Borneo, rapidly expanding to become an independent station with personnel doing a one year tour and aircraft rotated from the Singapore squadrons. These became virtually permanent detachments of up to 30 aircraft of nine types including the PR.7s and B.2s. By the middle of 1965, the height of the conflict, the station was working a full seven day week with some 2,500 movements a month, an incredible total.

As ever in time of tension the cry went up for PR and 81 Squadron was soon heavily involved in low level recce. The Squadron went on standby on the 10th December

and the next day started coastal and road recce of possible infiltration areas and trouble spots. On the 11th, WH780 struck a 90 ft radio mast at Brunei during a low pass and had to land at Labuan with a damaged wing, returning to Tengah some time later after a wing change.

During 1962, 45 Squadron re-equipped with B.15s, the first aircraft, WH969, arriving on 2nd September. By December all the B.2s had gone. The Squadron was given no time to settle down as the rebellion in Brunei broke out on 6th December. At first the B.15s were only called on to act as high speed transports from Singapore to Labuan for senior commanders, however by February the Squadron was on standby for bombing ops. The same month gunsights arrived for the aircraft so RP work-up began with crews doing 20° dives and firing at 1500 yards.

RP training was concentrated on for a few months with a favourite being a low level sortie to Song Song range for a live shoot, land at Butterworth to refuel and re-arm and then back to Song Song for another spate of rushing at the ground, then back to Tengah. One of the most 'enjoyable' ranges was Asahan where the targets were AFVs and tanks. As with the NEAF Squadrons, firepower demos for 'all and sundry' were a regular feature. Dave Pells, a Nav on 45 Squadron, recalls one such demo laid on for the Chief of the Defence Staff ... 'Our part was to rocket a landing craft anchored in China Rock Bay. This landing craft was 'squeezed' out of the army, the only spare one East of Suez. We had a live practice the day before. The brief was to aim short of the craft. Our three-ship formation lined up. The Boss was first and aimed short. The second aircraft's rockets straddled the landing craft and by the time we were lined up the target had sunk. The following day CDS saw three bunches of 48 rockets hitting the sea because there was no other target available!'

1963 started with severe weather throughout Borneo which not only restricted operations but caused widespread flooding and led to a 'hearts and minds' campaign of food drops and evacuations with 81 Squadron providing useful photo information. Otherwise, 1963 looked like being a quiet year. However, towards the end of the year there were fears that the lives of Britons in Indonesia might be in danger and so in September the British community in Djakarta was evacuated to Singapore. Indonesian aircraft, including B-25 Mitchell bombers, were regularly flying over Malaysian territory. FEAF established an Air Defence Identification Zone (ADIZ) around the borders of Sabah and Sarawak. In order to police this zone Javelins and Hunters were deployed to Labuan and Kuching in Borneo.

In Borneo there was an increase in the number of guerilla raids across the Kalimantan border into Sabah and Sarawak although at this stage Indonesian regular forces were not directly involved. The only way to watch this 800 mile frontier was to build a series of forts and to supply them by air and in this respect the helicopter forces came into their own. The other vital element was the work of PR and the effort expended on the Borneo survey paid dividends as commanders had accurate up to date maps and photographs from which to work. Added to this was the tactical photography from lower levels which produced excellent imagery and allowed border crossing points to be easily identified and to keep a watch on the jungle tracks and isolated longhouses. To quote one recent analysis of the period, 'The range and endurance of the Canberra was so much superior to any previous PR aircraft that not only could a great deal of work be completed in each sortie but the high speed of the aircraft permitted the results to be processed and issued to those requiring the information with the minimum loss of time. Tactical intelligence could not have been gained or updated in any other way than by aerial photography and, although other aircraft than the Canberra carried cameras for specific purposes, the contribution of 81 Squadron was even greater than it had been during the earlier operations in Malaya'.

In mid 1964 the situation flared-up again and escalated rapidly with the presence of Indonesian regulars. The PR Canberras began an intensive period of sorties during September when Indonesian paratroopers dropped in the Labis area. All leave was cancelled and crews recalled as the Squadron stood at readiness. A reinforcement of three aircraft from 58 Squadron had arrived in June to ease the workload and a programme of medium level photography in the Singapore area commenced, interspersed with specific SR and TR tasks.

This was the pattern for the next three years with periods of tension and standby broken by periods of 'normality' and a training routine. Reinforcement detachments were also a regular feature from now on with aircraft from 58 Squadron, 39 Squadron and 13 Squadron taking it in turns to help out. The final schedule was:

58 Sqn	June 1964	- April 1965
13 Sqn	April 1965	- August 1965
58 Sqn	August 1965	- December 1965
13/39 Sqn	December 1965 -	
58 Sqn		- August 1966

These detachments were usually three aircraft plus crews.

It was very much the same on-off story for 45 Squadron. The Squadron left Singapore on 'strategic deployment' to Kuantan on 17th September but were suddenly recalled to Tengah in mid October to assume the 'highest state of readiness'. This lasted until the end of the month with restricted flying, although a number of 'special' sorties were called for using a specially modifed B.6 (WH976).

From December onwards, 45 Squadron maintained a small detachment at Labuan as a show of strength with the aircraft flying regular border patrols. On the 26th one of the few live weapons attacks ever made by a Canberra took place when one aircraft made RP attacks on Indonesian positions at Kukup near the Johore Straits. The period of operations officially ceased in February 1966 but aircraft were rotated at Labuan as a 'presence', with the entire Squadron operating from there from time to time. During one such detachment the aircrew were holding a party on Pappen Island when a signal arrived at Labuan recalling two aircraft to Tengah as soon as possible. The signal was flown to the beach by helicopter and the crews ferried back to the airfield. Both aircraft were airborne for Tengah within two hours of the signal arriving at Labuan.

Dave Pells was operating from Labuan. . 'Whilst on detachment in Labuan, we participated in an army exercise and were being controlled by an Australian FAC, close to the border, who reported that we were being 'fired on by the Indonesians.' We left but there were no holes in the aircaft. The maps of Borneo when we arrived in Labuan had normal detail along the coasts, and had the rivers marked, but the rest was plain yellow with the words 'relief data unknown' printed on them. We spent a few low level navex's looking for the town and airfield at Sepulot in Sabah. We always failed and when the new maps arrived we discovered why. Sepulot had been moved by 40 nautical miles!'

The increase in tension led to a decision to bring into effect additional reinforcement plans and the four Canberra squadrons of the Akrotiri strike wing were called on to provide a squadron-strength (six to eight

aircraft) detachment in rotation. In September 1964, 73 Squadron was ordered 'to prepare to detach for an indefinite period to Tengah because of deteriorations in relations between Malaysia and Indonesia.' It was envisaged that if called on to take part in active ops it would be in Close Air Support (CAS) role under Forward Air Controller (FAC) direction so all crews had to convert to SDB and brush up on their RP. Eight aircraft went to Tengah via Gan and Butterworth and so began a 15 month commitment to FEAF. 73 Squadron were relieved by 32 Squadron in late November and used the B.16s left by 73. After almost interminable briefings and a bit of local familiarisation flying the detachment settled into the FEAF social and operational situation. The latter revolved around low level nav, RP and SDP at China Rock and Asahan ranges plus tactical work-ups and delivery trials, including a 300 ft/300 kts 'pop-up' technique. Tactical exercises were flown as four-ships against 20 Squadron Hunters and with FAC work over the jungle. In January 1965 all aircraft were restricted to 2.5 g as cracks were appearing in the main spars, this being attributed to age rather than vigorous evasion and tactical flying. After a pleasant detachment the Squadron returned to Cyprus in February.

Top: **45 Squadron B.15 line-up at Tengah in the early 1960s. Each aircraft has its clip-on sunshade in an effort to keep cockpit temperatures down. It was all to little avail, as in the hot, humid climate of the Far East the interior of the aircraft soon became unbearable - the only solution was to get airborne as soon as possible.** *Dave Pells*

Above: **PR.7 WH791 being prepared for a sortie June 1962. The flash crate is being wheeled under the flare bay.**

Opposite page, top: **45 Squadron four-ship over the Borneo coastline.** *Dave Pells*

58 Squadron PR.7s at Butterworth on one of the frequent recce reinforcements by UK and Middle East PR squadrons.

B.15 XK641, with yet another version of 45 Squadron camel motif, on detachment to Labuan 1966. Labuan, an island off Brunei, was the scene of regular squadron detachments. *Dave Pells*

81 Squadron PR.7 WH778 comes to a sad end, being broken up at Tengah, 1969. The aircraft suffered a heavy landing in December 1968 and was considered not worth repairing. The Squadron disbanded in January 1970 after 12 years of PR.7 ops in FEAF.

It was 249 Squadron's turn next but not for them the delights of Tengah and Singapore, for after a few days at Tengah it was off to the jungle strip at Kuantan. It came as a bit of a shock after tales of Singapore night life, to be thrust into the jungle proper to live in tents - but at least beds, electric light and iced beer were provided so the aircrew at least were totally satisfied! Training in low level jungle nav and FAC work continued around periods of armed standby for CAS and maritime recce. This standby usually involved two to four aircraft sitting on the pans in the 4.5 inch flare fit with full HE RP pods. One new crew had the misfortune to arrive on the Squadron at Kuantan and having stepped from the transport aircraft were greeted with a pile of jungle kit, told to dress up, given guns and sent off into the jungle to join the Squadron in rounding up terrorists. The rest of the Squadron meanwhile was enjoying the 'set-up' with an iced beer!

One of the problems of Kuantan was the short runway with tall trees on the approaches which combined with high temperatures meant that the Canberras could not get airborne with full war load and full tip tanks. Since all likely targets were at short range the decision was taken to fly with empty tips.

Fortunately, the discomfort of Kuantan was short-lived and it was back to Akrotiri in July. Two months later 73 Squadron were back for their second stint and decided that Kuantan was not so bad as they had been led to believe, the natives were friendly and a vigorous programme of visits was organised to tin mines, rubber plantations and the like. The nine-hole golf course saw many an improvised competition while others took advantage of a shuttle service to the beach areas, a favourite for B-B-Qs. Crews detached to Labuan from time to time for FAC work in North Borneo. The weeks passed quickly amidst a flurry of sporting prowess. The hard-pressed groundcrew sweated buckets to keep the aircraft serviceable in a climate that did not suit advanced-technology aircraft, as the Squadron engineering officer liked to refer to his charges. November came and there was a joyful handover to 32 Squadron although the latter were also back in Cyprus by Christmas bringing the NEAF involvement to an end.

Relations were eventually normalised by the Bangkok Agreement of 11th August 1966 and the period of 'Confrontation' came to an end. The end of the conflict meant that life returned to normal for the FEAF units with the daily round of training and exercises. Dave Pells again - 'Life on a FEAF bomber squadron was fairly gentle. It consisted of starting work at 8 am and finishing at 5 pm, Monday to Friday. Sometimes dawn take-offs would be called for with an 0430 take-off and night flying meant an 1830 take-off.'

Both units took part in regular station and Command exercises and in joint Commonwealth and navy exercises. For 81 Squadron this meant a monthly flying total averaging 300 hours in 2-3 hour sorties, although this was boosted by trips to Gan, the Cocos Islands, Australia and Hong Kong. The latter was a favourite, as it still is, and was a regular destination especially as some aircraft servicing was done by HAEC (Hong Kong Aircraft Engineering Corporation). Squadron detachments to Hong Kong took place two or three times a year, usually for one week, with the Canberras continuing their normal training routine of combined attacks by working with the Hunters of 28 Squadron. Bombing and RP work was done at the Port Shelter range.

With the end of confrontation, 45 Squadron began to concentrate on two more roles. The first of these was LABS with techniques and training on exactly the same lines as in RAFG or the UK. For a few months from November 1964 LABS training dominated all Squadron training as crews completed their initial work up. After this period it was into a routine similar to that of the other strike squadrons with rotation of role to maintain currency. A few years later 45 Squadron became the third Canberra unit to be equipped with the AS.30 guided missile. As early as October 1965 a Nord Aviation representative had visited Tengah to discuss the setting up of a simulator but the first aircraft was not modified until August the following year. By December 1966 three aircraft were ready to go but it was decided that no live firing should take place until an airborne simulator was available. The process dragged on but in September 1967 five

observers flew in 103 Squadron Whirlwinds for live firing of AS.11 missiles at China Rock as work up for AS.30 firing. At long last Exercise *Hotshot* saw five aircraft at Labuan for live firing. Twenty missiles were launched and scored an average CEP of 24 yards. Over the next two years the Squadron sent regular 'Hotshot' detachments to various ranges, although Woomera became the favoured location for controlled trials.

Disbandment

In November 1968 the Singapore Air Force was established at Tengah with Cessna 172 trainers and ex RAF Hunters, yet another signal that the withdrawal from the Far East was likely to be brought forward to 1970 from the original plan of 1975 as part of Government defence plans. One benefit was the lifting of the speed restrictions because the PR.7s were destined for disposal after the Squadron disbanded and there was therefore no need to conserve fatigue life. This led to a general increase in low level tactical flying with mixed formations of Canberras and Hunters against the Lightnings of 74 Squadron. It also meant that stocks of weapons could be more freely used, particularly the AS30 missiles which would have no further use after the disbandment. So from a situation where crews were lucky to get one or two live firings a year it was virtually a free-for-all as stocks were fired off. Many consider

A very atmospheric shot – you can almost hear the engines of the 45 Squadron B.15s as they taxi out! *Dave Pells*

this period to have been one of the most interesting and enjoyable in their flying careers.

In March 1969 the squadrons took part in Exercise *Crowning Glory*, the last major British and Commonwealth exercise in the Far East. The run-down began almost immediately with RAF Seletar ceasing operations at the end of March. However, 81 Squadron had a good last year with some successful surveys and a larger than usual number of 'Rangers'. The plan was for the Canberra squadrons to disband in January and as a parting gesture 81 Squadron flew exactly 81 hours that month before disbanding on the 16th. They were soon followed by 20 Squadron and 45 Squadron, these units gave a joint flypast of six aircraft each at dusk on the 18th February 1970. The once bustling Tengah was now virtually emptied of aircraft and another Canberra era came to an end.

Following the disbandment of the resident squadrons and the dismembering of FEAF, Canberras continued to deploy to and operate throughout the Far East because PR aircraft of 58, 13 and especially 39, Squadrons continued with the standing recce tasks of Gan, Singapore and Hong Kong. Within a few months of the closure, 58 Squadron were at Tengah trying to complete the few outstanding miles of Borneo survey. Gradually the area became the preserve of 39 Squadron with its PR.9s although in later years 13 Squadron's PR.7s took part in the major task of monitoring the 'boat people' around Hong Kong in the late 1970s and early 80's. Even after the disbandment of the final Canberra PR squadron the area has not been ignored and aircraft of No 1 PRU continue to have a SR role in the area.

Chapter Six

Diversity - Home and Abroad

Back in the UK - Diversity

By 1962 the boom period of Canberra usage was over in the UK as the Bomber squadrons disbanded or re-equipped with the trio of V-bombers. A few hectic years and the Canberra bomber wings had vanished.

It was an end and a beginning. It was certainly the end of the Canberra as a bombing element of Main Force Bomber Command, although it continued as a 'straight' bomber in the NEAF and FEAF areas and as an interdictor/bomber in these theatres and in RAFG for several more years. Its future in the UK was to be diverse and at times unusual. Only in the recce role did a front-line operational squadron remain in the UK. 58 Squadron remained operational until 1970 and then 39 Squadron on its return from Malta the

same year, until May 1982 when it became the last operational Canberra squadron in the RAF to disband, bringing to an end over 30 years of front-line service for the type.

However, it was the 'second line', 'support' and 'facility' squadrons which took the UK Canberra squadrons into another twenty years of service with a variety of roles and mark conversions. The situation following the loss of the bomber wings left a total of only three squadrons: 51 Squadron at Wyton continuing their 'radio calibration' duties; 58 Squadron at Wyton in the recce role and 245 Squadron at Tangmere as part of Signals Command in the radar calibration role. Over the ensuing fifteen years the situation changed as more squadrons became involved in calibration and 'other duties' as the task increased.

PR Rules

For 58 Squadron it was very much a continuation of their well established role of 'day and night visual and photo reconnaissance' with a UE of eight PR.7s and PR.9s; quite a large squadron with 46 aircrew and 130 groundcrew. The first unit to receive the PR.9, by February 1961 they had flown over 1,000 hours with the aircraft and were most impressed with the extra performance in speed, height and manoeuvrability. To take advantage of the service ceiling of the PR.9, crews were fitted with partial pressure helmets and equipment - essential above 50,000 ft when pressure breathing might be necessary, to ensure an adequate supply of oxygen.

The PR.9 prototype, converted PR.7 WH793. *via B. Robertson*

The first true PR.9, XH129, over the Short Bros & Harland Ltd airfield at Sydenham.
via B. Robertson

The PR.9 was the result of a contract for a development of the PR.7 using the more powerful Avon 206 (RA24) engines of 11,250 lb st to give the aircraft an operational height in excess of 60,000 ft and so put it beyond the range of missiles and fighters. The aircraft was to be designated High Altitude PR.9 (HA PR.9) and was the UK equivalent of the American U-2 spy plane. The necessary increase in wing area was achieved by increasing the chord inboard of the engines, in effect 'filling-in' the area between the engines and the fuselage, and a slight increase in wingspan.

Initial design work was done at English Electric but Napiers were subcontracted to modify PR.7 WH793 as the test aircraft, which made its first flight in the new configuration on 8th July 1955. Although it did not live up to the performance expectations it showed promise and so the concept was pursued. The nose area was redesigned giving the pilot a fighter-type bubble canopy, similar to the B(I)8 but hinged at the rear and with access via a removable ladder on the port side. The navigator's compartment was separated from the pilot and his access was through a hinged opening nose section. This combination gave the PR.9 its unique crew arrangement and made the pilot the 'rear' crew member!

The first aircraft of this series, XH129, was built by Shorts and made its first flight on 27th July 1958. Flight trials progressed reasonably well until the pre-evaluation structural test sortie, designed to be a limiting test for the airframe. In the 5g turn the aircraft went out of control and crashed into the sea; the pilot ejected but the observer, who had no ejection seat, was killed. With much effort the aircraft was recovered from the sea and investigation revealed that the wing surfaces had peeled back from the wing skin attachments causing the wing to 'fail'. Modifications, including a bang seat for the navigator, were incorporated into the eighth aircraft, XH136.

Beamont took time off his Lightning trials to flight test the new PR.9. After a few work-up sorties he took the aircraft for the structural test on 20th January 1960. This time there were no problems, the aircraft behaved perfectly. From then on it was a smooth introduction into service although later the PR.9 was to acquire a fierce reputation as an unforgiving aircraft.

On 58 Squadron it was a period of trials on systems as the capabilities of the PR.9 were explored at both ends of the envelope, from 60,000 ft to low level high speed by day and high level night flashing. As light relief the Squadron undertook a number of exotic surveys. A typical survey det for 58 Squadron was Operation *Sabadilla* in September 1962 which called for three PR.7s to complete a survey of British Guiana and Trinidad in a three-month period. Unfortunately, the weather had other ideas and only 60% was covered to 'acceptable photographic cover'. It was not until 1964 that the squadron had the chance to return to complete the job.

The detachment was based at Piarco Civil Airport, Trinidad for Operation *Thicket* and consisted of four crews and forty-seven groundcrew, including a section from the Royal Engineers Survey Liaison Staff based at Wyton. The first sorties were flown on 31st August to British Guiana. Using three-man crews to counter the standard problem of map reading over the jungle, one nav used the 'Green Satin' and passed info to the other who lay in the nose and did as much visual navigation as possible. Each flight block was flown - on an east-west heading - with frequent interruptions while the aircraft was repositioned over a reliable visual feature to take errors

out of the nav kit. And so it went, battling the persistent low cloud until, at last, the survey was virtually complete. Trinidad was much easier and two-man crews were used. It had been a 'routine' survey - exhausting (socially) and, at times, very frustrating to arrive in the task area and find it covered in cloud!

Just as the aircrew and groundcrew were getting used to the PR.9 and its little foibles, it was decided that all PR.9s were to be transfered to 39 Squadron by the end of 1962. With no reduction in the tasking it meant that the PR.7s worked twice as hard and the navigators even harder as some of the low level work in the PR.7 required two navs per aircraft. From time to time additional aircraft were acquired for special tasking such as the 'air sampling task' for Cambridge University in February 1964 for which the Squadron operated B.6 WT206.

The reinforcement commitment to FEAF was increased in late 1964 because of rising tension in the area and three aircraft were detached to assist 81 Squadron at Tengah. Flying a route Wyton-El Adem-Djibouti-Aden-Gan-Tengah, all aircraft were in place just 53 hours after the first aircraft had left Wyton, despite bad weather en route. The FEAF detachment clocked up an average 100 hours operational flying a month until relieved by a 13

A pair of brand new silver PR.9s at Sydenham before delivery. Shorts were responsible for the redesign of the PR.9 nose section and associated alterations to the navigator's Station. *via B. Robertson*

Squadron detachment in April 1965. On arrival in the UK there was just time for ejection seats to be modified to Mk.II standard (0-90 seat with single handle operation and automatic sequence) before it was back to Tengah again from August to December 1965 and once more from June to August 1966. With three aircraft in the Far East and others away on survey detachments Wyton was very much a transient home for the PR.7s. Those that were around picked up the odd 'special' such as police co-operation sorties in October over the border areas between Manchester and Sheffield searching for the graves of victims of a suspected mass murder. The TV and press showed great interest in the sorties, filming all aspects right up to analysis of results. Similar police work was undertaken years later by 39 Squadron using the vertical IRLS (Infra Red Line Scan) camera system. This usually entailed flying a very low level (150 ft) search of a small area looking for 'missing persons', the idea being that body heat would show up on the IR film.

Other specials for 58 Squadron included filming and tracking the *Torrey Canyon* oil slicks in March 1967 and a series of photo-chase sorties to film Blue Steel drops from a Vulcan. Amongst the frequent informal tasks were those referred to as 'OBJs' (Old Boy Jobs), these ranged from requests by archaeologists for photographs of their 'digs' to photographing the C-in-C's favourite golf course! This was the other PR - Public Relations!

As part of the general 'tone down' of the RAF, the silver PR.7s were repainted in camouflage scheme during 1967. During its last few years the Squadron conducted a series of very interesting trials one of which involved the use of a film that was processed in flight within the F95 camera. Despite initial favourable results nothing came of the trial, a pity as one of the aims in TR is to get film to the Photographic Interpreters (PIs) and prints to the requesting agency as quickly as possible. The ideal is a real-time relay whereby pictures are transmitted to a ground station rather than having to wait for the aircraft to return to base. Undoubtedly the new film would have saved time. Subsequently, on exercises 39 Squadron was rightly proud of its ability to have 'film on the table' within four minutes of the navigator leaping out of the aircraft.

Above: **Rare shot of a pair of PR.9s getting airborne during one of the FEAF reinforcement detachments. With the Avon 206 engines the PR.9 had almost twice the power of earlier marks.**

Below: **PR.9 XH174 of 39 Squadron at Wyton in 1982. This view illustrates the unique crew access. The canopy is held partially closed by a strut on the right-hand side. On the extreme right is the optical flat for the F.96 oblique camera, to the left of the ladder is the port F.95 camera.** *S. G. Richards*

Opposite page: **58 Squadron PR.7 being refuelled on Luqa during Exercise *Sunspot* . 1963.** *58 Squadron Records*

Top left: **58 Squadron survey detachment to Trinidad and British Guiana – at Piaico airfield, Trinidad, November 1962.**
Top right: **39 Squadron PR.9 in its second home, a Norwegian valley.** *R. W. Davies*

Above left: **XH137 of 39 Squadron – low vis markings.**
Above right: **58 Squadron aircrew sit back and admire their impressive new PR.9s.**
Adjacent: **XH167 of 58 Squadron.**

Below: **PR.7 WH794 of 58 Squadron, late 1960s. The Squadron's PR.7s were in silver finish: WJ821 was the first camouflaged aircraft to appear in August 1966.**
M. F. Sketchley

Top: **Bob Orchard loading kit into the pannier of a 58 Squadron PR.7 at Wyton, February 1966. The pannier fitted into the flare bay and was useful for carrying personal kit plus aircraft spares. It was important to remember not to open the bomb doors if the pannier was loaded – or risk spreading your kit over the countryside (and it happened!)**

Above: **PR.7 WJ825 of 58 Squadron at Akrotiri, October 1969. It was the norm for there to be a visiting or 'passing through' PR Canberra at almost every base worldwide, throughout most weeks of the year.** *R. Walker*

Below: **39 Squadron PR.9s, led by XH168, over Norway. On its return to the UK in October 1970, 39 Squadron became TR/SR unit for war deployment to the Northern Flank, using Oerland in Norway as a detachment base.**

In October 1968, 58 Squadron began the routine survey work of Northern Ireland; although at first this consisted of individual tasks covering specific small areas, it expanded to include regular vertical survey of major areas plus special tasks as requested. In later years aircraft flew sorties using IR False Colour film which detected the difference between living and dead vegetation - very useful against camouflaged targets but in this context able to detect buried arms caches and the like.

In the midst of its hectic worldwide tasks came the news that the Squadron was to disband when one of the NEAF recce squadrons moved to the UK. The run down began in early 1970 when WH802 was 'retired' to Bruggen as a gate guard. Flying continued up to 30th September with 39 Squadron arriving from Malta the following day with its PR.9s to become the UK recce squadron. Although 58 Squadron was disbanded, a Wyton Canberra detachment was established at Honington to provide 'a limited operational reserve during the transition phase of October'. This disbanded on 23rd October with the PR.7s having been ferried at various times in the month to Shawbury for storage. However, two aircraft 'in full war fit' were flown to Wyton to remain at 'the disposal of the Station Commander'.

Due to a shortage of PR.9s two PR.7s arrived back at Wyton to allow 39 Squadron to take on most of 58 Squadron's tasks while retaining many of its own worldwide commitments. Within a year the Squadron had been allocated to the Northern Flank of NATO and in September 1971 deployed for the first time to its new FOB (Forward Operating Base) at RNoAF Oerland at the mouth of the Trondheim fjord. Oerland became a second home for the Squadron with two major detachments a year when the entire Squadron took over part of the Norwegian base and exercised its war procedures flying the length and breadth of Norway and Denmark. Oerland was ideal for the PR.9 operations as aircraft could easily reach the extreme north or extreme south of the operational area. Lone PR.9s flying over snow-field or fjord became a regular sight as up to eight aircraft were tasked on SR or TR tasks. Each aircraft and crew was capable of virtually autonomous operation. Routine use was made of other RNoAF airfields to practise aircrew servicing on the aircraft and interpretation of photography. There can be no doubt that Norway is one of the most inspiring countries in which to fly, the scenery is truly breathtaking as you speed over the glassy waters of a fjord or the remote stillness of a snow-field or glacier.

Two detachments and one or two *Sharp Focus*'(one aircraft, three day detachment to a specific base) a year and crews soon became well-versed in operating in Norway.

The classic nose shot of the PR.9 showing the offset position of the pilot's canopy. The lens in the centre of the nose houses the forward facing F.95 camera.
S. G. Richards

This experience level and the capability of the PR.9 to fly a three hour low level sortie made the contribution of 39 Squadron to NATO enormous. This was enhanced in the late 1970s when most of the PR.9s were fitted with an improved navigational system consisting of a Decca TANS (Tactical Air Navigation System) computer, an improved Doppler and an accurate heading system of Master Reference Gyro. At the same time, the aircraft were given a radar warning receiver (RWR) and the night capability was improved by installation of an IRLS podded camera which fitted into the flare bay. The only external sign of the changes was the RWR aerials on the tail fin.

Having both a tactical and strategic role kept the Squadron very busy and gave great variety of flying to the aircrew. One day a crew would be flashing around the valleys in Wales on a low level exercise looking for the tiniest of bridges to photograph and report on; the next day they might be on the first leg of the transit to Hong Kong or Belize. It was not quite so hectic for the groundcrew although ground support was invariably arranged for major detachments as well as when aircraft went unserviceable 'down route'. In the latter case one or more relevant tradesmen would leap onto a civilian flight and joyfully deliver spares or 'on the spot' advice!

It was not unheard of for the aircraft to go unserviceable in one exotic location or another and require the attentions of said tradesman. However, the situation developed whereby the aircraft took with it a complete range of spares for radios, nav kit and fuel pumps, so that the time stuck anywhere could be cut down as much as possible. In theory, the crew was capable of changing any of the items although the prospect of changing a fuel pump at some of the stopover points did not generally appeal! One essential part of the pack up was a soft-faced hammer with which to 'encourage' reluctant items to work. It was remarkably successful on the starter system. Another vital piece was a large roll of black tape with which to seal-up the aircraft in tropical areas. This involved taping around the canopy and nose to keep out the torrential rain. If this was not done you were quite likely to find a convincing puddle under the nav's bang seat in the morning.

When the RAF finally said farewell to its base in Malta, 13 Squadron arrived at Wyton with its complement of PR.7s and

the old rivals were together again. However, each squadron kept its own specific area of operations - 39 squadron the Caribbean, Far East and Northern Europe, 13 Squadron the Med, Africa and Southern Europe. Even so, 13 managed to 'poach' a task in the Far East when 39 was unable to meet a requirement for shipping surveys of the sea areas around Hong Kong during the first rush of 'Boat People'. Such sorties helped to control the flood of illegal immigrants and also saved a number of people whose boats were unable to complete the journey and who were rescued following information from the crew.

The creation of a Wing Recce Cell at Wyton brought joint tasking for the squadrons on UK tasks. It was advisable when programmed on a task sortie to get to briefing before the other squadron in order to pick up the best of the tasks! For day to day tactical training each squadron ran its own 'Trip of the Day', usually a 2-3 hour low level sortie with four or five targets (bridges, dams, electronics and the like). There were occasional inter-Squadron competitions with both flying the same targets and timing points. This could have its hairy moments if one crew elected to fly a particular target using the port camera and another crew the starboard camera and the time on target (TOT) was the same!

13 Squadron PR.7 WT537 at Wyton, August 1979, the squadron having returned from Malta the previous year.

39 Squadron operated PR.7s for a limited period to boost the PR.9 strength. Here a PR.7 is on detachment to Tengah in mid 1971 for Operation *Mandau*, the survey of Borneo. Over the featureless jungle, two navs were a great advantage. Rear – Hally Hardie, Jim Meir, Derek Watson, John Morgan. Front – Dick Turner, Phil Keeble.
Phil Keeble

It was a full and interesting existence for both units with plenty of flying on a variety of tasks and a good sprinkling of overseas detachments and Rangers. 250-300 hours a year was an accepted norm per crew with about 40% of the total being at low level. Although the PR.7 had the edge in range and endurance, the same amount of fuel and less thirsty engines, the PR.9 had a far superior all-round performance. It is interesting to compare the PR.9's capability with some other 'modern' aircraft ... the PR.9 could fly at 540 kts at low level, albeit not very comfortably, and could operate at 60,000 ft plus. A favourite occupation of crews was to ring up a fighter station,

especially a Phantom unit, and offer them a high level training target, invariably the phone went very quiet when a figure of 55,000 ft was mentioned! An alternative sport was to visit a Jaguar base and watch the natives struggle off the end of the runway using full reheat. When it was time to depart the PR.9 would leisurely lift off a little way down the runway and go into a steep climb. Such stories are legion but the authors would hate to be accused of bias!

It continued like this until the final rundown of front-line Canberra strength started. In mid 1981 13 Squadron was reduced to half strength prior to complete disbandment the following January. A number of PR.7s were transferred to 100 Squadron to add to the growing collection of Canberra marks being operated by that squadron. 39 Squadron then followed a similar path when there was a reduction to half strength in January 1982 and disbandment in May. The 'half squadron' which was left in May 1982 was renamed 1 PRU (Photographic Reconnaissance Unit), resurrecting an old wartime designation. This unit, still based at Wyton, took on 39's SR and survey tasks but was not established for the tactical role. It continued to operate on a world wide basis and was rarely short of tasks – if anything they were on the increase!

Usual PRU strength was five PR.9s, all of

Top: **Updated PR.9 at Wyton. 39 Squadron's aircraft went for a series of modification updates from 1976 onwards. The outward sign of this work being the aerial housings (front and back of the fin) for the Radar Warning Receiver seen here on XH175.**

Above: **XH175 again but this time on the strength of No.1 PRU - note the unit marking on the fin. The PRU was formed out of the half-strength 39 Squadron**

Below: **The 231 OCU formation team in the mid 1960s; aircraft of the day are WJ637, WH920, WJ714 and WH641:A. Flying a close formation sequence was no easy task with four Canberras but it certainly looked impressive from the ground.**

which have received enhanced nav kit with the fitting of a modern nav aid, 'Omega'. Following a general trend towards low visibility camouflage all of the aircraft were given an overall matt finish of hemp/eggshell, slightly paler on the underside. This followed a similar paint job on one of 360's T.17s although the latter was given a gloss finish which proved somewhat more durable than the matt version. The new finish took some getting used to but the crews said the aircraft seemed to fly just a little faster! There are plans to further enhance the capability of the sensors, one possible development was the CASTOR (Corps Airborne Stand-off Radar) system but reports in the aviation press towards the end of 1987 suggested that this had been abandoned but that trials were taking place on an ASTOR system. It remains to be seen what system, if any, will be fitted to the PR.9s to take them into the next century for as yet no possible follow on aircraft has been suggested.

It was announced by Strike Command that 1 PRU would be retitled 39 (1 PRU) Squadron with effect from 1st July 1992. With Wyton due to close at the end of 1994, a move to Waddington is rumoured.

231 OCU

At Bassingbourn the job of providing aircrew for the depleted number of operational squadrons continued but with an increased emphasis on the low level role-training which had been introduced in late 1960. This reflected the increased low level nature of Canberra ops and the higher proportion of Interdictor marks entering service.

However, it was not until early 1961 that a proper low level package was included in the Long Bomber Course and the PR course, when crews flew at 250 ft on dual exercises and 1000 ft when solo. At the same time Gee was being phased out and LABS techniques introduced. It was a period of upheaval at the OCU and in May 1960 'A' and 'B' squadrons amalgamated into a single squadron of two flights. Further contraction of aircraft strength led to the amalgamation of these into a single flight in November 1961, as Bomber Squadron. C Flight remained, as before, the Reccce flight. A few years later the names were changed to reflect the changes in the operational roles of front-line Canberra squadrons, Bomber Squadron became Strike Squadron and PR

Above: **A nice shot of a T.4 at Cottesmore, September 1973, in the short-lived red and white training livery. WT488 was attached to 360 Squadron.** *S. G. Richards*

Below: **An unidentified 231 OCU Canberra poses as a Russian aircraft in the summer of 1967 for the film** *Billion Dollar Brain.*

Squadron became Recce Squadron. This change took effect in August 1964.

The previous year the decision had been taken to civilianise Technical Wing by contracting out aircraft servicing to Airwork Services. The change-over commenced in April 1963 and continued to September when the task was officially handed over to Airwork. The ensuing six months were chaotic with aircraft serviceability dropping dramatically until a series of 'show-downs' brought changes and matters improved.

Brian Crook and John Craven went through the PR OCU as a crew in late 1964/1965 before being posted to 39 Squadron. Brian Crook well remembers the five month course: 'The flying phase started with five dual famils in the T.4 for circuit work, general handling and asymmetric flying. This was followed by a solo T.4 trip before a pre-solo dual check in the PR.3 - with first the student and then the QFI taking it in turns to quiver on the rumble seat! Then came the bulk of the PR conversion with twelve PR.3 navexs, high level photo and low level trips with targets. Then, five T.4/PR.3 night trips before the T.4 pre final handling ride and the final handling check with the OC.'

Throughout the 1960s the OCU remained part of No.1 Group except for the period 1st March 1965 to 1st November 1967 when it was part of 3 Group. A bit of light relief in the summer of 1967 was a role in the film 'Billion Dollar Brain' when a number of aircraft were painted with Soviet red star markings and were filmed being bombed-up and scrambling. It was unfortunate that the Arab-Israeli war broke out at the same time and some overseas commentators took the presence of Canberras in this guise as proof of British participation in the war!

Aircraft strength continued to drop until by late 1966 the OCU was operating an average of eleven B.2s, nine PR.3s and sixteen T.4s. The following November it was announced that because of the impending reduction in the Canberra force the role of Bassingbourn would reduce and that by mid 1969 the station would close. The end came even earlier than planned and in May 1968 the OCU ceased flying from Bassingbourn saying farewell to this historic station on the 19th and flying to their new home at Cottesmore. After an eight year sojourn in Rutland the OCU moved again, in February 1976 to Marham, having in the meantime ceased PR conversion and lost its PR.3s. From now on all aircrew went through either a full conversion course or a short refresher course. Role training, PR for example, was done at squadron level.

Life continued as normal at Marham with four T.4s and two or three B.2s, two of the latter being designated B.2T because of a change in nav fit which gave them a Green Satin doppler and a GPI.IV. There were, however, fewer courses and fewer students, reflecting the continued run-down of Canberra strength with the withdrawal from the Near East and Far East. The demise of the Interdictor squadrons in Germany resulted in a reduction in the low level training and the OCU no longer taught weaponry. It was still a very traditional course with an intensive bout of groundschool on the aircraft and its systems and for the navs the 'delights' of the very out of date nav fit. Students were roughly 50:50 first tourists and ex-Canberra aircrew returning to flying after a ground tour. For the staff crews a tour on the OCU was invariably a 2-3 year period between squadron tours. The OCU remained a general course as the Canberra roles for which students were destined was too diverse to be covered. Whenever possible pilots and navs destined for the same squadron were crewed together for the student sorties. With the decision to concentrate all Canberra units at Wyton, the OCU moved across in July 1982 and took over the accommodation vacated by 39.

Aircraft strength in 1986 was two T.4s (WH848 and WJ879) and two B.2s (WJ731 and WE113), but the OCU also operated the T.4s which were on the strength of the station's flying squadrons, thus virtually doubling the complement.

After major fatigue problems with the T.4s, the OCU had to borrow aircraft from the Royal Navy and for a while these silver finished aircraft with orange dayglo bands were a familiar sight at Wyton.

231 OCU was once an organisation of a size that merited its own Station and although reduced to reside in a corner of the airfield at Wyton in more recent years it continued to maintain the excellent tradition that has seen it produce many thousands of aircrew over the years. Even in the late 1980s first tourists were still being sent to the Canberra.

The 'scheduled' run-down of Canberra units in the early 1990s began with the announcement that 100 Squadron would start to re-equip with Hawks in October 1991. Although it was anticipated that the OCU UE would be affected, it was the unexpected 'operational requirements' of Operation Granby that brought about the premature disbandment of 231 OCU on 15th December 1990. Even though by mid-1991 a review was under way, the OCU did not reform, instead, the CAST (Canberra Standardisation and Training) Flight had been formed informally at Wyton with a number of Staff crews and aircraft allocated as required. The rather abrupt demise of this proud unit occurred only a little more than a year before it would have celebrated 40 years of continuous association with the Canberra.

231 OCU B.2 WE113 'BJ' at Valley, August 1989. *S. G. Richards*

T.4 WJ874 doing circuits at Brize Norton, June 1985. Transferred from RAF to RN charge in November 1969 the aircraft went into service with the FRU. It was loaned to 231 OCU in May 1986 and was still in use at Wyton in August 1991. *S. G. Richards*

Royal Navy

The Navy was not one of the major users of the Canberra, no doubt mainly due to the aircraft's unsuitability for Carrier ops (the authors don't know of any plans to ever try such a feat!) However, various Canberras have been used by the Navy at home and overseas.

728B Squadron was one of only two units to operate the unmanned variant of the Canberra, the actual designation used by the Navy being U.14, which was a development of the U.10 fitted with PR.9 type hydraulic flying controls.

Six of these aircraft were used by the Squadron (coded '590' to '595') at Hal Far, Malta, on Seacat and Seaslug GW (Guided Weapon) trials. The first aircraft arrived on 25th May 1961. Aircraft serials ran '590' (WH921), '591' (WD941), '592' (WH720), '593' (WJ638), '594' (WH704) and '595' (WH876). All aircraft were painted overall white with wide black bands around the outer part of the wings.

WH720 made its first pilotless flight in August 1961 and the Squadron entered a short but intensive period of trials on the guidance systems of the missiles. Only one U.14 was shot down during the trials when '590' (WH921) was brought down by a missile fired from HMS *Girdle Ness* on 6th October 1961. The Squadron disbanded in December 1961 and the remaining aircraft returned to the UK where they became D.14s; the change of nomenclature being brought about by the change in the 'U' designation from 'Unmanned' to 'Utility'.

776 FRU (Fleet Requirements Unit) received the first TT.18 (WK123) in September 1969 and for a number of years the unit, operated by Airwork Services Ltd,

Above: **D.14 WH921 '590' of 728B Squadron was the only aircraft actually shot down – on 6th October 1961.**

Below: **D.14 WH921 again. The unmanned Canberras of 728B Squadron, Hal Far, were used as targets for guided missile trials.**

flew target facilities duties in the south coast weapons ranges from their base at Hurn. The unit crest was a Penguin standing on a target drone. 776 operated four or five TT.18s and a T.4 (WJ866), although B.2 WK142 was on strength for a while.

It was a relatively short-lived venture and on 30th November 1972 the unit was disbanded. In reality it moved to Yeovilton to join the FDS (Fighter Direction School) to form a single larger unit called FRADTU (Fleet Requirements and Air Directional Training Unit).

This unit was also operated by Airwork and used a mix of aircraft which included Canberra B.2s, T.4s and, especially, TT.18s on the same range of duties as the two separate units had previously performed. Little changed until November 1973 when the first of a new Canberra variant, the T.22, was delivered to replace the ageing Sea Vixens. The T.22 was a re-worked PR.7 equipped with an 'off the shelf' radar for airborne radar instruction and the mark

had made its first flight from Samlesbury in September 1973.

By the middle of the following year the unit's title had changed to FRADU, 'Training' having been dropped. Canberra strength consisted of seven TT.18s, five T.4s and six T.22s. However, numbers settled down to a norm of nine TT.18s, seven T.22s and a couple of T.4s. The unit performed very similar tasks to those of 7 Squadron and became a regular sight in the south-coast ranges and weaving in and out of evading frigates and destroyers on naval exercises. The next major change came about in 1985 when the T.22s were retired, the last one, WH780 - '853', leaving on 22nd September. A number of TT.18s were retired at around the same time and most of the redundant airframes went into store at St Athan. Since then Canberra strength on FRADU has been further reduced as 'executive twin-jets' (Falcons) have been bought - much more pleasant to fly but not as much fun!

TT.18s of FRADU at Yeovilton, June 1986. FRADU took over all RN facilities duties in late 1972 and gradually acquired a number of Canberra variants. *S. G. Richards*

Note the Penguin badge on B.2 WJ717 of 776 FRU, the Navy target facilities unit operated by Airwork Services. *MAP*

TT.18 WH887 of FRADU seen at St Mawgan in 1985. *R. C. B. Ashworth*

The prototype T.22, WT510 in primer, seen here on the occasion of its first flight – 28th June 1973. These aircraft were reworked PR.7s equipped with a radar. *BAC/AW/37137*

T.22 WH780 '853' of FRADU. *MAP*

U.10 WH733 on test from Sydenham. Most of the U.10s were destined for the LWRE at Woomera, Australia, where they were used for a variety of weapons trials. *Short Bros AC/2/3529 via B. Robertson*

Weapons Research Establishment

This joint UK/Australia trials unit, based at Salisbury, South Australia, was originally formed during 1947 as the Long Range Weapons Establishment. It was intended for the development and testing of inter-continental ballistic missiles. The base airfield was Edinburgh Field, whilst the testing range was nearly 300 miles away at Woomera.

The name was changed in 1955 to the Weapons Research Establishment to reflect the declining interest in ballistic missiles and the developing interests in more general weapons testing.

Canberras were used in considerable numbers, both at Edinburgh Field and at Woomera. The Canberra U.10 developed by Short Bros & Harland (see page 183) was used as a target aircraft. Seventeen of these were sent out from the UK; the first, WD961, made its initial operational flight on 25th June 1959, whilst the last, WH705, arrived during July 1962.

Each aircraft was fitted with a 'control supervisory panel' whereby the pilot could 'fly' the aircraft using a series of control buttons and indicator lamps. However, in fully automatic mode the U.10 was controlled by a master controller via his VHF radio link in the control van. During critical phases, such as take-off and landing, he could hand-over to two operators, one for the pitch control and one for the azimuth. The aircraft also had a number of automatic functions tied in to speed and attitude and it deployed a drogue parachute on landing. An explosive charge was positioned to sever the tail should it be necessary to destruct the aircraft. Specialised telemetry equipment was fitted to assess missile 'miss' distances as most firings were done with dummy warheads to test the guidance rather than the actual killing power. A number of live firings were made resulting in numerous Canberra casualties.

Most surviving U.10s were returned to the UK where they became D.10s, for the same reason that the U.14s became D.14s; ie the change of the 'U' designation from 'Unmanned' to 'Utility'.

Many other Canberras were operated by the RAF in Australia either on the series of nuclear tests or on weapons trials with the WRE. Amongst the latter were those which were used by 12 JSTU on the Blue Jay trials in late 1965. Of these aircraft, WH700 stayed on for Red Top, Jindivik and various other range duties with the WRE. At the end of its useful life it became derelict at Edinburgh Field until acquired for display at Parafield. WK165 was allocated to

WK165 in use with the WRE.
via R. C. B. Ashworth

A pilotless take-off by WD961 at Woomera.
Shorts

the WRE on 25th November 1955 and was used as an air to air photo platform on missile trials and as a trials platform for various bomb and fuse developments. It was eventually Soc (struck off charge) at Edinburgh Field on 13th February 1970. Photographs have appeared of this aircraft sporting variously-coloured missile silhouettes on the starboard side of its nose which probably reflect its part in air to air missile firings. At one stage it was given a non-standard pointed nose, no doubt for a radar system of some sort. This aircraft has also been acquired for preservation in recent years and is now with the Eureka Aviation Museum.

A T.4 in WRE use was WD954 which went on MoA charge from 11th January 1960 and was used at Woomera as a missile tracking aircraft. It was grounded by undercarriage problems and, although overhauled, was struck off charge at Edinburgh on 13th February 1970. Just prior to this date it was seen in use with the ATU in RAAF markings. Like its sister aircraft it too has been preserved and now resides at the Warbirds Aviation Museum, Mildura. This aircraft also sported nose art, the tally being twenty missile and seven bomb silhouettes on the port side of the nose.

By the early 1970s the Canberra was no longer used by the WRE. In fact, the UK commitment had decreased to such an extent that on 3rd April 1978 the site was renamed the Defence Research Centre and was dealing with essentially Australian projects.

Nuclear Tests

UK-based Canberra squadrons played an important part in the series of British Atomic tests in the 1950s when it was recognised that the performance of the Canberra would enable high altitude readings to be obtained for analysis.

One of the first such involvements was in October 1953 with operation *Hot Box* at Woomera when an aircraft was specially equipped to fly through the atomic cloud to examine effects on the aircraft and crew as well as to collect samples of radioactive dust. The crew consisted of Group Captain D. Wilson, the RAF's radiologist, Wing Commander G. Dhenin, a 'flying' doctor, plus the navigator. The highly-polished aircraft was given a unique nose emblem of white swan of England facing a black swan of Australia above the sea and separated by the RAF medical branch symbol of a serpent entwined about a rod.

76 Squadron line-up at Weston Zoyland during preparations for the Monte Bello atomic Task Force, 1956.

Squadron Leader J. G. Wynne and personnel of 76 Squadron in front of one of the unit's B.2s at Wittering 1954-55.
via Ron Webb

Dust collectors were fitted in special wing-tip tanks and the crew given protective clothing for their trip into the unknown. After a number of postponments for weather, suitable conditions at last prevailed and the test went ahead. Seconds before the detonation the aircraft turned away from the firing point but as the mushroom cloud rose, the Canberra turned and flew through the edge of the cloud to test the safety of the radioactive level. Having decided it was not 'too hot', the crew headed for the middle of the cloud. As expected, the aircraft was bounced around by the turbulent core of the cloud but emerged safely on the other side. Another run was made above the cloud and then one below and then it was time to head back to the airfield. The crew considered the after-landing 'processing' the worst part of the whole event. They taxied the aircraft around to the parking area, climbed out to strip off and stood under the waiting showers to be decontaminated until cleared by the monitors.

This was to be the pattern of future Canberra involvement with special collecting equipment, usually in modified tip tanks, together with radiological monitoring equipment. Met flights and PR were also carried out.

In November 1953 the first of the specialist units was formed at Wyton, designated 1323 Flight, with radiological monitoring duties around the world. The unit was involved with air sampling around the UK to read levels of atmospheric radiation for research purposes.

Two years later, 1st November 1955, 1323 Flight became 542 Squadron following the disbandment of that unit as a Canberra PR squadron on 1st October at Wyton. In practise the units were combined on 3rd October and carried on the work of the specialist flight with a UE of seven B.2s 'adapted for special tasks'. The operational policy of the unit was 'to carry out special tasks as directed' and this led to a wide variety of detachments to such places as Gibraltar, Kinloss and Goose Bay in Canada.

A non-flying detachment was sent to Weston Zoyland to prepare for the Squadron's occupation of this new 'special' base, the move taking place on 15th December.

The previous month 76 Squadron had moved there from Wittering to re-equip with seven special B.6s as the Canberra element of Task Group 308/5. One B.6 was loaned to 542, WJ764 - actually a 101 Squadron aircraft, and in turn 76 borrowed three B.2s. Both units were formed to carry out the same roles of special ops and nuclear cloud sampling.

In March 1956 'C' Flight of 542 Squadron moved to Australia with three, later four, B.6s, which were split two and two at Laverton and Darwin. This became a permanent detachment with periods of quiet interspersed with periods of activity during the actual tests. Both units acted independently of each other flying their own areas and routes when tasked but regular liaison visits were made to keep some degree of contact. A variety of special equipment was fitted to the aircraft the most important of which were the wing-tip collection tanks which could be opened to take air samples when required, although some earlier versions had fixed inlets. Although low level sorties were sometimes called for, the main area of ops for the Canberras was the higher levels with orbits at 20,000 ft, 40,000 ft and 47,000 ft.

It was a similar story for 76 Squadron with a detachment based in Australia to provide cloud sampling aircraft for specific tests. Aircraft were sent to various test sites and the Squadron took part in all the main tests, the schedule being:

1. Operation *Mosaic*, March 1956 on the Monte Bello islands, aircraft based at Pearce.
2. Operation *Buffalo*, Autumn 1956 at Maralinga, aircraft based at Edinburgh near Adelaide. The Squadron, except for one crew, returned to the UK but in February 1957 returned to Edinburgh Field to start training for the *Grapple* series of tests at Christmas Island.
3. April 1957 until June, Christmas Island.
4. Operation *Antler*, September-October 1957 at Maralinga.
5. *Grapple X,* November 1957.
6. *Grapple Y,* March 1958.
7. *Grapple Z,* August 1958.

The Air Task Force for Maralinga consisted of ten Canberras, two Valiants, eight Varsity, four Hastings and two helicopters. Edinburgh Field was used as the main base with certain aircraft moving forward to operate from Maralinga as appropriate.

The cloud sampling at the Maralinga tests was done by two aircraft which got airborne twenty minutes before the firing (tower or air-drop) and took-up pre-determined orbits ready to enter the cloud. One aircraft entered the cloud while the other, (back-up), aircraft photographed the sampler entering and leaving the cloud. Then it was back to base for the samples to be removed for use at Maralinga and for onward transmission to AWRE Aldermaston. The survey Canberras took over and tracked the cloud until it was over the sea, ascended too high or dispersed and undetectable.

On the *Grapple* tests the B.6s had two roles: firstly, low level recce of the area and ground zero from 2,000 ft fifteen minutes after the burst to note the sea wave, visibility, surface state of the island and such like; and secondly, to collect air samples at high altitude. In the hope of collecting very high altitude samples two aircraft were fitted with rockets (WT207 with Double Scorpion and WT208 with DH Spectre). Unfortunately, WT207 disintegrated at 56,000 ft over England during acceptance trials and so her sister aircraft was limited to more normal operations.

Having penetrated the cloud as directed by 'Sniff Boss', the lead aircraft, the sampler would fly through taking samples and monitoring radiation levels at various parts of the cloud. When complete it was back for decontamination and packaging of the samples for depatch to the UK - by express Canberra, 72 hours was allowed for this movement but it was often completed in 24! Decontamination usually meant a long soak under the shower and crews were rotated back to the UK if personnel radiation levels rose above a certain level.

The samplers were not the only Canberras involved in the *Grapple* tests. PR.7s of 100 Squadron took part in *Grapple X* and PR.7s of 58 Squadron in *Y* and *Z*. The job of the PR.7s was weather recce and photography. At dawn an aircraft would get airborne to conduct a high level met flight into cloud type, structure, temperature and wind velocity. Radio reports were sent back every twelve minutes to enable 'Go' or 'No-Go' decisions to be made about firing.

Meanwhile back in the UK the main part of 542 Squadron continued its sampling duties when and where required. In March 1957 the Squadron moved to Hemswell and a year later the Australian detachment was halved, leaving just two aircraft operating out of Laverton. With a new UE of five B.2s and two B.6s (in Australia), the Squadron moved again in July, to Upwood. It was a short-lived arrangement as on 1st October 1958 it was renumbered as 21 Squadron, with the Australian detachment becoming 'C' Flight 21 Squadron. This unit took part in the last series of *Hot Toddy* in Australia in October.

76 Squadron returned to the UK in November 1959, moving to Upwood at about the same time. By early the next year they were down to five aircraft and were finally disbanded on 31st December.

This virtually brought to a close the Canberra's involvement in the nuclear tests, the aircraft having done a variety of tasks that no other single aircraft type could have covered.

100 Squadron took its PR.7 flight to Christmas Island in 1957 as part of the Atom test air group. The aircraft were primarily used for weather recce and cloud tracking.

For the *Grapple* series of tests 58 Squadron deployed to Christmas Island.
58 Squadron records

Swifter Flight

In 1960 a special flight was formed at El Adem to investigate the effects of high-speed, low-level flight on aircraft structures and the aircrew. This had a dual purpose in that it provided data for use in the TSR.2 programme and also gave additional general information on such flight profiles. Six B.2s were used by Swifter Flight (WD950, WF890, WH648, WJ573, WH664 and WJ576) and each was specially strengthened for the rigorous test programe as well as being fitted with recording instruments. A seventh B.2, WJ608, was also used but was probably not given the additional strengthening.

Flight profiles demanded high speed (350 kts) sorties at 100-600 ft both day and night. Crews were attached to Swifter Flight from the Canberra squadrons of the Akrotiri wing and were subjected not only to the rigours of low level ops but also to various trials by Institute of Aviation Medicine (IAM) on heat, fatigue etc. The plan was to fly 1000 hours in the notional one-year period of the trial.

Swifter aircraft were given a white band around the centre fuselage, and carried a 'swift' emblem on the fin.

On completion of the trial three aircraft were converted to T.17 standard (WF890, WH664 and WJ576).

RAF Flying College/College Air Warfare

The RAF Flying College at Manby was amongst the first RAF units to receive Canberras. The College, renamed the College of Air Warfare (CAW) in 1965, had a long and distinguished association with the aircraft, which they operated from both Manby and Strubby in Lincolnshire.

The most 'notable' work done by aircraft from Manby was that undertaken by the *Aries* series of aircraft. *Aries I* was a Lancastrian and *Aries II* and *III* Lincolns but it was recognised that the Canberra presented opportunities to extend the limits of research and B.2 WH699 was acquired as *Aries IV*. This aircraft was in use by the RAFFC from 1953-59. During its first two years at Manby it undertook a series of spectacular flights, culminating on 14/15th October 1954 with the first British jet flight across the North Pole.

In June 1956 *Aries V*, PR.7 WT528, joined the research stable and it was soon in record-breaking form. After service with the RAF this aircraft was reworked by BAC and exported to India in 1964 as a PR.57 (BP746).

The last Canberras with the CAW were retired by May 1966.

Central Fighter Establishment

The All-Weather Wing of the Central Fighter Establishment was using an unidentified Canberra by February 1955, as an airborne target in interception trials. On 28th March 1955, B.2 WH921 of the CFE made a forced landing at Marham with the port main wheel retracted, sustaining only slight damage – this may have been the aircraft in use a month or so earlier.

PR.7 WT529 was attached to the Station Flight by January 1956, though sadly the aircraft crashed at Sudbrooke, Lincs on the 16th of that month, killing the two-man crew of Wing Commander A.B. Cole DFC AFC, OC Tactics Branch and Squadron Leader P. Needham AFC, the night tactics specialist of the CFE.

In May 1956, the All-Weather Development Squadron (AWDS) received B(I)6 XG554 for tactical evaluation trials. These trials never really got underway and at the end of July, XG554 was transferred to Bomber Command, together with the task.

Exercise *Stronghold* took place in September 1956 and the units of the CFE participated in their reserve squadron role. Attached to the AWDS, which formed a night fighter squadron under the 176 Squadron number plate, were two MoS Canberras, one of these with AI.Mk.18 radar and the other AI.Mk.20 radar. After the exercise both aircraft returned to the MoS (at Pershore).

The Target Facilities Squadron of the CFE operated six T.11s and a T.4 from West Raynham between 10th August 1961 and 20th March 1963 and this period is dealt with in greater depth later in this chapter under 'Waving the Flag'.

The CFE itself moved on to Binbrook on 12th October 1962. The DFCS followed on 13th November after completing its current course. This left the TFS at West Raynham (together with 85 Squadron – Javelin FAW.8s), where it remained until 20th March 1963, at which time the TFS was renamed 85 Squadron and the CFE association with the Canberra ended.

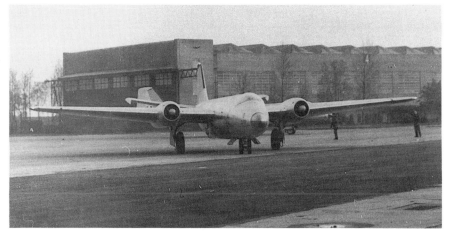

Two overseas tours were carried out by the CFE using the Canberra PR.7. The photographs show two (unidentified) aircraft leaving West Raynham on 31st October 1955 for a tour of Australia at the invitation of the RAAF. This tour was led by the CFE Commandant, Air Commodore J.

Grandy DSO. The lower photo shows the two aircraft of the second tour at West Raynham prior to leaving for Burma, in November 1957. This was led by the then Commandant, Air Commodore E. L. Colbeck-Welch, seen on the right of the small group photo taken in Burma.

Central Flying School

The Central Flying School (CFS) has the task of ensuring that standards of flying knowledge and routine practical flying skills are maintained.

Although the exact nomenclature tends to vary, an Examining Wing has Directing Staff that go out and test people in the field. Usually this entails an annual visit to each squadron where they fly with as many squadron pilots as possible. Essentially they are standardising the work of the 'CFS Agent' – the fully operational pilot on the strength of each squadron who is also a QFI. It is this agent of the CFS that is tasked with maintaining routine and practical flying skills to required standards and this is achieved by regular check-rides and the six-monthly Instrument Rating (IR) tests for all the Squadron pilots. The service nick-name of 'trappers' seems to be applied universally to all CFS Agents, QFI and Directing Staff alike!

It should be borne in mind that over a period of time, nomenclature such as 'Examining Wing' come and go and it is not easy to pin these changes down. For instance, from mid-1957 onwards this particular term was said to have fallen into disuse at CFS, having been superceded by 'CFS Directing Staff' – yet this too appears relatively short lived and was in turn superceded by 'Standards Wing'. The term 'Examining Wing' is said to have been reintroduced in March 1966 long after the Canberra had left CFS.

At Little Rissington in the summer of 1957, No.1 Squadron of CFS were operating three Provost Flights and No.2 Squadron two Vampire Flights. The Jet Provost T.1s were acquired from Hullavington for staff conversion, towards the end of 1957.

On 10th July 1957 the CFS Type Squadron came into operation to provide type experience for those students with a limited flying background. The Type Squadron was made up of a Hunter Flight

WT480, one of the CFS T.4s, seen at Thorney Island in May 1960.

(detached at Kemble), a Meteor and Communications Flight and an embryo Canberra Flight (both at Little Rissington).

In mid-August 1957 the first of three Canberra T.4s (WJ991) arrived at Little Rissington. However, it seems certain that the CFS had been involved with the Canberra before this time – as a memorable photograph of WE112, along with a RAF Sabre and Meteor night fighter, appeared in a 1954 magazine, and it is believed that odd aircraft were loaned to the Examining Wing from such units as the RAF Handling Squadron at Manby.

WJ991 was joined by WT480 during 1958 and by WD944 in 1959 and these were soon to acquire the code-letters CB, CC and CA respectively, displayed on the aircraft in the period flying-training style, ie astride the fuselage roundel.

In December 1954 the CFS Commandant of the time, Air Commodore J.N.H. Whitworth and his CFI, Wing Commander P.W. Gilpin, made the longest overseas tour in the history of the School, in a pair of Canberras. They called at the RAAF Station at East Sale to visit their counterpart to the CFS, and at the RNZAF CFS at Wigram before returning home via Indonesia, Thailand, Burma, India and Pakistan.

The CFS Canberra era drew to a close towards the end of 1962 but not before the fuselage codes of the three T.4s had been changed to 21, 22 and 20 respectively.

Other RAF Users

Throughout this book the authors have tried to give at least fleeting mention of all Canberra users – not an easy task considering the extensive use of the aircraft – not only by squadrons but by a variety of trials units (see Chapter 9) and central flying establishments. Certain units seem to have a very dim past, mainly due to lack of preserved records – for example the Bomber Command Development Unit and Bomber Command Holding Unit.

The BCDU has already been mentioned in its early years when 100 Squadron carried out the Canberra trials for this unit. However, when the BCDU moved to Finningley it retained a Canberra element to continue weapons and weapons systems trials until disbanded in December 1968.

The BCHU, or to give it its original title 'Bomber Command Air Crew Holding Unit', is an even more enigmatic organisation and was based at Coningsby from January 1958 for a period of approximately two years. The primary job of the unit with its B.2s and T.4s was exactly as the title suggests – to provide a unit where Canberra aircrew, awaiting postings following the late 1950s rundown of the Bomber Command Canberra force, could undertake continuation training to maintain flying currency.

The Bomber Command Acceptance and Modification Unit at Lindholme dealt with Canberras from 1953, with both a trials role for installations and an aircraft modification role. The following year the name was shortened to Command Modification Centre and in September 1956 the unit moved to Hemswell.

Mention must also be made of the various ferry units which had the job of delivering aircraft to and from MUs, although much of this work was also undertaken by squadron aircrew.

The RAF Handling Squadron operated from Manby between 1949 and 1954. This unit usually received the second or third production model of a new aircraft entering service so that its handling qualities could be assessed and the Pilot's Notes written. The second prototype Canberra B.2 (VX169) arrived at Manby on 3rd March 1951 for this purpose as did the fourth production B.6 during 1954.

It is worth highlighting again that many stations, both Canberra and non-Canberra, had Canberras attached for pilot Continuation Training (CT) and/or Instrument Flying Training (IFT). Likewise some Group and Command Communications Units in the UK and overseas had at least one Canberra amongst their diverse fleet.

Many units had a very transitory relationship with the aircraft, such as the 2nd TAF Development Unit at Ahlhorn, which ran from April to September 1953, investigating night interdictor roles for the Canberra in Germany.

Other squadrons borrowed aircraft whilst awaiting delivery of their allocated types – all of which goes to complicate an already complex picture.

Ground Instructional Airframes

In essence there are three possible fates for any redundant aircraft: storage or conversion for sale overseas (not many aircraft types fit the latter consideration, the Canberra and the Hunter being notable exceptions); the breaker's hammer; or, use as a Ground Instructional airframe. The Canberra has been used extensively as a G/i airframe with aircraft going to six of the Schools of Technical Training - No.1 SoTT at Halton, No.2 at Cosford, No.4 at St Athan, No.9 at Newton, No.10 at Kirkham and No.12 at Melksham. Aircraft so used were given 'M' serials, a long-running special numerical sequence, suffixed (or ocasionally prefixed) by the letter 'M' – for 'Maintenance' presumably.

Usage depended on the particular trade specialisation of the SoTT but all technical aspects were involved from airframe to avionics. Barrie Trump remembered avionics training on Canberra airframes at Cosford . . . , 'the staff would "arrange" for a particular piece of equipment to develop a snag and then let the trainee sort out the problem. Despite the age of some of the equipment fitted to the Canberras, the principles were the same and it provided useful "hands-on" training.'

So, even in its 'grounded' state the Canberra has been an invaluable training aid for thousands of technicians. Of course, it was not only Canberras that were used for this work and a look at the 'books' of some of the SoTTs provides a catalogue of RAF aircraft history.

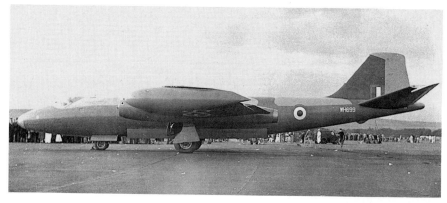

Below: **Note the Swifter Flight marking on the fin of Canberra WJ608 and the white forward and centre fuselage used on these trials aircraft.** *MAP*

Top: **B.2 WH699 *Aries IV* was used by the RAF Flying College out of Manby and Strubby between 1953 and 1959. On 17th September 1955 she visited West Malling.** *J. D. R. Rawlings*

Above: **One of the least known of Canberra activities was that of Swifter Flight which operated seven B.2s on high speed low-level trials in the early 1960s. WJ576 is seen here refuelling at El Adem.** *MAP*

Waving the Flag

The Canberra was an excellent all-purpose airframe and its stability and performance made it an ideal aircraft for use by the Target Facilities Squadron as a target towing aircraft.

Thus began one of the longest 'careers' of the Canberra and one that is still going strong with 100 Squadron at Wyton where they have a remarkably diverse collection of aircraft marks.

There are two basic elements to this task: one is where the aircraft itself acts as a target for either ground systems (SAMs), or fighters (GCI and PI); the other is when the aircraft tows a banner for someone to shoot at! No less than three squadrons were involved in the Target Facilities role - 85 Squadron from March 1963-1975, 7 Squadron from July 1970-January 1982 and 100 Squadron from 1972 to date. In the

early 1970s, 56 Squadron operated a small number of Canberras as their own TF flight at Akrotiri.

Eight B.2s were converted into the T.11 radar target role the work being done by Boulton Paul. The trials installation aircraft was WJ734 and work involved fitting an AI radar in a modified nose section. The primary role of these aircraft when they entered service was as airborne AI trainers for such aircraft as the Javelin. The T.11s served initially at Leeming with 228 OCU from 1959 until that unit disbanded and the aircraft transferred to the CFE at West Raynham on 10th August 1961, to form the Target Facilities Squadron (TFS). In the main the TFS flew airborne target sorties for the Lightning Squadrons but it also provided similar service for the Bloodhound Mk.1 surface-to-air missile squadrons. Many sorties were

Top: **WH639 of the RAF Flying College as part of the static display at the 1953 Royal Review, Odiham. Note the Chipmunk T.10 WZ865 coded JV of RAFC Cranwell, in the background.** *J.D.R.Rawlings*

Above: **A great many diverse units operated Canberras in one form or another. Ex 57 Squadron B.2 WH878 is seen here with the Bomber Command Holding Unit at Coningsby, 30 August 1958.** *R.Sturtivant*

Opposite: **56 Squadron operated Lightnings in Cyprus but also had a flight of Canberras for its own TF flight. T.4 WE188 carries the squadron 'fighter' markings on the nose. In the background is 13 Squadron PR.9 XH174.**

B.2 WJ681 of 56 Squadron at Cottesmore, for the type's 25th Anniversary celebration, 22nd May 1974. The squadron markings are much more conservative on this aircraft!

also flown in support of Bloodhound Mk.2 development trials at North Coates and for the Day Fighter Combat School, also at West Raynham and part of the Central Fighter Establishment. The TFS had a UE of six Canberra T.11s in April 1962 and T.4 WT485 arrived from Samlesbury on 2nd May. T.11 WH714 arrived from 5 MU on 7th November, whereas XA536 left for Boulton Paul's at Seighford on 24th February 1963, for modifications to the navigator's ejection seat.

With effect from 20th March 1963 the TFS was renumbered as 85 Squadron and was soon to move to Binbrook – the advance party doing so on 29th April. The main party followed on 2nd May, the Squadron's six T.11s (WH714, WH724, WH903, WH904, WJ610 and WJ975) flew in formation and they were joined by their T.4 WT485 later in the day. From Binbrook the Squadron continued in the role of the TFS acting as targets for the Lightning squadrons and the Bloodhounds of 25 (SAM) Squadron at North Coates. Some of the T.11s still had the Mk.17 AI sets fitted so the Squadron was able to carry out active radar search, known as 'Jim Crow' sorties, for incoming raids during exercises. This was, however, very much viewed as a 'bonus' and not one of the squadron's main tasks. An ever increasing number of tasks brought an increase in UE to nine Canberras and six Meteors and by February 1964 target towing had been added to the list of jobs.

A typical month would call for 170 or so programmed task sorties of which 40-50 would be cancelled, mainly because of unsuitable weather or by the user unit (e.g. the Lightnings). While demanding at times, it was not the most exciting of flying and as a bit of light relief the CO requested Rangers to Germany and Gibraltar. Clearance was eventually given for up to two Rangers a month to Bruggen or Gib. PIs particularly were noted for their boredom with the aircraft flying 'racetracks' in the designated area, frequently out over the North Sea, at the beck-and-call of the GCI site.

In July 1965, 228 OCU, the night fighter conversion school, was re-formed at Leuchars with Javelins and also three T.11s with AI sets still fitted. This unit used the Canberras as radar trainers until August the following year.

In the meantime, 85 Squadron had started to operate yet another mark of Canberra, the T.19. These were converted T.11s, the conversion entailed removing the 'Airpass' radar from the remaining eight aircraft. Aircraft were converted at various places over a period of some four years. The first aircraft (WH724) was completed in 1965 and the last (XA536) in 1969.

The aircraft were beginning to show signs of old age - and too many conversions - and cracks were starting to appear. Partly because of this and partly because of an increasing demand from fighter and SAM units the Squadron UE was increased to 14 aircraft in February 1968. At the same time the task was extended to provide target facilities for the RAFG Lightning squadrons. This involved detaching a crew to an RAFG station for three or four days and although the job was the same as in the UK it was still appreciated as a change of scenery.

One of the major problems of going anywhere in the B.2 (or any of its derivatives) was the lack of cockpit conditioning. The heat problem has already been mentioned but the cold problem was just as bad if not worse. There was no way of heating the cockpit area so at 40,000 ft with an outside air temperature of minus 60° it became *very* cold inside the aircraft. You could tell it was getting really cold when you had to scrape ice off the instruments before you could read them! A number of ways were devised to provide heating - not for the aircraft but for the crew. Life was not too bad for the pilot under his greenhouse as the sun's effects at 40,000 ft made him quite warm, except for his feet. However, for the rear cockpit occupants it was rather like sitting in a deep freeze. This led to the development of the electrically heated suit.

If full suits were not available, or through individual preference, just a pair of electically heated socks were worn. Although excellent they did provide the odd problem ranging from holes burnt in woollen socks to gently roasted toes! The most unpleasant sensation was 'asymmetric foot' when only one of the socks worked! A favourite navigator's trick was to sit beside the pilot and without being

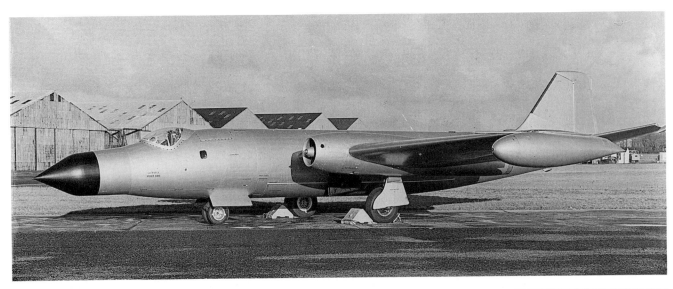

This page from the top:
T.11 WH904 of 85 Squadron, Binbrook, September 1964. *Tony Hancock*

228 OCU formation: the Canberra T.11s are WJ610/G and WJ975/E, the Javelins are coded S, V and U, and the nearer of the Meteor NF.14s is WS837. *Flight 41302s*

A publicity shot featuring TT.18 WJ632, the first target towing conversion.

Opposite: **WJ734 was the t/i aircraft for T.11. Production conversions could not carry tip tanks.** *BAC/AW/5809*

T.11 XA536 in use with the Leuchars Target Facilities Flight.

Close up of the T.11 nose on WH904.

85 Squadron T.19 WH714, the day following its hydraulic failure at Binbrook, 19th June 1968. Note the electricity pole already replaced between the wheel tracks!

caught, unplug his socks and plug yours in. The gradual onset of cold toes proved most amusing!

85 Squadron was so overtasked by the end of the 1960s that it was obvious that at least one more facilities squadron would be needed. The Squadron took part in a great many TACEVALS acting as targets for the particular unit being assessed and started sending detachments to the Med for Adexs in Malta and Cyprus. The last Meteor left the Squadron in October 1970 and two months later the B.2s were modified for banner towing to work with the Lightning Mk.6s on an air-to-air gunnery programme. The first proving flights were made in April with cine sorties, the system being treated as an interim measure pending entry into service of another Canberra conversion. In May the Squadron acquired the first three of its 'new' aircraft, TT.18s, giving a total aircraft strength of twenty-two aircraft, although a third were away at any one time on mod programmes. The Squadron never got to grips with operating the TT.18 and although three aircraft were on strength they were never available and passed to other units before they were used. Many records do not note this event and 85 Squadron was not an official *user* of the TT.18.

85 Squadron was not the first unit to operate the new mark as 7 Squadron had reformed at St Mawgan on 1st May 1970 with seven TT.18s in the target facilities role. The TT.18 was yet another B.2 conversion with a total of twenty-three aircraft being converted by either English Electric or Flight Refuelling Ltd. The first aircraft flew from the FR Ltd airfield at Tarrant Rushton on 14th April 1970.

The TT.18 was equipped with two Rushton winches, one under each wing, suitable for Rushton Mk.2 targets or conventional sleeve targets. Crews were initially sent to Tarrant Rushton for a conversion course but because of delays the formation ceremony for 7 Squadron was put back to 1st July. Part of the problem was caused by the use of contract servicing, by Airwork Ltd, first with a difficulty in recruiting a work force and then when the assembled work force imposed an overtime ban! Nevertheless, the first operational sorties were flown in June with 7 Squadron being on the receiving end of live firings of Tiger Cat SAMs and Lightning 30 mm Aden cannon shells. On 1st July the Squadron was declared operational, an event recorded in the ORB: 'All the crews on the Squadron have now been fired at and have since overcome their initial surprise and fright at being able to hear and feel the guns firing.' Throughout the years of being fired at there have been numerous occasions of crews receiving severe jolts as 30 mm shells flashed past the cockpit. On such occasions the occupant of the offending aircraft would be left in no doubt

as to his transgression and would be liable to a hefty bar bill! There has been the odd fortunate occasion when the attacker was making a cine run only and returned with excellent film of the Canberra as he shot past the banner on the wrong attack angle.

On 7th December 1972 one crew had an 'interesting' experience in WJ680. Flight Lieutenant D. Burgess and his nav, Pilot Officer G. Burns, had completed half of a post-Minor air test and had set the aircraft up for a critical speed run at 3,000 ft - full power on the starboard engine and the port throttled back - critical speed was found to be 175 kts rather than the normal 155 kts. Power was increased on the port engine and reduced on the starboard engine and the aircraft started to roll to the right. The pilot was unable to apply left rudder and to put on full left aileron trim. The aircraft increased its roll - and was also now in a dive. Full power was applied to the port engine and the starboard throttled back and gradually the wings were levelled and the aircraft put into a climb - having at one stage been below 1,000 ft. At this stage the crew informed ATC of the problem and whilst climbing to 10,000 ft decided that the problem must be the rudder jammed fully right. Attempts to free the rudder were unsuccessful and Bruce Bull, in a second Canberra vectored to the scene, confirmed that the problem was as suspected and that the top hinge of the rudder appeared to have sheared. Investigation showed that WJ680 could be controlled at 150-160 kts with heavy left aileron. The decision was made to attempt a landing at St Mawgan ... 5,000 ft overhead the airfield the nav banged out as agreed and landed safely to the north of the airfield. With the undercarriage selected down and the aircraft set up for a radar approach the idea was to maintain 150 kts until touchdown. As the Canberra settled onto the runway and aileron control was lost the aircraft veered off onto the grass and headed off towards a line of buildings and trees. So, undercarriage was selected 'up',

the aircraft yawed left, slithered to a stop and was promptly shut down. The pilot received an AFC for his skill. WJ680 flew again in April 1975.

85 Squadron were also involved with 'waving the flag' for the fighters to shoot at, especially on detachments to Cyprus for Armament Practice Camps (APCs). The decision was taken to reduce the Squadron to half strength at the beginning of 1972 and on the 28th January the Squadron moved back to West Raynham to hand half of its aircraft and crews over to form a new 100 Squadron.

All three TF squadrons continued to be shot at by an ever increasing variety of missiles and guns. The overseas APCs, usually to Cyprus or Decimomannu (Sardinia), were looked on as the highlight of the banner-towing calendar. In 1989, 100 Squadron is still involved with APCs for the Phantoms and Tornado F.3s which detach to Cyprus for an intensive air-to-air gunnery programme. Because of the number of APCs it has become a virtual permanent detachment of two-three aircraft and four-five crews at Akrotiri on a rotational basis. Each crew tends to do a six week stint, just long enough to soak up the sun (and a fair bit of Kokinelli). Likewise there is a 'permanent' detachment of groundcrew. The aircrew have their own accommodation block – suitably decorated with squadron symbology – which is the scene of excellent parties.

Opposite: **TT.18 WK143 releasing one of its Rushton targets.** *FR Ltd M2938*

TT.18 WJ639 of 7 Squadron at St Mawgan 1974 showing official Squadron badge - the seven stars of the 'Plough' on a blue disc, on the fin. *S. G. Richards*

Below: **Close up of the Rushton winch pack and target on TT.18 WK123.**

The 'flag' or banner is a 30 ft by 6 ft piece of material with a large black 'aiming' spot on it, the material being held taut and level by a spreader bar. This is attached by a 30 ft strop and 900 ft length of nylon rope to the poor old Canberra. All three 100 Squadron types, B.2/E.15/PR.7, were modified to tow banners; this involved fixing a hook (and strengthening) in the rear of the bomb bay. The banner was laid out on the runway and hooked up to the aircraft. With the banner attached the aircraft was limited to 180 knots. From Akrotiri the Canberra took the banner to the range out over the sea and flew racetracks or figure-eight patterns depending on the firing aircraft and the type of shoot. The Lightnings preferred the figure-eight as they could put two aircraft on the banner at once. Each aircraft used bullets with different colour paint so the holes, if any, could be credited to the right crew! It was generally boring for the nav with two one-and-a-half to two-hour trips a day and very little to do except watch for boats which strayed into the range, it was very much a pilot-orientated task. However, both crew could distinctly hear the fighters on the live runs - the 'vroom-whoosh' of the Phantom gatling gun and the more staccato note of the Lightning cannon.

A figure 7 superimposed on a Rushton target is an early unofficial 7 Squadron marking, seen here on TT.18 WJ715, in 1970.

85 Squadron's 'Farewell to Binbrook' parade, January 1972, includes WH904, WD948, WJ603 and WH670.

Banners were frequently adorned; on a 92 Squadron shoot the banner went off with a painting of a Jaguar on it in 'appreciation' of the recent 92 Squadron 'kill' in Germany. At other times it was adorned with a weird and wonderful assortment of clothing of which the least said the better!

On return to the airfield the Canberra would fly low over one side of the runway and drop the banner which was then recovered by a ground party.

Towards the end of the APC and after they had achieved the required classification scores, some fighter crews flew against 'evasion' banners whereby the Canberra pilot would impart a 'little' movement in the banner and give the fighter a moving target! One way of keeping new navs amused during the shoots was to get them to fill in a stats form of rounds fired by each fighter on each pass. One such nav was made to take the stats to the fighter squadron for the whole of the

detachment - and then they told him it was a wind-up!

Apart from their sojourns in the sun, 100 Squadron crews saw much of Europe with frequent NATO tasking and exercises, plus the ubiquitous Lone Rangers whenever these could be fitted into the hectic schedule. For much of 1973 the Squadron had a hefty commitment of detachments to Lossiemouth as silent targets to help 8 Squadron work up to operational status with its Shackletons.

In mid January 1972, 7 Squadron received six B.2s to help cope with the level of tasking. However, within three years five of these had been declared write-offs because of severe corrosion and so two T.19s were acquired from 85 Squadron when that unit disbanded in 1975. Other aircraft and personnel of 85 Squadron went to 100 Squadron for the move to Marham on 5th January 1976, giving the Squadron a mix of B.2s, T.4s, E.15s and T.19s which it kept until 1980 when the T.19s were taken off strength.

While 85 and 100 Squadron saw most of the SAM and air-to-air work, 7 was much more involved with the Royal Navy. The naval gunnery work was primarily for the 4.5 inch guns which are fitted to most RN warships. For this work the aircraft towed a sleeve target, rather like a large orange windsock, with, usually, an 8,000 ft tow. Up to three days a week were booked by the Navy for this work, almost always in the Wembury Range off the south coast. The guns were not cleared to fire until the Canberra had turned and was going back over the ship. In the 'clear' period they usually managed ten rounds or so.

Regular detachments to Kinloss of two or three aircraft flew target sorties for the Army and RAF Regiment Rapier units during their live firing practices in the Hebrides missile ranges. The target was towed at the end of a 20,000 ft cable, with a standard pattern flown at 1,800 feet giving a target height of 500 feet to simulate low level target aircraft. The same basic pattern was used for night shoots although instead of releasing purple smoke, the target was lit by a flare. Night sorties carried two navigators, one for each winch. Each target had six flares and on one occasion all six were set off in a fireworks display when the aircraft was hit by lightning! This was the most unusual way to lose a target, more common reasons being problems with the winches which involved the cutting of the cable, at other times the targets were actually shot off! The Army was a major user of the Squadron's services in various ranges throughout the UK, especially Salisbury Plain. At weekends the Territorial Army fired its Bofors guns against the towed targets.

The Squadron never really recovered from the serviceability problems as by the mid 1970s the TT.18s were also getting old and worn out. With aircraft away on refurbishment or modification, it was unusual for the Squadron to have more than half its aircraft available.

For a variety of reasons it was decided to disband 7 Squadron and from early 1981 aircraft left to find new homes; some went to FRADU, some went to Samlesbury for storage and six went to join 100 Squadron at Wyton, as did the last T.4. By the middle of December there were no aircraft left and the Squadron disbanded on 7th January 1982.

This gave 100 Squadron yet another boost in size, to which it added five PR.7s from 13 Squadron when that unit disbanded at Wyton in January 1982. This made 100 Squadron one of the largest squadrons in the RAF and gave it a diverse selection of Canberras - each with their own little quirks. Tasking continued, as it still does, at a phenomenal rate. November 1983 was a typical month with 100+ PIs, 22 RN tasks, army tasks, flight checking in Gibraltar, TACEVAL support, banner towing for UK and overseas tasks, AEW Nimrod trials, naval exercises, and Rangers - and this is not an exhaustive list!

The PR.7s retained full PR capability but on a day-to-day basis only the low level oblique cameras were fitted. At first there

7 Squadron TT.18 WJ721 showing the yellow/black 'don't shoot me' stripes.
Max Collier

Like most Canberra squadrons, 100 Squadron kept a T.4 on strength for pilot check rides and continuation training. T.4 WJ880/T is seen here at St Mawgan 1974.
S. G. Richards

was no PR conversion and only E.15 qualified crews flew the PR.7s.

In 1989 100 Squadron was diverse, busy - and content. The roles were varied and crews got a lot of flying and a fair number of detachments.

In September 1991, 100 Squadron began to re-equip with Hawks and were due to have a full UE of twelve by the end of the year. The Hawks will tow the banners for fighter gunnery but cannot operate the podded Rushton winch. The unit's E.15 and two PR.7s were originally slated to go to 360 Squadron but by the end of January 1992 the PR.7s had seemingly transferred to the PRU. The B.2s and TT.18s were withdrawn towards the end of 1991 and early in 1992 were in open storage on the north side of Wyton airfield, being progressively scrapped, due it is believed, to the monitored east-west disarmament programme.

Wiggly Amps

From the mid 1950s Canberras had been used, by 527 Squadron, 'to provide the flying effort required for the air calibration and performance testing of Control and Reporting radar installations in the UK, and when directed for similar installations in 2 ATAF.' This role was taken over by 245 Squadron at Tangmere in August 1958 as part of Signals Command. The 'bread and butter' work was the daily calibration runs in the north and south areas, to ensure that the UK air defence C & R radars were set up. Other calibration duties of radars, communications and IFF were carried out as required by the air defence units, such as Boulmer GCI site, airfields and RN ships, and, later, the Bloodhound SAM sites. When an airfield radar was being calibrated, the normal sortie profile was to fly with a crew of four, pilot and navigator

plus an Air Traffic Controller and a radar controller both of whom would be dropped off at the airfield. The aircraft then flew patterns along particular radials so that the radars could be calibrated. This normally took about four sorties of accurate but boring flying.

In the meantime there were occasional 'good deals' such as a three aircraft detachment to Malta in June 1961 to calibrate the airfield radars. In October the Squadron virtually doubled in size when B Flight was formed with six B.2s from Upwood in readiness for a major new NATO task. At the end of the year the Squadron learnt that it was to carry out a programme of flight checking on the NATO Long Range Early Warning radar chain being built from the North Cape of Norway to Turkey. Mobile first-line servicing team and support teams were organised for operations from FOBs (Forward Operating Bases), while the home base Shorts civilian contract workforce was also increased. The first of the new detachments operated from RNoAF Gardermoen in January-February 1962 to work on the first radar station. The task dragged on until April because of weather and equipment problems, although for 245 Squadron it was an on-off arrangment with a great deal of hanging about. At last the detachment moved on to Skrydstrup in Denmark to calibrate the Danish radar, a task which was completed in June. It was on to Germany next, operating out of Bruggen, for two stations and then back to Bodo, Norway, for a bit more of the Norwegian chain. For the other half of the Squadron back in the UK it was a period of chaos as crews were posted to V-bomber OCUs, at one stage only the CO and one other pilot had been with the Squadron for more than a year. The Squadron was re-united at Tangmere in December for rest and re-equipment ready for the next half of the EW chain in the Near East.

A quick break for Christmas and off to Aviano, Italy and then on to Ankara, Turkey in March. In the midst of this hectic activity came a severe shock. At morning briefing at Tangmere on 19th April 1963 the Station Commander stood up and announced that since 0001 that morning 245 Squadron had ceased to exist! With immediate effect the Squadron was re-numbered as 98 Squadron following the disbandment of that unit as a Thor unit. In March 1963, 98 Squadron received a number of E.15s - which were essentially converted B.15s with an enhanced electronic fit.

The collapse of the Thor organisation brought another squadron number into the Canberra world when 151 Squadron was renumbered 97 Squadron on 25th May 1963. On the 30th the unit's aircraft arrived at Coltishall, a temporary move while the runway at Watton was being resurfaced. The initial UE gave the Squadron one B.6, four B.2s, two Varsities and a Hastings. The Canberras went to 'B' Flight and were soon engaged on similar sorties to her sister squadron. The third crew member was designated 'Spec Op' (Special Operator) and was not carried on all sorties, although the majority required his presence for the specialist equipment used on EW/ECM training.

In February the following year the CO went to the Ministry of Aviation for a conference on flight trials for the T.17, a Canberra mark being developed to fulfil this EW training role.

Above: **100 Squadron E.15 WH972/CM.**

Opposite page: WJ975 as a T.19 of 100 Squadron, at Marham, 8th October 1979.

TT.18 WJ682 at Waddington 17th June 1978 shows the pattern of the diagonal black and yellow stripes.

Below: **100 Squadron's PR.7s were 'picked up' from 13 Squadron when that unit disbanded in 1981. They were later used for general facilities duties rather than recce work. Note the complete lack of underwing markings on WH779/CK.**
S. G. Richards

Bottom: **245 Squadron was one of the Signals Command units involved in radar calibration duties. B.2 WH670 seen here in 1961, finally served with 100 Squadron and when offered for sale in September 1991 had flown 10,003 hours (did any other Canberra exceed this?) Sadly it was scrapped in situ a few weeks later.** *MAP*

Opposite page: **WH642 of 'C' Flight, 151 Squadron, mid-August 1962.** *D. Watkins*

Mod B.6 WH945 of 97 Squadron at Watton, 1966. The squadron re-equipped with Canberras, Hastings and Varsities in May 1963 for 'Special Duties' and ECM training. *MAP*

This view of WK102 shows to good effect the 'lumps and bumps' of the ECM nose of the 360 Squadron T.17.

This page:
T.17 WF890 Marham, July 1969. *P. Birtles*

A fine study of WK162, a 98 Squadron B.2. Note the fuselage legend. *P. March*

Canberra 25th Anniversary at Cottesmore. 360 Squadron T.17s A, B, C, & G in the foreground; visitors in the background.

The decision to produce a dedicated ECM/EW aircraft for RAF and RN tasks led to the concept of a joint-service squadron as both services realised the importance of this type of training for operatonal units. Samlesbury carried out B.2 to T.17 conversions which included bomb bay mods for ECM equipment, new power supplies and a wierd 'lumpy' nose incorporating aerial horns. Twenty-three aircraft were converted but none ever entered service with 97 Squadron. The Squadron continued to have an input into the T.17 programme, including the final acceptance conference in May 1965, but had to make to do with its B.6 and B.2s (B Flight strength was one T.4, one B.6 and five B.2s). Meanwhile, jamming exercises with fighters, especially Lightnings and Sea Vixens, Air Defence and Naval radars continued apace providing one of the best training aids available at the time. Towards the end of the year the facility was extended to the RAFG Lightnings, and Luftwaffe F-104s on an opportunity basis. Nothing concentrates the fighter pilot's mind like having his lovely radar tracking picture wiped out by jamming! The Soviet capability in this field meant that such training for all NATO units required even greater resources than were, or are, available.

In September 1966 there was a big ceremony at Watton when Air Chief Marshal the Earl of Bandon presented standards to 97, 98 and 115 Squadrons. The sad part was that within two weeks 97 Squadron lost its Canberra flight to the newly formed 360 Squadron.

360 Squadron was the outcome of the idea of a joint-service squadron and was joint funded and manned by RAF and RN personnel, the latter having a 25% 'share'- and providing every fourth CO.

The Squadron formed at Watton on 1st April 1966 to operate 'in the ECM role in the UK' with plans for a second similar squadron, 361 Squadron, to form at Watton and deploy to the Far East. 361 duly formed on 2nd January 1967 but never received any aircraft. From February the aircrew flew sorties with 360 squadron aircraft and in May the CO of 361 assumed responsibility for administration and the engineers took over the servicing of some of the 360 Squadron aircraft. The Squadron disbanded on 14th July 1967, a casualty of the accelerated withdrawal from the Far East.

Although formed in January, the 'Joint RAF/RN Trials and Training Squadron' was not confirmed as 360 Squadron until September, with 831 Squadron as Naval element.

The same month, on the 19th, the prototype T.17, WJ977, arrived on the Squadron for EW trials but was gone again within a few days. Planned delivery of T.17s slipped again and it was then that 360 took over the aircraft and duties of 'B' Flight 97 Squadron, in October, using seven B.2s and a B.6. The first Squadron T.17 eventually arrived in December and by July strength was fourteen T.17s and 360 was in full swing as one of the most in demand of RAF units. The main role for the Squadron was, and is, providing EW environment training for air, sea and land units. In essence this means making life as difficult as possible for the GCI controller of the fighter pilot by jamming radar and communications and by spoofing. Jamming by electronic means, active radar jammers, or by dropping chaff makes it far harder to locate and track the target aircraft so that other techniques have to be developed.

One of the best angles from which to view the Canberra, here T.17 WF916.

T.17 WD955 at Cottesmore in May 1974. 360 Squadron was at Cottesmore from March 1969 to August 1975 when the unit moved to its current home, Wyton. Note the stylized '360' over a flash, on the fin.

The ability to operate in an EW environment is vital - even more so in the 1990s than in the 1960s. At times Squadron observers flew in the Lightnings to assess the effect of the particular types of jamming and to try and devise improvements in equipment and techniques for both 'hunter' and 'hunted'. Demand was such that detachments were sent to Europe and the Med on ECM training tasks. On exercises Squadron aircraft often provided ECM screening for the attacking recce and strike Canberras, a service much appreciated by the recipients and the cause of much frustration to the air defence units.

The joint RAF/RN aircrew complement is evident on the occasion of Sqn Ldr Mike Phillips' last sortie on 360 Sqn, in a T.4, 23rd July 1982. *via Tony Close*

T.17A WH646 of 360 Squadron, Wyton caught at St Mawgan, April 1987, in the new hemp scheme. *R. C. B.Ashworth*

And so the task continued, the Squadron operated from Cottesmore from April 1969 until August 1975 and then moved to its present location, Wyton. Continual improvements were made to the EW fit of the aircraft to keep pace with developments in air defence systems and aircraft and thus ensure continued training value.

While very few Canberra marks have been thought of as comfortable, the T.17 together with the T.4 is certainly the least comfortable. With so much equipment on board and two crew in the rear compartment area it is very crowded and at times very hot. For the nav it was a case of getting the Specialist Operator to the task area and bringing him back again at the end. The most interesting jobs were usually those which involved manufacturers trials.

The T.17 has now appeared in a new guise as the T.17A with an updated set of ECM equipment and a new paint scheme of hemp. In 1989, the job had not changed at all but as 'enemy' kit had become more sophisticated and with greater ECCM capability too, the kit of the 'Spoofer' had to be improved or training value greatly reduced. With its new electronic fit the 360 Squadron Canberras are quite capable of going on for another 15 years.

Conclusions

This 'post Bomber Command' period has already covered some 25 years, a time when the Canberra was finally withdrawn from overseas service and from front-line service, a time when the adaptability of the airframe led to numerous conversions into specialist roles.

In the late 1980s there were still some 60 Canberras in RAF service performing a wide range of support and trials roles. RAF Canberras are still seen worldwide and will continue to be so until the late 1990s when the last of the Canberra Squadrons is due to disband. What more fitting tribute could there be to the excellence of the design than the celebration of the types 40 year 'Jubilee' anniversary in May 1989.

A 'Golden' Anniversary perhaps?

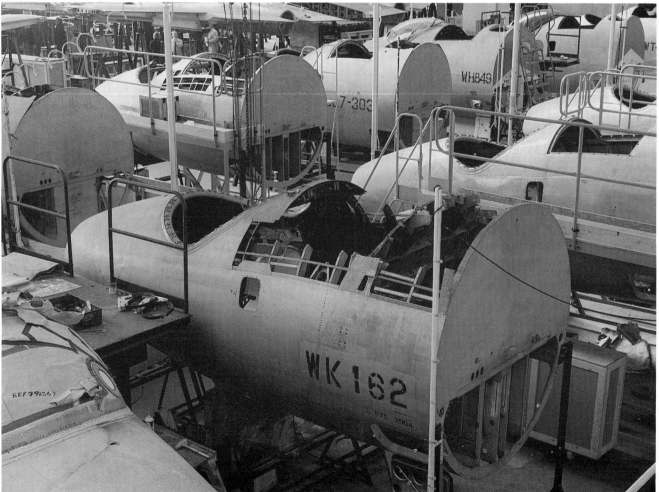

Chapter Seven

Canberra International

The Canberra was a great export success and also has the distinction of being one of the few British aircraft designs to be adopted by the United States. Canberras have been used by fourteen foreign air forces, seeing active service in many parts of the world, and this does not include the US and Pakistan who used the Martin B-57 Canberra. Over the years these sales have been worth some £80 million, much of it coming from the sale of refurbished RAF aircraft. Canberra sales fall into two categories: first, those nations which bought the aircraft soon after its entry into RAF service and who wanted it as a conventional medium level bomber; and, second, those nations that saw the appeal of the aircraft in the late 1960s and early 1970s as a COIN (Counter Insurgency) aircraft capable of carrying a large and varied weapons load.

Much interest was generated in the early years by the tours of RAF Canberras to various parts of the world, with the express purpose of public relations (showing the flag) and promoting sales interest. A classic example of this was the tour of South America in October 1952 when no opportunity was lost to display the aircraft to the full and to give rides to senior military and government officials. In other cases, such as Sweden, an interest was expressed by the 'buyer' so the RAF flew an aircraft out for the potential customer to take a closer look at it. The same policy prevails today with the Tornado putting on finery and visiting potential customers. With the run-down of RAF Canberra strength came the option for nations to buy refurbished ex RAF aircraft, possibly modified slightly to suit user needs. This brought jet interdictor/bomber aircraft within the budget of many nations and it was an area of sales that BAC/BAe exploited. The BAC Canberra brochure of that era makes interesting reading: a modified extract appears overleaf.

New Canberras for old. These views of the BAC workshops at Samlesbury show how busy the Canberra market was as 'new' marks were created and export versions completed. The views opposite are circa 1977, whilst that below was taken in 1970. *BAC via B. Robertson*

The Canberra today . . .

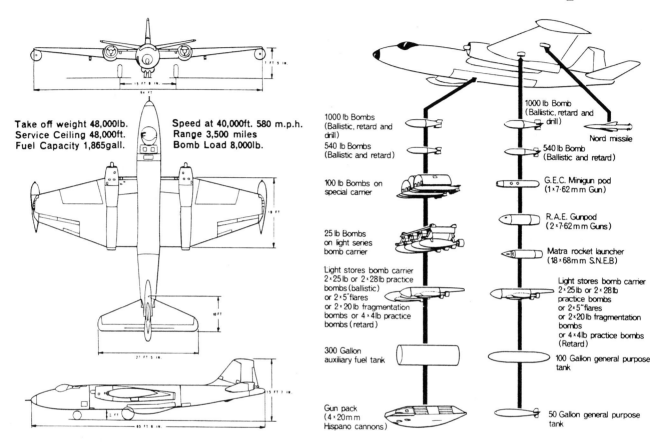

Take off weight 48,000lb.
Service Ceiling 48,000ft.
Fuel Capacity 1,865gall.

Speed at 40,000ft. 580 m.p.h.
Range 3,500 miles
Bomb Load 8,000lb.

1000 lb Bombs (Ballistic, retard and drill)

540 lb Bombs (Ballistic and retard)

100 lb Bombs on special carrier

25 lb Bombs on light series bomb carrier

Light stores bomb carrier 2×25 lb or 2×28lb practice bombs (ballistic) or 2×5″flares or 2×20 lb fragmentation bombs or 4×4lb practice bombs (retard)

300 Gallon auxiliary fuel tank

Gun pack (4×20mm Hispano cannons)

1000 lb Bomb (Ballistic, retard and drill)

Nord missile

540 lb Bomb (Ballistic and retard)

G.E.C. Minigun pod (1×7·62mm Gun)

R.A.E. Gunpod (2×7·62mm Guns)

Matra rocket launcher (18×68mm S.N.E.B)

Light stores bomb carrier 2×25 lb or 2×28lb practice bombs or 2×5″flares or 2×20 lb fragmentation bombs or 4×4lb practice bombs (Retard)

100 Gallon general purpose tank

50 Gallon general purpose tank

The Canberra has proved an outstandingly successful military aircraft and is in use today on tactical bombing, day-and-night interdiction, counter-insurgency and various anti-personnel missions, as well as photo-reconnaissance, pilot training and target towing duties.

New marks, constructed during refurbishing of B.2s have recently entered RAF service for special duties in operational roles extending throughout the 1970s, and other refurbished marks have entered service with two new air forces, bringing to sixteen the number of countries now flying this highly versatile aeroplane.

Its continued use on operational duties for many years is thus assured.

Although no longer in continuous production, Canberras released from operational service in the RAF are being rebuilt in the original BAC production factories for export with a renewed operational life.

Performance

The performance and capabilities of the Canberra adequately match the requirements of present day counter-insurgency operations and the more sophisticated missions of modern 'brush fire' actions.

Continuous development has given the aircraft a very powerful low-level strike capability, using guns, rockets and retarded bombs in combination up to an 8,000 lb load. Long range at high weapon loads makes the Canberra particularly suitable for internal security roles by allowing adequate time to be spent over the target area for search and positive identification before making the attack. Ease of handling and excellent manoeuvrability facilitate flying at low level over difficult terrain and permit a high degree of accuracy in delivery. The Canberra also has the merit of low vulnerability to retaliatory ground fire during low-level attack.

When equipped with the latest series bombsight, using Doppler input, an 8,000 lb bomb load can be delivered accurately from high level to distant targets using cruise climb techniques to obtain maximum range.

An economical interdictor reconnaissance bomber — for use through the 1970's

Typical Weapon Loads

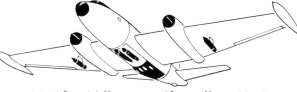

Internal: Gunpack 4x20mm cannons 4 Flares or 100 on special carrier
External: 36 SNEB 68mm rockets

Internal: 6 Ballistic or 4 Retarded bombs
External: 36 SNEB 68mm rockets 2 Nord missiles

Internal: 24x4lb Practice bombs, retarded or 12x5" Flares
or 12x20lb Fragmentation bombs or 12x25lb Practice bombs, ballistic
or 12x28lb Practice bombs, ballistic
External: 2 Ballistic or 2 Retarded bombs

Internal: 6 Ballistic or 4 Retarded bombs
External: 2 Ballistic or 2 Retarded bombs

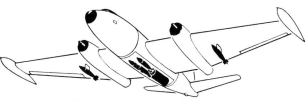

Internal: 3 Ballistic or 2 Retarded bombs 300 Gallon auxiliary fuel tank
External: 2 Ballistic or 2 Retarded bombs

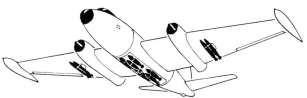

Internal: 6 Ballistic or 4 Retarded bombs
External: 4 Reconnaissance flares

Left and above:
Part of the Canberra brochure of the early 1970s (rearranged to fit our format).

Below: **The first Argentina B.62 carries the British Civil Registration it wore for the 1970 Farnborough Air Show.** *BAC/AW/1303m*

Four Canberra Mk.20s of No.1(B) Sqn RAAF, on exercise at Darwin, mid 1955. They include A84-207, 209 and 208. *via R. Bonser*

Argentina

The Fuerza Aerea Argentina was late to join the Canberra owners club but like half of the club its Canberras have seen active service. The decision was taken to equip No.1 Escuadron de Bombardeo of Grupo 2 de Bombardeo, part of 11 Brigada Aerea, at General Justo Jose de Urquiza airfield, with refurbished ex RAF Canberras. The initial order was for six B.62 (B.2) bombers and two T.64 (T.4) trainers. The bomber order was increased to ten and deliveries began in November 1970, with the first three aircraft delivered on the 16th of that month. The remainder were delivered in batches as they became available and the order was completed on 9th September 1971. One aircraft, B-103 (ex WJ713) was written off 22nd November 1971 but otherwise the FAA seemed to settle down well with the new type. Most initial training was done in the UK at 231 OCU, including weapons training.

Argentina was one of the nations which went for the appeal of the aircraft as a multi role aircraft, for its capability as a bomber in the event of any external trouble and for its suitability as a COIN aircraft in the event of internal disturbances. Like all other South American users, Argentina has kept details of its Canberra operations classified. However, over the years the aircraft have received variations to their weapons capability and the addition of simple EW systems. It is possible that the aircraft have been used on internal 'security' operations during the periods of unrest in Argentina. Chile has always been perceived as the main 'external' enemy and the Canberras were no doubt allocated targets in Chile as part of the overall air plans. The best documented operational use of the aircraft was during the Falklands conflict when small formations of Canberras, sometimes escorted by Mirages, made a number of attacks on the RN Task Force and on the land forces in the final stages of the battle. Grupo 2 Canberras deployed to the naval base at Trelew and flew their first combat sorties on 1st May 1982. Later on they operated out of Rio Gallegos having positioned there from Trelew for each mission.

The original operational concept was for hi-lo-hi missions to suit the Canberra's range and its vulnerability, the crews were in no doubt as to the threat posed by the various elements of the Task Force. By late April the Squadron was in place at Trelew with six B.62s and the two T.64s and, in common with the rest of the FAA, at a high state of readiness. There have been suggestions that Canberra missions were mounted over South Georgia at the end of April but the first confirmed operational sorties by FAA Canberras took place on 1st May with two three-aircraft missions being launched. The first had an uneventful shipping search while trying to carry out their orders to locate and attack British shipping. However, the second raid was picked up on radar and was intercepted by a flight of Sea Harriers. Having made their initial approach at high level, the Canberras had descended low over the sea and were running in below 100 ft under a layer of cloud. The Sea Harriers closed in and one Canberra (B-110) was hit by an AIM-9L and crashed into the sea with the loss of both of the crew. The aircraft was shot down by Lieutenant Curtis in Sea Harrier XZ451. A second aircraft was engaged but reports vary on the outcome of the AIM-9L launch, some sources claim that the missile missed the aircraft while others state that it hit the Canberra on the wing but that the aircraft, although damaged, was able to make it back to the mainland.

After this disastrous start it was decided to abandon the day low level shipping strikes and the Canberras had a quiet war until a new profile was introduced for high-level night bombing of troop positions on the islands. The first such raid took place on 29th May with blind-bombing, normally under the control of the Stanley CIC radar, of pre-determined target areas around San Carlos. There were also night low level missions and flying around the islands at 100 ft at night was certainly looked on as hazardous! Although not achieving many direct results these night missions brought some success in disturbing the rest of the British troops – no-one likes to have 1,000 lb bombs dropping on them from the night sky. The only proven Canberra success was an anti-shipping sortie on 8th June when two aircraft attacked the tanker *Hercules* to the north of the islands. One bomb hit the ship but failed to explode; however, the ship was later scuttled.

A second Canberra was lost late in the conflict to a surface-to-air missile fired by one of the Task Force ships and a recent article has been published which is an account by the pilot of this Canberra.

On Sunday 13th June a number of Canberras were detached to Rio Gallegos on standby to fly night supporting missions for the troops defending Port Stanley (Peurto Argentino). On receipt of the tasking order, two B.62s were readied for action as were two Mirage IIIEAs which were to act as fighter escort. The Canberras took off around 9pm and set course for Mount Kent, climbing to 36,000 ft. Some while later the Mirages took off to rendezvous with the bombers over the Falklands. The Mirages held steady some 30 kms behind the bombers while the latter positioned to the south of Mount Kent for the bomb run from 36,000 ft. Both aircraft ran in and dropped their loads, with unknown results, and made a 180 turn to escape the area. Just after the escape turn the lead aircraft (B-108) was hit by a SAM, probably a Sea Dart fired by HMS *Exeter* . . . 'a tremendous explosion, followed by an extremely violent jolt. The missile had hit

the lower front section of the fuselage and the effects were immediately felt: cockpit explosive decompression, tail elevator broken, and the No.1 fuel tank on fire.' The pilot did his best to control the aircraft, reduce speed and prevent a spin and as the aircraft passed 13,000 ft ordered the navigator to eject. With no response and the aircraft passing 7,000 ft he himself ejected. He was eventually picked up by a British helicopter and was repatriated at the end of the conflict. His had been the last FAA sortie of the war.

The Squadron had lost two aircraft during its thirty-five operational sorties, twenty-five of which were at night, with a total ordnance drop of 100,000 lbs of bombs. Two additional aircraft had been ordered (a B.92, ex WH914 and a T.94 ex XH583) from BAe in 1981 but were not delivered prior to the conflict and conversion by BAe had barely started.

The FAA lost another aircraft in an accident in August 1982 thus reducing the Canberra fleet to about five B.62s and two T.64s. The remaining aircraft are still in operational service but their limitations in the face of sophisticated weapons systems has been shown and post-war improvements were made to the ECM fit which up until then had comprised a simple chaff/flare dispenser and underwing ECM pod.

Australia

Australia was one of only two nations to licence-build the Canberra, the other being the United States. The Australian market had been targeted as a possible from early on, partly because they had the same desire to replace ageing Lincoln bombers as the did the RAF. Some commentators have even suggested that the decision to name the A1, 'Canberra', was to 'encourage' the Australian government to buy the aircraft. Interest was expressed as early as 1949 and by 1951 firm plans were in hand for Australia to build B.2s at the Government Aircraft Factory (GAF) at Fisherman's Bend, Melbourne. It was intended to build the basic B.2 but give it wing integral fuel and improved navigation kit and designated Mk.20. Two B.2s

B.62 B-108 of Argentine Air Force (FAA), seen at Warton 1971. This was the second Canberra to be lost during the Falklands conflict when it was brought down on a high level night bombing sortie. *P. A. Tomlin*

(WD939 and WD983) were purchased as training aircraft and re-serialled A84-307 and A84-125 respectively.

A84-307, flown by an Australian crew, set up an unofficial record for the fastest jet aircraft time England to Australia, flying the 10,200 miles from Lyneham to Darwin in just 21 hours flying time, arriving on 5th August 1951. The B.2 with its silver finish and black fin was the centre of attention on its arrival and was met by a crowd of dignitaries including the Prime Minister. The press were kept a respectable distance back and very few details were released about the aircraft. A84-125 arrived on 16th March 1952 and in a little more than a year the first GAF built aircraft was flying, A84-201 making its first flight from the company airfield at Avalon on 29th May 1953. This aircraft, and the second production example, were entered in the 1953 New Zealand Air Race. A84-201 came second in the speed section to one of the RAF PR.3s.

The first twenty-seven aircraft produced were similar to the RAF B.2s with Avon 101 engines, but all subsequent aircraft were given Avon 109s and were, therefore, more like the B.6. All were designated Mk.20 in RAAF service.

Production was serialled A84-201 to A84-248, the last aircraft made its first flight on 2nd July 1958 and was delivered on 30th September. The factory then produced seven T.4 variants, designated Mk.21, by converting five of its own Mk.20s plus the original two B.2s. The five converted Mk.21s were A84-201/3/4/5/6, all of these being completed between June 1958 and October 1959. Two additional T.4s (WT491 - A84-501 and WT492 - A84-502) were acquired direct from the UK in mid 1956, for conversion training.

In 1953 the first two Lincoln squadrons, 2 Squadron and 6 Squadron, re-equipped with Mk.20s at Amberley, followed by 1 squadron which re-equipped in July 1958. All three squadrons had the same primary role of light bomber but also carried out PR and various other duties. Ten years later the Australian Canberras were in action in one of the most remarkable scenarios in which Canberras have ever been involved. As early as 1962 Australia had been involved with the situation in Vietnam and had sent in a team of military advisers. The scale of involvement, as with the US forces, increased as the problem grew worse and by 1965 Australian ground troops were in action. On 22nd December 1966 the decision was announced to 'deploy to South Vietnam a squadron of eight Canberra bomber aircraft. These will be positioned to operate in support of our ground forces.'

On 19th April 1967 2 Squadron flew its aircraft to Phan Rang, 150 miles NE of Saigon, to operate alongside two squadrons of B-57s. Four days later the Squadron flew its first ops with eight aircraft, at hourly intervals, attacking targets with 500 lb bombs. The Squadron was tasked to provide eight aircraft in every 24-hour period, seven days a week for operations in any of the four Corps areas. The first day, 23rd April went as planned with the Boss, Wing Commander V. J. Hill, first away to attack a VC supply dump and camp in the south of the Mekong Delta. 2 Squadron was in business!

Initially, missions were restricted to 'Combat Sky Spots' (CSS) where the Canberras would bomb from high level on direction from a ground radar site – shades of TDP in Malaya? During the first full month of ops, the Squadron attacked 400 targets, often in support of the Australian Task Force – with an accuracy that became the envy of their American counterparts.

The Squadron commander was in favour of tactical work for his Squadron in co-operation with ground or airborne FACs and in September permission was given for these 'Boomer' missions. Initial bomb damage assessments gave a 100% hit rate and feedback from the ground troops was all in favour of this very visible form of air support. From mid November about half of the Squadron workload was daylight FAC work.

Top: **WD939 flew out to Australia as A84-307 in August 1951, to be used as a training aircraft for the RAAF.** *J. D. R. Rawlings*

Above: **Canberra Mk.20 A84-228 of No.2 Sqn RAAF, at Singapore 13th October 1961.** *C. T. Cunningham via C. J. Salter*

Above: **Licence built Canberra Mk.20 A84-218 of No.1(B) OCU, seen at Avalon, March 1968.** *MAP*

Conversion to Canberras began in 1953 when 2 Squadron gave up its Lincolns. This 2 Squadron line-up is at Butterworth, Malaysia in November 1966. *R. Walker*

In the period up to December, the Squadron flew nearly 2,000 sorties against more than 3,000 targets, thanks to a very high serviceability rate (about 97%!), a tribute to the groundcrew. The other 2 Squadron speciality was accuracy, any bombing error of greater than 60 yards was looked into in detail and if put down to an equipment problem was rectified immediately. This attention to detail gave the Squadron an error average that was envy of the other attack squadrons and made them very popular with the ground forces! They were the only level bombing squadron in the operational area and this ability to drop accurately from a low, level pass meant that 2 Squadron could operate under very low cloud bases that often prevented the US attack aircraft from getting into the target area. However, whenever possible bombing was done from 3,000 ft to negate the problem of ground small arms fire. One of the most frequent damage repairs done by the groundcrew was on fragmentation damage from the aircraft's own 500 lb or 750 lb bombs. Wing Commander Evans, the CO, explained other advantages of the Canberra: 'Whereas the fighters can spend only about 15 minutes over a target we can hang about for about an hour and a half. It gives the Forward Air Controller time to have a look for another worthwhile target in the area. The FAC's have often expressed amazement that we can stick around so long. We prefer to bomb from 3,000 ft but about 20% of our daylight missions are being flown to a minimum of 1,000 ft. FACs, flying in unarmed single engined Bird Dogs mark targets with smoke and direct the attacks. When possible they follow up the raid with an on-the-spot bomb damage assessment.'

The Squadron took part in the major defence and break-out from Khe Sanh and in countering the Tet offensive in the Mekong Delta. From early 1970 the Canberras began interdiction of lines of communication in the northern part of South Vietnam, mainly against the winding road through A Shan Valley.

Such intensive operations were bound to incur losses. On the night of 3rd November 1970, A84-231 failed to return from a ground support mission, after a successful bomb run radio contact was lost.

The CO, Wing Commander J. Downing, and his navigator, Flight Lieutenant A. Pinches, settled into their bomb run on a target in the north of the country on 14th March 1971. The navigator saw a SAM pass close to the aircraft and moments later there was a tremendous explosion and the aircraft went out of control (it was probably an SA-2 Guideline missile, the commonest in service with the Communist forces, although a number of SA-3 Goa systems were also used). A quick Mayday call and both crewmen ejected, landing safely in the jungle but separated by the dense undergrowth. Next day both were rescued by an American 'Dustoff' helicopter.

Operations continued unabated, but with a healthy respect for those areas protected by SAM systems, until 9th May 1971 when the Squadron made its last series of raids prior to withdrawal. The last bomb went on A84-244 and carried the words:
'76389th and Last Bomb
Compliments to 'Charlie'
From No.2 Squadron
RAAF UC Dai Loi'
In June the Squadron said farewell to Vietnam and returned to Amberley. In a few short years they had established an outstanding reputation for themselves and for the Canberra.

The same year, 1 Squadron and 6 Squadron re-equipped with F-4s and 2 Squadron, as the sole remaining Canberra unit, became a target-tow, recce and general purpose unit. It was like rolling the RAF's 100 Squadron, 39 Squadron and 7 Squadron into one and crews certainly had a very varied life. Norman Gray was a nav on the Squadron from 1975 to 1981 and he remembers the frequent detachments – some good and some not so good. One of the best was the Indonesian survey, *Gading V*, in 1976: . . . 'We were based at Kemojan airport in Jakarta and had a floor of a downtown hotel for our three-month stay. The detachment consisted of two aircraft with crews, who changed twice during the period, plus seventeen groundcrew. The job was survey of Sumatra and the daily routine pleasant . . . depart the hotel at 0530 for a met brief and flight planning session at 0600. One aircraft would launch at about 7 o'clock and be back about 11 and, unless the weather was so good that a second sortie was of benefit, that was it – back to the hotel for lunch and a lazy afternoon around the pool!'

Above: **Mk.20 of 2 Squadron during the Vietnam period. Good shot of the wing tip bomb pylon unique to RAAF Canberras.** *RAAF*

Below: **A84-229 at Oshkosh in August 1991; wearing US civil marks N229CA (at fin root) - the result of an exchange that saw a Ventura go to the RAAF Museum.** *J.M.G.Gradige*

A84-226, of No.1(B) Sqn RAAF, Amberley, Queensland, April 1965. *via R. Bonser*

'The target-towing job could be almost as good . . .'the Squadron was responsible for both towing targets for air-to-air gunnery and for acting as a radar target. In both cases we deployed to the appropriate fighter base and operated from there. The two main bases for this were Williamstown, New South Wales and Butterworth, Malaya. A normal deployment was three crews to fly a total of eight sorties a day. The Butterworth deployment was a 3-4 week stint with all the delights of Penang and the surrounding area.'

During his five and a half years on the Squadron, Norman cannot recall more than a month or so when the whole Squadron was together at Amberley.

2 Squadron performed this wide range of roles until mid 1982 when these duties were taken over by modern 'executive-jet' type aircraft.

Chile
Chile is the most recent nation to receive Canberras and a certain amount of mystery surrounds the acquisition of the aircraft. On 15th October 1982 three PR.9s, ex 39 Squadron aircraft which had been stored at St.Athan since the disbandment of that Squadron in May 1982, were flown out of RAF Wyton by Chilean crews, escorted by the Fuerza Aerea Nacional de Chile's Boeing 707. These aircraft, XH167, XH166 and XH173 were intended to enhance the PR capability of the Chilean Air Force and enable Chile to keep a close eye on Argentinian activity. Conversion to the aircraft was supervised by aircrew of 39 Squadron/No.1 PRU in order to put across both the limitations and capability of the PR.9. Very little is known about the use of these aircraft in Chile although border surveillance using the stand-off oblique cameras is no doubt the primary task. One aircraft has been lost in a flying accident and although the cause has not been announced early indications are of aircrew error.

Ecuador
In May 1954 Ecuador ordered six new B.6s to equip a light bomber squadron, Escuadron de Bombardeo 2123, at Quito. Deliveries started in early 1955, in pairs, with aircraft serialled BE-801 to BE-806. In the early 1960s the aircraft were re-serialled, details of which are in the appendices.

The aircraft had a very unremarkable career with the Fuerza Aerea Ecuatoriana but have performed a wide range of duties including, in the early 1970s, providing fast-jet training for pilots for the twelve Jaguars acquired by the FAE. By 1979-80, only three of the Canberras were still in active service, having been back to BAC at least once for refurbishment. One aircraft en route to the UK had to force land in Ireland and later continued its journey by sea. In 1981 the three remaining aircraft were phased out of service and put into store.

Ethiopia
Ethiopia was one of those nations which saw the appeal of the Canberra as a COIN type aircraft in the late 1960s and decided to buy four refurbished ex RAF B.2s. These aircraft, designated B.52, were all delivered in the latter half of 1968, serialled 351 to 354. It was originally anticipated that the Imperial Ethiopian Air Force would want a further six to eight aircraft to form a full squadron but no further orders materialised. It was not a happy association. There were frequent aircraft problems, including reports of at least two wheels-up landings causing airframe damage which, because of poor technical back-up, may have rendered the aircraft unusable. A somewhat turbulent political situation did little to ease the situation and one aircraft was lost when a pilot defected to a neighbouring country. The fate of the remaining aircraft is not known although a recent defence analysis suggested that both were still operating although this seems a little unlikely.

France
One of only three European buyers of the Canberra, France, like the other two customers, saw the Canberra as a useful trials and testbed aircraft. Four B.6s and two B(I)6s were ordered in 1954 and the first three were aircraft originally destined for the RAF but diverted to meet the overseas order (F763 started as WJ763, F779 as WJ779 and F784 as WJ784). The remaining three aircraft were straight off the production line, F304, F316 and F318, although the last two were to B(I)6 standard. The order was complete by 1955 and the aircraft began an interesting and varied life with military and civil trials units.

In February 1956 one aircraft was fitted with a Turbomeca Gabizo reheated turbojet of 2,400 lb st under the fuselage. Generally, the aircraft were used for high altitude experimental work and weapons testing. In the latter role extensive use was made of Canberras to test the Aerospatiale series of air-to-surface missiles such as the AS.12 and AS.30, with aircraft operating from Colomb-Bechar (in Algeria) and Cazaux. F316 was first used as a radar testbed and in this capacity undertook development work on AI Thomson/CSF Cyrano AI and various missile radars. It then went to Cazaux for use by the 'Armes et Engins' section on missile testing, primarily for the development of the Matra 530 and Super 530 AAMs. F304 was, like F316, used for radar development before being retired in 1972. F763 also operated out of Cazaux but as a calibration aircraft for the range at Landes. F779, which was later fitted with a Mk.8 nose, spent the whole of its working life at Cazaux as a missile platform for the Nord missile series AS.12, AS.20 and AS.30 but also took part in the Matra 530 trials. However, F784 was based at Bretigny and used principally as an equipment testing aircraft.

Chile received three PR.9s in late 1982, including '341' (ex XH166). One has since been lost in a flying accident. *via S. Scott*

Below left: FAE B.6 BE-805 made an unscheduled visit to Ballykelly, en route to BAC for refurbishing, 1962. *R. C. B. Ashworth*

Lower left: B.52 351 of the Ethiopian Air Force, one of only four refurbished ex RAF B.2s bought by Ethiopia in 1968.

Below right: B.6 F763/AM was ex RAF WJ763.

Lower right: Close-up of Matra R.530 AAM on underwing pylon of F779 (ex WJ779).

Bottom: F316 was one of six Canberras used by France's CEV on equipment and weapons trials at Cazaux. Other aircraft on the ramp include WGAF F-104, KE508. *via French Embassy*

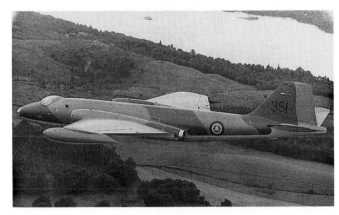

India

The Indian Air Force has been far and away the largest foreign user of the Canberra with over 100 aircraft acquired since 1958 and utilized in the full range, except nuclear, of Canberra roles.

An initial order was placed in 1957 for 80 aircraft, valued at £20 million (roughly 1.25 Tornados at current prices), consisting of 65 B(I)58s, equivalent to the B(I)8, eight PR.57s, equivalent to the PR.7, and seven T.54s, equivalent to the T.4. Although the aircraft were basically the same as their RAF equivalents there were a number of modifications, including autopilot, improved nav kit, radio altimeter and such like — items which RAF crews would have liked on their own aircraft. The first deliveries were made in April 1957 and the first of the bomber squadrons, No.5 Squadron, equipped in 1958, followed in 1959 by the other two bomber squadrons, 16 Squadron and 35 Squadron. Two of these light bomber squadrons still operate the B(I)58. No.106 Squadron formed with PR.57s towards the end of 1959 and about eight of these aircraft were still in use with the PR unit in 1987 operating from Agra, about 100 miles south of Delhi.

The final squadron to form, No.6 Squadron, had an unusual role for the Canberra, that of maritime support and anti-shipping. Most military experts now agree that the best way of attacking ships is with stand-off missiles but 6 squadron still operates in this role from Pune near Bombay, although IAF Jaguars are now taking on the anti-shipping role.

To maintain front-line strength, further orders were placed during the 1960s and 1970s. The simplest way to cover this is to list the deliveries as far as is known: 1963 - six B(I)58s and one T.4 (September).

A pristine pair of Indian AF B(I)58s on test from Warton. *EE Co AW/FA/166*

PR.57 IP991, the IAF PR.7 variant, seen at Woolsington in 1958. *MAP*

1964 - two PR.57s ex RAF PR.7s WT506 and WT528. 1965/66 - three T.4s ordered but only one delivered. 1969 - ten B.66s (ex RAF B.15/B.16s) ordered in October and delivered the following year. 1970 - eight B(I)12s and two T.13s bought from the RNZAF. (October) 1971 - two PR.57s. 1975 - six T.4s, delivered between June/September.

IAF B.66 F1028 on test out of Warton.
BAC AW/FA 595

B(I)58 IF976 of the Indian AF is similar to the RAF B(I)8. In 1957 India placed an order for 80 Canberras, by far the largest single overseas order. Additional orders have taken the total to over 100 aircraft of various marks.

The trainers were originally operated by an OCU at Agra but the remaining aircraft are probably held on individual squadron inventories.

Apart from owning one of the largest collections of Canberras, the IAF has also seen active service with these aircraft on more than one occasion, in 1961 in the Congo and then in the India-Pakistan wars of 1965 and 1971. The latter are also noteworthy as being the only Canberra v Canberra wars, the PAF being an operator of the B-57 Canberra.

The IAF converted a number of its T.4s into TT.18 equivalents under the title TT.418, although they are also referenced as TT.18s. In recent years India has been trying to re-equip its Canberra and Hunter squadrons and to this end is now a major user of Soviet aircraft. In the first instance Jaguar aircraft were acquired in limited numbers to replace Hunters and B(I)58s of 5 Squadron (1981) whilst HAL (Hindustan Aeronautics Ltd) has been manufacturing Jaguars to re-equip other squadrons, including 16 Squadron. The maritime strike Canberras of 6 Squadron were being joined (1987) by a flight of Sea Eagle equipped Maritime Jaguars. The Canberra will continue to serve the IAF into the next decade with 106 Squadron and 35 Squadron, the latter in the ECM role.

Indian Air Force Congo Operations
Following the very sudden granting of independence from Belgium in 1960, the newly-formed Congolese Central Government faced a rebellion in the mineral-rich province of Katanga which had declared itself independent. With revolt spreading and attacks being made on European property the Government called for United Nations assistance. The UN then called on member states to provide military forces and India responded with troops and aircraft. Hunters were at first considered because of the UN directive not to carry or drop bombs. However, Canberras were chosen and No.5 ('Tuskers') Squadron was sent with their B(I)58s, which were better than Hunters in that they carried four 20 mm cannon with 525 rounds per gun, had a longer endurance and, most importantly, had a navigator to find targets in the remote areas where operations were likely to take place. Six aircraft, plus support personnel, arrived at Leopoldsville in October 1961 as part of the UN force which included Ethiopian F-86 Sabres, Swedish Saab J.29s and a variety of transport aircraft.

As the only long range offensive aircraft available, it was not long before 5 Squadron was called on to make a series of decisive attacks. In early December the six Canberras, operating in pairs, made attacks on the rebel airstrip at Kolwezi and on Katangese troop concentrations in the

surrounding area. The effects were devastating. Wing Commander Suares led the pair attacking the airstrip:

'I took out the light aircraft with my 20 mm cannon on the first low level pass whilst Flight Lieutenant P. Gautan, flying the second Canberra, destroyed the Fouga Magister. We made a rapid turn and, on my second pass, I concentrated on the heavy transports and the control tower. During the second run I saw that we had stirred up a hornets nest of activity. Katangese soldiers were running about everywhere, and scores of muzzle flashes told me that we were flying through a curtain of bullets. On the third and final pass I saw that all the parked aircraft and the control tower were ablaze, so we both hammered away at the stacked fuel barrels, the adjacent hangars and the buildings.'

Back to base at Kamina airfield for a QTR (Quick Turn Round) and off to Kolwezi again:

'On my first pass I flew low over the bulk petrol stores without firing . . . I turned around for a second pass, firing a one-second burst. Since our cannon shells were loaded alternately with high explosive and incendiary shells, only one hit was needed to 'whoosh' off the entire line of storage tanks. On the third pass I concentrated on anything that had survived the previous attacks. As before, we were flying through an angry hail of small arms fire, and as I pulled up I heard the ominous bang as my

PR.57 P1099 (also wearing manufacturers flight test registration G27-184) at Samlesbury 1971. Note the ex 213 Squadron B(I)6s in the background.
BAe AW 31348

aircraft was hit in the nose area. My navigator was struck in the upper thigh. I pulled up through cloud and set course for Kamina, set the controls to automatic and climbed down and forward to render first aid.'

This is a classic account of this type of mission and it highlights the significant danger of small-arms fire, plus one of the more unusual advantages of an autopilot.

From then on, into January, it was intensive operations with armed reconnaissance, interdiction of supply routes and CAS, often with the help of ground FACs. The fire support given by the Squadron was also a major factor in the battle for Elizabethville. From mid January 1962 activity reduced and photo-reconnaissance became the main role until the Squadron returned to India a few weeks later.

IAF Canberras were back in action the following year during the little known 'Security action' entitled operation *Vijay* in Goa. Aircraft from 35 and 16 Squadrons made a number of raids on 18th December 1961 dropping 1,000 lb bombs. It was decisive and the armed resistance was ended.

IAF Canberras took part in the United Nations action in the Congo. Here, IF898, a B(I)58 of 5 Squadron flies over Kolwezi. 'Tuskers' provided the teeth of the air element to support Indian ground forces.

India-Pakistan Wars

When war broke out between India and Pakistan on 6th September 1965 it became the first conflict in which both sides used Canberras. Both sides of the war are considered here rather than split consideration of operations into two sections. Most detailed reports are from the PAF side as the IAF maintains a tight security regarding its operational strength and capability.

At the start of the war the IAF had approximately fifty-three B(I)58s and seven PR.57s operational and the PAF some twenty-five B-57 Canberras, including a few recce types. The autumn war followed a minor conflict which had broken out in disputed Kashmir in February-April of the same year.

IAF Canberras were probably involved in ground support missions in the week leading up to the full blown war from 6th September. From then on, the Canberras of both sides were involved with interdiction, CAS and recce tasks. The PAF concept of employment was 'harassment of enemy air bases carried out by single bomber raids repeated a number of times every night to keep the enemy's air bases under constant air attack alerts.' Thus began a series of raids against each others airfields, night interdiction, or more correctly – Counter Air, an excellent role for the Canberra. For the PAF the list of targets included airfields at Pathankot, Adampur, Halwara, Ambala and Jamnagar, with a standard tactic being four aircraft against each airfield at 5-10 minute intervals to cause the maximum disruption. Bomb delivery was from a pull up to 12,000 ft then into a shallow dive to pull out at about 6,000 ft. Daylight strikes were a little trickier and approaches were made at 200 ft with 'skip' bombing being a favourite technique against heavily defended targets such as Ambala.

The night of 6th September was typical of the pattern and started with the order for as many B-57s as possible to deploy to Peshawar for operations. Two waves of three aircraft each were tasked against Jamnagar airfield, routing along the coastline at 200 feet and descending even lower on approach to avoid radar detection. All pulled up to and dived on the target to release their 4,000 lb bomb load. Throughout the night a 'shuttle' of raids by single aircraft was maintained – one aircraft failed to return. A similar raid by four aircraft went in against Adampur airfield whilst five aircraft, led by Wing Commander Akhtar, attacked Pathankot airfield. In his account he recalls the inbound route flown at 250 feet by the light of a newish moon followed by the pull up to 7,000 ft and the dive on the target (at the airfield beacon which had been left on!) ... 'Heavy AAA lit up the target and I aimed along the runway towards the centre. I released my bombs at about 3,000 ft and all eight dropped. From there I didn't pull up but carried on diving at about 360 kts to exit low level at around 400 kts.'

The B-57s also went after other targets such as bridges and radar sites. 14 Squadron operating from East Pakistan also made a number of Counter Air strikes, including one very succesful strike on 7th September against the airfield at Kalaikunda. They found fourteen Canberras and a number of Hunters on the ground and claimed ten Canberras destroyed and others damaged. A second raid on the same target did not go so well and one aircraft was shot down.

A total of 195 B-57 missions were flown of which all but twenty were against airfields or radar installations. The pace of operations had reduced after the hectic first night but the 'standard' targets were attacked on an almost nightly basis. One of the most daring raids was that against the IAF Canberra airfield at Ambala – deep in Indian territory. A mission on 8th September was aborted when the aircraft failed to find the target but a pair on 18th September was more successful. Squadron Leader Najeeb Khan flew the lead aircraft ... 'On our first run in I released the four 1,000 lb bombs from the fuselage bomb bay, without apparent results, and the second time I dropped the wing bombs. The results were fairly discourag-ing with very little to show for our attacks; we subsequently discovered that our bombs were skipping much further than we had anticipated. In fact they seemed to bounce like tennis balls!'

Meanwhile, the IAF Canberras were doing exactly the same thing carrying out day and night raids on airfields with one to ten aircraft on each raid. The Squadrons from Agra went in at high level to bomb Rawalpindi and Sargodha which were defended by F-104s and the results were poor. The Indian Canberras attacked PAF airfields on all but three nights of the war but results were very variable. One attack by a single aircraft against Peshawar on 13th September went very well, the aircraft approached at low level and then pulled up to 2,000 ft over the runway to drop its 4,000 lb bomb near a large group of B-57s. The latter were very lucky to escape with light damage having been sheltered by a small building. Daylight strikes were often escorted by Gnats, usually against high value targets such as radar stations. One such raid on 21st September against the radars at Badin caused serious damage to the site, the attacking aircraft having plastered the area with 4,000 lb bombs, RPs and 20 mm cannon fire.

The PAF also operated an ELINT unit, 24 Squadron, using two RB-57Bs and an RB-57F to monitor and fix radar sites and at times to home attacking forces onto such sites. The RB-57F was modified to carry and drop a 4,000 lb bomb from 67,000 ft (!), a role which was practised but not used operationally.

The overall effectiveness of the Canberras of both sides in the conflict is hard to assess as details are still very limited. During the war the PAF lost four B-57s, including one RB-57B (11th September shot down in error by own AAA near Rahwali). IAF losses are not known but PAF claims include kills by F-86 (15th September) and F-104 (21st September) as well as AAA units.

The 14-day war of 1971 started with a PAF air strike on 3rd December which brought a rapid response from the Canberras of 5 Squadron 'Tuskers' who mounted night sorties on the first three nights of the war. This was followed by inderdiction and CAS missions against a wide range of targets with the Canberra once more proving both its accuracy and resilience to ground fire. It was a very inconclusive conflict which ended as rapidly as it began.

The US arms embargo had affected the spares situation for the B-57s and only some 15 aircraft were available. Nevertheless these aircraft carried out an intensive interdiction campaign against a string of IAF airfields. Losses have not been documented but various references speak of six crews lost over enemy airfields plus an RB-57 destroyed in a hangar at Masroor (5th December), one shot down by a Mirage (4th December) and one brought down by the Sargodha (PAF) AAA (5th December). IAF missions followed a similar pattern but there are no details of losses.

Iraq

In August 1959 the sale of of eight to ten Canberras to Iraq was authorised. The proposal was for servicing to be done by the Indian Air Force, at least in the early years, and in July 1960 an IAF technical team visited Iraq. The sale fell through following a coup which brought an anti-British regime to power.

New Zealand

The Royal New Zealand Air Force (RNZAF) was unique in that it acquired a squadron of Canberras on loan from the RAF. As part of the Commonwealth Strategic Reserve, No.75 Squadron formed in August 1958 operated from Tengah with fifteen B.2s during the period of *Confrontation*, working very closely with its RAF counterparts. The operational involvement was very similar to that of 45 Squadron with day and night sorties, singleton and formation.

In early 1962, 75 Squadron handed back its B.2s and returned to its old home base at Ohakea where it took over a number of Vampires and Canberras and operated as the Bomber OCU.

In February 1958 the RNZAF placed an order for eleven aircraft comprising nine B(I)12s, equivalent to the B(I)8 but with an autopilot and modified nav kit much like the IAF aircraft, and two T.13s, equivalent to the T.4. The first B(I)12 was actually B(I)8 WT329 destined for the RAF but sidetracked and re-serialled NZ6101, the remainder, including an order for a further two B(I)12s, were new aircraft off the production line and were serialled NZ6102-6111. The two T.13s were serialled NZ6151 and 6152 respectively, the first was a new aircraft and the second an ex-RAF T.4, WE190.

The aircraft were destined to equip 14 Squadron and the first four aircraft arrived in October 1959, followed by two more in December and the remaining one early in 1960. Delays in delivery of the T.13s led to the hire of two T.4s from the RAF, WJ859 and WJ864, which were collected from Australia in February 1960. NZ6101 crashed during an air display at Christchurch on 2nd November 1960 and NZ6104 crashed into the sea off Singapore in November 1964.

From November 1959 to February 1960 the Squadron acted as the BOCU until, on 1st March, it was re-activated as a light bomber/interdictor unit, receiving its first aircraft on 1st May. Then began a round of tours of New Zealand showing off the new aircraft, whilst at the same time working up to operational status. The Squadron had to use Vampires for RP training as the B(I)12s did not become RP capable until December 1961. Trials then began with two pylon-mounted Microcell glass fibre rocket launchers with 37 rockets each. Gradually the Squadron achieved operational status in all its roles, including anti-

shipping, and took part in deployment exercises to Singapore as part of the Commonwealth reinforcement. A typical anti-shipping exercise often started with a call to arms from a maritime Sunderland which had located the 'enemy' shipping. Directed to the area by the Sunderland, the Canberra would position itself for a low level RP strike.

It was generally agreed that such exercises were great fun as long as you took care to avoid the various aerials and other appendages which sprouted from most ships!

The T.13s eventually arrived in early

Above: **T.13 NZ6152 at Ohakea, November 1970. The polished surface of the engine nacelle is blackened by the starter cartridge exhaust.** *RNZAF G3/5096*

Opposite, from the top: **B.2 WF915 of 75 Squadron, 1959, wearing standard squadron markings of a Kiwi superimposed on a map of New Zealand. (This aircraft crashed in the Malayan jungle in October 1961.)** *Chris Salter collection*

As part of the Commonwealth Strategic Reserve, 75 Sqn RNZAF was equipped with RAF B.2s, including WH666, on a loan basis.

B(I)12s of 14 Squadron RNZAF in company with B.15s of 73 Squadron RAF over Malaya. All remaining RNZAF Canberras were sold to India in 1970.

1962, NZ6151 in February and NZ6152 in April, and the RAF T.4s were returned to the UK.

The OCU was incorporated into 14 Squadron as 'C' flight in October 1962, giving a strength of ten B(I)12s and two T.13s. Two years later they were given camouflage paint schemes ready for deployment to the operational theatre. In September 1964 the Squadron moved to Singapore on armed standby because of the *Confrontation* with Indonesia (see Chapter 5), and the following month went to the forward base at Labuan in Borneo. They were back at Tengah a week later, some said because of the political sensitivity of having an RNZAF squadron in the 'front line'. 14 Squadron stayed in the FEAF area until the end of

Confrontation and in March 1965 moved to Butterworth. The final month was a sad one as NZ6104 crashed during a low level RP attack at China Rock range. After 18 months at Butterworth the Squadron left to return to Ohakea 1966.

Back in New Zealand, the Squadron continued its training as before but the decision had been taken to phase out the Canberras, which duly took place in July 1970.

The remaining aircraft were offered for sale and were bought as a 'job lot' by the Indian Air Force. Eight B(I)12s and two T.13s were duly transferred in November 1970.

During its years of service, the B(I)12 was liked by the aircrew for its good all round performance, the visibility (for the pilot) and the 'punch' of the cannon and RPs. As a way of life it was as attractive as it was to (most) RAF crews, for instance, the final trip on the OCU ... 'Final trip was to Fiji, hotel and other expenses paid, out Friday and back Sunday. All we had to do was get there, refuel and service the aircraft, stay out of trouble and get back!' On the Squadron there was the usual list of Lone Rangers, the favourite destinations being Hong Kong and the Phillipines.

Peru

The Fuerza Aerea del Peru was another of the early customers with an order for eight B(I)8s in November 1955, with the first aircraft being delivered in May the following year. As was common practice, the first four aircraft were diverted from RAF deliveries to meet overseas customers orders as quickly as possible. These first

four 474 (WT343), 475 (WT348), 476 (WT367) and 478 (XH206) were followed by four aircraft off the production line, 479-482. One aircraft, 479, was written off soon after arrival (23rd September) and a second, unknown aircraft on 11th June 1959. The remaining six were reserialled in 1960 and a replacement bought in 1960 joined the same serial list, 206-212. 210 crashed 8th April 1963 and 207 8th February 1972.

Another order was placed for delivery in 1966 and comprised six refurbished ex RAF B.2s (WJ974, WJ976, WK112, WH726, WH868 and WE120), serialled 233-238, and delivered as B.72s, and two refurbished T.4s (WH659 and WJ860), serialled 231-232, all the aircraft having been refurbished by BAC.

The FAP equipped two Canberra squadrons as part of Grupo de Bombardeo 21 at Jorge Chavez International Airport, Lima, although they also operated from Limatombo.

Despite the apparently high accident rate of the B(I)8s, the FAP was happy with its Canberras. A further order was placed in 1968 for three B.56s (ex RAF B.6s) and three B(I)56s (re-worked ex RAF B.6s). This order was followed by a single T.4 in 1973 and a batch of B(I)68s ordered in 1973. The latter comprised eleven ex RAF aircraft converted by Marshalls, deliveries commenced in March 1975 with the last aircraft, ex-XM278, being delivered in July 1978 via Tenerife.

In December 1991 five B(I)12s were purchased from the SAAF to supplement an estimated fifteen Canberras still remaining in service.

B.56 240 (G27-97) for FAP, Warton 1969. Note the ASM under the wing – Peruvian Canberras were equipped with a wide range of weapons options. *BAC/AW/24136*

The Canberra remains in operational service as an important element in the front-line strength of the FAP. As with all the South American users, information on aircraft employment and strength is hard to come by. However, it seems likely that the aircraft's roles include COIN, for which a wide range of weapons are available, and strategic bomber. The former is almost certainly the most important of the two and squadron training is said to concentrate on this role.

Rhodesia/Zimbabwe

In 1957 the Royal Rhodesian Air Force (RRAF) ordered eighteen Canberras as part of the Federal Empire Defence commitment. This order consisted of three T.4s and fifteen B.2s, the T.4s being B.2 airframes fitted with new T.4 nose sections by the RAF MU at Samlesbury. All aircraft were taken from RAF stocks and the first sixteen Rhodesian crews were trained at Bassingbourne by 231 OCU, with a planned output of four crews a month.

The first four aircraft flew in formation over Salisbury before landing at New Sarum and 5 Squadron formally came into being on 13th April 1959. The original intention had been to form two (5 and 6 Squadron) high altitude bomber squadrons but in the event only 5 Squadron operated the Canberra. The aircraft were painted silver overall with Federal markings and serial numbers RRAF159 to RRAF176 were allocated.

Although the aircraft were intended as high altitude bombers, the RRAF approached English Electric shortly after the aircraft were delivered with a request for the installation of rocket rails on the aircraft belly behind the nose wheel bay. The response was that the fuselage was not stressed for this installation, which would invalidate the aircraft warranty. The result of this response was that the modification was designed and installed by the RRAF at New Sarum.

A pair of RRAF Canberras being bombed up. Both wear the early silver scheme and RRAF markings.

The first long flight was made in September 1959, when six aircraft had a one month detachment operating with the RAF Canberra wing at Akrotiri, Cyprus. In the early 1960s an increased emphasis on counter-insurgency operations led to further use of rockets, together with the development of a bomb box which was carried in the bomb bay and contained a large number of 20 lb fragmentation bombs.

1961 saw two further detachments to the Middle East with two aircraft going to Aden and two to Bahrein. On these detachments they operated with 8 Squadron, RAF on Operation *Sea Sheik*. The first Canberra accident occured during the same year when RRAF171 landed wheels-up – the aircraft was repaired however and continued in service until it was written-off on 20th

October 1969. 1963 was an eventful year, a new serial number system was introduced whereby aircraft serial number was derived from the primary role of the type rather than a simple sequential listing. Thus, bombers received the RRAF 200 block, with the B.2 aircraft becoming RRAF200 to RRAF214, while the T.4s became RRAF215 to RRAF217. No.5 Squadron took part in another detachment to the Middle East during which it won the Middle East Bombing Trophy, against stiff opposition from the RAF Canberra units.

The year also saw the end of the Central African Federation. As part of the dissolution exercise, the aircraft of the RRAF were shared between that force and the new Zambian Air Force. The majority of the aircraft, including the Canberras, remained in Rhodesia and the national markings changed from the three assegais of Federation on RAF Type D roundels to a single large assegai on a Type C roundel. At the same time, a dark earth / dark green camouflage was applied.

The Rhodesians announced UDI on the 11th November 1965 and by early 1966 the United Nations had applied comprehensive mandatory sanctions against Rhodesia – one result of which was the loss of 25 Avon engines which were in the UK for overhaul at the time.

In 1967 the first major terrorist incursions took place across the *Zambesi* from Zambia and into the Zambesi Escarpment of Rhodesia. No.5 Squadron's Canberras were involved in anti-terrorist operations (Operation *Nickel* and Operation *Cauldron*). The range of the aircraft was further enhanced in 1968 with the fitting of two additional bomb bay fuel tanks. One widely reported operation at this time was the elimination of terrorist training camps in Zambia. A Rhodesian Hunter circled over the principal Zambian Air Force base and challenged any ZAF aircraft to move (non did) while the Canberras dealt with the terrorist camps.

Not all the Squadron's tasks were so warlike. One ongoing task was the systematic aerial survey of Rhodesia, part of the country was photographed each year and the whole country re-photographed every five years. The aircraft also flew lifesaving courier missions, a typical one being a flight to Johannesburg to collect serum for the treatment of a man who had been bitten by a rare type of snake.

Prior to UDI, all jet engine overhauls were done in the UK, however, sanctions meant that the Rhodesian Air Force had to become self sufficient. The challenge was met and by 1970 all major Avon overhauls, a 1000 man-hour task, were carried out at New Sarum. Another local improvisation was starting the engines using compressed air to turn the engine to self-sustaining RPM – a much cheaper method than using the starter cartridges at $10 a time (an air start was about 30c!).

Rhodesia declared itself a Republic in 1970, the national markings became a green roundel with a white centre containing a gold lion holding an elephant's tusk, a green/white/green fin flash and the serial number prefix changed from RRAF to R.

1971 saw the harmonisation of the low level bomb sights, which eliminate the need for calibration bombing with a subsequent saving in time and bombs (and improved accuracy). This system was used to good effect in 1972 during Operation *Hurricane* when the Squadron made daily armed flights over the operational area. By the end of the seventies, eight aircraft were grounded due to various major structural problems. The most common was the 'Frame 21' defect and the grounded aircraft were cannibalised to produce three additional aircraft (R2516, R2158 and R2519). The latter was unique in that it had a solid nose cone, locally produced and with three optical flat panels as stocks of the normal perspex nose had run out.

The Canberras continued in service throughout the bush war and it is a tribute to the strength of the airframe that, although numbers became much depleted, there is no record of any aircraft being brought down by the terrorist forces. The war finally ended in 1979 and Rhodesia became Zimbabwe in April 1980, when the national markings became a yellow Zimbabwe bird carried only on the fin, the R prefix being deleted from the serial number at the same time. Two further Canberras (2250 and 2215) were obtained, both being ex RAF (delivered from Marham on 25th March 1981) and both remaining in RAF camouflage. They were grounded by 1986 and the story of the Canberras of Rhodesia and Zimbabwe came to a close in September 1987 when the surviving aircraft were offered for sale by public tender in Harare.

Much of the above section was contributed by aviation historian Neil Gaunt, an ex-Rhodesian Canberra technician.

RRAF B.2 in dark camouflage – note the 'unofficial' rocket rails under the nose.
via A. Thomas

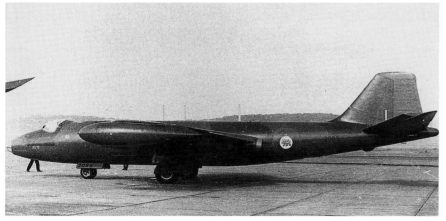

Originally WJ571, this is camouflaged Rhodesian AF B.2 2085 at Durban, 1970.

South Africa

The South African Air Force (SAAF) ordered six B(I)12s in 1961, the last of these, serial 456, was the last production Canberra. Deliveries began the following year to the newly re-formed 12 Squadron at Waterkloof. Three ex RAF T.4s (WJ991, WJ864 and WJ617) were ordered early in 1963, making the highest trainer : operational Canberra ratio of any air force! The first two aircraft were delivered on 30th September 1963. All deliveries were complete by the end of 1964 and the Squadron declared operational in the interdiction and PR roles.

All aircraft started with an all-over silver paint scheme, with the T.4s also having high visibilty dayglo bands. However, in the mid 1970s the B(I)12s were repainted in PRU blue, with the T.4s receiving the same treatment in 1978.

Details of operational service are sparse due to the anti-guerilla ops undertaken by the SAAF, but it is certain that 12 Squadron's Canberras have played their part. As with the RRAF the Canberra proved an excellent workhorse in the anti-guerilla environment where its range, payload and survivability made it a better low level attack aircraft than lighter or more sophisticated aircraft. SAAF Canberras have been used on many cross-border missions to strike at the guerilla training camps in the neighbouring 'front-line' states of Namibia and Angola; the stealthy approach and massive firepower proving of great value, although one was lost when the pilot was killed by ground fire.

The five surviving B(I)12s were modernised in 1987/88 to provide improved weapons payload and delivery accuracy. The Canberras were placed in storage in 1990 and five B(I)12s were sold to Peru in December 1991.

Above: **Rhodesian Air Force B.2 of 5 Squadron in the late 1970s. Note the lack of markings.** *via A. Thomas*

Below: **B(I)12 453 of 12 Squadron SAAF at Pretoria, February 1970. SAAF B(I)12, 456, was the last production Canberra.**

Bottom: **Three B(I)12s and a T.4 of SAAF 12 Squadron during the 30th anniversary flypast. Aircraft carry virtually no markings other than a small three-number black code on the rear fuselage.** *SAAF photo*

Sweden

Sweden signed a contract for two ex RAF B.2s in 1959 at a cost of £100,000 each, to include the training of two pilots and four technicians. They were designated Tp52 (Transport Aircraft 52), WH711, serialled 52001 arrived on 1st February 1960 and WH905, serialled 52002, on 5th March 1960. Stationed at the F8 wing at Barkaby, near Stockholm, both were involved with research duties of various kinds and as electronic intelligence platforms. Both made their last flights on 23rd January 1973, 52001 is preserved in a private museum and 52002 in the Flygvapen-museum at Malmen. The latter aircraft logged nearly 1400 hours in Swedish service.

Venezuela

The first overseas sale of Canberras was made to the Fuerza Aerea Venezolana, which was to become the major operator of the type in South America with marks fulfilling bomber, interdictor and recce roles. In January 1953 an order was placed for six B.2s and the first aircraft, 1A-39,

arrived at Maracay 1st April 1953 flown in by an RAF crew. Beamont used this aircraft to fly a number of displays on the first two days of the month. The rest of the deliveries were made by civilian crews of 'Silver City Airways', as well as 12 Squadron crews from Binbrook. Early 1957 brought another order, for eight B(I)8s and two T.4s, all of which had been delivered by February 1958. A third large order, the first for refurbished aircraft, was placed for twelve B.2s and two PR.3s. Aircraft were sent back to Samlesbury for refurbishment at various times but in 1978 the FAV started small-scale modifications, radio and armament, on its own aircraft.

Below: **B(I)8 4B-39 for Venezuela on test from Warton.** *Flight 35290s*

Bottom left: **Venezuelan B.2 1339, ex WH649, is seen at Warton around 1966.**

Bottom right: **Sweden operated two ex RAF Canberras in the ELINT/SIGINT role. Tp 52001 was ex RAF B.2 WH711. It was retired in January 1973, to a private museum.**

The Canberras equipped two squadrons, Esc 38 and Esc 39, of Grupo de Bombardeo 13 at Barcelona.

Other orders were placed and existing aircraft converted over the years until the FAV inventory had no less than seven marks in service: B.2, B(I)88, T.4, T.84, B.82, B(I)82 and PR.3/PR.83 - in reality, variations on the B.2, PR.3, T.4 and B(I)8. They were equipped with the full range of air to ground weapons including ASMs.

Over the years at least nine aircraft have been lost and at one stage in the late 1970s the FAV requested the services of an RAF QFI and navigator for a few months to have a look at the training routine and suggest improvements in any problem areas. In 1986 an RAF PR.9 on survey duties in the Caribbean paid a courtesy visit to Barcelona to celebrate the FAV's long association with the Canberra.

Grupo de Bombardeo 13 finally withdrew its remaining seven B.82s, one PR.83, two T.84s and one B(I)88 late in 1990. The Canberras had been well liked by crews, who found them excellent low level aircraft for their primary roles of interdiction and CAS.

Wearing the third of its series of four codings (not including the original RAF serial), D-9569 gets airborne from Filton in September 1975. *Austin Brown*

FAV B.82 1233 at Greenham Common, 1979. *R. Bonser*

West Germany bought three Canberras for trials and experimental work in 1961. One of them, 99+36, has been stuck on a pylon at Sinsheim since 1984.

The other two aircraft, in a rather fetching brick-red (orange) colour scheme, were fitted with a package of high-grade cameras in the bomb bay for survey photography and oblique surveillance work. Fitted out to German standards of nav kit and instruments, they were most 'un-Canberra' like in their interior appearance, with neat panels of modern instrumentation and no Canberra 'smell' (it is noticeable that most aircraft have a distictive 'smell' to the interior and the Canberra most certainly has!)

The aircraft reverted to Luftwaffe markings in 1977 - few aircraft have ever been re-serialled so often - but the crews were still civilian, mainly ex Luftwaffe. 99+36 has been on static display at Sinsheim since 1984. The orange Canberras have been fairly frequent visitors to the UK and have been seen at a good many air shows. One Canberra is reported to have made a belly landing during 1991. TT.18 WK123 (ex 100 Squadron) was delivered to MilGeoAmt Ingolstadt on 8th January 1992 as a spares source and its wings had been fitted to 99+34 by July 1992.

A summary of the aircraft produced and/or remanufactured for overseas users, is included in an Appendix.

West Germany

Germany, like France, acquired the Canberra purely as a trials and experimental aircraft. Three refurbished ex RAF aircraft, WK130, WK137 and WK138, were delivered to Erprobungstelle 61, based at Oberpfaffenhofen near Munich, in 1961 after overhaul and modification by Marshalls. The aircraft then had an interesting and varied career and no less than four changes of serial numbers! These aircraft were initially employed on target-towing duties; they moved to Manching in October 1966.

The Canberras were transferred to the West German Defence Ministry, in civil markings, and then two were loaned to the Military Geographic Service. One served with DFVLR, the German Aerospace Research Institute, for high altitude calibration duties, work connected with microwave and infra-red radiometry and recovery and test of rocket payloads.

Chapter Eight

B-57 Canberra - The American Angle

One of the greatest achievements of the Canberra was that it broke into the American market! It then proved as popular with crews and as versatile in its uses as it did in RAF service, seeing operational service during the Vietnam war.

The stalwart tactical bombers of the Second World War, such as the B-26 Invader, were by 1950 in urgent need of replacement and the USAF were as embarrassed for modern aircraft in the Korean War as were the other Western nations. As a result of these problems a committee was formed to evaluate all British, American and Canadian aircraft that roughly met the specifications for a new night interdictor bomber. A further proviso was that it had to come from an existing design because of the time scale. The list eventually comprised the Martin XB-51, of which there were two flying, the North American B-45 Tornado, already in service with Tactical Air Command, the North American AJ-1 Savage, already in Fleet service, the CF-100 Canuck from Avro Canada and the English Electric Canberra.

Evaluation teams toured the companies in the late summer of 1950 to obtain initial assessments. A team led by Brigadier-General Albert Boyd, Air Materiel Command, visited the UK in August-September and Beamont flew a snappy display for them at the USAF MU at RAF Burtonwood on 17th August. The team moved to Warton in September to observe flight trials and look at the aircraft in more detail. At the end they pronounced themselves impressed and thought the aircraft suitable for three USAF roles: all-weather fighter; TR aircraft; and, medium to high altitude short-range bomber. In essence it was an aircraft the Americans found hard to classify as it was too large to be a fighter and to small to be even a 'light' bomber. This, added to the general American reluctance to buy anything foreign, meant that the Canberra would have an uphill struggle.

A 'fly-off' contest planned for November was delayed until the following February as this was the first date that the Canberra would be available. The committee reported in December 1950 that both the Canberra and the XB-51 were suitable for the USAF requirement and proposed that sufficient Canberras be bought to equip two light bombardment groups until sufficient XB-51s were available, at which point they would replace the Canberras. Detailed negotiations took place and enquiries made as to English Electric's ability to supply up to 300 aircraft off the production line. The answer was a reserved yes as it would inevitably affect the rate of deliveries to the RAF at a crucial phase in the build up of the new bomber wings. They were costed at $1,474,000 apiece, to be delivered to RAF standard although this would involve substantial re-working to bring them to USAF standard before entry into service; for instance, the addition of forward armament, a new bombing system and flight instruments.

However, English Electric agreed to authorise licence production, probably the only workable solution in the circumstances. It also meant that redesign work could be done to incorporate USAF requirements at the production stage. The Glenn Martin company agreed to carry out the contract and the design was given the designation B-57 Canberra.

In the meantime, WD932, a production aircraft, was flown to Andrews AFB, Washington, on 21st February by an RAF crew. This, the first direct jet crossing of the Atlantic, brought yet another distance/speed record for the Canberra. Beamont took over the aircraft the next day ready for the fly-off on 26th February.

The 'rules' stated that each aircraft had a ten minute slot for a routine to include a tight turn in each direction, slow speed and high speed runs and a short-field landing. While some pilots were worried about completing the sequence in the specified time, Beamont had decided to complete the sequence quickly and then 'improvise' for his remaining three or four minutes! Although some of the entrants had the edge over the Canberra in specific areas, for example the XB-51 was 100 kts faster, they were all totally outclassed by the agile performance of the English Electric aircraft.

The short-field landing went slightly wrong when the tyres burst on the grit-covered ice of the runway but the aircraft came to a stop with no damage.

The decision was announced soon after: 'The Canberra comes closest to fulfilling the night interdictor profile because of its excellent characteristics of endurance, range, manoeuvrability and the visibility provided from the nose section.'

The official promulgation was made on 23rd March 1951 and Glenn Martin received a contract for 250 B-57A Canberras for the night interdictor bomber role. It was specified that all licence-built aircraft should be called Canberra but over the years this was forgotten or ignored. The decision made, the pace increased and detailed production plans made. Five sub-contractors were signed up to produce over half of the components, including a licence-built version of the 7,200 lb st Sapphire - the J65 Sapphire to be built by the Wright Aeronautical Corporation.

The first drawings arrived in June and were promptly redrawn to reflect the design changes and American measurements. WD932 was delivered to the Martin works in Maryland as a pattern aircraft and trials platform. The designers were already looking to the future and proposed a 'super Canberra', a swept-wing high subsonic aircraft incorporating features of the Canberra and the XB-51, although this came to nothing.

Meanwhile, WD932 was bought and another B.2, WD940, arrived in September, having captured the Aldergrove-Gander record en route. It retained its RAF markings for about a year until re-serialled '117352' (actually the 17,352nd aircraft purchase allocated in the 1951 fiscal year). WD932 also retained RAF markings never getting its '51-17387' serial as it crashed on 21st December 1951 during a trial. This accident was caused by wing structural failure and was one argument used in the case put forward by certain Air Force circles to either change the structural design or give up on the Canberra.

About the same time a design change was made which would have appealed to many RAF crews - the navigator's position was moved out of its 'black hole' and into tandem with the pilot under an enlarged bubble canopy. The main reason for the change was the perceived unsuitability of the standard Canberra for ground-attack work because of restricted visibility for the pilot and distortion of the gunsight, problems which the new layout removed. Furthermore, the navigator was able to see out! Other changes included improved avionics plus waist-fuselage airbrakes in place of the wing airbrakes.

WD940 being used by Martin as the B-57 Canberra pattern aircraft (51-17352) at Baltimore, 1951. *GLM Co P46380*

B.2 WD932 which Beamont flew in the February 1951 'fly-off' to decide which of the contending aircraft was to be awarded the USAF contract. The aircraft was later bought by Martin as one of the pattern aircraft. *GLM Co P40837*

WD940 was given the new cockpit lay-out for detailed design consideration but it never flew again and was later scrapped. The new layout was designated B-57B and the changes were incorporated in the already running production line after completion of the B-57A and RB-57A series. The first B-57A made its first flight on 20th July 1953 and was handed over on 20th August. Like its RAF counterpart, the B-57 Canberra rapidly became a multi-role design and this was reflected in the production contracts placed with Martin. The original contract was for 177 aircraft and this was followed in 1953 by a more detailed set of orders for thirty-eight B-57C dual control aircraft, 258 B-57Bs, of which forty were built as B-57Ds. The final order came in the 1955 budget for sixty-eight B-57E target tow aircraft. With overlapping and superceding orders the final production run was 403 aircraft in six different variations. Production was complete by February 1957 but over the years aircraft were uprated and modified although not to the same extent that the RAF modified and re-modified its Canberras! With the B-57G, the Canberra was at last given the range of sensors and weapons it truly needed to fulfil the night interdictor/intruder role.

Another design feature that would have been useful in the RAF interdictor versions was the rotating bomb bay, which was excellent for use with LABS as it allowed a high entry speed into the manouevre, whereas RAF aircraft were limited by the speed restrictions of the bomb doors. The only RAF aircraft to have a similar rotating bomb bay development was the Buc-caneer, in the late 1950s. Another change was the addition of eight fifty-calibre M-3 machine guns in the wings, a standard American fit which was more convenient than the RAF interdictor gun pack but nothing like as potent. From production aircraft ninety-one onwards, however, the machine guns were replaced by a pair of 20 mm M-39 cannon in each wing.

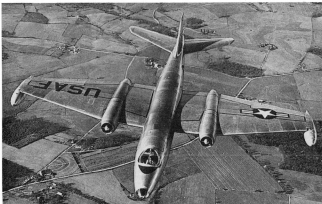

Top: **The huge production facility for B-57s at the Maryland factory.** *GLM Co P50220 via Bruce Robertson*

Above left: **B-57A in polished metal finish.**

Above right: **Line-up of RB-57As including 52-1435/36/38 and 42.** *GLM Co P50312*

The B-57A had so few changes from the basic Canberra that it was only two years before the first aircraft took to the air, handling and behaving just like its counterpart. Only eight B-57As came off the production line, the major batch of these early aircraft, sixty-seven total, being modified during production into RB-57A recce aircraft. It was these aircraft that went into service first, equipping the 363rd Tactical Recce Wing at Shaw AFB, South Carolina from 1954. The same year the first bomber unit, 345th Bomb Group, started its work up, at first with a number of RB-57As for type conversion and then receiving its B-57Bs. Two further recce units formed in Europe, the 10th and 66th TRWs, in the mid 1950s, each receiving a limited number of RB-57As.

However, the first unit to be fully B-57 equipped was the 461st BG(tactical) at Hill AFB. Entry into service accelerated as units around the world re-equipped, the 38th BG in France and the 3rd BG in Japan made up the total of four Bomber Groups, all having traded-in their outdated B-26 Invaders.

The RB-57A was powered by two 7220 lb st Wright YJ65-W-1 jet engines, similar in performance to the B.2 Avons but with a different contour giving a pronounced bulge in the forward part of the engine.

By 1958 all three operational units had said goodbye to their RB-57As in favour of other types. The aircraft went to the ANG units or, in some instances, went to civilian and Government test agencies.

The 'OCU' duties for the BGs were performed by the 3510th Combat Crew Training Wing at Randolph AFB, Texas which was one of the first units to acquire the trainer variant. The operational units sent batches of aircrew to Randolph for conversion training. The crews from 3rd BG ferried aircraft back to Japan after the course - the ferry flight itself being quite an achievement, including a five hour thirty minute leg to Hawaii. There were four more legs before the aircraft arrived at Johnson AB near Tokyo.

Above: **An excellent underside view of the B-57A showing the rotary bomb bay.** *GLM Co P51137R*

Below: **B-57B 53-3958 of 501st TBS, 345th TBW – the first unit to receive this night intruder model.** *MAP*

Bottom: **RB-57B 52-1580 'G' of 71st BS, based at Laon in France but seen here at Kastrup, in Denmark, 1957.** *MAP*

It was then a similar pattern of work to that of the Bomber Command squadrons with exercises and tours. The B-57s often took the part of the 'enemy' and caused great difficulties to the defenders.

It was a fairly short-lived world-wide establishment as by 1958 the B-57s had been withdrawn from Europe, although the 345th deployed to Turkey in the latter half of the year during a crisis in Lebanon. This unit later moved to Japan but disbanded in June 1959 leaving the three squadrons of the 3rd BG as the only B-57 bomber units. These squadrons had a nuclear role throughout South-East Asia and because of Japanese policy refusing the storage of nuclear weapons one squadron was based, on rotation, in Korea where there were nuclear storage facilities. This situation prevailed until April 1964 when it was proposed to retire the B-57s and hand them over to the Air National Guard.

However, the growing crisis in South-East Asia brought a drastic change to these plans and the 8th and 13th Bombardment Squadrons moved to Clark AFB, Philippines, and by the end of April were on operational standby.

Vietnam War

Following French withdrawal from Vietnam in 1957 the Communists continued to make gains in the south. American military advisers were first sent into the area in 1959 and by 1963 numbered 15,000. The following year American combat aircraft were in operation and by the end of 1965 ground forces were in place bringing total American strength to 181,000, a figure that gradually increased to half a million.

On 4th August 1964 the B-57s were ordered to deploy to Bien Hoa in South Vietnam. The remainder of 1964 did not go well. Two aircraft were written off on the deployment itself and further disaster struck when five aircraft were destroyed during a Viet Cong (VC) mortar attack. Meanwhile the squadrons could not hit back as they were limited to unarmed recce sorties because of the Geneva Accord which stated that no new weaponry, in this case jet aircraft, could be introduced into the area.

It was not long before such niceties were forgotten in the face of continued VC gains as the pace of the conflict increased. The Canberras were ordered into action in February and the following month were cleared to bomb targets beyond the borders of South Vietnam. During this period the B-57s were employed on CAS and interdictor sorties, achieving good results while losses remained low - one aircraft being lost in March and one in April.

With the B-57B (this is 52-1493) Martin had 'Americanised' the Canberra and introduced a new crew layout with the tandem seating under a bubble canopy. This close-up shows how much better was the visibility, especially for the navigator (!) in this variant. The flat plate windscreen was a great advantage in the ground attack game. *GLM Co P51443 via Bruce Robertson*

Camouflaged B-57B '21571' with 8th BS 'PQ' tail code. Note the Davis Monthan storage code 'BM027' on nose.

The 461st BG at Hill AFB was the first unit to be fully equipped with B-57Bs. Here '21556' is seen visiting Prestwick.

Various techniques for night interdiction of supply routes, the vital life-lines of the VC forces, were tried. First attempts used one aircraft to locate the target and drop parachute flares while the second aircraft made a guns and bombs attack. This developed into a complex mixed formation employing a C-130 'Blind Bat' flare ship, two B-57s, an EF-10B Skynight ECM aircraft and a follow-up RB-57E of the 'Patricia Lynn' unit to photograph the results, although this latter element was soon discontinued. There were never enough aircraft available to do anything more than scratch the surface of the problem and the supply routes were never closed down.

The misfortunes continued and in May 1965 a fully bombed-up aircraft (nine 500 lb bombs in the bomb bay and four 750 lb bombs under the wings) exploded at Bien Hoa killing twenty-eight personnel and destroying ten aircraft. Replacement aircraft were obtained from the ANG and the squadrons continued to operate from Da Nang. The range of tasks was formidable as was the selection of weapons available and the B-57s were in constant demand for their accuracy. They also achieved an excellent reputation for their reliability and ruggedness.

The same year, B-57s were handed to the Vietnamese Air Force (VNAF) but by August 1966 they had ceased operating the aircraft. With a reduction in strength, the USAF B-57s were rotated, a squadron at a time, between Da Nang and Clark for 60 day periods. In October 1966 the operational detachment moved to Phan Rang and remained there until September 1969 when B-57s were finally withdrawn from the combat zone.

Despite the odd mishap the B-57 had served well in Vietnam.

B-57D

Twenty of the production run of B-57Bs were given oversized wings (106 ft span), 10,000 lb st J57 engines and designated RB-57D for the daylight high altitude recce role equivalent to the PR.9, and a stop-gap measure pending the introduction of purpose-designed high-altitude recce aircraft such as the U-2. The first deliveries were made in April 1956 to the 4028th SR Squadron at Turner AFB and later that year six aircraft went to Yokota, Japan. These aircraft belonged to SAC and were code-named *Black Night*. They greatly improved the recce cover previously obtained by the RB-57As of the 6021st at Yokota, although much of the work that they did is still clothed in secrecy. However, it certainly involved ELINT/SIGINT collection as well as the more standard role of air sampling.

During the Taiwan Straits Crisis of 1959 a number of these aircraft operated out of Taiwan in Chinese Nationalist markings and one is known to have been shot down.

Below: **8th BS B-57B 53-3882 was a late 1959 Tengah visitor from Okinawa. Note the 45 Sqn 'flying camel' fin 'zap'.** *Roger Evans* **T.4 equivalent B-57C '53840' served with 4424 Combat Crew Training Squadron.** *MAP*

53-3964 is a fairly anonymous RB-57D-4 with BA 'Buzz' prefix to last three. *MAP*

Opposite: **This B-57E close-up shows the neat back-end target stowage.** *Martin P56308 via Bruce Robertson*

Bottom: **Single-seater RB-57D-1 53-3977 effectively illustrates the extended wings of this model.**

Europe was another theatre which received frequent visits from detachments of RB-57Ds, usually from the Group B (AAR) batch of aircraft which could carry out very long missions. These aircraft operated out of Rhine Main AB and the sole RB-57D-1 was used by this detachment from time to time. By 1959 it was virtually a permanent detachment allocated to the 7407th Support Squadron.

The RB-57D was also unusual in that it was a one-man crew aircraft. The first six were of this standard design whilst the next seven were one-man crew but were also given air-to-air refuelling capability (AAR), both designated simply RB-57D. The remaining seven aircraft of the series were AAR-capable two-crew versions, designated RB-57D-2. One single-seat AAR-capable example (53-3963) was designated RB-57D-1 and given additional radar sensors - evidenced by its long nose and various fuselage bumps.

The oversized wings proved prone to structural failure, fortunately usually on landing, so some aircraft went into storage while others were converted to other duties. The wing problems continued and following the loss of '973' at 50,000 ft through wing failure, the aircraft went back into storage. However, the high altitude task remained and after more wing modifications the aircraft were brought back into service and, with even more ECM kit, became EB-57Ds. These aircraft furnished Air Defense Command with a high-altitude target for training purposes and went initially to the 4677th DSES to join the standard B-57Ds already

being operated by that unit. RB-57Ds saw service with a number of specialised units - NASA operated a few aircraft for high altitude tests and others went to the 1211 Test Squadron (Sampling) of the Air Weather Service (later designated 58th Weather Research Squadron) as WB-57Ds.

As with the RAF Canberras, the RB-57Ds proved a useful platform from which to undertake nuclear cloud sampling and the 4077th aircraft took part in many tests in the late 1950s and early 1960s.

So they remained until they were once again placed in storage in mid 1970.

B-57E
Sixty-eight B-57Es were built by Martins as target towing aircraft, for which they had a modified tail section equipped with two target canisters and tow reels in the bomb bay. On task, the B-57s were usually accompanied by a T-33 as a spotter aircraft which would check the target from time to time. When the target was considered to be of no further use it was cut free. Having been duly fired at by their own side for years, twelve aircraft were converted into bombers when the need arose for 'straight' B-57s for use in Vietnam. At least

two became RB-57Es equipped with avionics and sensors for use as TR aircraft. These latter arrived at Tan Son Nhut in May 1963 and, equipped with a wide range of optical and IR cameras, were soon heavily involved on a variety of recce missions. By the end of the year three more aircraft had joined the 'Patricia Lynn' outfit as Detachment 1, assigned to the 33rd TG, although in August 1965 they were assigned to the 6250th Combat Support Group.

With frequent changes and updates of the kit, including one aircraft with Terrain Following Radar, the unit remained operational until August 1971, having lost two aircraft to ground fire during the war for thousands of hours spent over North and South, Cambodia and Laos. Yet again the Canberra had proved to be an excellent aircraft for the job and was well liked by its crews - not least for its ability to absorb a great deal of small-arms fire without critical damage.

Some aircraft were later converted to EB-57Es, the first E denoting their role as EW aircraft with numerous black boxes for EW/ECM training (like the RAF T.17s) missions.

Above: **The RB-57F had an even more extensive wing area and a span of 122 ft! Like most other examples, 63-13291 (a rebuilt B-57B 52-1574) served with the 58th WRS.**

Below: **'Mothballed' RB-57Fs at the Davis Monthan storage area, 1982 – as were many other B-57 variants. Visible, left to right: 63-13294, '91, 63-13301 (MAC tail-band), 63-13296, '88, '95.** *MAP*

Bottom: **WB-57F 63-13296 of the 58th WRS, 1973. The starboard wing droops almost to the runway. The type suffered excessive wing stress and by 1974 had been retired into storage.** *MAP*

RB-57F

Another variant designed for the high altitude recce task, the RB-57F was given a 122 ft wing span, a wing area of 2,000 sq ft! The aircraft was described as 'a long-endurance, high-altitude aircraft, a versatile diagonistic vehicle designed to handle world-wide aerial policing of the nuclear test ban treaty, air sampling, upper air weather data collection and multi-sensor reconnaissance, while retaining a weapons delivery capability.'

All the aircraft were modified from existing airframes, although the wings were of new design. Wings were built up a three spar pattern with honeycomb sandwich panels for strength and lightness. The 'droop' on the wings meant that there was every chance of the wingtips scraping the ground on take-off, to alleviate repair problems the wingtips were easily detachable for repair in the field! The wings had numerous built-in hardpoints for stores such as fuel tanks, air sampling ducts and specialised equipment giving role flexibility.

After a first flight on 23rd June 1963 the variant entered service and was soon seen around the world on intelligence gathering tasks. To provide adequate thrust for the desired performance the aircraft were fitted with two detachable pod-mounted J60 engines under the wings. However, for normal take-offs the power of the main engines, a pair of Pratt & Whitney TF33-P-11 turbofan engines each giving 18,000 lb thrust, was more than enough. The J60s gave an additional 3,300 lb thrust each. Performance was excellent with operational altitudes in excess of 100,000 ft and an endurance of ten hours using internal fuel, which could be extended using additional fuel tanks. However, it suffered wing structure problems as its sister variant had the same wings. Those aircraft operated by the 58th Weather Recce Squadron for the collection of weather data were later designated WB-57F. Most RB-57Fs were destined for use by the Air Weather Service and began this role in June 1964, being equipped with an extensive range of sensors and samplers to record atmospheric data. This aircraft operated very much on a world wide basis and, like the RB-57Ds, was also used for nuclear cloud sampling.

Despite the loss of one aircraft in December 1965 and another in November 1966 the aircraft continued in the high altitude role. Two aircraft were used in Pakistan during the 1965 war with India. These aircraft were notionally operated by 24 Squadron of the PAF but it is thought that they were operated by or for the CIA on intelligence tasks. One aircraft was damaged by an SA-2 missile.

By July 1974 most aircraft were in storage but some remained in use with NASA on high altitude trials.

B-57G

With the realisation that modern sensors were vital to the night interdiction role in Vietnam, the B-57G was developed to fulfil the requirement for a self-contained night attack aircraft for the disruption of supply routes. To meet this requirement a number of B-57Bs were given new nose sections incorporating sensors and tracking systems - resulting in a very ugly though high-tech nose profile!

In late 1969 sixteen aircraft were withdrawn from service in Vietnam and sent back to Baltimore for these mods, which included installation by Westinghouse of the sensor systems. The first Air Force acceptance flight took place in July 1969.

The 13th BS was reformed and with eleven aircraft moved to Uban, Thailand in September 1970 to become part of 11th TFW. From the very first it was a success. With its FLR, IR and Low Light TV systems and cockpit readouts, combined with 'smart' weapons such as Laser Guided Bombs (LGBs), the aircraft was a superb night intruder. No flares to give it away, just sneak up and plant an LGB on the target. 'Smart' weapons were the keynote of these aircraft although it could also deliver unguided bombs with exceptional accuracy. Prowling along the known supply routes at night it could detect and accurately attack the supply convoys that were the lifelines of the VC. Unfortunately it was too little and too late.

Only one aircraft was lost and that involved a mid-air collision with an O-2A in December 1970. By April 1972 the Squadron had withdrawn to Clark and the aircraft later went to the ANG, although they were soon phased out because of equipment serviceability problems.

Air National Guard

RB-57As of the 363rd TRW were handed over to the Air National Guard in 1958 to equip four squadrons and start what was to be a twenty-four year 'Canberra' period for the ANG.

In April 1958 the 117th TRS of the Vermont ANG (code 'KS') received a complement of RB-57As and as more aircraft became available expanded to Group status in October 1962 as the 190th TRG. Operating from NAS Hutchinson and, later, Forbes AFB the unit used these aircraft until 1972 when they changed role and re-equipped with the sophisticated B-57G as the 117th TBS/190th TBG. However, within two years the B-57Gs were paid off and the unit acquired a number of EB-57s and became a 'Defence Systems Evaluation' unit (117th DSES/190th DSEG). Another short-lived period as in July 1978 the B-57s were replaced by KC-135As.

There was a second DSES B-57 unit operating at the same period, the 134th DSES/158th DSEG using EB-57Bs and Es from June 1974 to 1982 when it re-equipped with F-4s. This saw the end of ANG B-57 employment.

The ultimate B-57 was the B-57G, a high-tec Canberra full of sensors for all-weather/ night ops in Vietnam. This example is 53-3860 ex 'FK' Kansas ANG. *R. Walker*

Standard USAF practice was to hand older types to ANG units as soon as they were released from front-line service. The B-57s saw extensive ANG use over a 24 year period. 52-1446 is a RB-57A of Kansas ANG, 117TRS at Forbes AFB, May 1968. Note the '0-' serial prefix, denoting an aircraft over 10 years old! *MAP*

RB-57A 52-1459 of Michigan ANG's 172 TRS.
MAP

B-57C 53-3856 serving with 134th DSES,
Vermont ANG, 1977. *MAP*

Kansas ANG B-57B 52-1502 of 117 DSES.
MAP

RB-57A 52-1490 of Arkansas ANG. *R. Walker*

The 'heyday' had been in the 1960s with four other TR units similar to the 117th. The 154th TRS of the Arkansas ANG ('AR') had received RB-57As in March 1958 along with a few RB-57Bs. They became part of the 189th TRG in October 1962 operating from Little Rock AFB. Two other units formed in 1958. The 165th TRS (Kentucky ANG) acquired RB-57Bs which it operated until July 1965, with Group status as 123rd TRG from October 1962. The 172nd TRS (Michigan ANG) acquired RB-57As in April 1958 which it then operated until 1971. The final TRS unit to form was the 192nd TRS/152nd TRG (Nevada ANG) with its RB-57Bs from March 1961 to October 1965.

Most of the units received additional aircraft during their operational period including a number of RB-57Cs and RB-57Es. The only other ANG unit to operate the 'Canberra' was the 149th FIS which in the late 1950s received one RB-57B to work with its F-86s.

Pakistan Air Force

The PAF was the only foreign user, other than the fleeting use by the VNAF and the 'appearance' of aircraft in Taiwanese markings, of the B-57. In 1952 the PAF stated a requirement for two light bomber squadrons and the Air Staff proposed to buy twenty Canberras from English Electric in 1953 with a further thirty-three planned for 1954. Whilst these negotiations were taking place the PAF began setting up the necessary infrastructure and training

programme. However, the political situation changed and the order was not confirmed. Instead, a Mutual Defense Assistance Pact was signed with the U.S. to include provision of a wing of Douglas B-66 bombers. This was subsequently changed to twenty-four B-57Bs and two B-57Cs, destined for No.31 wing at Mauripur.

No.7 Squadron received ten B-57Bs and one B-57C in June 1960 with her sister squadron, No.8, receiving a similar complement two months later. Two years later (December 1962) No.24 Squadron started to operate the high altitude RB-57F variant.

The operational use of the PAF B-57s is covered in the previous chapter under 'India-Pakistan Wars'.

Chapter Nine

Trials and Special Duties

There has rarely, if ever, been an aircraft so extensively used for trials and experimental work as the Canberra. The well designed airframe with a relatively low wing loading provided the ideal aircraft for testing the new generation of jet engines just being introduced. It also had the performance necessary to effectively try out the new equipment, weapons and systems being designed at this time as well as offering the various Government Establishments a vehicle for general research.

In previous chapters we have seen brief instances of squadron-level trials instituted either from higher authority or as a squadron 'good idea' that was pushed up the line. Within this category came the navigation kit trials on such things as Decca and Blue Shadow and weapons trials including AS.12 and AS.30. Added to this are all the tactical trials which squadrons are continually doing to improve the operational efficiency of their weapons system (i.e. aircraft, crew and weapons).

We can now look at some of the many Canberras used by the industry and the Establishments which were involved with the basic development of the aircraft and new equipment. Under each Company the aircraft details are covered by aircraft serial order rather than in order of use.

The work undertaken by Canberras in the trial/development field was so varied and extensive that it would require a rather large book to present a detailed survey. Hence, we have summarised the main involvement of the aircraft and highlighted a few specific examples.

The Industry

Armstrong Siddeley Motors Ltd

Armstrong-Siddeley Motors Ltd received WD933 at their Bitteswell test facility early in 1951 for the installation of two 7,220 lb st Armstrong-Siddeley Sapphire ASSa.3 engines. These were first flown on 14th August 1951 but after a limited amount of flying were replaced by later 8,300 lb st ASSa.6 engines, the aircraft taking to the air again during April 1952. Finally, two of the more powerful Sapphire ASSa.7 units, each giving 10,300 lb st were fitted and a first flight with these was made from Bitteswell on 13th August 1954. This aircraft

eventually came to grief in a spectacular accident at Bitteswell on 10th November 1954 when test pilot James Starky was making an emergency landing. The aircraft belly landed at high speed, flipped over onto its back and slid inverted across the airfield. Both the pilot and observer, Peter Taylor, were saved by their ejection seat headrests.

Further development of the ASSa.7 was undertaken with three more B.2s. WK141 was transferred from RAF charge on 14th January 1955 and first flew with its new engines on 7th May. It was later fitted with an A-S Viper 8 engine under the starboard wing, with which it first flew during September 1958. This engine was in due course replaced by a later Viper 11. WK141 was disposed of by Bristol-Siddeley from Filton in March 1963 and was moved to the fire compound at Prestwick. WK163 was

transferred to Armstrong-Siddeley without charge on 28th January 1955 and made its first flight with ASSa.7s later in the year. This aircraft left to go to Napiers during October 1955 in order to have a Double Scorpion rocket motor fitted.

Earlier, in 1953, the first of the three additional B.2s, WV787, had arrived at Bitteswell when it was transferred without charge on 31st May 1953. The new engines had been fitted and the aircraft flown during March 1954. After completing its flying with Armstrong-Siddeley, the aircraft had Avons refitted and went on to serve Ferrantis and the A&AEE in a long career of experimental flying.

WD933 in use by Armstrong-Siddeley for Sapphire ASSa.3 engine trials.

WK141 was used as a Viper engine testbed at Bitteswell and Filton. *BS.E42007*

A.V. Roe

Although A.V. Roe & Co Ltd of Manchester were called upon to produce B.2 aircraft in 1951 they did no development flying other than production testing. Their first Canberra flew on 25th November 1952 from Woodford piloted by J.D. (Johnny) Baker.

Boulton Paul

A great deal of specialist modification work to Canberras was done by Boulton Paul Aircraft Ltd, located at the RRE Defford and later at their own airfield at Seighford, where they also carried out experimental work under contract.

The third prototype Canberra, VN828, arrived during 1955 for modifications and was fitted with a Mk.8 type cockpit section and a nose radome housing AI.Mk.18 radar.

Canberra B.2 WH671 came on loan to Boulton Paul on 24th December 1952 for engine de-icing trials.

In order to provide a radar training aircraft, B.2 WJ734 was delivered for trials installations. The conversion involved fitting an extended nose radome containing AIRPASS (Airborne Interception Radar and Pilot's Attack Sight System). Eight more conversions followed for use by the RAF as the Canberra T.11 and two similar aircraft were converted for the Swedish Air Force as the Tp.52.

WH967, which had been modified from B.6 to trials installation for the B.15 by Marshalls of Cambridge, was transferred to Boulton Paul for handling trials with the Nord AS.30 missile.

WJ643, a B.2 used by Ferranti, went to Seighford in February 1956 to have a Mk.8 nose fitted and was returned to Ferranti in February 1957.

Boulton Paul were subcontracted by the Ministry of Defence to work on a project study for a flying classroom during April 1963 and three B.2s were used in connection with this work, WH868, WJ645 and WJ647. The scheme was abandoned and all three aircraft were sent to 15MU at Wroughton.

One other interesting trial undertaken by Boulton Paul was the use of WK161 for anti-radar development along with Balliol T.2 WG125.

Bristol Aero-Engines Ltd

The first Canberra B.2 to be used by Bristol Aero-Engines Ltd for trial engine installation work was WD952 which arrived at Filton on 13th December 1951. The Avon engines were replaced by a pair of Olympus 99s rated at 8,000 lb st – these were in fact Bristol B.Ol 1/2Bs, normally rated at 9,750 lb st but derated because of Canberra airframe limitations: a first flight with these engines was made on 5th August 1952. Mounting the Olympus caused difficulties because the big engine projected a long way ahead of the wing resulting in c-of-g problems. These were

overcome and the installation then proved to be trouble-free. Two large 'auto-observer' cameras were fitted in the bomb bay. This aircraft established a new world height record on 4th May 1953 when Wing Commander W.F. Gibb, Bristol's chief test pilot, reached an altitude of 63,668 ft. Later type Olympus 101s of 11,000 lb st were tested and, in 1955, Olympus B.Ol.II (Olympus 102s) of 12,000 lb st were fitted. With these engines the height record was again broken when Walter Gibb, flying

solo, reached a height of 65,876 ft. This aircraft later crashed near Filton (12th March 1956) and was eventually broken up at Colerne.

A second B.2, WH713, was also fitted with Olympus engines. This aircraft was transferred to Filton on 2nd January 1957 after serving with 15 Squadron. Olympus 104 engines of 13,000 lb st were fitted and the aircraft was used for engine silencer tests before being scrapped at Filton on 7th September 1959.

WK163 which had previously been with Armstrong-Siddeley and Napiers went to Bristol Siddeley for testing long and short life Viper engines. After this it went on to the RRE at Pershore.

De Havilland

A number of Canberras were used by the various companies comprising the de Havilland group at Hatfield.

The second prototype, VN813, was converted for D.H. Engine Co by Folland Aircraft Ltd during 1956 to have the D.H. Spectre rocket motor fitted in the lower rear fuselage. This became the first aircraft flown in Britain with a fully controlled rocket motor. The first 'cold' airborne firing of the Spectre was on 18th December 1956 and the first 'hot' firing during February the following year. The second Canberra to be used for Spectre trials was

a B.6, WJ755, which arrived at Hatfield on 13th June 1957.

The first Canberra B.2 to be delivered to Hatfield for trials work was WD992. This was delivered to D.H. Propellers Ltd on 28th April 1952 for missile develoment and remained at Hatfield testing guidance systems until it was eventually scrapped on 14th June 1965.

After being used by Rolls-Royce at Hucknall for Avon development, WF909 was delivered to Hatfield to have a 7,000 lb st D.H. Gyron Junior DGJ.1 engine fitted to the port side only. It flew with this engine on 28th May 1957 and shortly afterwards the starboard engine was also installed. Subsequently the port nacelle tested the full Buccaneer intake. The aircraft remained based at Hatfield until broken up there during 1962.

WH700, a B.2, had been used by 27

Squadron but was loaned to D.H. Propellers during September 1955, being taken off RAF charge on 9th December 1955. This was used for Blue Jay installations and went out to WRE in Australia for air firing trials. In 1987 this aircraft was current with the Parafield Museum, South Australia.

Also on C(A) charge for D.H. Propellers Ltd was B.2 WH735 which was fitted with a nose scanner for guided missile trials and was involved with Javelin development.

B.2 WJ644 was delivered to D.H. Propellers for Blue Jay testing in September 1956 and was later used by the company for Red Top installation trials. Another missile test aircraft, B.2 WK135, was taken from RAF charge on 25th August 1954 and delivered to Hatfield for Blue Jay trials. B.2 WJ978 was transferred to the company on 26th February 1957 for the same programme.

Above: **WF909 was originally used by Rolls-Royce for Avon development, then transferred to de Havilland engines for the installation of a Gyron Junior engine in the port nacelle. The difference in tail pipes can be clearly seen in the photograph.** *DH Engines via R. Bonser*

WD992 being used by DH Propellers, June 1962, for missile development. *P. Birtles*

Opposite: **A hybrid aircraft, VN828 – the third prototype, seen here in 1955 with a Mk.8 cockpit and experimental AI.Mk.18 radar after modification by Boulton Paul.**

WD952 being used by Bristol's as the Olympus test bed. This aircraft twice broke the world altitude record. *Bristol Aero Co.*

Second prototype VN813 engaged in a ground run of the variable thrust *Spectre 5* rocket engine, being developed for the SR.53 *DH 20A*

A special Joint Services Trials Unit (No 12 JSTU) was formed at Hatfield in early 1956 of RAF, RN and company personnel to carry out evaluation of the Blue Jay missile (which later entered RAF service as the Firestreak.) Firing trials were scheduled to take place in Southern Australia, at Woomera range, with the aircraft based at Edinburgh Field. Four of the aircraft, WH700, WJ978, WJ644 and WK135 were prepared for the trial and in July 1956 an advance party sailed to Australia to prepare facilities and test procedures. John Alton, a Flight Lieutenant engineer member of the team, recalls . . .

'The Canberra proved to be a very successful launching platform. It permitted the pilot to concentrate on achieving an accurate firing position relative to the target whilst the other crew member carried out other pre-launch functions. The launch system black boxes were easily fitted in accessible positions in the bomb bay and a missile pylon was fitted under each wing outboard of the engine.'

Missile firings were made against either a Jindivik drone target or, for live warhead evaluation, a Meteor drone.

Canberra PR.9 XH132 was modified by Short Bros and Harland as the SC.9 for use as a Red Top missile trials aircraft. It spent many years at Hatfield before going to the RRE at Pershore on 21st January 1972.

English Electric / BAC

As the designers of the Canberra, the English Electric Co. (EE Co) retained all the prototype aircraft, as well as the first production B.2, for extensive development flying.

The prototype VN799, having made its first flight at Warton on 13th May 1949 stayed there for some time before going to A&AEE Boscombe Down and the RAE at Farnborough. The second aircraft, VN813, fitted with RR Nene engines made its first flight on 9th November 1949 at Warton and remained there on development work until going to Rolls-Royce at Hucknall in November 1950. VN828, the third aircraft,

made its first flight at Samlesbury on 22nd November and was retained until used for trials at Telecommunications Research Establishment (TRE) Malvern. The fourth prototype, VN850, first flew on 20th December 1949 and, amongst other trials, this aircraft was used for tip tank testing until it too went to Hucknall in October 1950.

Making its first flight on 21st April 1950, the Canberra B.2 prototype VX165 stayed with EE Co test flying for a while but it crashed at Boscombe Down on 15th August the following year. The second B.2, VX169, also spent a considerable time at Warton, and visited the RAF Handling Squadron at

Above: **Another missile trial, this time XH132 at Hatfield, February 1967 in use with Hawker Siddeley Dynamics for Red Top missile trials.** *P. Birtles*

Below: **WJ644 firing a de Havilland Firestreak air to air guided missile at high altitude on the Aberporth range in South Wales.** *DH Co 10535A*

Bottom: **WH700 operating with 12 JSTU on Firestreak firing trials from Edinburgh Field, Australia, December 1959. Note the Firestreak under the port wing.** *J. Alton*

Above: **BAC's B.2 G-ATZW (WD937) seen near Llanbedr, June 1967.** *A. Pearcy*

Below: **B.2 WD953 in use by Ferranti's at Turnhouse, April 1962.** *W. Bishop*

Bottom: **B.2/B.8 WJ643 with AIRPASS nose, Ferranti Flying Unit, Turnhouse.**

Manby and the A&AEE, before going to the RAE during September 1954. The first production B.2, WD929, which made its first flight on 8th October 1950 remained with the company for some time, as well as being the star at the official naming ceremony at Biggin Hill in January 1951. It later spent some time with the RAE and was ultimately converted to a U.10 target aircraft.

As B.2 production got underway, WD934 was retained on loan for a short while for development and display flying, before being delivered to 101 Squadron at Binbrook on 14th September 1951. Prior to that, on 29th June, WD937 was transferred without charge to EE Co for permanent trials work. This aircraft was ultimately used by the company as a support aeroplane and as such was put on the civil register as G-ATZW making its first flight with these marks on 28th October 1966. It made its last flight on 10th November 1967 and was then withdrawn from use.

WD958 was on loan to EE Co from 7th December 1951 until its departure to 23 MU on 2nd May 1953, whilst the next aircraft on the line, WD959, was also loaned to the company from 31st December 1951 until leaving for Rolls-Royce during December 1953.

WJ565, Handley Page built B.2 was used to test the trial installation of the belly gun pack planned for the interdictor marks. However, WT307 was the first production model of the B(I)6 and made its first flight on 31st March 1955, being retained until collection on 22nd October. The true interdictor version, the B(I)8 first flew on 8th June 1955 and was collected on 1st November.

The fifth production Canberra PR.9, XH133, was used at Warton for trials installations, one of which was on the suitability of the F49 camera.

In 1969 BAC used WE121 as a chase aircraft during Jaguar test flying at Warton. At Fairford, BAC borrowed B.2 WJ627 from the RRE, when needed, for use as a chase aircraft for Concorde test flying between 1968 and 1972. A third chase aircraft was used, B.6 WH952, this time as the MRCA (Tornado) chase aircraft during test flying from Warton in 1975.

Ferranti

Ferranti Ltd were heavily involved with radar experiments and the Ferranti Flying Unit (FFU) operated no less than eight Canberras, all on loan from the Ministry. The only trials aircraft owned by the Company was the prototype Meteor NF.14 WM261, registered as G-ARCX.

The B(I)8 prototype, VX181, arrived at the FFU at Turnhouse on 4th April 1956 for AI target trials and remained there for some time before going to 15 MU for storage on 16th October 1957. In serial order but, in fact, the last Canberra to enter service

Above: **AIRPASS equipment being loaded in the nose of one of the Ferranti trials Canberras at Turnhouse.** *Ferranti*

Below: **B(I)8 with LRMTS in nose, trials aircraft operated by Ferranti Flying Unit.**

with the FFU was WD947 which did not arrive until 23rd December 1966 and left just under a year later on 31st October.

WD953 arrived on 30th October 1961 having previously been with A&AEE. It remained in use with the FFU until 13th February 1969 when it was transferred to the RRE at Pershore.

After serving with 100 Squadron at Wittering, B.2 WJ627 arrived at Turnhouse on 4th August 1959 for research and development of airborne electronic equipment and was transferred to MoS charge on 17th July 1961. It remained with Ferrantis until 9th September 1963 when it left to continue similar work with the RRE.

WJ643 was taken into immediate MoS charge on 7th September 1954 and delivered to the FFU on 21st September for target experiments. The aircraft was sent to Boulton Paul at Seighford in February 1956 to have a Mk.8 nose fitted and was returned to Turnhouse the following February. The Company installed AIRPASS equipment in the nose, a system which was being developed for the EECo Lightning. A first flight was made with this fitted during January 1958. In 1966 the aircraft was further modified to have a B.8 wing and to have Avon RA.7 engines fitted in place of the RA.3s. INAS (Inertial Navigation and Attack System) was installed for testing as part of the Harrier programme. The aircraft moved with the FFU from Turnhouse to West Freugh during February 1969 and then went to the RAE at Farnborough in December 1969 to have a laser installation fitted in the nose. It returned to West Freugh the following year but went back to Farnborough again in 1972 to serve with the RAE.

B(I)8 WT327 was delivered to Boulton Paul on 31st August 1955 and was modified to carry AI.Mk.23 radar in the nose as well as additional trials equipment. It was delivered to the FFU on 28th August 1956 to act as a testbed for Lightning systems. The aircraft was returned to Boulton Paul at Seighford for modifications on 2nd April 1963 when the nose was again modified, this time to take Forward Looking Radar (FLR) in connection with TSR.2 development. WT327 returned to Ferranti on 8th February 1964 and remained with the Company until delivered to the RRE at Pershore on 12th April 1966.

After being used by Armstrong Siddeley for Sapphire testing, WV787 was transferred to the FFU in January 1958. A B.8 forward fuselage was fitted and this aircraft was used for radar development with a Buccaneer nose radome until 2nd December 1963 when it went to the A&AEE at Boscombe Down.

The modified PR.9 (SC.9) XH132 was attached to the FFU for a few months in 1961, 30th May to 14th September, for specific trials.

In the fourteen years that Canberras were used by the FFU they carried out a wide range of sensor trials for the advanced generation of aircraft entering service in the 1970s on intercept radars, ground mapping and attack radars and other equipment and sensors such as Laser Ranger and Marked Target Seeker (LRMTS).

Flight Refuelling

The Canberra became the first British jet aircraft to be equipped as a tanker for in-flight refuelling when a B.2, WH734, was loaned to Flight Refuelling Ltd by the MoS. The aircraft was taken off RAF charge on 31st July 1954 and sent to Tarrant Rushton for modifications which included a hose drum unit (HDU) in the back part of the bomb bay for high-speed flight trials on the latest probe-and-drogue systems. The conversion was done at Tarrant Rushton and, in the words of the Company, proved 'how simply a bomber can be turned into a tanker without fuss and bother.' The bomb-bay HDU was connected to existing fuel, hydraulic and electrical systems and all that was needed was a 7 inch by 8 inch control panel in the cockpit.

The initial trials were carried out using a Meteor F.8 as a receiver aircraft but a

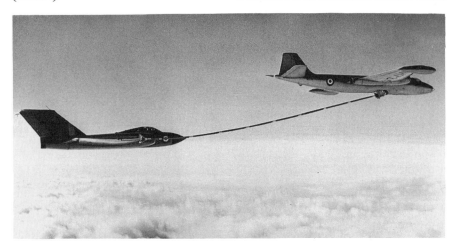

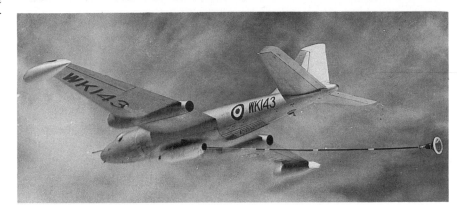

WH734 refuelling a Javelin during AAR trials. The HDU is installed in the bomb bay.

WH734 of FR Ltd at Llanbedr with nose probe fitted, January 1964. *A. Pearcy*

WK143 being used by FR Ltd for AAR trials of the buddy-buddy system, using a pod under the fuselage. *FR Ltd*

variety of other types were used in testing the probe-and-drogue system. WH734 later had a nose probe fitted so that it became a tanker/receiver and was used in testing the 'buddy-buddy' system of refuelling with WK143. Such a development could have been of great value in the tactical tanker role in RAFG and could have made use of redundant B.2 airframes as the bomber force declined.

WH734 was further modified to have a Rushton target winch fitted under the port wing and a mounting pylon to take a Beech AQM.37A Stilletto supersonic target drone under the starboard wing. This aircraft was still being used by the RAE at Llanbedr on Flight Refuelling Ltd charge in 1986.

WK143 had been in use since 10th March 1955 and was used for a variety of refuelling experiments. It too had a nose probe fitted together with a HDU in the bomb bay. This aircraft was converted by the Company to a TT.18 with Rushton winches.

To improve the towed target performance offered by the Meteor, B.2 WJ632 was modified to take a Rushton winch under each wing. This aircraft was used by FRLtd for development work until it went to the A&AEE in 1968. It was replaced by WH718 which was used for trials during 1969 and 1970. Initially eighteen B.2s were converted to TT.18s, some by EE Co and others by FRLtd.

The Company received B.2 WE121 from RRE Pershore on 6th May 1974 for modification for use by the RAE at Llanbedr. This included fitting a Rushton winch under one wing and the mountings for a AQM.37A Stilletto under the other wing. The aircraft had been grounded by early 1980.

WK128 arrived by road from Pershore early 1977 and was rebuilt to incorporate modifications for Stilletto trials.

Folland

Folland Aircraft at Hamble carried out a considerable amount of sub-contract work with the Canberra doing one-off modifications for trials work. They also developed an ejector seat and to test this Canberra B.2 WJ725 was put on Ministry of Aircraft charge on 7th July 1960 for a test seat to be installed and trials carried out.

Handley-Page Ltd

In a similar position to the Avro company, Handley-Page Ltd of Cricklewood also produced Canberra B.2 aircraft, commencing work in 1951. Their first B.2 flew from Radlett on 5th January 1953, and only production testing was carried out.

Marshalls of Cambridge

This Company was heavily involved with Canberra modification and overhaul work. Apart from the various routine overhauls the company also carried-out one-off trials installations. Amongst these was B(I)8 WT333 which was delivered to them

as a new aircraft on 23rd March 1956 for various trials installations for RAE Farnborough. These included a Smiths Mk.19 autopilot and a power rudder stabiliser. The aircraft later returned to Marshalls for further mods, including LABS equipment which had been designed by Marshalls in conjunction with the RAE Weapons Department. The aircraft then went to the A&AEE.

The Company was also responsible for developing revised radio fit and armament modifications for the B.6, which were installed in B.6 WH967. Equipment included U/VHF radio, Radio Compass, Blue Silk, Decca Navigator and Roller Map. The mods were so extensive that new mark numbers were introduced as the B.15 and B.16, the latter having Blue Shadow equipment fitted.

Canberras were also overhauled, modified and tested for export to overseas Air Forces by Marshalls; one of the bigger tasks being the refurbishment and conversion of eleven B(I)8s to B(I)68s for the Peruvian Air Force in the mid 1970s.

Martin Baker

Martin Baker Ltd of Denham carried out ejector seat trials using B.2 WD962. When the Company introduced the automatic ejector seat it was necessary to make actual ejections in flight as part of the testing programme. Testing conditions in the UK were difficult, so it was decided to carry out a series of tests at Castel Benito airport in Tripoli. The transit flights established another Canberra record with the journey being made in 2 hours 44 minutes on 18th February 1954. All ejection seat tests were made at low level and successful results were obtained using dummies. No 'live' tests were made.

Installation problems with ejector seats for the three crew members of the Canberra made escape from the aircraft difficult. There was a metal hatch cover over the two navigators' heads and this had to be jettisoned before ejection. Martin Baker developed a special seat for the Canberra, the Mk.2C and to test this a B.2, WK126, serving with 9 Squadron was sent down to Chalgrove and fitted with the latest seat together with a frangible glass fibre hatch cover. After a test firing on the ground, the aircraft, flown by Company test pilot Captain J.E.D Scott made an airborne test on 19th January 1956. The seat top smashed the hatch cover during the ejection and the dummy was undamaged. The seat operation was fully automatic.

More recently, Martin Baker have been using WH876 in connection with parachute trials at Chalgrove. The aircraft moved there in mid 1985 from the A&AEE at Boscombe Down where it had been involved on tests of the latest version of the Mk.10 rocket-powered seat, in this instance for the Harrier GR.5.

Napier

D Napier and Son Ltd, a member of the English Electric Co Group, carried out conversion of PR.7 WH793 to become the prototype for the PR.9. The converted airframe made its first flight on 8th July 1955 at Luton Airport at the hands of Mike Randrup, Napier's test pilot. WH793 had the increased wing area and bigger engines of the production aircraft but retained the PR.7 cockpit and nose. It was later used by the RAE at Bedford.

B.2 WK163 arrived at Napier's works at Luton Airport in late 1955 having previously been with Armstrong Siddeley at Bitteswell. Napier's installed a Double Scorpion NScD1/2 rocket motor at the rear of the bomb bay and the first flight with this unit was made on 20th May 1956. This aircraft achieved another world height record on 28th August 1957 when Mike Randrup and Walter Shirley took it to 70,310 ft. The Double Scorpion was intended as a power booster for the English Electric Company's P.1, then under development.

Rolls-Royce

Rolls-Royce Ltd used a considerable number of Canberras for testing engines, silencers and reheat units. As a safeguard against the failure of the Avon engine, the second prototype, VN813, had been fitted with RR Nene engines. After test flying with EE Co this aircraft was transferred to Rolls-Royce at Hucknall in November 1950 where it carried out Nene development flying until August 1952. It then went on to the TRE at Malvern.

VN850, the fourth prototype, arrived a month prior to VN813 and was used extensively for RR Avon RA.2 testing until it crashed on Bulwell Common near Hucknall on 13th May 1951.

The second production aircraft, WD930, arrived at Hucknall on 22nd August 1951 after a short spell with the RAF Handling Squadron at Manby. The Avon RA.3s were replaced by RA.7s, which were in turn replaced by RA.14 units. The first flight with the latter was made during July 1953 and the aircraft appeared at the SBAC show at Farnborough that year with these engines. Shortly afterwards Avon RA.26 engines were fitted and, finally, Avon RA.29s were test flown during 1956. These engines were being developed for the Comet 4 airliner and a series of silencers were tested during the early part of 1958. This aircraft was scrapped at Hucknall during August 1960.

Rolls-Royce had carried out some early reheat experiments using Meteor F.4 RA435 fitted with Derwent engines. To continue this work B.2 WD943 was delivered to Hucknall on 12th October 1951 and Avon engines with reheat were fitted. These engines, designated Avon RA.7R were later replaced by more powerful RA.14Rs.

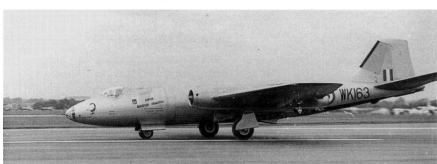

This airframe continued to serve the Company until July 1957 when it went to 23 MU and was eventually sold as scrap.

WD959 arrived at Hucknall after a couple of years with EE Co. This aircraft was also used on the reheat trials and was fitted successively with Avon RA.7R, RA.14R and RA.24R engines. The latter units were being developed for the Lightning and resulted in large nacelles extending a long way aft of the trailing edge of the wing. WD959 left Rolls-Royce in October 1959 and went to the RAE as an instructional airframe, 7620M, but soon moved to No.12 SoTT at Melksham (30th October 1959).

Another direct delivery to Rolls-Royce was WF909 which arrived in July 1952 straight off the production line. This was used for Avon development and surge testing both with RA.3s and RA.7s. This aircraft went on to de Havilland's at Hatfield for Gyron Junior installation.

WH671 arrived at Hucknall during June 1954 and was fitted in turn with Avon RA.24, RA.28 and RA.29 engines. The first flight with the RA.24s was made on 12th December 1955. The aircraft's working life ended in November 1961 when it was broken up for scrap.

Initially delivered to the Handling Squadron at Manby and then serving with 617 squadron, WH854 moved to Hucknall so that Avon relighting tests could be carried out. On completion of this series the aircraft went on to the RRE at Defford.

Short Bros and Harland

Short Bros and Harland Ltd at Belfast became involved in Canberra production in 1951 when the 'panic' orders to increase production rates on the B.2 were placed. The first B.2, piloted by Tom Brooke-Smith, flew out of Sydenham on 30th October 1952 with the Company involved in production and production testing rather than trials. However, when the requirement arose for a pilotless target version of the Canberra, Shorts was awarded the contract to develop and produce a suitable aircraft.

The Napier 'Double Scorpion' rocket engine can just be seen at the rear of the bomb bay on WK163. This aircraft was used to capture the world height record in August 1957 at 70,310 ft.

WK163 again, at Farnborough, the month after it took the record. Note the 'nose art' of a scorpion and height record details.

WD930 being used for silencer trials. *RR HP 23999*

The camera caught most of this fairly low pass by WD930, fitted out for testing and development of the Comet silencer unit, Hucknall, April 1958. *RR H3182*

A standard B.2, WJ624, was flown into Belfast for conversion into a trials aircraft, making its first flight as such on 11th June 1957. It operated at Belfast, interspersed with long periods grounded for mods, until its last known flight on 18th September 1961. Shorts converted a further seventeen B.2s to pilotless U.10 variants, all of which were delivered to weapons ranges in Australia. A further six conversions were made to U.14 standard, which were similar to the U.10 except for the fitting of hydraulic servo-assisted controls and were for target use by the Royal Navy.

Further production of Canberras at Belfast included the PR.9, the first of these flying on 27th July 1958. The fourth aircraft was retained by Shorts as a special conversion designated by Shorts as the SC.9 and intended for trials with the Red Top missile being developed by de Havillands at Hatfield. The Company was also responsible for on-going 'Major' servicing of the PR.9 fleet.

PR.3 WE146 was received for modification as a launch platform for the AQM.37A Stilletto supersonic target to join the fleet of Canberra launch aircraft at RAE Llanbedr. The aircraft was delivered in 1968.

Opposite: **Rolls-Royce used a great number of Canberras over the years as engine test beds. WH671 arrived at Hucknall in June 1954 and went on to test the Avon RA.24, .28 and .29 engines. It is seen here at Hucknall in April 1961 only months before it went for scrap.** *RR HP6475*

Another RR development aircraft, WD959 which tested Lightning reheat units extending well beyond the trailing edge of the wing. Photographed at Wymeswold Febuary 1955. *RR HN1925*

After serving with 76 Squadron, WJ987 was delivered to Shorts in November 1956 for conversion to U.10. It was the first full conversion for radio control. *SB&H*

Vickers Armstrong

Vickers Armstrong (Aircraft) Ltd was involved with weapons development and used several Canberras in this field.

WD933 was allocated to Vickers on 13th April 1951, the day after it was collected from EE Co, but four months later it was transferred to Armstrong Siddeley for Sapphire engine installation.

WD935 was delivered to Wisley on 8th August 1951 for use on guided weapons installations. It was modified in the works at Hurn to be used in connection with Vickers type 888 Red Dean guided missiles. It first flew with under wing carriers fitted on 14th October 1953 and carried under wing

stores for the first time in January 1954. Wing reinforcing was needed because of the weight of the Red Dean missile. A brake failure after a series of roller landings at Wisley on 21st September 1955 resulted in the unexpected arrival of the aircraft on the A3 London-Portsmouth road! Vickers test pilot Peter Marsh had a lucky escape when the aircraft dropped about fifty feet off the end of Wisley's runway into a ditch on the side of the road. The Canberra remained at Wisley after this and was used for GEC bomb trials until it was delivered to the BCDU at Wittering on 11th September 1959.

The next Canberra delivered to Vickers was WD942 which arrived at Wisley on C(A) charge on 28th September 1951. It was modified as the Vickers type 692 and prepared for a flight to Australia. For this, the RAAF serial A84-2 was applied and the aircraft left Wisley on 12th March 1952. Red Dean trials were carried out by

Vickers at the WRE in Australia from March 1952. This aircraft was transferred back to RAF charge on 6th December 1956 but remained in Australia until ferried back to 15 MU on 3rd October 1957.

WD956 was another Canberra allocated to Vickers for Red Dean testing. It arrived from EE Co and was used until 30th April 1957 when it too went to 15 MU at Wroughton. The final Canberra used for weapons testing was WH660 which arrived on 31st May 1953.

Considerable work was done on the Red Dean project which was intended as a weapon for the thin wing Javelin development to Specification F.153D. Gloster's were not happy at the time being taken to develop the weapon, nor the increase in its weight during this period. However, the cancellation of F.153D in July 1956 also brought an end to the Red Dean weapon and to the use of the Canberra in this connection.

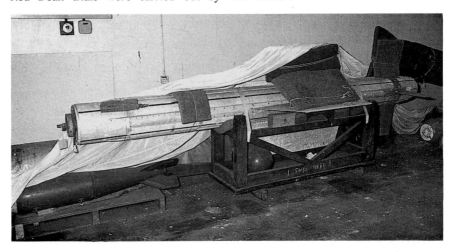

Above: **Probably all that remains of the *Red Dean* missile programme, in the museum store at Cardington, 1989.**

Below: **WD935 was used for Red Dean guided weapons trials by Vickers Armstrong. It had a varied career,** including signals development work at Watton (note radar nose) and was preserved at the St Athan museum – seen here as it arrived in its original black/grey scheme, prior to being resprayed in a later Bomber Command scheme of grey/green upper and blue undersides. *S. Pope*

MoD Establishments

A&AEE Boscombe Down

The various Ministry establishments received Canberras for a great many purposes. Early aircraft went to the A&AEE at Boscombe Down for Service acceptance trials and development flying, whilst VX169, WD930 and WE112 were used by the RAF Handling Squadron at Manby. Canberras were in continuous use with the A&AEE from 1950 to 1985 and all the various marks have been tested there, although in many cases the visits have been short-lived. Three particular aircraft are of interest. The first of these, WJ638, had been modified as a D.14 drone aircraft for use with 728B Squadron Royal Navy in Malta but having survived its time as a target drone returned to the UK and was delivered to Pershore store on 11th November 1961. After a short rest WJ638 moved to the A&AEE on 27th June 1962 where the radio control was removed and

the aircraft reverted to a B.2. There were further modifications for ejector seat tests which continued into the mid 1970s after which the aircraft was retired and sent to the fire dump at Predannack, Cornwall on 5th January 1978.

WH876 had also been a drone target with 728B Squadron; it survived and returned to the UK in December 1961 and was put into store at Pershore. During 1963 the aircraft was reworked as a B.2 and joined the Bomber Maritime Test Squadron at the A&AEE in March 1964. It was used for target towing and by 1971 a nose probe had been fitted, although this was never a 'wet' system. During the mid 1970s it was carrying out ejector seat tests having replaced WJ638 which had previously been used for this work. It remained at Boscombe until it went to Martin Baker at Chalgrove in mid 1985 to carry out work on parachute trials.

The third aircraft was WV787 which had already been used by Armstrong Siddeley for engine testing and Ferranti in connec-

tion with radar developments. After arrival at Boscombe in 1967 it was fitted out as a tanker aircraft to carry out de-icing trials for other types of aircraft on test. Apart from a spray bar being fitted beyond the rear fuselage, water could be sprayed out of pipes close to the engine exhausts. A rearward facing close-circuit television was fitted behind the bomb-bay so that the test aircraft flying in the spray could be filmed. WV787 was also used as an aerodynamic test bed for the Canberra T.22, the Buccaneer nose fitted being similar to that proposed for the new mark. During the mid 1970s WV787 was used for air to air photography and it remained at Boscombe until August 1984. It was then disposed of to the Battle Damage Repair Flight at Abingdon but before being destroyed this interesting aircraft was saved by the Newark Air Museum who were able to buy it for preservation. It was moved to their site at Winthorpe, Newark in late 1985.

Two other long term residents of Boscombe were the two T.4s used jointly by the A&AEE and the Empire Test Pilot's School (ETPS). WJ865 and WJ867, both of which had previously been with 231 OCU, were used for a variety of tasks and by mid 1975 were in a rather fetching overall grey and white finish with a light blue stripe down each side. WJ865 was in use until late 1981 when it was moved to the RAE at Farnborough for apprentice training (6th January 1982). The other T.4, WJ867, stayed until 1984 when it was moved by road to the BDR Flight at Abingdon.

By the mid 1970s the school was also using B.2 WK164 which carried white lettering on an overall shiny black finish.

The rugged, adaptable airframe of the Canberra made it an ideal aircraft for use at ETPS.

WJ638 in use with the A&AEE as an ejection seat test bed. In this case note that there are two ejection seat rails showing.
R. C. B. Ashworth

The A&AEE fleet of eight Canberras on the unique event of all being airborne at the same time – which took a little planning in order to find sufficient pilots.

RAE Farnborough

The RAE at Farnborough has had a long and varied connection with the Canberra starting with the original prototype VN799. This aircraft arrived at Farnborough in March 1951 and began a series of auto-pilot trials until it crashed on 18th August 1953 while operating with the Blind Landing Experimental Unit (BLEU) from Martlesham Heath.

A great many other aircraft have been operated by the various elements of the RAE and have been fitted with many non-standard items, including wing-tip bomb racks and camera pods, radome noses, underwing weapon pylons, nose refuelling probes and gust research probes. The RAE has been involved with all the development problems and has carried out weapons trials, runway slush experiments at Thurleigh (Bedford), aquaplaning trials, radar testing and many other still unspecified tests. The Experimental Flying Squadron (EFS) specialised in weapon trials and in the late 1970s such trials included the Stingray torpedo, rocket pods, 1000lb bomb fusing and Cluster Bomb Units (CBU), plus a device called the LSPTV (Low Speed Parachute Test Vehicle). The inventory in 1975-78 comprised six aircraft: B(I)6s WT308 and WT309, painted all over white with pillar-box red nose and tail and the RAE badge on one side of the nose, although this scheme was later changed to the MoD(PE) red/white/blue 'raspberry ripple' scheme; T.4s WH844 and WJ992; B(I)8 WJ643 – the hybrid B.2/B.6/B(I)8 which had previously been used by Ferranti; and, PR.3 WE173 which belonged to the Met Flight.

WT333 B(I)8 of A&AEE, carrying out Microcell Rocket Trials, 1958. This aircraft had the nose of WK135 fitted during 1976 and is currently on charge to RAE.

A&AEE B.2 WH876 seen at Abingdon in September 1965 doing a message pick up! The poles supporting the guide wire can just be seen but the pick up hook is lost underneath the aircraft. *J. B. Collinson*

The RAE's Western Squadron (hence the 'W' formation by personnel) pose for the camera at Farnborough, 1975. The Canberras are B(I)6 WT308 and T.4 WH844. The Hunter T.7 is XL563. *via Vic Avery*

The A&AEE's B.2/B.8 hybrid WV787 was involved in trials as an icing tanker: note the rear spray bar assembly. Seen at an IAT occasion in the mid-1980s. *R. Bonser*

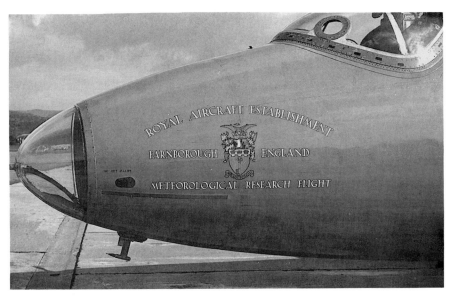

The Institute of Aviation medicine (IAM) has been involved with the medical problems of high speed and high altitude flight as well as that of disorientation. The Meteorological Research Flight has been concerned amongst other things with gust research at high and low level as well as new instrumentation for Met data collection. One of the research programmes necessitated PR.3 WE173 being based at Buckley Field, Denver, Colorado during March 1973 to carry out tests on Clear Air Turbulance (CAT). This aircraft had previously seen service with RAF squadrons before being loaned to the RAE in the early 1960s. It was struck off RAF charge on 15th May 1969 and continued to serve with the RAE until withdrawn in March 1981. This was the last flying PR.3 and sadly ended its days with the BDRF at Coltishall, having been flown there on 4th March 1982.

This page: **Close-up of the nose of WJ582 showing the RAE crest.** *A. Pearcy*

Opposite: **Canberra T.4 WJ992 of the Blind Landing Experimental Unit seen landing at Bedford, 7th October 1958. WJ992 still serves the RAE at Bedford.**

RAE Met Research Flight B.2 WJ582 at Llanbedr in October 1960. *A. Pearcy*

Here, WT333 of RAE wears a specialised nose to reflect particular trials.
F. G. Swanborough

RAE's XH568 in mid-'60s, with long pointed nose probe and interesting fin 'zaps'.

WH657 of the RAE was at Cranfield in June 1966 to carry out slush trials under the control of the College of Aeronautics. Its colour scheme of white with 'arctic' red areas on the nose, rear fuselage and wings was similar to that seen on a number of RAE aircraft over the years.

One Canberra was engaged on Met research that was not an RAE aircraft. B.2 WH872 was attached to 202 Squadron, Coastal Command, at Aldergrove from early 1957 to February 1958 to extend the vertical range of the Met recce flights to above 45,000 ft – well beyond the capability of the Squadron's Hastings! The aircraft was given extra nav kit for its Atlantic flights plus an assortment of Met recording equipment. Brian Hunt, then Met leader on the Squadron, recalls his happy memories of the Canberra . . .

'Just the three of us used to fly on the sorties, which started off as local descents from max height over Aldergrove in order to check our instruments against the radio-sonde balloon as it came up. Having got the temperature corrections, etc sorted out and the pilot 'trained' in doing what the Met observer wanted him to do, we then started to branch out into the North Atlantic and do the same thing with the weather-ship radio-sonde. The final stage was to latch in with the routine Hastings flight and do an extended vertical sounding. Most of the routes were triangles from Aldergrove, with soundings at the two furthest corners. The Hastings would go off to take its readings and descend to low level at the second turn. The Canberra meanwhile would have cooled its heels at Aldergrove to give the Hastings a chance to get well out over the sea, then take off and cruise climb to max height, descending and climbing again as required to get the soundings. In the weather ship phase we used to liven up the crews of the ships by almost removing their masts on several occasions!'

B.2 WH657 arrived at the RAE on 5th June 1953 and amongst the various tests this aircraft carried out were fuel systems development for the National Gas Turbine Establishment. From early 1962 to March 1966 it was used for tracking British satellites in northern latitudes, carrying the nose legend 'UK-USA Co-operation Space Project NASA.' During 1966 WH657 was carrying out slush trials at Cranfield under the control of the College of Aeronautics. It went onto RFD Ltd at Godalming, and in 1986 was bought by Booker Air who loaned it to the Brenzett Museum in Kent.

The PR.9 prototype, WH793, was used by the RAE who fitted a nose probe to carry instrumentation. The aircraft was in service with the establishment until broken up at Farnborough in August 1975.

B.2 WH912 was involved in a series of trials which involved visible modification to its nose outline. At one time the aircraft was being used to develop the AIRPASS system. It also spent time with Ferranti but eventually ended its life derelict at Luton.

B.6 WH952 was used by various sections of the RAE, including the IAM and the Met Research Flight. It left Farnborough in December 1972 and was later used by BAe as a chase aircraft at Warton.

B.2 WK135 was used for runway slush trials at Thurleigh in 1966 after which it went to Pershore and gave up its nose section to WT327 in 1969. The remains of the aircraft had already gone to the fire dump at Pershore.

The BLEU operated T.4 WE189 which had special blind landing equipment fitted. Unfortunately, the aircraft crashed whilst on test from Martlesham Heath killing both crew.

Over a period of 25 years a total of thirty five Canberras in a variety of standard and non-standard marks were operated by the RAE on a wide range of duties.

TRE, RRE; TFU, RRFU; RRS, ARS.

The Telecommunications Research Establishment at Malvern, renamed the Radar Research Establishment (RRE) in 1953, carried out many experiments with Canberras flown initially by the Telecommunications Flying Unit (TFU) based at Defford. This unit was renamed the Radar Research Flying Unit (RRFU) in 1955, but remained based at Defford until 1957 when it moved to Pershore, six miles away. In 1977 it was decided to economise on flying and all RRFU aircraft were transferred to the Royal Aircraft Establishment at Bedford. There, the unit became the Radar Research Squadron (RRS) of the RAE. All aircraft were moved to Bedford by December 1977. The RRS remained in existance until the end of 1988 when it amalgamated with the Flight Systems Squadron at Bedford. On 1st January 1989 the Aerospace Research Squadron (ARS) was formed and fifty years of flying by a unit dedicated solely to flying for the Government's principle radar research unit came to an end.

In April 1991 a major reorganisation saw the Royal Aerospace Establishment relinquish its Royal Charter and become absorbed into the new Defence Research Agency (DRA). Similarly, the RSRE (Royal Signals and Radar Establishment) no longer exists.

In February 1951, WD929, the first production B.2, was the first Canberra to be delivered to the TFU. The Canberra went on to become the most numerous type flown post-war by the unit, and between 1951 and 1977 more than forty Canberras were used on a great variety of radar trials. Some aircraft spent only a few weeks with the organisation whilst others spent their whole working life involved with radar research. The Canberra proved to be so extremely adaptable that it became the standard high performance radar flight trials aircraft. Many sported radomes of various shapes and sizes and some grew humps and bumps to house non standard equipment; others, however, showed no external sign of their experimental nature.

After a period with EE Co and Rolls-Royce, the second prototype VN813 went to the TRE at Defford in 1951 and stayed some months before going on the D.H. Engine Co. The third prototype VN828 also arrived at Defford in 1951 and spent the major part of its working life with the RRE. It suffered Cat.4 damage on 10th June 1953 when the aircraft overran the runway whilst making a flapless landing after an engine failure. The aircraft was rebuilt by Boulton Paul to incorporate a B(I)8 cockpit together with a nose radome housing AI.Mk.18 radar. It was completed

RRE fleet for AI.Mk.18 radar development: Third prototype VN828 (nearest), WJ646 and WH660.

RRE PR.7 (mod) WH774 with dorsal observer's position aft of the cockpit.

in 1955 and returned to the RRE. Testing continued here until the aircraft was further modified to become the Canberra T.11 test-bed, making its first flight as such on 29th March 1958. It was eventually scrapped at Pershore after its last flight on 14th December 1961.

Though VX181 was to be seen at Pershore, it was only flown in on 11th June 1969 after its useful life at A&AEE and was used as a ground training airframe. As mentioned previously, WD929 was the first Canberra to arrive at TRE when it flew in on 9th February 1951. It only remained a few weeks as it was back with EE Co by early April. Similarly, WD930 visited Defford for a few weeks during the summer of 1951. The third production aircraft WD931 arrived during 1958 after some years at the RAE. This aircraft remained working at the RRE until retired following its last flight on 24th February 1965. It was struck off charge on 13th March 1965 and relegated to apprentice training and was finally burnt at Pershore during fire training in June 1969.

WD963 arrived at Defford on loan as a new aeroplane on 11th January 1952. After development trials it was delivered to the RRF at Upwood on 14th July 1952 for service trials with Blue Shadow before being taken on charge by 109 Squadron at Hemswell.

PR.3 WE147 arrived for trials work in 1953 and after various installations made its final flight 23rd February 1968. It was officially retired in August, dismantled in November and finally removed to the AWRE at Shoeburyness during December 1969. Loaned to the RRE in 1952, WF892 only had a short working life as it crashed just after taking off from Exeter following a bird strike on 23rd October 1953.

B.2 WF917 was transferred from RAF charge on 31st May 1953 and delivered to Defford for RRE use. Apart from a short period on loan to the RAE between 24th January and 17th April 1962, it remained at the RRE until retired during 1968. It was sold to BAC and flown out of Pershore 22nd November 1968. Two other B.2s which spent most of their time with RRE were WG788 and WG789. The first was collected for C(A) on 25th August 1952 and was on MoS charge from 31st May 1953 working experimentally on various trials until making its final flight at Pershore 23rd December 1968. Its nose was removed, reworked and then fitted to XH568 in 1970. The RRE made great use of the ability to remove and refit the Canberra's nose. This enabled a cockpit and

nose section to be modified with new installations and only fitted to the aeroplane when ready for flight testing. This feature prevented aircraft being grounded for long periods for modifications to take place. The latter aircraft, WG789, served for some time with 231 OCU at Bassingbourn before being taken onto MoS charge for use at the RAE on 6th February 1956. It was delivered to Boulton Paul at Defford later in the year but was operated by the RRFU from 9th June 1959 on guidance systems trials. Apart from periodic loans to BAC for use as a chase aircraft for Concorde testing at Fairford, WG789 remained with the RRE until transferred to the RAE at Bedford on 1st November 1976.

Another new aircraft collected for C(A) was B.2 WH638 which went initially to BP at Defford. After installation and development work it was handed over to the RRE during 1953 for testing and from 27th October 1954 passed on to 100 Squadron.

WH660 was another B.2 received during 1954 and had AI.Mk.18 installed. After further AI development work as well as guided weapons trials the aircraft was retired after its last flight on 31st January 1970, and broken up during 1971.

More radar trials were carried out by B.2 WH702 which arrived at Defford in 1953. This was eventually retired during 1968 and sold to BAC who flew it out of Pershore on 5th November 1968.

Two other residents with the RRE were PR.7s WH774 and WH776. These both had visible modifications from standard; WH774 having a dorsal observers position aft of the cockpit and WH776 having bulges on both sides of the rear fuselage each housing three cameras. WH774 stayed with the RRE until flown to Bedford to join the RAE on 16th August 1976, whilst WH776 made its last flight 30th April 1970 and was withdrawn to provide spares. A further PR.7 WH777 also spent two years at Defford from 1954 to 1956.

One of only two T.4s used by the RRE, WH854 arrived in 1958 as a B.2 and was used as a target aircraft. It was converted to a T.4 and was in use with the RRE until transferred to ETPS on 14th December 1961. It was flown in from A&AEE to Pershore 3rd March 1969 which proved to be its last flight. It was retired at Pershore during August and broken up there during November 1969. Another target aircraft was B.2 WH857 which spent a few months with the RRFU during 1961.

An unusual aircraft to be delivered to the RRE was WH945 which arrived at Defford from Binbrook 29th April 1957 complete with 'Suez' stripes. An extra long nose with anti-submarine radar was installed and after trials the aircraft was delivered to 100 Squadron at Wittering on 30th April 1959. WH953 was a B.6 which was delivered new to Defford on 28th January 1955. It was transferred from RAF charge on 2nd February and was modified to take AI.Mk.20 in a short conical nose. After a period of testing, the aircraft was modified during 1958 to have a long nose radome, which increased the fuselage length by some four and half feet. This aircraft was flown to the RAE at Bedford 16th December 1976 and still serves there with the ARS.

Next in serial order was WJ627, another B.2, received from the Ferranti flying unit on 9th September 1963. This Canberra was also loaned as needed to BAC as a chase aircraft during the testing of Concorde. WJ646 was also a B.2 and was transferred off RAF charge 16th September 1954 and delivered direct to Defford. It was converted by Boulton Paul to carry AI.Mk.18 in an extended B(I)8 nose unit. It flew on various other trials until making its final flight 18th December 1968. It was officially retired during 1969 and was dismantled and removed by road to Boscombe Down on 16th December 1970.

Taken off RAF charge on 9th December 1955, WJ679 was another B.2 to spend most of its life with the RRE, much of it as a special target aircraft. WJ679's last flight was 13th October 1967. It was retired during 1968 and broken up during December.

Loaned from the RAF after serving with 109 Squadron, B.6 WJ770 was delivered to Defford during 1955 for installations and trials. After completion the aircraft was delivered to the RRF at Wyton during 1956.

Used as a jamming aircraft for guided weapons trials, B.2 WJ990 arrived at the RRE during 1963 and after five years was flown out to 15 MU at Wroughton on 30th April 1968. The only other T.4 to be used by RRE arrived from the RAE 27th September 1962. This was WJ992, also a converted B.2, and was the last Canberra to leave the RRFU at Pershore when it was flown back to the RAE at Bedford 1st November 1977. It is still in use with the ARS at Bedford.

Flown in during 1963 B.2 WK119 was modified as a jamming aircraft and worked for the RRFU until flown out to 15 MU at Wroughton 29th January 1968. Much earlier, B.2 WK120 had been transferred from RAF charge on 9th December 1955 and was modified for trials at Defford. It was the last of the RRFU Canberras to transfer from Defford to Pershore, doing so on 9th October 1957. After a long spell of trials it made its last flight at Pershore on 21st January 1968 and was later broken

up there. WK121 had been taken from RAF charge on 21st April 1954 and though allotted to BP at Defford it was transferred to the RRE on 13th December 1955. It remained in use as a target aircraft for two years until leaving during 1957. In use with 100 Squadron at Wittering, the RAF loaned B.2 WK123 to the RRE for trials for a period during 1955 and 1957. After this it was returned to the unit at Wittering. WK128, another B.2, arrived at Pershore during 1958 and was used initially as a jamming aircraft. After further research work it was withdrawn from use in May 1975 and was eventually dismantled in February 1977 and removed by road to Tarrant Rushton for Flight Refuelling Ltd. This aircraft still serves at Llanbedr. In the same production series, B.2 WK129 also went to Defford in 1955. After a relatively short working life it flew into high ground at Carnedd, Llewelyn in North Wales on 9th December 1957.

After being used by Bristol Siddeley for testing Viper engines, WK163 moved to Pershore in 1959 and began a long association with radar testing. It was rebuilt at Pershore during 1968 and 1969 when it was fitted with B.6 wings and engines. Its original nose was fitted to WT327 during 1969, and later during 1972 WK163 received the nose from XH568. This again demonstrates the flexibility of the Canberra nose units. On 1st July 1976 it was the first of the RRFU Canberras to be transferred to the RAE at Bedford, where it served until 1986.

B(I)8 airframes have also played their part in the research programmes. WT327 was received from Ferranti on 12th April 1966 after it had been used for TSR.2 development work. During 1969 and 1970 it was fitted with the B.2 nose and cockpit removed from WK135 and became, in effect, a B.6. This was modified to incorporate a LRMTS and the aircraft flew again in April 1971. During 1972 the reworked nose from WK163 was fitted and except for a short spell with the A&AEE, this aircraft served solely with the RRE until being handed over to the RAE at Bedford on 25th April 1977, where it continues to serve with the ARS.

Two other B.6s have given long service to the RRE. The first, XH567, arrived at Pershore in 1961 and amongst other trials was used in the development of the sideways looking radar for the TSR.2. It was flown to Bedford on 16th December 1976 and continues in use with the ARS. The second aircraft, XH568, did not arrive until 1967, after it had been used by the RAE at Farnborough. It was converted to long nose configuration by fitting the nose removed from WG788 and suitably modified. The original nose went in turn to WK163. This Canberra was also flown to the RAE, but a month earlier, on 18th November 1976, and it too still serves at Bedford.

WH945 was received by RRE from Binbrook in early 1957, still wearing the Suez Crisis markings from its days with 12 Squadron as a standard B.6. *via M.Nolan*

Canberra B.6 WH953 wearing the RAE 'raspberry ripple' scheme. *F. G. Swanborough*

Finally, the SC.9 XH132 spent the latter part of its life on radar trials at Pershore. It arrived 21st January 1972 and remained nearly five years until flown to Bedford 18th November 1976. It continued flying with the RRS at Bedford until its final flight to St Mawgan 24th September 1986 for use by the BDRF there. A sad end to an interesting aeroplane.

Torpedo Development Unit
The Torpedo Development Unit (TDU) at Gosport received B.2 WH661 and carried out parachute mine trials between July 1953 and March 1955. After this the aircraft served with the RAE for a number of years.

Many other Canberras were used over the years for a great many tests and trials, this chapter has recorded a number of the more interesting histories. Much of the development work, especially that involving weapons and radar, is still of an unknown nature and will no doubt remain classified for a number of years. However, the importance of the Canberra in the field of trials and experimentation cannot be doubted.

Above: A fine study of WK163 in service with the RRE. *R. Henry*

B.6s XH567 and '568 have spent their entire careers with the RAE and/or RRE. *R. Henry*

Canberras in Colour

At first glance you might be forgiven for thinking this was the prototype Canberra on an early test flight, but in fact it is one of Wyton's T.4s, WT478, doing a splendid job of pretending to be VN799 on the occasion of the 40th Anniversary celebrations in May 1989. Amongst the crew for this flight was 'Bee' Beamont – who else! For further details of this event see pages 209-211. *T. Malcolm English*

Above: **VX181, the PR.3 prototype, was another Canberra that spent its career as a test/trials aircraft and is seen here, circa 1964, in a very attractive scheme that included the inscription 'Bomber & Maritime Test Squadron' – an element of the A&AEE.** *R. Bonser*

Below: **In 1967, PR.3 WE146 was adapted by Shorts (as the SD.1) to act as a launch aircraft for the American-built Beech AQM-37A supersonic target drone, itself modified for British use as the SD.2 *Stiletto* (right). WE146 was on the books at RAE Llanbedr when it went to the 25th Anniversary celebrations at Cottesmore in May 1974. Judging by the 'nose art' it appears to have made a creditable 26 *Stiletto* firings by then.** *R. Bonser*

B.2 WP515 in the 'Bomber Command 1' black/grey scheme, in the early 1950s. *via D.M.Sargent*

Canberra B.2 WJ713 was in the static line-up at RAF Syerston for the 'Battle of Britain' Open Day on 19th September 1959. It was believed to be a College of Air Warfare machine. Note the small unit badge on the nose and the red (arctic?) areas on fin, tailplane and outer wing panels. *R.Bonser*

B.2 7590M (ex WH668) at the 4 SoTT St Athan Open Day, 8th October 1961, in the 'Bomber Command 2' paint scheme of medium sea grey/light sea grey upper surfaces with PRU blue under surfaces. Note the 10 Squadron red 'speed bird' on the nose and the Honington Wing 'rising pheasant' on the fin. *M.P.Marsh*

No.1 SoTT instructional airframe '18' is actually 7387M ex-WD999, which served at Halton from November 1956 until eventually dismantled in 1978. Taken on 18th April 1972, this scene will evoke many memories: the staff NCO instructor in the white coat, the trainees under instruction, the trolley acc etc. On the fin is the 'Black Swan' emblem of 103 Squadron and on the nose a variation of the 551 Wing marking, plus the pennant of Squadron Leader Shuster.

B.2 WK145 was photographed at around mid-day in the static line-up at RAF Gaydon's 'Battle of Britain' Open Day on 19th September 1964. Note the red/white 98 Squadron markings on the nose and the more orange-looking areas on the fin and outer wing. *M.P.Marsh*

231 OCU B.2 WJ677 in the light grey with red day-glo strips scheme, photographed at Cottesmore in 1970. Note the leopard's head crest on the fin and the serial number repeated on the nose wheel door. *MAP*

B.2 WJ731 'BK' in the final 231 OCU scheme, landing at Wyton, 2nd May 1990. 231 OCU was disbanded in the following December due to the requirements of Operation *Granby* but '731 continued on with 231's eventual progenitor, the Canberra Standardisation and Training (or CAST) Flight. *J.B.E.Hale*

T.4 WE192 in the short-lived red and white 'non operational' livery, circa 1973. *via D.M.Sargent*

This July 1969 photograph shows T.4 7636M (ex-WJ878) in the early training colour scheme, silver with yellow trainer bands around the rear fuselage and wings, as well as displaying the No.1 SoTT airframe code '19'. This machine had spells with the A&AEE, RAE and EECo interspersed with service at 231 OCU, from where it was flown, to Halton for use as an instructional airframe in May 1960. *B.Lewis*

T.4 WJ879 'BH' of 231 OCU overflies RAF Wyton on 2nd May 1990. Note the colour scheme, the Type B roundels and the absence of underwing serials. *J.B.E.Hale*

Canberra B.6 (BS) WJ770 of the Radar Reconnaissance Flight based at Wyton. Note the red areas on the fin, tailplane and wing-tips applied as a safeguard against a forced landing in the arctic, also the unit's green lightning flash on the fin. Note the 'Heath Robinson' fuel catcher (?) too! Although not wholly in focus this is indeed a rare photograph, believed to have been taken in 1958 – probably during '770's second spell with the RRF. *Neville Franklin collection*

B.6 (BS) WJ781 of 9 Squadron attended an Open Day at the RCAF base at Langar, Notts on 8th July 1961, only five days before the Squadron disbanded. The distinctive 'Blue Shadow' modification can be seen on the fuselage side. *R. Bonser*

B(I)6 WT313 spent all of its service career with 213 Squadron whose 'hornet' emblem adorns the fin. It is seen here staked out at Teversham, Cambridge Airport, sometime in 1967. It was SoC in the October of the following year. *B. Lewis*

Canberra PR.3 WE172 of 231 OCU Bassingbourn begins its display at Coventry Airport, Baginton, on the occasion of the National Air Races, 18th August 1962. *R. Bonser*

PR.7 WJ815 at the Abingdon 'Battle of Britain' Open Day, 6th September 1967. The distinctive 58 Squadron 'owl' motif has appeared in several variations over the 'PR' years; here it is in stencilled form, at other times it has been superimposed on a white disc. Note also the red starter 'bullet'. *R. Bonser*

WT530, one of the Malta based 13 Squadron PR.7s, attended the 25th Anniversary Canberra celebration at Cottesmore on 22nd May 1974. *R. Bonser*

PR.7 WT519 of 100 Squadron on the runway at Wyton, 17th June 1987. Note the towing banner being laid out alongside. *J.B.E. Hale*

This Shorts-built PR.9, XH133, spent seven years on various trials before entering squadron service. It is seen here at Warton on 11th June 1966, whilst on BAC Flight Trials. In the background is the sole Reid and Sigrist RS.4 Desford trainer, G-AGOS. XH133 was placed in storage at St Athan in 1982 and had been moved to the scrapping area by mid 1992. *B.Lewis*

PR.9 XH165 displays its 39 Squadron fin marking at the Finningley 'Battle of Britain' Open Day, 19th September 1980. It had previously served 58 and 13 Squadrons and later it went to 1 PRU. It was placed in storage at St Athan in September 1987 and was noted in the scrapping area in September 1992. *B.Lewis*

1 PRU PR.9 XH135 'AC' taxies in at Wyton on 18th April 1989. *J.B.E.Hale*

The latest squadron number-plate changes announced by Strike Command in the wake of the 'peace dividend' meant that 1 PRU would become No.39 (1 PRU) Squadron in July 1992. The newly named unit's fin marking was evident on XH169 'AC' on 15th August 1992. *J.B.E.Hale*

16 Squadron adopted a shark's mouth marking towards the end of its B(I)8 period as evidenced here on WT332. A white skeletal figure of 'the Saint' was also sometimes on the fin. At other periods, this unit's B(I)8s were seen with crossed-keys on a white disc on the port side (ie WT345 in 1967) and a Squadron badge on the starboard side (ie XM262 in 1970). Larger rear fuselage serials and the rear fuselage black/yellow band were also worn on these latter two occasions.

WT332 B(I)8 'M' of 3 Squadron, Geilenkirchen, RAF Germany, was a guest at the Finningley 'Battle of Britain' Open Day, on 16th September 1967. Note the code on the nose wheel door and large rear fuselage serial (compared to the previous photograph). *C.J.Salter*

B.15 WH960 in use as a g/i airframe at No.2 SoTT Cosford in May 1982. Although allocated 8344M it still sports its service serial number and 32 Squadron colours. The white strip, on the fin below the code, probably once had XXXII superimposed upon it, as did others on the unit. The aircraft was on offer for sale in September 1991. *R.Bonser*

Seen here at Boscombe Down on 7th September '67, is one of the Akrotiri Strike Wing's B.15s – WH948. Later in the day it was to participate in a Firepower Demonstration on the Larkhill range. This particular machine was later converted to an E.15 (see opposite page). *B.Lewis*

98 Squadron E.15, WH948 complete with unit colours on the nose and black Cerberus on the fin, on approach to its home base at Cottesmore, 1st September 1972. Some aircraft of this unit wore a single figure code (usually the last digit of the serial) in white above the fin flash. *B.Lewis*

Radar target trainer T.11 WH904 of 85 Squadron approaches its home base of Binbrook in 1967/8 (the precise date is unknown). Although this example does not carry a letter code, some others did, in black, above the fin flash. *via R.Bonser*

T.19 WJ975 'X' of 100 Squadron at the Leuchars 'Battle of Britain' Open Day, on 14th September 1974. Its home base at this time was West Raynham. *B.Lewis*

The T.22s were re-worked PR.7s with an 'off the shelf' radar for aircrew radar instruction. WH801 was the first example delivered to FRADTU and is seen here at the Cottesmore 25th Anniversary gathering in May 1974. *R.Bonser*

Opposite page:
Camouflaged 360 Squadron T.17 WK111 'B' photographed in the Autumn of 1973. *via R.Bonser*

Another 360 Squadron T.17, WJ630 'ED' at Wyton, 5th September 1988, in the 'hemp' scheme. *J.B.E.Hale*

360 Squadron T.17A WD955 'EM' – the oldest Canberra still in regular RAF service – had acquired an attractive fin marking at this time, 9th November 1991. *J.B.E.Hale*

This page, from the top:
Operated by Airwork Services Ltd for the Royal Navy, 776 FRU TT.18 WK126 in the sun at Hurn, 10th September 1971. Sadly, no sign of the 'Penguin' unit marking. *B.Lewis*

7 Squadron TT.18 WJ721 was another of the participants at the Cottesmore 25th Anniversary gathering, 22nd May 1974. *R.Bonser*

A rather wet Royal Navy FRADU TT.18 WJ717 '841' at Yeovilton, 28th June 1977. Note the remains of a fin flash – presumably a hangover from its former career with the Royal Air Force. *B.Lewis*

By 4th June 1980 the FRADU TT.18s had exchanged their red rear fuselage band for a yellow one. This is WJ636, at Yeovilton. *J.B.E.Hale*

100 Squadron TT.18 WK127 'CS' lands at Wyton, 17th July 1986. *J.B.E.Hale*

This 100 Squadron TT.18, WJ636 'CX' had acquired a black fin and rudder when photographed on 2nd August 1990. *J.B.E.Hale*

A Manching-based WTD-61 crew took 99+34 to Fürstenfeldbruck Open Day on 18th July 1992. They confirmed that it had been fitted with the wings of former 100 Squadron TT.18 WK123 'CY'. *WTD-61*

Nice air-to-air of 99+35 of the Militarische Geographisches Amt, based at Jever. *WTD-61*

Opposite page: **This Indian AF 6 Squadron trio, photographed on 27th November 1990 over the Arabian Sea near Pune, comprises B(I)66 F1021, 'TT' Q1792(?) and B(I)12 IF930. The latter still wears the triangular nose patch of its former operator – No.1 TTU.** *P.Steinemann, Skyline APA*

Indian B(I)58 IF922 from No.1 Target Towing Unit, based at Pune, in a striking targeting scheme for work with naval ships. Photographed 27th November 1990 – from a MiG-29! *P.Steinemann, Skyline APA*

Unique view of all three German Canberras during their 'D' serials phase, taken at Wahn.

South African Air Force 'Can' T.4 457 – 31 years old and looking good when recorded on this low pass. Note the glazed nose and low visibility markings. It was eventually retired in 1990 and passed to the SAAF Museum at Swartkop. *SAAF*

Martin EB-57B 52-1564 on the ramp at Andrews AFB in May 1981. Its markings suggest it belonged to the 134 DSES, Vermont ANG. The unit name 'The Green Mountain Boys' painted on the chaff dispenser pod has connections with the spirited local militia at the time of the American Revolution. *J.Grech collection*

International Air Tattoo '79, held at Greenham Common, was notable for coinciding with so many anniversaries, including the Phantom's 21st, the Lightning's 25th and the Canberra's 30th! Amongst the latter was '1233' from one of the major overseas users – the Fuerza Aerea Venezolana. This was one of 23 B.2/ B(I)2 aircraft that returned to BAC for modernisation and refurbishment between 1975 and 1980. This particular machine was redelivered as a B.82 on 27th June 1979 – a matter of only three days after this photograph was taken. This event was also notable for the rain! *B.Lewis*

Canberras have been used for a multitude of tasks over the years, including ejection-seat trials by Martin Baker Limited. Here, WH876 tests yet another seat . . .

WV787 spent all its working life as a trials vehicle before eventually being preserved at the Newark Air Museum. It had been used by the A&AEE for icing trials (note the spray bar under the rear fuselage) prior to attending the Greenham Common Air Tattoo in July 1981. *J.Grech*

Above: **Completed in 1959 as a PR.9, XH132 underwent extensive modifications by Shorts and was redesignated SC.9. Thus began a test career that would eventually span 36 years. It is seen here at Hatfield, 1st July 1969, whilst with Hawker Siddeley Dynamics** . *B.Lewis*

Below left: **XH132 then went to the RRE to conduct missile homing head trials. It also acquired a new paint scheme to reflect its change of ownership – as evidenced here, when it was seen participating in the 25th Anniversary celebrations at Cottesmore, on 22nd May 1974.** *R.Bonser*

Below right: **In December 1976, XH132 was transferred to the RAE and soon received their 'raspberry ripple' colours – in which guise it attended an Open Day at Wyton on 15th July 1984. Retired to BDRF duties at St Mawgan in September 1986, it was reported to have been repainted but was broken up on site during 1992, in spite of efforts to preserve it.** *J.B.E.Hale*

Above: **The RAE (and now the DRA) at Llanbedr have utilised Canberras for a variety of trials and duties throughout the career of this illustrious type, many of them in connection with the Aberporth range. Here the attractively painted WK128 is seen on approach to its home airfield, on 16th May 1990.** *J.B.E.Hale*

Left: **This pleasing four-ship formation is representative of the Wyton Canberra Wing in the mid 'eighties – pre-'hemp' days. The 231 OCU T.4 leads a 360 Squadron T.17, 100 Squadron B.2 and a 1 PRU PR.9 past the tower, in some style.** *RAF Wyton*

Below: **100 Squadron began to shed its Canberras in favour of Hawks with effect from October 1991. This photograph, taken during the transition phase, features TT.18 WJ682 'CU' and Hawk T.1A XX247 'CM' – both in the unit's colours.** *via J.B.E.Hale*

Chapter Ten

40 Years of the Canberra
– 13th May 1989 –

The unique character of the Canberra was emphasised by the 40th Anniversary celebrations which took place at RAF Wyton on the weekend 12-14th May 1989. The intention was to gather as many ex-Canberra personnel together as possible but it rapidly became evident that this would have run into many thousands and so the reluctant decision was made to limit the event to Canberra aircrew and engineering officers. Even so, the enquiries flooded in by the hundred and eventually about 1400 people attended the event. A formal dinner was held in the officers Mess – the list of Air Rank officers alone was testament to how widespread was the Canberra's net. The stories flowed thick and fast as indeed they did also at the infomal gathering for those not attending the dinner – enough stories to fill a volume twice the size of this. The authors have stowed many away ready for the 50th anniversary of the Canberra and the re-issue of this history! However, the most fascinating aspect was the age range – a look across the room from groups aged 60 (they had been in their early '20s when, fresh-faced, they joined the first Bomber Command Canberra squadrons) to groups still in their early '20s linked by the fact that they had all flown this remarkable aircraft. There is no other aircraft type that this could apply to now or in the past. The Canberra is without doubt unique.

The celebrations continued on Saturday 13th, 40 years to the day since VN799 first took to the sky and the Canberra era began. A hangar had been arranged for the main event with aircraft and equipment displays plus a history and photographic display for each squadron. This latter area became the focus of attention for the entire morning as crews were re-united after 30 years apart. Yet more stories were swopped, often prompted by the sight of a particular photograph. Amidst this amicable chaos the authors made new contacts and were grateful to have sight of many photographs some of which we have been able to include in this history. The Canberra photo archive is an on-going concern and we would be delighted to hear from anyone with items concerning the Canberra.

The afternoon was devoted to a flying display – opened by a recreation of the first flight with one of Wyton's T.4s (WT478) doing a splendid job of pretending to be VN799. Although the blue paint was not quite right the overall effect was perfect, as was that on the reserve aircraft!

Aircraft and equipment, plus photographic displays for each squadron proved a major attraction at the reunion . This was the scene in one small part of the hangar on the Saturday. The PR.9 is XH174 of 1 PRU.

The crew for the re-enactment of VN799's first flight (in WT478) comprised 'Bee' Beamont (centre), Squadron Leader Dave Watson (right) and Flying Officer Baker .

The crew for this flight consisted of 'Bee' Beamont (who else!), Squadron Leader Dave Watson (longest serving Canberra pilot) and navigator, Flying Officer Baker (the 'newest' Canberra navigator). A number of other aircraft took part in the display including the Mosquito and Vulcan but the closing session was all Canberra. The OCU put up a four-ship, the *Green Marrows* – the first time this has been seen for many years, the PR.9 did its usual astounding display, there was a mixed Wyton formation and an attack profile by a pair of TT.18s. Tremendous stuff and a fitting tribute to the Canberra!

However, there was no pause as it was on to the official reception in another of the Wyton hangars where champagne, marching bands and speeches brought the official side of the day to a close. In the evening the Officers Mess hosted its largest ever party with no less than 1200 guests. Even in the early hours of the morning stories were still in full flow and a 'competition' was being run, by word of mouth, as to who had the most Canberra hours – the highest appears to be around 8000 but another record which takes some beating is that of 3500 hours in the T.4!

A few hours rest and it was off to Bassingbourn for the last party of the weekend. To many this was little short of a pilgrimage, back to the home of the Canberra. It was a most appropriate way to wind up what had been a unique event.

As with all such events a number of commemorative items were produced, one of the finest being a 24″x33″ print of a pair of Canberras. This print, from a painting by Robert Taylor, shows a B.2 (WE113) and a T.4 (WH849) over the twin-canals, an area that all Canberra aircrew know well. It is a most evocative print and is full of life. Details of this limited (1000 numbered and signed) edition can be obtained from the publisher of this book, Midland Counties Publications, Unit 3, Maizefield, Hinckley Fields, Hinckley, Leicestershire, LE10 1YF.

From the top: **The 'spare' VN799 – in reality 231 OCU T.4 WJ877 (and also painted blue) sits quietly in the line of static Canberras, on the Friday afternoon.** *C.J.Salter*

This impressive air to ground photo reveals the forty Canberras assembled to celebrate the occasion. The far line consists mainly of 100 Squadron and the PRU, while the OCU, 360 Squadron, visiting machines and the 'spare' VN799 are in the nearer line.

100 Squadron TT.18 WK118 'CQ' holds the foreground as the Friday enthusiasts do the rounds. *C.J.Salter*

231 OCU put up the four-ship 'Green Marrows' on the Saturday.

TT.18 WK123 'CY' was on the strength of 100 Squadron. *C.J.Salter*

B.2/TT.18 WH734 was from RAE Llanbedr. *C.J.Salter*

This 360 Squadron T.17A (WH902/EK) was under tow and in the process of being marshalled into the line up, on the Friday afternoon. *C.J.Salter*

During the afternoon of Friday 12th May, several hundred jubilant enthusiasts were privileged to gain admission to RAF Wyton to view the assembled Canberras and other aircraft types sent as representatives of former Canberra units. For the record, details of the individual aircraft present on that occasion follow:

Static – WT478 (normally 'BA', painted as 'VN799/P') Canberra T.4, 231 OCU; XS605 Andover E.3, 115 Sqn; XT668/S Wessex HC.2, 72 Sqn; XT897/CC Phantom FGR.2, 228 OCU; XV869 Buccaneer S.2B, 12 Sqn; XX766/EC Jaguar GR.1, 6 Sqn (special marks); ZE116/AL Tornado GR.1, 9 Sqn; ZD714/BE Tornado GR.1, 14 Sqn; ZA470/FL Tornado GR.1, 16 Sqn; ZA600/CM Tornado GR.1, 17 Sqn; ZA542/JA Tornado GR.1, 27 Sqn; ZD747/DK Tornado GR.1, 31 Sqn; ZA559/L Tornado GR.1, 617 Sqn; ZE789/DD Tornado F.3, 11 Sqn; ZA714/EX Chinook HC.1, 7 Sqn; N907FR Falcon 20, FR Ltd.

Canberra Line-up – WH670/CB, WP515/CD Canberra B.2's; WT509/CG, WT519/CH, WT538/CJ, WH779/CK Canberra PR.7's; WH972/CM, WH981/CN, WH983/CP Canberra E.15's; WK118/CQ, WK124/CR, WJ680/CT, WJ682/CU, WJ715/CV, WH718/CW, WJ636/CX, WK123/CY Canberra TT.18's, all 100 Sqn; WK111/EA, WJ630/ED, WH664/EH, WF890/EJ, WF916/EL, WJ986/EP Canberra T.17s, 360 Sqn; WJ607/EB, WJ633/EF, WH646/EG, WH902/EK, WJ981/EN Canberra T.17As, 360 Sqn; XH168/AB, XH169/AC, XH131/AF, XH135/AG Canberra PR.9's, 1 PRU; WT480/BC, WJ877 (normally /BG, also painted as 'VN799/P'), WE113/BJ, WJ731/BK, WJ866/BL, WJ874/BM Canberra T.4's, 231 OCU; WH734 Canberra B(TT).2, RAE Llanbedr; WK142/848 Canberra TT.18, FRADU. 'AB', 'AC', 'AF', 'AG', 'EB', 'ED', 'EF', 'EG', 'EJ', 'EK', 'EL', and 'EN' were in the hemp colour-scheme.

Hangar Display – WD955/EM Canberra T.17A, 360 Sqn; XH174 Canberra PR.9, 1 PRU; WH848 Canberra T.4 (fuselage, ex / BD 231 OCU).

Elsewhere – XV191 Hercules C.1P, LTW (for press use); XW664 Nimrod R.1P, 51 Sqn; XX182 Hawk T.1, 4 FTS; XX350 Hawk T.1, TWU/234 Sqn; XZ591/S Sea King HAR. Three/234 Sqn; ZA774 Gazelle AH.1, AAC; 10979/AR gy/bk A-10A, 10 TFW; RR299/HT-E (G-ASKH) Mosquito T.3, BAe; WK127/FO Canberra TT.18, BDRF; WJ817/FU Canberra PR.7, ex BDRF, on dump.

Main Gate – WH773 Canberra PR.7 (8696M, 13 Sqn marks); WT305 Canberra B.6 (mod) (8511M, 51 Sqn marks); XH170 Canberra PR.9 (8739M, 39 Sqn marks).

The only based Canberras not noted were B.2 WJ567/CC and E.15 WJ756/CL (definitely still current, noted on 21.4) of 100 Sqn, and T.4's WH849/BE and WJ879/BH of 231 OCU.

Sadly, Gp Cpt Reginald McKendrick, Wyton Station Commander and architect of these celebrations, lost his life in the accident to Canberra T.4 WJ877 at Wyton on 18th March 1991.

Appendix One

Canberra Records

During its first ten years the Canberra was always in the news for breaking speed and height records and by 1958 no less than nineteen point-to-point and three height records had been officially recognised. There were a number of other records achieved but in the absence of 'official' observance they went unrewarded.

POINT-TO-POINT RECORDS

21st February 1951
Atlantic crossing (Aldergrove to Gander)
B.2 WD932 in 4 hours 37 minutes.
Sqn Ldr A. E. Caillard, Flt Lt Haskett and
Flt Lt A. J. R. Robson.
Unofficial.

31st August 1951
Atlantic crossing (Aldergrove to Gander)
B.2 WD940 in 4 hours 18 minutes.
Wg Cdr R. P. Beamont, D. A. Watson and
R. H. T. Rylands.
Average speed 481.12 mph.

18th February 1952
London to Tripoli (Castel Benito)
B.2 WD962 in 2 hrs 41 mins 49.5 secs.
Sqn Ldr L. C. E. Devigne, Flt Lt P. A. Hunt.
Average speed 538.12 mph.

26th August 1952
Double crossing of Atlantic
(Aldergrove to Gander and back)
VX185 in 10 hrs 3 mins 29.28 secs.
Wg Cdr R. P. Beamont, Peter Hillwood
and Dennis Watson.
Average speed 411.99 mph.

26th August 1952
Atlantic crossing (Gander to Aldergrove)
VX185 in 3 hrs 25 mins 18.13 secs.
Average speed 605.52 mph.

25th Sept 1952
UK to Luqa and back
6 hours 5 minutes.
AVM Dermot Boyle, Fg Off R. B. Brownlow,
and Sgt T. Cramp.   Unofficial.

28th September 1952
London to Nairobi (Eastleigh)
WD987 B.2 of 12 Squadron
9 hours 55 minutes 16.7 seconds.
Wg Cdr H. P. Connelly (OC Flying, Binbrook),
Sqn Ldr D. Clare and ACM Sir Hugh P. Lloyd.
Average speed 427.3 mph.

27th January 1953
London to Karachi (Mauripur)
PR.3 VX181 in 8 hrs 52 mins 28.2 secs.
Flt Lt L. M. Whittington, Flt Lt J. A. Brown.
Average speed 441.8 mph.

27/28th January 1953
London to Darwin
VX181 in 22 hours 21.8 seconds.
Flt Lt L. M. Whittington, Flt Lt J. A. Brown.
Average speed 391.2 mph.

8th October 1953
London to Iraq (Basra)
PR.3 WE139 on New Zealand Air Race
5 hours 11 minutes 5.6 seconds.
Flt Lt R. L. E. Burton, Flt Lt D. H. Gannon.
Average speed 544.3 mph.

8/9th October 1953
London to New Zealand
(Christchurch) Air Race,
WE139 in 23 hrs 50 mins 42 secs.
Flt Lt R. L. E. Burton, Flt Lt D. H. Gannon.
Average speed 494.48 mph.

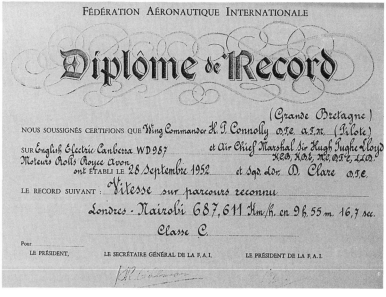

8/9th October 1953
London to Ceylon (Colombo)
PR.7 WH773 in 10 hrs 25 mins 21.5 secs.
Wg Cdr L. M. Hodges, Sqn Ldr R. Currie
Average speed 519.5 mph.

17th December 1953
London to South Africa (Capetown)
WH699 *Aries IV* 12 hrs 21 mins 3.8 secs.
Wg Cdr G. G. Petty, Sqn Ldr T. McGarry and
Sqn Ldr J. McD Craig.
Average speed 486.6 mph.

19th December 1953
Capetown to London
WH699 *Aries IV* 13 hrs 16 mins 25.2 secs.
Wg Cdr A. H. Humphrey, Sqn Ldr D. Bower
and Sqn Ldr R. F. B. Powell.
Average speed 452.8 mph.

14/15th October 1954
Norway to Canada
1st British jet flight over North Pole.
WH699 *Aries IV* in 6 hours 43 minutes.
Wg Cdr A. H. Humphrey, Sqn Ldr D. Bower
and Flt Lt F. R. Wood

28th February 1955
Scampton to Cyprus (Nicosia)
4 hours 13 minutes.
AVM J. R. Whitley.   Unofficial

28th June 1955
Ottawa to London
WH699 *Aries IV* in 6 hrs 42 mins 12 secs.
Sqn Ldr I. G. Broom.
Average speed 496.82 mph.

Opposite page: **FAI Diploma for the London-Nairobi record.** *Wg Cdr D. Clare*

VX185, the B.5 prototype, with its Atlantic record flights nose art. *BAC SE310*

This page, from the top: **PR.7 WT504 returns to Wyton five days after its non-stop Wyton-Khormaksar flight on 24th October 1955.**

B.2 WD932 leaves Aldergrove 21st February 1951 on its record-breaking flight. *via Flt Lt A. J. R. Robson*

PR.3 WE139, victor in the London-New Zealand Air Race, complete with race number and nose legend, 1953. *BAe SG726*

23rd August 1955
London to New York
PR.7 WT528 in 7 hrs 29 mins 56.7 secs.
Capt J. Hackett, Peter Moneypenney.
Average speed 461.12 mph

23rd August 1955
New York to London
PR.7 WT528 6 hrs 16 mins 59.5 secs.
Average speed 550.35 mph.

23rd August 1955
London to New York to London
PR.7 WT528 14 hrs 21 mins 45.5 secs.
Average speed 481.52 mph.

24th October 1955
Wyton to Khormaksar
PR.7 WT504 58 Squadron
in 7 hours 45 minutes.
Sqn Ldr E. J. Holloway, Fg Off Broom.
Unofficial.

16th February 1956
London to Cairo
B(I)8 in 3 hours 57 minutes 18.9 seconds.
Peter Hillwood and Dennis Watson
Average speed 551.8 mph.

25th May 1957
Tokyo to London
PR.7 WT528 *Aries V*
in 17 hrs 42 mins 2.4 secs.
Wg Cdr W. Hoy, Flt Lt P. J. Lageson
and Flt Lt J. J. L. Denis.
Average speed 335.7 mph.

22nd February 1958
Washington to Caracas
4 hours 10 minutes 59.7 seconds.
Delivery of T.4 2E-39 by Capt J. Hackett,
P. Moneypenney and FAV officer.
Average speed 492.95 mph.

HEIGHT RECORDS

63,668 ft – 4th May 1953.
WD952 with Bristol Olympus engines.
W. F. Gibb.

65,890 ft – 29th August 1955.
WD952 with Bristol Olympus engines.
W. F. Gibb.

70,310 ft – 28th August 1957.
WK163 with Scorpion rocket motor.
Mike Randrup.

Appendix Two

Canberra Variants
and Projects Summary

The alpha-numeric sequence included in the first column of the following tabulated data is essentially a 'Company type number' derived from the Society of British Aircraft Constructors' standard drawing office system of designations for British aircraft, instigated in the late 1940s. It consisted of one letter (or in some cases two) representing the initial of the design firm, followed by two characters (one alphabetical and one numerical) representing the aircraft for which the design had been prepared. These latter two characters constituted the 'type number'.

English Electric were allotted the company prefix 'E' under this system, and 'A1' was the 'type number' of the first aircraft on which the standard system was employed (. . the second would be 'A2', the ninth 'A9', the tenth 'B1' and so on), hence 'E.A1'. In similar fashion, Short Bros, who were responsible for some Canberra development design, used company designator 'S' to prefix their drawing references, e.g. 'S.C9'.

British service designations take the form of a role letter prefix to a model number, e.g. B.Mk.6 – where 'B' indicates 'Bomber', 'Mk' (mark) the normal standard and '6' the sixth major model/ variant. This is frequently abbreviated to B.6, or even B6.

Designation details	Serial	F/f date
E.A1 1st prototype (spec B3/45)	VN799	13.5.49
2 x 6000 lb st RR Avon RA.2		
E.A1 2nd prototype	VN813	9.11.49
2 x 5000 lb st RR Nene R.Ne.2		
E.A1 2nd prototype DH Spectre dev.	VN813	18.12.56
2 x 5000 lb st RR Nene +		
1 x 7000 lb DH Spectre DSpe1		
E.A1 3rd prototype	VN828	22.11.49
2 x 6000 lb st RR Avon RA.2		
E.A1 4th prototype	VN850	20.12.49
2 x 6000 lb st RR Avon RA.2		
E.A3 B.2 prototype (spec B5/47)	VX165	23.4.50
2 x 6500 lb st RA.3 (101)		
E.A3 B.2 – 1st production (EECo)	WD929	8.10.50
2 x 6500 lb st RR Avon RA.3 (101)		
B.2 – Avon development		
2 x 7590 lb st RA.7	WD930	8.51
2 x 9500 lb st RA.14	WD930	.7.53
2 x 10000 lb st RA.26	WD930	.54
1 x 10000 lb st RA.26 (stbd) +		
1 x 10500 lb st RA.29 (port)	WD930	8.56
2 x 9500 lb st RA.7R	WD943	.51
2 x 11500 lb st RA.14R	WD943	
B.2 – Sapphire development		
2 x 7590 lb st ASSa3	WD933	8.51
2 x 8300 lb st ASSa6	WD933	4.52
2 x 10300 lb st ASSa7	WD933	8.51
2 x 10300 lb st ASSa7	WK141	4.52
B.2 – Olympus development		
2 x 8000 lb st Olympus 99	WD952	5.8.52
2 x 11000 lb st Olympus 101	WD952	
2 x 12000 lb st Olympus 102	WD952	.55
B.2 – 1st production (Short Bros)	WH853	30.10.52
2 x 6500 lb st RR Avon RA.3 (101)		
B.2 – 1st production (A.V. Roe)	WJ971	25.11.52
2 x 6500 lb st RR Avon RA.3 (101)		
B.2 – 1st production (Handley Page)	WJ564	5.1.53
2 x 6500 lb st RR Avon RA.3 (101)		
B.2 – Scorpion development	WK163	2.5.56
2 x 6500 lb st RR Avon RA.3 +		
1 x 6000 lb Double Scorpion NScD1/2		
B.2 – Gyron Junior development	WF909	28.5.57
1 x 6500 lb st RR Avon RA.3 (stbd) +		
1 x 7000 lb st Gyron Junior DGJ1 (port)		

Designation details cont'd	Serial	F/f date
B.2 – Viper development	WK163	9.58
2 x 6500 lb st RR Avon RA.3 +		
1 x 2470 lb st Viper ASV.7R		
E.A2 PR.3 prototype (spec PR31/46)	VX181	19.3.51
2 x 6500 lb st RR Avon RA.3 (101)		
PR.3 – 1st production	WE135	31.7.52
2 x 6500 lb st RR Avon RA.3 (101)		
S.D1 PR.3 – Beech AQM-37A launch acft		.67
2 x 6500 lb st RR Avon RA.3 (101)		
E.A4 T.4 prototype (spec T2/49)	WN467	12.6.52
2 x 6500 lb st RR Avon RA.3 (101)		
T.4 – 1st production	WE188	31.7.52
2 x 6500 lb st RR Avon RA.3 (101)		
E.A6 B.5 prototype (spec B22/48)	VX185	
2 x 6500 lb st RR Avon RA.3 (101)		6.7.51
2 x 7500 lb st RR Avon RA.7 (109)		15.7.52
E.A7 Swept wing Canberra project,	—	
not proceeded with.		
B.6 – 1st production	WJ754	26.1.54
2 x 7500 lb st RR Avon RA.7 (109)		
B(I)6 – 1st production	WT307	31.3.55
2 x 7500 lb st RR Avon RA.7 (109)		
B.6 (BS) conversion with two seats	—	
only and Blue Shadow equipment		
PR.7 – 1st production	WH773	16.8.53
2 x 7500 lb st RR Avon RA.7 (109)		
B(I)8 prototype (Spec IB.122)	VX185	23.7.54
2 x 7500 lb st Avon RA.7 (109)		
B(I)8 – 1st production	WT326	8.6.55
2 x 7500 lb st Avon RA.7 (109)		
PR.9 prototype	WH793	8.7.55
2 x 10500 lb st RR Avon 206		
PR.9 – 1st production	XH129	27.7.58
2 x 11500 lb st RR Avon 206		
S.C9 PR.9 – modified (Red Top missile)	XH132	2.5.61
2 x 11500 lb st RR Avon 206		
S.C4 U.10 – prototype conv. (later D.10)	WJ624	11.6.57
2 x 6500 lb st RR Avon RA.3		
T.11 prototype conversion	WJ610	29.3.58
2 x 6500 lb st RR Avon RA.3		
B(I)12 (ex WT329)	NZ6101	.59
2 x 7500 lb st RR Avon RA.7		
T.13	NZ6151	14.11.60
2 x 6500 lb st RR Avon RA.3		
S.C6 D.14 – 1st conversion	WH921	28.3.61
2 x 6500 lb st RR Avon RA.3		
B.15 – 1st conversion	WH961	4.10.60
2 x 7500 lb st RR Avon RA.7		
E.15 (B.15 conversion)	—	—
2 x 7500 lb st RR Avon RA.7		
B.16 – 1st conversion	WT302	.60
2 x 7500 lb st RR Avon RA.7		
T.17 – 1st conversion	WJ977	9.9.65
2 x 6500 lb st RR Avon RA.3		
T.17A – 1st conversion	WD955	.86
2 x 6500 lb st RR Avon RA.3		
TT.18 – 1st conversion	WJ632	21.3.66
2 x 6500 lb st RR Avon RA.3		
T.19 – 1st conversion	WH724	.65
2 x 6500 lb st RR Avon RA.3		
Mk.20 – 1st Australian production	A84-201	29.5.53
2 x 6500 lb st RR Avon RA.3		
Mk.20 – 28th a/c onwards	A84-228	22.3.56
2 x 7500 lb st RR Avon RA.7		
Mk.21 (Australian conversion)	A84-201	17.6.58
2 x 6500 lb st RR Avon RA.3		
T.22 – 1st conversion	WT510	28.6.73
2 x 7500 lb st RR Avon RA.7		

Marks 22-24 were originally for Australian production.

Export Versions:

B.2	– West Germany	YA+151	.66
B.2	– Sweden (Tp52)	52001	.59
B.2	– Rhodesia (Zimbabwe)		.59
B.2	– Venezuela - some B(I)2		.53
PR.3	– Venezuela		.66
T.4	– India		.58
T.4	– Rhodesia (Zimbabwe)		.59
T.4	– Venezuela		.58
T.4	– South Africa		.64
B.6	– Equador		.55
B.6	– France		.55
B(I)8	– Peru		.56
B(I)8	– Venezuela		.57
PR.9	– Chile		10.82
B(I)12	– South Africa (later to Peru)		3.8.63
B(I)12	– New Zealand (later to India)		.59
T.13	– New Zealand (later to India)		.60
B.52	– Ethiopian B.2		.67
B.56	– Peru B.6		.69
B(I)56	– Peru		.69
PR.57	– Indian PR.7		.58
B(I)58	– Indian B(I)8		.58
B.62	– Argentine B.2		.70
T.64	– Argentine T.4		.71
B(I)66	– Indian B.15/16		.70
PR.67	– Indian PR.7 - later update.		.70
B(I)68	– Peru B(I)8		.75
B72	– Peru B.2		.66
T.74	– Peru T.4		.66
B(I)78	– Peru B(I)8 later update		
B.82	– Venezuelan B.2 reworked		.77
B(I)82	– Venezuelan B(I)2 reworked		.78
PR.83	– Venezuelan PR.3 reworked		.78
T.84	– Venezuelan T.4 reworked		.78
B(I)88	– Venezuelan B(I)8 reworked		.77
B.92	– Argentina - later update. Not completed		
T.94	– Argentina - later update. Not completed		
TT.418	– T.4 converted in India to TT.18		

American Production:

B-57A - 1st production		52-1418	20.7.53
2 x 7220 lb st Wright J65-W-1			
RB-57A		52-1426	10.53
B-57B - 1st production		52-1493	28.6.54
2 x 7220 lb st Wright J65-W-5			
B-57C - 1st production		53-3825	30.12.54
2 x 7220 lb st Wright J65-W-5			
RB-57D - 1st production		53-3963	.11.55
2 x 11000 lb st P&W J57-P-37A			
B-57E		55-4234	16.5.56
RB-57F - 1st conversion		63-13286	23.6.63
2 x 18000 lb st P&W TF33-P-11 +			
2 x 3300 lb st P&W J60-P-9			
B-57G			7.69

CANBERRA PROJECTS

The English Electric Company Limited carried out many in-house projection design studies to develop their aircraft and between the late 1940s and early 1964 allocated company project identity numbers within a sequence P.1 to P.45 (not part of the SBAC standard drawing office system). Known Canberra project development numbers are:

P.2   Variant for bomber intruder role. May 1950.
P.4   Development with redesigned nose. May 1951.
P.12   All-weather fighter variant.
P.13   Guided weapon target variant.
P.16   Night fighter variant for Indian Air Force.
P.21   PR.9 with two Rolls Royce RB.133. August 1957.
P.28   Clipped-wing variant.
P.38   Bomber/reconnaissance variant for South Africa.

Appendix Three

RAF Canberra Squadrons,
their markings and Maintenance Units

Sqn	Mk.	Dates used	Location	Dates based
3	B(I)8	Jan 61 - Jan 72	Geilenkirchen	Jan 61 - Jan 68
			Laarbruch	Jan 68 - Jan 72
6	B.2	Jul 57 - Dec 59	Akrotiri	
	B.6	Nov 59 - Jun 62		
	B.16	Feb 62 - Jan 69		
7	B.2	May 70 - Dec 81	St Mawgan	
	TT.18	May 70 - Dec 81		
9	B.2	May 52 - Dec 55	Binbrook	May 52 - Jun 59
	B.6	Sep 55 - Jul 61	Coningsby	Jun 59 - Jul 61
10	B.2	Jan 53 - Jan 57	Scampton	Jan 53 - May 55
			Honington	May 55 - Jan 57
12	B.2	Mar 52 - Mar 59	Binbrook	Mar 52 - Jul 59
	B.6	Dec 54 - Jul 61	Coningsby	Jul 59 - Jul 61

Sqn	Mk.	Dates used	Location	Dates based
13	PR.7	May 56 - Dec 61	Akrotiri	May 56 - Sep 65
	PR.9	Jul 61 - Aug 76	Luqa	Sep 65 - Jan 72
			Akrotiri	Jan 72 - Oct 72
	PR.7	May 72 - Dec 81	Luqa	Oct 72 - Oct 78
			Wyton	Oct 78 - Dec 81
14	B(I)8	Dec 62 - Jun 70	Wildenrath	
15	B.2	Mar 53 - Apr 57	Coningsby	Mar 53 - May 54
			Cottesmore	May 54 - Feb 55
			Honington	Feb 55 - Apr 57
16	B(I)8	Mar 58 - Jun 72	Laarbruch	
17	PR.7	Jun 56 - Dec 69	Wahn	Jun 56 - Mar 57
	PR.3	Jun 56	Wildenrath	Mar 57 - Dec 69
18	B.2	Aug 53 - Jan 57	Scampton	Aug 53 - May 55
			Upwood	May 55 - Dec 58
	B.2	Dec 58 - Feb 60	Finningley	Dec 58 - Feb 60
21	B.2	Sep 53 - Jun 57	Scampton	Sep 53 - Jun 55
			Waddington	Jun 55 - Jun 57

Continuing the long tradition of being photographed with their aircraft are groups from 40 Squadron at Wittering in 1954 *(top)* **and 44 Squadron, at Coningsby in 1953.** *Latter via Vic Avery*

Sqn	Mk.	Dates used	Location	Dates based
21	B.6	Oct 58 - Jan 59	Upwood	Oct 58 - Jan 59
27	B.2	Jun 53 - Dec 56	Scampton	Jun 53 - May 55
			Waddington	May 55 - Dec 56
31	PR.7	Mar 55 - Mar 71	Laarbruch	
32	B.2	Jan 57 - Aug 61	Weston Zoyland	Jan 57 - Feb 57
			Nicosia	Feb 57 - Mar 57
	B.15/16	Jul 61 - Feb 69	Akrotiri	Mar 57 - Feb 69
35	B.2	Apr 54 - Sep 61	Marham	Apr 54 - Jul 56
			Upwood	Jul 56 - Sep 61
39	PR.3	Jul 58 - Nov 62	Luqa	Jul 58 - Oct 70
	PR.7	Oct 70 - Mar 72	Wyton	Oct 70 - May 82
	PR.9	Oct 62 - May 82		
	PR.9	Jul 92 -	Wyton	Jul 92 -
	PR.7	Jul 92 -		
40	B.2	Oct 53 - Dec 56	Coningsby	Oct 53 - Feb 54
			Wittering	Feb 54 - Oct 56
			Upwood	Oct 56 - Dec 56
44	B.2	Mar 53 - Jul 57	Coningsby	Mar 53 - Apr 53
			Marham	Apr 53 - May 54
			Cottesmore	May 54 - Feb 55
			Honington	Feb 55 - Jul 57
45	B.2	Dec 57 - Dec 62	Coningsby	Dec 57
	B.15	Sep 62 - Feb 70	Tengah	Dec 57 - Jan 70
50	B.2	Aug 52 - Oct 59	Binbrook	Aug 52 - Dec 55
			Upwood	Dec 55 - Oct 59
51	B.2	Aug 58 - Mar 60	Watton	Aug 58 - Mar 63
	B.6	Aug 58 - Jul 74	Wyton	Mar 63 - Oct 76
	B.6	Jan 76 - Oct 76		
56	B.2	Dec 68 - 75	Akrotiri	
57	B.2	May 53 - Dec 57	Coningsby	May 53 - May 54
			Cottesmore	May 54 - Feb 55
			Honington	Feb 55 - Dec 56
			Coningsby	Dec 56 - Dec 57
58	PR.3	Dec 53 - Oct 55	Wyton	
	PR.7	Dec 54 - Sep 70		
	PR.9	Jan 60 - Dec 62		
59	B.2	Aug 56 - Dec 57	Bruggen	Aug 56 - Oct 57
	B(I)8	Feb 57 - Jan 61	Geilenkirchen	Nov 57 - Jan 61
61	B.2	Aug 54 - Mar 58	Wittering	Aug 54 - Jul 55
			Upwood	Jul 55 - Mar 58
69	PR.3	May 54 - Jun 58	Laarbruch	
73	B.2	Mar 57 - May 62	Akrotiri	
	B.15	Mar 62 - Mar 69		

Sqn	Mk.	Dates used	Location	Dates based
76	B.2	Dec 53 - Dec 55	Wittering	Dec 53 - Nov 55
	B.6	Nov 55 - Dec 60	Weston Zoyland	Nov 55 - Apr 57
			dets Australia	Dec 55 - Dec 60
			Hemswell	Apr 57 - Jul 58
			Upwood	Jul 58 - Dec 60
80	PR.7	Jun 55 - Sep 69	Laarbruch	Jun 55 - Jul 57
			Bruggen	Jul 57 - Sep 69
81	PR.7	Jan 58 - Jan 70	Tengah	
82	PR.3	Nov 53 - Nov 54	Wyton	
	PR.7	Oct 54 - Sep 56		
85	B.2	Apr 63 - Dec 75	West Raynham	Apr 63 - Apr 63
	T.11	Mar 63 - Apr 69	Binbrook	May 63 - Jan 72
	T.19	Aug 65 - Dec 75	West Raynham	Feb 72 - Dec 75
88	B(I)8	Jan 56 - Dec 62	Wildenrath	
90	B.2	Nov 53 - May 56	Marham	
97	B.2	May 63 - Jan 67	Watton	
	B.6	May 63 - Jan 67		
98	B.2	Apr 63 - 71	Tangmere	Apr 63 - Oct 63
	E.15	Aug 70 - Feb 76	Watton	Oct 63 - Apr 69
			Cottesmore	Apr 69 - Feb 76

This 61 Squadron B.2 photographed at Upwood in July 1955 conceals its individual identity but displays the Lincoln Imp marking on the fin. *Malcolm Freestone*

Bottom: **58 Squadron group and PR.7 at Christmas Island during the *Grapple* tests in 1958.**

Sqn	Mk.	Dates used	Location	Dates based
100	B.2	Apr 54 - Sep 59	Wittering	Apr 54 - Sep 59
	B.6	Aug 54 - Sep 59		
	B.2	Feb 72 - Dec 91	West Raynham	Feb 72 - Jan 76
	E.15	Jan 76 - Dec 91	Marham	Jan 76 - Jan 82
	T.19	Feb 72 - May 80	Wyton	Jan 82 - Dec 91
	PR.7	Jan 82 - Dec 91		
	TT.18	Dec 81 - Dec 91		
101	B.2	May 51 - Jun 54	Binbrook	
	B.6	Jun 54 - Jan 57		
102	B.2	Oct 54 - Aug 56	Waddington	Nov 54 - Dec 54
			Gutersloh	Dec 54 - Aug 56
103	B.2	Nov 54 - Aug 56	Gutersloh	
104	B.2	Mar 55 - Jul 56	Gutersloh	
109	B.2	Jul 52 - Feb 55	Hemswell	Jul 52 - Jan 56
	B.6	Sep 54 - Jan 57	Binbrook	Jan 56 - Jan 57
115	B.2	Jan 54 - Jun 57	Marham	
139	B.2	Nov 52 - Jul 55	Hemswell	Nov 52 - Jan 56
	B.6	Feb 55 - Dec 59	Binbrook	Jan 56 - Dec 59
149	B.2	Mar 53 - Aug 56	Coningsby	Mar 53 - May 54
			Cottesmore	May 54 - Aug 54
			Ahlhorn	Aug 54 - Sep 54
			Gutersloh	Sep 54 - Aug 56
151	B.2	Jan 62 - May 63	Watton	
	B.6	Jan 62 - May 63		
192	B.2	Jan 53 - Aug 58	Watton	

Sqn	Mk.	Dates used	Location	Dates based
192	B.6	Jul 54 - Aug 58	Watton	
199	B.2	Mar 54 - Dec 58	Hemswell	Mar 54 - Oct 57
			Honington	Oct 57 - Dec 58
202	B.2	Apr 57 - Feb 58	Aldergrove	
207	B.2	Mar 54 - Mar 56	Marham	
213	B(I)6	Mar 56 - Dec 69	Ahlhorn	Mar 56 - Aug 57
			Bruggen	Aug 57 - Dec 69
214	PR.7	not equipped	Laarbruch	Jun 55 - Aug 55
245	B.2	Aug 58 - Sep 63	Watton	Aug 58
			Tangmere	Aug 58 - Apr 63
249	B.2	Sep 57 - Nov 59	Akrotiri	
	B.6	Nov 59 - Mar 63		
	B.15/16	Nov 61 - Feb 69		
360	B.2	Apr 66 - Jul 67	Watton	Apr 66 - Mar 69
	T.17	Dec 66 - date	Cottesmore	Mar 69 - Aug 75
	E.15	c.Jan 92 -	Wyton	Aug 75 - date
361		not equipped	Watton	Feb 67 - Jul 67
527	B.2	Aug 53 - Aug 58	Watton	
	PR.7	Apr 56 - Jun 56		
540	PR.3	Dec 52 - Oct 54	Benson	Dec 52 - Mar 53
	PR.7	May 54 - Mar 56	Wyton	Mar 53 - Mar 56
	B.2	Jun 53 - Sep 54		
542	PR.7	Jun 54 - Oct 55	Wyton	May 54 - Dec 55
	B.2	Nov 55 - Oct 58	Weston Zoyland	Dec 55 - Apr 57
	B.6	Nov 55 - Oct 58	Hemswell	Apr 57 - Jul 58
	PR.7	Nov 55 - Oct 58	dets Australia	Mar 56 - Jan 59
			Upwood	Jul 58 - Dec 58
617	B.2	Jan 52 - Apr 55	Binbrook	
	B.6	Dec 54 - Dec 55		

The control tower at Butterworth, Malaya, provides an interesting backdrop for this 101 Squadron group photograph, taken in May 1955 during their first deployment for the Malayan emergency.

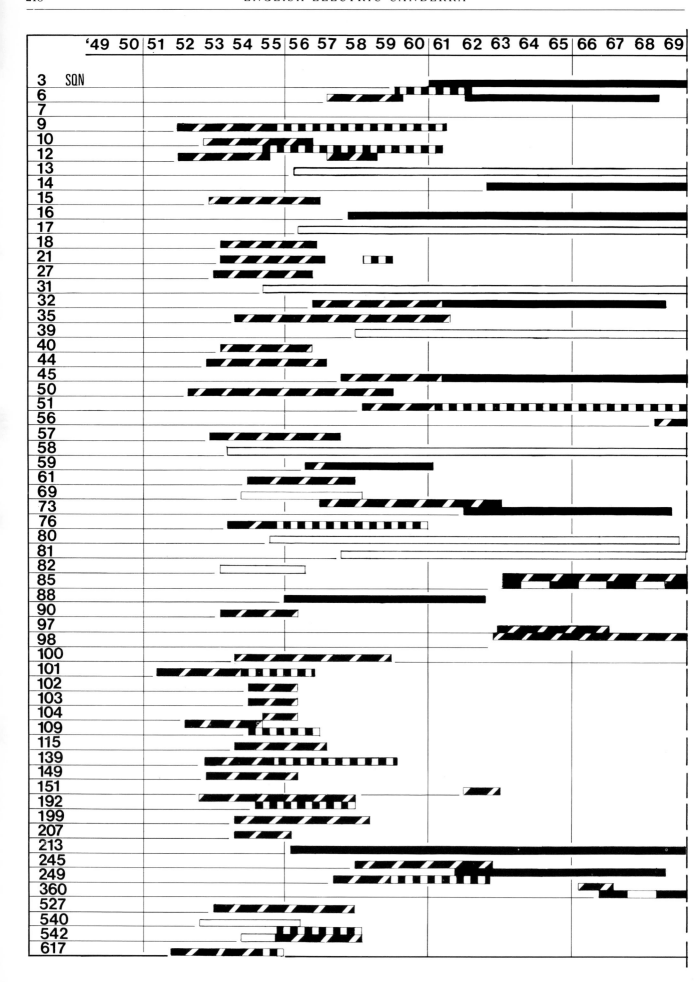

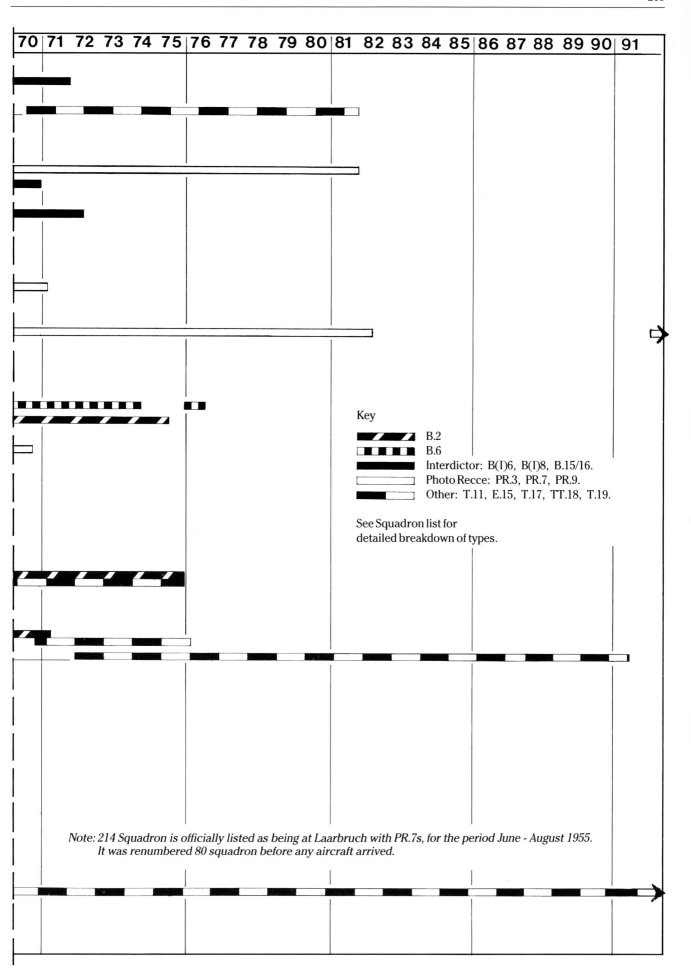

Key

B.2
B.6
Interdictor: B(I)6, B(I)8, B.15/16.
Photo Recce: PR.3, PR.7, PR.9.
Other: T.11, E.15, T.17, TT.18, T.19.

See Squadron list for
detailed breakdown of types.

*Note: 214 Squadron is officially listed as being at Laarbruch with PR.7s, for the period June - August 1955.
It was renumbered 80 squadron before any aircraft arrived.*

CANBERRA UNIT MARKINGS

General Aircraft Colour schemes – During its very long and continued service, the Canberra has carried a wide range of overall colour schemes. The following aircraft and squadron listings cover the majority of schemes other than the specialist unit and trials schemes. Squadron markings were the subject of much variation, often at the instigation of a new 'Boss', in response to such events as special detachments or squadron exchanges. Most squadron aircraft at one time or another carried a miniature squadron badge and combination of other items such as Union Jacks or temporary devices.

Overall Aircraft Scheme

Bomber Command 1 – grey/black
Bomber Command 2 – medium sea grey/light sea grey upper surfaces with PRU blue under surfaces.
Bomber Command 3 – overall silver.
18 Group – the T.17s and PR.9s at Wyton carry an overall hemp (or, according to some descriptions, eggshell) finish in matt or gloss (1988-89).

Units

3 Squadron – horizontal green bar with yellow outline on fin and rudder; maroon and black cockatrice on white disc centred on the green bar, superceded by red and grey cockatrice later.
6 Squadron – red winged tin opener on tip tanks; dark blue and red Gunners stripe on fin of B.2 and B.6; red tin opener on white disc on fin, flanked by red and blue stripe on B.16s.
7 Squadron – Rushton target in dayglo on fin, a blue figure '7' later superimposed. Plough in white on dark blue disc on fin.
9 Squadron – blue lightning flash on nose; later a green bat on blue circle on fin; finally a blue fin grey/green bat and yellow/red IX on white disc.
10 Squadron – red 'speedbird' on nose; red bow with black arrow on tip tanks. Later a red winged black arrow on tip tanks.
12 Squadron – gold lightning flash on nose; later a red fox on fin. Later a painted fox's head on a white disc on a green fin.

13 Squadron – a black lynx's head superimposed on a grey dagger on a white disc on fin.
14 Squadron – yellow winged crest of a Red Cross of St George on a shield carried on fin. Later a smaller version carried on the nose with three blue diamonds on either side in white rectangles.
15 Squadron – horse shoe on fin with red hunting horn. Later a white rising pheasant outline on fin.
16 Squadron – black fuselage waistband with yellow edges in line with and same overall width as fuselage roundel. White 22 inch diameter circle on nose, outlined with 1 inch diameter yellow ring and with yellow and black crossed keys insignia superimposed. Later black/yellow crossed keys insignia on fin. Later an outline 'saint' on fin. Some had 'sharkmouth' on nose.
17 Squadron – blue zigzag on white disc on fin; also blue zig zag on white rectangle on nose.
18 Squadron – blue speed bird on nose; winged horse on tip tanks, winged horse on white disc on fin.
21 Squadron – red crossed keys on nose; later crossed keys on tip tanks.
27 Squadron – red cheat line full length of fuselage.
31 Squadron – yellow star on black disc on fin; later a shaded star used.
32 Squadron – blue and white diagonals on tip tank and fin - B.2. Brass hunting horn suspended on a blue bow on white disc on nose flanked by blue and white stripes - B.15.
35 Squadron – blue tip tanks, black horses head with yellow wings on fin; later yellow and green winged horses head on fin. This followed by a black horses head with yellow wings, on white shield superimposed on a yellow lightning flash outlined in black on the base of the fin.
39 Squadron – black and yellow triangles on tip tanks, white 'V' on blue nose wheel doors carried over from 69 Squadron - PR.3.

Green winged bomb on white disc on fin - PR.9; later dull red winged bomb on fin. Finally green winged bomb on red fin disc.
40 Squadron – gold and blue chequer board on fin with blue disc in centre.
44 Squadron – horse shoe on fin with yellow hunting horn; later a white rising pheasant on fin.
45 Squadron – blue flying camel with red wings on white fin disc.
50 Squadron – orange lighting flash on nose; later horizontal sword in light blue with yellow handle, surmounted by '50' in red on tip tanks.
51 Squadron – small red goose on fin and on wing tip tanks. Royal Air Force Signals Command inscription in black along fuselage above roundel. Later dayglo flying goose on white disc on fin.
56 Squadron – Firebird on nose flanked by red/white chequers.
57 Squadron – Horse shoe on fin with yellow hunting horn; later red and blue phoenix on fin.
58 Squadron – black owl on white disc on fin - PR.3; later red owl on white disc - PR.9.
59 Squadron – red exclaimation mark superimposed on white triangle with red outline on fin.
61 Squadron – blue and gold chequerboard on fin, unknown coloured disc in centre. Later red Lincoln Imp on fin; later on tip tanks.
69 Squadron – white 'V' on blue nose wheel doors.
73 Squadron – blue demi talbot hound with red or yellow maple leaf on its shoulder on a white shield on fin. Dark blue/light blue/dark blue arrow strips on tip tank.
76 Squadron – black lion superimposed on white rose on fin. Later a dingo badge on fin.
80 Squadron – yellow bell on azure disc on fin.
81 Squadron – dagger superimposed on a star on white fin disc.
82 Squadron – black crest on fin, also red and green nose wheel doors diagonally divided.
85 Squadron – red and black checks on either side of fuselage roundel; later also white hexagon on black disc on fin.
88 Squadron – yellow and black serpent with red and white tongue on fin.
90 Squadron – yellow fin flash, white tip tanks. Golden leaping hind on fin for exercise *Excessive.*
97 Squadron – no known markings.
98 Squadron – white zigzag on red rectangle on either side of squadron badge on nose. Later a black cerberus outlined in white on fin.
100 Squadron – gold and blue chequers on fin with green disc in centre; also skull and cross bones insignia on fin of some aircraft. Later a white skull and cross bones on green disc outlined in white on fin.
100 Squadron – reformed unit 1972. Skull and cross bones on green disc centred on gold and blue checkered fin.
101 Squadron – white lightning flash on nose; later black and white lightning flash on nose - B.2. Also Roman '101' in yellow on black disc on fin - B.6.

102 Squadron – red lion carrying a blue bomb, on fin.
103 Squadron – black swan on fin.
104 Squadron – no known markings.
109 Squadron – yellow flash on fin. Later yellow flash outlined in black on fin.
115 Squadron – green tip tanks.
139 Squadron – red flash outlined in white on fin.
149 Squadron – horse shoe with lightning entwined on fin.
151 Squadron – no known markings.
192 Squadron – no known markings .
199 Squadron – Hemswell fin flash (colour not known). Blue waves and two yellow swords on white disc on fin.
207 Squadron – red tip tanks.
213 Squadron – Hornet in black, yellow and white on fin. Later a smaller version flanked by orange and black bars on nose.
245 Squadron – no known markings.
249 Squadron – yellow tip tanks with black and red assegai on which a white disc carried a black trotting elephant. Later, yellow tip tanks with yellow fin flash outlined in white.
360 Squadron – a blue '360' pierced by a red lightning flash on white back ground on fin; later a blue trident surrounded by red, yellow and white wings on fin. In 1984 a red bar either side of the fuselage roundel carrying a yellow lightning flash was introduced. Fin badges later deleted.
527 Squadron – no known markings.
540 Squadron – fin markings not identified.
542 Squadron – diagonal black bar on nose wheel door.
617 Squadron – red lightning flash on nose.

Binbrook Wing – lightning flash on nose.
Hemswell Wing – triangular flash on fin.
Scampton Wing – speedbird on nose.
Wittering Wing – checker boards on fin.
Marham Wing – coloured tip tanks.
Cottesmore Wing – horse shoe with hunting horn on fin.
Waddington Wing – Lincoln City coat of arms on fin.
Honington Wing – rising pheasant on fin.
551 Wing – red smoke cloud with blue lightning flash on nose.
Radar Reconnaissance Flight – green lightning flash outlined in white on fin.
Swifter Flight – dark blue swift on pale blue diamond on red arrow on fin.
No.1 PRU – dark blue/light blue world globe outlined in white.
231 OCU – snarling cheetah's face on fin; later a yellow and black cheetah's head on white shield on fin. This was followed by rampant cheetah in yellow with black spots and a red collar and chain on white disc on fin.
Akrotiri Station – white shield outlined in black with pink flamingo superimposed.
Akrotiri Strike Wing – pink flamingo with black lining detail superimposed with white lightning flash on fin, below a blue 'sea' with white wave crests.

CANBERRA MU LIST

The following list of Maintenance Units which in one capacity or another have handled Canberras is constructed from the SD161 location of RAF units. MUs have played a fairly central role in the Canberra story as modification centres and storage locations from which squadrons collected their aircraft and to which aircraft went for short or long-term storage between squadron service or pending disposal. Obviously, some MUs were more important than others for the Canberra, some being involved only on the fringes and for a matter of months, others, like 15 MU at Wroughton and 19 MU at St Athan, over very many years. St Athan still performs this role with a fair number of airframes in storage – a sort of mini Davis-Monthan where aircraft are 'mothballed' for possible re-use.

5 MU Kemble	27 MU Shawbury	45 MU Kinloss	60 MU Dishforth
15 MU Wroughton	30 MU Sealand	49 MU Sealand, Faygate,	71 MU Bicester
19 MU St Athan	32 MU St Athan	later Colerne	103 MU Akrotiri, dets at Safi
20 MU Aston Down	33 MU Lyneham	54 MU Cambridge,	(Malta) and Limassol
22 MU Silloth	34 MU Shawbury	later Honington	389 MU Seletar
23 MU Aldergrove	39 MU Colerne	58 MU Sutton Bridge	390 MU Seletar
			431 MU Bruggen

Appendix Four

Canberra Operations - Malaya and Suez

MALAYAN EMERGENCY 1955 - 1959

No Canberra PR sorties are included as they are too numerous to mention. All bombing sortie details are based on Squadron ORBs. See map page 95.

101 Squadron (Feb - June 1955)

Date	Acft	Weapons	Target
23 Feb	3	6 x 1000 lb	
24 Feb	2	6 x 1000 lb	
25 Feb	4	6 x 1000 lb	
28 Feb	3	6 x 1000 lb	AM
1 Mar	5 sts	6 x 1000 lb	AM
4 Mar	2	6 x 1000 lb	
4 Mar	2	6 x 1000 lb	Datum
7 Mar	4 sts	6 x 1000 lb	Datum
8 Mar	4	6 x 1000 lb	AM
9 Mar	2	6 x 1000 lb	AM
9 Mar	4 sts	6 x 1000 lb	Night Datum
10 Mar	4 sts	6 x 1000 lb	Night AM
11 Mar	3 sts	6 x 1000 lb	Night AM
22 Mar	4 sts	6 x 1000 lb	North of Butterworth
23 Mar	2 sts	6 x 1000 lb	North of Butterworth
24 Mar	4 sts	6 x 1000 lb	North of Butterworth
25 Mar	4 sts	6 x 1000 lb	AM. North of Butterworth
30 Mar	2	6 x 1000 lb	AM. North of Butterworth
2 Apr	4	6 x 1000 lb	
7 Apr	4 sts		AM
22 Apr	3		AM
23 Apr	3	6 x 1000 lb	Datum
25 Apr	4	6 x 1000 lb	3 Datum; 1 AM
26 Apr	5 sts		2 Datum; 3 AM
27 Apr	3 sts		Datum
7 May	3		AM. Ipoh
8 May	3		AM
14 May	3		
19 May	3		Datum
31 May	3		AM

617 Squadron (June - Oct 1955)

Date	Acft	Weapons	Target
21 June	3	6 x 500 lb	AM
22 June	3	6 x 500 lb	AM. 8nm E of Butterworth
23 June	2	6 x 500 lb	Datum
24 June	3	6 x 500 lb	Datum. S. Patiang
27 June	2	6 x 1000 lb	AM. Ipoh
27 June	1	4 x 1000 lb	AM. Thai
	2	6 x 1000 lb	border
29 June	1	6 x 1000 lb	AM. Bongsu
	2	4 x 1000 lb	AM. Bongsu
4 July	3	9 x 25 lb	AM. Bongsu
5 July	3	12 x 25 lb	AM. Bongsu
13 July	2	6 x 1000 lb	Datum. Negri Sembilan
14 July	3	6 x 1000 lb	Datum. Negri Sembilan
14 July	3	6 x 1000 lb	AM. Bongsu
15 July	3	6 x 500 lb	Datum. Port Dickson area.
16 July	3	6 x 500	Datum. Port Dickson area.
30 July	3	6 x 1000 lb)	
30 July	3	6 x 1000 lb)	
31 July	3	6 x 1000 lb)	AM Mentakab
31 July	3	6 x 1000 lb)	area
1 Aug	3	6 x 1000 lb)	
2 Aug	4	6 x 500 lb	AM Tapah Rd
11 Aug	3	6 x 1000 lb	Datum
23 Aug	3	6 x 1000 lb	AM. 15nm NE of Ipoh.
29 Aug	2	6 x 500 lb	AM. S. Bongsu
30 Aug	2	6 x 500 lb	AM. S. Bongsu

12 Squadron (Oct 1955 - Mar 1956)

Date	Acft	Weapons	Target
1 Nov	3	6 x 500 lb	Practice strike
2 Nov	3	3 x 500 lb	Practice strike
8 Nov	3	3 x 500 lb	Practice strike
22 Nov	6	500/1000 lb	Johore
24 Nov	7	6 x 1000 lb	Perak
25 Nov	6	6 x 1000 lb	Perak
27 Nov	7	6 x 1000 lb	Cameron Highlands
28 Nov	7	6 x 1000 lb)	
30 Nov	5	6 x 1000 lb)	
1 Dec	5	6 x 1000 lb)	
2 Dec	5	6 x 1000 lb)	
2 Dec	5	6 x 1000 lb)	Seremban
3 Dec	5	6 x 1000 lb)	area
3 Dec	5	6 x 1000 lb)	
4 Dec	7	6 x 1000 lb)	
5 Dec	6	6 x 1000 lb)	
10 Dec	7	6 x 1000 lb)	
20 Dec	4	6 x 1000 lb	Cameron Highlands
1956			
9 Feb	4	1000 lb	Kajang area
10 Dec	6	1000 lb	Johore
11 Dec	6	1000 lb	Ipoh
16 Feb	6	1000 lb	
16 Feb	5	1000 lb	
20 Feb	5	1000 lb	
21 Feb	4	1000 lb	Johore
21 Feb	6	1000 lb	Johore
24 Feb	5	1000 lb	Ipoh
3 Mar		1000 lb	Night Johore

9 Squadron (Mar - June 1956)

Date	Acft	Weapons	Target
7 Apr	5	6 x 1000 lb	
16 Apr	2		
23 Apr	3		
27 Apr	3		
21 May	3	6 x 500 lb	
12 June	6	6 x 1000 lb	
13 June	3		
18 June	7	6 x 1000 lb	
21 June	2		
23 June	5	6 x 1000 lb	
24 June	2	6 x 500 lb	

101 Squadron (June - Aug 1956)

Date	Acft	Weapons	Target
21 June	6	6 x 1000 lb)	
22 June	4	6 x 5000 lb)	Datum.
23 June	6	6 x 1000 lb)	Seremban
23 June	1	6 x 1000 lb)	area
24 June	2	6 x 500 lb)	
29 June	6 sts	6 x 500 lb	AM. Chikus Forest Res.
2 July	3	6 x 500 lb	Besout Forest Reserve
2 July	3	6 x 500 lb	Besout Forest Reserve
8 July	3	6 x 500 lb	AM. CT crops Perangin area
12 July	3	6 x 500 lb	AM. Bongsu
17 July	3	4 x 500 lb	AM. Gunong Liang East
20 July	3	6 x 500 lb	AM. Melukot Hill
21 July	1	6 x 500 lb	AM. N. of Kluang
25 July	3	500 lb	AM. Behrang Forest Res.
31 July	3	500 lb	AM. Bubu Forest Res.

45 Squadron (Mar 1958 - Aug 1959)

Date	Acft	Weapons	Target
18 Mar	4	6 x 1000)	
19-22 Mar	4	6 x 1000 lb)	AM
19-22 Mar	4 x 4	6 x 1000 lb)	Op. *Ginger*
27-30 Mar	5 x 4	6 x 500 lb)	Yong Peng
27-30 Mar	2 x 1	6 x 500 lb)	area
4 June	2	6 x 1000 lb	Tanjong Kualang
6 June	5	6 x 1000 lb	Pahang border

Date	Acft	Weapons	Target
7 June	5	6 x 1000 lb	
13 June	5	6 x 1000 lb	Kota Tinggi
20 June	5	6 x 1000 lb	Johore area
24 June	5	6 x 1000 lb	Ipoh
10 July	4	4 x 1000 lb)	TDP. North
10 July	3	4 x 1000 lb)	Selangor
14 July	6 sts	6 x 500 lb)	TDP.
15 July	3	6 x 500 lb)	Penggarang
17 July	10 sts	6 x 500 lb	TDP.
22 July	4 sts	6 x 500 lb	TDP.
23 July	9 sts	6 x 500 lb	TDP. Telok Anson
24 July	5	6 x 1000 lb	TDP.
26-27 July	11 sts	6 x 500 lb	TDP. Penggaram
31 July	5 sts	6 x 500 lb	TDP. Layang Layang
1 Aug	5 sts	6 x 500 lb	TDP. Nth Kota Tinggi
3 Sept	5	6 x 1000 lb	TDP. East of Ipoh
30 Sept	5	6 x 1000 lb	TDP. Nth ?
9 Nov	9 sts	6 x 500 lb	TDP. Sth Johore
14 Nov	5	6 x 500 lb	FD. Rasa
8 Dec	5 sts	6 x 500 lb	TDP. Nth of Selangor
1959			
13 Aug	3	6 x 1000 lb)	TDP. 30m E. of
17 Aug	3	6 x 1000 lb)	Kuala Lumpur

SUEZ OPERATIONS 1956

The data concerning Canberra Ops during the Suez crisis is reconstructed from Squadron ORBs. No PR sorties are listed.

Date	Acft	Weapons	Target
12 Squadron	**(B.6s to Luqa, Sept)**		
31 Oct	3	4 x 1000 lb	Almaza
1 Nov	6	4 x 1000 lb	Cairo West
1 Nov	6	4 x 1000 lb	Fayid
4 Nov	9(?)	4 x 1000 lb	El Agami shore battery

Date	Acft	Weapons	Target
101 Squadron	**(B.6s to Luqa, Sept)**		
31 Oct	1	4 x 1000 lb	Abu Sueir
1 Nov	4	4 x 1000 lb	Kasfareet
4 Nov	7	4 x 1000 lb	Huckstep
139 Squadron	**(B.6s to Nicosia, Sept)**		
31 Oct	2 x 4	⌖ mark	Almaza
1 Nov	2	⌖ mark	Inchas
1 Nov	4	⌖ mark	Cairo West
2 Nov	2 x 4	⌖ mark	Luxor
3 Nov	4	⌖ mark	Huckstep
3 Nov	2 x 2	⌖ mark	Almaza
4 Nov	4	⌖ mark	Huckstep
5 Nov	2 x 2	⌖ mark	Port Said - DZ
5 Nov	2	⌖ mark	Huckstep
109 Squadron	**(B.6s to Luqa, Oct)**		
31 Oct	3		Almaza
1 Nov	3		Cairo West
1 Nov	2		Cairo Intl.
4 Nov	4		El Agami
4 Nov	2		Huckstep
15 Squadron	**(B.2s to Nicosia, Oct)**		
31 Oct	4		Almaza
31 Oct	3		Kabrit
1 Nov	1		Abu Sueir
1 Nov	3		Cairo West
1 Nov	5		Luxor
2 Nov	3		Cairo Radio DL
2 Nov	5		Luxor
3 Nov	8		Almaza Barracks
5 Nov	6		Huckstep
10 Squadron	**(B.2s to Nicosia, Oct)**		
31 Oct	8	6 x 1000 lb	Almaza

No others detailed in Squadron records.

Date	Acft	Weapons	Target
61 Squadron	**(B.2s to Nicosia, Oct)**		
1 Nov	1(?)	6 x 1000 lb	Abu Sueir
1 Nov	5	6 x 1000 lb	Inchas DL
1 Nov	3	6 x 1000 lb	Fayid
2 Nov	4	6 x 1000 lb	Cairo Radio DL
2 Nov	4	6 x 1000 lb	Luxor DL
3 Nov	8(?)	6 x 1000 lb	Nifisha MY DL
5 Nov	7	6 x 1000 lb	Huckstep DL

Date	Acft	Weapons	Target
9 Squadron	**(B.6s to Hal Far, Oct)**		
31 Oct	6	4 x 1000 lb	Abu Sueir
1 Nov	4	4 x 1000 lb	Kasfareet
2 Nov	7	4 x 1000 lb	Huckstep
4 Nov	2	4 x 1000 lb	Huckstep DL
18 Squadron	**(B.2s to Nicosia, Oct)**		
31 Oct	4	⌖ mark	Kabrit
1 Nov	4	⌖ mark	Abu Sueir
1 Nov	4	⌖ mark	Fayid
1 Nov	4	⌖ mark	Kasfareet
2 Nov	2	⌖ mark	Cairo Radio DL
2 Nov	4	⌖ mark	Huckstep
3 Nov	5	2:⌖ mark / 3:6 x 1000 lb	Ismailia
4 Nov	4	⌖ mark	Agami Island
5 Nov	2	⌖ mark	Para DZ
5 Nov	2	⌖ mark	Huckstep
27 Squadron	**(B.2s to Nicosia)**		
1 Nov	8	6 x 1000 lb	Inchass
1 Nov	8	6 x 1000 lb	Luxor
2 Nov	4	6 x 1000 lb	Cairo Radio - low level day
2 Nov	3	6 x 1000 lb	Luxor
3 Nov	6	6 x 1000 lb	Ismalia Rlwy
5 Nov	6	6 x 1000 lb	Huckstep
44 Squadron	**(B.2s to Nicosia)**		
1 Nov	2	6 x 1000 lb	Cairo West
1 Nov	3	6 x 1000 lb	Fayid
2 Nov	5	6 x 1000 lb	Cairo Radio - low level day
2 Nov	3	6 x 1000 lb	Luxor
3 Nov	5 or 6	6 x 1000 lb	Almaza Barracks
5 Nov	6	6 x 1000 lb	Huckstep

Key

⌖	Target mark	AM	Auster Mark
Sts	Sorties	DL	Daylight
MY	Marshalling Yards		

61 Squadron detachment at Nicosia during the Suez crisis. *Malcolm Freestone*

Appendix Five

Technical Details

	B.2	PR.3	T.4	B+B(I)6	PR.7	B(I)8	PR.9	B.15
DIMENSIONS								
Height to top of fin	15ft 7in	15ft 7in	15ft 7in	15ft 7in	15ft 7in	15ft 7in	15ft 7in	15ft 7in
Length overall	65ft 6in	66ft 8in	65ft 6in	65ft 6in	66ft 8in	65ft 6in	66ft 8in	65ft 6in
Span without tip tanks	64ft	64ft	64ft	64ft	64ft	64ft	67ft 10in	64ft
Span with tip tanks	65ft 6in	65ft 6in	65ft 6in	65ft 6in	65ft 6in	65ft 6in	67ft 10in	65ft 6in
WEIGHTS (lb)							57,500 with tips	
Max take off	42,000 (later 46)	46,000	38,000	55,000	55,000	56,750	53,300 without	
Max landing	31,500 (later 40)	40,000	31,500	40,000	40,000	40,000	40,000	
Total fuel	14,650	2417 gal	14,650 (tips)	2788 gal	3305 gal	23,207	22,000	
ENGINES								
Rolls Royce Avon	Mk.1 (RA.3)	Mk.1 (RA.3)	Mk.1 (RA.3)	Mk.109 (RA.7)	Mk.109 (RA.7)	Mk.109 (RA.7)	Mk.206 (RA.29)	Mk.109 (RA.7)
	6500 lb st	6500 lb st	6500 lb st	7500 lb st	7500 lb st	7500 lb st	11250 lb st	7500 lb st
	Single breech	Single breech	Single breech	Triple breech	Triple breech	Triple breech	3 shot (2 gal)	Triple breech
	Cartridge start	Cartridge start	Cartridge start	Cartridge start	Cartridge start	Cartrige start	AVPIN start	Cartridge start
	No anti-icing	No anti-icing	No anti-icing	Ineffective anti-icing	Ineffective anti-icing	Ineffective anti-icing	Efficient anti-icing	Ineffective anti-icing

Limitations:	RPM	JPT°C	RPM	JPT°C	RPM	JPT°C	RPM	JPT°C	RPM	JPT°C	RPM	JPT°C	RPM ±.5	JPT°C	RPM	JPT°C
Maximum	7800	600°C	7800	600°C	7800	600°C	7950±50	680°C	7950±50	680°C	7950±50	680°C	100% ±.5	750°C	7950±50	680°C
Maximum intermediate	7600	565°C	7600	565°C	7600	565°C	7750	620°C	7750	620°C	7760	620°C	97.5%	720°C	7750	620°C
Maximum continuous	7400	530°C	7400	530°C	7400	530°C	7500	575°C	7500	575°	7500	575°C	95%	705°C	7500	575°C
Ground idle	2750±100	500°C	2750±100	500°C	2750±100	500°C	2750±100	530°C	2750±100	530°C	2750±100	530°C	31%± 30 100% – 8000 RPM	625°C	2750±100	530°C

Oil Pressure	Min at idle: 3 psi Min at 7400 rpm : 15 psi	Min at idle: 3 psi Min at 7400 rpm : 15 psi	Min at idle: 3 psi Min at 7400 rpm : 15 psi	Min at 7500: 15 psi Normal at 7500 : 20 psi	Min at 7500: 15 psi Normal at 7500 : 20 psi	Min at 7500: 15 psi Normal at 7500 : 20 psi	'Dolls Eyes' black At 45% rpm	Min at 7500: 15 psi Normal at 7500 : 20 psi

CREW POSITIONS	B.2	PR.3	T.4	B+B(I)6	PR.7	B(I)8	PR.9	B.15
Access	Side door	Side door	Side door with right pilots seat hinged at top to swing fwds to give access to rear and aft to give access to front seats.	Side door	Side door		Pilot: Rear hinged opening canopy. Navigator: side hinged nose section.	Side door
Pilot(s)	Seat slightly offset to left under 'standard' bubble canopy. Mk.1C ejection seats later replaced by Mk.2CA. Canopy jettisonned for escape.		2 x Mk.3 CT seats under standard canopy.	As B.2	1CN, later 2CA1 Mk.2 ejection seat.	Canopy replaced by fixed 'Fighter-type' offset to port but over original pilots position. Mk.2CB seat.	Mk.3CS Mk.2 seat raised and moved rearwards to pressure bulk-head. Canopy similar to B(I)8 but opens to give access.	As B.2
Navigator(s)	Ejection seat Mk.5 same as pilots. And positioned at rear off cabin against pressure bulk-head. Seat behind pilot for 1st Nav with fold down chart table and Nav instruments. Bombers have 2nd seat for 2nd Nav/Bomb aimer/AEO. Passageway at side of pilot gives access to prone position for weapon aiming/vert photo/low level nav. Perspex nose fitted with optical flat, offset in bombers to allow room for bomb sight. Metal hatch above seats jettisonned for escape. Folding Rumbold seat alongside pilot for extra BA crew member or for Nav to use at low level.	Single Mk.2CA seat at rear. No perspex nose. No prone position.	As B.2		1CN, later 2CA2 Mk.4 ejection seat.	At normal station Nav has hinged bucket seat which can swivel into 4 positions facing	Mk.4QS Mk.2 seat in front of pilot under francible hatch. No access to pilot, no prone position or transparent nose. Periscope mounted in floor caves x 1 1/2, 30° adjustable fore and aft through the vertical.	As PR.7

B(I)8 continued:
either forwards to give access to the prone position, backwards to reach the pilots position, right to allow emerg egress and left to face chart table. In latter position it could be folded and stowed. For t/o and landing the Nav had a seat to right of and below the pilot. In emerg, Navs parachute (Mk.8) was on stbd wall and clipped onto chest harness, static line operated chute. Door jettisonned in normal way but bottle deployed a wind break.

SEATS
All Ground level 90 kts (simplified list)

Mk.1C — Very basic seat. Top handle only. No leg restraint system. Feet had to be brought back into stirrups with thigh guards to support legs. This could be folded for access. Separate harness for parachute and seat. Manual height adjustment. With early seats harness and parachute deployment was done manually. Seats were later modified to release the harness automatically but it was still up to crew member to extract himself out of the seat thus allowing a barometic control to deploy the parachute at 13000ft.

Mk.2 — Bottom (alternative) handle introduced as were leg restraints. Seat now fully automatic with parachute deployment from seat. Negative 'G' strap introduced as lap straps alone insufficient. Two settings available for barometric control unit. For use in mountainous areas.

Mk.3 — Combined seat/parachute harness. Thigh guards omitted. Manual separation from seat achieved by guillotine – PEC.

Mk.4 — Same as Mk.3 but due to lack of space seat motored up and down by actuator.

Note: Pilots with a thigh length of more than 26.5 inches are not allowed to fly the Canberra as there is insufficient clearance from the cockpit coaming in the event of an ejection.

HEATING/ PRESSURISATION
All marks pressurised to '½ height + 2': e.g. at 40,000ft the cabin height should be 22,000ft; above 46,000ft the cabin HT is maintained.
Cabin temperature is adjusted manually but in all marks except PR.9 is inadequate for long flights at high level. It is common for the cabin to be covered in ice. Electrically heated clothing was tried but later discarded although wiring and plugs remain in some aircraft. PR.9 is fitted with an air ventilated suit system which can blow warm or cool air as set individually by crew members for AVS but full system seldom fully operational.

FLIGHT LIMITATIONS
The following limits applied to all Canberra marks:

	IAS	Mach			IAS	
Max speed:	450	0.75	Below 15,000ft	Undercarriage:	180	(1951 rules) max
		0.79	Between 15,000 to 20,000ft		190	(1955 onwards) max
		0.84	or when nose up trim change occurs		170	Normal lowering
			(for PR.9 450/.84 or nose up trim	Flaps:	145	(1951 rules)
			regardless of height).		160	(1955 onwards)
With tip tanks:	365	0.79	Below 25,000ft			
		0.80	Above 25,000ft			
Bomb/Flare	300	0.75	(1951 rules)	'G' Limits	No mention in early Pilots Notes	
doors open:	350	0.75	Below 40,000ft (1955 onwards)	1955 –	B.6	4g without tips
		0.80	Above 40,000ft			3g with tips
Airbrakes:					PR.9	3¾ max
2 position	nil	nil		'G'-Limits varied with aircraft weight and use		
3 pos (mid)	nil	nil		of aileron – also dependant on the fatigue life		
3 pos (full)	400	0.75	12,500ft to 25,000ft	of the aircraft.		
		0.79	Above 25,000ft			

	B.2	PR.3	T.4	B+B(I)6	PR.7	B(I)8	PR.9	B.15

FUEL SYSTEM

B.2: Three fuselage tanks feed to the engines by electric LP pumps (2 per tank) and engine driven HP pumps. Fuel balance is achieved by manual selection of pumps. Tip tanks can be fitted which feed into the rear (3) tank under engine bleed air pressure.

Tank capacities:
1- 512 gals
2- 317
3- 545
2 x 250 gal drop tanks 500
Total: 1874 gals

PR.3 / T.4:
4000 lb
2500
4250
3900
14650 lb

B+B(I)6:
	gals
Tank 1	535
Tank 2	325
Tank 3	540
Integs	900
Tips	488
Total	2788

PR.7: As PR.9

B(I)8: As B.15

PR.9: 5 fuselage tanks. 1-4 – top tanks; 5 - rear

Top	960	7392	7680
Rear	540	4158	4320
Belly	417	3210	3336
Integs	856	6591	6848
	2773	21351	22184
Tips	488	3757	3904
	3261	25108	26088

B.15: 3 fuselage tanks as per B.2 + integs + opt bomb bay tank (300 gal)

Fuel SG		.77	.80
Caps 1	520	4004	4160
2	317	2441	2536
3	540	4158	4320
Integs	856	6591	6848
	2233	17194	17864
Tips	488	3757	3904
BB	293	2256	2344
	3014	23207	24112

HYDRAULICS

B.2: 31 pint reservoir feeds 2 eng driven pumps. 2 accumulators 1350 psi. System pressure 2500-2550 psi. services: U/c, flaps, airbrakes, bomb doors, Wheel brakes. Emergency hand pump at stbd side pilots seat. Wheel brakes controlled by hand lever on control column.

PR.3: As B.2

B+B(I)6: Same as B.2 except reserves only 16 pint + system pressure 2200-2700 psi. Maxarets.

PR.7: 2 x Pumps Lockheed Mk.9. Cut in 2200 psi. Cut out 2700 psi. Thermal Relief 3450±100. Resv 2 gals.

B(I)8: 2 x Pumps Lockheed Mk.9. Cut in 2200 psi. Cut out 2700 psi. Thermal Relief 3450±. Resv 2 gals. Toe brakes with Maxarets.

PR.9: 4 x Integral 180 Mk.27 offload pressure 2750. Max (relief) press 2900. Therm Relief, 3450±100. Set v system 2 pumps. 25 gals resv. Control System 2 pumps 2 x resvrs each 7pts. Toe brakes with Maxarets.

B.15: As B.6/PR.7

ELECTRICS

B.2: 2 x 6kW 28 volt DC generators one per engine. Cut in rpm 4150 aft cut out 3500-4000. Full output above 5000.

PR.3: As B.2 Cut in at 1700 rpm. Full output 3000 rpm.

B+B(I)6: 2 x 6kW 28v Gen driven through auto 2 speed gearboxes. Cut in/out 1700 rpm. Full power 3000 rpm.

PR.7: 2 x 9kW 28v Gen (type 519) Auto 2 speed.

B(I)8: 2 x 9kW 28v Gen (type 519) Auto 2 speed.

PR.9: 2 x 12kW 28v Gen with constant speed drive providing full power at all Eng speeds.

B.15: 2 x 6kW 28v Gen

B.2: AC - 115v 400c/s No's 2+3 Inverters; 115v 1600c/s No's 4+5 Inverters

PR.3: As B.2

B+B(I)6: AC - 115v 400c/s No's 2+3 Inv; 115v 1600 (?) No's 4+5 Inv

PR.7: AC - 115v 400c/s 3 ∅ No's 1+2; 115v 400c/s 1∅ No's 6, 7, 8; No's 4, 5 - 1600c/s.

B(I)8: AC - 115v 400c/s 3∅ No's 1+2; 115v 400c/s 1∅ No's 6, 7, 8

PR.9: AC total of 8 inverters all except No.5 providing 115v 400c/s. No. 5 - 1600c/s

B.15: AC - 115v 400c/s No's 1+2; 115v 400 1∅ No's 5, 6, 8

	B.2	PR.3	T.4	B+B(I)6	PR.7	B(I)8	PR.9	B.15
RADIOS Initial equipment of all marks only VHF but later fits of V/UHF sets such as PTR 175	Original fit 2 x 12(?) channel VHF with intercom	Original fit 2 x 12(?) channel VHF with intercom	VHF/UHF	Original fit 2 x 12(?) channel VHF with intercom	Original fit 2 x 12(?) channel VHF with intercom. Later - HF/UHF/VHF	Original fit 2 x VHF (10 ch TR85 and TR86) Mod 3404 added ARC 52 UHF. Mod 4320 changed both of above for IX PTR175H Stdby UHF (ARI 23057)	VHF/UHF	
NAV/RADAR EQUIP. Great variation over the years even within a/c of the same mark.	Rebecca - ARI 5610 GEE-H - ARI 5829 Orange Putter rear warning - ARI 5800 ILS/Zero reader	Rebecca - ARI 5610 GEE-H - ARI 5829 Orange Putter rear warning - ARI 5800 ILS/Zero reader Green Satin Radio Altimeter Radio Compass GPI.IV	Rebecca - ARI 5610 GEE Mk.3 Orange Putter rear warning - ARI 5800 ILS/Zero reader Later: Tacan API Radio Compass	Rebecca - ARI 5610 GEE-H - ARI 5829 Orange Putter warning - ARI 5800 ILS/Zero reader Green Satin Radio Altimeter Radio Compass GPI.IV	Rebecca - ARI 5610 GEE-H - ARI 5829 Orange Putter warning - ARI 5800 ILS/Zero reader Green Satin Radio Altimeter Radio Compass GPI.IV Later: Twin VOR DME Doppler 72m	Blue Silk GPI Mk.4 with Roller Map DECCA IFF Mk.10. Radio Compass ILS Radio Altimeter Rear warning equipment	Green Satin GPI Mk.4 TANS IFF Mk.10. Radio Compass. OMEGA ILS/Zero reader. Auto pilot coupled to ICS. Radio Altimeter + Radar Altimeter RWR	
CAMERAS	1 vert bomb score camera F24 PR role: Day - 1 x F24 Night - 2 x F97+ flashes		nil	F24 vert G45 gun camera in stbd wing ldg edge PR role: 2 x F97 + flashes. Target marker: TI's	F95 in nose (optional) instead of gun sight. F24 in rear fuselage aft of bomb bay. G45 in stbd leading edge. *PR.9 cont'd:* Mk.4 fitted into pod in flare bay for survey work. Other pod mounted cameras available for high altitude work. F97 cameras for night photo. IRLS pod.	Fan of 3 x F95 low-level cameras mounted within the pressure cabin. 3 x air conditioned camera bays. Originally used F52 but replaced by F96. Focal lengths up to 48″. Gyro stabilised F49	
		Day - 6 x F52, 1 x F49 Alternate - 4 x F52, and 1 x F49 Survey - 1 x F49 Night - 2 x F89+ flash crate			Day - 6 x F52, 1 x F49 Alternate - 4 x F52, and 1 x F49 Survey - 1 x F49 Night - 2 x F89+ flash crate Low level - F95			
WEAPONS	Max bomb load 10,000 lb. Practical load - 6,000 lb. (Usual 6 x 1000 lb) Various bombs up to 2 x 4000 lb	Photo flashes	Nil	Max bomb load 10,000 lb. Practical load - 6,000 lb. (Usual 6 x 1000 lb) Various bombs up to 2 x 4000 lb	Photo flashes	4 x 20mm Hispano cannon in under-belly gun pack (rear of bomb bay). Flares carried at front of bomb bay. Pylons outboard of engines for bombs or rockets. Special wpn 1650 lb	5 x 8″ High alt photo flares. Flare pack of 1.75 inch photo flashes for low alt night photo.	B.15/16 standard bomb loads or underwing pylon stores - RPs or AS 30 missile. E.15 Nil

B(I)6 – B6 with gun pack fitted into rear of bomb bay – special doors enabled reduced load of bombs/flares to be carried in front of bay. Mk.3N reflector gun sight above pilots coaming. 4 x 20mm Hispano cannon Max 3 secs burst per 10 secs.

Gun/bomb/camera controls on right hand grip.

Mk.3N replaced by SFOM.

Note:

The technical data presented above is an attempt to draw together, in tabular form, data which covers the various marks, and derivative marks, of the Canberra. The choice of marks has been dictated by those which involve major changes to engine, airframe or performance. Most other marks are covered, in general terms, by reference to the mark from which they were developed.

The story is never simple - for example, to cover the different radio fits of the B.2 over its 40 year life would require too large a space; the list is therefore, by necessity, incomplete; rather, it encapsulates various periods of various marks. All data is based upon 'Pilots Notes' and 'Flight Reference Cards', as issued to the aircrew, for each mark. Even here the figures are often not very consistant! As an amendment was issued to one of these documents it was quite likely to change an element of data from one of the sections below, unfortunately not all editions of these documents are extant.

The authors would be delighted to hear from readers who have managed to 'hold on' to copies of Pilots Notes and FRCs - we are trying to build a collection to cover every option.

Appendix Six

Canberra Cockpits

The main text of this book contains details of many elements of the individual cockpit layouts for various Canberra marks plus 'operators comments' on the same. This appendix gives an overview of each cockpit in turn although it is not always possible to include mention of every small change of avionics fit and not every mark of Canberra is included; to do so would take another book! For the pilot end of the empire there is often little to say for each cockpit as B.2 derivatives tended to keep a 'standard' B.2 layout of controls and instruments and so to avoid repetition only significant changes are mentioned. Major changes of equipment to suit new roles tended to be fitted in the back and so the nav cockpits are much more varied.

Canberra B.2
Pilot: The best way to examine the set up in the cockpit is to run through the office in the standard left to right format, although not every small piece of kit will be mentioned. On the left hand side were the bomb door controls, radios and intercom, throttles and fuel management (HP Cocks), trimmers and the oxygen regulator. In all the many B.2 variants and modifications that were produced little of this basic layout changed although changes in equipment did take place. The forward portion was divided up into a number of panels with the main one being the flight instrument panel directly in front of the pilot – and partly hidden by the control column! Standard 1950s flight instruments were fitted to almost all versions of the

Canberra (a sore point with those who flew the PR.9 when far superior items were available but not used). The G4B compass was tucked away in the lower half of the panel and was one of the most difficult instruments to scan because of the control column. The standby compass in the early B.2s was a P.12 but within a few years this gave way to the almost universal E.2 which was quite adequate for its intended purpose of a cross-check for the main compass and as a 'get you home' standby.

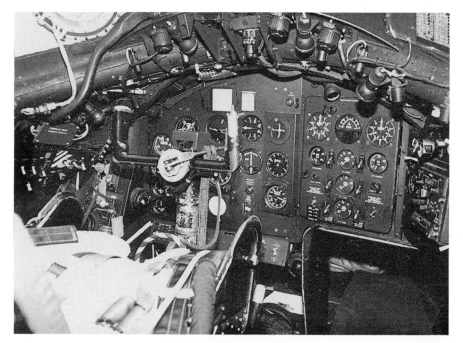

This is as typical a Canberra cockpit as you will get. The spectacle control column with the parking brake control in the middle, instrument panels divide into flight instruments in front and the engine panel to the right.

There have been a variety of 'standard' fits in the Nav empire of the B.2. The one shown here is the post bomber period as all bombing kit has been removed. The main instruments visible are the usual run of flight instruments – altimeter, ASI, and below them the Compass and Air Position Indicator.

To the left of the main compass were the ASI, Machmeter and the Turn and Slip indicator. Above the compass was the artificial horizon – the primary blind flying instrument and therefore centrally placed. To the right of this was the RCD (Rate of Climb and Descent Indicator). To the right of the flight instrument panel was the engine panel with JPT, RPM and oil pressure indicators as well as fuel gauges, LP cock and pump switches. The engine starter system was on a small panel below the main flight instrument panel with a master starting switch and port and starboard starter pushbuttons. Only two things stick in the mind about starting Canberra engines: the first is the cloud of smoke and choking fumes from the cartridge starter; the other is the impressive speed with which the engine creates a sheet of ice over the intake if the temperature and humidity are within certain bands. If the engine is not shut down very rapidly on the signal by the groundcrew then it is likely that the ice will break up and go down the engine. Icing was a problem at any time for most versions of the Canberra

because the aircraft had little anti-icing protection for the engines – except for the PR.9 which had effective engine anti-icing.

Back in the cockpit ... the final front panel, on the extreme right, carried the engine fire extinguisher buttons and engine fire warning lights plus pressurisation/temperature controls and indicators.

On the side of the panelling between the two cockpits was the electrical control panel (ECP); the front face carried fuel cock and pump circuit breakers in a position such that the pilot could operate them with his right hand. In front of this on a pedestal was the socket for the hydraulic handpump, the handle for which was stowed by the entrance door. In the event of a hydraulic failure this system could be used to pump the undercarriage down by hand and, if required, the flaps as well. This was easier said than done because this could take considerable effort and time even with pilot and nav taking it in turns!

As with all early marks of Canberra the ejection seat was the somewhat basic type 1C which was operated by a single firing handle at the top of the seat – the 'face

screen handle'. To eject, the pilot pulled the handle down to bring a protective blind down over his face and operate the seat firing cartridge. The seat then rose up the attachment rail and the drogue gun was fired by a static line attached to the aircraft. This deployed a drogue parachute to slow down and stabilise the seat and allow the occupant to release his harness and, when clear of the seat, operate his parachute.

Within a few years of its entry into service the B.2 started a long history of minor internal changes which make it almost impossible to talk of a 'standard' B.2-type cockpit layout. However, the basic arrangement of instrument panels and controls remained similar to that of the early version described above. Ejection seats also changed as improved automatic seats became available and most received the Mk.2CA1 seat.

Navigator: As mentioned above long-serving airframes such as the B.2, went through a series of mods, equipment and role changes which make it hard to define a standard. However, in general terms the

Opposite: **Although not a standard cockpit, this RRE aircraft does feature some of the basic equipment of the 1950s such as Gee and Blue Silk.** *R. Henry*

The pilot's end of the T.4. There are duplicated flying controls but the instrument layout is reasonably standard. The 'student' sits in the left-hand seat.

The right-hand seat is pivoted to swing forwards to let the nav climb into his black hole and back to let the pilots in. In this view the seat is back, giving access to the 'student' seat. On a pilot 'running change', the instructor would stay strapped in while the student pilots swapped over – a tricky little manoeuvre, especially at night!

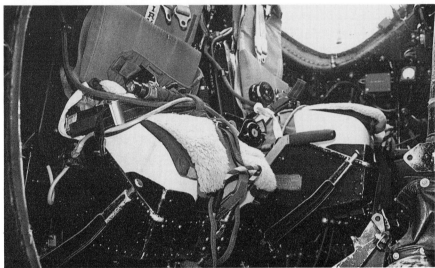

small plotting table was positioned in front of the navigator plotter and above it was ranged the nav and avionics fit. This fit could include Gee-H controls and indicator, Rebecca (or, later, an ILS control), Orange Putter, compass and basic flight instruments. The starboard side held the main bombing control panel and switchery although the actual bomb release was in the nose (with a second release button on the pilot's panel, though this was later moved to the control column.) The master control for the 'bombing' camera was above the bomb panel.

It was, for the period, quite a neat and well arranged cockpit but it was not particularly comfortable – mainly due to the uncomfortable bang seat, crowded conditions and lack of temperature control.

By the time that Ken Delve flew in the B.2s at 231 OCU in 1976 they had changed to reflect their more general purpose role. The B.2Ts were equipped with the Green Satin doppler and a GPI.IV as the main nav fit in addition to TACAN – a luxurious fit some would say! The fold-up nav table was still there, covered in perspex and the scribblings of previous occupants of the seat as well as various helpful bits of paper barely descernable under the doodles. A 1,000 mn navex was just as boring, and cold, as it must have been back in 1951 although you could always unstrap and change places with the pilot.

Canberra T.4

Pilot: The T.4, of course, was an aircraft 'beloved' by generations of Canberra aircrew – it was cramped, uncomfortable and was the scene of numerous exciting events such as IRTs, Flight Commanders checks and Night Asymmetric Checks (NACs), all of which conspired to be a real pain! The lack of comfort was due mainly to the requirement that the aircraft should be easily modified from the original B.2 design – hence the side-by-side ejection seats in the front. The left hand side of the cockpit was, essentially, a B.2 and to make it a 'trainer' a second set of controls was added along with another seat for the instructor. The entertainment and exer-

tion required to manipulate the seat has already been mentioned. It was at its worst on a 'running change' when one student pilot, or more likely a squadron pilot on a check ride, would taxy the aircraft to a suitable spot, apply the brakes, unstrap and climb out of the door by crawling over the instructor - who had moved his seat and opened the door. The replacement pilot would then do the reverse. The poor old nav in the back could suffer a long and arduous night sortie while numerous squadron pilots got their 'ticks on the board'!

John Clemons, as a QFI on 39 Squadron, spent more than his fair share of time strapped into the T.4. ... 'With a single seat the view out of the streamlined canopy was surprisingly good. Move the seat to the right or left (as in the T.4) and the pilot's head needed to be touching the canopy in order to see out, not too difficult when wearing a leather or cloth flying helmet but very tricky with the advent of the bulkier bone-dome. Possibly the worst combination was a Mk.2 helmet on a taller then average pilot where the head had to

be canted sideways by about 30 degrees to see out at all, and then only with one eye! Add to this the DV panel on both sides right in the line of sight and it will be obvious that the pilots had to lean inboard to an alarming degree. This put unrelenting pressure on the inboard buttock and hence the 'numb bum' syndrome; to fly an asymmetric overshoot at the end of a long check ride inflicted a degree of pain that is burned indelibly into the memory!'

Few pilots have anything good to say about the T.4 although it was without doubt an essential aircraft in the Canberra inventory, particularly in the early days when pilots were converted from heavy piston-engined aircraft to jets.

One of the best comments ever made about the beast was by a 39 Squadron pilot on an annual check ride. When approaching the dispersal point and facing another T.4 parked on the pan, the examiner asked, 'what would you do if the brakes failed now.' The reply, as quick as a flash was 'open up the throttles and take out two of the ....!' That really sums up the aircrew approach to the T.4!

Navigator: Having struggled into the back by squeezing behind the right-hand seat, the Navigator is in one of the proverbial Canberra 'black-holes'. There is plenty of room as there is only one ejection seat, a Mk.2CA2 (1CN in the earliest production T.4s), on the left-hand side. As ejection seats go this is not the most comfortable variety, partly because of the arrangement of parachute straps and seat straps which requires the navigator to put on the brown parachute straps first and then the blue seat straps whilst at the same time trying to get the two locking boxes in comfortable positions. Having settled in, a scan around the office reveals not a lot because the T.4 had very little of anything in the back!

The avionics fit, if such it can be called, varied from nothing to the luxury of a radio compass, TACAN and Air Position Indicator (API). Of these the TACAN was the only really useful item and was very accurate because a set of vernier scale readouts was provided. However, it was only rarely that the Navigator had to do any true navigating in the back of the T.4 because the aircraft spent most of its time flying around the airfield local area on pilot checks or on beacon-to-beacon Instrument Rating Tests (IRTs). Sometimes the aircraft were taken further afield and it was a case of back to basic nav techniques of Dead Reckoning. As with most other marks of Canberra this is a somewhat simplistic analysis as the T.4 had differing fits from time to time and even squadron to squadron. At one stage in the 1960s some T.4s were equipped with Rebecca and Decca Mk.1 (Air).

Canberra B.6

Pilot: The B.6 cockpit was a little more ordered than the B.2 in that switches had been grouped together into a Take-off panel on the port side. This contained all the essential switchery for fuel cocks and fuel transfer, heaters, demist, intercom and battery with the instruction that 'all switches are to be set UP for take-off'. Otherwise, the left-hand side of the pilot's cockpit was similar to the B.2.

Front panels again were very similar to the B.2 except for a slight shifting around of instruments, the 'blind-flying' panel was re-organised to make the instruments easier to see. A radio altimeter was fitted on the left side of the frontpanel with a height band selector below the indicator and a set of three 'limit' lights to the left of the panel. This was a great aid to safe low level operations and all that was missing was an audio warner.

Navigator: No appreciable changes.

Canberra PR.7

Pilot: The major difference in the pilot's office from the bomber versions was the addition of camera controls and indicators.

Opposite: **PR.7 pilot empire. The straps hanging over the controls are the leg restraint straps of the ejection seat. Take-off panel on the left and flight instruments and engine panels in front.**

Nav Station in the PR.7 with plotting table, flight instruments and nav equipment.

Back of the PR.7 on right hand side.

Right: **The view (!) from the nose of a PR.7. Camera controls on the left.** *Brian Crook*

A dramatic view of the pilot's 2CA1 ejection seat in the PR.7.

Most instrument and control panels reflected only minor changes, if any at all. On the left side an extra switch was provided to control the camera doors, with an associated 'doors open' indicator (a white 'dolls-eye'); also, a photoflash jettison switch. Directly in front of the pilot were controls for the F.49 camera and the F.95 cameras (on the left pillar of the control column) as well as indicator lights for camera exposure and flash release.

Navigator: Like so many of the Canberra marks the PR.7 received a variety of equipment fits during its service life although many of the basics, especially camera equipment, changed little. There was only one seat fitted in the rear, a 2CA2 of various marks, mainly due to a lack of room on the right hand side because of equipment boxes. By the mid 1970s the avionics fit was quite reasonable with twin VOR, DME, a GPI.IV and a Doppler 72M (ex Vulcan), plus flight instruments such as ASI and Altimeter. Most of this was positioned above the standard hinged table. On the left hand side was a Radio Compass and intercom box. On the right were doppler boxes and inverters. The camera controls were on the right of the central panel and, unlike the PR.9, the port and starboard F.95 camera magazines could not be changed in flight.

The PR.7 had a sextant mounting but the sextant was rarely carried, although Steve Norrie, a nav on 13 Squadron, recalls that it was sometimes used on ADEXs for air combat so that the crew could look behind them!

Whilst this was the office the work-room was down in the nose. The prone position was the same as in the other marks and the aircraft had the standard pair of 'grab' handles and cushioned floor. The camera controls were repeated in the front and there was a doppler read-out of drift and groundspeed. Over the flat portion of the perspex nose was the 'banana' sight which the nav used for tracking photo targets. This curved piece of black metal, painted yellow on the edges, (hence banana) took a little while to get used to but with a bit of practise became second nature. It was attached by wires to a control by which the drift could be set making it into a drift sight.

Because the nose position was used for high-level photo work there was a second oxygen regulator and one of the trickiest operations was transferring from the oxygen supply at the back, into a hose by the door and then into the nose regulator.

The few PR.7s in use with 100 Squadron in 1991 had no specific photo task but were used as general work-horses including target towing. All the camera switchery was in place but the banana sight had gone and there was now a hook release mechanism in the rear cockpit. It was one of the best-loved aircraft on the Squadron because of its avionics fit and the extra performance. The additional range of the PR.7 was not usually needed and the aircraft were invariably flown less tip tanks. One exception to this was Flight Checking when the tip tanks were fitted in order to give the standard radar signature against which the radar performance is calibrated.

Canberra B(I)8

Pilot: The B(I)8 was very much a pilot's aeroplane and was well liked by all who flew it. This was largely due to the excellent visibilty from the bubble canopy – and the variety of roles which the aircraft performed, most of which were at low level. Basic instrument layout had changed little from previous marks other than those items connected with the weapons fit.

Navigator: For the reasons already discussed in Chapter 3 it was not so well liked by the navigators although most now remember it with affection. The seat was a stow-away affair which went under the small nav table facing the starboard side of the aircraft. Avionics consisted of a Blue Silk doppler, GPI.IV, radio compass and a Decca 1 Air, which was quite a reasonable fit for the area and roles of the B(I)8. The table occupied about a third of the cockpit area and was at the feet of the pilot, which Dudley Brown recalls 'was a good place from which to tie the pilot's boot laces together! However, there was another seat on the right hand side of the bulkhead with a full restraining harness and in theory the nav was to strap-in this seat for take-off and landing and after that he could move around. It was also a good place to sit to observe the pilot's instrument panel.'

Like other marks the B(I)8 had a mattress in the nose, although this sometimes went missing and the floor was very uncomfortable and, if the aircraft hit turbulence, quite painful! The grab handles were useful on some of the more extreme antics such as LABS. Most of the time at low level was spent in the nose and the visibility was excellent, helped by the additional side panel windows. There was little kit in the nose other than a compass repeater and a Decca roller map, which was little used because of the prep time required on the route maps. There was no bomb sight as weapons delivery was done by the pilot.

Canberra PR.9

Pilot: The PR.9 pilot was in many ways the envy of the Canberra force both because of the undisputed performance of his aircraft and the luxury of a decent canopy and an autopilot!

On the ground the canopy could be held open with a strut, a real boon in hot weather, and it was closed by pulling down on two handles while an electric motor inserted four locking pins. Because the canopy was offset to the left of the fuselage the view downwards to the right was somewhat restricted but in all other directions it was superb, aided by two rear view mirrors mounted on the windscreen arch. Unfortunately, the ejection seat was set a little too close to the vertical which left the pilot almost hanging in his straps - resulting in back problems that plagued some PR.9 pilots throughout their tours.

Within the cabin were several reminders of the PR.9's ancestry as a Canberra with 'standard' instrument layouts, although the right-hand side was different with a 'fold-away' panel for the fuel controls and indicators. At the rear of the starboard console were a set of controls unique in the Canberra world to the PR.9. These were the selector switches for the power controls and the autopilot. This latter was extremely useful on high level transits where it did all the work but could also be used one channel at a time during a photo run to provide a height lock whilst leaving the ailerons and rudder free for track corrections.

Around the coaming were a row of warning lights for the power controls, there being no manual reversion. John Clemons . . . 'To fly the PR.9 was a joy, the power controls were light and precise and the responsiveness and power of the engines was legendary. With full internal fuel you could take off with only 90% rpm and still make 40,000 ft in 8 minutes!

Pilot end of the PR.9 in the pre-mod state (no TANS readout).

Opposite: **The front panel of the Navigators station before the mod programme of the late 1970s. Bottom right – Green Satin doppler, left – GPI Mk.IV. The large circular central object is the periscopic viewer.**

The PR.9 navigator's operational panel – i.e the camera controls and fuses. An additional control box was fitted above the main panel when one of the podded systems was fitted into the flare bay.

Indeed there was so much power available and the aircraft was so responsive that a favourite ploy when bounced by a fighter at low level was to throw a 4g evasive turn while closing the throttles to slow down to 200 knots or so, thus causing him to overshoot, and then out-accelerate him as he tried to match your speed, ah! those were the days . . .'

Navigator. Unlike his other half, the Navigator in the PR.9 was often greeted with 'how the hell do you stand being locked up in there!' This was a reference to the unique seating arrangement of the PR.9 whereby the hinged nose swung open, the nav climbed in and strapped-in facing forward on his 4QS ejection seat and the nose swung closed again with a resounding clang!

From this position at the sharp end of the aircraft the Nav was surrounded by equipment on all sides. Visual reference was by means of two small rectangular windows, one on each side, which were positioned so that a PR run using the oblique F.95 cameras would, in theory, put the target in such a position that the nav could see it and make a visual report (VIS-REP).

This was not always the case as a last minute jink or a wing down or up to get the correct positioning of the target one-third of the way up the frame of the photo often gave the Nav no chance to even glimpse the target. However, forward view was somewhat better through the periscope which gave a field of vision of 60 degrees, a reasonable amount at low level. This recce sight was really designed for high level PR work and could be moved

through various positions from fully forward, to vertical and even to look at the underneath of the aircraft. In the vertical position it was used for photo survey work in the same way that the PR.7 banana sight was used. This was great at reasonable heights but when a low level vertical task came in that required the aircraft to fly at 1,500 ft or so the allowable error in following the planned survey line was very small and an accurate Small Area Cover (SAC) was a feat of great concentration for both of the crew! The backwards part of the sight was useful on ADEXs because it allowed the Nav to scan below and behind the aircraft for the sneaky fighter!

The left hand consoles carried the camera controls, a series of camera selectors and controls for all the aircraft cameras plus any podded systems carried in the flare bay. The flare pistol sat high up on the left hand side but was rarely used; it was intended for use in the event of a communications failure. Apart from the odd flare fired through boredom or to celebrate a particular event it was redundant. There was a trial at one stage to see if chaff cartridges could be fired from the pistol but the only trial ones fired went down the port engine and had no effect on the tracking radar!

The right hand console was communications, power supplies and 'odds and ends' such as the radio altimeter. All avionics were on the front panels around the recce sight. Like all Canberras the PR.9 Nav empire was badly served by flight instruments, having only the basic ASI, and altimeter and no attitude indicators - which would have proved very useful and perhaps averted some of the Canberra accidents. Apart from the GM.7 compass there were very few other instruments except for the nav fit. This consisted of a radio compass, TACAN, Green Satin doppler and good old GPI.IV. In the late 1970s the equipment was greatly improved by replacing the Green Satin/GPI with a Reference Gyro, new doppler and TANS. This enhanced the nav capability greatly and along with the introduction of IRLS as a passive night sensor gave the PR.9 a realistic night capability. At the same time, and as part of the same modification programme, aircraft were fitted with an RWR.

The port and starboard F.95 cameras were just behind the level of the ejection seat and magazines could be changed in flight, the starboard one being a little trickier as the camera was mounted upside down. The biggest problem with camera selection was interpreting the wishes of the pilot as you rushed in to the target. By tradition the pilot operated the camera because he was in a better position to see the target and assess when to switch the camera on and off. At the planning stage the crew would try to arrange it so that the target went down the left hand side of the aircraft - better view for the pilot - and hence plan to use the port camera. On the way in the pilot would call for the camera he wanted to use . . . it was not unusual for the Nav to select said camera only to see the aircraft bank the other way, resulting in a good sequence of sky pictures! One solution was to select all three cameras!

By dint of the seating arrangement there was no physical link between the two crew but in the event of an intercom failure the Nav was provided with an extending rod with a clip on the end; the idea was to put a message in the clip, bash the pilot on the toe with it and wait for the reply! Boredom is a wonderful thing . . . on one high level transit in some part of the world the pilot decided to wake the Nav up. He unstrapped and climbed down into the 'well' on the right hand side. By wriggling forward he was able to get his arm far enough forward to tap the Nav on the shoulder. The shock a tap on the shoulder at 50,000 ft when no-one can reach you is, to say the least, startling!

The best answer when faced with the question of life in the black hole is to list the exotic places the black hole has taken you to in the last year.

Above: **Front end of a 73 Squadron B.15 with the somewhat crowded cockpit arch with the LABS indicators. Compare with the E.15.**

Below: **E.15 Front cockpit.**

Canberra E.15

Navigator: The general arrangement was à la B.2 with side by side ejection seats, in this case the 2CA2 Mk.4. The cockpit area was very cramped due to the amount of equipment and access was made trickier because of the cabin cooling pipe which left a rather narrow tunnel for the Navs to crawl through. Dick Frost, a Nav on 100 Squadron, recalls that this made it quite difficult and uncomfortable for the Navs when they were wearing immersion suits and that because of this the E.15 was disliked on low level sorties.

The left hand side had few items other than the standard hatch systems, oxygen regulator and a poor radio compass. Most of the kit was installed above and to the right of the small nav table with a Blue Silk doppler, GPI.IV, compass, Tacan and Decca. For a Canberra this was a large amount of nav kit but it also created the space problems as well as generating a fair amount of heat – which was good at high level but not so welcome at low level.

Opposite: **Navigator's position in E.15.**

Apart from minor changes to instrumentation and layout, the TT.18 front cockpit is fairly standard.

The main feature of the Nav station in the TT.18 is the twin control panels for the winches. These two identical panels are on the right, above the plotting table.

The E.15 was also well equipped with good comms, two radios plus HF radio and AUTOCAT – a system which could transfer one radio to another. This was great for spoofing fighters as you could transmit one radio to block the fighter's transmissions.

The E.15s on 100 Squadron were used for the full range of Squadron tasks from banner towing to Flight Checking and were often specified for the latter task because of their more comprehensive nav fit.

Canberra TT.18

Navigator. Another B.2 variant with sparse nav kit – radio compass, API and TACAN, although it also had the luxury of a single VOR. The basic arrangement was B.2 standard, except for 2CA2 seats and all that really distinguished the TT.18 was the extra window on the starboard side and the winch controls. Each window was provided with a Morris Minor car wing mirror so that the Nav could watch the operation of the winches. The winch control packs were identical to the flight refuelling packs fitted in other aircraft and simply had different labels! The winches and cables were reasonably reliable but the cable could be cut if required by hitting the 'press to test' on the panel.

Dick Gilbert, on 7 Squadron, was one who still used the good old electric socks from time to time, usually on a flog down to Gibraltar, and remembers the trick of poaching the pilot's supply if sitting up the front of the aircraft.

Appendix Seven

Canberra Production
for the British Services

English Electric A1 Prototypes (4 acft) to Spec B3/45
Later known as Canberra B. Mk.1.
Contract 6/Acft/5841/CB6(b). Placed 7 January 1946.
Serial numbers allocated 10.12.45.
VN799 (P) f/f 13.5.49 at Warton. EE Co. A&AEE.. 27.10.49. RAE
for MK.IX Auto pilot trials. AIEU type 'D' auto pilot
17.2.53. Cr when engines failed at 300ft on approach
1.5 miles SE of Sutton Heath, Woodbridge, Suffolk
18.8.53. (2k) Soc 23.9.53.
VN813 2(P) f/f 9.11.49 at Warton. EE Co. RAE 12.4.50. EE Co
12.5.50. RR Hucknall Nene dev 30.11.50. RRE for ARI
5844 trials 11.9.51. RR Hucknall, Nene dev 15.8.52.
DH Engine Co – Spectre dev 8.6.53. Follands
Chilbolton for Spectre installation under sub-
contract 24.6.53. DH Engine Co Hatfield for trials
9.7.54. Sold to Enfield Rolling Mills 21.12.59 for scrap.
VN828 3(P) f/f 29.11.49 at Samlesbury. EE Co for aerodynamic dev 27.4.51. TRE 'Green Satin' mods
14.11.51. BP Defford for AI Mk.18 mods 21.5.54. RRE
17.1.56. Last flight 14.12.61. Acft retired and
dismantled and nose to WJ643. Soc 18.1.62. Still
derelict at Pershore 9.63.
VN850 4(P) f/f 20.12.49. EE Co. RR Hucknall for Avon dev
6.10.50. Cr at Bulwell Common, Hucknall, Notts.
13.6.51. Cat.5 (3k). Soc 1.10.51.

**VN813, the 2nd prototype, at Farnborough in
September 1957, was the first Canberra to be
fitted with the DH Spectre rocket motor.**

**PR.3 prototype VX181 wore the distinctive A&AEE
fin crest, a neat fuselage cheatline and '181' on
the nose wheel door, when seen in the twilight of
its career, at Malta, c.1967.** *MAP*

Canberra Prototypes (5 acft ordered, only 3 built).
Spec B5/47 Bomber (2 acft built, 2 cancelled) known as
B. Mk.2.
Spec PR.31/46 Photo-Reconnaissance (1 acft) as PR. Mk.3.
Contract 6/Acft/2000/CB6(b). Placed 1948.
Serial numbers allocated 22.1.48.
VX165 B.2(P) f/f 21.4.50. EE Co. A&AEE. Performance and
handling 8.11.50. EE Co 18.11.50. A&AEE 12.12.50.
EE Co 2.5.51. A&AEE 25.5.51. Stall warning on
approach, starboard engine picked up first and acft
yawed, rolled and port wing struck runway; acft
came to rest on runway at Boscombe Down, 15.8.51.
To EE Co Warton 4.9.51. Soc 28.3.52.
VX169 B.2 2(P) f/f 2.8.50. EE Co. A&AEE for Armament trials
24.3.51. EE Co 15.8.52 for automatic 'window'
launcher mods. RAE for flight trials 22.4.53.
Marshall's for radio mods 11.5.56. RAE for trials
12.10.56. To PEE Shoeburyness 4.5.60. Soc 5.5.60.
VX173 Cancelled - airframe became WD929
VX177 Cancelled - airframe became WD930
VX181 PR.3(P) f/f 19.3.51. EE Co. A&AEE handling and PR
trials 6.11.51. RAE Radio compass tests 8.12.51. EE Co
27.12.51. A&AEE 18.3.52. EE Co for Australia trials
mods 11.11.52. A&AEE 2.1.53. UK-Australia record
27.1.53. At LRWE. BP Defford for t/i low altitude PR
role equipment 4.4.54. EE Co for Cat.4R survey
26.3.56. BP Seighford for F46 Mk.I camera t/i A&AEE
for trials 15.8.58. A&AEE trials of Ferranti and Litton
inertial platforms 3.4.62. A&AEE trials of F.126
camera and Sperry vertical gyro 18.9.67. Released
2.1.69 and equipment moved to WF922. Flown to
Pershore 11.6.69 and used as ground training acft for
emergency services. B/u and scrapped at Pershore
9.69; burnt 1972.

Canberra B.5 Prototype (1 acft) to Spec B22/48
Contract 6/Acft/4689/CB(b). Placed 1950.
Serial numbers allocated 22.1.48 for original PR.3 2(P).
VX185 Begun as PR.3 2(P). Completed as B.5(P).
F/f 6.7.51 at Samlesbury. Loaned to EE Co 9.9.51.
CS(A) at EE Co 23.4.52, preparations for transatlantic
record, made 26.8.52. To Warton for conv to B(I)8
28.1.54. Contract No.6/Acft/9195/CB6(b). F/f as B(I)8
23.7.54. A&AEE 4.5.55. Ferranti as Target for AI Radar
6.4.56. To Shorts Belfast re PR.9 dev 10.4.58. BP
Seighford for t/i 29.6.59. Allotted to St Athan as G/i
10.10.59. Became 7631M and delivered 9.2.60. To BAC
Filton 5.61 and B/u there 30.4.64.

Canberra B.2 (70 acft)
Contract 6/Acft/3520/CB6 (b). 130 acft (part). March 1949.
Serial numbers allocated 23.6.49.
Production by English Electric Co, Preston.
WD929 F/f 8.10.50. EE Co. Aw/cn 9.2.51. TRE Defford for radio
tests 9.2.51. EE Co Warton 15.3.51. TRE Defford for
'G-H' tests 5.4.51. RAE Special nav and bombing
project 20.6.51. Napiers, Luton – rocket installation
for F23/49 30.8.55. EE Co for major o/h 14.4.56. Shorts
Belfast 15.7.57. Conv U.10 under Contract
6/Acft/12392/CB6(b) at Rochester. WRE 19.5.59.
Cr at WRE 15.10.59.
WD930 Aw/cn 8.3.51. Handling Squadron. RRE. RR. for RA.7
dev on MoS charge 22.8.51. Later RA.14 and RA.26.
Reallocated RA.29 dev 5.2.60. Scrapped at Hucknall
8.60. Sold to R H Bushells as scrap 19.7.61.
WD931 Aw/cn 22.3.51. RAE 27.3.51 bombing dev. AV Roe for
t/i bomb carrier 23.12.52. RAE 11.5.53. AV Roe
Woodford 1.2.54. RAE for bomb dev trials 23.11.55.
RRE high altitude radar target 28.2.58. Last flew
24.2.65. Soc Pershore 13.5.65. Used for fire practice
until 1969. Nose section in Cosford Museum 6.92.
WD932 Sold to MoS, sold to EE Co, sold to CSA. Aw/cn
20.2.51. 6 months loan to USAF 20.2.51. Atlantic
record 21.2.51. Cr at Centreville, Maryland, USA
21.12.51 whilst on trials with Martins. US serial
51-17387 allotted but not worn. Pattern acft for
Martin B-57A to contract AF33(038)-022617.
Replaced on contract by WG788.
WD933 Aw/cn 12.4.51. C(A) loan to AS Bitteswell for
Sapphire dev 13.4.51. Cr at Bitteswell 10.11.54. W/o.
WD934 Aw/cn 13.4.51. C(A) loan to EE Co. 101. 231 OCU. Nea
at 15 MU 21.11.61. Ss 1.7.64.
WD935 Aw/cn 8.5.51. C(A) charge for VA Wisley for control of
guided bombs 8.5.51. VA 'Red Dean' trials 23.6.55.
Allotted A84-1 for WRE trials. Ntu as acft stayed
in UK. BCDU Wittering 11.9.59 for Service trials.
VA for mods 19.4.60. BCDU Finningley 9.5.60 for
continuation of trials. Returned to Air Ministry
charge 8.7.60 at CSE. 151. 97.360. To St Athan for
storage 23.11.71. To St Athan museum 18.4.75.
Allotted 8440M in 1976. Sold at auction 9.89 to Air
Support Service (£7500). Scrapped 23.11.89. Nose
section retained at Kew.
WD936 Aw/cn 25.5.51. 101. 102. 6. SF Khormaksar. RAF Safi
(Malta) 19.1.58. Nea at 33 MU 27.8.58. G/i as 7589M
25.9.58. No.1 RS 30.10.58. Soc at Locking 28.10.63.
WD937 Aw/cn 29.6.51. EE Co without charge 29.6.51 for t/i
work. A&AEE for powered rudder tests 17.12.54.
EE Co Warton 24.1.55 for aerodynamic research.
A&AEE 24.10.56. EE Co 16.7.57 t/i jettisonable plastic
tip tanks. 17.7.58 investigation of cabin pressure with
canopy off. 28.10.58 tailplane actuator tests. 24.6.59
LABS bombing deflector trials. Allotted 7611M
23.9.59 ntu. 15.10.59 photo and chase duties re TSR2
dev. Sold to BAC 18.10.66 and registered G-ATZW.
Wfu 10.11.67. B/u at Samlesbury '68.

WD938 Aw/cn 26.6.51. 101. 231 OCU. Nea 28.1.69. B/u at 15 MU 9.70. Ss 10.6.71.

WD939 Aw/cn 1.8.51. To RAAF as A84-307 1.8.51. 6 Sqn RAAF. To assist RAAF training in Australia. LWRE. Conv Mk.21 f/f 26.9.58, del 7.11.58. 1 Sqn RAAF. 2 Sqn RAAF. 1(B)OCU RAAF. 2 Sqn RAAF. Displayed at No.1 Central Ammunition Depot RAAF, Kingswood, NSW. Replaced on contract by WP514.

WD940 Aw/cn 31.8.51. To USA as pattern acft for Martin B-57A. Atlantic record 31.8.51. USAF 51-17352 to contract AF33(038)22617. Nose reworked as test layout for B-57B. Scrapped at Sampson AFB, New York. Replaced on contract by WG789.

WD941 Aw/cn 15.8.51. 101. 12. 40. Marshall's Cambridge 15.2.56 for t/i of T.M. Bomb type E. 23 MU 9.6.59. Shorts Belfast 3.5.60 for conv U.14 f/f 27.4.61. 728B Sqn RN. Flown to Pershore for storage 11.12.61. Ss and b/u on site 10.63.

WD942 Aw/cn 25.9.51. C(A) loan to VA Wisley 28.9.51. Modified to VA type 692. To LRWE as A84-2 with VA. 'Red Dean' trials 14.1.55. Ret to Air Min charge 6.12.56 but retained on loan in Australia with 12JSTU. Reverted to WD942. Ret to UK 3.10.57. MoS for trials at AWRE Shoeburyness 16.4.62.

WD943 Aw/cn 12.10.51. RR for Avon reheat dev 17.10.51. Nea at 23 MU 7.7.60. Ss 20.11.62.

WD944 Aw/cn 28.9.51. 101. Conv T.4. CFS. SF Coningsby. CFS. Handling Sqn. SF Laarbruch. SF Bruggen. 14. 98. 360. 7. 98. Sold to BAC 19.2.76.

WD945 Aw/cn 17.9.51. EE Co for mods 17.9.51 A&AEE 18.12.51. BP for mods 30.6.52. RAE 'Blue Devil', 'Red Cat' trials 31.5.53. TRE 'Green Satin' dev 10.8.53 A&AEE 31.7.55. RAE instrument flight trials 30.11.55. RAE target marker 20.11.56. RAE 'Green Flax' dev 31.7.57. A&AEE escort trials aircraft at Bahrein 28.8.58. Soc as spares at Boscombe Down 8.5.64.

WD946 Aw/cn 25.10.51. 101. 9. 73. Nea at 23 MU 24.1.63. Ss 1.7.64.

WD947 Aw/cn 25.10.51. RAE. Armament dev 14.11.51. AIEU/RAE Martlesham Heath 12.12.51 for bomb dev. RAE 9.7.64 for satellite systems dev flying ballistic trajectories. Ferranti Turnhouse for radar discrimination trials 23.12.66. 15 MU for storage 31.10.67. Soc for spares 22.4.71.

WD948 Aw/cn 12.10.51. 101. 102. 45. 75 RNZAF loan. 85. 100. FFS Manston 1.3.77, allotted 8530M.

WD949 Aw/cn 31.10.51. 101. 103. Nea at 15 MU 21.11.56. Soc for fire fighting at Bassingbourn 6.4.63.

WD950 Aw/cn 31.10.51. 101. 231 OCU. Swifter flight. Nea at 15 MU 21.11.61. Soc for fire fighting 17.6.63.

WD951 Aw/cn 2.11.51. CSDE. 231 OCU. JCU Hemswell. 139. 40. 61. 15. To C(A) charge 30.4.57. Shorts Belfast. Conv U.10 f/f 28.7.58. Handling Sqn. WRE Australia. Destroyed by missile 20.7.59.

WD952 Aw/cn 30.11.51. C(A) charge 13.12.51. Bristol Aero Engines Ltd. Olympus test-bed. B.Ol.1/2B f/f 5.8.52. Altitude record to 63,668 ft 5.53. Re-engined B.Ol.11 1955. Altitude record 65,876 ft 29.8.55. Cr nr Filton 12.3.56. B/u at Colerne 9.56.

WD953 Aw/cn 23.11.51. 237 OCU. 231 OCU. To C(A) charge 17.12.51 for RAE fuse and bomb dev. Ferranti Turnhouse 12.9.61 as target acft for 'Indigo Corkscrew'. 11.7.67 target acft for Harrier nav/attack system. Flown to Pershore for storage 13.2.69. Declared Nea 8.69 and dismantled. Sent to RAE Bedford 5.8.70 where burned.

WD954 Aw/cn 12.12.51. C(A) charge 12.12.51. To A&AEE for tropical trials in Kenya 14.5.52. Ret to RAF charge. Conv T.4. SF Hemswell. SF Upwood. 76. To Edinburgh Field for pilot training 18.12.59. MoA charge 11.1.60. Woomera range tracking acft. ATU Edinburgh Field, Australia. Soc 13.2.70. To Warbirds Aviation Museum, Mildura 30.11.74. Note. B.2 nose as g/i at No.2 RS Yatesbury 1960. FFS Manston. 71 MU. To Lincs Aviation Museum, Tattershall 1971. Lincolnshire Aviation Heritage Centre '88. To the Cockpit Collection, Chadwell Heath, Essex 6.89.

WD955 Aw/cn 7.12.51. 101. 617. 21. SF Waddington. 245. 98. Conv T.17. 360. Conv T.17A 5.87. 360, current as 'EM' 8.91.

WD956 Aw/cn 7.12.51. C(A) at EE Co for t/i of mods 7.12.51. VA Wisley for 'Red Dean' dev. 13.1.54. VA Weybridge to 15 MU 30.4.57. Nea at 15 MU 22.11.61. Ss 30.12.64.

WD957 Aw/cn 19.12.51. 231 OCU. 149. Nea at 15 MU 22.4.61. To Colerne for fire fighting 20.8.65.

WD958 Aw/cn 7.12.51. C(A) charge at EE Co t/i of mods 7.12.51. A&AEE flight clearance trials 26.8.52. Shorts Belfast 29.9.55. EE Co Warton for fatigue tests 7.5.57. Allotted for g/i at No.2 RS Yatesbury as 7460M 16.7.57 ntu. Soc 18.7.57. Ss 7.7.61.

WD959 Aw/cn 21.12.51. EE Co loan. RR Hucknall 12.53 for Avon RA.7R and RA.24R dev. To RAE as 7620M 20.10.59. No.12 SoTT Melksham. Soc there 7.10.64.

WD960 Aw/cn 28.12.51. EE Co loan to Farnborough. RAE. Flying accident Llandow; Cat.5 30.4.52 and soc.

WD961 Aw/cn 21.12.51. 617. 61. 15. to C(A) charge 26.4.57. Shorts Belfast. Conv U.10 f/f 7.9.58. Handling Sqn. RAAF 24.11.58, WRE. Destroyed by missile 9.6.59.

WD962 Aw/cn 31.12.51. loan to RAE arrived 2.1.52. Ejection seat tests. To MoA charge 7.5.53. Soc 6.7.61 and b/u at RAE.

WD963 Aw/cn 11.1.52. TRE Defford for 'Blue Shadow' t/i 11.1.52. RRF Upwood for service trials 14.7.52. 109. TRE loan. RRF. TRE. 109. 139. Conv T.4. 75 RNZAF loan. 45. 81. 45, ditched in sea 2 miles from Tengah, after engine failure, 29.6.67, Cat.5

WD964 Aw/cn 31.1.52. 617, dived into ground and blew up when tail actuator failed, Tealby, Lincs 9.12.52. (2k).

WD965 Aw/cn 31.1.52. 617. 10. 15. 44. Ss at 15 MU 7.9.70.

WD966 Aw/cn 31.1.52. 617. 231 OCU. RAFFC. CAW. 85, loan to 231 OCU. Cat 5(c) 20.8.70. Nea 16.9.70, St Athan. Soc 1.10.71.

WD980 Aw/cn 19.2.52. 617. 50. 15. 44. SF West Raynham. 57. BCHU. 230 OCU. 100. Nea at 15 MU '69. To FFS Catterick 4.1.71. Soc 4.1.77.

WD981 Aw/cn 19.2.52. 231 OCU, lost canopy and dived into ground near Newmarket, 24.6.54, Cat.5 (3k).

WD982 Aw/cn 19.2.52. 617. Engine blew up whilst starting at Binbrook. Acft Dbr 15.6.54, Cat.5

WD983 Collected by RAAF as A84-125 to assist training. Left Hurn 16.3.52. 6 Sqn RAAF. Conv Mk.21 f/f 9.2.59, del 10.6.59. 1 Sqn RAAF. 2 Sqn RAAF. 1(B)OCU RAAF. ARDU. In store at No.3 Acft Depot 7.85. Replaced on RAF contract by WP515.

WD984 Aw/cn 29.2.52. 617. Cr during a snowstorm whilst on GCA approach to Binbrook 27.3.52, Cat.5 (3k).

WD985 Aw/cn 4.4.52. On charge to 12 Sqn 7.4.52, fuel switched off in error and belly landed near Sealand 8.4.52 whilst on delivery by 4 Ferry Pool crew!

WD986 Aw/cn 6.3.52 (last acft in black/grey scheme). 617. 100. Nea at 15 MU 22.11.61. To Watton for fire fighting 14.4.63. Soc 17.7.63.

WD987 Aw/cn 2.3.52 (first acft in mod 312 Medium Sea Grey/ Light Sea Grey upper surface, PRU Blue lower surface). 12. 231 OCU. Nea at 15 MU 24.1.63. Ss 27.4.64.

WD988 Aw/cn 4.4.52. 12. 32. 73. Nea at 15 MU 11.7.61. Scrap to AWRE at Shoeburyness 2.5.62.

WD989 Aw/cn 4.4.52. 12. 100. 73. Lost power on one engine on t/o, swung off runway at Mehrabad, Iran 1.7.58. Soc 26.9.58.

WD990 Aw/cn 10.4.52. 12. 540. 12. 9. 27. SF Waddington. Nea at 15 MU 22.11.61. To g/i at Colerne 10.62, allotted 7764M. Sold to BAC 8.7.66. G27-120. Conv to B.52 for Ethiopia as 354. Del 2.11.68.

WD991 Cr on first test flight at Cottam, nr Preston 25.3.52. Replaced on contract by XA536.

WD992 Aw/cn 24.4.52. C(A) charge at DH Propellers Ltd Hatfield for 'Blue Jay' tests 28.4.52. Released 6.5.64. Ss to Cambria Acft Spares Ltd 14.6.65.

WD993 Aw/cn 24.4.52. 12. 44. Nea at 15 MU 22.4.61. Sold to BAC 14.7.65. Conv to B.2 for Venezuela as 1364, del '67. BAC for overhaul '75. G27-260. Conv to B.82 and returned to Venezuela 3.5.78 as 1364.

WD994 Aw/cn 24.4.52. 12. Flew into hill on GCA to Binbrook, at Sixhills, Lincs 10.11.52, Cat.5 (3k).

WD995 Aw/cn 24.4.52. 617. 103. 249. 32. Cr after collision with Javelin XH906 during practise interception, Akrotiri 26.10.61. Soc 20.11.61, Cat.5 (3k).

Sapphire 7 testbed WD933 was engaged on relight tests on 10.11.54 when one engine failed to relight and the other was accidentally inactivated. In the subsequent forced landing within Bitteswell airfield boundary, made with u/c retracted, misted windscreen and no power or R/T comms, the aircraft flipped over upon contact with the runway intersection. See page 173.
Armstrong-Siddeley via D.M.Sargent

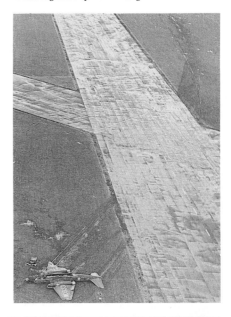

WD996 Aw/cn 24.4.52. 12. 27. 57. To g/i Little
Rissington as 7802M 12.3.63.

WD997 Aw/cn 30.4.52. 9. 21. SF Waddington. 231 OCU. Nea
23 MU 24.1.63. Ss 27.4.64.

WD998 Aw/cn 30.4.52. 9. Soc 11.6.63. To Wyton for fire
fighting 6.63.

WD999 Aw/cn 30.4.52. 9. 103. No.1 SoTT as 7379M 17.10.56 -
cancelled. To No.1 SoTT as 7387M 27.11.56.
Dismantled 7.78. Ss 9.80.

WE111 Aw/cn 16.5.52. 9. 617 for Suez crisis 11.56. Conv T.4.
13. SF Akrotiri. ITF Akrotiri. 6, flew into sea on
approach to Akrotiri 24.4.62, Cat.5 (2k).

WE112 Aw/cn 19.5.52. Handling Sqn. CFS. RAFFC. CAW. Sold
to BAC 10.10.69. G27-180. Ss 1974.

WE113 Aw/cn 30.5.52. Del 9.6.52. 231 OCU. 245. 98. 85. 100.
231 OCU as 'BJ' 8.91. In open storage at Wyton 23.1.92.

WE114 Aw/cn 30.5.52. 231 OCU, dived into ground on night
overshoot at Bassingbourn 24.7.57.

WE115 Aw/cn 26.5.52. 231 OCU. Ss from 15 MU 14.2.64.

WE116 Aw/cn 30.5.52. 231 OCU. Cr into ground returning
from night navex, near Thirfield, Herts 20.8.52,
Cat.5 (3k).

WE117 Aw/cn 26.5.52. 231 OCU. 32 MU. Cr when both engines
cut on test flight 3 miles ENE of Llanelli, Carmarthen
13.1.58, Cat.5(1k).

WE118 Aw/cn 30.5.52. 231 OCU. RRF. 231 OCU. 207. Conv T.4.
SF Hemswell. SF Binbrook. SF Coningsby. 231 OCU.
Soc 25.10.71 at 15 MU. Remains to FFS Catterick.

WE119 Aw/cn 30.5.52. 231 OCU. Cr 3 miles SE of Ware, Herts -
lost control at height 20.12.54, Cat.5 (2k).

WE120 Aw/cn 5.8.52. 231 OCU. Sold to BAC 14.7.65.
Refurbished and sold to Peru as 238, del 5.12.66.

WE121 Aw/cn 13.6.52. 231 OCU. ETPS 29.8.63. A&AEE for
radio interference and TACAN trials 1.7.69. BAC
Warton 10.10.69 - chase acft for Jaguar until 14.7.72.
RRE for o/h and conv to target towing role 1972-74.
Used as required as Concorde chase acft. FR Ltd
6.5.74 for target towing trials. RAE Llanbedr 30.12.74.
Grounded due to fatigue 2.79. FR Ltd for cannibal-
isation 14.12.79. RAE BDR research 26.6.80. Parts to
P&EE Foulness 31.10.80. Rear fuselage to Abingdon
28.8.86. Remainder at P&EE. Sold for scrap 12.90.

WE122 Aw/cn 13.6.52. 231 OCU. 245. 98. Conv TT.18. FRADU.
To St Athan store 25.2.87. To RAE Llanbedr 8.87,
current 5.91.

**B.2 WD999 of 9 Sqn seen during a Coronation
Flypast practice in July 1953. The 'white' part of
the colour scheme was allegedly a hangover from
trials at Woomera.** *via Owen Temple*

**Any 103 Squadron Canberra photograph is a
rarity. Just how WD995 got into this situation at
Gutersloh on 30.6.55 we do not know, but it was
repaired and flew again.** *via Wg Cdr W. Bonner*

WD947 of the RAE, Llanbedr, 10.5.61. *A. Pearcy*

Canberra PR.3 (27 acft)
Contract 6/Acft/3520/CB6(b). 130 acft (part). March 1949.
Serial numbers allocated 23.6.49.
Production by English Electric Co, Preston.
WE135 F/f 31.7.52. Allotted CS(A) for t/i work 5.11.52.
Aw/cn 27.11.52. Att 541. A&AEE. EE Co. Ex loan
26.5.54. 58. 237 OCU. 231 OCU. 39. 231 OCU. Loan to
85. Soc 5 MU 18.11.72. Catterick for fire fighting.
WE136 Aw/cn 27.11.52. 540. 231 OCU. 237 OCU. 231 OCU. Nea
at 33 MU 25.1.63. Ss 16.12.66.
WE137 Aw/cn 28.11.52. A&AEE handling trials 3.12.52. To
RAF Wyton 18.5.53. 540. 82. 69. 39. 237 OCU. 231 OCU.
Soc at 5 MU 15.11.72. To FFS Catterick.
WE138 Aw/cn 31.3.53. A&AEE. 58. 69. 39. Nea at 33 MU and
ss 16.12.66.
WE139 Aw/cn 30.1.53. Handling Sqn. 540. Winner UK-NZ Air
race. 69. 39. 231 OCU. To RAF Museum Henlow
24.4.69 as 8369M. To RAF Museum, Hendon as
WE139. Current.
WE140 Aw/cn 17.2.53. 540. 231 OCU. 237 OCU. 231 OCU. B/u
at 15 MU and ss 7.9.70.
WE141 Aw/cn 11.3.53. 540. 231 OCU. Dismantled at 15 MU
and soc 1.10.71. To FFS Catterick.
WE142 Aw/cn 27.3.53. 540. 231 OCU. B/u at 15 MU 7.70, soc
and ss 7.9.70.
WE143 Aw/cn 30.10.53. 540. 58. 231 OCU. RRF. 231 OCU.
Cr on asymmetric approach to Bassingbourn 23.6.58,
Cat.5 (1k).
WE144 Aw/cn 18.5.53. 540. 82. 58. 69. 39. 231 OCU. Soc at
19 MU 16.6.72, remains to Special Procurements
Executive, Corsham, Bath, 1973. RAF Rudloe Manor
for fire fighting.
WE145 Aw/cn 18.5.53. 540. IAM. G/i at No.2 SoTT, Cosford
1.64. Allotted 7843M 13.4.64. Repainted as WE143
24.6.68, corrected to WE145. School of Photography,
Cosford. Cosford Museum allotted 8450M ntu. To fire
dump, Wyton as 7843M 4.78. Allotted 8597M 1979.
B/u and removed 12.81.
WE146 EE Co. SBAC show 9.53. Aw/cn 9.10.53. To MoS for
RAE for camera trials 14.10.53. RAE Met Flt. RAE.
Shorts Belfast 2.8.66. Conv to SD.1. RAE Llanbedr. Soc
spares for fire fighting at Llanbedr 29.4.75
WE147 Aw/cn 30.6.53. MoS charge. TRE 1.7.53 for 'Green
Satin' and 'Blue Study' trials. RAE 1.7.53. RAE Met Flt.
RRE Doppler trials for TSR2 17.1.62. Last flight

23.2.68. Soc for spares 16.4.69. Dismantled 11.69.
AWRE Shoeburyness 12.69.
WE148 Aw/cn 30.9.53. 540. 58. 39. Nea at 15 MU 31.1.63,
b/u 2.69, ss 20.6.69. Wroughton for fire fighting.
WE149 Aw/cn 29.9.53. 540. Lost power and cr on approach
to Wyton 12.8.54. Cat.5 (2k).
WE150 Aw/cn 9.10.53. 231 OCU. 237 OCU. 231 OCU. B/u at
15 MU 7.71, soc 29.9.71 and remains to FFS Catterick.
WE151 Aw/cn 23.10.53. 231 OCU. 237 OCU. 231 OCU. Nea at
33 MU 23.6.65. Ss 16.12.66.
WE166 Aw/cn 30.9.53. 231 OCU 27.10.53 to 23.10.56. 237 OCU
23.10.56. 231 OCU 11.6.63 to 7.5.69. B/u at 5 MU 7.70.
Ss 18.1.71.
WE167 Aw/cn 30.10.53. 540. 82. BP for night photo
installation 16.12.55. A&AEE flight trials 28.6.56.
15 MU 26.4.57. BP Seighford for wing tip photo flash
cartridge 10.11.58. EE Co Warton for trials 16.3.60.
A&AEE for trials 22.4.60. BP Seighford 28.4.60. 15 MU
7.9.60. Nea at 15 MU 30.1.63, ss 12.5.67.
WE168 Aw/cn 9.10.53. 540. 69. 39. 231 OCU. Soc 13.5.69. FFS
Manston. Static display Manston 28.7.69. Allotted
8049M. Scrapped 2.90, to Hanningfield, Chelmsford.
Nose to Glen Mitchell, Colchester for exhibition 2.90.
WE169 Aw/cn 6.11.53. 82. 69. 39. 231 OCU. Soc 15.5.69.
To FFS Manston.
WE170 Aw/cn 21.10.53. 540. 58. Force landed after engine
failure on GCA to Wyton 21.12.54. Cat.5
WE171 Aw/cn 30.10.53. 231 OCU. 237 OCU. 231 OCU. Sold
to BAC 7.7.65. Conv to PR.3 for Venezuela as 2444. Del
28.10.66 (39th Sqn FAV).
W/o at Maracay 9.3.76.
WE172 Aw/cn 9.10.53. 231 OCU. 237 OCU. 231 OCU. Sold to
BAC 20.5.65. Conv to PR.3 for Venezuela as 2314.
Del 26.8.66. (39th Sqn FAV). BAC for o/h '76. G27-264.
Conv to PR.83 and ret to Venezuela as 2314 13.9.78.
Wfu at El Libertador 10.90.
WE173 Aw/cn 6.11.53. 82. 58. SF Upwood. 69. 39. MoS charge
for RAE. Met Flt. 231 OCU. Soc 15.5.69. RAE Met Flt.
Withdrawn 31.3.81. To Coltishall 4.3.82 as 8740M, for
fire practice.
WE174 Aw/cn 13.11.53. 82. C(A) free loan for BP trial mods
12.11.59, A&AEE 15.8.60. 69. 39. 231 OCU. Soc 15.5.69.
To FFS Manston 18.5.69.
WE175 Aw/cn 13.11.53. 82. 58. 39. 231 OCU. Soc 13.5.69. To
Wattisham fire dump 13.5.69.

Canberra T.4 (8 acft)
Contract 6/Acft/3520/CB6(b). 130 acft (part). March 1949.
Serial numbers allocated 23.6.49.
Production by English Electric Co, Preston.
WE188 f/f 31.7.52. Aw/cn 2.10.53. SF Hemswell.
SF Waddington. SF Upwood. 231 OCU. SF Upwood.
231 OCU. 56. SF Wyton. 100. 231 OCU. 360. 231 OCU.
Sold to BAC 19.11.81. In store at Samlesbury 1986.
Acquired by Solway Avn Society, Carlisle. 6.88.
WE189 Aw/cn 30.10.53. AIEU for type D auto pilot dev 9.11.53.
Marshall for installation of PR.7 type nose 28.9.55.
AIEU 22.11.55. Cr at Martlesham Heath, Cat.5 28.9.56.
Soc 12.4.57.
WE190 Aw/cn 27.11.53. A&AEE. SF Wyton. EE Co. Conv by BP
to T.13 for RNZAF as NZ6152. Del 3.2.61. 14 RNZAF.
Bomber OCU RNZAF. Sold to India 11.70.
WE191 Aw/cn 24.12.53. 231 OCU. 237 OCU. 231 OCU. 245.
Sold to BAC 24.5.65. Conv for IAF as Q497 in 1969.
Order cancelled. To 5 MU for storage. Re-Sold to BAC
1.2.78. By road to Samlesbury 10.78. To Warton in
sections '88. Airfield Fire Services.
WE192 Aw/cn 5.1.54. 231 OCU. 3. 231 OCU. 39. 231 OCU. 360.
231 OCU. 7. 231 OCU. Sold to BAC 26.11.81. Storage
at Samlesbury. Solway Avn Society, Carlisle 1988.
WE193 Aw/cn 30.1.54. 231 OCU. SF Upwood. 231 OCU. TFS
West Raynham. 85. 39. 85. 231 OCU. Sold to India as
Q1791 del 23.7.75.
WE194 Aw/cn 19.2.54. 231 OCU. 237 OCU. SF Wyton. 14. SF
Laarbruch. 31. Soc 10.11.71 at 15 MU.
WE195 Aw/cn 27.2.54. 231 OCU. 237 OCU. SF Wyton. 231
OCU. Sold to India as Q1792 del 18.6.75.

**231 OCU PR.3s WE136, WE172 and WE140 and
others were temporarily snowbound at their
Bassingbourn base when this delightful scene
was captured for posterity on 3.1.62.**

Above: **Souden near Exeter, on 23.10.53, was the scene of a tragic accident as a result of a bird strike on the RREs WF892 following take off.**

ATDU B.2 WH661 at Thorney Island, Sept 1954. Note the wingtip camera bulge. *J.D.R.Rawlings*

Below: **WG788 of the RRE was one of only two Canberras to have serials in the 'WG' range. They were replacements for two B.2s diverted off an early contract and sold to the USA. Both WG788 and WG789 spent their working lives on test duties with various research establishments.** *via M.Nolan*

Canberra B.2 (18 acft)

Contract 6/ACFT/3520/CB6 (b). 130 acft (part). March 1949.
Serial numbers allocated 28.4.50.
Production by English Electric Co, Preston.

WF886 Aw/cn 20.6.52. 231 OCU. 90. 6, destroyed by fire after EOKA bomb attack on hangar at Akrotiri 27.11.57. Cat.5.

WF887 Aw/cn 20.6.52. 231 OCU. 115. SF Khormaksar. G/i at Watton, allotted 7637M 2.6.60. Fuselage to CSDU Swanton Morley.

WF888 Aw/cn 24.6.52. 231 OCU. Cr when engine cut at 500ft on take-off, hit ground near Steeple Morden, Herts 19.12.52. Cat.5 (3k).

WF889 27.6.52. 231 OCU. Cr when acft dived into ground during night sortie, 2 miles N of Bassingbourn 16.2.53. Cat.5 (3k).

WF890 Aw/cn 5.8.52. 231 OCU. Swifter Flight. Conv T.17 del to Watton 19.5.67. 360. Conv T.17A. 360, current as 'EJ' 8.91.

WF891 Aw/cn 30.6.52. Watton. 109. 12, cr when engine failed on take off and acft hit GCA vehicle, Binbrook 2.4.54. Cat.5 (2k).

WF892 Aw/cn 30.6.52. RRE for installation and trials of 'Blue Shadow' side-ways looking radar 1952-53. Cr at Souden, near Exeter 23.10.53 after birdstrike on take-off. Cat.5 (2k).

WF907 Aw/cn 4.7.62. 9. 100. allocated to No.1 SoTT as 7380M 17.10.56 - cancelled. G/i to No.1 SoTT as 7386M 27.11.56. To fire dump Halton '68, burnt 5.71.

WF908 Aw/cn 11.7.52. 9. 18. 231 OCU. Soc at 15 MU 7.2.64. To Manston for non-destructive training as 7828M 7.2.64. FFS Manston 13.3.67.

WF909 Aw/cn 17.7.52. RR Hucknall 18.7.52 for Avon development. Hatfield 8.12.55 for DH Gyron Junior dev. B/u at Hatfield 1962. Sold to Cambria (Acft Spares) Ltd 8.2.63. Remains at Staravia, Ascot '64.

WF910 Aw/cn 29.7.52. 231 OCU. Cr after both engines cut on climb out from GCA at Lakenheath. Acft hit the ground 500 yds short of runway at Mildenhall when trying to make a forced landing 4.11.53.

WF911 Aw/cn 29.7.52. 231 OCU. Sold to BAC 21.5.69. G27-161. Scrapped at Samlesbury '76.

WF912 Aw/cn 31.7.52. 231 OCU. Ss 27.4.64.

WF913 Aw/cn 31.7.52. 231 OCU. Ss 1.7.64.

WF914 Aw/cn 13.8.52. 109. 6. 73. 6. Sold to BAC 29.3.65. Conv B.2 for Venezuela as 1233. Del 7.66.(40th Bomber Sqn FAV). To BAC for o/h '77. G27-302. Conv B.82 and ret 27.6.79 as 1233. Wfu at El Libertador 10.90.

WF915 Aw/cn 15.8.52. 109. 115(?). 231 OCU. 75 RNZAF loan. Cr in Malayan jungle 26.10.61. Cat.5.

WF916 Aw/cn 15.8.52. 9. 50. 115. 207. 44. 15. 44. SF Binbrook. 12. 9. Conv T.17 del to 15 MU 28.12.69. 360. A&AEE for pressure error measurements 3.8.70. Ret Cottesmore 12.10.70. 360, current as 'EL' 8.91.

WF917 Aw/cn 22.8.52. TRE Defford for top radar cover tests 25.8.52. To GW(A) charge for 'Orange Cocktail MTS' 28.2.56. RAE 'Violet Banner' trials (infra-red homing device) 9.10.59. ETPS 24.1.62. RRE Pershore for preparation for ECM trials 17.4.62. High altitude

target 7.11.62. BAC Samlesbury conv of special radar fit 29.11.63. RRE Pershore for 'Bloodhound Mk.2' trials 7.4.64. Marshall's for major o/h and aerial installation 2.3.67. RRE 22.11.67. Soc 5.9.68. Sold to BAC 22.11.68. G27-128. Dismantled 1.71 and scrapped.

Canberra PR.3 (7 acft)

Contract 6/Acft/3520/CB6 (b). 130 acft (part). March 1949.
Serial numbers allocated 28.4.50.
Production by English Electric Co, Preston.

WF922 Aw/cn 13.11.53. 82. 58. 69. 39. Loan to MoA 18.5.61. BP Seighford for mods 18.5.61. Marshall's for t/i & flight trials of survey cameras 15.3.63. 15 MU 25.7.67. A&AEE for trials of Lindholme gear for PR.9 fit in NEAF 11.6.68. A&AEE for camera mods and Sperry vertical gyro. 2.1.69. To MoA charge 31.1.69. RRE for o/h 10.12.70. A&AEE for new photo equipment 26.8.71. Sold to BAC and del to Marshall's 25.3.75. B/u at Cambridge. Nose to Lincoln Field Vintage and Historic Acft Collection, Bushey 1981. Fuselage to Midland Air Museum, Coventry 6.84. Current.

WF923 Aw/cn 26.11.53. 82. 58. 231 OCU. 237 OCU. 231 OCU. Nea at 33 MU 26.3.63. Ss 16.12.66.

WF924 Aw/cn 27.11.53. 82. 58. 69. 39. 231 OCU. Soc 12.5.69. To fire dump Tangmere.

WF925 Aw/cn 15.1.54. 82. 237 OCU. 231 OCU. Soc at 15 MU 29.8.68 for fire fighting at Benson. Fuselage on fire dump Benson 2.69.

WF926 Aw/cn 29.1.54. 82. 69. 39. Cr into sea on GCA, 19 miles ENE of Luqa, Malta 21.1.60. Cat.5 (2k).

WF927 Aw/cn 5.11.54. 69. 16. 39. 231 OCU. Soc at Cottesmore 16.5.69 - to fire dump.

WF928 Aw/cn 26.2.54. 82. Cr when acft caught fire and broke up after photo flash exploded, Sandbanks Range 3.6.54. Cat.5 (2k).

Canberra B.2 (2 acft)

Contract 6/Acft/3520/CB6(b). 130 acft (part).
Replacements for WD932 and WD940 diverted off contract.
Serial numbers allocated 4.8.50.
Production by English Electric Co, Preston.

WG788 Aw/cn 25.8.52. To BP Defford for 'Blue Sugar', 'Blue Study', 'Green Garland' (Infra-red fuse for Firestreak missile) trials 25.8.52. TRE Defford 16.11.53. GW(A) charge 28.2.56 for 'Green Garland' and 'Blue Sky' dev. RRE for 'Sea Dart' trials. 8.7.68. Final flight 23.12.68. Released 12.2.69. Nose to XH568 1970. Fire Dump Defford 1970. Soc for fire fighting 25.2.71.

WG789 Aw/cn 29.8.52 231 OCU. To MoS charge 6.2.56 for use by BP at Defford for 'Red Dean' computer trials 6.2.56. BP Seighford for guided weapons guidance system 1.6.59. RRE Pershore for 'Sea Dart' guidance system trials 1959/71. BAC Fairford as Concord chase acft 8.7.71 to 6.8.71. RRE storage 6.8.71. RRE for 'Sea Eagle' guided weapon homing head carry trials 6.10.72. RSRE Bedford 1.11.76. Soc at Bedford 23.2.82 used by apprentices. Scrapped 1986 and taken by road to Burgess Hill W.Sussex.

Canberra B.2 (86 acft)

Contract 6/Acft/5786/CB6(b) 215 acft (part). 20 Sept 1950.
Serial numbers allocated 20.9.50.
Production by English Electric Co, Preston.

WH637 f/f 26.8.52. Aw/cn 29.8.52. 231 OCU. CAW. 35. 9. Conv T.4. 13. SF Akrotiri. ITF Akrotiri. SF Akrotiri. Soc at St Athan 17.11.72.

WH638 Aw/cn 12.9.52. To BP Defford for 'Green Satin' installation 15.9.52. TRE 'Green Satin' flight trials 6.2.53. A&AEE service trials 1.7.53. 100 Sqn for trials 27.10.54. 249. 32. 73. Sold to BAC 27.8.66. G27-117. Conv B.52 for Ethiopia as 351. Del 24.7.68.

WH639 Aw/cn 25.9.52. RAFFC. Cr when acft broke up in the air 2.5 miles SW of Doncaster, 24.6.54. Cat.5 (2k).

WH640 Aw/cn 26.9.52. 109. 104, cr when acft hit ground 3000 yds short of r/w on approach to Gutersloh, Germany 24.9.55. Cat.5 (3k)

WH641 Aw/cn 25.9.52. 231 OCU. 85. Cr when acft spun into ground during practice asymmetric landing at Wattisham 27.7.70. Cat.5 (2k)

WH642 Aw/cn 26.9.52. 50. 103. 527. CSE. 245. 98. 97. 360. Soc at 19 MU 23.1.75. To Catterick for fire fighting.

WH643 Aw/cn 26.9.52. 50. 100. 40. 90. 207. Soc 17.6.63. To Cottesmore for fire fighting.

WH644 Aw/cn 30.9.52. 109. 104. 59. Sold to Rhodesia and del 7.4.59 as RRAF173 (5 Sqn), renumber RRAF214 in 1963 and R2514 in 1969. Zimbabwe AF as 2514 in 1980.

WH645 Aw/cn 30.9.52. 109. 207. 115. 542. 75 RNZAF. TFS West Raynham. Ss 15.5.64.

WH646 Aw/cn 30.9.52. 50. 10. 45. 75 RNZAF. 45. Conv T.17. Del RAF Watton 3.4.67. 360. Conv T.17A. 360, current as 'EG' 8.91.

WH647 Aw/cn 30.9.52. 50. 249. 73. Sold to BAC 29.3.65. Conv B.2 for Venezuela as 1131, del 2.66. (40th Bomber Sqn). To BAC for o/h 21.7.75, G27-257. Conv B.82 ret 28.9.77 as 1131.

WH648 Aw/cn 24.10.52. 231 OCU. RRF. 231 OCU. Swifter Flight. Soc at 15 MU 13.7.64 and ss.

WH649 Aw/cn 17.10.52. 139. 57. 44. 12. Sold to BAC 29.3.65. Conv B.2 for Venezuela as 1339. del 30.9.66 (40th Bomber Sqn). To BAC for o/h '75, G27-259. Conv B.82 ret 16.3.78 as 1339. Wfu at El Libertador 10.90.

WH650 Aw/cn 24.10.52. 109. 139. 104. 249. Soc at 23 MU and ss 1.7.64.

WH651 Aw/cn 24.10.52. 139. 109. Conv T.4. FTU. FECS. 81. 45. 81. Soc at 19 MU 14.2.72.

WH652 Aw/cn 31.10.52. 50. 76. 32. To MoA charge 20.9.60. Shorts Belfast. Conv U.10. f/f 12.12.61. To WRE Edinburgh Field, Australia, 23.2.62. No.1 ATU. Destroyed by missile at Woomera 12.2.64.

WH653 Aw/cn 24.10.52. 50. Sold to Rhodesia and del 7.4.59 as RRAF160 (5 Sqn). Renumber RRAF201 in 1963 and R2051 in 1969.

WH654 Aw/cn 31.10.52. 50. 32. Soc at 23 MU and ss 27.4.64.

WH655 Aw/cn 31.10.52. 139. 57. 249. Cr when u/c jammed up and acft belly landed at El Adem 29.8.58.

WH656 Aw/cn 13.11.52. 139. 109. Cr when acft lost power on overshoot, Scampton 23.8.54. Cat.5 (2k).

WH657 Aw/cn 7.11.52. 231 OCU. NGTE Farnborough for high altitude engine problems 4.6.53. RAE for parachute stabilizing systems 29.7.60. Used for tracking British satellites in joint UK-USA project 1962-66. College of Aeronautics 3.6.66 for slush trials. RFD Ltd 30.4.69 on loan. Sold to RFD 29.11.77. Booker Air for preservation 1986. Del to Brenzett, Kent 12.87.

WH658 Aw/cn 7.11.52. 109 (?). 139. 104. 59. Conv T.4. Sold to Rhodesia as RRAF174, del 20.3.61 (5 Sqn). Renumber RRAF215 in 1963 and R2155 in 1969. Zimbabwe AF as 2155 in 1980.

WH659 Aw/cn 13.11.52. 139. 12. 90. Conv T.4. SF Laarbruch. 16. 3. Sold to BAC 10.11.65. Refurbished and sold to Peru as 231. Del 21.5.66. W/o 6.10.71.

WH660 Aw/cn 21.11.52. To MoA charge for VA Wisley, for 'Red Dean' tests 28.11.52. RRE AI Mk.18 development 1954/58. AI research 1958/61. Guided weapons trials 1961/67 and 'Sea Dart' carry trials 1967/70. Last flight 31.1.70. Retired 12.70, to fire dump, Pershore. B/u 1971.

WH661 Aw/cn 21.11.52. Transferred from RAF charge 28.11.52. RAE 28.11.52, ATDU 4.7.53, RAE parachute mine trials 17.3.55. Soc 5.5.60. To P&EE Shoeburyness.

WH662 Aw/cn 21.11.52. 12. Sold to Rhodesia and del 10.3.59 as RRAF161 (5 Sqn). Renumber RRAF202 in 1963 and R2502 in 1969. Zimbabwe AF as 2502 in 1980.

WH663 Aw/cn 25.11.52. 139. Cr on overshoot at Corringham, nr Gainsborough, Lincs 19.3.53. Cat.5 (2k)

WH664 Aw/cn 1.12.52. 231 OCU. Swifter Flight. To BAC for conv T.17. Del Watton 31.7.67. 360 as 'EH' 8.91. Authorised for disposal 12.6.91. In open storage at Wyton, minus rear fuselage, 23.1.92.

WH665 Aw/cn 28.11.52. 10. 45. 75 RNZAF. To BAC for conv T.17. Del Watton 13.3.67. 360. Soc Wyton 1.12.82. G/i to No.2 SoTT, Cosford as 8763M ntu. BAC Samlesbury 28.4.83. Moved to Rolls-Royce Technical College, BAe, Filton 10.88. Fuselage still present 6.90.

WH666 Aw/cn 12.12.52. 10. 45. 75 RNZAF. TFS West Raynham. 56. 100. To Zimbabwe as 2250, del 20.3.81.

WH667 Aw/cn 12.12.52. 10. 45. 85. 100. Cr on take off, after engine blew up, Akrotiri 7.11.80. Cat.5 (2k).

WH668 Aw/cn 18.12.52. 10. 21. 10. 100. 57. G/i at No.4 SoTT as 7590M 30.9.58. Soc at St Athan 28.10.63.

WH669 Aw/cn 19.12.52. 10. Cr when acft dived into ground on overshoot, Dilhorne, Staffs 27.3.53. Cat.5 (3k)

WH670 Aw/cn 19.12.52. 192. 527. 245. 98. 85. 100, last flown (as 'CB') 11.90 (10003 hrs). On offer for sale at Wyton 9.91. Reported scrapped at Wyton by 23.1.92.

Ex-360 Squadron T.17 WH664 being broken up at Wyton, January 1992. The large (light blue) cross on the forward fuselage, is an indicator that it has been condemned for breaking and although not confirmed, may be connected with the implementation of the East-West disarmament agreement. *MAP*

WH671 Aw/cn 18.12.52. BP on loan, engine de-icing trials. 24.12.52. Transferred from RAF charge 8.8.53 whilst with BP. RR for Avon RA.14 dev 9.6.54. RA.24 handling 1.10.59. Released 17.3.61. B/u 11.61.

WH672 Aw/cn 23.12.52. 10. Sold to Rhodesia as RRAF162, del 10.3.59. (5 Sqn). Renumber RRAF203 in 1963 and R5203 in 1969, Zimbabwe AF as 5203 in 1980.

WH673 Aw/cn 9.1.53. RAFFC. BP Seighford for 'Blue Silk' t/i 28.3.61. CAW 14.5.63. 15 MU storage 18.7.66. G/i at RAE Farnborough 7.11.73. Parts to AWRE Foulness 1.80, last noted 6.89.

WH674 Aw/cn 31.12.52. 10. 104.59. Conv T.4. Sold to Rhodesia as RRAF175, del 28.3.61. (5 Sqn). Renumber RRAF216 in 1963. Cannibalised late '70s: parts possibly used in R2516, in which case passed to AFZ in 1980.

WH695 Aw/cn 23.1.53. 2TAF TDU. 1323 Flt. 542. 21. SF Upwood. No.1 SoTT as 7657M 20.10.60.

WH696 Aw/cn 16.1.53. del to St Athan by 2 FU. Cr when acft dived into ground near Twyford, Berks on delivery flight by 3(LR)FU 27.1.53. Cat.5 (1k)

WH697 Aw/cn 26.1.53. 2TAF TDU. 1323 Flt. Force landed in sea off Ailinglapalap, Marshall Islands 11.3.54. Salvage impractical, engines removed and acft destroyed Cat.5.

WH698 Aw/cn 27.1.53. 192. 51. B/u at 15 MU 2.69. Fuselage to FFS Catterick. Soc 4.1.71.

WH699 Aw/cn 30.1.53. RAFFC, 'Aries IV'. Cr after take off, Strubby, Lincs 28.11.59. Cat.5 (1k). The 'WH699' depicted at Cranwell is really WJ637.

WH700 Aw/cn 30.1.53. 2TAF TDU. 1323 Flt ntu. Loan to C(A) 8.9.55. DH Props for 'Blue Jay' t/i 9.9.55. C(A) charge 9.12.55. Allocated to 'Blue Jay' JSTU at WRE Australia 16.10.56, despatched from Hatfield 4.2.57. 12 JSTU. 'Red Top'/Jindivik trials 30.12.59. Safety acft 'Blue Steel' trials 5.2.60. Released 1.12.60. Soc at Edinburgh Field 13.2.70. To Air Museum Parafield, SA 1982. Lincoln Nitshke Military and Historical Aircraft Collection, Greenock, South Australia 1990.

WH701 Aw/cn 30.1.53. 2TAF TDU. 1323 Flt. 542. 21. SF Upwood. G/i No.4 SoTT as 7659M 25.7.60.

WH702 Aw/cn 16.2.53. RRF. Off RAF charge 25.7.57. RRE 'Red Setter' sideways looking radar trials 1954/56. 'Green Satin' trials 1955/56. G-Band experimental radar dev Soc 5.9.68. Sold to BAC, despatched 5.11.68. G27-127. Conv B.62 for Argentina as B105, del 26.5.71. (1 Sqn).

WH703 Aw/cn 16.2.53. 231 OCU. 85. 100. 231 OCU. 100. G/i at Marham as 8490M 29.3.76. To BDRF Abingdon, last noted 8.89.

WH704 Aw/cn 20.2.53. 231 OCU. To MoA charge 15.6.60 Shorts Belfast. Conv U.14 f/f 4.7.61. 728B FAA 5.9.61. To Pershore for storage 5.12.61. Soc 20.9.63 and used for apprentice training. Used for fire practice and b/u at Pershore 1966.

WH705 Aw/cn 20.2.53. 231 OCU. 115. 139. 231 OCU. To MoA charge 29.9.60 Shorts Belfast. Conv U.10 f/f 19.4.62. Despatched Belfast for WRE, Edinburgh Field, 4.7.62. No.1 ATU. Destroyed by missile 28.4.65.

WH706 Aw/cn 20.2.53. 617. Conv T.4. 33MU. RAE/SME for indirect vision trials for future acft. 13.9.56. 33 MU 26.3.57. FECS. 45. 81. 45. Soc and b/u at 19 MU 7.7.72.

WH707 Aw/cn 27.2.53. 44. Sold to Rhodesia as RRAF163, del 5.5.59. (5 Sqn). Renumber RRAF204 in 1963 and R2504 in 1969. Zimbabwe AF as 2504 in 1980

WH708 To Venezuela as 1A-39, del '53. (39 Sqn). W/o 24.4.56.

WH709 To Venezuela as 2A-39, del '53. (39 Sqn). To EE Co for o/h 2.59, ret to FAV. Renumbered 6315. To BAC for o/h '68, G27-159, ret 6.8.69. To BAC for o/h '77, G27-303, ret 11.7.79 as 6315. Wfu at El Libertador 10.90.

WH710 Aw/cn 27.2.53. C(A) charge 27.3.53 for RAE Armament Dept for mine dev. ARDU trials flight, Australia for bomb ballistics 10.6.53. Allocated A84-3 by RAAF 13.6.53. Ret to UK 7.58. Reverted to WH710. Marshall's Cambridge for removal of long range tank 4.7.58. Shorts Belfast 22.7.58. Conv U.10, f/f 9.8.60. Despatched Belfast for WRE Edinburgh Field 30.9.60. No.1 ATU. Destroyed by missile 26.5.65.

WH711 Aw/cn 17.3.53. 149. 88. 213. Sold to BAC 29.7.59. Sold to Sweden. Conv by BP to Tp52 as 52001, del 1.2.60. (F8 Wing). Last flight 23.1.73. To F3 Wing, Malmen. To Air Museum, Ugglarp '73. Current.

WH712 Aw/cn 30.4.53. 57. CFS. 57. Sold to BAC 29.3.65. Conv B(I)2 for Venezuela as 1425, del 12.66. (40th Sqn). To BAC for o/h '77, G27-306. Conv B(I)82 and ret 7.11.79 as 1425. Wfu at El Libertador 10.90.

WH713 Aw/cn 26.3.53. 149. To C(A) charge 2.1.57. Bristol Engine Co. - Olympus test-bed. Scrapped at Filton 7.9.59. Soc 26.5.60. Sold to R.J. Coley.

WH714 Aw/cn 27.3.53. 44. Conv T.11. 228 OCU. TFS West Raynham. 85. Conv T.19. 85. Cr in landing accident (brake failure), Binbrook 19.6.68. Cat.5. Fire dump and burnt 10.69.

WH715 Aw/cn 30.3.53. EE Co for fuel trials. RAE. A&AEE high altitude aircrew clothing tests 9.10.56. BP Defford 'Orange Putter' t/i 31.12.56. BP Seighford flight trials 8.4.58. A&AEE 10.12.58. RAE West Freugh for bomb and fuses trials 17.5.60. RAE Farnborough 21.6.61. ETPS 3.62. Cr near Crewkerne, Somerset 1.10.68. Cat.5 (1k). Soc 12.5.69.

WH716 Aw/cn 30.4.53. 231 OCU. Cr when acft dived into ground at night 2.5 miles SSW of Stowmarket, Suffolk 10.5.55. Cat.5 (3k).

WH717 Aw/cn 31.3.53. 44. Cr when both engines flamed out. Acft landed but port u/c collapsed and acft went into runway over-shoot area at Watton 1.5.57. Cat.5

WH718 Aw/cn 31.3.53. 10. 44. Conv TT.18. Ex-BAC Samlesbury 28.8.68. A&AEE for TT.18 production check 4.10.68. FR Ltd Tarrant Rushton 11.2.69. BAC Warton for rudder research 6.10.69. A&AEE 17.6.70. FR Ltd Tarrant Rushton for Rushton winch trials 1.3.72. 7. 100 as 'CW' 8.91. Authorised for disposal 15.7.91. Open storage at Wyton 9.91. Fin removed by 23.1.92.

WH719 Aw/cn 13.4.53. 44. Sold to BAC 25.11.65. G27-101. Conv B.56 for Peru as 244, del 4.6.69.

WH720 Aw/cn 30.4.53. 57. To MoA charge 10.5.60. Shorts Belfast. Conv U.14, f/f 18.5.61. Del 3.7.61 to 728B FAA. To Pershore for storage 5.12.61. Released 26.3.63. Soc 20.9.63. Derelict, b/u and Ss to R.J. Coley 10.63.

WH721 To Venezuela as 3A-39, del 53. (39 sqn). To EE Co for o/h 4.8.58. ret and renumber 6409. To BAC for o/h '68, G27-158, ret 9.5.69. To BAC for o/h '78, G27-304. Conv B.82 and ret 22.8.79 as 6409. Preserved at Generalisimo Francisco de Miranda AB, Caracas 10.90.

WH722 To Venezuela as 1B-39, del '53. (39 Sqn). W/o at Bocodel Rio 8.11.54.

WH723 Aw/cn 30.4.53. 231 OCU. RAE/Armament Dept 13.9.55. WRE/JSTU 15.11.55. RAE. G/i at Weeton as 7628M 8.1.60. G/g Upwood 4.60 marked as 'WJ642' in 35 Sqn markings. Assigned to RAE 4.5.78 ntu. AWRE Foulness. Sold for scrap 12.90.

WH724 Aw/cn 30.4.53. 15. Conv T.11. 228 OCU. TFS West Raynham. 85. Conv T.19. 85. 100. Soc 30.4.76. Fire dump Shawbury, burnt shell by 11.87.

WH725 Aw/cn 22.5.53. 15. 50. Soc 8.3.72. To IWM store Duxford 5.72. Refurbished as 50 Sqn acft for display at IWM 9.73. Current.

WH726 Aw/cn 22.5.53. 540. 58. Sold to BAC 1.2.66. Refurbished and sold to Peru as 236, del 21.9.66.

WH727 Aw/cn 29.5.53. 231 OCU. SF Khormaksar. Sold to BAC 21.5.69. G27-162. Conv B.62 for Argentina as B107, del, 26.5.71. (1 Sqn). Cr Panama 1.7.83.

WH728 Aw/cn 28.5.53. 27. Cr on take off, after engine failure at Kasfareet, Egypt 11.3.55. Cat.5

WH729 Aw/cn 28.5.53. 27. 21. 9. To MoA charge 8.10.57. Shorts Belfast. Conv U.10, f/f 20.10.59. Despatched from Belfast 18.11.59. WRE. Destroyed by missile 14.4.64.

WH730 Aw/cn 11.6.53. 27. 21. 57. Sold to BAC 29.3.65. Conv B(I)2 for Venezuela as 1437, del 3.67. (40 Sqn). To BAC for o/h '77, G27-307. Conv to B(I)82 and ret 7.2.79.

WH731 Aw/cn 11.6.53. 15.50. Soc and allotted to Manby for fire fighting 4.2.64.

WH732 Aw/cn 10.7.53. 27. 21. SF Binbrook. 12. 9. Sold to BAC 29.3.65. Conv B(I)2 for Venezuela. Used for stores clearance trials as G27-3 before delivery. Del as 1529 4.67. (40 Sqn). To BAC for o/h '75, G27-263. Conv B(I)82 and ret 14.6.78, as 1529.

WH733 Aw/cn 10.7.53. 27. 21. 57. To C(A) charge 8.10.57. To Shorts Belfast for conv U.10, f/f 30.6.59. Despatched to WRE 18.9.59. Cr on landing 30.11.59.

WH734 Aw/cn 26.6.53. Del FR Ltd at Tarrant Rushton 2.7.53 (with 2.41 hrs flying time recorded) for use as trials acft. Released from RAF charge 31.7.54. Conv to tanker/receiver 5.55. Conv to TT role (to carry stiletto supersonic targets and Rushton winch system) 4.76. RAE Llanbedr as target trials aircraft 6.78. A&AEE 7.78. RAE Llanbedr 4.79, in use as B.2/ TT.18, total hours still only 1250 by 9.89. Still in use 7.91.

WH735 Aw/cn 26.6.53. C(A) charge for DH Propellors Ltd. Hatfield for AI Mk.18 Scanner. 15.7.53. F23/49 air conditioning equipment dev. 16.4.58. G/i at No.2 RS as 7623M 1.12.59. FFS Catterick 3.8.65.

WH736 To Venezuela as 2B-39, del '53. (39 Sqn). To EE Co for o/h '59. ret and renumber as 3246. To BAC for o/h '68, G27-157, ret 6.69. To BAC for o/h '78, G27-309. Conv B.82 and ret 15.4.80 as 3246. Wfu at El Libertador 10.90.

WH737 To Venezuela as 3B-39, del 14.7.53. (39 sqn). To EE Co for o/h 17.8.58, ret. W/o Maracaibo 17.4.63.

WH738 Aw/cn 30.6.53. RAE (on loan re NZ race). 1323 Flt. Missing on transit flight from Momote to Kwajalein in Marshall Islands 23.2.54. Cat.5 (3k).

WH739 Aw/cn 16.7.53. 101. 50. SF Upwood. 75 RNZAF. 45. 85. 100. Soc at 19 MU 27.7.76.

WH740 Aw/cn 16.7.53. 18. 40. SF Upwood. 75 RNZAF. Conv T.17. 360. Soc at Wyton 1.12.82. G/i at No.2 SoTT as 8762M '83. For sale 9.91. To E.Mids AeroPark 1.92.

WH741 Aw/cn 7.8.53. 109. 100. 61. 73. 6. Soc 31.9.63. at 103 MU Akrotiri.

WH742 Aw/cn 14.8.53. 21. 9. To C(A) charge 25.11.57. Shorts Belfast. Conv U.10, f/f 11.12.59. WRE. Destroyed by missile 17.7.62.

WH715 '27' was one of at least seven B.2s or T.4s used by the Empire Test Pilots School at Farnborough from 1954 onwards. The School moved to Boscombe Down 29.1.68 and thereafter the aircraft were shared with the A&AEE. *MAP*

Canberra PR.3 (1 acft WH772) and **PR.7** (23 acft)
Contract 6/ACFT/5786/CB6(b). 215 acft (part). 20 Sept 1950.
Serial numbers allocated 20.9.50.
Production by English Electric Co., Preston.

WH772 F/f 29.1.54. Aw/cn 26.2.54. 82. 58. 231 OCU. Soc at
15 MU 27.11.68. Fuselage to Benson for fire fighting.

WH773 First prod PR.7, f/f 16.8.53. Aw/cn 10.9.53. 540. 82. 31.
80. 58. 13. Soc at Wyton 9.6.81. To 2331 (ATC) Sqn as
8696M 9.81. G/g Wyton. Dismantled 2.90 to Vallance
Byways, Charlwood '90.

WH774 F/f 28.10.53. Aw/cn 20.11.53. To MoS charge 20.11.53
for RAE. RRE for IR radiometer trials 1960-69; RRE for
satellite tracking station calibration 1970-76 (took
over from WH776). Loaned as required for Concorde
chase acft by BAC at Fairford 1972. RAE 16.8.76.
Dismantled 8.87, wings taken away, rest to fire dump.

WH775 Aw/cn 31.12.53. Loan to CS(A) for A&AEE handling
trials 11.1.54. EE Co 5.8.54. 82. 13. 31. 17. 31. Allotted
8128M at Bruggen for G/i at Wildenrath 11.3.71. BAC
for o/h 18.3.76. Reverted to WH775. 13. Holding flight.
Allotted 100. ntu. Last flight 29.1.82 (5372.20 hrs).
St Athan for storage 10.2.82. G/i at No 2 SoTT 30.7.85.
Allotted 8868M 11.85. For sale 5.91, current 6.92.

WH776 Aw/cn 19.2.54. C(A) on loan 11.3.54 for RAE altimeter
Mk.6 trials. UHF, VHF trials '55. MoS charge 31.8.55.
RAE for TACAN, 'window' phases 2 and 3 10.5.60, RAE
Llanbedr 18.3.66. RAE Farnborough 14.4.66. Released
12.3.69. RRE for satellite tracking station calibration
19.6.69. Last flight 30.4.70. Soc for spares at Pershore
29.7.71; cut up and burnt 3.77.

WH777 Aw/cn 25.2.54. RR Hucknall for engine surge
investigation 25.2.54. To C(A) charge 11.3.54. RAE
for 'Blue Study' dev 24.9.54. RRE for 'Blue Study'
fitment and trials 1.12.54. Marshall's for mods
17.6.55. RAE 7.2.56. 15 MU 31.8.56. Ret to RAF charge.
RAE camera trials 30.4.57. 15 MU 20.6.57. 81. St Athan
for storage 1.71. Sold 30.11.81. Parts to South Wales
APS at Rhoose, Cardiff 1982.

WH778 Aw/cn 19.2.54. Handling Sqn. A&AEE. 31. 13. 81.
Nosewheel collapsed on landing and acft went off
r/w, Tengah 20.12.68. Soc at Tengah 27.3.69.

WH779 Aw/cn 27.3.54. 542. 13. 80. 31. Allotted 8129M at
Bruggen for G/i at Wildenrath 11.3.71. 19 MU for
storage. o/h at St Athan 1973. Reverted to WH779. 13.
Holding flight, 100 as 'CK' 8.91. Reported transferred
to 1 PRU by 23.1.92.

WH780 Aw/cn 31.3.54. 542. 58. 527. 82. C(A) loan to BP
Defford 18.7.56. A&AEE 14.11.57. 81. To RN charge
15.2.71. Conv T.22 and del to RN 15.2.74. FRADU. To
St Athan store 2.86, on offer for sale 5.91.

WH790 Aw/cn 31.3.54. 540. 542. 82. 58. Cr on GCA in bad
weather, 11 miles ESE of Goose Bay, Canada 16.5.57.
Cat.5 (2k).

WH791 Aw/cn 31.3.54. 542. 82. 58. 81. Allotted 8165M and
8176M at St Athan ntu. Soc as scrap, 11.2.72.
Cancelled. To Cottesmore as Gg as 8187M 13.10.72.
Marked as 'WH717' 4.73. but corrected 5.74, current
7.91.

WH792 Aw/cn 20.4.54. EE Co 26.4.54 mods for TEU Khartoum
for tropical trials. A&AEE 3.8.54. Marshall's for t/i of
IFF Mk.10 10.2.55. A&AEE 22.4.55. Marshall's for
Mk.10 auto pilot 11.8.55. EE Co Warton flight trials of
Mk.10 auto pilot 6.12.56. Marshall's for reversion to
standard 14.6.57. BP Seighford 20.2.58. 17. 31. 17. 31.
Decoy acft at Laarbruch as 8095M 30.4.70. Last noted
1.77.

WH793 Aw/cn 23.4.54. To Napiers on MoS charge 26.5.54.
Conv PR.9(P), f/f 8.7.55. EE Co. A&AEE 22.4.58. EE Co
Warton 9.5.58. RAE Bedford for gust research 8.3.61.
Indian National Aeronautical Laboratory Bangalore
for Monsoon trials 20.6.72. RAE 9.10.72. Released
7.2.73. BAC Fairford as Concorde chase acft 10.8.73.
RAE Farnborough for storage 11.3.75. Soc 25.4.75 at
Farnborough. Despatched to Bedford.

WH794 Aw/cn 18.6.54. 540. 82. 58. 13. To BDRF Abingdon as
8652M 15.7.80. Soc 22.3.83. Allocated to Otterburn
range 22.3.83. Still at Abingdon 9.83. By road to FFS
Catterick 1.84. Still at Catterick 4.88.

WH795 Aw/cn 30.4.54. 542. 540. 58. 81. Cr when acft landed
too fast, burst tyre and left r/w - going through a sea
wall at Kai Tak, Hong Kong 5.8.68. Soc at Hong Kong
23.8.68. Cat.5.

WH796 Aw/cn 17.5.54. 542. 82. 542. 100. 58. 13. MoA. 58.
SF Wyton. 39. St Athan for storage 7.71. Sold 30.11.81.
Nose with Humberside APS 11.82.

WH797 Aw/cn 13.5.54. 542. 58. 81. To RN charge 15.2.71. Conv
T.22. FRADU. To St Athan store 27.2.85, on offer for
sale 5.91.

WH798 Aw/cn 20.5.54. 542. 100. 17. 80. 13. 17. 31. Decoy acft
at Bruggen as 8130M, '71. To St Athan store. Sold
30.11.81. Parts to South Wales APS, Rhoose 16.7.82,
last noted 9.88.

WH799 Aw/cn 27.5.54. 542. 82. 58. 82. Shot down by Syrian
Meteor over Suez 6.11.56. Cat.5

WH800 Aw/cn 30.6.54. 540. 82. 58. 80. 31. Sold to BAC 2.10.69,
G27-183. Conv PR.57 for India as P1098, del '71.

WH801 Aw/cn 28.5.54. 540. 58. 13. 31. 17. To RN charge
15.2.71. Conv T.22 del 16.11.73 (first T.22 del). On
FRADU. To St Athan store 6.9.85, on offer for sale 5.91.

WH802 Aw/cn 14.7.54. 540. 58. 81. 58. Decoy acft at Bruggen
as 8067M 27.2.70, last noted 8.78.

WH803 Aw/cn 30.6.54. 540. 17. To RN charge 15.2.71. Conv
T.22. FRADU. To St Athan store 31.5.84, on offer for
sale 5.91.

WH804 Aw/cn 16.7.54. 540. 58. 17. 31. Decoy acft at Laarbruch
as 8126M 8.1.71, last noted 1.77.

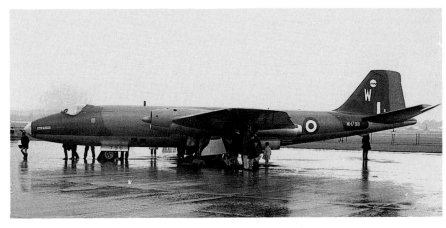

**Above: PR.7 WH798 'W' of 17 Squadron serves as
a shelter for a few brave spectators at the Benson
'Battle of Britain' air show, 14.9.68.** *MAP*

Below: **PR.9 Prototype WH793 in use by the 'Aero
Flight', at Luqa 9.10.72, only two days after its
official book transfer to the RAE.** *A. Coleman*

Canberra T.4 (12 acft)

Contract 6/Acft/5786/CB6(b). 215 acft (part). 20 Sept 1950.
Serial numbers allocated 20.9.50.
Production by English Electric Co., Preston.

WH839 F/f 24.2.54. Aw/cn 27.2.54. 231 OCU. 151. 97. 360.
Handling Sqn. 231 OCU. Conv T.4 for India as Q1795,
del 23.9.75.

WH840 Aw/cn 19.3.54. 231 OCU. Att 88. 245. 151. 97. BP
Seighford for t/i of radio mods 6.11.64. A&AEE. 3. SF
Bruggen. SF Laarbruch. SF Bruggen. SF Laarbruch.
To St Athan store '70. Eng Sqn St Athan and allocated
8350M. Soc at St Athan 3.4.74. G/g at Locking 8.4.74.
Sold to Staffordshire Aviation Museum, moved to
Seighford 1.91.

WH841 Aw/cn 19.3.54. 231 OCU. SF Geilenkirchen. 213.
A&AEE 22.9.67. RAF Germany 29.12.67. SF Bruggen.
SF Wildenrath. Soc and b/u at St Athan 16.8.72.

WH842 Aw/cn 31.3.54. 231 OCU. 88. 80. SF Bruggen. Soc at
5 MU 23.11.71. FFS Catterick '72.

WH843 Aw/cn 31.3.54. 231 OCU. SF Geilenkirchen. 59. 31. SF
Laarbruch. 16. 231 OCU. 7. Soc and b/u at St Athan
26.11.71.

WH844 Aw/cn 23.4.54. 231 OCU. To MoA charge 27.11.62.
RAE Farnborough 1.66. Store at Farnborough 2.86.
Allocated for BDR at Abingdon 17.9.86 as 8914M. ntu.
Dismantled and removed by road 19.1.88 to Pendine
ranges.

WH845 Aw/cn 13.5.54. 231 OCU. Sold BAC 14.7.65 for conv to
T.4 for India as Q496. Ready for del 12.66 - order
cancelled. Stored 5 MU. Re-sold to BAC 14.8.72,
G27-224. Conv T.74 for Peru as 246.

WH846 Aw/cn 7.5.54. 231 OCU. 3. SF Laarbruch. 100. St Athan
store '77. Sold to BAe 29.1.82. Store at Samlesbury
5.85. To Yorkshire Air Museum, Elvington, York 6.88,
current 5.91.

WH847 Aw/cn 17.5.54. 231 OCU. 45. Sold to BAC 25.6.65,
G27-116. Conv T.4 for India as Q495.

WH848 Aw/cn 3.6.54. SF Marham. SF Binbrook. SF Gaydon.
232 OCU. 231 OCU. CAW. 231 OCU. Loan to 7. 85. 100.
13. 7. 231 OCU. Wfu 2.8.88. Soc. Cat.5 for robbing of
spares 10.88. CSF less tail unit 2.89, tail section to
BDRF Abingdon 2.89.

WH849 Aw/cn 25.5.54. Del to SF Marham 27.5.54, SF
Coningsby. SF Binbrook. RAE. 76. 231 OCU. 85. 360.
100. 231 OCU. 7. 231 OCU, current as 'BE' 8.91.

WH850 Aw/cn 14.6.54. 15. SF Honington. SF Cottesmore. 88.
14. SF Wildenrath. SF Laarbruch. 231 OCU. St Athan
store 21.6.72. Sold to BAe 26.11.81. Store at
Samlesbury 12.86. Macclesfield Historical Avn Soc,
Chelford '88, current '90.

Canberra B.2 (60 acft)

Contract 6/Acft/5790/CB6(b). 100 acft (part). 20 Sept 1950.
Serial numbers allocated 20.9.50.
Production by Short Bros & Harland, Belfast.

WH853 1st prod acft, f/f 30.10.52. Aw/cn 28.11.52. Del 12.52.
10. 45. Cr when acft stalled on take off and hit trees,
Tengah 18.11.58. Cat.5 (2k).

WH854 Aw/cn 12.12.52. Handling Sqn. 617. 90. MoA charge
2.4.58. Conv T.4. RRE 2.4.58 for FCT and target
aircraft. ETPS 14.12.58. RAE soft ground arrestor
trials 9.12.66. A&AEE 4.12.67. Del RRE on final flight
3.3.69. Soc 11.3.69. Sold for scrap 4.6.70. Nose section
to Martin-Baker at Chalgrove 11.69, last noted 6.86.

WH855 Aw/cn 24.3.53. 149. Sold to Rhodesia as RRAF164
5.5.59. (5 Sqn). Renumber RRAF205 in 1963 and
R2055 in 1969. Zimbabwe AF as 2055 in 1980.

WH856 Aw/cn 26.2.53. 44. SF Honington. Conv TT.18. 7.
FRADU. To BDRF Abingdon as 8742M 2.3.82. Ss to
Park Aviation Supply 31.1.86.

WH857 Aw/cn 16.3.53. 44. MoA. RRE as target acft for 'Orange
Yeoman' ground radar trials 23.2.61. CSE. 98. 151. 97.
Cr on asymmetric approach to Watton 3.5.66. Cat.5
(2k).

WH858 Aw/cn 30.3.53. 44. 73. Ss at 23 MU 27.4.64.

WH859 Aw/cn 28.4.53. 57. 27. SF Waddington. 231 OCU.
MoA charge 20.6.61.

WH860 Aw/cn 30.4.53. 57. 27. 21. SF Khormaksar. MoA charge
23.9.60. Shorts Belfast. Conv U.10, f/f 10. 4.62. WRE.
No.1 ATU. Destroyed by missile 24.5.64.

WH861 Aw/cn 18.6.53. 27. Conv T.4. 69. 39. SF Akrotiri. 56. 7.
Ss 19 MU 15.10.70.

WH862 Aw/cn 30.6.53. 231 OCU. Sold to BAC 29.3.65. Conv B.2
for Venezuela as 1511, del 2.67. (40 Sqn). To BAC for
o/h '75, G27-261. Conv B.82, ret 8.9.77 as 1511. Wfu at
El Libertador 10.90.

WH863 Aw/cn 29.5.53. To CSE charge for IAM/RAE. High
Altitude fire investigation. 29.3.57. EE Co ECM trials
3.7.63. A&AEE. BAC for reversion to standard 10.6.65.
Ret to RAF charge 28.6.66. Conv T.17. 360. Soc 29.5.81.
To BDRF Marham as 8693M 16.6.81. Cut up 6.90.

WH864 Aw/cn 30.6.53. 231 OCU, cr after take-off, 1 mile W of
Bishop Stortford, Herts 11.11.54. Cat.5 (2k).

WH865 Aw/cn 30.6.53. 231 OCU, cr when acft flew into
ground on night approach to Bassingbourn 14.8.57.
Cat.5 (1k).

WH866 Aw/cn 10.7.53. 18. 115. SF Binbrook. 9. To 15 MU for
storage 13.11.58. Ss 1.7.64.

WH867 Aw/cn 31.7.53. 18. 44. Sold to Rhodesia as RRAF159
2.6.59. (5 Sqn). Renumber RRAF200 in 1963 and
R2005 in 1969.

WH868 Aw/cn 11.8.53. 109. 139. BAC. used in connection with
a project study for a flying classroom 4.63. Sold to
BAC 1.2.66. Refurbished and sold to Peru as 237,
del 22.10.66. W/o 4.7.81.

WH869 Aw/cn 27.8.53. RAFFC. 527. 245. 98. 7. Rescue training
at Abingdon as 8515M 1.2.77, last noted 9.90.

WH870 Aw/cn 30.9.53. 90. 35. 207. 213 (?). 32. SF Akrotiri.
73. 249. CAW (?). To 15 MU for storage 10.65. Ss at
15 MU 20.12.66.

WH871 Aw/cn 31.8.53. 40. 44. Sold to Rhodesia as RRAF165
2.6.59. (5 Sqn). Renumber as RRAF206 in 1963 and
R2065 in 1969.

WH872 Aw/cn 30.9.53. 40. 10. 15. 202. 32. 249. To BAC for T.17
conv 25.8.66. Del 15 MU 29.3.68. Loan to MinTech
28.2.69. St Athan 23.4.69. 360. Acft aquaplaned at
Bedford 30.11.81. G/i at Bedford 15.3.82. To fire dump.

WH873 Aw/cn 7.10.53. 76, cr into ground on night approach
to Wittering 16.8.54. Cat.5 (3k).

WH874 Aw/cn 8.10.53. 76. 50. SF Upwood. 45. Conv T.17. 360,
cr in collision with T.4 WJ862 over
Sutton-in-Ashfield, Notts 29.1.71. Cat.5.

WH875 Aw/cn 30.10.53. 76. 32. 73. Sold to BAC 21.5.69,
G27-163. Conv B.62 for Argentina as B109, del 9.9.71
(1 Sqn).

WH876 Aw/cn 30.10.53. 115. 207. 73. MoA charge 23.8.60.
Shorts Belfast. Conv U.14 f/f 10.8.61. 728B FAA.
Pershore store 3.12.61. Conv B.2 at Pershore. A&AEE.
Conv U.10. A&AEE. With MB at Chalgrove 8.85. Store
at A&AEE 7.88. Dismantled 1.90.

WH877 Aw/cn 30.10.53. 231 OCU. RAFFC. Sold to BAC 29.3.65.
Conv B.2 for Venezuela as 0129, del 12.65. (40 Sqn).
To BAC for o/h '75, G27-301. Conv B.82 ret 18.6.80 as
0129. Wfu at El Libertador 10.90.

WH878 Aw/cn 30.10.53. 57. CFS. 57. 75 RNZAF. RAFFC. CAW.
85. Soc 7.1.72.

WH879 Aw/cn 27.11.53. 50. Soc 1.5.63. Wittering for fire
fighting.

WH880 Aw/cn 27.11.53. 90. 50. SF Upwood. Sold to BAC 8.7.66,
G27-99. Conv B56 for Peru as 242, del 9.4.69. W/o
13.12.72.

WH881 Aw/cn 30.11.53. 1323 Flt. RAE/IAM. 1323 Flt. 542. 21.
SF Upwood. Sold to BAC 29.3.65. Conv B(I)2 for
Venezuela as 1280, 11.66. (40 sqn). To BAC for
o/h '77, G27-305. Conv B(I)82 ret 16.5.79 as 1280.

WH882 Aw/cn 30.11.53. 90. 40. SF Wittering. 45. Collided with
WJ983 in cloud, cr at Kotatingo, S.Malaya 13.12.57.
Cat.5 (3k).

WH883 Aw/cn 31.12.53. 115. 50. SF Upwood. Sold to Rhodesia
as RRAF166, del 7.4.59. (5 Sqn). Renumber as
RRAF207 in 1963. W/o

WH884 Aw/cn 23.12.53. 1323 Flt. 542. 21. SF Upwood. G/i at
No 12 SoTT as 7658M 20.10.60. Scrapped 24.4.64.

WH885 Aw/cn 30.12.53. 115. 90. 6. MoA charge 29.9.60. Shorts
Belfast. Conv U.10 f/f 10.4.62. WRE. Destroyed in
accident 1.4.64.

WH886 Aw/cn 31.12.53. 207. 44. 73. Sold to BAC 21.5.69,
G27-164. Conv B.62 for Argentina as B108, del 9.9.71.
(1 Sqn). Grupo 2. Shot down by Sea Dart missile from
HMS *Exeter*, S of Mount Kent, Falkland Islands 14.6.82.

WH887 Del 29.1.54. 1323 Flt. 542. 21. SF Upwood. Conv TT.18.
RN charge 27.11.69. FRU. FRADU. Loan to FR Ltd.
FRADU. St Athan store 27.11.86. FRADU 10.12.86.
St Athan store, FRADU current 7.92 as '847'.

WH902 Aw/cn 1.12.53. 1323 Flt. 542. 21. SF Upwood. To BAC
for conv T.17. Del 15 MU 3.1.68. 360. Conv T.17A. 360,
current as 'EK' 8.91.

WH903 Aw/cn 31.1.54. 617. 102. To BP Seighford for conv to
T.11 4.12.64. 228 OCU. TFS West Raynham. 85. First
conv T.19; f/f 6.66. 85. 7. Allotted 8584M for fire
practice at Marham 21.12.77. B.2 nose at Charlwood,
Sussex 10.89.

WH904 Aw/cn 31.1.54. 207. 35. Conv T.11. 228 OCU. TFS West
Raynham. 85. Conv T.19. 85. 7. Sold 4.6.80 to
Marshalls. To Newark Air Museum 9.85, current. 9.91.

WH905 Aw/cn 29.1.54. 207. 115. SF Binbrook. 12. 9. 12. Sold
to BAC 15.2.60. Conv Tp52 for Sweden as 52002, del
5.3.60. (F8 Wing). Last flight 23.1.73. F3 Wing at
Malmen. Air Force Museum, Malmen, current.

WH906 Aw/cn 26.2.54. 207, cr when acft flew into trees on
approach to Marham 3.12.54. Cat.5 (3k).

WH907 Aw/cn 26.2.54. 15. 61. 50. 231 OCU. Soc at 19 MU
27.11.73. To West Raynham for fire fighting.

WH908 Aw/cn 26.2.54. 44. 18. 61. RAFFC. To 15 MU for storage
1968. Soc at 15 MU 31.3.71. Fuselage to FFS Catterick.

WH909 Aw/cn 31.3.54. 35. Ss 1.7.64.

WH910 Aw/cn 19.3.54. 35. 61 during Suez crisis and 1956/7 at
Luqa/Nicosia. 35. Soc at 15 MU 21.5.64. Allocated
High Ercall as G/i. Burnt on Ouston fire dump.

WH911 Del 24.3.54. 35. 98. In store at St Athan 8.77. Soc and
b/u at St Athan 9.83. Nose at Park Aviation, Faygate,
Sussex '90.

WH912 Aw/cn 31.3.54. To MoA charge 31.3.54. RAE. VT-fuse
trials 2.4.54. Hunting Engineering, Luton for Vickers
weapons dev 1.12.60. Released 18.12.62. Derelict at
Luton and sold to Staravia 16.9.63.

WH913 Aw/cn 31.3.54. 100. 35. 245. 98. Sold to BAC 23.2.68,
G27-114. Conv B.62 for Argentina as B104, del 26.2.71.

WH914 Del 2.4.54. 100. 61. 50. 76. 35. 231 OCU. Sold to BAe
12.10.81, G27-373. Conv B.92 for Argentina, part
converted 4.82 but not del because of Falklands War.
Put into store as G27-373. Stored dismantled at
Samlesbury. Scrapped 1988.

WH915 Aw/cn 25.5.54. 61, cr at Wigginton, 2 miles SSE of
Tring, Herts 8.3.57. Cat.5 (3k).

WH916 Aw/cn 18.5.54. 617. 103. 12. 35. Ss 1.7.64.

WH917 Aw/cn 28.5.54. 27. 10. 50. Ss 27.4.64.

WH918 Aw/cn 31.5.54. 61. 35. ss 1.7.64.

WH919 Aw/cn 18.5.54. 231 OCU. 18. 35. 231 OCU. A&AEE
frangible hatch trials 27.2.61. 231 OCU. To 60 MU
Leconfield for mods as Nav and t/i; 6.3.70. A&AEE
avionics retrofit (B2(T) acft) 4.2.71. 231 OCU. Soc
at Marham 1.4.76.

WH920 Aw/cn 25.5.54. 44. 18. 35. 231 OCU. SOC at St Athan
27.1.72.

WH921 Aw/cn 31.5.54. CFE. CF West Raynham. MoA charge
30.3.60. Shorts Belfast. Conv U.14 f/f 28.3.61. 728B
FAA. Shot down by Sea Slug missile from HMS
Girdleness, Malta 6.10.61.

WH922 Aw/cn 29.6.54. 61. 50. 45. 75 RNZAF. 45. Soc and b/u at
15 MU 23.12.70. Fuselage to FFS Catterick 12.70.

WH923 Aw/cn 30.6.54. 61. 100. 61. 50. 231 OCU. Soc at 19 MU
31.8.73.

WH924 Aw/cn 7.7.54. 61. 50. Soc at 15 MU 14.12.70. To FFS
Catterick 12.70.

WH925 Aw/cn 30.9.54. 207. 18. 35. BCDU Finningley. 231 OCU.
Soc 3.11.60. To Catterick for fire fighting.

WH944 Aw/cn 30.9.54. Del 8.54 139. 10. 35. 231 OCU, swung
off r/w when tyres burst at Waddington 13.5.68. Cat.5.

**B.2 WH878 'A' of 85 Squadron on finals to
Binbrook in November 1970. Squadron chequers
and fin marking are red/black, serial (repeated
on nose wheel door) and fin code are in black.**

**B.6 WH952 at Kinloss 1969, when reportedly on
strength of RAE/Institute of Aviation Medicine.**
MAP

**White B.6 WH962 of 76 Squadron at Alice Springs,
1957.** *C.H.Donne*

**A successful wheels-up landing for WH974 of
9 Squadron. The nav has blown his hatch (just
behind the canopy) – standard practice in such
cases. It is now up to the groundcrew to recover
the aircraft!**

**Although based at Edinburgh Field Australia, for
a period, 76 Squadron B.6s often operated from
New Zealand. Note the stylised 'dingo' marking
on the fin of WH980, 1959.** *R.W.Kerr via C.J.Salter*

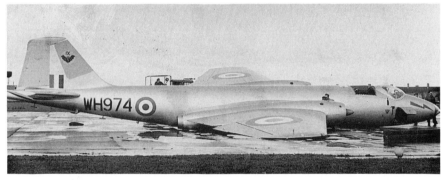

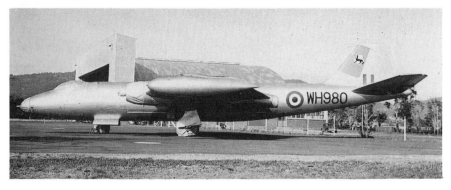

Canberra B.6 (40 acft)

Contract 6/Acft/5790/CB6(b). 100 acft (part). 20 Sep 1950.
Contract revised 2 April 1953 to alter original contract for B.2 variant to B.6.
Serial numbers allocated 20.9.50.
Production by Short Bros & Harland, Belfast.

WH945 Aw/cn 29.10.54. Del 11.54. 101. 12. RRE 29.4.57 for modification for joint RRE/Bomber Command trials requirement. Nose length increased by 56". Modified to have ASV Mk.21 (anti submarine radar) 'Blue Silk' and GEE 3. Del to 100 Sqn Wittering for service trials 30.4.59. CSE. 151. 97. 360. 15 MU store 1968. Soc at 15 MU 1.10.71.

WH946 Aw/cn 29.10.54. 617. 542. 21. 76. SF Coningsby. Allotted g/i as 8185M 15.2.72. To Army training area Ewyas Harold, Hereford. Ss to Lovaux (Northwest) Ltd '82. Fuselage to Bomber County Museum, Cleethorpes 21.4.84. Fuselage to scrapyard near Grimsby 6.87, rest at museum. Nose only moved to Hemswell Aviation Society, Hemswell, '88.

WH947 Aw/cn 29.10.54. 617. SF Binbrook. 12. Conv B.15. 32. ASW. Soc at 103 MU 14.2.68.

WH948 Aw/cn 31.10.54. 101. 12. Conv B.15. 32 (?). 249 (?). 73. 45. 98. Conv E.15. 98. 100. Starboard engine fire, acft abandoned and cr 7 miles NW of Coltishall 15.8.77. Cat.5.

WH949 Aw/cn 5.11.54. 617. 542. 21. 76. SF Coningsby. BCDU Finningley. Soc at 15 MU 7.9.70.

WH950 Aw/cn 31.12.54. 617. cr on asymmetric approach to Mauripur, Pakistan 18.10.55. Cat.5.

WH951 Aw/cn 26.11.54. 617. 9. 12, brakes failed on landing, overshot and hit wall, Luqa 7.3.57. Cat.5

WH952 Aw/cn 27.1.55. From RAF charge 2.2.55. A&AEE Marshalls for fatigue investigation 13.2.63. Marshalls for wing pylon installation 21.8.64. RAE Bomb bay door buffeting 24.11.64. A&AEE ERU trials 14.9.70. RAE 23.9.70. WRE for BL755 release trials 13.1.71. RAE 13.4.71. BAC - MRCA chase acft 19.7.74. RAE Bedford for apprentice training 9.6.76. Soc 13.7.76. Wfu at Bedford 4.82. By road to Woolwich for preservation 16.4.86. At Royal Arsenal West, Woolwich, current 2.91.

WH953 Aw/cn 28.1.55. RRE Defford 28.1.55. From RAF charge 2.2.55. RRE for AI Mk.20 installation and trials 1956-58. RRE Pershore mod to long nose standard 1959. RRE exp single dish CW AI radar 1961/63. RRE with exp FM1 CW radar (conv of CW AI previously fitted) 1963/69. RRE research for JP236 AEW 1969/71. RRE with Marconi exp prototype AI for Tornado fighter 1975/77. RSRE Bedford 16.12.76, last noted 8.92.

WH954 Aw/cn 7.12.54. 617. 9. 109. 12 (?). 9. Conv B.15. 73. Sold to BAC 6.3.69, G27-167. Conv B.66 for India as IF1021, del '70.

WH955 Aw/cn 22.12.54. 617. 9. 109. 9. SF Coningsby. Conv B.15. 32. 45. Soc at 19 MU 29.10.76.

WH956 Aw/cn 11.2.55. 12. 139 (?). Conv B.15. 73. 32. 249. 6. 249. 32. 73. 45. Cat.5 damage 15.7.69. Soc 29.12.69.

WH957 Aw/cn 31.1.55. 617. 542. 21. SF Upwood. SF Hemswell. Conv B.15. 32. ASW. 98. Conv E.15. 98. 100. To St Athan store 1.82. G/i at No.2 SoTT 30.7.85, 8869M allotted 11.85, on offer for sale 9.91.

WH958 Aw/cn 31.1.55. 617. SF Binbrook. 12. Conv B.15. 45. Birdstrike on take-off, overshot r/w into sea at Kai Tak, Hong Kong 17.8.64. Cat.5

WH959 Aw/cn 17.2.55. 12. Conv B.15. Handling Sqn. 45. ASW. 45. Sold to BAC 16.5.69. G27-177. Conv B.66 for India as IF1022, del '70.

WH960 Aw/cn 3.2.55. 12. 9. Conv B.15. 32. ASW. 32. Last flew 31.1.69 (3419 hrs). G/i at No.2 SoTT, allocated 8344M 3.1.73, on offer for sale 9.91.

WH961 Aw/cn 25.2.55. 9. Conv B.15. 73. 45. No.1 SoTT. Sold to BAC 16.5.69, G27-178. Conv B.66 for India as IF1023, del 11.70.

WH962 Aw/cn 25.2.55. School of AvMed. 76. Soc at 15 MU 29.9.71. To Catterick for fire fighting.

WH963 Aw/cn 16.3.55. 12. Conv B.15. 45. Soc at 19 MU 20.9.72.

WH964 Aw/cn 18.3.55. 12. Conv B.15. 73. 32. 249. ASW. 98. Conv E.15. 98. 100. Last flown 27.1.82 (6165.15 hrs). To St Athan store 10.2.82. G/i at No.2 SoTT 30.5.85. 8870M allotted 11.85. On offer for sale 5.91.

WH965 Aw/cn 24.3.55. 12. 9 (?). 12. Conv B.15. 45. Allotted 8015M at 15 MU '69. Ss 13.4.70.

WH966 Aw/cn 30.3.55. 617. 542. 21. SF Upwood. Conv B.15. 32. BAC for t/i AS30 systems 6.1.66. A&AEE for CA clearance 4.7.66. ASW 1.9.66. 45. Soc 20.9.76. St Athan.

WH967 Aw/cn 31.3.55. 12. 100. 12. To Marshalls for B15 t/i. C(A). A&AEE, BP for AS30. Cr into sea 2 miles N of Wheelus AFB, Libya after explosion in wing 22.6.66. Cat.5.
WH968 Aw/cn 5.4.55. 12. Conv B.15. 32 (?). 73. 45. Soc at 19 MU 29.10.76.
WH969 Aw/cn 29.4.55. 9. Conv B.15. 45. MoS charge 29.11.68. PEE, Shoeburyness.
WH970 Aw/cn 19.5.55. 12. Conv B.15. 32. ASW. Soc at St Athan 25.6.76.
WH971 Aw/cn 31.5.55. 12. Conv B.15. 32. ASW, cr landed during undershoot at Akrotiri 24.4.68. Cat.5
WH972 Aw/cn 22.9.55. 9. Conv B.15. 32. ASW. 98. Conv E.15. 98. 100. Cr. on approach to Kinloss 27.6.90.
WH973 Aw/cn 31.5.55. 9. Conv B.15. 32 (?). ASW. 73. BAC allotted G27-176 but acft not released by RAF. Conv E.15. 98. Cr at Lobthorpe, Cottesmore, Leics 5.10.71 after control failure. Cat.5
WH974 Aw/cn 31.5.55. 9. Conv. B.15. 73. 45. Soc at No.1 SoTT 16.3.73. Fire dump Wittering.
WH975 Aw/cn 28.10.55. RAE Aero flight 8.4.60. Handling Sqn 15.3.62. To 15 MU 2.69. Soc 1.12.71.
WH976 Aw/cn 10.8.55. 76. BCDU. 58. 45. Soc at 15 MU 29.11.71. FFS Catterick.
WH977 Aw/cn 26.8.55. 9. Conv B.15. 73. 45. Soc at 19 MU 1.1.74. FFS Catterick.
WH978 Aw/cn 29.7.55. 76. Soc at 15 MU 1.10.71.
WH979 Aw/cn 31.8.55. 76. Soc at 15 MU 1.10.71.
WH980 Aw/cn 31.8.55. 76. Soc at 15 MU 1.10.71.
WH981 Del 8.9.55. 9. Conv B.15. 73. ASW. 45. 98. Conv E.15. 98. 100. MoD (PE). 100 as 'CN' 8.91. In open storage at Wyton 23.1.92.
WH982 Aw/cn 28.9.55. 9. Force landed after engine failure on take-off, Idris, Libya 14.9.59. Cat.5
WH983 Aw/cn 30.9.55. 9. Conv B.15. 73. ASW. 98. Conv E.15. 98. 100, last flown (as 'CP') 11.1.90 (8157 hrs). On offer for sale at Wyton 9.91. Reported scrapped by 23.1.92.
WH984 Aw/cn 17.10.55. 9. SF Binbrook. 9. Conv B.15. Handling Sqn. 32/73. ASW. Last flew 11.3.69 (2303 hrs). G/i at No.2 SoTT as 8101M 11.8.70, on offer for sale 9.91.

Canberra B.2 (100 acft; 75 built, 25 cancelled)
Contract 6/Acft/5943/CB6(b). October 1950.
Serial numbers allocated 27.10.50.
Production by Handley Page Ltd., Radlett.
WJ564 1st Prod acft f/f 5.1.53. Del 12.3.53. 149. 249. Ss 1.7.64.
WJ565 Aw/cn 31.3.53. C(A) A&AEE Bombing trials 9.4.53. BP Defford for gun pack t/i 14.4.54. A&AEE. Conv T.17. 360. To St Athan store 2.81. Last flown (as 'CL') 2.11.81 (3509 hrs). G/i at No.2 SoTT as 8871M 11.85, on offer for sale 9.91.
WJ566 Aw/cn 31.3.53. 44. Conv T.4. 73. SF Akrotiri. ITF Akrotiri. 32. SF Akrotiri. 73. FR Ltd. 7. Soc at St Mawgan 7.8.75. Fire dump. Moved to Predannack 9.76, fire fighting training by SAH Culdrose.
WJ567 Aw/cn 31.3.53. 149. 59. 45. 75 RNZAF. 45. MinTech for A&AEE silent target duties 27.7.68. 85. 100 as 'CC' 8.91. In open storage at Wyton, partly dismantled, 23.1.92.
WJ568 Aw/cn 24.4.53. 57. RAE Bedford bomb carrier trials 13.6.56. To 15 MU as aircraft unsuitable 3.7.56. Conv T.4. 231 OCU. Sold to BAC 8.12.67. To Marshall's, Cambridge for systems trials.
WJ569 Aw/cn 30.4.53. 149. 59. 231 OCU. Sold to BAC 8.7.66. To Marshall's, Cambridge. B/u Cambridge 5.71.
WJ570 Aw/cn 30.4.53. 149. 59 (?). 139 (?). 45. TFS West Raynham. Sold to BAC 30.4.65. Conv B.2 for Venezuela as 1183, del 30.4.66. (40 sqn). BAC for o/h '75, G27-258. Conv B.82, ret 7.7.77 as 1183.
WJ571 Aw/cn 21.5.53. 540. 139. 104. Sold to Rhodesia as RRAF167, del 5.5.59. (5 Sqn). Renumber as RRAF208 in 1963 and R2085 in 1969. Zimbabwe AF as 2085 in 1980.
WJ572 Aw/cn 21.5.53. 27. 21. Sold to Rhodesia as RRAF168, del 10.3.59. (5 Sqn). Renumber as RRAF209 in 1963 and R2059 in 1969. Zimbabwe AF as 2059 in 1980.
WJ573 Aw/cn 22.5.53. 540. 1323 Flt. 542. SF Upwood. Swifter Flt. G/i Tech College, Henlow 20.10.60. Allotted 7656M 21.12.60. RAF Museum Henlow 9.63, last noted '86.
WJ574 Aw/cn 4.6.53. 540. 57. Sold to BAC 5.12.69, G27-182. Conv TT.18. RN charge 4.10.74. FRADU. Det Key West NAS, Florida 31.10.78. FRADU. To St Athan store 29.5.85. FRADU, current 7.91.
WJ575 Aw/cn 12.6.53. 15. 57. Cat.5 (c) fire. Soc 15.4.57.
WJ576 231 OCU. Swifter Flt. MoA. BP Seighford ECM trials 15.7.63. Off MoA charge 8.6.65. To BAC for conv T.17. Del Watton 1.5.67. 360. To St Athan store mid 1970s. B/u at St Athan 5.83. Fuse to S.Wales APS, Rhoose 7.83.
WJ577 Aw/cn 26.6.53. 231 OCU. RAFFC. Ss 27.4.64.
WJ578 Aw/cn 31.8.53. 21. SF Waddington. Sold to Rhodesia as RRAF169, del 10.3.59. (5 Sqn). Renumber as RRAF210 in 1963 and R2510 in 1969. W/o 16.11.71.
WJ579 Aw/cn 30.6.53. 27, cr when acft dived into ground from 40,000 ft. Eastnor, Hereford 17.6.54. Cat.5 (3k).
WJ580 Aw/cn 14.7.53. 231 OCU. SF Khormaksar. MECS; Cat.5 (c) 28.1.64. Soc 22.5.64.
WJ581 231 OCU. Conv T.17. 360. To St Athan store mid 1970's. Sold 9.3.83.
WJ582 Aw/cn 21.7.53. RAE Met Flt 24.7.53. BP Defford for installation of equipment 31.3.55. RAE 27.6.55. Cr into sea E of Leuchars 21.2.62.
WJ603 Aw/cn 24.7.53. 18. 115. 35. 6. 98. 85. 98. 85. 100. Last flown 12.80. (6012 hrs). BDRF Wattisham as 8664M 15.12.80, on offer for sale 5.91.
WJ604 Aw/cn 31.8.53. 21. 9. MoA charge 8.10.57. Shorts Belfast for conv U.10 f/f 20.11.59. Del from Belfast 9.12.59. WRE. Destroyed due to control failure 18.2.64.
WJ605 Aw/cn 18.9.53. 18. 40. SF Upwood. 75 RNZAF. 45. Caught fire and broke up during bomb run at China Rock ranges, 26 miles E Changi, Singapore 16.4.62. Cat.5 (2k).
WJ606 Aw/cn 16.9.53. 40. Sold to Rhodesia as RRAF170, del 2.6.59. (5 Sqn). Renumber as RRAF211 in 1963. Cannibalised and parts used in R2516. See WH674.
WJ607 Aw/cn 31.10.53. 18. 44. 35. SF Upwood. Conv T.17. Del 15 MU 2.11.67. 360. BAC Warton for t/i fit 21.1.81. Ret to 360 30.4.81. Conv T.17A. 360, current as 'EB' 8.91.
WJ608 Aw/cn 11.9.53. 231 OCU. Swifter Flt. NECS. Cat.5 (c) 28.1.64. Soc 22.5.64.
WJ609 Aw/cn 23.9.53. 21. 139. To Shorts Belfast for U.10 conv 8.10.59. Conv cancelled 31.3.59. RAE Llanbedr trials 7.9.59. as 'Shepherd' acft for U.14 trials and Jindivik trials 7.9.59. Released by C(A) 22.11.60. To 23 MU Aldergrove 7.2.61. Sold to BAC 21.5.69, G27-165. Conv B.62 for Argentina as B106, del 26.5.71. (1 Sqn)
WJ610 Aw/cn 30.9.53. 101. 50. 9. Conv T.11. Handling Sqn. 228 OCU. TFS West Raynham. 85. 228 OCU. 85. Conv T.19. 85. 100. Cr after take-off, West Raynham 26.6.72. Cat.5
WJ611 Aw/cn 30.9.53. 101. 102. 59. MoA for A&AEE. 245. 98. 7. Soc at 23 MU 30.11.76. Allotted 8451M ntu.
WJ612 Aw/cn 13.11.53. 101. 149. 59. Sold to Rhodesia as RRAF172, del 7.4.59. (5 Sqn). Renumber as RRAF213 in 1963.
WJ613 Aw/cn 30.1.54. 101. 102. 59. Conv T.4. Sold to Rhodesia as RRAF176, del 20.3.61. (5 Sqn). Renumber as RRAF217 in 1963 and 2175 in 1969. Zimbabwe AF as 2157 in 1980.
WJ614 Aw/cn 30.4.54. 35. 6. RAFFC. 98. 85. 100. Conv TT.18. RN charge 25.2.72. FRADU. To St Athan store 31.1.87. Ex St Athan 28.10.87. FRADU, current 7.92 as '846'.
WJ615 Aw/cn 30.1.54. 12. 50. Cr when acft flew into high ground at night, Lochnager, Aberdeenshire 22.11.56. Cat.5 (2k).
WJ616 Aw/cn 8.1.54. 199. 1321 Flt. 199. 18. CSE. 151. 97. 360. Sold to BAC 23.2.68, G27-111. Conv B.62 for Argentina as B101 (G-AYHO for 1970 SBAC show), del 17.11.70 (1 Sqn).
WJ617 Aw/cn 13.1.54. 21. Conv T.4. 228 OCU. TFS West Raynham. Sold to BAC 11.3.63. Conv T.4 for S.Africa as 459, del 4.64. (12 sqn).
WJ618 Aw/cn 30.1.54. 207. 32. 73. B/u at 33 MU 10.66. Ss 15.12.66.
WJ619 Aw/cn 31.12.53. 27. SF Waddington. 231 OCU. Sold to BAC 21.5.69, G27-166. Conv B.62 for Argentina as B110, del 9.9.71. (1 sqn). Grupo 2. Shot down by an AIM-9L from Sea Harrier, 150 miles NNW of Port Stanley 1.5.82.
WJ620 Aw/cn 8.1.54. 115. 50. SF Upwood. 50. 61. 527. 98. 85. Soc at 19 MU 21.3.75. FFS Manston 6.75.
WJ621 Aw/cn 27.2.54. 57. CF West Raynham. MoA charge 13.3.58. To Shorts Belfast for U.10 conv f/f 22.1.60. Del from Belfast 29.2.60. WRE. No.1 ATU, cr on approach 17.12.64. Cat.5.
WJ622 Cr when controls jammed, flew into railway embankment at Radlett, pre-del test flt 25.2.54. Cat.5.
WJ623 Aw/cn 21.1.54. 101. 9. 50. SF Upwood. MoA charge 7.3.58. To Shorts Belfast for U.10 conv f/f 11.3.60. Del from Belfast to Benson 24.5.60. WRE.
WJ624 Aw/cn 31.3.54. HP. 45 MU. To Shorts Belfast 6.9.55. To MoA charge 9.12.55 for initial conv U.10 f/f 11.6.57. RAE Bedford for trials 13.1.58. To RAE Llanbedr for evaluation 15.10.59. Conv U.14 at Llanbedr. Last recorded flight 18.9.61. Derelict Belfast '64.
WJ625 100. 21. SF Waddington. 231 OCU. Conv T.17. 360. Cr into sea after take-off, Gibraltar 3.8.83. Cat.5.
WJ626 Aw/cn 31.3.54. 149. 249. 73. 249. 13. Cat.5 (c) 21.1.64 at 103 MU. Soc 6.4.64.
WJ627 Aw/cn 23.3.54. 149. 100. To Ferranti Turnhouse as target for AI Mk23. 2.7.59. MoS charge 17.7.61. RRE Pershore for evaluation 8.4.63. Ferranti 19.8.63. RRE jamming acft for guided weapons trials 9.9.63. BAC Samlesbury for special radar fit 5.12.63. RRE 24.4.64. BAC Filton for training Concorde pilots 1.7.68. Concorde chase acft from 18.12.69. RAE Bedford for nylon barrier trials 28.9.73. Soc for fire fighting 14.7.75.
WJ628 Aw/cn 5.3.54. 35. 104. 249. 32. 73. Soc at 15 MU 31.3.71. FFS Catterick.
WJ629 Aw/cn 20.4.54. 40. 32. 6. Conv TT.18. 7. FRADU on RN charge 24.6.81. Chivenor for crash rescue training as 8747M 24.3.82, noted 7.90. Nose at N. Weald 6.92.
WJ630 Aw/cn 31.3.54. 100. 45. 75 RNZAF. 45. Conv T.17 del Watton 1.5.67. 360, current as 'ED' 8.91.
WJ631 Aw/cn 30.4.54. 207. 115. 9. 12. 76. 231 OCU. 85. Loan to 360. 85. Soc at 15 MU 1.10.71. Catterick for FFS.
WJ632 Aw/cn 20.4.54. 90. 40. SF Wittering. 45. To Marshalls Cambridge for initial conv TT.18 14.10.64. BAC Warton for t/i of long length TT System 16.6.65 f/f 21.3.66. FR Ltd for flight trials of FR winch 7.7.66. A&AEE trials 11.4.68. Cr when acft abandoned on test flight, 3.5 miles SE Bridport, Dorset 2.5.70. Cat.5.
WJ633 Aw/cn 31.3.54. 100. 231 OCU. Conv T.17 del 15 MU 30.10.67. MoD(PE). 360. To Samlesbury to become last T.17a, returned to 360 19.10.87, current as 'EF' 8.91.
WJ634 Aw/cn 13.5.54. 61. 76. 35. Ss at 23 MU 1.7.64.
WJ635 Aw/cn 30.4.54. 100. 50. 35. 245. 98. 7. SOC at St Mawgan 7.8.75, fire dump, scrapped 2.87.
WJ636 Aw/cn 31.5.54. 104. 61. 35. To BAC for conv TT.18 31.10.67. Del 27 MU 6.3.69. RN charge at 27 MU 3.10.69. FRU. FRADU. To St Athan store. 100 as 'CX' 8.91. In open storage at Wyton 23.1.92.
WJ637 Aw/cn 21.5.54. 35. 61 (loan). 35. 231 OCU. Allotted 8755M '82, RAFC Engineering Flt, Cranwell 20.9.82. Displayed outside Trenchard Hall 3.83. Painted as 'WH699 Aries' by 2.84, current 8.91.
WJ638 Aw/cn 31.5.54. 102. 35. To MoA charge and del to Shorts Belfast 30.5.60. Conv U.14 f/f 13.6.61. 728B FAA Hal Far 8.8.61. To Pershore store 12.12.61. Conv B.2. To A&AEE for ejector seat trials 27.6.62. To RN Culdrose for Predannack fire dump 5.1.78.
WJ639 Aw/cn 31.5.54. 57. Conv TT.18. To BAC Warton for t/i and flight test of banner target towing capability 26.2.71. A&AEE 8.7.71. BAC Samlesbury for mods 21.9.71. FRL for t/i mods 24.1.73. 7. Sold to BAe 9.12.81. Store at Samlesbury. Acquired by North East Aircraft Museum, Sunderland 6.88.
WJ640 Aw/cn 31.8.54. 231 OCU. 192. 51. To BP Seighford for t/i 19.12.62. 51. 85. BAC Samlesbury for height encoding altimeter 7.8.71. Off MoA charge 24.11.71. 85. 100. Last flown 14.9.81 (5928.05 hrs). G/i at No.2 SoTT as 8722M 6.11.81, on offer for sale 5.91. Dismantled and departed by 7.8.91.
WJ641 Aw/cn 2.7.54. 109. 40. 50. 231 OCU. 7. Soc at St Mawgan 12.1.76. Fire dump. To Predannack 9.76 for fire fighting training by SAH Culdrose.
WJ642 Aw/cn 30.6.54. 61. 35. To 15 MU Store 26.9.61. Soc at 15 MU 14.12.70. FFS Catterick. 'WJ642' as G/g at Upwood from 4.60 was really WH723.
WJ643 Aw/cn 31.8.54. To MoS charge 7.9.54 for Ferranti Turnhouse. AI dev. BP Defford for AI Mk.23 dev 16.2.56. Ferranti Turnhouse 18.2.57. Loaned to CFE West Raynham for trials 29.8.58. A&AEE for AI MK.23 training for pilots involved with F23/49 dev 13.11.58. Ferranti Turnhouse 19.2.59. Ferranti for Harrier nav/attack system dev 3.5.66. RAE West Freugh for RAE trials of Ferranti nav/attack system 18.2.69. RAE Farnborough for Jaguar laser ranging system and weapon aiming research 24.12.69. RAE West Freugh 1970. To Cranfield for installation of retraction mechanism re FLIR equipment 12.6.75. RAE Farnborough flight trials 2.12.75. C.I.T. Cranfield 22.12.75. RAE 14.1.76. Soc at Farnborough 9.81. To PEE Shoeburyness. Extant 6.89.

WJ644 Aw/cn 23.9.54. To MoS charge 27.9.54. To DH
Propellors, Hatfield for 'Blue Jay' dev. BP Defford
'Blue Jay' mods 20.12.54. DH Props 'Red Top'
launching platform 24.6.59. 12 JSTU. EECo Warton t/i
for drag launched banner mods 23.1.62. Marshall's
Cambridge for t/i 2.1.64 – later cancelled. Sold to BAC
17.3.65. Dismantled at Samlesbury 1966. Sold for
scrap 12.90.

WJ645 Aw/cn 30.8.54. 21.57. BAC used in connection with a
project study for a flying classroom 4.63. Ss 12.5.67.

WJ646 Aw/cn 14.9.54. To MoS charge 16.9.54. To BP Defford
for AI Mk.18 dev. RRE Defford for AI Mk.18 trials
5.12.56. RRE for Hughes UK-71N Tracking equipment
installation 21.5.65. RRE trials of moving target
indicator equipment 23.9.65. RRE trials AMTI/AEW
programme 29.7.68. Last flight 17.12.68. Released
and allotted to A&AEE for fire fighting 5.2.69.
Removed by road to Boscombe Down 16.12.70. Soc
2.2.71. Reassembled at A&AEE with wings from
WK120, but burnt out at A&AEE 1.73.

WJ647 Aw/cn 28.9.54. 15. 61. 527. BAC for a project study for
a flying classroom 1.4.63. Sub contract to BP. B/u at
15 MU and ss 20.12.66.

WJ648 Aw/cn 6.10.54. 207. 18. 35. 45. Ss 20.12.66.

WJ649 Aw/cn 27.10.54. 231 OCU. Cr when starboard engine
flamed out on approach, Bassingbourn 8.7.59.
Cat.5 (3k).

WJ674 Aw/cn 27.10.54. 61. 100. 40. 50. 35. 231 OCU. Cr on
practice asymmetric approach and hit ground near
Fox Inn, South Witham, Cottesmore 2.8.73. Cat.5 (1k).

WJ675 Aw/cn 30.11.54. 102. 40. 50. 85. B/u at 15 MU and
ss 13.4.70.

WJ676 Aw/cn 30.11.54. 149. 40. 50. 35. 245. Last flown 10.62
(2267 hrs). G/i at No.12 SoTT as 7796M 13.12.62.
Station museum, Colerne '63 as WJ676. G/g RAF
Hospital Wroughton 2.2.76, on offer for sale 5.91.

WJ677 Aw/cn 31.12.54. 103. 40. 50. 231 OCU. 7. Flown to
Yeovilton for fire dump 26.11.75. Soc 27.11.75. Nose
extant 4.91 outside FAA Museum.

WJ678 Aw/cn 31.1.55. To C(A) charge 4.2.55. Marshall's
Cambridge for t/i. To 15 MU 31.8.55. Marshall's
t/i of interdictor role mods 11.2.56. A&AEE for
clearance for trials 14.11.56. CEPE at Namao,
Edmonton, Canada for winterisation trials 28.11.56.
Marshall's 4.5.57. To 15 MU 13.11.57. 85. 100. To
BDRF Abingdon 26.6.85. Allotted 8864M 11.85,
current 5.91.

WJ679 Aw/cn 16.2.55 del 15 MU. To C(A) charge 9.12.55. for
RRE Defford for AI research. RRE high altitude
ground and airborne exp radar research 16.4.58.
Special target with tip tank mounted searchlight.
RRE guided weapon fuse trials 6.7.66. Last flight
13.10.67. Dismantled at Pershore 12.68. To PEE
Shoeburyness 13.1.69. Soc 29.1.69. Sold for scrap
12.90.

WJ680 Aw/cn 25.3.55. 104. 103. 59. Conv TT.18 del 30.5.68. 7.
100 as 'CT' 8.91. In open storage at Wyton 23.1.92.

WJ681 Aw/cn 22.4.55. 527. 245. 98. 85. 100. 56. 231 OCU. Loan
to 100. 231 OCU. G/i for crash rescue training,
Brawdy as 8735M 8.1.82, last noted 6.87.

WJ682 Aw/cn 29.4.55. Del 5.55. SF Upwood. 50. SF Upwood.
35. RAE Llanbedr for dropping radar reflective
parachute targets over Cardigan Bay for
'Bloodhound' firings 4.10.61. 33 MU 2.4.62. . 98. Conv
TT.18 del 27 MU 17.1.69. FRL for TT trials 21.1.71. To
St Athan 14.6.71. FRL 9.8.71. St Mawgan 28.2.72. 7. 100
as 'CU' 8.91. In open storage at Wyton 23.1.92.

WJ683 to WJ707 - cancelled HP production - 25 acft.

WJ580, a 231 OCU B.2, at Turnhouse 'Battle of
Britain' air show 1959. *Ian G. Stott via C. J. Salter*

Rare 104 Squadron 'thunderbolt' fin marking on
B.2 WJ628 at Gutersloh 20.2.56. *Sqn Ldr D. Sawden*

WJ641, a B.2 of 50 Squadron. *MAP*

E.15 WJ756 '6' of 98 Squadron was at the 25th
anniversary event at Cottesmore, 22.5.74.

B.6 (mod) WJ775 was probably on the strength of
51 Squadron when this was taken. *Paul Fehloner*

Canberra B.2 (26 acft)
Contract 6/Acft/5786/CB6(b). 20 September 1950
Serial numbers allocated 27.10.50.
Production by English Electric Co, Preston.

WJ712 Aw/cn 11.8.53. 139. RRF. Handling Sqn. Sold to BAC 8.7.66, G27-100. Conv B.56 for Peru as 243, del 2.5.69.

WJ713 Aw/cn 24.8.53. RAFFC. CAW. 85. 360. Sold to BAC 23.2.68, G27-112. Conv B.62 for Argentina as B102 (G-AYHP for 1970 SBAC show), del 17.11.70 (1 Sqn).

WJ714 Aw/cn 14.8.53. 139. 109. 231 OCU. 360. 98. Sold to BAC 23.2.68, G27-113. Conv B.62 for Argentina as B103, del 17.11.70 (1 sqn). Cr on take-off from General Urquiza airfield 22.11.71.

WJ715 Aw/cn 31.8.53. 21. 10. 21. 50. 76. 50. 231 OCU. 75 RNZAF. To BAC for conv TT.18. Del 27 MU 1.69. FRL for trials at West Freugh 2.3.70. RAE West Freugh 13.3.70, FRL 1.4.70. 7. 100 as 'CV' 8.91. Authorised for disposal 12.7.91. Open storage at Wyton 9.91. Rudder missing by 23.1.92.

WJ716 Aw/cn 31.8.53. 9. Cr when both engines cut on overshoot, Binbrook 26.11.53. Cat.5.

WJ717 Aw/cn 31.8.53. 15. 61. To BAC for conv TT.18 7.9.67 del 27 MU 18.12.68. RN charge at 27 MU 30.9.69. FRU. FRADU det Key West NAS, Florida 31.10.78. FRADU 8.80. To St Athan store 21.2.85. Allotted 9052M for engine training at St Athan '90, current 5.91.

WJ718 Aw/cn 11.9.53. 207. 35. 115. 61. Sold to BAC 4.11.69, G27-181. Scrapped at Samlesbury '76.

WJ719 Aw/cn 24.9.53. 35. 50. 35. 245. 98, u/c retracted whilst taxiing at Samsun, Turkey 29.4.63. Acft flown home with u/c locked down but deemed beyond repair. To Laarbruch for fire fighting.

WJ720 Aw/cn 18.9.53. 40. Cr on night GCA approach at North Elmham, Norfolk (15 miles from Marham) 24.7.54. Cat.5 (3k).

WJ721 40. 50. Conv TT.18. FRU. 7. Sold to BAe 19.11.81. Sold to Pennine Aviation Museum, Bacup '88.

WJ722 Aw/cn 30.9.53. 21. 50. CAW. 98. 85. 98. Ss to Lovaux (North West) Ltd, Macclesfield 1983.

WJ723 Aw/cn 28.9.53. 21. 50. MoA for A&AEE 2.12.59. Target to test and calibrate equipment for Sea Vixen, NA39, Lightning and Javelin trials. 15 MU 18.3.60. (Replaced by WK121). B/u at 15 MU and Soc 1.10.71.

WJ724 Aw/cn 30.9.53. 15. 61. 50. Allotted 8127M at 15 MU ntu. B/u at 15 MU and Soc 1.10.71.

WJ725 Aw/cn 14.10.53. 40. 50. SF Upwood. 35. Marshall's Cambridge 4.6.58 for installation of special parachute assembly to stabilize man-dummy during free-fall from high altitude. Folland Acft Co Benson 25.7.58. Marshall's 23.8.58. Benson for preparation for ferry to Australia 8.9.58. WRE for flight trials of parachute assembly. Ret to Marshall's Cambridge 30.6.60 for restoration to standard. Sold to R. J. Coley as scrap 7.7.61.

WJ726 Aw/cn 16.10.53. 76. 35. Ss 27.4.64.

WJ727 Aw/cn 23.10.53. 40. 50. 45. Ss 14.2.64.

WJ728 Aw/cn 29.1.54. 9. 18. 61. 50. 231 OCU. 100. To RAE for apprentice training 18.2.76. B/u at Farnborough 3.84.

WJ729 Aw/cn 30.10.53. 139. 32. 6. B/u at 15 MU and Soc 1.10.71.

WJ730 Aw/cn 13.11.53. BP Defford for t/i of low level night PR conv set 30.11.53. A&AEE for trials 18.8.54. MoS charge 31.12.54. Napiers Luton for installation of gas generating system 1.9.55. BP for removal of previous system 24.7.57, (del Luton-Defford 2.9.57). BP flight trials of F-97 Mk.2 camera from 14.7.58. ETPS Farnborough 18.3.59. Lost control and cr following practice engine failure on take off, Farnborough 25.10.62. Cat.5. Soc 12.2.63.

WJ731 Aw/cn 24.11.53. Del 3.12.53. 76. 90. 50. 231 OCU. 7. 231 OCU, current as 'BK' 8.91.

WJ732 Aw/cn 30.11.53. 10. 27. 50. 35. Ss 27.4.64.

WJ733 Aw/cn 31.12.53. 18. 27. 18. 61. 50. Ss 30.6.71.

WJ734 Aw/cn 3.12.53. 18. BP Defford for t/i of T.11 conv 20.8.56. A&AEE for handling trials 21.5.58. BP for regularisation of A&AEE mods to AI Mk.17 13.11.58. Del to Seighford 11.12.58. Released 6.9.60. To 60 MU Dishforth 14.8.62. Soc 29.8.62. To PEE Shoeburyness.

WJ751 Aw/cn 8.1.54. 115. 18. 61. 35. B/u at 15 MU and ss 7.9.70.

WJ752 Aw/cn 8.1.54. 115. 18. 61. 35. To RN charge 8.7.71. Ret to RAF charge 4.2.72. 5 MU. Soc 3.3.72 at Lyneham for fire fighting

WJ753 Aw/cn 8.1.54. 115. 18. 61. 85. 100, Swung off runway after heavy landing, Marham 19.6.78. Soc Cat.5 (c) 23.6.78.

Canberra B.6 (31 acft)
Contract 6/Acft/5786/CB6(b). (part). 20 September 1950
Serial numbers allocated 27.10.50.
Production by English Electric Co, Preston.

WJ754 1st prod acft f/f 26.1.54. Aw/cn 26.2.54. MoA air fleet at Warton 26.2.54. A&AEE 6.4.54, Cat.3 acc 30.4.54. Replaced by WJ755. RR Hucknall for Avon RA.7 surge tests 27.8.54. To 15 MU Wroughton 27.7.55. 49 MU Sealand 1.11.55. 76. 1439 Flt. 76. Sold to BAC 14.11.67, G27-98. Conv B(I)56 for Peru as 241, del 19.3.69.

WJ755 Aw/cn 31.3.54. MoA air fleet at Warton 31.3.54 for t/i of gun sight etc. for night interdiction. A&AEE 4.5.54 to replace WJ754 after accident. Released 12.5.54.and ret to Warton. Marshall's Cambridge for mods 29.12.54. A&AEE for ILS & IFF Mk.10 trials 1.12.55. Marshall's for invertor cooling tests 6.3.56. A&AEE invertor cooling trials re ILS IFF Mk.10 13.12.56. Marshalls 7.3.57. DH Engine Co. Hatfield 13.6.57. Follands Chilbolton 15.7.57 for conv to Spectre rocket flying test-bed. DH Engine Co. Hatfield for flight trials 23.4.59. Sold to Cambria Acft Spares for scrap 8.2.62.

WJ756 Aw/cn 30.3.53. Del 33 MU 7.5.54. 101. 9. Bristol's at Filton for conv B.15 31.7.61. 15 MU 6.6.63. BAC Samlesbury 25.11.64. HQ. NEAF early 1965. 32. ASW. 7 Eng Sqn St Athan 15.1.69. RAF Watton 22.6.70. 98. Conv E.15. 98. 100 as 'CL' 8.91. On major service at Hurn 1.92.

WJ757 Aw/cn 20.3.54. Handling Sqn. 76. Sold to BAC 14.11.67, G27-97. Conv B(I)56 for Peru as 240, del 3.3.69.

WJ758 Aw/cn 30.3.54. 101. 12. Cr when hydraulic leak meant wheels-up landing at Ta Kali, Malta 12.12.57.

WJ759 Aw/cn 31.3.54. 101. 9, cr during LABS loop Tarhuna, Libya 24.11.60. Cat.5 (3k).

WJ760 Aw/cn 30.4.54. 101. 12. Conv B.15. 73. ASW. Sold to BAC 12.3.69.

WJ761 Aw/cn 30.4.54. 101. 9. hit parked acft (WH973) at Luqa 18.3.59. Cat.5.

WJ762 Aw/cn 23.4.54. 101. 12. Conv B.15. 73. ASW. 6 (?). Sold to BAC 27.2.69. Scrapped at Samlesbury 7.76.

WJ763 French Air Force as F763 '54. Centre d'Essais en Vol. CEV c/s F-ZJAM. Musée de l'Air, Le Bourget '84.

WJ764 Aw/cn 25.4.54. 101. 12. Conv B.15. 73. ASW. Sold to BAC 11.9.69. G27-179. Scrapped at Samlesbury '76.

WJ765 Aw/cn 31.5.54. 101, landed wheels-up at Binbrook 13.9.54 Cat.5. G/i at No.10 SoTT as 7158M 8.11.54. G/i at No.12 SoTT as 7158M 31.12.57. Soc at 33 MU 4.9.59. Ss 3.61.

WJ766 Aw/cn 31.5.54. 101. 9. 139. 9. Conv B.15. 45. Sold to BAC 14.4.69. Scrapped '76.

WJ767 Aw/cn 30.6.54. Mod to B.6(BS). 109. 139. Cr into sea off Spurn Head, Yorks on night approach to Binbrook 16.1.58. Cat.5 (3k).

WJ768 Aw/cn 2.7.54. Mod to B.6(BS). 109. SF Binbrook. 139. BCDU. 51. Flown to Akrotiri for fire fighting 9.7.74.

WJ769 Aw/cn 30.6.54. Mod to B.6(BS). 109. 139, port engine caught fire after t/o, Nav and Observer ejected, pilot crash landed at Idris, Libya 3.10.57, Cat.5. Front fuselage allotted 7546M as G/i at Binbrook 26.11.57.

WJ770 Aw/cn 16.7.54. Mod to B.6(BS). 109. RRE Defford for 'Yellow Aster' t/i. RRF Wyton for service trials 4.1.56. Ret to Hemswell 12.1.56. 109. RRF. Conv B.16. 249. 6. Cr into hills in fog at Sinopoli, Calabria, Italy 11.3.68. Cat.5 (3k).

WJ771 Aw/cn 13.8.54. Mod to B.6(BS). 109. 139. 6. 12. Conv B.16. 6. Cr when acft disintegrated at 5000 ft, 15 miles S of Khartoum 16.7.64. (3k).

WJ772 Aw/cn 16.7.54. Mod to B.6(BS). 109. 139, disappeared after take-off from Malta en route to El Adem 22.4.58. Acft discovered in desert 160 miles SSE of Gabes, Tunisia 8.2.59. Cat.5.

WJ773 Aw/cn 27.8.54. Mod to B.6(BS). 139. 249. Conv B.16. 249. ASW. 249. Soc at 5 MU 1.10.71. FFS Manston.

WJ774 Aw/cn 31.8.54. Mod to B.6(BS). 139. 6. Conv B.16. 249. 32. 249. ASW. Soc at 19 MU 17.12.71. To Oakington for FF '72.

WJ775 Aw/cn 31.8.54. Mod to B.6(BS). 192. 51. G/i CSDE. 5.9.74. Allotted 8581M '77. Current 6.91.

WJ776 Aw/cn 31.8.54. Mod to B.6(BS). 139. 6. Conv B.16. 6. ASW. Sold to BAC 5.3.69. G27-171. Conv B.66 for India as IF1028.

WJ777 Aw/cn 10.9.54. Mod to B.6(BS). 139. 6. 249. Conv B.16. 6. ASW. 249. Soc at 5 MU 10.5.72. FFS Manston 6.72.

WJ778 Aw/cn 30.9.54. Mod to B.6(BS). 139. 6. Conv B.16. 249. ASW. Sold to BAC 20.2.69, G27-169. Conv B.66 for India as IF1029.

WJ779 French AF as F779 '54. Centre d'Essais en Vol. Later fitted with Mk.8 nose section. CEV c/s F-ZJAN. Replaced on contract by XJ249.

WJ780 Aw/cn 12.11.54. Mod to B.6(BS). 109. 139. 249. Conv B.16. 6. ASW. Sold to BAC 21.8.69, G27-174. Conv B.66 for India as IF1025.

WJ781 Aw/cn 29.10.54 Mod to B.6(BS). 109. 139. 9. 249. Conv B.16. 6. ASW. BAC allocated G27-175 '69. but acft not released. Soc at 5 MU 1.10.71. FFS Manston '72.

WJ782 Aw/cn 29.10.54. Mod to B.6(BS). 109. 139. Conv B.16. 249. ASW. Soc at 5 MU 1.10.71. FFS Manston '72.

WJ783 Aw/cn 6.11.54. Mod to B.6(BS). 109. 139. 249. Conv B.16. 249. ASW. 32, port wheel disintegrated on take-off and acft went into barrier at Akrotiri 31.7.68. Cat.5. Soc 31.1.70.

WJ784 French AF as F784 '54. Centre d'Essais en Vol. CEV c/s F-ZJPK, later F-ZJAK. Replaced by XJ257.

Canberra PR.7 (11 acft)
Contract 6/Acft/5786/CB6 (b). (part). 20 September 1950.
Serial numbers allocated 27.10.50.
Production by English Electric Co, Preston.

WJ815 Aw/cn 13.7.54. 540. 82. 58. 13. To BDRF Coningsby as 8729M 8.12.81. Extant 4.91.

WJ816 Aw/cn 16.7.54. 31. Sold to BAC 2.10.69, G27-184. Conv PR.57 for India as P1099, del 27.8.71.

WJ817 Aw/cn 16.7.54. 58. 17. 80. 58. 13. BDRF Wyton as 8695M 9.6.81. To Fire Section early '89. Coded 'FU2', amended to 'FU', current 5.91.

WJ818 Aw/cn 26.8.54. Marshall's Cambridge for MK.1 auto-pilot mods 26.8.54. RAE for flight trials 4.4.55. 58 Sqn Wyton for service trials 6.2.56. 13. Wheel-up landing Akrotiri 16.1.59. Cat.5.

WJ819 Aw/cn 31.8.54. 82. 542. 58. B/u at 27 MU and ss 11.11.69.

WJ820 Aw/cn 24.9.54. 82. 58. 100. 13. MoA at Marshalls for ejector seat check fitting 7.3.61. 15 MU 13.4.61. RAE for moving topographical display dev 3.7.61. 15 MU 25.1.62. 58. Cr, wheels up 5.10.64. Cat.5.

WJ821 Aw/cn 13.9.54. 82. 58. 13, force landed at Bedford 8.80. Allotted 8668M 13.1.81. By road to Bassingbourn 1.4.81. G/g at Allenbrooke Barracks 7.5.81, current 12.90.

WJ822 Aw/cn 28.9.54. 100. 58. 13. 58. 81. Cr after aborted take-off due to engine failure, Tengah 29.5.69. Cat.5.

WJ823 Aw/cn 29.9.54. 82. 58. Collided with Lockheed T-33A 56-1604 on night flight. Cr near Ellington, Hunts 12/13.6.58. Cat.5 (3k).

WJ824 Aw/cn 30.9.54. 82. 58. 100. 58. Cr into high ground at night, 4 miles E of Udale, Cumberland 29.1.63. Cat.5 (2k).

WJ825 Aw/cn 30.9.54. 82. 58. 100. 58. SF Wyton. 13. BDRF Abingdon as 8697M 10.6.81. Honington 22.8.84. FFS Catterick 24.10.85.

Canberra T.4 (25 acft)
Contract 6/Acft/5786/CB6(b). (part). 20 September 1950
Serial numbers allocated 27.10.50.
Production by English Electric Co, Preston.

WJ857 Aw/cn 18.6.54. SF Wittering. 231 OCU. Sold to BAC 5.7.68.

WJ858 Aw/cn 16.6.54. 149. 69. 13. Destroyed in hangar fire, EOKA bomb attack, Akrotiri 27.11.57. Cat.5.

WJ859 Aw/cn 25.6.54. SF Scampton. SF Waddington. SF Coningsby. (B)OCU RNZAF. Sold to BAC 3.10.62. Conv T.54 for India, del 9.63.

WJ860 Aw/cn 30.6.54. SF Binbrook. 231 OCU. 245. 98. Sold to BAC 10.11.65. Refurbished and sold to Peru as 232, del 18.4.66.

WJ861 Aw/cn 30.6.54. 35. SF Marham. SF Weston Zoyland. SF Wyton. SF Laarbruch. 31. 231 OCU. 85. 100. 7. 39. PRU. 231 OCU. MoD(PE). 231 OCU. St Athan for storage as 'BF' 23.9.87 – last flight: 5814.50 hrs. On offer for sale 9.91.

WJ862 Aw/cn 13.8.54. SF Scampton. SF Upwood. SF Binbrook. SF Upwood. CSE. 151. SF Bruggen. SF Laarbruch. 360. 98. 231 OCU, cr on formation with WH874, hit ground 1.5 miles S of Mansfield, Notts 29.1.71. Cat.5.

WJ863 Aw/cn 13.8.54. SF Cottesmore. SF Honington. 15 (loan?). 231 OCU. SF Akrotiri. 360. 231 OCU. Sold to BAC 13.11.75. Nose to Marshall's for systems trials 6.1.76. Other parts used in o/h of Venezuela T.4 0621 during '77.

WJ864 Aw/cn 31.8.54. SF Wittering. SF Gaydon. 232 OCU. (B)OCU RNZAF. Sold to BAC 11.3.63. Conv T.4 for S.Africa as 458, del 4.64. (12 Sqn).

WJ865 Aw/cn 2.9.54. ETPS/A&AEE. To RAE Farnborough at end of fatigue life as G/i for apprentice training 5.11.81. Soc 15.1.82. Last noted in store at RAE 10.88.

WJ866 Aw/cn 10.9.54. SF Wyton. RAFFC. 231 OCU. To RN charge at 27 MU 13.11.69. FRU. FRADU. Loan to 231 OCU 13.5.83. Ret to RAF charge 1.4.86. 231 OCU. MoD(PE) loan. 231 OCU, current as 'BL' 8.91.

WJ867 Aw/cn 30.9.54. ETPS Farnborough 30.9.54. ETPS Boscombe Down 21.1.68. Grounded at end of fatigue life 2.79. To fire dump Newton as 8643M 12.79. To BDRF Abingdon 10.84. To FFS Catterick 31.1.86, last noted 4.88.

WJ868 Aw/cn 12.10.54. 149. SF Gutersloh. 59. SF Geilenkirchen. 59. 16. 3. SF Laarbruch. SF Bruggen. SF Laarbruch. Conv T.4 for India as Q1796, del 4.8.75.

WJ869 Aw/cn 27.10.54. SF Gaydon. 232 OCU. 231 OCU. Loan to RN. FRADU. 231 OCU. To Zimbabwe as 2215, del 25.3.81.

WJ870 Aw/cn 17.11.54. 102. 31. SF Laarbruch. 213. SF Ahlhorn. 213. SF Bruggen. 231 OCU. Loan to RN. FRADU. 231 OCU. Loan to 7. 231 OCU. 360. 231 OCU. To St Mawgan for BDRF as 8683M 16.4.81, last noted 12.87.

WJ871 Aw/cn 26.11.54. 231 OCU. Cr 2 miles W of Stilton, Hunts 24.2.56. Cat.5 (2k).

WJ872 Aw/cn 30.11.54. 231 OCU. SF Akrotiri. ITF Akrotiri. 32. 13. 360. Soc at Wyton 18.5.76. G/i at No.1 SoTT as 8492M 5.76. To AWRE Foulness (less nose) 10.8.81. Nose to 327 (ATC) Sqn, Kilmarnock 24.9.81.

WJ873 Aw/cn 20.12.54. 231 OCU. 237 OCU. SF Wyton. C(A). 51. Soc at 15 MU 6.10.71. B/u.

WJ874 Aw/cn 24.12.54. SF Gaydon. SF Binbrook. SF Coningsby. 231 OCU. Handling Sqn. To RN charge at 27 MU 12.11.69. FRU. 231 OCU 22.4.86. In open store at Wyton 2.88. Active 231 OCU 12.89, current as 'BM' 4.92.

WJ875 Aw/cn 24.12.54. SF Wyton. 230 OCU. 231 OCU. 230 OCU. 231 OCU. Sold to BAC 27.3.68, G27-122. Conv T.64 for Argentina as B112, del 26.2.71. (1 Sqn).

WJ876 Aw/cn 31.12.54. SF Scampton. SF Binbrook. 1 Group Comms Flt. SF Waddington. 231 OCU. Handling Sqn. SF Akrotiri. 39. SF Akrotiri. 13. 56. 13. 39. 13. 7. Soc at St Mawgan 7.8.75. To Predannack for FF by SAH Culdrose 9.76. Nose to RAF EF Abingdon, current '90.

WJ877 Aw/cn 12.1.55. SF Hemswell. SF Binbrook. SF Upwood. SF Binbrook. SF Coningsby. 231 OCU. 58. 51. 231 OCU. 51. 85. 51. 98. 51. 231 OCU. 360. 231 OCU. 13. MoD(PE). 13. SF Wyton. 100. 231 OCU. Painted pale blue and 'VN799' to represent 1st prototype for 40th anniversary event, 13/14.5.89. Cleaned 17.5.89 and returned to correct serial and standard colour scheme. Cr. on take off from Wyton 18.3.91.

WJ878 Aw/cn 28.1.55. To C(A) for Marshalls. t/i of mods peculiar to T.4 10.2.55. 231 OCU. EECo Warton for tail plane actuator mods 23.3.56. A&AEE 9.5.56. EECo for aerodynamic investigation re Canberra flight restrictions (trim tab settings etc) 28.5.56. RAE for trials 29.6.56. 231 OCU. Flown to No.1 SoTT 10.5.60. G/i at No.1 SoTT as 7636M 1.6.60. Ss '74.

WJ879 Aw/cn 31.1.55. Del 23 MU 8.2.55. SF Wittering. SF Hemswell. SF Wittering. SF Finningley. SF Wyton. 58. 231 OCU. 58. 39. 7. 231 OCU. 7. 231 OCU, current as 'BH' 8.91.

WJ880 Aw/cn 23.2.55. 104. SF Gutersloh. SF Laarbruch. EECo, to Marshall's for t/i of LABS. A&AEE for flight trials 25.9.62. Marshall's for mods 19.11.62. RAF Germany 23.4.63. SF Laarbruch. 16. 60 MU. 56. 100. 85. 7. G/i at No.1 SoTT as 8491M 2.7.76. Tail section to BDRF Abingdon 24.9.81. Nose allotted to 2408 (ATC) Sqn at Hornchurch and moved to North Weald late '82. Fuselage to AWRE Foulness 9.84. Sold for scrap 12.90. Nose to South Yorkshire Air Museum, Firbeck '90.

WJ881 Aw/cn 28.2.55. 231 OCU. Loan to Ferry Sqn. CAW (?). SF Akrotiri. ITF Akrotiri. SF Akrotiri. Soc at 5 MU 23.11.71. FFS at Catterick 4.72.

Canberra B.2 (100 acft); 75 built, 25 cancelled
Contract 6/Acft/5990/Cb6(b). 10 November 1950
Serial numbers allocated 10.11.50.
Production by A.V.Roe, Woodford

WJ971 1st prod acft f/f 25.11.52. Aw/cn 27.2.53. 139. 104. 59. Sold to BAC 8.7.66, G27-119. Conv B.52 for Ethiopia as 353. Del 10.10.68.

WJ972 Aw/cn 30.4.53. 15. 6. 32. 6. Sold to BAC 29.3.65.

WJ973 Aw/cn 17.4.53. 149. 6. B/u at 15 MU and ss 1.7.64.

WJ974 Aw/cn 30.4.53. 15. 57. Sold to BAC 1.2.66, G27-76. Refurbished and sold to Peru as 233, del 22.11.67.

WJ975 Aw/cn 30.4.53. 231 OCU. 35. 44. Conv T.11. 228 OCU. TFS West Raynham. 85. Conv T.19. 85. BAC Warton for flight trials and refurbishment 8.6.71. 100. 7. 100. Sold to Marshall's 21.5.80. To Bomber County Museum, Cleethorpes '83. Moved to Hemswell 3.88, current with Hemswell Aviation Society, Hemswell 9.91.

WJ976 Aw/cn 28.5.53. 15. 44. 12. 9. Sold to BAC 1.2.66, G27-77. Refurbished and sold to Peru as 234, del 4.8.66. W/o 18.12.69.

WJ977 Aw/cn 12.6.53. 15. 57. 21. 139. SF Binbrook. 9. 139. MoA. BP Seighford for initial conv T.17 26.6.63. BAC Samlesbury 13.8.63, f/f 9.9.65. A&AEE for T.17 C(A) clearance 6.5.66. Trials with 360 Sqn Watton 19.9.66. BAC Samlesbury for special fit 23.6.67. Tests on aerial system 1.2.68. 15 MU 21.3.68. 360. Rescue training at Wyton as 8761M 1.12.82. Dump 11.87. Gone by 3.88.

WJ978 Aw/cn 17.7.53. 18. 207. DH Propellors Hatfield for 'Blue Jay' trials 29.3.56. Ex RAF Charge 26.2.57. 12 JSTU at WRE 30.5.57. Reallotted 'Red Top' / Jindivik trials 30.12.59. Instrument checking and 'Blue Steel' range safety acft 5.2.60. 'Red Top' trials 28.4.60. Soc 31.7.62.

WJ979 Aw/cn 9.7.53. 18, cr when acft lost power on approach to Scampton 23.2.54. Cat.5.

WJ980 Aw/cn 9.7.53. 18. 115. SF Binbrook. 139. Sold to BAC 29.3.65. Conv B.2 for Venezuela as 1371, renumbered before delivery as 2001, del 3.67. (40 Sqn). To BAC for o/h '75, G27-262. Conv B.82, ret 1.2.78 as 2001.

WJ981 Aw/cn 14.8.53. 103. 88. 44. 75 RNZAF. 45. CAW. To BAC for conv T.17. Del Watton 5.5.67. 360. First conv T.17A. 360, current as 'EN' 8.91.

WJ982 Aw/cn 24.8.53. RAFFC, cr landed on approach to Manby 28.9.53.

WJ983 Aw/cn 28.8.53. 21. 45, cr after collision with WH882 in cloud over Pontian, Singapore 13.12.57. Cat.5 (1k).

WJ984 Aw/cn 31.8.53. CSE. 98. 97. 360. Soc 21.3.75. G/i at St Athan.

WJ985 Aw/cn 11.9.53. 15. 104. Ss 12.5.67.

WJ986 Aw/cn 30.9.53. 40. 90. 115. 542. 75 RNZAF. 45. To BAC for conv T.17. To RAF Watton 2.3.67. 360, current as 'EP' 8.91.

WJ987 Aw/cn 30.9.53. 76. MoA charge 23.11.56. To Short Bros for conv U.10. Flight trials 4.2.58. WRE 14.3.59. Destroyed by missile 17.10.59.

WJ988 Aw/cn 5.10.53. 76. SF Weston Zoyland. 75 RNZAF. 45. To BAC for conv T.17. Del Watton 12.66. 360. Birdstrike on t/o Watton 20.11.68, pilot raised u/c to stop. Cat.5. Soc 7.3.69.

WJ989 Aw/cn 19.10.53. RAFFC. Sold to BAC 8.7.66. Stored at Marshall's until b/u '71.

WJ990 Aw/cn 28.10.53. 76. 40. BP Seighford for 'Orange Putter' t/i 1.5.59. 15 MU 31.8.60. RRE Pershore for 'Bloodhound' trials 18.6.63. BAC Samlesbury for Special radar fit 5.11.63. RRE Pershore as jamming acft for 'Bloodhound' trials 5.3.64. Marshall's for aerial installation 1.11.66. RRE for Bloodhound trials 22.9.67. 15 MU 30.5.68. MoD(PE) 15.5.75. To AWRE Foulness. Sold for scrap 12.90.

WJ991 Aw/cn 28.10.53. 76. Conv T.4. CFS. SF Coningsby. CFS. Sold to BAC. Conv T.4 for S.Africa as 457, del 2.64. (12 Sqn).

WJ992 Aw/cn 30.10.53. 76. Conv T.4. From RAF charge 17.1.57 for Martlesham Heath. BLEU/RAE 7.6.57. RRE Pershore for crew training 27.9.62. RAE Bedford 1.11.77, current 8.92.

WJ993 Aw/cn 20.11.53. 90. 207. 6. Ss 1.7.64.

WJ994 Aw/cn 19.11.53. 115. 329. 12.9.12. RAE for Guided Weapon Recovery System 10.3.59. RAE flight trials 29.5.61. ETPS 11.7.61. Cr when u/c collapsed on roller landing at Farnborough 1.4.63. Cat.5.

WJ995 Aw/cn 16.12.53. 90. RAE Bedford for barrier trials 3.7.56. Hunting Percival Thurleigh 17.12.56. RAE for uprating Mk.13 arrestor gear 6.3.57. MoS charge 30.4.57. RAE aquaplaning trials. Non flyable acft 17.4.59. Released Cat.5 22.11.63. Soc 12.63. Broken up and scrapped at Bedford '67.

WK102 Aw/cn 30.11.53. 207. 75 RNZAF. 45. To BAC for conv T.17. Del Watton 23.3.67. 360. Soc 18.2.83. G/i at No.2 SoTT as 8780M, on offer for sale 9.91.

WK103 Aw/cn 9.12.53. 76. 32. 73. 32. Soc 30.9.65. FFS Catterick '66.

WK104 Aw/cn 24.12.53. 90. 32. 6. 249. 32. 73. SF Akrotiri. 73. Sold to BAC 5.8.66, G27-118. Conv B.52 for Ethiopia as 352. Del 12.9.68.

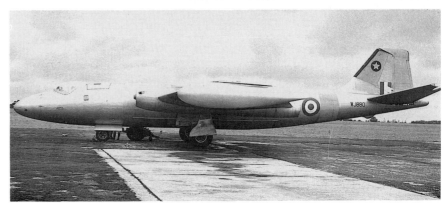

T.4 WJ876 was in use with No.1 Group HQ Communications Flight when photographed at Lindholme in 1957. *MAP*

T.4 WJ880 of 31 Squadron visited Bovingdon on 5th August 1958, whereupon it was photographed by the seemingly ever present Arthur Pearcy.

WK105 Aw/cn 31.12.53.90, cr into ground near Wereham on approach to Marham 25.4.54. Cat.5 (3k).

WK106 Aw/cn 31.12.53.50.90.207. Conv T.11.228 OCU.85. 228 OCU.85. Conv T.19.85.100. Soc at Marham 16.3.76. Allotted 8504M ntu. B/u and removed by 2.77.

WK107 Aw/cn 22.1.54.12.44(?).15. MoA charge, to Short's Belfast conv U.10 29.9.60. f/f 28.1.62. WRE 6.3.62. Destroyed by missile 17.11.65.

WK108 Aw/cn 26.1.54.617.103. Sold to Rhodesia as RRAF171. del 2.6.59. (5 Sqn). Renumber as RRAF212 in 1963 and R5212 in 1969. W/o 28.12.69.

WK109 Aw/cn 29.1.54.9.6. Ss 1.7.64.

WK110 Aw/cn 29.1.54.115. SF Binbrook. 12. To MoA charge, to Short's Belfast for conv U.10 19.3.59, f/f 20.4.60. WRE 30.5.60. Destroyed by missile 23.11.62.

WK111 Aw/cn 12.2.54. RAFFC. 202.32.73. To BAC for conv T.17. Del Watton 2.6.67.360, current as 'EA' 8.91.

WK112 Aw/cn 12.2.54.27. SF Waddington. Sold to BAC 29.3.66. Refurbished and sold to Peru as 235, del 30.1.67. W/o 8.8.68.

WK113 Aw/cn 25.2.54.617.102.249.6. B/u at 23 MU and ss 27.4.64.

WK114 Aw/cn 18.3.54.35.76.32, cr into sea at Limasol Bay, Cyprus 8.7.57. Cat.5 (4k). Soc 7.8.57.

WK115 Aw/cn 26.2.54.90.32.103 MU 11.11.60. Soc at 103 MU 30.4.61.

WK116 Aw/cn 31.3.54.231 OCU. CAW.85.100, both engines failed on take-off, cr into sea 5 miles from Akrotiri 25.2.82. Crew ejected safely.

WK117 Aw/cn 31.3.54.18.207.90.18.73. B/u at 15 MU and ss 14.2.64.

WK118 Aw/cn 12.4.54.103.59. CAW. To FRL for conv TT.18. 3.70.7.100 as 'CQ' 8.91. In open storage at Wyton 23.1.92.

WK119 Aw/cn 31.3.54.103. NECS. MoA for RRE Pershore. Jamming acft 'Bloodhound' Mk.II ECM dev. BAC Samlesbury for special fit 27.9.63. Pershore 4.10.63. RRE Bloodhound trials. 15 MU 29.1.68. 7. Soc at St Mawgan 7.8.75. To fire dump. B/u 1984. Nose at Wyton 5.89.

WK120 Aw/cn 1.4.54. RRE Defford on loan 17.10.55 for 'Blue Label' dev. Ex RAF charge 9.15.55. Also equipped for 'Blue Streak' dev 5.56. Last Radar Research Flying Unit Canberra to leave Defford 9.10.57. RRE Pershore range measuring device for 'Lighthouse' 9.10.59. Target acft 29.9.65. Last flight 2.1.68. Nea 4.4.68. Soc at Pershore 24.3.69.

WK121 Aw/cn 15.4.54. Ex-RAF charge to BP Defford for 'window' launching equipment 21.4.54. RRE high speed 'window' dropping. AI Mk.18 telemetry 23.6.55. Replaced WJ723 at A&AEE as target acft and equipment calibration 16.2.60. Soc 2.2.73. Fuselage to RAE Farnborough. To AWRE Foulness and Sold for scrap 12.90.

WK122 Aw/cn 26.4.54.61.15. Conv TT.18. A&AEE radio proving trials 4.4.68. 15 MU 6.9.68. 7. Sold to BAC 10.11.81. By road to Flambards Triple Theme Park, Cornwall 24.5.88.

WK123 Aw/cn 30.4.54.100. BP Defford 'Blue Study' Cat and Mouse t/i 15.7.55. RRE flight trials 'Blue Study' 30.12.55. A&AEE flight trials 'Blue Study' and photo equipment installation 14.2.56. A&AEE for Lindholme ASR Gear investigation 3.12.56. 15 MU 21.4.58. BAC for project study for flying classroom 4.63. Npw. 15 MU. BAC for o/h and conversion to TT.18 25.4.67. Del to 27 MU 7.5.68. To RN charge 6.9.69. FRU. FRADU. St Athan store. 100, as 'CY' 8.91. To MilGeoAmt at Ingolstadt, 8.1.92 (for spares?)

WK124 Aw/cn 27.5.54.103.59.213. To BAC for conv TT.18. Del to 27 MU 1.69. FRU. 7. 100. Allotted 9093M for Crash rescue training at FFS Manston and flown in 26.3.91.

WK125 Aw/cn 21.5.54.76. SF Upwood.35, cr after engine failure, acft force landed El Adem, Libya 6.3.58.

WK126 Aw/cn 1.6.54.9.100. To BAC for conv TT.18 25.4.67. Del 27 MU 21.5.68. To RN charge at 27 MU 13.11.69. FR Ltd for missile trials and R&D flying 19.6.70. Airwork. Hurn for FRU 2.11.70. FRADU. To St Athan store '89, FRADU 1.90, St Athan store 10.90, current 7.91.

WK127 Aw/cn 27.5.54.10. Conv TT.18. 7. 100, accident 13.12.88, acft w/o for spares. To BDRF Wyton 2.89. Coded 'FO' 1989. Allotted 8985M 1989, current 5.91.

WK128 Aw/cn 18.6.54. BP Defford 1954. RRE as jamming acft for 'window' launching trials 1958. Ex-RAF charge 13.3.59. RRE Guided Weapon fuse research and laser trials. Wfu 1975. By road to FR Ltd Tarrant Rushton 2.77. O/h and mods for Beech AQM-37A Stiletto trials. RAE/FR Ltd Llanbedr 10.78, current at Llanbedr 7.91.

WK129 Aw/cn 18.6.54. RRE Defford for AI Mk.20 19.4.55. ETPS 19.4.55. RRE AI Mk.20 trials 24.8.55. RRE Guided Weapon terrain measurements 28.2.56. Cr into high ground at Carnedd, Llewelyn, Wales 9.12.57. Cat.5 (2k).

WK130 Aw/cn 23.6.54.35.98. Sold to BAC 28.3.66. Conv B.2 for West Germany as YA+151. del 10.66. Renumbered 00+01 in 1968, D9569 in 1970 and 99+36 in 1976. Preserved displayed on pylon at Siusheim '84, current.

WK131 Aw/cn 15.7.54.57. G/i at No.1 SoTT as 7912M 24.5.66. To Halton fire dump '73.

WK132 Aw/cn 30.6.54.61.15. G/i at No 1 SoTT as 7913M 27.6.66. To Halton fire dump ,73.

WK133 Aw/cn 15.7.54.35.76.35.50.35.245.98. B/u at 15 MU and ss 13.4.70.

WK134 Aw/cn 11.8.54.102.59. G/i at No 1 SoTT as 7914M 9.8.66. To Halton fire dump '73. To FFS Catterick 9.74.

WK135 Aw/cn 20.8.54. From RAF charge 25.8.54 for DH Hatfield 'Blue Jay' installation. 12JSTU Edinburgh Field Australia 8.11.56. Ret to Hatfield 2.12.58. Reallotted 'Red Top' launch acft 27.5.60. Released 30.6.62. RAE Bedford for effects of slush on landing and take off 13.11.62. Released 30.6.64. Allotted College of Aeronautics Cranfield 10.3.66. Cancelled 5.4.66. Soc 27.1.67. To fire dump Pershore.

WK136 Aw/cn 31.8.54. 231 OCU, cr when tailplane actuator failed. Stowmarket, Suffolk 26.9.55. Cat.5 (1k).

WK137 Aw/cn 31.8.54.102.59. Sold to BAC 28.3.66. Conv B.2 for West Germany as YA+152, del 10.66. Renumbered 00+02 in 1968, D9566 in 1970 and 99+34 in 1976, current.

WK138 Aw/cn 23.9.54.102.59. Sold to BAC 28.3.66. Conv B.2 for West Germany as YA+153, del 10.66. Renumbered 00+03 in 1968, D9567 in 1970 and 99+35 in 1976, current.

WK139 Aw/cn 30.9.54.90. B/u at 15 MU and ss 13.4.70.

WK140 Aw/cn 30.9.54.50.115. B/u at 15 MU and ss 20.12.66.

WK141 Aw/cn 30.9.54. EE Co. From RAF charge 14.1.55. AS Bitteswell Sapphire Sa.7 dev 14.1.55. Reallotted to Viper ASV.3, ASV.8 and ASV.11 engine dev in wing pod 13.1.59. BS Engines Filton (on closure of Bitteswell) 18.9.59. Released 15.1.63. Soc 8.3.63. To MoA Prestwick for fire fighting.

WK142 Aw/cn 27.10.54.115.207.90.98(?). FRU. To RN charge 22.9.69. To BAC for conv TT.18 27.6.72. To RN charge at Yeovilton 5.3.73. FRADU, last noted 12.90.

B.2 WK116 of 100 Squadron at Luqa in November 1973, in the red/white scheme. On 2nd June 1976 it went to Samlesbury as the first 'Long Term Fleet' overhaul candidate. *F. Coleman*

WK143 Aw/cn 29.10.54. To FR Ltd. 10.3.55 for probe and FR pack experiments with WH734. Conv TT.18. FR Ltd trials acft. Llanbedr fire dump 8.89, current 7.91.

WK144 Aw/cn 31.10.54. 527. 245. 98. 85. G/i at St Athan as 8689M 29.4.81. Fire dump 9.90.

WK145 Aw/cn 26.11.54. 527. 245. 98. 7. To MoD(PE) charge 4.12.75. RAE. Llanbedr 2.76, to fire dump 8.77.

WK146 Aw/cn 30.11.54. 102. 59. B/u at 15 MU and ss 12.5.67. Nose to RAF Abingdon, last noted '90.

WK161 Aw/cn 24.12.54. RAE for special armament trials 14.7.55. To MoA charge 9.12.55. BP Defford for radar absorbant materials assessment trials 14.1.57. BP special target for air to air radar dev 12.62. BP for removal of special coating 11.63. Sold by MoA to Cambria Acft for spares 14.6.65.

WK162 Aw/cn 31.12.54. 527. 245. 98. 85. 100, cr on t/o, Alconbury 8.8.85. Cat.5. By road to Wyton allotted 8887M for crash repair at Wyton, gone by 3.88.

WK163 Aw/cn 21.1.55. From RAF charge 28.1.55 for AS Bitteswell for Sapphire Sa.7. Napier for Double Scorpion installation 20.5.56. Height record of 70310 ft 28.8.57. BS Filton for testing short and long-life Viper. RRE for Infra-red linescan dev 1959. Canberra B.6 wings and engines fitted at Pershore 1968. Original nose to WT327 1969. Nose from XH568 fitted 1972. First Radar Research Flying Unit Canberra to be handed over to RAE Bedford 1.7.76, current 8.92.

WK164 Aw/cn 11.2.55. Westland Acft Merryfield for air conditioning equipment 1.11.55. MoA charge 9.12.55. BP Defford 23.10.56. FR Ltd Tarrant Rushton for trials 8.11.57. Marshalls Cambridge for liquid oxygen equipment 12.5.58. A&AEE 27.11.59. To RAF charge 9.12.77. 100. P&EE Foulness. 7.82. Rear fuselage to Abingdon 28.8.86. Other remains at P&EE and sold for scrap 12.90. Nose retained.

WK165 Aw/cn 28.2.55. From RAF charge 12.12.55. WRE trials 31.1.56 also for airborne photography of weapons. No.4 JSTU from 2.63. Released 1.12.69. Soc at Edinburgh Field 13.2.70. To Eureka Aviation Association/Ballarat Aviation Museum, 9.2.85. Incomplete, under restoration to static 1990.

WK166 to WK190 Cancelled

Canberra T.4 Prototype (1 acft) to Spec T2/49
Contract 6/Acft/6265/CB6(b). 2 February 1951.
Serial number allocated 2.2.51.
Production by English Electric Co, Preston.
WN467 F/f 12.6.52. EE Co. A&AEE 11.11.52. EE Co Warton for t/i's 29.1.53. Ex C(S) charge 6.1.53. To 231 OCU 6.6.53. SF Binbrook. SF Wittering. SF Honington. 231 OCU. 16. SF Bruggen. Soc at 15 MU 9.11.71 and b/u.

Canberra B.2 (2 acft)
Contract 6/Acft/3520/CB6(b). 130 acft (part). March 1949.
Replacements for WD939 and WD983 diverted off contract.
Serial numbers allocated 28.2.51.
Production by English Electric Co, Preston.
WP514 Aw/cn 31.7.51. 101. 9. 73. Destroyed by fire in hangar after EOKA attack, Akrotiri 21.11.57. Cat.5
WP515 Aw/cn 7.3.52. 12. 617. 12. 231 OCU. RAFFC. CAW. 85. 100. Last flight 23.8.89 (9066 hrs). To St Athan for storage 10.89. Partially dismantled by 5.91. On offer for sale 9.91.

Canberra B.2 (50 acft)
Contract 6/Acft/6446/CB6(b). March 1951.
Serial numbers allocated 28.2.51.
Intended Production by Handley Page Ltd, Radlett.
WS960 to WS999 - cancelled
WT113 to WT122 - cancelled

Canberra B.2 (50 acft)
Contract 6/Acft/6447/CB6(b). March 1951.
Serial numbers allocated 28.2.51.
Intended production by A.V.Roe & Co Ltd, Woodford.
WT140 to WT189 - cancelled

Canberra B.6 (50 acft; 9 built, 41 cancelled)
Contract 6/Acft/6448/CB6(b). March 1951.
Original contract for B.2 variant. Revised to B.6.
Serial numbers allocated 28.2.51.
Production by Short Bros & Harland Ltd, Belfast.
WT205 Aw/cn 31.10.55. 9. EE Co for conv B.15 21.7.61. Loan to CS(A) 10.12.62, Marshall's Cambridge for t/i's 10.12.62. A&AEE for clearance trials 19.4.63. Marshall's 16.7.63. A&AEE armament trials 13.7.64. Marshall's 22.6.66. A&AEE 20.10.66. Marshall's t/i for practice bomb carrier 19.12.66. A&AEE 18.4.67. MoA charge from 30.1.69. A&AEE ballistic trials 26.3.71. Release 7.6.72. Soc 31.8.72. Allotted to RAE 31.8.72. Flown to Farnborough 28.9.72. Conv ground effect vehicle. Broken up for Scrap.
WT206 Aw/cn 30.11.55. Task Force 308. 76. 51. 58. 45. Soc 1.10.71.
WT207 Aw/cn 30.11.55. Task Force 308. 76. Ret to UK 3.12.57. Napiers Luton for Double Scorpion installation. Del ex conv to 76 Sqn Hemswell 2.4.58. Engine caught fire at 56,000 ft (crew bailed out and survived). Cr at Monyash, Derbys 9.4.58. Cat.5.
WT208 Aw/cn 23.1.56. Task Force 308. 76. Napiers Luton for Double Scorpion installation 21.10.57. Dispatch ex conv to 76 Sqn Hemswell 17.3.58. Ret to Napiers Luton for removal of Double Scorpion 14.7.58. SF Binbrook. Conv B.15. 45. Sold to BAC 14.11.67, G27-96. Conv B(I)56 for Peru as 239, del 3.2.69.
WT209 Aw/cn 17.2.56. SF Binbrook. 9. Conv B.15. 45, wheels up landing, Tengah 1.2.68. Cat.5
WT210 Aw/cn 22.2.56. 101. 109. 101(?). 12. Conv B.15. BAC for mods 8.6.64. A&AEE for Electromagnetic compatability trials 14.12.64. BAC Samlesbury 11.2.65. 73. ASW. Sold to BAC 19.2.69, G27-168. Conv B.66 for India as IF1020, del '70.

WT211 Aw/cn 29.2.56. SF Binbrook. 12. Conv B.15. 45. Soc at Cottesmore 1.3.72.
WT212 Aw/cn 29.3.56. MoA. IAM/RAE. Soc 1.12.74. B/u at Farnborough.
WT213 Aw/cn 30.3.56. Del 4.56. SF Binbrook. 9. Conv B.15. 32. 73. 32. 45. Cat.5 acc 17.3.69. Soc 22.4.69.
WT214 to WT224 - cancelled.
WT250 to WT279 - cancelled.

Canberra B.6 (6 acft)
Contract 6/Acft/6445/CB6(b). 190 acft (part). 28 Feb 1951.
WT304 - WT306 transferred to contract 6/Acft/5786/CB6(b) as replacements for diverted aircraft.
Serial numbers allocated 28.2.51.
Production by English Electric Co, Preston.
WT301 F/f 9.11.54. Aw/cn 30.11.54. Mod B.6(BS). 192. 51. Soc 12.7.74. To DEODS Chattenden, Kent 7.74, last noted '90.
WT302 Aw/cn 30.11.54. Mod B.6(BS). 139. A&AEE. MoA at Marshall's Cambridge for t/i's for B16. A&AEE for C(A) release as B.16 29.8.61. Marshall's 4.10.61. A&AEE for Electromagnetic compatability (EMC) trials 11.12.61. Marshall's for t/i's and major inspection 10.9.62. A&AEE flight trials of mods 24.3.65. Marshall's for return to standard 21.5.65. Del 23 MU 19.10.65. 249. Sold to BAC 10.7.69, G27-172. Conv B.66 for India as IF1026, del '71.
WT303 Aw/cn 30.11.54. Mod B.6(BS). 139. NEAF Comms Sqn. 249(?). SF Coningsby. 12. Conv B.16. 6. ASW. Sold to BAC 25.2. 69. G27-170. Conv B.66 for India as IF1024, del '70.
WT304 Aw/cn 29.4.55. Mod B.6(BS). SF Binbrook. 139, cr at night during target marking exercise, El Adem, Libya 2.6.59. Cat.5 (3k).
WT305 Aw/cn 11.5.55. Mod B.6(BS). 192. 51. BP for mods to B.6(mod) 1967. 51. Marshall's Cambridge for 'Project Zabra' 11.4.73. BAC Warton for flight trials 16.5.73. RRE for installation of Infra-red Sensor and flight trials 17.7.73. Ret to Wyton 2.4.75. 51. Allotted 8511M 15.11.76. G/g Wyton 5.7.77. Cut up and scrapped 10.89.
WT306 Aw/cn 13.5.55. Mod B.6(BS). 139. 6. Conv B.16. 249. ASW(?). Sold to BAC 25.2.69. B/u at Samlesbury 9.76.

'Night Arrival' by WK125 of 35 Squadron, El Adem, 6th March 1958, crewed by Flt Lt Ashworth, Fg Off Dockar and Fg Off John Hyde. *via Sqn Ldr John Hyde*

WP515 of 231 OCU c.1957, in black/grey scheme.

Canberra B(I)6 (19 acft)

Contract 6/Acft/6445/CB6(b). 19 acft (part). 28 Feb 1951.
Serial numbers allocated 28.2.51.
Production by English Electric Co, Preston.

WT307 B(I)6 f/f 31.3.55. EE Co. Aw/cn 22.4.55. MoS at Warton 22.4.55. A&AEE check handling 12.7.55. BP 13.7.56. A&AEE 17.7.56. Marshall's 9.12.57. SF Bruggen. 213. Sold to BAC 11.12.69. B/u at Samlesbury '76.
WT308 Aw/cn 27.5.55. From RAF charge 9.12.55. RAE. In store at Farnborough 10.88.
WT309 Aw/cn 30.6.55. Handling Sqn. From RAF charge 28.2.58. RAE. A&AEE, in store A&AEE 6.90.
WT310 Aw/cn 30.6.55. 213, mid air collision with WT315 and cr 1 mile E of Elbergen, W.Germany 15.1.62. Cat.5 (3k).
WT311 Aw/cn 15.7.55. 213. SF Bruggen. 213. A&AEE for EMC trials 27.11.62. To Bruggen 19.12.62. 213. Sold to BAC 8.12.69, in store 5.76.
WT312 Aw/cn 31.8.55. 213. A&AEE for clearance of 25lb practice bombs in LABS 9.10.58. To Bruggen 28.1.59. 213. Sold to BAC 8.12.69, in store 5.76.
WT313 Aw/cn 9.9.55. 213. W/o 26.9.68 and Soc 14.10.68.
WT314 Aw/cn 31.8.55. 213. Decoy acft at Bruggen as 8069M 11.12.69. Fire dump '71.
WT315 Aw/cn 23.9.55. 213. SF Wildenrath. 213. During formation flight, WT310 went above WT315 to photograph it, lost sight of each other, collided and cr 1 mile E of Elbergen, 15.1.62. Cat.5 (2k).
WT316 Aw/cn 23.9.55. C(A) charge Warton for t/i mod 25.11.55. To 15 MU 24.4.56. SF Bruggen. 213. MoA at Marshall's for t/i mods 15.3.65. To RAF Germany 4.3.66. 213. Sold to BAC 11.12.69. In store 5.76.
WT317 Aw/cn 31.10.55. 213. Sold to BAC 11.12.69. In store 5.76.
WT318 Aw/cn 22.11.55. 213. Sold to BAC 8.12.69.
WT319 Aw/cn 22.11.55. 213. SF Laarbruch. BAC Samlesbury 1960. A&AEE Decca equipment trials 14.10.60. To RAF Germany 21.2.61. 213. Marshall's for t/i's 21.6.67. RAF Germany 15.7.67. 213. Sold to BAC 8.12.69. To BAC Filton for apprentice training 10.76.
WT320 Aw/cn 29.11.55. 213. Sold to BAC 11.12.69. In store 5.76.
WT321 Aw/cn 30.12.55. 213. BP Seighford t/i mod 16.9.59. RAF Germany 7.3.60. 213, cr on recovery from LABS, in woods near Varrelbusch W.Germany 10.5.60. Cat.5.
WT322 Aw/cn 17.1.56. 213. Marshall's for t/i of Decca/Doppler equipment 17.7.58. A&AEE 'Blue Silk' Decca installation assessment 28.5.59. RAF Germany 29.7.59. 213. BCDU Wittering. Marshall's for t/i of nose camera 15.2.60. A&AEE flight assessment 5.5.60. Marshall's 22.6.60. RAF Germany 23.3.61. 213. Marshall's 11.5.61. A&AEE for UHF and EMC trials 4.5.62. Marshall's for t/i's 8.8.62. Reversion to standard acft 12.2.63. RAF Germany 5.7.63. 213, cr when acft rolled onto its back and dived into ground at Nordhorn range, W.Germany 23.2.67. Cat.5 (3k).
WT323 Aw/cn 27.1.56. 213. Sold to BAC 11.12.69. B/u at Samlesbury 7.76.
WT324 Aw/cn 27.1.56. 213. Cr, birdstrike on asymmetric approach to Bruggen, at Roermond, Holland 14.7.65. Cat.5 (3k).
WT325 Aw/cn 17.2.56. 213, cr after collision with Victor B(K).1A XH646 over Holt, Norfolk 19.8.68. Cat.5 (3k).

Canberra B(I)8 (30 acft)

Contract 6/Acft/6445/CB6(b). 190 acft (part). 28 Feb 1951.
Serial numbers allocated 28.2.51.
Production by English Electric Co, Preston.
Acft marked * subcontracted to and built by Short Bros.

WT326 1st prod acft f/f 8.6.55. MoS Charge 15.7.55 at Warton Aw/cn 21.7.55. A&AEE Handling Sqn 7.11.55. Cr when acft spun into ground near Salisbury, Wilts after t/o from Boscombe Down 27.11.55. Cat.5. (2k).
WT327 Aw/cn 31.8.55. BP Seighford for installation of AI Mk.23 for TSR2 dev. BP Defford 21.9.55. C(A) charge 9.12.55. Ferranti at Turnhouse for dev and flight trials 2.8.56. BP Seighford 2.4.63. for installation of FLR equipment as t/i for TSR2. Ferranti for dev and flight trials 8.2.64. RRE Pershore 12.4.66. RRE Pershore for synthetic aperture radar research 12.1.67. Nose from WK135 fitted 1969, replaced by nose from WK163 in 1971 incorporating LRMTS. F/f during April 1971. A&AEE 27.11.76. RRE 7.2.77. Flown out to RAE Bedford 25.4.77, current 8.92.

213 Squadron B(I)6 WT319 in the early silver colour scheme. Pilot on this occasion was Flying Officer N. Hargreaves.

WT328 Aw/cn 31.10.55. To C(A) charge for EE Co 31.10.55. A&AEE 6.2.56, cr into sea off Shoreham, Sussex after tailplane actuator failure 7.5.56. Cat.5.
WT329 Aw/cn 13.1.56. MoS Charge at Warton 13.1.56. Record flight London-Cairo 16.7.56. Tropical trials at Aden A&AEE Handling Sqn 12.11.56. 23 MU 5.4.57. Warton to Marshall's Cambridge for mods 27.5.57. BP Seighford 9.4.58. for sale and conv B(I)12 for RNZAF as NZ6101. Handling Sqn A&AEE for B(I)12 pilots notes 27.7.59. BP Seighford 27.8.59. Del to 23 MU 3.12.59 for del to New Zealand. (14 Sqn). Cr on overshoot at Christchurch Airport 2.11.60.
WT330 Aw/cn 31.1.56. Handling sqn. 59. 3. A&AEE for carriage and release of flares trials 4.5.62. RAF Germany 23.7.62. 3. 16. 3, cr following engine failure on take-off at Akrotiri 10.11.65. Soc 18.3.66. Cat.5.
WT331 Aw/cn 29.2.56. 88. Crash landed after losing control during asymmetric overshoot at Sharjah 5.7.59. Cat.5. Soc 14.8.59.
WT332 Aw/cn 14.2.56. 88. SF Laarbruch. 16. 3. 16. Allotted 8200M 22.5.72. Soc 6.6.72. Decoy acft at Bruggen. Removed to Nordhorn range as target '80.
WT333 Aw/cn 21.3.56. To C(A) on loan 23.3.56. To Marshall's for t/i Mk.10 auto pilot and various t/i's. RAE Armament Dept for LABS dev and flight trials 30.7.56. Marshall's for LABS mods and other t/i's. To C(A) charge 13.3.59. A&AEE 19.3.59 for rocket firing trials. Marshall's for more t/i's and major o/h. RAF Germany 13.7.65 for t/i and flight trials of drop tanks. A&AEE for flight clearance of drop tanks 7.2.66. WRE, Edinburgh Field 24.5.66 for armament trials. RRE Pershore for 'Sky Flash' guided weapon homing head dev 21.7.69. 27 MU for storage 8.9.70. RRE Pershore 24.2.72. Mod to long nose B.6 configuration in 1976 by fitting nose from WK135 modified. Flown to RAE Bedford 18.5.77, current 2.91.
WT334 Aw/cn 9.3.56. 88. 16, cr 3 miles N of Nordhorn range after bomb run 16.2.60. Cat.5 (2k). Soc 22.2.60.
WT335 Aw/cn 21.3.56. 88. Handling Sqn, 88, cr near Hochneukirch, W.Germany, 8.9.59. Soc 8.9.59.
WT336 Aw/cn 27.3.56. 88. 14. 3. 14. 3. 16. Decoy acft Gutersloh 4.72. Soc 8.6.72.
WT337 * Aw/cn 31.7.56. 88. 14. 16. 14. 16. Soc 6.6.72. Decoy acft at Bruggen until '77. To Nordhorn range as target.
WT338 Doc to India as B(I)58 IF906, del 14.2.58.
WT339 Aw/cn 29.3.56. 88. 14. 3. 16. Allotted 8198M 22.5.72. G/i at Eng Dept Cranwell 9.6.72. Soc 9.6.72. Dumped at Cranwell 2.82. Fire dump Barkston Heath '87, last noted 8.90.
WT340 * Aw/cn 28.8.56. 88. 16. MoA. 16. 3. Nea at St Athan 9.5.72. Sold to Marshall's 17.12.73. Conv B(I)58 for Peru. Tested as G-52-6, del '75 as 251.
WT341 Aw/cn 25.4.56. 88. 16. 14. 16. 3. Nea at St Athan 10.5.72. Soc 6.2.73. Little Rissington Fire Section 6.2.73.

WT342 * Aw/cn 28.9.56. 88. 3. 16. 3. 16. 3. Nea at St Athan 10.5.72. Sold to Marshall's 8.11.73. Conv B(I)68 for Peru. Tested as G-52-4, del 15.5.75 as 249.
WT343 Doc to Peru as 474, del 25.5.56. (21 Grupo). Later
WT344 Aw/cn 25.4.56. 88. 16. 88. 16. Sold to BAC 10.1.69, G27-145. Conv B(I)68 for Peru as 245, del 16.7.71. Cr in Brazil 30.6.72.
WT345 * Aw/cn 31.10.56. 59. 3. 14. 16. 14. 16. Soc 23.4.71. G/i as 8150M. Decoy at Laarbruch 13.5.71.
WT346 Aw/cn 17.5.56. 88. Loaned to MoA for A&AEE for EMC tests 21.6.62. RAF Germany 3.7.62. 88. 14. 3. 16. Allotted 8197M 22.5.72. Soc 8.6.72 and moved to Colerne museum 17.6.72. To Cosford museum 4.76, current.
WT347 * Aw/cn 31.10.56. Loan to C(A). Marshall's for t/i 13.12.56. RAE to check t/i 6.2.57. Marshall's 1.3.57. 49 MU for special fit 21.3.57. SF Wittering 30.5.57. 100 Sqn 1.6.57. A&AEE with bomb bay deflector for LABS practice bombs re bomb bay buffetting 18.3.59. C(A) loan 21.8.59. EE Co for flight trials of LABS deflector 23.8.59. A&AEE for C(A) release, practice bomb 21.9.59. BCDU Wittering 17.12.59. BCDU Finningley 1.3.60. A&AEE for LABS trials with 1650 lb and 2000 lb weapons 26.5.60. MoA loan 17.8.60. EE Co. 22.12.60. 16. 14. 3. Nea at St Athan 11.5.72. Soc 3.1.73. FFS Catterick.
WT348 Doc to Peru as 475, del 12.6.56. (21 Grupo). Later renumbered 207. W/o 8.2.72.
WT362 Aw/cn 31.5.56. 88. 14. 3. Nea at St Athan 11.5.72. Soc 23.1.73. FFS Catterick. Nose section extant 4.88.
WT363 * Aw/cn 10.1.57. 59. 3. 88. 14. 16. 14. Collided with XM278 whilst formation flying and cr near Roermond 11.6.68.
WT364 Aw/cn 31.5.56. On loan to C(A) Samlesbury 21.8.56. A&AEE radio and nav assessment 27.9.56. Marshall's for IFF Mk.10 'Orange Putter' 'G' Scope 12.3.57. A&AEE 27.8.57. Ex C(A) loan 22.5.58. 33 MU 22.5.58. 16. 59. 3. Nea at St Athan 11.5.72. Sold to Marshall's 28.11.73. Conv B(I)68 for Peru. Tested as G-52-5, del 21.7.75 as 250.
WT365 Aw/cn 15.6.56. 88. 14. 16. Nea at 23 MU 16.4.71. Soc 8.10.71. Scrapped 1.72.
WT366 * Aw/cn 16.1.57. 59. 88. 14. 16, acft stalled and crashed one mile N of Xanten, Germany 5.10.71. Cat.5 (2k). Soc 11.10.71.
WT367 Doc to Peru as 476, del 2.7.56. (21 Grupo). Cr 11.6.59(?)
WT368 Aw/cn 29.6.56. 88. 16. 88. 14. 16. 16. 3. Nea at St Athan 11.5.72. Sold to Marshall's 25.10.73. Conv B(I)68 for Peru. Tested as G-52-2, del 8.3.75 as 247.

Canberra B.6 (75 acft; 6 built, balance cancelled)

Original Contract 6/Acft/6445/CB6(b), part. 28 Feb 1951.
All 6 acft built transferred to Contract 6/Acft/5786/CB6(b). as replacements for diverted aircraft.
Serial numbers allocated 28.5.51.

Production by English Electric Co, Preston.

WT369 Aw/cn 24.12.54. Mod B.6(BS). 139. 249. Conv B.16. 6.
    ASW. 249, cr when port u/c leg collapsed on landing,
    Luqa 26.8.68. Cat.5.

WT370 Aw/cn 20.12.54. 617. 139. 249. Conv B.15. 45,
    cr on overshoot from roller landing Kuantan, Malaya
    23.9.64.

WT371 Aw/cn 7.1.55. Mod B.6(BS). 139, cr short of r/w on
    asymmetric approach to Nicosia 6.11.56. Cat.5 (3k).

WT372 Aw/cn 14.1.55. Mod B.6(BS). 139. 12. 139. 6. Conv B.16.
    6. Cat.4R 10.5.66. Soc 23.8.66.

WT373 Aw/cn 11.3.55. Mod B.6(BS). SF Binbrook. 139. 6. Conv
    B.16. 6. 249(?). ASW. Sold to BAC 5.8.69, G27-173.
    Conv B.66 for India as IF1027.

WT374 Aw/cn 10.2.55. Mod B.6(BS) Marshall's Cambridge,
    testing application of mods to B.6(BS) 16.2.55. 15 MU
    22.7.56. 139. SF Binbrook. 139. 249. Conv B.16. 249. 6.
    Sold to BAC 20.2. 69. Scrapped at Samlesbury '75.

WT375 to WT387 - cancelled.

WT397 to WT422 - cancelled.

WT440 to WT469 - cancelled.

Canberra T.4 (20 acft; 18 built, 2 cancelled)
Contract 6/Acft/6445/CB6(b). 190 acft (part). 28 Feb 51.
Serial numbers allocated 28.5.51.
Production by English Electric Co, Preston.

WT475 F/f 26.2.55. Aw/cn 28.2.55. SF Binbrook. SF Waddington.
    231 OCU. 1 Gp Comms Flt. 231 OCU. Soc 25.5.67 at
    Marshall's. 71 MU dump 7.67 at B/u at Bicestor

WT476 Aw/cn 18.3.55. SF Waddington. 231 OCU. 90 Gp
    (loan?). Sold to BAC 27.3.68, G27-121. Conv T.64 for
    Argentina as B111, del 26.2.71. (1 Sqn).

WT477 Aw/cn 31.3.55. SF Wyton. BCHU, cr out of cloud
    during approach, 2.5 miles E of Hemswell 13.6.58.
    Cat.5 (3k).

WT478 Aw/cn 31.3.55. Del 15 MU 7.4.55. 231 OCU. SF Akrotiri.
    39. 13. 360. 100. 231 OCU. Painted pale blue and
    'VN799' to represent 1st prototype for 40th
    anniversary event, 13/14.5.89. Cleaned 17.5.89 and
    reverted to correct serial and standard colour
    scheme, as BA/231 OCU. Open storage at Wyton 9.91
    and 23.1.92.

WT479 Aw/cn 15.4.55. SF Upwood. SF Wildenrath. 88. 17. 14.
    Soc at St Athan 1.1.74. To FFS Catterick.

WT480 Aw/cn 30.4.55. Del 33 MU 2.5.55. 102. CFS. 231 OCU. 7.
    13. 7. 231 OCU. 7. 360. 231 OCU, current as 'BC' 8.91.

WT481 Aw/cn 30.4.55. 13. 32. SF Akrotiri. 39, cr into sea 35
    miles SW of Malta 2.6.65. Cat.5 (3k).

WT482 Aw/cn 27.5.55. 103. SF Gutersloh. SF Wildenrath. SF
    Wahn. 17. 88. SF Bruggen. 231 OCU. 85. 231 OCU.
    Flown to Luqa 21.4.75. for Malta War Museum Soc
    6.1.76. Not displayed and acft scrapped at Hal Far
    12.82. Nose section to Wyton by 7.82. Later marked
    '160 CSE'. Nose to Charlwood Sussex 21.6.89, then
    Stratford Aircraft Collection, Long Marston 9.89,
    last noted 9.90.

WT483 Aw/cn 13.6.55. 69. SF Laarbruch. 69. SF Laarbruch. 16.
    231 OCU. 39. 231 OCU. Sold to BAC 11.11.81.
    Dismantled 88. Moved to BAe Filton 10.6.88. To
    Stratford Aircraft Collection, Long Marston 3.10.88,
    last noted 9.90.

WT484 Aw/cn 24.6.55. SF Laarbruch, cr near Empel,
    Germany 10.8.56. Cat.5 (3k).

WT485 Aw/cn 30.6.55. 231 OCU. TFS West Raynham. 85. 231
    OCU. Sold to India as Q1793, del 9.9.75.

WT486 Aw/cn 30.6.55. SF Wildenrath. 88. 17. 14. SF
    Wildenrath. G/i at No.2 SoTT as 8102M 21.8.70. To
    apprentice training school 23 MU '75. Derelict by '80.
    To fire dump Belfast Airport.

WT487 Aw/cn 12.7.55. SF Wahn. 17. SF Wildenrath. 17. 231
    OCU. Sold to India as Q1794, del 20.8.75.

WT488 Aw/cn 23.8.55. CSE. 527. 245. 98. 360. SF Wyton.
    231 OCU. 360. 231 OCU. 98. 360. 231 OCU. 360. 98. 360.
    Sold to BAe 13.11.81. Dismantled '88. Nose section to
    Dunsfold 6.88. Current with fire section 5.91.

WT489 Aw/cn 31.8.55. SF Binbrook. 231 OCU, cr after t/o.
    Steeple Morden, Cambs 17.4.67. Cat.5 (3k).

WT490 Aw/cn 16.9.55. SF Wyton. 231 OCU. Soc and b/u at
    19 MU 7.7.72.

WT491 Aw/cn 23.9.55. Sold to RAAF as A84-501 and del 5.4.56.
    1(B)OCU.

WT492 Aw/cn 7.10.55. Sold to RAAF as A84-502 and del 3.5.56.
    1(B)OCU. Withdrawn from service 12.68 and
    presented to Lord Mayor of Melbourne's children's
    holiday camp at Portsea, Melbourne, S. Australia.

WT493 to WT494 - cancelled T.4

The above two views of WT327 reflect the change in profile that can occur due to the interchange of a front fuselage. The upper view was taken when in use by Ferranti's and the other at Coltishall in 1971, when with the RRE and fitted with WK135's nose! Nowadays it looks different again. *MAP*

WT331 of 88 Squadron was unfortunate enough to become 'unstuck' (or should it be 'stuck') when control was lost during an asymmetric overshoot at Sharjah 5th July 1979. It was the end for '331, as it was declared Cat.5 (unrepairable) and was struck off charge approximately five weeks later.

Canberra PR.7 (40 acft)
Contract 6/Acft/6445/CB6(b). 190 acft (part). 28 Feb 1951.
Serial numbers allocated 28.5.51.
Production by English Electric Co.
WT503 F/f 1.10.54. Aw/cn 29.10.54. 58. BP Seighford for Decca
Mk.8. equipment 23.5.60. A&AEE flight trials 20.3.61.
BP Seighford t/i mod F95 cameras 6.7.61. 58.
A&AEE camera bay heating system investigation
19.8.63. 58. Marshall's t/i survey cameras 21.3.66. 58.
Soc at St Athan 1.10.71 and b/u.
WT504 Aw/cn 29.10.54. 58. 100. 58. Cr 11.5 miles NNE of
Wyton 24.10.60, following total loss of electrics. Cat.5.
WT505 Aw/cn 30.11.54. 58. Cr into high ground near Calder
Bridge, Cumberland 20.1.56. Cat.5 (2k).
WT506 Aw/cn 30.11.54. 58. Sold to EE Co 16.11.62. Conv
PR.57 for India as BP745.
WT507 Aw/cn 10.12.54. 58. 527. 58. A&AEE. 58. 17. 31.
Allotted 8131M at 431 MU Bruggen for G/i at
Wildenrath 11.3.71, ntu. G/i at No.1 SOTT Halton as
8548M 24.3.77. B/u '82. Nose to 384 (ATC) Sqn at
Mansfield, other parts to PEE Foulness. Sold for scrap
12.90.
WT508 Aw/cn 10.12.54. 31. 13, destroyed in hangar fire after
EOKA bomb attack, Akrotiri 27.11.57. Cat.5.
WT509 Aw/cn 31.12.54. Del to 45 MU 24.1.55. 31. 17. 80. 58.
A&AEE Radio trials 12.11.74. 23 MU 21.2.75. 13. 100
as 'CG' 8.91. Reported transferred to 1 PRU by 23.1.92.
WT510 Aw/cn 31.12.54. 31. 80. 31. To RN charge 15.2.71.
Conv T.22(P) f/f 28.6.73. BAC. A&AEE for T.22 release
30.8.73. FRADU. To St Athan store 16.7.85, current
5.91.
WT511 Aw/cn 31.12.54. 31, hit trees and cr after double
engine failure at low level, 5 miles NW of Munster,
Germany 8.11.61. Cat.5 (2k).
WT512 Aw/cn 28.1.55. 58. 100. 58. Allotted 8093M 20.3.70.
Decoy acft at Wildenrath.
WT513 Aw/cn 31.1.55. 31. 17. 31. Allotted 8065M 30.4.70.
Decoy acft at Laarbruch.
WT514 Aw/cn 11.2.55. 31. 80. 31. Allotted 8132M by 431 MU
Bruggen 11.3.71. Decoy acft at Wildenrath.
WT515 Aw/cn 31.3.55. 31. EE Co. 31. MoS at Seighford for t/i
mods 12.11.59. RAF Germany 21.3.60. 31. BP Seighford
for t/i mods 21.6.63. RAF Germany 31.1.64. 31. Wing
hit refueller when acft was being marshalled at
Ingolstadt, Germany 2.5.66, Cat.5. Soc 9.5.66.
Laarbruch fire dump.
WT516 Aw/cn 31.3.55. 80. 31. 17. 31. Allotted 8068M 30.4.70.
Decoy acft at Laarbruch.
WT517 Aw/cn 31.3.55. 80. Soc at 15 MU 2.11.70 and ss.
WT518 Aw/cn 31.3.55. 31. 80. 31. Allotted 8133M at 431 MU
Bruggen for G/i at Wildenrath 11.3.71, ntu. Storage at
St Athan. Allotted 8691M as G/i at CTTS St Athan
30.4.81. Dismantled at St Athan. Rear fuselage to
Wales Air Museum July '83.
WT519 Aw/cn 15.4.55. Del to 33 MU 19.4.55. 31. MoD(PE).
A&AEE flight trials 10.7.73. 60 MU 23.11.73. . 13. 100
as 'CH' 8.91. In open storage at Wyton 23.1.92.

**Even the Upwood Station Flight T.4 WT479 had
acquired in-theatre 'Suez stripes' when it visited
Nicosia in December 1956.** *Malcolm Freestone*

WT520 Aw/cn 29.4.55. 80. 31. 17. 31. 17. 31. Allotted 8094M '70
ntu. Soc 18.10.71. Allotted 8184M as G/i Manby.
Moved to School of Recruit Training Swinderby 3.74.
as background for parades. Moved to fire dump area
8.91. Scrapped. Nose at Burntwood, Staffs by 11.91.
WT521 Aw/cn 29.4.55. 80. 31. Allotted 8134M 11.3.71
by 431 MU Bruggen. Decoy acft at Wildenrath.
WT522 Aw/cn 11.5.55. 80. 31. 80. Soc 27.10.69. Honington fire
dump.
WT523 Aw/cn 27.5.55. 31. 17. 31, birdstrike 25.2.71. Allotted
8135M 11.3.71 by 431 MU Bruggen. Decoy acft at
Laarbruch.
WT524 Aw/cn 27.5.55. 80. 31. Allotted 8136M 11.3.71 by
431 MU Bruggen. Decoy acft at Laarbruch.
WT525 Aw/cn 23.6.55. 80. 17. To RN charge 15.2.71.
Conv T.22. FRADU. To St Athan for store 1.3.85, on
offer for sale 5.91.
WT526 Aw/cn 27.6.55. 80, cr when acft broke up near
Gescher, Germany 20.2.58. Cat.5 (2k).
WT527 Aw/cn 30.6.55. 80. 17. BAC Warton UHF installation
4.10.65. A&AEE flight trials 15.3.66. RAF Germany
6.6.66. 31. Allotted 8137M 11.3.71 by 431 MU Bruggen.
Decoy acft at Laarbruch.
WT528 Double-Atlantic record flight 23.8.55. Aw/cn 27.9.55.
RAFFC. 'Aries V'. Sold to BAC 13.11.62. Conv PR.57
for India as BP746.
WT529 Aw/cn 12.8.55. SF West Raynham, cr after t/o. 5 miles
N of Grantham, Lincs 16.1.56. Cat.5 (2k).
WT530 Aw/cn 17.8.55. 13. 80. 58. 13, cr after engine failure on
t/o, Luqa 7.12.78. Cat.5.
WT531 Aw/cn 9.9.55. 31. 80, cr into mountain 4 miles E of
Berriedale, Caithness 2.2.66. Cat.5 (2k).
WT532 Aw/cn 23.9.55. 80. 17. 80. 13. 31. 58. SF Wyton. 13. To
BDRF Coltishall as 8728M 7.12.81. Reprieved as
WT532 17.2.82. MoD(PE). RAE Bedford. Last flight
29.2.85 (7285 hrs). G/i No.2 SoTT Cosford 1.4.86.
Allotted 8890M. On offer for sale 9.91.
WT533 Aw/cn 29.9.55. 17. 31. 17. Allotted 8066M 30.12.69.
Decoy at Gutersloh. Decoy at Wildenrath.
WT534 Aw/cn 31.10.55. 31. 80. 17. G/i at No.1 SoTT as 8549M
'77. To fire dump Halton '81. Nose to Abingdon
29.3.82 and then to 489 (ATC) Sqn, Birmingham. To
492 (ATC) Sqn, Shirley 9.87.
WT535 Aw/cn 21.10.55. 17. To RN charge 15.2.71. Conv. T.22.
FRADU. To St Athan store 17.12.84, on offer for sale
5.91.
WT536 Aw/cn 31.10.55. 17. 13. 31. 80. Allotted 8063M
19.11.69. Last flown 1.12.69 (2425 hrs). G/i at No.2
SoTT 2.12.69. 8070M allotted in error and cancelled,
on offer for sale 5.91. Cut up 8.91. Nose and tailplane
only to Bruntingthorpe 31.8.91.
WT537 Collected 29.12.55. 17. 31. 13. Sold to BAC 9.11.81.
G/g at Samlesbury 2.87.
WT538 Aw/cn 30.11.55. Del to 15 MU 2.12.55. 17. 13. 17. 80. 31.
80. 31. 13. 100 as 'CJ' 8.91. In open storage at Wyton
23.1.92.
WT539 Aw/cn 20.1.56. Doc to EE Co 11.3.57. Conv PR.57 for
India as IP986.
WT540 Aw/cn 17.1.56. 13, cr, engine failure on finals, Akrotiri
26.8.59. Cat.5.
WT541 Aw/cn 17.2.56. Doc to EE Co 17.1.57. Conv PR.57 for
India as IP988.
WT542 Aw/cn 29.3.56. Doc to EE Co 28.2.57. Conv PR.57 for
India as IP987. Used VT-EEM during 7.76.

Canberra B.2 (1 acft)
Added to Contract 6/Acft/3520/CB6(b) in 1951.
Serial number allocated 1.6.51.
Production by English Electric Co, Preston.
WV787 Aw/cn 26.8.52. AS Bitteswell 1.9.52. for Sapphire Sa.7
reheat. From RAF charge 31.5.53. BP Seighford for
mods 5.6.58. Ferranti for NA39 radar 28.10.59.
Canberra T.22 aerodynamic test-bed. FR Ltd for
installation of spray facility 6.12.73. A&AEE for
filming Jaguar and icing trials 19.7.75. To BDRF
Abingdon 23.12.83. allotted 8799M. Newark Air
Museum 10.85, current 9.91.

Canberra B.2 (1 acft)
Added to Contract 6/Acft/3520/CB6(b).
Replacement for WD991, which crashed on test flight.
Serial number allocated 29.5.52.
Production by English Electric Co, Preston.
XA536 Aw/cn 30.4.53. 50. 15. 228 OCU. Conv T.11. 228 OCU.
TFS West Raynham. 85. EE Co for t/i mods 26.2.63. 85.
RRE for S-Band Clutter measurements with standard
AI Mk.17 26.10.64. Ret to Binbrook 10.5.65. 85. Loan to
228 OCU. 85. Conv T.19. 85. 7. 100. Allotted 8605M
30.8.78. To BDRF Abingdon. 9.78. Fire dump 27.11.80.

Canberra B(I)6 (1 acft)
Added to Contract 6/Acft/6445/CB6(b). 1954.
Replacement B.6, built as B(I)6.
Serial number allocated 24.5.54.
Production by English Electric Co, Preston.
XG554 Aw/cn 29.2.56. CFE. 213. Sold to BAC 8.12.69. B/u at
Samlesbury '76.

Canberra PR.9 (9 acft)
Contract 6/Acft/11158/CB6(b). 77 acft (part). 31 July 1954.
Serial numbers allocated 21.7.54.
Contract placed with English Electric Co, Preston.
Production by Shorts Bros & Harland Ltd, Belfast.
Transferred on MoS contract 6/Acft/14027/CB6(b). Nov 1956.
XH129 F/f 27.7.58. Shorts Belfast. Aw/cn 11.9.58. EE Co
Warton for type handling 11.9.58. Cr off Lancs coast
whilst on EE Co test 9.10.58. Cat.5 (1k).
Soc 19.5.59.
XH130 Aw/cn 3.6.59. EE Co Warton 3.6.59. A&AEE 1.7.59.
Shorts Belfast performance trials 23.12.59. A&AEE
Autopilot and performance trials 25.2.60. Shorts for
mods 29.9.60. 13. Cr at Hal Far on approach to Luqa,
Malta 25.9.63. Cat.5 (2k).
XH131 Aw/cn 4.3.59. EE Co Warton for flight checking 5.3.59.
Shorts Belfast 17.3.59. EE Co Warton 30.7.59. Shorts
for engineering trials 29.9.59. Tropical trials at
Bahrein 16.12.59. EE Co/Shorts 20.1.60. A&AEE
16.2.60. Shorts 14.4.60. EE Co Warton fatigue
investigation of wing/fuselage joint 28.7.60.
Shorts for C(A) release mods 2.12.60. A&AEE for
flight trials 7.5.63. Shorts 15.8.63. Del 15 MU 2.4.64.
AHQ Malta 6.64. AHQ Akrotiri 4.11.64. AHQ Malta
11.64, ex MoA fleet charge 18.1.66. 13. 39. 1 PRU.
To Shorts for o/h 5.11.90.
XH132 Aw/cn 9.6.59. To MoS charge 31.3.60. Rebuilt as Short
SC.9. DH Props. HSD. RRE for 'Sky Flash' guided
weapon homing head dev 21.1.72. RAE 1.12.76. To
BDRF St Mawgan 24.9.86, last noted 12.91, reported
allocated for disposal.
XH133 Aw/cn 17.9.59. A&AEE day photo trials 18.4.60. Shorts
Belfast 25.7.60. A&AEE night photo trials 1.12.60.
Shorts 18.1.62. A&AEE F96 oblique cameras 18.2.63.
Shorts 26.8.63. A&AEE camera bay heating 1.1.64.
Shorts 29.7.64. A&AEE fuel pump waxing trials
11.3.65. Shorts t/i of F95, and F49 cameras 9.8.65.
BAC Warton flight trials 18.3.66. A&AEE flight trials
28.6.66. Malta for 13 Sqn 27.9.66. A&AEE 13.6.67 Malta
for 39 Sqn 12.12.67. 1 PRU. Last flew 29.6.82 (5991
hrs) to St Athan for storage. On offer for sale 9.91.
XH134 Aw/cn 9.10.59. A&AEE 9.10.59. Shorts Belfast 2.11.59.
58. 39. A&AEE for t/i's 31.12.71. RAF Wyton 22.8.73.
39. 1 PRU, current as 'AA' 8.91.
XH135 Aw/cn 23.12.59. Del Handling Sqn Boscombe Down
23.12.59. Shorts Belfast 18.3.60. Del 15 MU 2.5.61. 58.
13. 39. St Athan for store 2.82. 1 PRU, current as 'AG'
8.91.
XH136 Aw/cn 30.12.59. MoA. 58. 13. 39. A&AEE. 1 PRU.
Allotted 8782M 8.2.83. G/i at No.2 SoTT 6.83. On offer
for sale 9.91, current 6.92.
XH137 Aw/cn 31.12.59. 58. 13. 39, cr on approach to Wyton
3.5.77. Cat.5 (2k).

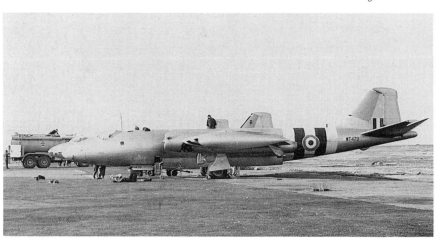

Canberra B.6 (20 acft; all later cancelled)
Contract 6/Acft/11158/CB6(b). 77 acft (part). 31 July 1954.
Serial numbers allocated 31.7.54.
Contract placed with English Electric Co, Preston.
XH138 to XH151 - cancelled B.6 production.
XH158 to XH163 - cancelled B.6 production.

Canberra PR.9 (23 acft; 14 built 9 cancelled)
Contract 6/Acft/11158/CB6(b). 77 acft (part). 31 July 1954.
Contract placed with English Electric Co, Preston.
Serials numbers allocated 31.7.54.
Production by Short Bros & Harland Ltd, Belfast,
transferred on MoS Contract 6/Acft/14027/CB6(b). Nov 1956.
Order reduced to 23 PR.9s in March 1958.
XH164 Aw/cn 31.12.59.58.13, cr on approach to Luqa 7.1.69.
Cat.5 (2k).
XH165 Aw/cn 4.3.63.58.13.39.1 PRU. St Athan store 22.9.87:
last flight (7715 hrs). On offer for sale 9.91.
XH166 Aw/cn 16.3.60.58.13.39.13.39.1 PRU. To Chile as
341 15.10.82.
XH167 Aw/cn 11.8.60.58.39.13.39.13.39.1 PRU. To Chile as
342 15.10.82.
XH168 Aw/cn 29.4.60. Del 15 MU 4.5.60.58.39.13.39. A&AEE
20.5.76,39. A&AEE 2.9.76.39. To St Athan for store
11.81.1 PRU, current as 'AB' 8.91.
XH169 Del 15 MU 4.8.60.58.39. MoD(PE).13.39.1 PRU,
current as 'AC' 8.91.
XH170 Aw/cn 29.7.60.58. MoA.39. Allotted 8739M to G/g
Wyton 7.82, current 8.91.
XH171 Aw/cn 4.8.60.58. MoA.39.13.39. Allotted 8746M. G/i
at No.2 SoTT 13.7.82, last noted 6.92.
XH172 Aw/cn 23.9.60.58.39.13, lost control and cr 3 miles
E of Akrotiri 6.10.72. Cat.5 (2k).
XH173 Aw/cn 30.9.60.58.13.39.13.39.1 PRU. To Chile as
343 15.10.82.
XH174 Aw/cn 4.10.60.58.39. Min Tech.39.13.39.1 PRU to
St Athan store 24.5.89, still there dismantled 5.91.
Cockpit section at RAE Bedford 10.91.
XH175 Aw/cn 5.10.60.58.39. Loan to A&AEE.39.1 PRU to
St Athan store 25.1.89, current 5.91.
XH176 Del 2.11.60.58.39.13.39. Det A&AEE, cr on test flight,
Chilmark, Wilts 25.5.78.
XH177 Aw/cn 30.12.60.58.13. Cat.4R 14.12.65. Re-Cat.5 (c)
7.4.66 due to cracks in main spar. Soc 5.7.67 at Luqa.
Nose at Wales Aircraft Museum, Cardiff '90.
XH178 to XH186 - cancelled.

Canberra B(I)8 (25 acft)
Contract 6/Acft/11158/CB6(b). 77 acft (part). 31 July 1954.
Serial numbers allocated 31.7.54.
Production by English Electric Co, Preston.
Acft marked * subcontracted to and built by Short Bros.
XH203 F/f 11.9.56. Doc to India as B(I)58 IF896,
del 8.58 (5 Sqn).
XH204 * Aw/cn 8.2.57.59.3. Cr when controls jammed. 8
miles NE Wesel, Germany 9.5.67.
XH205 Doc to India as B(I)58 IF897.
XH206 Doc to Peru as B(I)68 478. Del 1.7.56 (21 Grupo).
XH207 Aw/cn 12.10.56.59, cr in bad weather 3 miles S of
Sorpe dam, Germany 4.3.59. Cat.5 (2k). Soc 4.3.59.
XH208 * Aw/cn 13.3.57.59.3. Allotted 8167M and Soc 13.8.71.
Decoy acft at Bruggen.
XH209 Aw/cn 31.10.56. EE Co for t/i mod for LLBS. Sub-
contracted to Marshall's 4.1.57. C(A) loan 19.3.57.
RAE Farnborough Armament Dept 3.7.57. Marshall's
15.8.57. Ex C(A) loan, 15 MU 5.9.57.59. Handling Sqn
27.1.58.59.16. Allotted 8201M 22.5.72. Soc 8.6.72.
Decoy acft at Gutersloh.
XH227 Doc to India as B(I)58 IF899.
XH228 * Aw/cn 19.3.57.59.3. Nea at St Athan 16.5.72. Soc
22.2.73 and del to FFS Catterick.
XH229 Doc to India as B(I)58 IF900.
XH230 Doc to India as B(I)58 IF901.
XH231 * Aw/cn 11.4.59. EE Co for t/i mods sub-contracted to
Marshall's 26.4.57.33 MU 6.6.57.59. RAE Armament
Dept for 2000 lb TMB Electric system trials 27.8.57 on
C(A) loan. RAF Germany 16.9.57.59.3.88.3, cr near
Osnabruck, Germany 3.2.65. Cat.5 (2k). Soc 15.3.65.
XH232 Doc to India as B(I)58 IF902.
XH233 Doc to India as B(I)58 IF903.
XH234 * Aw/cn 30.4.57.59.3.16. Nea at St Athan 30.6.72. Sold
to Marshall's 22.1.74. Conv B(I)68 for Peru, tested as
G-52-7 and del 22.10.75 as 252.
XH235 Doc to India as B(I)58 IF904.
XH236 Doc to India as B(I)58 IF905.
XH237 Doc to India as B(I)58 IF907.
XH238 Doc to India as B(I)58 IF908, del 20.2.58.
XH239 Doc to India as B(I)58 IF909.
XH240 Doc to India as B(I)58 IF910.
XH241 Doc to India as B(I)58 IF911.
XH242 Doc to India as B(I)58 IF912.
XH243 Doc to India as B(I)58 IF913.
XH244 Doc to Venezuela, del 4.6.57 as 4A-39 (39 Sqn).

Canberra B.6 (4 acft)
Contract 6/Acft/11313/CB6(b). 1954.
Serial numbers allocated 21.9.54.
Production by English Electric Co, Preston.
XH567 Aw/cn 31.1.55. To MoA charge. RAE/ATDU trials
1956-57. RRE for SLAR dev for TSR2. Also Phantom
recce pod dev. Flown to RAE 16.12.76, current 8.92.
XH568 Aw/cn 23.2.55. To MoA charge. RAE. RRE for Sea Skua
guided weapon homing head trials. Conv to long
nose configuration during 1970 by fitting nose ex
WG788 modified. Flown to RAE 18.11.76, current 8.92.
XH569 Aw/cn 11.3.55. Mod B.6(BS). RRF. Force Landed at
Woodhurst near Wyton after engine exploded,
24.7.56. Cat.5.
XH570 Aw/cn 1.4.55. Mod to B.6(BS). 139.249. Conv B.16.
249. ASW. B/u at 5 MU and Soc 1.10.71.

Canberra T.4 (2 acft)
Contract 6/Acft/11313/CB6(b). 1954.
Serial numbers allocated 21.9.54.
Production by English Electric Co, Preston.
XH583 F/f 1.2.55. Aw/cn 2.3.55. 231 OCU. SF Bruggen.
SF Laarbruch. 231 OCU. SF Larbruch. Sold to BAe
10.81, G27-374. Conv T.94 for Argentina, ready for del
4.82 but not del because of Falklands war. Stored
dismantled at Samlesbury. Scrapped 1988. Nose only
to North East Aircraft Museum, Usworth.
XH584 Aw/cn 18.3.55. 231 OCU. Soc at Bassingbourn 12.7.66
- out of fatigue life.

Canberra B(I)6 (2 acft)
Contract 6/Acft/5786/CB6(b). 215 acft (part). 20 Sept 1950.
Replacements for WJ779 and WJ784 diverted off contract.
Serial numbers allocated 7.10.54.
Production by English Electric Co, Preston.
XJ249 Aw/cn 29.3.56. 213, cr into a ridge at Silberhorn, Hartz
mts, Germany 30.12.57. Cat.5 (3k).
XJ257 Aw/cn 30.4.56. 213, u/c jammed up so wheels-up
Ahlhorn, Germany 9.4.57.

**A lovely portrait of XH135 'AG' of 1 PRU, in the
latest 'Hemp' colour scheme, circa 1988.**

Canberra PR.9 (11 acft; all later cancelled)
Contract 6/Acft/12164/CB(6). Placed 1955.
Serial numbers allocated 25.5.55.
Contract placed with English Electric Co, Preston.
Transferred to Short Bros & Harland. Later cancelled.
XK440 to XK443 - cancelled.
XK467 to XK473 - cancelled.

Canberra B.6 (1 acft)
Contract 6/Acft/12265/CB6(b) - (part). Placed 1955.
Serial number allocated 30.6.55.
Production by English Electric Co, Preston.
XK641 F/f 3.5.56. Aw/cn 11.5.56. SF Binbrook. 12. Conv B.15.
    45, cr after loss of control, hit high ground at Taseh
    Chini, Pahang, Malaya 4.4.66. Cat.5 (3k).

Canberra T.4 (2 acft)
Contract 6/Acft/12265/CB6(b) - (part). Placed 1955.
Serial numbers allocated 30.6.55.
Production by English Electric Co, Preston.
XK647 Doc to India as T.4 IQ994, del 4.58.
XK650 Doc to India as T.4 IQ995, del 4.58.

Canberra B(I)8 (3 acft)
Contract 6/Acft/6445/CB6(b) - (part).
Serial numbers allocated 21.12.55.
Replacements, added to contract 21 December 1955.
Production by English Electric Co, Preston.
XK951 Aw/cn 21.9.56. 88. 14. 16. 3. Nea at St Athan 30.6.72.
    Sold to Marshall's 22.6.73. Conv B(I)68 for Peru, test
    flown as G-52-3, del 15.4.75 as 248.
XK952 Aw/cn 31.8.56. 59.3. C(A) loan 24.3.63. A&AEE EMC
    trials 27.3.63, RAF Germany 9.4.63. 3. 16. MoA loan
    28.11.66. Ret 16 Sqn 31.3.67. 14. 16. Nea at St Athan
    16.5.72. To FFS Manston 6.4.73. Last noted at 71 MU,
    Bicester 4.4.73.
XK953 Doc to India as B(I)58 IF895.

Canberra B(I)8 (1 acft)
Contract 6/Acft/11158/CB6(b) - (part).
Replacement, added to contract 21 December 1955.
XK959 Doc to India as B(I)58 IF898.

Canberra T.4 (2 acft, both cancelled)
Contract 6 Acft/12265/CB6(b) - (part).
Replacement for XK647/XK650, added to contract 5 Feb 57.
Serial numbers allocated 5.2.57.
Intended production by English Electric Co, Preston.
XM228 and XM229 - cancelled by MoS. Sold by EE Co to
    Venezuela as 1E-39 and 2E-39.

**213 Squadron B(I)6 XJ257 in a spot of bother at
Valkenburg following an engine failure on take
off. Pilot was Fg Off Norman Hargreaves.**

**B.6 XK641 reveals an early 12 Squadron fin
marking at Binbrook in 1959.** *D.S.Glover*

Canberra B(I)8 (2 acft)
Contract 6/Acft/6445/CB6(b) - (part).
Replacements added to contract 5 February 1957.
Serial numbers allocated 5.2.57.
Production by English Electric Co, Preston.
XM244 Aw/cn 15.8.58. 16. 3. 16. 3. 16. Allotted 8202M 22.5.72.
    Soc at Laarbruch 8.6. 72. Decoy at Gutersloh. Fire
    dump 5.79, remains there 1990.
XM245 Aw/cn 29.8.58. BP Seighford 'Blue Silk' (Decca Mk.8)
    installation 17.9.58. A&AEE 1.9.59 for assessment of
    t/i. BP Seighford for further t/i 26.11.59. A&AEE
    22.3.61. BP Seighford 13.4.61 more t/i. EE Co for
    reconditioning 3.12.63. Aw/cn 18.6.64. 14. Marshall's
    for t/i 12.5.65. MoA loan 14.5.65. A&AEE for C(A)
    release trials 24.6.65. Marshall's 10.9.65 for further t/i.
    RAF Germany 21.3.66. 3. 16. Soc at Laarbruch 6.6.72.
    To Nordhorn range for use as target.

Canberra B(I)8 (18 acft)
Contract 6/Acft/11158/CB6(b) - (part).
Replacements added to contract 5 February 1957.
Serial numbers allocated 5.2.57.
Production by English Electric Co, Preston.
XM262 Aw/cn 19.9.58. 16. 3. Nea at St Athan 16.5.72. Soc
    23.3.73. To FFS Catterick.
XM263 Aw/cn 30.9.58. 16. 3. Nea at St Athan 30.6.72. Sold to
    Marshall's 13.3.74. Conv B(I)68 for Peru, test flown as
    G-52-10, del 10.77 as 255.
XM264 Aw/cn 31.10.58. 16. 3. 14. 16. Soc at Laarbruch 19.6.72.
    Allotted 8227M. Decoy acft at Laarbruch, preserved
    at Laarbruch 11.80, also noted 8.89. At Hermeskeil
    Museum, Germany by 10.91.
XM265 Aw/cn 23.10.58. 16. Marshall's for t/i of sub-miniature
    radio 10.3.64. A&AEE 19.10.64 for flight trials of radio
    compass t/i. RAF Germany 30.11.64. 16. Allotted
    8199M 22.5.72. Soc at Laarbruch 6.6.72. Decoy acft at
    Bruggen, last noted 4.88.
XM266 Aw/cn 31.10.58. 59. 3. cr 2 miles E of Tiverton, Devon
    21.11.61. Cat.5 (2k). Soc 22.11.61.
XM267 Aw/cn 31.10.58. 16. 3, cr on approach to Akrotiri
    15.12.70. Cat.5 (2k). Soc 1.4.71.
XM268 Aw/cn 12.12.58. 16. 3. Nea at St Athan 16.5.72. Soc
    8.3.73. FFS Catterick.
XM269 Aw/cn 21.11.58. SF Wildenrath. 88. 14. 16. Soc at
    Laarbruch 6.6.72. To Nordhorn for use as a target.
XM270 Aw/cn 12.12.58. 88. 16, cr on approach, Gutersloh
    5.6.66. Cat.5 (1k). Soc 5.6.66.
XM271 Aw/cn 30.12.58. 59. 3. MoD for t/i of PTR175 14.4.65.
    Marshall's for t/i 30.4.65. RAF Germany 14.9.65. 3. 16.
    Allotted 8204M 14.6.72. Soc 21.6.72. G/i at No.9 SoTT
    21.6.72. G/i at No.1 SoTT 6.2.74. Removed during '81.
    Fuselage to PEE Foulness 4.81. Sold for scrap 12.90.
XM272 Aw/cn 5.1.59. SF Wildenrath. 88. 14. A&AEE for
    armament trials 16.7.63. Ret to 14 Sqn 26.7.63.
    Further trials at A&AEE 12.8.63. Ret to 14 Sqn 23.8.63.
    (see XM275). 16. Soc 20.6.72. Marham for fire fighting.
XM273 Aw/cn 19.1.59. 88. 14. 3. Nea at St Athan 30.6.72. Sold
    to Marshall's 7.2.74. Conv B(I)68 for Peru. Test flown
    as G-52-8 and del 25.11.75 as 253.

XM274 Aw/cn 24.2.59. SF Bruggen. 3. 16. Soc at Laarbruch
    24.8.71. Allotted 8170M 26.8.71. Decoy acft at
    Laarbruch.
XM275 Aw/cn 6.3.59. SF Laarbruch. 16. A&AEE for Leapus
    flare trials 4.7.63. Ret to 16 Sqn 26.7.63. A&AEE for
    further trials 12.8.63. Ret to 16 Sqn 23.8.63. (Also see
    XM272). 16. 3. 16. Wattisham for fire fighting 19.6.72.
    Soc at Wattisham 20.6.72.
XM276 Aw/cn 6.2.59. C(A) loan 26.2.59. RAE for IBS trials
    26.2.59. EE Co for mods 28.3.60. 59.3. MoA loan
    26.9.66. Marshall's t/i harness restraints 26.9.66. RAF
    Germany 29.11.66. 3. Allotted 8178M 8.10.71 -
    cancelled. Nea at St Athan 16.5.72. Sold to Marshall's
    18.4.74. Conv B(I)68 for Peru. Test flown 23.11.77 as
    G-52-11 and del 28.1.78 as 256.
XM277 Aw/cn 27.2.59. SF Geilenkirchen. 88. 14. 3. 16. Soc
    23.6.72. Flown to Chivenor for FFS 28.6.72. Ss 10.1.75.
XM278 Aw/cn 27.2.59. 16. 14. 3. Nea at St Athan 16.5.72.
    Sold to Marshall's 3.4.74. Conv B(I)68 for Peru. Test
    flown as G-52-12 and del 5.7.78 as 757.
XM279 Aw/cn 26.3.59. 16. 3. Nea at St Athan 16.5.72. Sold to
    Marshall's 19.3.74. B/u for spares at Cambridge for
    B(I)68 contract.

Canberra B(I)8 (1 acft)
Contract KD/E/01/CB6(b) - (part). 5 March 1958.
Replacement for WT329 (to New Zealand as NZ6101).
Serial number allocated 5.3.58.
Production by English Electric Co, Preston.
XM936 Aw/cn 31.3.59. 59. 3. Nea at St Athan 30.6.72. Sold to
    Marshall's 11.2.74. Conv B(I)68 for Peru. Test flown
    as G-52-9 and del 27.1.76 as 254.

Canberra B(I)8 (2 acft)
Original Contract KD/E/01/CB6(b) - (part). 5 March 1958.
Contract Revised to KC/2R/Q8/CB9(c).
Serial numbers allocated 5.1.60. Doubtful whether ever worn.
Production from spares by English Electric Co, Preston.
XP289 Doc for RNZAF as B(I)12 NZ6110.
    Aw/cn 30.3.61. To RNZAF 18.5.61.
XP290 Doc for RNZAF as B(I)12 NZ6111.
    Aw/cn 14.4.61. To RNZAF 26.5.61.

SUMMARY OF CANBERRA PRODUCTION

UK built:		
	631	by English Electric Co.
	144	by Short Bros & Harland
	75	by Avro
	75	by Handley Page
	925	of which:
		9 were prototypes
		773 were for RAF/MoD
		143 were for export
Licence built:	48	Australia
	403	USA
	1376	Total

CANBERRA CONSTRUCTION NUMBERS

Canberras built by English Electric Co had no constructor's
number as such, but had a forward fuselage number, which
is often quoted as a construction number.

However, because front fuselages complete with the
cockpit assembly were changed from time to time, i.e. during
a refurbishing programme or a conversion such as a B.2
to a T.4, the number for a given airframe would change
accordingly. The forward fuselage numbers for EE Co built
Canberras were in the 71xxx series starting with 71001 for
the prototype VN799.

Aircraft built by A.V. Roe initially carried an Avro build
number, commencing with 6596 for their first B.2 WJ971.
These numbers were also carried on the nose portion of the
airframe but were not sequential with the serial numbers.

Handley Page B.2's had production numbers from HP151B
for WJ564 through to HP225B for WJ682, in sequence with
the allocated serial numbers. Short Bros & Harland production commenced at SH1610 for WH853 (their first B.2)
whilst SH1741 was their last PR.9, XH177.

However, as there was complete interchangeability of the
forward fuselage, an EE Co airframe could, for example, have
another manufacturers nose fitted during rebuild, thus,
there is no reliability on any of these nose numbers so far as
identifying a particular airframe is concerned.

Appendix Eight

British Mark Conversions

The aircraft of the British air arms are usually acquired as a result of manufacturers responding to a specification that originates as an Air Staff Requirement. Sometimes this results in a completely new aircraft, but on many occasions the requirement is met by a new variant of an existing design. The Canberra has proved to be a most suitable vehicle for adaptation to new roles and as a result, over the years, many have been modified to an extent that justified the creation of a new 'Mark' number.

B.2 to T.4

16 aircraft conversion programme for RAF.
EE built T.4 front fuselages. Most if not all, fitted by Short Bros & Harland Ltd, Belfast.

WD944	WD954	WD963	WE111	WE118	WH637
WH651	WH659	WH706	WH854	WH861	WJ566
WJ566	WJ568	WJ617	WJ991	WJ992	

3 more converted for Rhodesia: WH658 WH674 WJ613

B.2 to B.8

2 aircraft fitted with Mk.8 fronts (no Mk.8 operational equipment or gunpacks) for convenience of development radar fitment.
WJ643 (Ferranti) WV787 (A&AEE)

B.2 to U.10 (later D.10)

18 aircraft converted by Short Bros & Harland Ltd, Belfast.

WD929	WD951	WD961	WH652	WH705	WH710
WH729	WH733	WH742	WH860	WH885	WJ604
WJ621	WJ623	WJ624	WJ987	WK107	WK110

B.2 to T.11

Trials installation by Boulton Paul on WJ734.
8 true conversions for RAF use. Boulton Paul built the front fuselages by converting other B.2 noses – fitted by MUs.

WH714	WH724	WH903	WH904	WJ610	WJ975
WK106	XA536				

B.2 to U.14 (later D.14)

6 aircraft converted by Short Bros & Harland Ltd, Belfast.
WD941 WH704 WH720 WH876 WH921 WJ638

B.2 to T.17

24 aircraft converted by EECo Ltd, at Preston.

WD955	WF890	WF916	WH646	WH664	WH665
WH740	WH863	WH872	WH874	WH902	WJ565
WJ576	WJ581	WJ607	WJ625	WJ630	WJ633
WJ977	WJ981	WJ986	WJ988	WK102	WK111

B.2 to TT.18

18 aircraft converted initially by EECo Ltd, Preston and delivered 1968/69 (those in italics for Royal Navy, others for RAF).

WH718	WH856	*WH887*	WJ629	WJ632	*WJ636*
WJ639	WJ680	WJ682	WJ715	*WJ717*	WJ721
WK118	WK122	*WK123*	WK124	*WK126*	WK127

4 further conversions by EECo, delivered 1974.
WE122 *WJ574* *WJ614* *WK142*
1 conversion by Flight Refuelling Ltd, about 1975 – WK143.

B.2 to B(TT)2

Unofficial designation but quite commonly used for any aircraft modified to tow targets of various types.
WD948 WE113 WH666 WJ640 WJ753 WK162 WP515

B.2 to B.2E

A&AEE special radio fit for solo flying. Unofficial designation.
WK164

B.6 to B.6 (mod)

Local modifications at RRE based on T.11 type front fuselage.
WH945 WH953 WH946

B.6 to B.6 (BS)

Modifications by Boulton Paul Ltd. Blue Shadow equipment.

WJ767	WJ769	WJ770	WJ771	WJ772	WJ773
WJ774	WJ776	WJ777	WJ778	WJ780	WJ781
WJ782	WJ783	WT302	WT303	WT304	WT306
WT369	WT371	WT372	WT373	WT374	XH569
XH570					

4 aircraft modified as ELINT 'Listeners' for 51 Sqn.
WJ768 WJ775 WT301 WT305

B.6 to B.15

Trials installation by Marshall's of Cambridge on WH967
38 production conversions by Bristol Aeroplane Co. at Filton and some by EECo Ltd, Samlesbury.

WH947	WH948	WH954	WH955	WH956	WH957
WH958	WH959	WH960	WH961	WH963	WH964
WH965	WH966	WH967	WH968	WH969	WH970
WH971	WH972	WH973	WH974	WH977	WH981
WH983	WH984	WJ756	WJ760	WJ762	WJ764
WJ766	WT205	WT208	WT209	WT210	WT211
WT213	WT370	XK641			

B.6(BS) to B.16

1 trials installation conversion by Marshall's.
19 production conversions by Marshall's of Cambridge.

WJ770	WJ771	WJ773	WJ774	WJ776	WJ777
WJ778	WJ780	WJ781	WJ782	WJ783	WT302
WT303	WT306	WT369	WT372	WT373	WT374
XH570					

Ferranti Flying Unit's WJ643 at Turnhouse. It has had a B.8 front fuselage fitted and AI.Mk.23 (Lightning) radar for system trials. *via C. J. Salter*

Canberra U.10 WJ621 basks in the sun at Luqa in 1960. *MAP*

PR.7 to T.22

7 aircraft converted by BAC at Preston.
WH780 WH797 WH801 WH803 WT510 WT525 WT535

B(I)8 to B.6

2 Establishment aircraft reworked for trials use, not to full B.6 operational standard – just front fuselages.
WT327 WT333

T.11 to T.19

Removal of radar equipment from 8 T.11s.

WH714	WH724	WH903	WH904	WJ610	WJ975
WK106	XA536				

U.10 to U.14

Conversion by RAE Llanbedr.
WJ624

D.14 to B.2

Converted back to B.2 by RRE.
WJ638

D.14 to B.2

1 aircraft eventually converted back to near B.2 by A&AEE.
WH876

B.15 to E.15

Electronic fit to 8 B.15 aircraft.

WH948	WH957	WH964	WH972	WH973	WH981
WH983	WJ756				

T.17 to T.17A

Change of electronic fit to 6 aircraft by BAe Samlesbury.
WD955 was t/i aircraft, then to full standard. Others –
WH646 WH902 WJ607 WJ633 WJ981

Appendix Nine

Instructional Airframe Numbers and 'Class B' Markings

INSTRUCTIONAL AIRFRAME NUMBERS

Since 1921, RAF airframes and engines used for instructional purposes have been organised into a simple numerical sequence for each, with 'M' and 'E' suffix letters respectively to denote the series. The FAA have used a similar system since 1942, albeit with an 'A' (for aircraft) prefix.

The allocation of a 'M' number (sometimes referred to as a 'Maintenance' or 'Ground Instructional' serial) usually meant that the aircraft was grounded thereafter, although, almost inevitably, there have been the odd exceptions.

There follows a listing of known 'M' numbers allocated to RAF Canberras, together with the relevant service serial, issue dates (where known) and comments.

Serial	P/i	Issue date	Remarks
7158M	ex WJ765	8.11.54	No. 10 SoTT Melksham.
7379M	ex WD999	17.10.56	1 SoTT Halton - cancelled see 7387M.
7380M	ex WF907	17.10.56	1 SoTT Halton - cancelled see 7386M.
7386M	ex WF907	27.11.56	1 SoTT Halton.
7387M	ex WD999	27.11.56	1 SoTT Halton.
7460M	ex WD958	16.7.57	Allotted to No. 2 Radio School Yatesbury, ntu (not taken up).
7546M	ex WJ769	26.11.57	Allotted at Binbrook - front fuselage only.
7589M	ex WD936	25.9.58	1 Radio School Locking.
7590M	ex WH668	30.9.58	4 SoTT St Athan.
7611M	ex WD937	23.9.59	ntu.
7620M	ex WD959	20.10.59	RAE. To Melksham.
7623M	ex WH735	1.12.59	2 Radio School, Yatesbury.
7628M	ex WH723	8.1.60	Weedon. To Upwood Gate as 'WJ642', April '66.
7631M	ex VX185	9.2.60	4 SoTT St Athan.
7636M	ex WJ878		1 SoTT Halton.
7637M	ex WF887	2.6.60	CSE Watton.
7656M	ex WJ573	20.10.60	RAF Tech College, Henlow.
7657M	ex WH695	20.10.60	1 SoTT Halton.
7658M	ex WH884	20.10.60	1 SoTT Melksham.
7659M	ex WH701	8.9.60	4 SoTT St Athan.
7764M	ex WD990	10.62	Colerne.
7796M	ex WJ676	13.12.62	12 SoTT Melksham.
7802M	ex WD996	12.3.63	Little Rissington.
7828M	ex WF908	7.2.64	Non destructive training, Manston.
7843M	ex WE145	13.4.64	School of Photography Cosford. Remarked WE143 24.6.68, later corrected to WE145. See 8450M & 8597M.

B.2 7913M, alias WK132, at No.1 SoTT Halton in 1968. Note the local code '6'. *MAP*

7912M	ex WK131	24.5.66	1 SoTT Halton.
7913M	ex WK132	24.5.66	1 SoTT Halton.
7914M	ex WK134	24.5.66	1 SoTT Halton.
8015M	ex WH965	13.5.68	
8049M	ex WE168	26.6.69	FFS. Manston.
8063M	ex WT536	21.11.69	2 SoTT Cosford. See 8070M.
8065M	ex WT513	15.10.69	Decoy at Wildenrath.
8066M	ex WT533	15.10.69	Decoy at Gutersloh.
8067M	ex WH802	15.10.69	Decoy at Bruggen.
8068M	ex WT516	15.10.69	Decoy at Laarbruch.
8069M	ex WT314	15.10.69	Decoy at Bruggen.
8070M	ex WT536		Allotted in error. See 8063M. Reallotted to Spitfire V EP120.
8093M	ex WT512	20.4.70	Decoy at Wildenrath.
8094M	ex WT520	20.4.70	At Manby. Cancelled 29.12.70. See 8184M.
8095M	ex WH792	20.4.70	
8101M	ex WH984	6.8.70	2 SoTT Cosford.
8102M	ex WT486	20.8.70	2 SoTT Cosford.
8126M	ex WH804	8.1.71	
8127M	ex WJ724	.71	Wroughton, ntu.
8128M	ex WH775	11.3.71	Allotted at Bruggen for G/i at Wildenrath, but acft o/h and reverted to WH775 1976. See 8868M.
8129M	ex WH779	11.3.71	Allotted at Bruggen for G/i at Wildenrath, but acft o/h and reverted to WH779 1975.
8130M	ex WH798	.71	Decoy at Bruggen.
8131M	ex WT507	11.3.71	At Wildenrath, ntu. See 8548M.
8132M	ex WT514	11.3.71	Decoy at Wildenrath.
8133M	ex WT518		Decoy at Wildenrath, ntu. See 8691M.
8134M	ex WT521	11.3.71	Decoy at Wildenrath.
8135M	ex WT523	11.3.71	Decoy at Laarbruch.
8136M	ex WT524	11.3.71	Decoy at Laarbruch.
8137M	ex WT527	11.3.71	Decoy at Laarbruch.
8150M	ex WT345	23.4.71	
8165M	ex WH791		At St Athan, ntu. See 8176M and 8187M.
8167M	ex XH208	13.8.71	Decoy at Bruggen.
8170M	ex XM274	26.8.71	Decoy at Laarbruch.
8176M	ex WH791		At St Athan, ntu. See 8165M and 8187M.
8178M	ex XM276	8.10.71	ntu. See G52-11 (Class B).
8184M	ex WT520	18.10.71	Manby. See 8094M.
8185M	ex WH946		Pontrilas Army Training area.
8187M	ex WH791		Cottesmore Gate Guard. See 8165M and 8176M.
8197M	ex WT346	22.5.72	Colerne Museum.
8198M	ex WT339	22.5.72	Engineering Dept, Cranwell.
8199M	ex XM265	22.5.72	Decoy at Bruggen.
8200M	ex WT332	22.5.72	Decoy at Bruggen.

8201M	ex XH209	22.5.72	Decoy at Gutersloh.
8202M	ex XM244	22.5.72	Decoy at Gutersloh.
8204M	ex XM271	14.6.72	Cottesmore.
8227M	ex XM264	6.72	Decoy at Laarbruch.
8344M	ex WH960	3.1.73	2 SoTT Cosford.
8350M	ex WH840		Locking Gate Guard.
8369M	ex WE139		RAF Museum Hendon.
8440M	ex WD935		St Athan.
8450M	ex WE145		ntu. See 7843M and 8597M.
8451M	ex WJ611		23 MU Aldergrove, ntu.
8490M	ex WH703	29.3.76	Marham.
8491M	ex WJ880	.76	1 SoTT Halton.
8492M	ex WJ872	.76	1 SoTT Halton.
8504M	ex WK106	.76	Marham, ntu.
8511M	ex WT305	15.11.76	Wyton.
8515M	ex WH869	1.2.77	Abingdon.
8530M	ex WD948	.77	Manston, ntu.
8548M	ex WT507	24.3.77	1 SoTT Halton. See 8131M.
8549M	ex WT534	.77	1 SoTT Halton.
8581M	ex WJ775	.77	CSDE Swanton Morley.
8584M	ex WH903	.77	
8597M	ex WE145		Fire Dump Wyton. See 8450M and 7843M.
8605M	ex XA936		Abingdon.
8643M	ex WJ867		Newton.
8652M	ex WH794	7.80	Abingdon.
8664M	ex WJ603	15.12.80	Wattisham.
8668M	ex WJ821	13.1.81	Bassingbourn.
8683M	ex WJ870	16.4.81	St Mawgan.
8689M	ex WK144	21.4.81	GD School St Athan.
8691M	ex WT518	30.4.81	CTTS St Athan. Fuselage only.
8693M	ex WH863	.81	Marham.
8695M	ex WJ817	9.6.81	Wyton.
8696M	ex WH773	9.6.81	2331 ATC Sqn Wyton.
8697M	ex WJ825	11.6.81	Abingdon.
8722M	ex WJ640	6.11.81	2 SoTT Cosford.
8728M	ex WT532	7.12.81	Crash Rescue Training, Coltishall, ntu. (Rescinded and reallotted 17.2.82). See 8890M.
8729M	ex WJ815	8.12.81	Crash Rescue Training Coningsby.
8735M	ex WJ681	8.1.82	Crash Rescue Trng, Brawdy.
8739M	ex XH170	.82	Gate Guard Wyton.
8740M	ex WE173	.82	Crash Rescue Training Coltishall.
8742M	ex WH856	3.82	BDR Abingdon.
8746M	ex XH171	.82	2 SoTT Cosford.
8747M	ex WJ629	15.3.82	Crash Rescue Training Chivenor.
8755M	ex WJ637	.82	Cranwell ground display as 'WH699'.
8761M	ex WJ977	1.12.82	Crash Rescue Training Wyton.
8762M	ex WH740		2 SoTT Cosford.
8763M	ex WH665		2 SoTT Cosford.
8780M	ex WK102		2 SoTT Cosford.
8782M	ex XH136	8.2.83	2 SoTT Cosford.
8799M	ex WV787	23.12.83	BDRF Abingdon.
8864M	ex WJ628	11.85	BDRF Abingdon.
8868M	ex WH775	11.85	g/i Cosford.
8869M	ex WH957	11.85	g/i Cosford.
8870M	ex WH964	11.85	g/i Cosford.
8871M	ex WJ565	11.85	g/i Cosford.
8887M	ex WK162	.86	Crash Rescue Training Wyton.
8890M	ex WT532	.86	g/i No. 2 SoTT Cosford. See 8728M.
8914M	ex WH844	17.9.86	BDR Abingdon, ntu.
8985M	ex WK127	.89	BDR Wyton.
9052M	ex WJ717	.90	4 SoTT St Athan.
9093M	ex WK124	.91	MoD Fire School, Manston.

'CLASS B' MARKINGS

'Class B' registration marks are allocated for a variety of reasons, including for experiment or test. Since 1948, Class B markings have consisted of the nationality letter (G for the UK) linked to the manufacturers identity number and in turn to an individual airframe number (e.g. G-27-1).

Although G-27 was allocated to the English Electric Company soon after the 'B' system was introduced, it was March 1967 before G27-1 was used on Lightning F.52 659 for Saudi Arabia. The system continued in use until 1985: G27-405 being the last. Since then export aircraft have done all their flying in air forces markings. Note that EECo always applied the Class B markings in the form G27-xxx, in contrast to the more usual G-27-xxx style.

The Class B markings were mainly used on Canberras intended for export. Application of the markings varied: sometimes it would be for a ferry flight following its re-purchase from the RAF by the manufacturers; more often it was done later, following an inspection and allocation to a particular refurbishing and/or remanufacturing programme.

The markings were either worn solely (i.e. when the aircraft was adorned in a primer paint scheme), in place of or in conjunction with a former military user serial or an intended user serial. The markings often continued to be worn for test flying prior to delivery. The first Canberra to use the 'B' system was G27-3 (ex-WH732), for stores clearance flying in March 1967, prior to delivery to Venezuela as 1529.

Details of the Class B markings known to have been applied to Canberras are as follows. The column headed 'Date' indicates when the 'B' system marking was first noted in use. It is probable that the appropriate 'B' serials were officially allocated much earlier, perhaps by as much as eighteen months in some cases.

Class B	Date	Serial	Remarks
G27-3	3.67	WH732	to Venezuela AF as 1529
G27-76	11.67	WJ974	to Peru as B.52 233
G27-77	7.66	WJ976	to Peru as B.56 234
G27-96	11.68	WT208	to Peru as B.56 239
G27-97	1.69	WJ757	to Peru as B.56 240
G27-98	2.69	WJ754	to Peru as B.56 241
G27-99	2.69	WH880	to Peru as B.56 242
G27-100	2.69	WJ712	to Peru as B.56 243
G27-101	3.69	WH719	to Peru as B.56 244
G27-111	3.70	WJ616	to Argentina as B.62 B101 (G-AYHO)
G27-112	7.70	WJ713	to Argentina as B.62 B102 (G-AYHP)
G27-113	8.70	WJ714	to Argentina as B.62 B103
G27-114	9.70	WH913	to Argentina as B.62 B104
G27-116	6.68	WH847	to India as T.4 Q495
G27-117	5.68	WH638	to Ethiopia as B.52 351
G27-118	6.68	WK104	to Ethiopia as B.52 352
G27-119	8.68	WJ971	to Ethiopia as B.52 353
G27-120	9.68	WD990	to Ethiopia as B.52 354
G27-121	10.70	WT476	to Argentina as T.64 B111
G27-122	12.70	WJ875	to Argentina as T.64 B112
G27-127	1.71	WH702	to Argentina as B.62 B105
G27-128	11.68	WF917	dismantled 1.71, scrapped
G27-145	6.71	WT344	to Peru as B(I)68 245
G27-157	4.69	2B-39 ex WH736	ex Venezuela for overhaul - delivered back as 3246
G27-158	4.69	3A-39 ex WH721	ex Venezuela for overhaul - delivered back as 6409
G27-159	6.69	2A-39 ex WH709	ex Venezuela for overhaul - delivered back as 6315
G27-160	2.71	4B-39	ex Venezuela for overhaul - delivered back as 0923
G27-161	10.69	WF911	broken up late 1975
G27-162	3.71	WH727	to Argentina as B.62 B107
G27-163	6.71	WH875	to Argentina as B.62 B109
G27-164	4.71	WH886	to Argentina as B.62 B108
G27-165	2.71	WJ609	to Argentina as B.62 B106
G27-166	7.71	WJ619	to Argentina as B.62 B110
G27-167	6.70	WH954	to India as B.66 IF1021
G27-168	8.70	WT210	to India as B.66 IF1020
G27-169	10.70	WJ778	to India as B.66 IF1029
G27-170	10.70	WT303	to India as B.66 IF1024
G27-171	11.70	WJ776	to India as B.66 IF1028
G27-172	12.70	WT302	to India as B.66 IF1026
G27-173	1.71	WT373	to India as B.66 IF1027
G27-174	2.71	WJ780	to India as B.66 IF1025
G27-175	5.69	WJ781	Ntu. Not released by RAF.
G27-176	5.69	WH973	Ntu. Not released by RAF.
G27-177	9.70	WH959	to India as B.66 IF1022
G27-178	9.70	WH961	to India as B.66 IF1023
G27-179	9.69	WJ764	scrapped 1976
G27-180	10.69	WE112	scrapped 1975
G27-181	10.69	WJ718	scrapped 1976
G27-182	12.69	WJ574	to Royal Navy as TT.18
G27-183	6.71	WH800	to India as PR.57 P1098
G27-184	6.71	WJ816	to India as PR.57 P1099
G27-224	12.72	Q496	to Peru as T.74 246 ex WH845
G27-254	9.77	0240	ex Venezuela for overhaul - delivered back as B.88 0240
G27-255	11.77	0269	ex Venezuela for overhaul - delivered back as B.88 0269
G27-256	1.78	0426	ex Venezuela for overhaul - delivered back as B.88 0426
G27-257	8.77	1131	ex Venezuela for overhaul - delivered back as B.82 1131
G27-258	5.77	1183	ex Venezuela for overhaul - delivered back as B.82 1183
G27-259	1.78	1339	ex Venezuela for overhaul - delivered back as B.82 1339
G27-260	3.78	1364	ex Venezuela for overhaul - delivered back as B.82 1364
G27-261	6.77	1511	ex Venezuela for overhaul - delivered back as B.82 1511
G27-262	1.78	2001	ex Venezuela for overhaul - delivered back as B.82 2001
G27-263	4.78	1529	ex Venezuela for overhaul - delivered back as B.82 1529
G27-264	8.78	2314	to Venezuela as PR.83 2314
G27-265	2.78	0621	ex Venezuela for overhaul delivered back as T.84 0621
G27-301	5.80	0129	ex Venezuela for overhaul - delivered back as B.82 0129
G27-302	5.79	1233	ex Venezuela for overhaul - delivered back as B.82 1233
G27-303	6.79	6315	ex Venezuela for overhaul - delivered back as B.82 6315
G27-304	6.79	6409	ex Venezuela for overhaul - delivered back as B.82 6409
G27-305	3.79	1280	ex Venezuela for overhaul - delivered back as B(I)82 1280
G27-306	10.79	1425	ex Venezuela for overhaul - delivered back as B(I)82 1425
G27-307	12.78	1437	ex Venezuela for overhaul - delivered back as B(I)82 1437
G27-308	12.79	0923	ex Venezuela for overhaul - delivered back as B(I)88 0923
G27-309	3.80	3246	ex Venezuela for overhaul - delivered back as B.82 3246
G27-310	1.80	0619	ex Venezuela for overhaul - delivered back as T.84 0619
G27-311	4.80	0453	ex Venezuela for overhaul - delivered back as B(I)88 0453
G27-373	10.81	WH914	for Argentina as B.92 - not delivered because of Falklands War
G27-374	10.81	XH583	for Argentina as T.94 - not delivered as above.

Marshalls of Cambridge (prefix G-52)

Class B	Date	Serial	Remarks
G-52-2	12.74	WT368	to Peru as B(I)68 247 - delivered 8.3.75
G-52-3	2.75	XK951	to Peru as B(I)68 248 - delivered 15.4.75
G-52-4	4.75	WT342	to Peru as B(I)68 249 - delivered 15.5.75
G-52-5	7.75	WT364	to Peru as B(I)68 250 - delivered 21.7.75
G-52-6	7.75	WT340	to Peru as B(I)68 251 - delivered 9.75.
G-52-7	9.75	XH234	to Peru as B(I)68 252 - delivered 22.10.75
G-52-8	10.75	XM273	to Peru as B(I)68 253 - delivered 25.11.75
G-52-9	9.75	XM936	to Peru as B(I)68 254 - delivered 27.1.76
G-52-10	7.77	XM263	to Peru as B(I)68 255 - delivered 11.10.77
G-52-11	10.77	XM276	to Peru as B(I)68 256 - delivered 28.1.78
G-52-12	4.78	XM278	to Peru as B(I)68 257 - delivered 5.7.78

D.H. Engines (prefix G-5)

Class B	Date	Serial	Remarks
G-5-22		VN813	Spectre trials, 1956. Not confirmed.

For a more detailed coverage of the British 'Class B' registrations we recommend *Under B Conditions*, published by Merseyside Aviation Society Ltd, 1978.

G27-179 (ex-WJ764) and G27-161 (ex-WF912) and others, in open storage at Samlesbury 1970. Unusually, neither were chosen for refurbishing and were scrapped in 1975-76. *MAP*

B(I)68 G-52-5 being reworked at Marshalls of Cambridge for the Peruvian Air Force (FAP), May 1975. *R. J. Starling*

Appendix Ten

Surviving ex-RAF Canberras

It is fortunate that enough interest has been generated by the Canberra for various public and private institutions to take an active part in preserving various examples. This list gives details of those surviving airframes (sometimes only major sections) not in service with any UK flying unit, at September 1991.

Serial	Mk	Location/Remarks
VX185	B.8	Science Museum, London (nose section).
WD931	B.2	425 (ATC) Sqn, Aldridge, Staffs (nose section).
WD935	B.2	Stored at Kew (nose section).
WD954	B.2	The Cockpit Collection, Chadwell Heath, Essex (nose section).
WE139	PR.3	RAF Museum, Hendon.
WE146	PR.3	Farnborough (cockpit section).
WE168	PR.3	Glen Mitchell, Colchester (nose section).
WE173	PR.3	Coltishall (Battle Damage Repair use).
WE188	T.4	Solway Aviation Society, Carlisle.
WE192	T.4	Solway Aviation Society, Carlisle.
WF911	B.2	Pennine Museum, Bacup (nose section).
WF922	PR.3	Midland Air Museum, Baginton.
WG789	B.2/6	Barry Parkhurst, Kew (nose section).
WH657	B.2	Air Museum, Brenzett, Kent.
WH665	T.17	BAe. Filton (fuselage section).
WH673	B.2	Foulness (fuselage section).
WH700	B.2	Lincoln Nitshke Aircraft Collection, Greenock, S.Australia.
WH703	B.2	Abingdon (BDRU).
WH724	T.19	Shawbury dump (nose section).
WH725	B.2	IWM, Duxford.
WH740	T.17	Cosford (2 SoTT). For sale 9.91.
WH773	PR.7	Vallance Byways, Charlwood.
WH774	PR.7	Farnborough (fire dump).
WH775	PR.7	Cosford (2 SoTT). For sale 5.91.
WH777	PR.7	Samlesbury (rear fuselage).

Serial	Mk	Location/Remarks
WH780	T.22	St Athan (storage). For sale 5.91.
WH791	PR.7	Cottesmore (gate guard).
WH794	PR.7	FFS Catterick (hulk).
WH796	PR.7	Hemswell Aviation Society, Hemswell (nose section).
WH797	T.22	St Athan (storage). For sale 5.91.
WH798	PR.7	Wales Aircraft Museum, Cardiff (rear section at Samlesbury).
WH801	T.22	St Athan (storage). For sale 5.91.
WH803	T.22	St Athan (storage). For sale 5.91.
WH840	T.4	Staffordshire Aviation Museum, Seighford.
WH844	T.4	Pendine Ranges.
WH846	T.4	Yorkshire Air Museum, Elvington.
WH848	T.4	Wyton dump (less tail unit).
WH850	T.4	Macclesfield Historical Aviation Society, Chelford.
WH854	B.2	Martin Baker Ltd (cockpit section).
WH869	B.2	Abingdon (BDRU).
WH872	B.2	Bedford (fire dump).
WH903	B.2	Vallance Byways, Charlwood (nose section).
WH904	T.19	Newark Air Museum.
WH911	B.2	Park Aviation, Faygate (front section).
WH952	B.6	Royal Arsenal West, Woolwich.
WH957	B.15	Cosford (2 SoTT). For sale 9.91.
WH960	B.15	Cosford (2 SoTT). For sale 9.91.
WH964	E.15	Cosford (2 SoTT). For sale.
WH984	B.15	Cosford (2 SoTT). For sale 9.91.
WJ565	T.17	Cosford (2 SoTT). For sale 5.91.
WJ573	B.2	Henlow (RAF Museum store).
WJ576	T.17	Wales Aircraft Museum, Cardiff.
WJ581	T.17	Wales Aircraft Museum, Cardiff (rear fuse).
WJ603	B.2	Wattisham (fire dump). For sale 5.91.
WJ629	TT.18	Chivenor (BDR).
WJ637	B.2	Cranwell (on display as WH699).

Serial	Mk	Location/Remarks
WJ639	TT.18	North East Aircraft Museum, Sunderland.
WJ640	B.2	Cosford (2 SoTT). For sale 5.91.
WJ676	B.2	RAF Hospital, Wroughton (gate guard). For sale 5.91.
WJ677	B.2	Outside FAA Museum, Yeovilton (nose section).
WJ678	B.2	Abingdon (BDRU).
WJ717	B.2	Engineering Training, St Athan.
WJ721	TT.18	Pennine Aviation Museum, Bacup.
WJ756	E.15	Cosford (2 SoTT).
WJ775	B.6	CSDE, Swanton Morley.
WJ817	PR.7	Wyton fire dump.
WJ821	PR.7	Allenbrook Barracks, Bassingbourne.
WJ857	T.4	Warton (nose section).
WJ861	T.4	St Athan (storage). For sale 9.91.
WJ862	T.4	Cambridge airport fire dump (nose section).
WJ865	T.4	RAE (storage).
WJ867	T.4	St Mawgan (BDR).
WJ870	T.4	FFS Catterick (hulk).
WJ872	T.4	327 (ATC) Sqn, Kilmarnock (nose section).
WJ876	T.4	RAF Abingdon (nose section).
WJ880	T.4	South Yorkshire Air Museum, Firbeck (nose section).
WJ975	T.19	Hemswell Aviation Society, Hemswell.
WK102	T.17	Cosford (2 SoTT). For sale 9.91.
WK122	TT.18	Flambards Triple Theme Park, Helston.
WK124	TT.18	MoD Fire Training School, Manston.
WK127	TT.18	Wyton (BDR).
WK144	B.2	St Athan dump.
WK145	B.2	Llanbedr dump (remains).
WK146	B.2	RAFEF Abingdon (nose section).
WK164	B.2	PEE Foulness (nose section).
WP515	B.2	St Athan (storage). For sale 9.91.
WT301	B.6	DEODS Chattenden, Kent.
WT308	B(I)6	RAE (storage).
WT309	B(I)6	A&AEE, Boscombe Down (storage).
WT339	B(I)8	Barkston Heath fire dump.
WT346	B(I)8	Cosford Aerospace Museum.
WT362	B(I)8	FFS Catterick (nose section).
WT482	T.4	Stratford Aircraft Collection, Long Marston (nose section).
WT483	T.4	Stratford Aircraft Collection, Long Marston.
WT486	T.4	Belfast Airport fire dump.
WT488	T.4	Dunsfold fire dump (nose section).
WT507	PR.7	384 (ATC) Sqn, Mansfield (nose section).
WT510	T.22	St Athan (storage). For sale 5.91.
WT518	PR.7	Wales Aircraft Museum, Cardiff (wings from WJ581).
WT520	PR.7	Swinderby. Sold 8.91.
WT525	T.22	St Athan (storage). For sale 5.91.
WT532	PR.7	Cosford (2 SoTT). For sale 9.91.
WT534	PR.7	492 (ATC) Sqn, Shirley (nose section).
WT535	T.22	St Athan (storage). For sale 5.91.
WT536	PR.7	Cosford (2 SoTT). For sale. 5.91.
WT537	PR.7	Samlesbury (gate guard).
WV787	B.2/8	Newark Air Museum.
XH132	S.C9	St Mawgan (BDR).
XH133	PR.9	St Athan (storage). For sale 9.91.
XH136	PR.9	Cosford (2 SoTT). For sale 9.91.
XH165	PR.9	St Athan (storage). For sale 9.91.
XH170	PR.9	Wyton (gate guard).
XH171	PR.9	Cosford (2 SoTT).
XH174	PR.9	St Athan (storage).
XH175	PR.9	St Athan (storage).
XH177	PR.9	Wales Aircraft Museum, Cardiff (nose section).
XM244	B(I)8	Gutersloh fire dump (remains).
XM264	B(I)8	Hermeskeil Museum, Germany.
XM279	B(I)8	South Yorkshire Air Museum (nose section).

Above: XM264 ex-16 Squadron Laarbruch B(I)8 (allotted 8227M), at Hermeskeil Aircraft Museum, Germany, in October 1991. *Paul Hare*

Below: B.2 WJ676 (7796M) guards the RAF Hospital entrance at Wroughton, in June 1986. It was listed for disposal in mid-1991. *S. G. Richards*

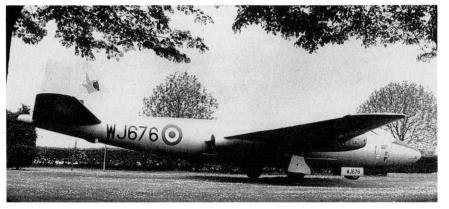

Appendix Eleven

Canberras Produced for Other Nations

ARGENTINA

First contract placed with BAC towards end of 1967, for twelve refurbished and modified ex-RAF aircraft (ten B.2s and two T.4s). Delivered as B.62s and T.64s between Nov 1970 and Sep '71. The British civil registrations G-AYHO/P were applied to B101/2 in anticipation of their appearance at the 1970 SBAC Show at Farnborough, prior to delivery. Class B marks allocated for pre-delivery test flights in UK.

B-101   ex WJ616, G-AYHO, G27-111. Del 17.11.70.
B-102   ex WJ713, G-AYHP, G27-112. Del 17.11.70.
B-103   ex WJ714, G27-113. Del 17.11.70. Cr 22.11.71.
B-104   ex WH913, G27-114. Del 26.2.71.
B-105   ex WH702, G27-127. Del 26.5.71.
B-106   ex WJ609, G27-165. Del 26.5.71. Cr?
B-107   ex WH727, G27-162. Del 26.5.71. Cr Parana
        1.7.83 (not W/o).
B-108   ex WH886, G27-164. Del 9.9.71. Shot down 13.6.82.
B-109   ex WH875, G27-163. Del 9.9.71.
B-110   ex WJ619, G27-166. Del 9.9.71. Shot down by
        Sea Harrier 1.5.82.

The two T.64s were:
B-111   ex WT476, G27-121. Del 26.2.71.
B-112   ex WJ875, G27-122. Del 26.2.71.

Second contract placed mid 1981, for two aircraft. These were prepared for delivery as a B.92 and T.94, but embargoed because of the Falklands dispute.
B.92   ex WH914, G27-373. Still stored at Samlesbury 1986.
         Dismantled later, but still stored.
T.94   ex XH583, G27-374. Still stored at Samlesbury 1986.
         Scrapped 1988.

B.62 B-102 (G-AYHP) is seen taking part in the 1970 Farnborough display before delivery to the FAA. Note the RP pod under the wing – reflecting its COIN capability, and the *Red Arrows* Gnats.

AUSTRALIA

Three B.2s were allocated RAAF serials for missile trials but remained on UK charge. Contract details are unknown.
A84-1   ex WD935. Remained in UK and serial ntu.
A84-2   ex WD942. Del 12.3.52. Loan only by UK MoD for
        trials at WRE Woomera. Returned to UK 3.10.57.
A84-3   ex WH710. RAAF serial allocated 15.6.53. Loan only.
        WRE Woomera. Returned to UK 11.57.

A contract was announced by the Australian Secretary of State for Air in January 1951 for two B.2 aircraft to be diverted off the first British production contract and supplied for familiarisation and performance handling trials prior to the licence production Mk.20 being available.
A84-125 ex WD983. To RAAF charge 16.3.52. Arr in Australia
        11.5.52, after 23 hrs 05 mins flying time delivery by
        Sqn Ldr P. Fisher and Flt Lt J. Sharp. Used briefly
        by ARDU before going to Amberley at end of May to
        join 82 Wing for conversion training. Conv to Mk.21
        by GAF, f/f 9.2.59, re-del 10.6.59. Retired at Amberley.
        Intended for National Aeronautical Collection,
        Laverton. On display at ARDU 1991.
A84-307 ex WD939. To RAAF charge 1.8.51, del Lyneham to
        Laverton over 4-day period beginning 5.8.51 by
        Wg Cdr D. R. Cuming and Flt Lt C. Harvey (total
        flying time 25 hrs 24 mins). Used for aircrew
        refresher training for a few days at Laverton before
        going to 82 Wing base at Amberley. Conv to Mk.21
        by GAF, f/f 26.9.58, re-del 7.11.58. Preserved at No.1
        Central Ammunition Depot, Kingswood, NSW.
Two further ex-RAF aircraft, this time T.4s, were sold to RAAF (by MoS?) as under. Decision to purchase was announced in Australia on 3.11.55. Contract details unknown.
A84-501 ex WT491. Del 6.4.56. To Portsea holiday camp
        11.66 – later scrapped.
A84-502 ex WT492. Del 3.5.56. Eventually relegated to g/i use
        at RAAF Wagga.

Licence production: Initially, a production order was placed for 48 aircraft to be built by the Government Aircraft Factory at Fisherman's Bend, near Melbourne to meet the requirements of RAAF Specification AC82. Production started in 1951 and the first aircraft (A84-201) flew from Avalon on 29.5.53. Deliveries were completed 16.12.58. These aircraft were initially referred to as B Mk.XXs by the GAF but as the Mk.20 by the RAAF. Prefix A84- was allotted, with aircraft numbered A84-201 to A84-248. The first twenty-seven were similar to the UK-built B.2s, using Australian-manufactured Avon RA.3 engines, whilst the remainder were completed with Avon RA.7s. There were differences however: externally the Australian-produced Mk.20s had the pitot tube moved from the centre of the nose glazing to a point below the nose. Structurally there were modifications to the airframe and undercarriage to permit operations at an AUW of 51,000 lb (some 6,000 lb heavier than the B.2 in 1950). Another structural modification involved the redesign of the wing leading edge to allow for the fitting of integral wing tanks, first fitted to A84-221 in 1955 for trials and to -224 onwards on manufacture. Earlier aircraft (except those converted to Mk.21) had them retro-fitted. There were also other changes, including extensive alterations to the radio and navigation aids for Australian operations and detail changes to the electrics (generators and cockpit lighting etc) and the provision of cartridge starting. Another significant difference was the reduction in crew from three (pilot, navigator, bomb aimer) on English Canberras to two (pilot and nav/bomb aimer combined) on the Australian examples. Five of the early aircraft (A84-201/-203/-204/-205/-206) and two of the B.2s (A84-125 and -307) were later modified as dual-control trainers by the GAF in response to RAAF Specification AC100, and as a consequence were re-designated Mk.21. Three Mk.21s were required for use by No.1 (Bomber) OCU in Amberley's No.82 Wing; three for use at the Central Flying and Air Armament Schools at East Sale and one in maintenance.

The reserved mark numbers 22 to 24 were not taken up by Australian production, as originally envisaged, and the Mk.22 was subsequently used in the UK for the T.22.

The Canberra Mk.20s saw operational service with No's 1, 2 and 6 Sqn's RAAF. They were operated for 28 years and in so doing became the longest serving combat type in the history of the RAAF. For the final 11 years of service they were used for training, target towing and cartographic surveys. The latter role required the fitting of appropriate (mod 769) equipment and A84-245 was the first conversion, completed Feb '73; others were A84-230, -232, -233, -234 and -238.

A84-201 f/f 29.5.53. First GAF-built example. Conv to prototype Mk.21 by GAF, f/f 17.6.58, re-del 4.9.58. Retired at Amberley. Extant as gate guard.

A84-202 f/f 25.8.53, del 27.8.53. Crashed Amberley, Qld 6.54 and w/o.

A84-203 f/f 19.11.53, del 23.2.54. Conv to Mk.21 by GAF, f/f 31.10.58, re-del 11.12.58. Placed in storage for Papua New Guinea Museum. Still in store at Amberley.

A84-204 f/f 5.3.54, del 8.7.54. Conv to Mk.21 by GAF, f/f 3.4.59, re-del 26.5.59. Sold to R. O. Keys 6.85.

A84-205 f/f 10.6.54, del 3.8.54. Conv to Mk.21 by GAF, f/f 20.11.58, re-del 10.2.59. Crashed Amberley 3.70.

A84-206 f/f 26.7.54, del 11.8.54. Conv to Mk.21 by GAF, f/f 14.10.59, re-del 11.3.60. Crashed Amberley 2.65.

A84-207 f/f 17.8.54, del 27.8.54. Soc 4.72. Incomplete airframe at WA Museum of Aviation, Jandakot, Geraldton, WA, 1990.

A84-208 f/f 8.9.54, del 15.9.54. Preserved at RAAF Museum Point Cook, Victoria.

A84-209 f/f 21.9.54, del 17.11.54. Placed in storage 12.68. Soc 11.71. To Camden Museum of Aviation, Narellan, NSW (cockpit and nose only).

A84-210 f/f 29.9.54, del 4.11.54. Minor landing mishap at Amberley 9.60. Repaired. Soc 11.71. Sold to Syd Beck, Mareeba, Qld. Beck Collection at Townsville, Qld, closed 1990, so whereabouts uncertain.

A84-211 f/f 12.11.54, del 7.12.54. Soc 11.71 and scrapped.

A84-212 f/f 22.11.54, del 8.12.54. Soc 11.71. Sold to Mr P. Hookway, later scrapped.

A84-213 f/f 14.12.54, del 23.12.55. Crashed Darwin, NT, 4.65 and w/o.

A84-214 f/f 11.1.55, del 21.1.55. Used for stress analysis by Aeronautical Research Laboratories, later scrapped.

A84-215 f/f 15.2.55, del 2.3.55. Soc 11.71. Fire dump Amberley.

A84-216 f/f 15.3.55, del 4.4.55. Soc 11.71. Scrapped.

A84-217 f/f 4.4.55, del 27.4.55. Soc 11.71. Sold to Mr P. Hookway, later scrapped.

A84-218 f/f 27.5.58, del 21.6.55. Soc 11.71. Sold to Mr P. Hookway, later scrapped.

A84-219 f/f 25.5.58, del 20.6.55. Soc 11.71. Extant Alex Campbell Park, Brymaroo, Qld.

A84-220 f/f 12.7.58, del 3.8.55. Soc 11.71. Destroyed in Karinga trials, Woomera, SA, 8.82.

A84-221 f/f 12.8.55, del 30.8.55. First acft with integral wing tanks. Soc 11.71. Destroyed in Karinga trials, Woomera, SA, 07.86.

A84-222 f/f 16.8.55, del 1.9.55. Soc 11.71 and scrapped.

A84-223 f/f 7.9.55, del 7.10.55. Soc 11.71. To Chewing Gum Field Museum, Tallabadgera, Qld – but museum closed 1989. To Bull Creek by 11.91.

A84-224 f/f 19.10.55, del 24.4.56. Soc 11.71 and scrapped.

A84-225 f/f 12.10.55, del 5.5.56. Soc 11.71. Preserved at Queensland Air Museum, Caloundra.

A84-226 f/f 28.10.55, del 24.4.56. Relegated to g/i use at RAAF Wagga. Extant 11.90.

A84-227 f/f 13.11.55, del 27.4.56. Soc 11.71. Sold to Mr P. Hookway, later scrapped.

A84-228 f/f 22.3.56, del 23.4.56. First with Avon Mk.109 (RA.7) engines. Shot down by SAM during mission on N/S Vietnam border 14.3.71.

A84-229 f/f 22.11.56, del 4.4.57. Allocated to RAAF Museum at Point Cook upon retirement (6.82). Flown to USA from Amberley 12.8.90 by owner and warbird restorer Steve Picatti (with Sqn Ldr G.Garley, RAAF, as navigator) in exchange for a Lockheed Ventura. Rgstd N20AN and then N229CA in USA. On show at Oshkosh EAA Convention, Aug 91.

A84-230 f/f 20.12.56, del 6.3.57. Flown on ops in Vietnam. Fitted with cartographic survey equipment. Presented to WA Air Force Assoc, Bull Creek, Perth Oct '83. Extant 1990. To Luskintyre by 11.91.

A84-231 f/f 30.5.56, del 7.6.75. Failed to return from a Combat Sky Spot bombing mission in Da Nang area, 3.11.70.

A84-232 f/f 31.5.56, del 12.6.57. Fitted with cartographic survey equipment. To ASTA (ex-GAF) for display, 1985.

A84-233 f/f 18.7.56, del 3.9.57. Flown on ops in Vietnam. Fitted with cartographic survey equipment. To Woomera 5.82. for use as Karinga bomb target – destroyed 7.82.

A84-234 f/f 24.7.56, del 17.9.56. Flown on ops in Vietnam. Fitted with cartographic survey equipment. Purchased by Mr N. Mason 1985. Nose section at RAAF Museum, Point Cook, Victoria.

A84-235 f/f 3.9.56, del 22.10.56. Flown on ops in Vietnam. Relegated to g/i use at RAAF Wagga.

A84-236 f/f 21.9.56, del 17.12.57. Flown on ops in Vietnam. Del 8.82 to RAAF Museum, Point Cook, Victoria (taxiable).

A84-237 f/f 5.10.56, del 22.5.58. Flown on ops in Vietnam. Destroyed in Karinga bomb trials, Woomera 8.82.

A84-238 f/f 25.10.56, del 24.4.58. Flown on ops in Vietnam. Fitted with cartographic survey equipment. Preserved on 'pole' at Willowbank caravan park nr Amberley, Qld.

A84-239 f/f 6.12.56, del 13.5.58. Cr Butterworth, Malaya 3.60 and w/o.

A84-240 f/f 10.1.57, del 21.4.58. Flown on ops in Vietnam. Flown to RNZAF Museum at Wigram in 1984.

A84-241 f/f 1.4.57, del 16.5.57. To Woomera, SA, 6.82 for Karinga trials. On display.

A84-242 f/f 6.6.57, del 2.8.57. Flown on ops in Vietnam. Retired at Amberley: intended for National Aeronautical Collection at Laverton .

A84-243 f/f 2.8.57, del 9.9.57. Suffered landing accident Butterworth, Malaya 8.58. Wfu and reduced to spares.

A84-244 f/f 9.9.57, del 14.10.57. Flown on ops in Vietnam. To Woomera 1.81 for use as target. Destroyed.

A84-245 f/f 16.10.57, del 29.11.57. Flown on ops in Vietnam. Fitted with cartographic survey equipment 11.72-2.73. To Aeronautical Research Laboratories, Fisherman's Bend 7.83 for display.

A84-246 f/f 22.11.57, del 17.12.57. Flown on ops in Vietnam. Used for stress tests. Scrapped.

A84-247 f/f 16.5.58, del 8.8.58. Flown on ops in Vietnam. Stored at Australian War Memorial, Canberra and/or Dunstan Military College.

A84-248 f/f 2.7.58, del 30.9.58. Flown on ops in Vietnam. Preserved at RAAF East Sale, Victoria. For sale 6.91.

At least five Canberras (A84-212, -218, -227, -209 and -217 respectively) are reported to have been allocated registration/callsign VH-PTQ. This is presumed to be connected with their after-service sale and storage at Essendon Airport.

CHILE

Three ex-RAF PR.9s were delivered direct from RAF Wyton.
341 ex XH166. Del 15.10.82.
342 ex XH167. Del 15.10.82.
343 ex XH173. Del 15.10.82.
One aircraft lost in a flying accident 24.5.83.

ECUADOR

One contract placed May 1954 for six new B.6 aircraft to be used by the Esquadrilla de Bombardeo of the FAE. The serial numbers were initially applied to the fins. They were later repeated on the nose but with a 'BE' prefix. Later in 1963, these serials were replaced by the forward fuselage construction numbers, although the 'BE' prefixes were retained with the last three of the new numbering sequence.

801 became BE-801 then 71390/BE-390.
802 became BE-802 then 71391/BE-391.
803 became BE-803 then 71402/BE-402.
804 became BE-804 then 71405/BE-405. Cr in Ireland during 1962. Ferried to EEco. Rpd & ret to Ecuador.
805 became BE-805 then 71411/BE-411.
806 became BE-806 then 71509/BE-509. Although seen as such in early 1974 this serial was later corrected to 71409/BE-409 (administrative error).

The three surviving aircraft were reported phased out during 1981, and placed into storage.

ETHIOPIA

One contract placed for four refurbished and modified ex-RAF B.2s. Class B marks were allocated for test flying and deliveries were between July-November 1968, as B.52s.

351 ex WH638, G27-117. F/f 6.68 and del 24.7.68.
352 ex WK104, G27-118. Del 12.9.68.
353 ex WJ971, G27-119. Del 10.10.68.
354 ex WD990, G27-120. Del 2.11.68.

FRANCE

One contract placed early 1954 for six new aircraft, three diverted from a RAF contract and three newly built. The first four were B.6s and the latter two to B(I)6 standard. All were used as either, engine, missile or radar test-beds.

F763 ex WJ763, del 8.54. CEV c/s F-ZXRK, later F-ZLAM. To Le Bourget by 1977. Preserved at Musée de l'Air.
F779 ex WJ779, del '54. CEV c/s F-ZLAN. Later fitted with Mk.8 nose (offset canopy). Wfu 1979.
F784 ex WJ784, del 1.55. EPNER c/s F-ZJPK, later CEV c/s F-ZLAK. Scrapped at Bretigny 1975-6.
F304 del 8.55 to CEV c/s FZLAL. Scrap Bretigny 1974.
F316 del 9.55 to CEV c/s FZLAT. Fitted with pointed nose for Cyrano II Missile trials installation. Wfu by 1979.
F318 del 12.55 to CEV c/s F-ZXRV later F-ZLAU. Wfu at Cazaux range 1975.

The 'F' serial prefix was eventually removed from most aircraft. The origin of the 304/316/318 numbers has been a source of confusion and has defied verification. They are thought not to be linked to the RAF 'WT' serialled machines nor to the '71xxx' forward fuselage numbering sequence.

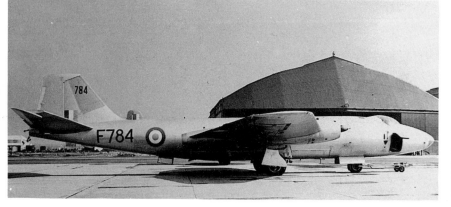

French B.6 F784, seen here in 1963, retained its 'F' prefix until 1969 at least. *MAP*

Opposite page: **Ethiopian B.52 '354' near Bake Hora, was hastily photographed from an airliner window.** *via Tony Haven*

This ADE (Air Defence Establishment?) developed 'ULKA', mounted on an Indian B(I)58 pylon, at Bangalore, was described as a 'rocket propelled missile target drone' at the time. *via F. G. Swanborough*

INDIA

First contract placed January 1957 for 68 new aircraft. Production by EECo at Preston comprised six T.4s, eight PR.57s and fifty-four B(I)58s. Of these, twenty-four were diverted off RAF contracts and test-flown in primer with RAF serials.
B(I)58s. These were based on the RAF B(I)8s but with autopilot, extra nav kit and other mods and were to serve with Nos 5, 16, and 35 Sqn, IAF. Boulton Paul modified WT338 as a trials aircraft for the Mk.58 special features, after which it was included as part of the initial batch.

IF895   ex XK953.
IF896   ex XH203.
IF897   ex XH205.
IF898   ex XK959.
IF899   ex XH227.
IF900   ex XH229.
IF901   ex XH230.
IF902   ex XH232.
IF903   ex XH233.
IF904   ex XH235.
IF905   ex XH236.
IF906   ex WT338.
IF907   ex XH237.
IF908   ex XH238.
IF909   ex XH239.
IF910   ex XH240.
IF911   ex XH241.
IF912   ex XH242.
IF913   ex XH243.
IF914 to IF934 inclusive.
IF960 to IF973 inclusive.
PR.57s. Eight new aircraft, based on RAF PR.7s but fitted with autopilot, extra nav kit, radio altimeter and other mods, for service with 106 Sqn IAF. Three aircraft diverted off British contract early 1957 and five built to order.
IP986   ex WT539.
IP987   ex WT542. Used VT-EEM 7.76.
IP988   ex WT541.
IP989 to IP993 inclusive.
T.4s. Six standard aircraft, two diverted from RAF contracts and four to order, for service with the Jet Training Wing.
IQ994   ex XK647. Del 4.58.
IQ995   ex XK650. Del 4.58.
IQ996 to IQ999 inclusive. '999 del 5.1.58.
First contract option for further twelve aircraft taken up July '57.
B(I)58s. Eleven new aircraft.
IF974 to IF984 inclusive. Last example (IF984) del 9.59.
T.4. One new aircraft.
IQ985
Second contract placed 1961 for six new B(I)58, built up from stocks of major assemblies manufactured before closure of production line. Deliveries during 1963.
BF595 to BF600 inclusive
Third contract placed with BAC late 1962 for three ex-RAF aircraft, i.e. two PR.57s (BP745/6) and one T.4 (BQ744).
BP745   ex WT506. Del Spring '64.
BP746   ex WT528. Del Spring '64.
BQ744   ex WJ859. Del 9.63.
Fourth contract placed 1965 for three ex-RAF T.4 aircraft. Delivery embargoed in 1966, acft to 5MU Kemble for storage.
Q495   ex WH847. To 5MU. To BAC Samlesbury mid '68. Test flown as G27-116. Del to India 7.68.
Q496   ex WH845. Not del. Bought by BAC. Sold to Peru as 246
Q497   ex WE191. Not del. bought by BAC. Stored by BAC at Samlesbury. Moved to Warton '88 for fire practice.

Fifth contract placed October 1969 for fourteen aircraft but subsequently reduced to twelve, i.e. ten B(I)66s and two PR.67s. Class B marks were allocated for pre-delivery test flights. Del between 10.70 and 8.71.
B(I)66 - ten refurbished ex-RAF B.15/B.16s.
IF1020   ex WT210, G27-168. Del 10.70.
IF1021   ex WH954, G27-167.
IF1022   ex WH959, G27-177.
IF1023   ex WH961, G27-178.
IF1024   ex WT303, G27-170.
IF1025   ex WJ780, G27-174.
IF1026   ex WT302, G27-172.
IF1027   ex WT373, G27-173.
IF1028   ex WJ776, G27-171.
IF1029   ex WJ778, G27-169.
PR.67s - two refurbished ex-RAF PR.7s to later standard.
P1098   ex WH800, G27-183.
P1099   ex WJ816, G27-184. Del 27.8.71.
Sixth contract placed 1975 for six T.4 aircraft, bought direct from RAF stocks at 5MU Kemble. Delivered between June-Sept '75. In India, these were modified to have target-towing equipment, and redesignated TT.418.
Q1791   ex WE193. Del 23.7.75.
Q1792   ex WE195. Del 18.6.75.
Q1793   ex WT485. Del 9.9.75.
Q1794   ex WT487. Del 20.8.75.
Q1795   ex WH839. Del 23.9.75.
Q1796   ex WJ868. Del 4.8.75.
In November 1970 ten fatigue life expired aircraft were bought from RNZAF, eight surviving B(I)12s and two T.13s.
B(I)12 - eight aircraft: NZ6102/03/05/07/08/09/10/11, but tie-ups with India AF serials are not confirmed.
F1183 to F1190 inclusive.
T.13 - two aircraft: NZ6151/52. Tie-ups not confirmed.
Q1191 and Q1192.

NEW ZEALAND

Initially loaned sufficient RAF B.2s to equip 75 Sqn. During the period July 1958 to January 1962 seventeen B.2s and three T.4s were used, mainly in Malaya, viz:
B.2s -   WD948, WF915, WH645, WH646, WH666,
WH739, WH740, WH878, WH922, WJ567,
WJ605, WJ630, WJ715, WJ981, WJ986,
WJ988, WJ102.
T.4s -   WD963, WJ859, WJ864.
First contract placed February 1958, via MoS, for eleven aircraft for use by 14 Sqn RNZAF, deliveries between Sep '59 and Mar '61. Contract No KD/E/01/CB6 (b) - part.
B(I)12 - nine modified versions of B(I)8 with autopilot, extra nav kit. WT329 used as trials installations acft '59 and then included in contract. Dates 'to RNZAF' quoted are probably hand-over dates. First four aircraft (6102-5) were handed over at RAF Upwood. Survivors sold to India Nov '70
NZ6101   ex RAF WT329. Aw/cn at 23 MU 3.12.59. To RNZAF charge 11.1.60. Cr at Christchurch NZ, 11.60.
NZ6102   Aw/cn and del ex-Warton to 23 MU 10.9.59.
To RNZAF charge 16.9.59. Sold to India 11.70.
NZ6103   Aw/cn and del ex-Warton to 23 MU 10.9.59.
To RNZAF charge 16.9.59. Sold to India 11.70.
NZ6104   Aw/cn and del ex-Warton to 23 MU 10.9.59.
To RNZAF charge 16.9.59. Cr off Malayan coast 30.11.64.
NZ6105   Aw/cn and del ex-Warton to 23 MU 17.9.59.
To RNZAF charge 24.9.59. Sold to India 11.70.

NZ6106   Aw/cn and del ex-Warton to 23 MU 30.9.59.
To RNZAF charge 14.10.59. Retd to UK (by air) with faulty main spar. To BAC 1.5.70. B/u at Samlesbury 5.76.
NZ6107   Aw/cn and del ex-Warton to 23 MU 16.10.59.
To RNZAF charge 2.11.59. Sold to India 11.70.
NZ6108   Aw/cn and del ex-Warton to 23 MU 30.11.59.
To RNZAF charge 11.1.60. Sold to India 11.70.
NZ6109   Aw/cn and del ex-Warton to 23 MU 15.1.60.
To RNZAF charge 25.3.60. Sold to India 11.70.
T.13 - two T.4 aircraft modified to have autopilot and extra fuel tank in bomb-bay, one ex-RAF and one new machine.
NZ6151   Aw/cn and del ex-Warton to 23 MU 13.12.60.
To RNZAF charge 30.1.61. Sold to India 11.70.
NZ6152   ex WE190. Aw/cn at 23 MU 3.2.61. To RNZAF charge 29.3.61. Sold to India 11.70.
Note: NZ6109 and NZ6151 were the last Canberras off the English Electric production line, closed at the end of 1959.
B(I)12 - Second contract placed on behalf of New Zealand, via MoS, early 1960 for two additional B(I)12 aircraft for use by 14 Sqn RNZAF. It was probably intended that these would be supplied as part of contract no KD/E/01/CB6(b), but RAF serial numbers XP289/290 were originally allocated to these aircraft, therefore they were probably officially diverted off contract no KC/2R/08/CB9(c). These two aircraft were built from the stock of major B.8 components produced speculatively following the closure of the production line.
NZ6110   Aw/cn and del ex-Warton 30.3.61. To RNZAF charge 18.5.61. Sold to India 11.70.
NZ6111   Aw/cn and del ex-Warton 14.4.61. To RNZAF charge 26.5.61. Sold to India 11.70.

PERU

First contract placed November 1955 for eight B(I)8 acft, four diverted from British contracts and four new build, for 21 Grupo FAP. Initially numbered 474 to 482, they were renumbered 206 to 212 1959/60.
474   ex WT343. Del 25.5.56. Later 206.
475   ex WT348. Del 12.6.56. Later 207. W/o 8.2.72.
476   ex WT367. Del 2.7.56. Cr 11.6.59 at Chiclayo.
478   ex XH206. Del 11.7.56. Later 209.
479   del 6.8.56. Cr 23.9.56 at Lima, during a display.
480   del 19.9.56. Later 210. Wheels-up landing 8.4.63 at Chiclayo.
481   del 1.2.57. Later 211.
482   del 20.3.57. Later 212.
Second contract placed late 1959 for one new B(I)8 built from stock major assemblies. Attrition replacement.
208   del 28.11.60.
Third contract placed 1965/6 for eight refurbished acft for service with second Canberra Sqn of Grupo 21.
T.4 - two ex-RAF T.4s. One or both aircraft may have been updated to T.74 standard in Peru, using kits supplied by BAC.
231   ex WH659. Del 21.5.66. W/o 6.10.71.
232   ex WJ860. Del 18.4.66.
B.2 - six ex-RAF B.2s. Class B marks for trials use. These aircraft may have been updated to B.72 standard out in Peru, using kits supplied by BAC.
233   ex WJ974, G27-76. Del 22.11.67.
234   ex WJ976, G27-77. Del 4.8.66. W/o 18.12.69.
235   ex WK112. Del 30.1.67. W/o 8.8.68.
236   ex WH726. Del 21.9.66.
237   ex WH868. Del 22.10.66. W/o 4.2.81.
238   ex WE120. Del 5.12.66.

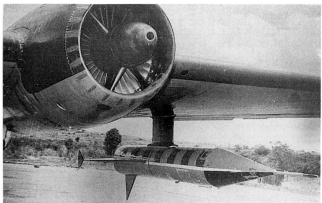

Fourth contract placed 1968 with BAC, for six refurbished aircraft made up of parts from a number of aircraft - mix and match - so that ex-RAF identities are a bit dubious; for example 3 acft had unused spare front fuselages and two others came from used spares stock. Del between Feb and June 1969. Class B marks allocated for test flying prior to delivery. *B(I)56* - three B.6 and three B.2s, all ex-RAF.

239   ex WT208, G27-96. Del 3.2.69. W/o 12.11.73.
240   ex WJ757, G27-97. Del 3.3.69
241   ex WJ754, G27-98. Del 19.3.69
242   ex WH880, G27-99. Del 9.4.69
243   ex WJ712, G27-100. Del 2.5.69
244   ex WH719, G27-101. Del 4.6.69.

Fifth contract placed 1969 for one refurbished and updated ex-RAF B(I)8 aircraft, redesignated B(I)68.

245   ex WT344, G27-145. Del 16.7.71. Cr Brazil 30.6.72.

Sixth contract placed c1971 with BAC for one refurbished ex-RAF T.4, redesignated T.74.

246   ex WH845, (intended for India as Q496 but del embargoed; bought back by BAC), G27-224. Del 2.73.

Seventh contract placed June 1973 with Marshalls of Cambridge for eight (later amended to eleven) refurbished and modernised ex-RAF B(I)8s. The centre fuselage structures were in fact refurbished by BAC at Samlesbury. Class B marks for test-flights. Redes B(I)68.

247   ex WT368, G52-2. Del 8.3.75.
248   ex XK951, G52-3. Del 15.4.75.
249   ex WT342, G52-4. Del 15.5.75
250   ex WT364, G52-5. Del 21.7.75.
251   ex WT340, G52-6. Del   .75.
252   ex XH234, G52-7. Del 22.10.75.
253   ex XM273, G52-8. Del 25.11.75.
254   ex XM936, G52-9. Del 27.1.76.
255   ex XM263, G52-10. Del 11.10.77.
256   ex XM276, G52-11. Del 28.1.78.
257   ex XM278, G52-12. Del 5.7.78.

Approx twenty Canberras were still in FAP service early in 1989 and this is thought to have dwindled to around fifteen by December 1991, at which point five B(I)12s were purchased from the SAAF. Ex-SAAF T.4 458 may join them.

RHODESIA

Order placed late 1957 for fifteen ex-RAF B.2s for use by 5 Squadron, RRAF. These were supplied direct from RAF stocks and serialled RRAF159 to 173 inclusive. Delivery dates were as follows: 161, 162 and 168 on 10.3.59; 169 on 12.3.59; 160, 166, 172 and 173 on 7.4.59; 163, 164 and 167 on 5.5.59; 159, 165, 170 and 171 on 2.6.59.

A further contract was placed early 1958 for three ex-RAF B.2 aircraft. These were modified to T.4 standard by fitting newly-built Mk.4 front fuselages at Samlesbury and were delivered as RRAF174 to 176 inclusive, on 20.3.61, 28.3.61 and 20.3.61 respectively.

In 1961 a new serialling sequence was introduced and following UDI this sequence was modified again, the prefix being shortened to 'R' and the unit number '5' being incorporated into the serial in a set pattern. At the end of the 1970's eight grounded aircraft were cannibalised to produce R2516, 2158 and 2519 and the survivors were passed to the AFZ in April 1980. We are indebted to Neil Gaunt, an ex Rhodesian Canberra technician for the following serial information:

RRAF 1st srs	RRAF 2nd srs	Rhodesian Air Force	Air Force Zimbabwe	ex-RAF
RRAF159	RRAF200	R2005		WH867
RRAF160	RRAF201	R2051	2051	WH653
RRAF161	RRAF202	R2502	2502	WH662
RRAF162	RRAF203	R5203	5203	WH672
RRAF163	RRAF204	R2504	2504	WH707
RRAF164	RRAF205	R2055	2055	WH855
RRAF165	RRAF206			WH871
RRAF166	RRAF207			WH883
RRAF167	RRAF208	R2085	2085	WJ571
RRAF168	RRAF209	R2059	2059	WJ572
RRAF169	RRAF210	R2510		WJ578
RRAF170	RRAF211			WJ606
RRAF171	RRAF212	R5212		WK108
RRAF172	RRAF213			WJ612
RRAF173	RRAF214	R2514	2514	WH644
RRAF174	RRAF215	R2155	2155	WH658
RRAF175	RRAF216			WH674
		R2516	2516	WH674/WJ606
RRAF176	RRAF217	R2175	2175	WJ613
		R2158		
		R2519		

SOUTH AFRICA

First contract placed 1961 or 1962. Six new B(I)12 aircraft, delivered late '63 - early '64, for use with 12 Squadron SAAF. Built from stocks of major assemblies, put in hand following closure of the EE production line. Known as 'Cans' by their SAAF crews, they were used extensively for low and medium level bombing and photo reconnaissance during the conflict along the Namibian and Angolan borders. One was lost after the pilot was hit by ground fire. The B(I)12s were modernised in 1987/88 to give improved weapons payload (+40%) and delivery accuracy.

451   f/f 31.8.63. Del 19.10.63.
452   del .11.63.
453   del 15.12.63.
454   del .1.64.
455   del .2.64.
456   f/f 30.2.64. Very last Canberra to be completed. Del .4.64.

Second contract placed early 1963. Three ex-RAF T.4 aircraft, delivered by early 1964, for use with 12 Squadron SAAF.

457   ex WJ991. Del .2.64. To SAAF Museum, Swartkop.
458   ex WJ864. Del .4.64. To Ysterplaat Museum
459   ex WJ617. Del .4.64. To SAAF Museum, Swartkop.

The Canberra force was placed in storage in 1990 as part of the SAAF defence cuts. Five B(I)12s were sold to Peru and left on delivery on 17.12.91. T.4s 457 & 459 went to Swartkop near Pretoria; 458 flew to Ysterplaat Museum near Cape Town 27.12.91 but is reported earmarked to go on to Peru in 1992.

SWEDEN

One contract. Two ex-RAF B.2s were ordered late 1959. Modified by Boulton Paul (externally similar to T.11) and used for radar and avionics flight test work by F8 Wing, with designation Tp52. Last flights 1973. Both preserved in Museums in Sweden.

52001   ex WH711. Del 1.2.60. To Ugglarp Museuem.
52002   ex WH905. Del 5.3.60. To Malmen AF Museum.

B(I)12 452 of 12 Squadron SAAF at Port Elizabeth August 1969. The all over silver finish gave way to a very distinguished blue in the mid 1970s. *R. Walker*

52002, ex RAF B.2 WH905, was operated by the Swedish Air Force for research duties and as an ELINT platform prior to retirement in the Flygvapenmuseum at Malmen. *Swedish Air Museum*

USA

The commencement of the Korean conflict and the shortcomings of the in-service ex-World War II Douglas B-26, prompted the urgent procurement of a light tactical bomber by the USAF. Following a flying demonstration and ground inspection at Andrews AFB in Feb '51, the Senior Officers and USAF Weapons Boards chose the Canberra as the best interim aircraft available for their night tactical intruder role. The US Air Staff directed AMC (procurement directive 51-135, 2.3.51) to arrange for domestic production. On 24.2.51 the Glenn L. Martin Company received letter contract AF 33(038)-22617 asking them to deliver 250 B-57s (Americanised version of the Canberra) between 11.52 and 10.53. This contract also authorised Martin to acquire Canberra manufacturing rights; the license agreement being finally signed on 8.5.51. The required design changes, loss of the first pattern aircraft and a major initial delay in the government furnished (Curtiss-Wright built) Armstrong-Siddeley Sapphire jet engines, all contributed to serious production slippage and contracts were altered as needs

changed. Martin built 403 B-57s eventually and in time EECo received royalties in excess of $3.5 million: another $1 million was paid for the two Canberra 'pattern' aircraft supplied.
Canberra - two ex-RAF B.2s diverted off first British production contract and supplied as pattern aircraft to USA:
51-17387ex WD932, del to USA 21.2.51. Test- flown for 41 hours by Martins between Apr-Oct'51. USAF pilots began test flying Fall'51. Crashed 21.12.51. USAF serial allotted but never carried.
51-17352ex WD940, del to USA 31.8.51 Test-flown for 4 hrs by Martins then disassembled and sections shipped to main subcontractors.
Licence production:
B-57A - Martin model 272. Serials 52-1418 to 52-1425. 8 built to contract AF33 (038) - 22617.
As Canberra B.2 but adapted to US production techniques; two 7220 1bst J65-W-5 jet engines (J-65-B-5 on early aircraft). Armament consisted of eight 0.5in guns, plus 5,000 1lb of bombs. Eight B-57-MA were built; the initial example made its first flight 20.7.53 and successfully underwent an official AF acceptance test on 20.8.53. It was immediately loaned back to Martin whose pilots test-flew it for 292 hours in 284 flights. On 19.6.57 it was transferred to NACA as NASA218. The other 7 were delivered in Dec'53 and extensive USAF testing began. The second machine was loaned to the Weather Bureau of the Dept of Commerce early in 1957 and following modification it was used in the National Hurricane Project as N1005: this machine was extant at George T. Baker Engineering School, Miami Airport, in 1972. By mid-1961 the B-57A no longer appeared in the Air Force inventory.
RB-57A - Martin model 272A, Weapon System 307L. Serials 52-1426 to 52-1492. 67 built to contract AF33(038)-22617.
As B-57A but with a camera installation aft of the bomb bay. Missions included day and night, high and low, visual and photographic reconnaissance besides day combat mapping. This version was totally unarmed and painted in high-gloss black to minimise detection from searchlights. It carried only a two-man crew (pilot and photo-navigator). The first of this version to be built flew in Oct'53; the type went into operational service in mid-54 with the 345th LBW at Langley AFB, Va, for transitional training and later deliveries went to the 363rd TRW at Shaw AFB, SC. The last 5 examples were delivered in Aug'54. Problems with engines, control system and wing fuselage attachment fittings were experienced, although the 'garden gate' mod had remedied the latter difficulty by Nov'54. These ills and lack of spares and equipment led to delayed aircraft assignments at home and overseas. The first two USAF Wings in W. Germany did not keep their RB-57As very long, both the 10th TRW at Spangdahlem AB and the 66th at Sembach AB began converting to RB-66s in late 1957. Ten RB-57As had been lost in accidents by 1958 and at end of 1970 only 2 remained on the active USAF list. Ten aircraft were converted to RB-57A-1 configuration for high-altitude reconnaissance under Project *Lightweight* (later called *Heartthrob*). This involved the removal of some equipment, fitting higher thrust J65-W-7 engines and a crew reduction from 2 to 1. This variant was 5,665 1bs lighter than the standard 48,847 lb aircraft and its service ceiling improved by 5,000ft. Completed in Aug'55, six -1s went to the 7499th Composite Sqn in USAFE and four to the 6007th CS in the Far East Air Forces. Two RB-57As were modified under *Hardtack* (also known as *Heartthrob Jr*) by replacing some equipment with the highly sophisticated Convair-developed AN/APS-60 Startack high altitude radar: these RB-57A-2s were delivered in Sep'57 (9 months late). Two RB-57A (mod) were handed over to Republic of China under Project *Large Charge*. In 1957 the Air Research & Development Command lent an RB-57A (possibly 52-1438 as N96) to Northrop Aircraft Inc, to study laminar flow boundary layer control. In the Spring of '58, a number of RB-57As were prepared by the Air Force, under temporary designation B/20 for atmospheric sampler missions. Another example (52-1435) was used mostly for flight evaluation purposes as an NRB-57A until retired in Dec '69, and several other RB-57A airframes were later used in the extensive rebuild RB-57F programme. The following have been preserved in Museums etc: 52-1426, 1456, 1475, 1482, 1485, 1488, 1492.
EB-57A - Martin model 272R. In the mid-1960s the Air Force gave the go-ahead for 32 (also reported as 12) RB-57As to be fitted with an ECM compartment in the bomb-bay. The first flew in Apr'66, the programme was completed in less than a year and ADC used them for ECM training until the early '70s - twelve were still in the operational forces in late 1971. Airframes reported to have been involved included: 52-1428, 1437, 1439/42, 1447/48, 1450, 1461, 1464, 1481/82(?), 1489.
B-57B - Martin model 272, Weapons System 307A.
This was the major production varient. 202 were built: Serials 52-1493 to 52-1594 (102) to contract AF33(038)-22617; 53-3859 to 53-3935; 53-3937 to 53-3939; 53-3941 to 53-3943; 53-3945 to 53-3947; 53-3949 to 53-3962 (100) to contract AF33(600)-22208.
Night intruder 'bomber' model with redesigned forward fuselage seating pilot and navigator in tandem; up to 6,000 1b of bombs in a modified bomb-bay with rotary doors and underwing pylons for eight 5-in rockets or two 500lb bombs. Wing armament eight 0.5inch guns, replaced by four M-39 20mm cannon from 91st example. These changes set back production targets; the first example did not fly until 18.6.54 and the first assignments to two US-based TAC Wings began in late '54 and early '55. Light bomb wings in France and Japan began to receive aircraft in mid- and late-55 respectively. A peak number of 18 B-57Bs was delivered in June 1955 and production ended with delivery of the last two in May'56. In Sep'56 a 3-phase improvement programme was initiated to bring the model to the required tactical standard. 52-1497 was used as the Bomarc missile nose test-bed; 52-1512, 1530, 1532, 1541, 1567 and 53-3883 were loaned to the SVAF in 1965/6; 52-1576 went to NASA as NASA809 (also reputed to be N637NA and N809NA at various times). Many B-57Bs were later converted to RB-57Fs or B-57Gs. One unidentified B-57B was extensively modified for Operation *Red Wing*, a special weapons test in the Pacific in 1956: it was later restored to its regular configuration. Six B-57Bs were modified during Aug/Sep'56 to perform sampler roles in the *Red Wing* tests and in Dec'57 four additional B-57Bs were also modified to monitor post-nuclear blast radioactive fall-out in the upper atmosphere. Following the *Red Wing* tests, these planes were all allocated to the AF Special Weapons Center at Kirkland AFB, New Mexico. In late 1957, ten B-57Bs were modified under project *Stardust*. This entailed removing all armament and fitting with the latest flying instruments. These were used by high-ranking officers for proficiency flying and transportation. In Sept'59, 25 B-57s were delivered to Pakistan under the Military Assistance Program: B.57Bs 53-3885, 3891, 3938/39, 3941/43, 3945/47, 3949/52, 3954/61 and B-57Cs 53-3834, 3846 and 3848. TAC hastily phased-out their B-57B/Cs between Apr'58 and 23.6.59, but PACAF elected to keep 2 squadrons (8th & 13thBS) at Johnson AFB, Japan until 1965, at which point they moved to Clark AB in the Philipines and small numbers soon flew missions from Bien Hoa and Da Nang Air Bases in South Vietnam. Martin reconfigured the following 8 B-57Bs for combat, late 1965: 52-1498/99, 1510, 1550, 1590, 53-3827, 3831 and 3838. From Dec 1967 to July 1968 three B-57Bs (52-1518, 1580 and 53-3860) were modified with a low-light television mounted in a pod under the left wing for the *Tropic Moon II* programme. More extensive mods for project *Tropic Moon III* resulted in 16 conversions to B-57G configuration (see below). The ANG flew recce-modded Bs until 1966 but their more recently acquired Gs (reconfigured Bs) went to Davis Monthan for storage in early '74. Quite a number of Bs were preserved: 52-1499/1500, 1504/5, 1509, 1516, 1519, 1526, 1548, 1551 (NASM) and 1584.
EB-57B - ECM conversion with similar fit to EB-57As, 22 airframes believed converted: 52-1499/1507, 1509, 1511, 1515/16, 1519/21, 1526, 1545, 1548, 1551, 1564, 1571, 53-3859(?).
JB-57B - 52-1540 and 1594 were converted for calibration of missile tracking cameras, also 52-1539 and 1562, fitted with a TM-76 *Mace* nose section housing ATRAN (Automatic Terrain Recognition and Navigation) radar, and used by 38thTMW to develop cruise missile guidance systems; these aircraft were initially given the non-standard designation MSB-57B (MS for Missile Simulator).
NB-57B: - 52-1496, 1498, 1580 and 1581 (and possibly 1493 and 1451 too) used for miscellaneous tests.
RB-57B - Several B-57Bs (including 52-1518, 1522, 1557,1559, 1570/1, 1589, 53-3860, 3920) were modified for photo-reconnaissance and allocated to ANG Squadrons.
B-57C - Martin model 272, Weapon System 307A. Serials 53-3825/3858, 3936, 3940, 3944 and 3948 (38) to contract AF33(600)-22208. Transition trainer version of the B-57B, with dual controls. Was to have been designated TB-57B but this rescinded in Aug'54. First example was flown 30.12.54 and the 38th and last was delivered in May'56. Due to their similarity most B-57B mods were applied to the B-57Cs. In 1955 four B-57Cs were allocated to ATC to help the transition training program. Other Cs went straight to tactical units and it was usual to find that 2 out of every 18 aircraft in a R/B-57 squadron were B-57Cs. 53-3838, 3849, 3929 and 3940 loaned to SVAF 1965/6. Phaseout followed the B's pattern and like TAC's B-57Bs the Cs were brought up to the reconnaissance configuration in 1958 for service with the ANG.
RB-57C - Photo-reconnaissance version of the B-57C for ANG service. At least 53-3831/2, 3841/2, 3851 and 53-3944 so converted. Three RB-57Cs were still on the ANG inventory in mid'73.
WB-57C - At least four B-57Cs were modified for weather reconnaissance tasks - 53-3832, 3844, 3850 and 3851.
B-57D - This model was originally ordered as part of the second Martin contract AF33(600)-22208, dated 4.11.53. Fifty-three aircraft were to be purchased but of these, 20 aircraft (53-3963 to 3982) were transferred in 1955 to the third contract as RB-57Ds and the remaining 33 aircraft (53-3983 to 4015) were cancelled.
RB-57D - Developed from a study completed in Dec'52 by the Wright Air Development Center. This high altitude daylight reconnaissance model featured a substantially altered B-57B fuselage, new extended span wings with optional tip radomes and a service ceiling of 65,000 ft. A total of 20 was built in four basic models, under contract AF33(600)-25825. All but the six 'Group A zeros' were equipped for In Flight Refuelling by KC-97s. First flight of the RB-57D was on 3 Nov 1955, first deliveries were made in the spring of 1956 and complete by March 1957. At least three Group A RB-57Ds wore the Nationalist Chinese markings (including 33-3981 - also marked as 5844) from 1959 to 1963: one is believed shot down. Four RB-57D Group B airframes 53-3970, 3972, 3974/75 were used in the RB-57F rebuild programme. In 1958, several 'zeros' (Group A and B models) were used for the Eniwetok Atoll bomb drop tests under operation *Hardtack* and in 1962 five black 'D's from the 4677 DSES and '973 from Wright-Patterson were assigned to Christmas Island under project *Dominic* for cloud sampling in the vicinity of the nuclear detonation test.
RB-57D Group A 'zero', (model 294), serials 53-3977/82 (6).
RB-57D Group B 'zero', (model 744), serials 53-3970/76 (7).
RB-57D-1 Group D, (model 796), serial 53-3963 (1) with IFR, AN/APG-56 and provision for nose or tail radomes.
RB-57D-2 Group C, (model 797), serials 53-3964/69 (6) with IFR provision, tail radome, ferret ECM and a crew of 2 (pilot & ECM operator).
Conflicting published information has also referred to the above as RB-57D-1-MA thru' - 4-MA respectively.
EB-57D - Folllowing structural problems with the RB-57D, (including the loss of a wing at 50,000ft by '973) most of the D's were put back into storage. But a continuing requirement for a high altitude target aircraft saw the emergence of the EB-57D (converted D-0s and D-2s) with updated ECM gear. These too were withdrawn by mid-1970 but '982 was retired to Tucson Air Museum. Nine are believed to have been converted including 53-3964/66, 68, 77 and 82.
B-57E - Basically as B-57C dual control model but without its combat gear and the inclusion of tow reel operating equipment mounted on the bomb bay door. It also had a full time power rudder and yaw dampers and a tail cone modified to accommodate the externally mounted target canisters. A total of 68 were built under contract AF33(600)-29645, with serials 55-4234 to 55-4301 (Martin model 272E). An order for 26 B-57Cs in the same contract was later cancelled. The first production aircraft flew on 16 May 1956. On 10 July'56 the AF cancelled SACs request for seven B-57E conversion to TRB-57E and confirmed that 64 B-57Es would go direct to the Air Defense Command - the 4 exceptions (minus tow-target equipment) went to the AF Flight Test School (first one delivered Oct'56). The model entered operational service in August 1956 and although a number of problems resulted in a minor program slippage, the last 'E' was delivered in Mar'57. In the mid-60s, all B-57Es (including converted B-57Bs) were equipped with the external AF/A372-1 tow target system. With the heavy attrition rate in Vietnam, 12 E's (and 8 B's) were returned to the Martin plant late in 1965 to be combat configured for tactical recce and light bomber roles. The twelve E's involved were: 55-4238, 4248, 4251, 4259, 4265, 4268/70, 4274, 4282, 4284/85. Only 9 B-57Es were still on the AF inventory by the end of June 1973. 55-4274 is preserved in the Pima Air Museum, Arizona and 55-4244 in the SAC Museum.
EB-57E - A sophisticated but relatively inexpensive conversion programme that provided ECM targets to ground and airborne radar systems. Operated in the 1960s by a number of Defence Systems Evaluation Squadrons based around the US and a few overseas. The last Air Force unit (17 DSES) finally gave up its aircraft in Dec'79 although the EB-57B Canberras of the 158DSEG, ANG survived into the early 1980s. Conversions to EB-57E standard are believed to include: 55-4239/42, 4247, 4253/54, 4260, 4263, 4266, 4275/76, 4278/81, 4287/88, 4290, 4292/96, 4298, 4300. 55-4279 has been reported to be preserved.

JB-57E - 55-4237 was converted from B-57E and used for temporary testing.

NB-57E - Four B-57Es (55-4257/58, 4262 and 4267) were used for permanent testing.

RB-57F - Six B-57Es (55-4237, 4243, 4245, 4249, 4257, 4264) were converted by General Dynamics for classified reconnaissance missions in Vietnam between May 1963 and August 1971 under project *Patricia Lynn*. These were fitted with two vertical cameras and an infra-red scanner in the bomb bay and a redesigned nose with a vertical and forward oblique camera.

TB-57E - A few B-57Es (and B-57Bs converted to Es) were modified and used for training, under this designation.

RB-57F - Extensively rebuilt strategic reconnaissance and air weather sampler version of the B-57B/RB-57D with a new 122ft span wing with anhedral tips, extended nose with additional electronic equipment, and two 16,500 lb st TF-33-P-11A engines plus two 2900 lb st J60-P-9s in detachable underwing pods. Seventeen B-57B-MA and four RB-57D-MA were rebuilt by General Dynamics (first example flew 23 June 1963) and the type was operational by Feb'64. New serial numbers were allocated as follows:

63-13286 ex 52-1589	63-13287 ex 53-3864	63-13288 ex 52-1539
63-13289 52-1527	63-13290 52-1562	63-13291 52-1574
63-13292 52-1594	63-13293 52-1583	63-13294 53-3935
63-13295 53-3918	63-13296 53-3897	63-13297 53-3900
63-13298 52-1536	63-13299 52-1573	63-13300 52-1427
63-13301 52-1432	63-13302 52-1433	63-13500 53-3972
63-13501 53-3975	63-13502 53-3970	63-13503 53-3974

Of the above, 63-13287 was lost with both crew members in the Black Sea on 14 Dec 1965, '297 was lost in Nov'66, another came apart at 50,000ft in mid'72, and one was nearly destroyed in a hangar at Karachi that was hit by a bomb from an Indian AF Canberra in December 1971.

WB-57F - A redesignation of the RB-57F. Used by 58 WRS in many parts of the world between June 1964 and July 1974. Most were placed in storage at Davis Monthan, but three machines, 63-13198, 13501 and 13503 were transferred to NASA where they became NASA 928, 925 and 926 respectively and were used into the early 1980s.

B-57G - This version was developed to fill the requirement for a self contained night attack system for use in Laos. Sixteen B-57Bs were withdrawn from Phan Rang and returned to Baltimore to receive 3 sensors under project *Tropic Moon III* - but initially referred to as *Night Rider*: forward looking APQ-139 radar, infra-red and low light level television plus a lasering device. These modifications were expensive (almost $49 million). TAC reactivated the 13th BS to fly these reconfigured aircraft. The operation, which was often criticised but proved an accurate weapon delivery method, lasted about two years and in April 1972 most of the Gs were stripped of their 'Tropic Moon' equipment and found their way to the 190 TBG of Kansas ANG at Topeka. After a further two years of service they were retired to Davis Monthan where they were eventually scrapped. The sixteen conversions were applied to: 52-1578, 1580, 1582, 1588, 53-3860, 3865, 3877/78, 3886, 3889, 3898, 3905/06, 3928/29 and 3931. Of these '905 was lost whilst on test in Dec 1969 and another was lost in Southern Laos on 12 Dec 1970, probably as a result of a collision with a Cessna 0-2A FAC airplane.

The first B.2s for Venezuela were delivered to Caracas by RAF crews from 12 Squadron, including Master Pilot Johnston and Flight Lieutenant Flavelle. This rare shot of either 1A-39 or 2A-39, was taken at Binbrook in March 1953, just prior to the departure. *via N. Sparkes*

VENEZUELA

First contract placed 27.1.53. Six new B.2 aircraft, diverted from second British production contract. Delivered March-July 1953 (first two by RAF crews via Gibraltar, others via Gander by Silver City crews). Used by 39 Bomber Sqn FAV.

1A-39	ex WH708. Del 20.3.53. W/o 24.4.56.
2A-39	ex WH709. Del 20.3.53.
	To EECo for o/h 2.59. Ret to FAV. Renumbered 6315.
	To BAC for o/h 1968. (G27-159). Re-del 6.8.69.
	To BAC for o/h 1977. (G27-303). Conv to B.82.
	Re-del 11.7.79 as 6315. Withdrawn 1990.
3A-39	ex WH721. Del 9.5.53.
	To EECo for o/h 4.8.58. Ret to FAV. Renumbered 6409.
	To BAC for o/h 1968 (G27-158). Re-del 9.5.69.
	To BAC for o/h 1978 (G27-304). Conv. B.82.
	Re-del 22.8.79 as 6409. Preserved at Generalisimo Francisco de Miranda, Caracas 10.90.
1B-39	ex WH722. Del 9.5.53. W/o 8.11.54 at Bocodel Rio.
2B-39	ex WH736. Del 5.6.53.
	To EECo for o/h 1959. Ret to FAV. Renumbered 3246.
	To BAC for o/h 1968. (G27-157). Re-del 6.69.
	To BAC for o/h 1978. (G27-309). Conv B.82.
	Re-del 16.4.80 as 3246. Wfu at El Libertador 10.90.
3B-39	ex WH737. Del 14.7.53.
	To EECo for o/h 8.58. W/o 17.4.63.

Second contract placed January '57. Ten new aircraft, eight B(I)8s (one diverted off a British contract) and two T.4s. Delivered June '57 to Jan '58 for use by 39th Bomber Sqn FAV.

4A-39	ex XH244. Del 4.6.57. Renumbered 3216.
	W/o at Corro 28.1.69
5A-39	Del 7.6.57. W/o at Charon 20.4.60.
4B-39	Del 19.6.57. Renumbered 0923.
	To BAC for o/h 1968. (G27-160). Re-del 1.4.71.
	To BAC for o/h 1977 (G27-308). Fully refurbished with revised radio and armament. Redesignated B(I)88. Re-del as 0923 12.3.80.
5B-39	Del 22.6.57. W/o near Corro 19.11.64.
1C-39	Del 13.11.57. Renumbered 0240.
	To BAC for o/h '75. (G27-254). Conv to B(I)88.
	Re-del as 0240 23.11.77. Cr 2.12.86
2C-39	Del 13.11.57. Renumbered 0269.
	To BAC for o/h 1975. (G27-255). Fully refurbished with revised radio and armament. Redesignated B(I)88. Re-del as 0269 4.1.78. Cr 14.11.78.
3C-39	Del 16.12.57. Renumbered 0426
	To BAC for o/h 1975. (G27-256). Conv to B(I)88.
	Re-del as 0426 22.2.78
4C-39	Del 11.1.58. Renumbered 0453.
	To BAC for o/h 1978. (G27-311). Conv to B(I)88.
	Re-del as 0453 21.5.80. Withdrawn 1990.

The two T.4s used two airframes cancelled by MoS - XM228 and XM229.

1E-39	Del 14.12.57. Renumbered 0619.
	To BAC for o/h 1977. (G27-310). Conv to T.84.
	Re-del as 0619 5.3.80. Withdrawn 1990.
2E-39	Del 14.2.58. Renumbered 0621.
	To BAC for o/h 1976. (G27-265). Conv to T.84.
	Re-del as 0621 12.4.78. Withdrawn 1990.

Third contract placed 1965. Fourteen RAF refurbished aircraft (twelve B.2s and two PR.3s). B.2s delivered between Dec '65 and April 67, all for service with 40th Bomber Sqn FAV. Four B.2s were fitted with a bomb bay gun pack and designated B(I)2 - see below. Most returned for modernisation and refurbishment as part of a 24 aircraft contract.

0129	ex WH877. Del 12.65.
	To BAC for o/h 1977 (G27-301). Conv to B.82.
	Re-del 18.6.80. Withdrawn 1990.

1131	ex WH647. Del 2.66.
	To BAC for o/h 1975 (G27-257). Conv to B.82.
	Re-del 28.9.77.
1183	ex WJ570. Del 30.4.66.
	To BAC for o/h 1975 (G27-258). Conv to B.82.
	Re-del 7.7.77.
1233	ex WF914. Del 7.66.
	To BAC for o/h 1977 (G27-302). Conv to B.82.
	Re-del 27.6.79. Withdrawn 1990.
1280	ex WH881. Del 11.66, as B(I)2.
	To BAC for o/h 1977 (G27-305). Conv to B(I)82.
	Re-del 17.5.79.
1339	ex WH649. Del 30.9.66.
	To BAC for o/h 1975 (G27-259). Conv to B.82.
	Re-del 16.3.78. Withdrawn 1990.
1364	ex WD993. Del 1.67.
	To BAC for o/h 1975 (G27-260). Conv to B.82.
	Re-del 3.5.78.
1425	ex WH712. Del 12.66, as B(I)2.
	To BAC for o/h 1977 (G27-306). Conv to B(I)82.
	Re-del 7.11.79. Withdrawn 1990.
1437	ex WH730. Del 3.67 as B(I)2.
	To BAC for o/h 1977 (G27-307). Conv to B(I)82.
	Re-del 7.2.79.
1511	ex WH862. Del 2.67.
	To BAC for o/h 1975 (G27-261). Conv to B.82.
	Re-del 8.9.77. Withdrawn 1990.
1529	ex WH732, (G27-3). Del 4.67 as B(I)2.
	To BAC for o/h 1975 (G27-263). Conv to B(I)82.
	Re-del 14.6.78.
2001	ex WJ980. Initially serialled 1371 - but changed to 2001 before acft del to Venezuela 3.67.
	To BAC for o/h 1975 (G27-262). Conv to B.82.
	Re-del 1.2.78.
2314	PR.3 ex WE172. Del 26.8.66.
	To BAC for o/h 1976. (G27-264). Re-des PR.83.
	Re-del 13.9.78. Withdrawn 1990.
2444	PR.3 ex WH171. Del 28.10.66. Slated for refurbishment in UK 1975, but crashed 9.3.76, so not updated (contract reduced by 1 to 23).

Grupo Aereo de Bombardeo 13 at El Libertador withdrew its remaining Canberras late in 1990; these being B.82 0129, 1233, 1339, 1425, 1511, 3246, 6315; PR.83 2314; T.84s 0619 (made the very last FAV Canberra flight), 0621; B(I)88 0453. B.82 6409 is preserved at Generalisimo Francisco de Miranda AB, Caracas, 10.90.

WEST GERMANY

(German Federal Republic).

One contract placed 1965 for three ex-RAF B.2 aircraft, for service with Erprobungstelle 61 for experimental work.

YA+151 ex WK130. Del 10.66. Renumbered 00+01 1968.
    Transferred to DFVLR. Renumbered D9569 1970.
    Allocated special duty regn 99+36 in 1976.
    Preserved at Sinsheim Museum.

YA+152 ex WK137. Del 10.66. Renumbered 00+02 1968.
    Transferred to Mil Geo Amt in 1970, and renumbered D9569. Allocated special duty regn 99+34 in 1978. Still in use 1992.

YA+153 ex WK138. Del 10.66. Renumbered 00+03 1968.
    Transferred to Mil Geo Amt in 1970, and renumbered D9567. Allocated special duty regn 99+35 in 1976. Still in use 1992.

ZIMBABWE

Eight B.2s and three T.4s were inherited from the Rhodesian Air Force (RhAF) when it became the Air Force of Zimbabwe (AFZ) on Independence Day, 18.4.80.

2051	B.2 ex WH653.
2502	B.2 ex WH662.
5203	B.2 ex WH672.
2504	B.2 ex WH707.
2055	B.2 ex WH855.
2085	B.2 ex WJ571.
2059	B.2 ex WJ572.
2514	B.2 ex WH644.
2155	T.4 ex WH658.
2516	T.4 ex WH674 (mainly).
2175	T.4 ex WJ613.

Two ex-RAF aircraft were supplied direct from RAF stocks, departing from Marham 25 March '81.

2250	B.2 ex WH666.
2215	T.4 ex WJ869.

Many of the above B.2s/T.4s were advertised for sale during 1988. Three Canberras were reported still at Harare, under shelters, in August 1991.

Appendix Twelve

Candid
Canberras

From the top: **16 Squadron B(I)8 XM269 acquired propellers for a farewell joke on a squadron engineering officer, May 1966** *(via Vic Avery).* □ **B.2 WD954 skirts Mount Kilimanjaro, Kenya, during tropical trials in 1952** *(EECo FA76).* □ **Canberra TT.18 WH887 '847' of FRADU over the Canberra cruise liner, near Gibraltar, 1987** *(via Ted Chapters).* □ **This low pass over the El Adem range by a 213 Squadron B(I)6 in March 1969 provides a good view of the gun pack – note the bystander too.** □ **This was the scene staged at Upwood on 9th October 1957 for 61 Squadron's Christmas card photo, however the faint markings on fins and tip tanks, leave a doubt as to true unit ownership.** □ **Finally yet another wind-up – or rather 360 Squadron T.17A WD955 sporting a 'sidewinder', at the 40th Anniversary gathering, 12th May 1989.**

Bangs, Prangs and Flashes ... *(this page anti-clockwise)*.. PR.7 WH791 jacked up on 21st June 1962 – the first occasion that 81 Squadron dropped photo flashes. □ A 45 Squadron B.15 WH948 engaged on 6 x 1000 lb drop, December 1969. □ A great many Canberras were safely delivered by the various ferry units, so it is perhaps a little unfair to show this B.2 WD985, which was 'dropped' by a No.4 Ferry Pool crew near Hawarden, 8th April 1952, whilst on delivery to 12 Squadron *(Alan Reed)*. □ A bird strike during a roller landing at Waddington in July 1973 to T.4 WT480/B resulted in a score quoted as Birds 1 - OCU nil (Crew OK). □ Eric Tilsley brings a 213 Squadron B(I)6 in for yet another, flashy low pass, in early 1969. □ As a key installation within Bomber Command's structure the OCU at Bassingbourn received a great many visits, and here a B.2 bomb load is under inspection by visiting Staff College Officers, 19th September 1957. □ Yet another bomb job, on 45 Squadron's flight line, in 1965. □ Finally 17 Squadron PR.7 WT533 with Sassoon '67 inscription, at Wildenrath *via D.Adams*

People and Places . . . *(from the top, clockwise)* . . **Aircrew from 69 Squadron (OC Wg Cdr V. C. Woodward DFC)** are grouped in front of the New Zealand Air Race winner WE139, one of their PR.3s, at Laarbruch in March 1958. □ **213 Squadron crews** planning the first sortie of 'Aircent 65', the 4th Tactical Weapons Meet, at Chaumont Air Base, France. □ **231 OCU** participated in *Winter Watcher* in Akrotiri, during October-November 1985. □ This group of **617 Squadron aircrew** was at Butterworth, Malaya in 1955 *(via K.M.Bawden)*. □ Two views of **139 Squadron's Caribbean Tour Display**, September 1955 – B.6 WJ774 is on the ground at Jamaica *(via Wg Cdr A.Ashworth and Wg Cdr W.Bonner)*. □ Finally, **David Robinson and Sqn Ldr John Harrington** of the **Radar Reconnaissance Flight at Wyton 1957** *(via Sqn Ldr David Robinson)*.

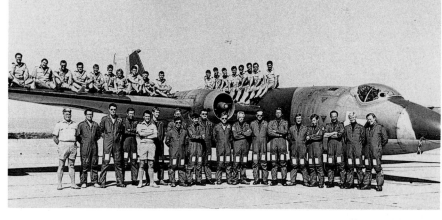

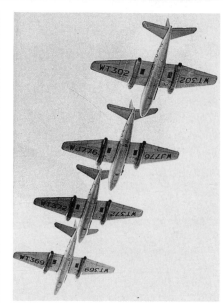

Threesomes ...*(anticlockwise from the top)*..**This 100 Squadron (BCDU) formation taken circa 1959 includes the only known photo of the unit's B(I)8 WT347, as well as B.6(mod) WH945 and Valiant B.1 WP214** *(via W/C W.Bonner).* □ **This Tengah trio snapped circa 1967, comprises a 45 Squadron B.15, a 64 Squadron Javelin FAW.9 (XH707/F) and a Hunter FGA.9 of 20 Squadron.** □ **There was a 58 Squadron detachment to Changi between March - June 1956 for operation** *Planters Punch,* **the PR.7s are WH790, 797 and 791.** □ **There could hardly be a more appropriate photograph with which to close our story . . . taken at Warton from the SAR Whirlwind XG597 on 16th July 1965, it focuses on three of the most impressive British aircraft of the post WW2 era – and all from the same stable! Canberra B.2 WD937 was in use as a chase plane for TSR.2 XR219 - the first of a type intended as a Canberra replacement but cruelly axed for political reasons. The Lightning F.6 is XR755, while prototype XA847 stands in the background, along with the company communication aircraft, Dove G-APSK and Heron G-AREC.** *BAC ref AW 15705*

Index

This selective index references only the chapters of the book; it is considered that the appendices are self-indexing. The same is to a large extent true of the chapters themselves and it is important to examine all of a particular chapter to obtain the full story of any incident or unit.